Management:
Concepts and Situations

HOWARD M. CARLISLE

Utah State University

SCIENCE RESEARCH ASSOCIATES, INC.
Chicago, Palo Alto, Toronto
Henley-on-Thames, Sydney, Paris, Stuttgart

A Subsidiary of IBM

Acknowledgments

The author gratefully acknowledges permission to reprint quotes and illustrative materials from the following sources: Chapter 1: p. 11—From *Towards a Unified Theory of Management* by Harold Koontz. Copyright © 1964 by McGraw-Hill, Inc., Used with permission of McGraw-Hill Book Company. pp. 24, 25—Reprinted with permission of *The Wall Street Journal*, © Dow Jones & Company, Inc. All Rights Reserved. Chapter 2: pp. 35, 36—From *General and Industrial Management* by Henri Fayol (1949, Sir Isaac Pitman & Sons Limited). Reprinted by permission of the publishers. Chapter 3: p. 60—Fig. 3-1, from *Situational Management* by Howard M. Carlisle. Used with permission of the American Management Associations. p. 61—Fig. 3-2, from *Situational Management* by Howard M. Carlisle. Used with permission of the American Management Associations. p. 66—Table 3-2, from *Situational Management* by Howard M. Carlisle. Used with permission of the American Management Associations.

p. 67—Fig. 3-3, from *Situational Management* by Howard M. Carlisle. Used with permission of the American Management Associations. p. 70—Fig. 3-5, from *Situational Management* by Howard M. Carlisle. Used with permission of the American Management Associations. pp. 72, 73—Table 3-3, from *Situational Management* by Howard M. Carlisle. Used with permission of the American Management Associations. p. 77—From J. Sterling Livingston, "Myth of the Well-Educated Manager," *Harvard Business Review,* January–February 1971, p. 84. Chapter 4: pp. 96, 97—Abridged from Kenneth E. Boulding, "General Systems Theory—The Skeleton of Science," *Management Science,* April, 1956, pp. 197–208. Chapter 5: p. 132—Reprinted with permission of *The Wall Street Journal,* © Dow Jones & Company, Inc. All Rights Reserved. Chapter 6: p. 148—From James B. Boulden, "A Systems Approach to Corporate Modeling," *Journal of Systems Management,* June 1973, pp. 14–20. Chapter 8: p. 189—Fig.

8-1, from *Situational Management* b[y] Howard M. Carlisle. Used with permissio[n] of the American Management Associa[-]tions. Chapter 9: pp. 220, 221—Reprinte[d] with permission of *The Wall Street Jou[r]nal,* © Dow Jones & Company, Inc. A[ll] Rights Reserved. Chapter 10: pp. 248, 249[—] From Dewitt C. Dearborn and Herbert [A.] Simon, "Selective Perception," *Soci[o]metry,* Vol. 21, 1958, pp. 140–143. pp. 25[6,] 257—From pp. 111–113 (as boxed inse[rt]) from *Organizations and Their Membe[rs]* by Jay W. Lorsch and John J. Morse. Cop[y]right © 1974 by Jay W. Lorsch and John [J.] Morse. Reprinted by permission of Har[per] & Row, Publishers, Inc. Chapter 11: p. 27[4—] Fig. 11-1 from *Individual in Society* [by] Krech, Cruchfield, and Ballachey. Co[py]right © 1962 by McGraw-Hill, Inc. U[sed] with permission of McGraw-Hill B[ook] Company. p. 276—Reprinted with per[mis]sion of *The Wall Street Journal,* © [Dow] Jones & Company, Inc. All Rights Reser[ved.]

(continued on page [ ]

Library of Congress Cataloging in Publication Data

Carlisle, Howard M.
    Management concepts.

    Bibliography.
    Includes indexes.
    1. Management.   I. Title.
HD31.C345   658.4   75-29382
ISBN 0-574-19230-1

Preface

This book deals with the problem of understanding organizations and making them more effective. No question is more vital to modern society than the problem of using resources and accomplishing goals in the context of the organization. Many of the crises of the 1960's and 1970's resulted from cumbersome organizations and ineffective management. The expansion in the size of organizations, the continued explosion of technological development, the accelerated pace of social change, and the increased complexity of society have all contributed to making the revitalization of organizations and improved management some of the great challenges of our era.

Needless to say, there is no shortage of books relating to organizations and their management. The proliferation of knowledge and the availability of information in this area have been as rapid as any. It therefore places the burden on the author of a new text to demonstrate the advantages of his material. Basically, I have attempted to develop a more realistic, useful approach to the problem of management through the following:

- A method that goes beyond an explanation of management concepts and techniques to an analysis of situations is used. The assumption is that *if* certain conditions exist, *then* specific concepts and techniques become appropriate for application. This diagnosis of situations is supplemented by a profile approach that points out management variables and illustrates their attributes (dimensions) in a relative fashion by using a scale ranging from low to high intensity. Using the profile, attributes are summarized in terms of how these measurements point to the need for a particular management technique.

- An approach emphasizing concepts and situations is incorporated throughout all of the major subjects covered. The recent popularity of this contingency approach to management has resulted in a rash of texts and literature on the subject. Generally, however, the contingency considerations of these texts are grouped within a few chapters or segments, so many of the topics remain essentially unchanged.

- The contingency approach emphasizes an analytical methodology of examining dependent relationships. This contrasts with the more descriptive constructs of traditional management. Actually, the text is an attempt to blend traditional management with contingency considerations. The process framework dividing management into planning, organizing, staffing, directing, and controlling functions is maintained throughout. (However, situational variables such as tasks, technology, and environmental factors receive greater coverage, with less emphasis on traditional subjects like organizational structure.)

· The book is strongly applications oriented. Many examples are provided, and each chapter has a section designating the implications that the information has for the practitioner. The two case incidents that follow each chapter are designed to help the student develop "hands-on" skills.

Situational analysis attempts to get away from the vague generalizations and simplifications that have hampered management theory in the past. Upon leaving his cabinet post, Daniel P. Moynihan stated, "One of the greatest weaknesses of Americans is the habit of reducing the most complex issues to the most simplistic moralisms." Contingency approaches attempt to overcome this by emphasis on identifying variables, understanding relationships, and acknowledging that management situations have multiple causes and consequences. It involves a facing up to the complexities of organizations.

This book represents the culmination of a long search process by the author. More than a decade ago, after ten years of experience as an administrator in business and government, I felt dissatisfied with management theory because it represented broad generalizations that often in practice did not fit. The appropriateness of management concepts tended to vary with the organization and with the situation. It is therefore most satisfying to participate in the development of approaches that recognize the uniqueness of organizations and seek to identify the relationship between organizational variables and the use of concepts and techniques.

The book is aimed at the introductory, junior-level course. It assumes that the student has had no previous formal training in management. To make the book more readable and to emphasize the applications aspects, few footnotes are used, and only a minimum of new jargon is introduced. It is also assumed that the book can be used in certain higher-level junior-college courses or as the initial course in an M.B.A. Program. It should also be of value in most management training programs.

A common outline embraces each chapter. A set of questions relating to the topics to be covered introduces the chapter. This is followed by the body of the textual material. Each chapter closes with a series of questions that forces the student to extend the materials presented. These are followed by the two case incidents. Several parts of the book end with "Manager Profiles," describing the actual background, duties, and affiliations of people in contemporary managerial positions.

The sequence of the outline is divided into eight parts. Following a brief explanation of the nature and history of management, a complete contingency model is presented in chapter 3. The balance of the book explores the variables of the model and relates them to planning, organizing, staffing, directing, and controlling concepts. After chapter 3 there is a discussion of decision making, and then the macro approach is adopted through analyzing the variables of the external environment. The focus then moves to that part of the internal environment of the firm where conditions are often determined or influenced by external factors. Internally, a building-block approach is used in which the basic element of organizations—the individual—is first examined. This is followed by exploring the tasks people perform, organizational structure, and the consequences of people interacting in groups. As more concepts are compiled, the problems of leadership in organizations are considered, and ultimately methods for planning and controlling operations are presented, which represent a return to broader, macro considerations.

One of the difficult problems to deal with, and where some apologies are involved, relates to acknowledging the role of women in management. The masculine gender is used in most instances in reference to *managers*. The sole reason for this is ease in writing style. "He/she" references are cumbersome and prove tiresome to the reader. However, in doing this, there is no intent to slight the equal, important role that women have in managing organizations.

As usual, acknowledgments are too numerous to fully elaborate. However, I would be remiss if I did not express appreciation to Bob Bovenschulte, the original SRA business editor, who intrigued me into writing the text. Bruce Caldwell, the current editor, also has provided incentive and an outstanding job in production. Monty Kast and Jim Rosenzweig, consulting editors, have been extremely helpful since the original conception of the manuscript, along with Carl Anderson, University of Maryland, Pat Connor, Oregon State University, Gene Dalton, Brigham Young, Paul V. Grambsch, University of Minnesota, Jerry Hunt, Southern Illinois University, Stephen Michael, University of Massachusetts, and John Newstrom and Bill Werther, Arizona State University, who reviewed the manuscript. Special thanks again go to my colleague, Krishna Shetty, who jointly explores with me many of the issues of managing organizations. Final bouquets go to Carol Miller and to my wife, Colleen, who typed most of the manuscript.

December, 1975   Howard M. Carlisle

Alternate Schedule of Topics

For those instructors who would prefer to cover planning, control, and budgeting earlier, the text is designed so that the following schedule may be used:

CHAPTERS
   1–9
   21–24
   10–20
   25

Contents

To Richard, Julie, Jana Lou, and Michael

PART I

Introduction and Background

The Nature of Management

How important are organizations to society?

How is *management* defined?

Why is management considered a process?

What responsibilities does the manager have for resource utilization?

What are the basic functions of management?

Why does management theory seem to concentrate on people?

What is the contingency approach to management?

Is management an art or a science?

THE IMPORTANCE OF ORGANIZATIONS

Organizations are the most important institutions in modern society. Essentially every human activity of significance is carried on through people functioning in organizations. This ranges all the way from the production of goods by companies to government by political organizations. All major achievements of society have been made possible through organized effort. Scientific advance, transportation systems, community development, and cultural events are all established and sustained through joint human endeavor. The human being's dominance over other forms of life has been achieved through a genius for harnessing resources and integrating human effort as a part of group activity.

Many would find reason to take exception to this interpretation of organizations, stamping it as an attempt to glorify the organization and downgrade the individual—our folklore is abundant with examples of the rugged individual who overcomes insurmountable odds to succeed. However, as important as individual rights and freedoms are in serving as the cornerstone of a democratic society, it cannot be denied that organizations dominate our existence, and that individuals can typically acquire substantial influence only through attaining power positions in organizations. Few individuals can or want to be a Robinson Crusoe, existing as a secluded island in the frenzied sea of organizational activity.

The primary reason that organizations fulfill this role is because they have proven to be the most effective means of fulfilling people's needs: business organizations provide a mass of goods and services that satisfy physical needs; governments foster an organized, regulated society fulfilling security and independence needs; social groups exist to satisfy man's need for acceptance and belonging.

As we shall examine in detail later, individual behavior is largely shaped by group identification and by personal interaction with others. Human behavior is social behavior and is comprehensive only in the context of the family, firm, school, church, government, peer groups, or other units comprising an organizational set. This pluralistic (multi-institutional) approach to society recognizes that political, economic, and social power are organizationally centered.

THE ROLE OF MANAGEMENT

If organizations are the great instruments of power and accomplishment in our society, it is management that makes them effective. The role of management is to plan, organize, integrate, and interrelate organizational activities and resources for the purpose of achieving common objectives. The responsibility of the manager is to direct the organization so that it is effective in goal accomplishment.

Management is considered to be the activating element. Managers assemble, arrange, and integrate the human elements and resources of an organization so that the resultant coordinated activity will optimize performance and need satisfaction. Unmanaged resources and uncoordinated effort result in confusion and drift; managed resources and co-ordinated effort have a synergistic effect where the simultaneous action of the separate elements becomes greater than the sum of the effects taken independently. Goals such as a higher standard of living and an improved quality of life are dependent on our capacity to direct and control massive organizations.

Defining Management

Management is a young discipline. As a result, limited specialized terminology has been developed and broad agreement over essentials is lacking, such as the definition of basic terms in the field. (Even the scope of the discipline is subject to argument.) However, most management theorists take the position expressed here that management deals with methods and means of effectively using the resources of an organization to achieve its established objectives. More specifically, management is defined as *the process by which the elements of a group are integrated, coordinated, and/or utilized so as to effectively and efficiently achieve organizational objectives.*

Implicit in this definition are five basic premises that serve as the foundation for the conceptualization of management theory and practice. These are:

1. Management is a process.
2. Management implies direction of a human organization.
3. *Effective* management is achieving desired results and making proper decisions.
4. *Efficient* management is prudent allocation and use of resources.
5. Management concentrates on goal-oriented activities.

Management as a Process

Traditionally management has been defined, and the associated principles have been developed, based on what managers do. Rather than considering management as a group of people, the discipline has focused on the *activities* managers are engaged in. Accordingly management is a *process*. It is still common in a colloquial sense to refer to "management" as the top executives in an organization who direct the administrative structure. This is a proper designation of the group that holds the leadership positions in the organization, but it is an incomplete designation of the field of management or the body of knowledge that comprises it. Management as a body of knowledge is normally considered to consist of the activities or processes that supervisors or leaders are engaged in as they direct the affairs of the organization. Since management is a process, it is necessarily dynamic and changing.

Management and Organizations

The second premise of management is that it deals exclusively with *human* organizations (an animal trainer is not a manager). A manager coordinates the activities of an organization so that goal achievement takes place. To do this he or she must necessarily direct and coordinate the activities of people. A manager is also a supervisor. (For the purposes of this text, the terms *supervisor* and *manager* are synonymous.) As such, he or she is in charge of subordinates. In some rare instances managers can exclusively direct or be in charge of materials, such as an inventory of finished goods, but even here they will normally at least have a secretary reporting to them.

Different terms are used regarding the level in the organization where the manager is located. The apex of the organization is represented by *top management* or the *chief executive officer*. The *first-line supervisor* is the lowest formal level of supervision, and *middle managers* are found in between.

Effective and Efficient Management

In accordance with our definition, a manager is concerned with effectively and efficiently achieving organizational objectives. *Effectiveness* implies making the right choices in terms of desired results. It involves competency in decision making that is related to establishing goals for the organization, selecting proper alternatives, and evaluating situations so decisions are made that enhance the organization. An effective business organization is one that is on the forefront of what is occurring within its industry.

Efficiency is the proper utilization of resources in the achievement of these goals or the implementation of these decisions. Efficiency deals exclusively with resource utilization. It involves achieving goals with the least waste or greatest economy of resources. Efficiency is, of course, one of the prime responsibilities of a manager in a business firm, since the margin between the cost of producing a product and the price received for it determines a firm's profit, which is the most common measure of the success of management. Resources in organizations take on a different importance in management, depending on the goals of the organization and the resources that are available to it. However, any manager who squanders resources is considered inefficient and not fulfilling his or her responsibilities to the organization.

Management and Goals

The final premise underlying management is that leaders are ultimately evaluated on how effective the organization is in achieving its objectives. Organizations exist because its members have certain common goals. The efficiency and productivity goals of management may not be the same as the income and occupational goals of different employees, but the goals are interdependent because the success of one set is normally dependent on the success of the other. Managers are selected to direct, coordinate, and control the organization in order to achieve its objectives.

Organizations do not have goals that exist apart from the individuals who comprise the organizations. On the other hand, the organizational goals are not simply a summation of individual ones—each individual will have personal goals somewhat different from those of the organization's. Organizational goals are established by individuals as a result of group processes that modify what each would do individually.

FIVE FUNCTIONS OF THE MANAGEMENT PROCESS

The functions that make up the management process serve as a convenient means to subdivide the management field. Accordingly, management has been dissected into subfields based on the managerial functions of *planning, organizing, staffing, directing,* and *controlling.* Different theorists or writers may use slightly different terms or, as is often the case, they may even combine or further divide these functions. However, the five functions enumerated continue to have wide acceptance as the basic elements of the management process.

An Example

The functions of management can be discerned in the following hypothetical, although frequently enacted, situation. Assume that the Apex Engineering Company submits a bid of $500,000 to perform research and development work for a government agency. Three months later the government accepts the bid, but some redefinition of the scope of work is involved, and a $460,000 contract is negotiated. When Apex receives the contract, they assign one of their top engineers, Paul Noonce, to manage the project. What responsibilities does Paul have in this position?

What functions must he perform as manager of the project? The answers to the questions involve a variety of activities that can be summarized under the headings of the five management functions:

PLANNING.   Initially he will review the goals of the program and determine whether they need to be modified, clarified, or further refined. Once the goals are clarified, he will review the work to be performed and establish the sequencing, timing, and distribution of resources required to accomplish the tasks outlined. Policies and procedures to guide the workflow will also be established. All of this constitutes the *planning* function of management.

ORGANIZING.   After Paul has reviewed the plan of work, he will then move to the next step of considering how to organize the project. Should he set up subgroups based on the functions to be performed or based on subprojects of the total work plan? What types of positions should be established and how is the work to be coordinated? What authority should be given to each manager? Each of these questions relates to the supervisor's responsibilities in relation to the *organizing* function of management.

STAFFING.   Once he has in mind how he wants to organize the work, Paul will then set about the task of finding individuals who have the sufficient skills and training to handle the duties relating to the positions established. This *staffing* function of management involves the problem of matching the individual skills with the demands of particular positions. It also involves developing and training people to handle these positions, and, once the organization starts functioning, it includes appraising individual performance.

DIRECTING.   After the plans have been developed, the organization established, and the personnel selected, the manager must take the initiative in starting operations and coordinating activities so that the entire project can begin to function. The manager must lead in the execution phase of the plans. He should establish an internal environment in which the members of the organization become committed to organizational objectives and one in which they enthusiastically cooperate in the group activities and in performing their assigned tasks. In handling this directing function, the manager is serving as the activating element in the organization.

CONTROL.   Once the project is underway, it is the final responsibility of Paul and the other managers to ensure that the work being accomplished is consistent with the existing plans. This *control* function involves a responsibility to adapt the organization to changing events and to monitor and regulate the activities of the organization consistent with existing plans and goals. If the operations are not obtaining the results desired, it is then the responsibility of the manager to make the necessary changes to achieve them. It is difficult to separate the planning and control functions in practice, even though it is common to segregate them in theory. Budget, planning, and reporting systems serve both planning and control functions.

Management versus Operations Functions

These five functions performed by Paul as director of the Apex Engineering Company project are the ones that have received all of the emphasis and study in the history of management thought. These are the functions that serve to identify the boundaries and separate into parts the body of knowledge called management. Management functions are contrasted with the *technical,* or *operations,* functions of a manager that relate to his career training in a field of specialization. Any manager has two sets of skills: those of planning, organizing, staffing, directing and controlling, plus technical or operations skills (such as engineering or accounting) that relate to the tasks performed as a part of the workflow in organizations.

Classifying the Functions

Functions are classified based on the activities an individual is engaged in at a particular time—not the title of the position. The Director of Marketing is a manager, but if he is engaged in closing a large sale with a customer, he is in that particular instance performing operations, not handling managerial functions. He must be engaged in one of the five management functions to be classified as performing managerial work.

This distinction is important in evaluating management operations. Too often managers devote too much time to performing technical work rather than managerial. They help the group by efficiently performing a portion of the operations involved in the workflow, but the group effort is inefficient because of lack of direction and coordination, resulting from inadequate supervision. This distinction is also important in evaluating the types of skills necessary for a particular executive position. Too often skill in management functions is played down when compared with technical qualifications. For example, often the most technically qualified engineer is selected to be the engineering supervisor, with secondary consideration being given to his managerial abilities.

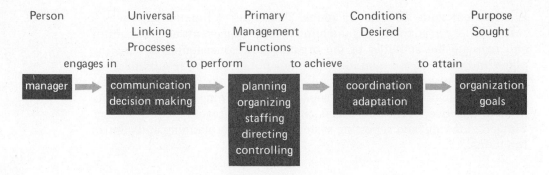

Fig. 1-1. The management process

The example of Paul Noonce accurately reflects the managerial responsibilities of directing the *internal* affairs of an organization. However, traditional management theory tends to ignore managerial responsibility for handling its *external* affairs. Organizations do not function in a vacuum but are subject to external organizations and forces that constitute the environment of the firm. The response of government officials to the work performed by Apex Engineering, technological improvements resulting from scientific advance, the actions of competitors, and many other such external influences need to be considered by Paul as he manages his particular project.*

COMPREHENSION OF THE
TOTAL MANAGEMENT PROCESS

The management process involves more than supervisors performing five basic functions. Managers must also be skilled decision makers and have unusual communication abilities. They require a broad understanding of the unit and how it is interrelated with other elements of the organization. They are also responsible for constantly shaping and modifying the organization so that it is successful in adapting to the changing conditions of its environment. Figure 1–1 displays the total management process taking all of these factors into consideration.

---

*Part IV of this text covers the macro-management problem of dealing with external considerations. These factors are coming to be recognized as an increasingly important dimension of management.

MANAGEMENT SKILLS

To behave effectively as a manager, the individual must develop abilities to think, to adjust, and to learn independently in a world of rapid change after leaving the campus. He must become an effective problem solver in the broad sense outlined above, prepared to make and implement decisions on unknown problems with unknown, yet to be developed, analytical tools. If this argument is correct, it says much about the role of the university in teaching both the managers of tomorrow and those of today who need to improve their performance, and about what we must know to do an effective teaching job. It emphasizes, rather than the teaching of today's best prevailing business practice, development of capacities like the following:

1. Orderly, rational, problem-solving ability
2. Understanding and repeated use of basic analytical concepts
3. Ability to learn from experience and to grow in understanding in a changing world
4. Ability to deal effectively with others, both in person and through written communication
5. Understanding of the role of business in the entire environment and sensitivity to the processes of social change

G. L. Bach, "Universities, Business Schools, and Business," contained in Harold Koontz (ed), *Toward a Unified Theory of Management* (New York: McGraw-Hill Book Company, 1964), p. 192.

The Linking Processes of Management

The manager is a person who, through the *linking processes* of communication and decision making, plans, organizes, staffs, directs, and controls an organization to achieve its goals and objectives. If successfully performed, the result is a coordination of organizational activities and external adaptation. Communication and decision making are also referred to as the *intervening* management processes because they connect and interrelate the five management functions. However, these two intervening processes are not solely associated with the management process. Individuals engaged in operations also make decisions and communicate with others as they perform their tasks, so these processes are not distinctively managerial. However, when an individual plans, organizes, staffs, directs, and controls *group* activities, he is engaged in functions that are exclusive to the management process. (An individual can plan and organize his own work, but since it does not involve a group it is not considered managerial.)

Communication and decision making are also referred to as the *linking* processes, because a manager can perform management functions (such as planning and organizing) only by making decisions and communicating these decisions to others. Communication and decision making are ubiquitous processes that relate to essentially everything a manager does. For those reasons they are extremely essential to the success of a manager and receive consideration along with the primary management functions in all comprehensive treatises on the management process.

**Integrative Conditions
Resulting from Managerial Action**

Coordination and adaptation are two other management-related processes that are difficult to conceptualize. They are separately identified, but in a literal sense they are conditions that result from actions taken relating to the basic management functions. Effective planning will contribute to coordination, as will effective organizing. If a manager fails to schedule work, coordination will break down. Many writers consider coordination to be the epitome of the management process and hence the essence of management. Certainly one major objective of performing management functions is to achieve internal coordination of all elements. However, coordination tends to imply a static situation involving a set of interrelated activities, whereas organizations are constantly changing in their process of adapting to external conditions. Adaptation to external forces is a true challenge to management.

The difficulty in evaluating coordination and adaptation from a management standpoint is that there are no processes or concepts that exclusively "coordinate" or "adapt." Coordination and adaptation are achieved only through the management functions of planning, organizing, staffing, directing, or controlling. No specific body of knowledge or set of management techniques relates exclusively to coordination or adaptation, since both conditions result from the manner in which the five primary management functions are performed.

MANAGEMENT AND RESOURCES

Another dimension of management is the burden of the responsibility to effectively and efficiently use the resources of the organization. A manager with as few as ten individuals reporting to him or her typically has the responsibility for well over $100,000 in resources. When the annual salaries of these workers are included along with the machinery, materials, working space, fringe benefits, support services, and other overhead costs, the magnitude of the manager's burden or responsibility for resource management becomes evident. In the case of a business firm, the owners place valuable resources in the hands of a manager and make him responsible for efficiently using these to achieve the specific goals of the organization. The supervisor is expected to obtain desired results, including protective custody and frugal use of these resources.

Influence of Economics

Traditionally, viewing a supervisor as a manager of resources has been one of the central themes of management philosophy. This results to a significant degree from the influence of the economists, especially the microeconomist. Economics developed as a discipline before management, so economic theory influenced the structure of management theory. Figure 1-2 is the basic microeconomic model. Input in the form of men, machinery, money, and materials are obtained by the organization. The organization then processes or transforms this input into goods and services that are the output of the organization. These goods and services then compete in the marketplace with those of other firms. How competitive a firm is in the marketplace depends to a degree on how efficiently it processes its resources in providing the output. Thus the emphasis is placed on internally managing an organization so as to minimize costs and maximize profits through efficient resource utilization.

    This model provides a convenient although incomplete view of the role of a manager. His responsibilities encompass more than using resources efficiently. However, it highlights one of his primary roles. As

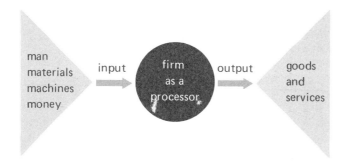

Fig. 1-2. Microeconomic model of a firm

Peter Drucker, one of the leading writers on management states, management "is the organ of society specifically charged with making resources productive."[1] All organizations use some resources, and for many, such as business firms, how efficiently they are used is a major factor in determining survival and growth. Accordingly, all managers need to be concerned with the resource utilization of their organization.

Evaluating Resource Utilization

Evaluating each resource or input of an organization for the purpose of identifying the problems associated with its efficient use is a useful exercise in understanding the rationale behind the development of management thought and practice. Resource utilization confronts a manager with considerations that have been instrumental in shaping the emphases that have developed in management theory and practice. For the purpose of this analysis, the matrix contained in table 1-1 is appropriate.

Table 1-1. Matrix on Managerial Use of Resources

	How well can a manager predict the resource?	How efficiently do managers utilize the resource?	What values are associated with use of the resource?	How much will the resource increase in value or grow?
Materials	Highly predictable	98% + in assembly work—Lower in other types	Primarily economic	No quantity increase—prices may change
Machines	Highly predictable	98% + in controlled environment	Primarily economic	No normal quantity increase
Money	Highly predictable	High but not as high as materials or machines	Primarily economic	Money has a time value and will increase
Men	Difficult to predict	Time: 40%–70% Skill: 10%–25%	Economic and Human	Normally men become much more valuable with experience

The traditional input classification is the "four m's": *materials, machines, money, and men.* More appropriate terms could be used, such

---

1. Peter Drucker, *The Practice of Management* (New York: Harper and Brothers, 1954), pp. 3–4.

as *people* for *men*. And vital resources (such as information) have been left out. Furthermore, man is not literally a resource but in one respect is a source of energy, just as oil or electricity is. However, the traditional designations are presented here for the purposes of examining historical trends—as well as for preserving the quality of alliteration. Regarding these resources, four questions basic to the management process are raised: How predictable are the resources? How efficiently are they used? What values are associated with their use? Which of the resources will grow or become of more value to the organization?

The Predictability of Resources

In attempting to summarize all management practice, such as has been done in table 1-1, it is easy to overgeneralize and therefore mislead the reader. The matrix has many shortcomings as a universal model, since it will not hold for all management situations. However, it is sufficiently consistent to represent the different characteristics or attributes of these resources as they are typically found in management practice.

Material is a good example. Through chemistry, metallurgy, engineering, and other sciences, sufficient knowledge of materials exists to modify or transform them in a predictable fashion. Copper is extracted from ore through a known, reliable process. Machine output can also be forecast with high accuracy. Most machines are sold under a warranty so that if they do not perform in accordance with their specifications they can be returned to the manufacturer. If a machine is purchased that is to stamp out five hundred parts in one hour, it will operate at that level or be returned. (However, be careful to note that if the operator does not properly use the machine, and the result is fewer parts, it is a man or people problem, not defective equipment.)

Money, however, is not as predictable as materials or machines since it depends on what is done with it. If it is used to purchase items that command a specific price, the use is predictable. If it is used for investment purposes where corporate securities are purchased to obtain future benefits, this is not as predictable.

But without question, man is the least predictable element of an organization. Two pounds of copper are essentially identical, but two individuals are not. They have different skills, different temperaments, and different interests. Not only are any two people different, but even the same person experiences at least slight changes in moods from day to day. The changes are normally small but inevitable. The contrast is found in the statement that "you can predict when water will boil but you cannot predict when a man will." Individuals tend to be relatively predictable on a group basis, but quite unpredictable on an individual basis—especially when compared with the other nonhuman resources.

The Efficiency of Resources

The efficient use of a resource is closely associated with its predictability. The constant nature of materials makes it possible for a firm to have a small "scrappage factor" or "in process loss" when materials are used in transformation processes. In routine assembly work (such as in an automotive plant), normally less than two percent of the components will be damaged or destroyed during the assembly process. This efficiency is lower in intermittent production (such as a carpenter making cabinets), and much lower in experimental activities associated with research and development, but generally the efficient utilization of materials is relatively high.

Machines are also efficiently used if the environment is controlled so that temperature, humidity, and other similar factors will not affect machine processing. Electric typewriters will usually work in a predictable way—it is the typist who introduces uncertainty in the typing process.

Money, of course, is not used as efficiently as materials or machines because of the predictability problem. However, organizations have made immense improvements in their money management as trained people in financial analysis have moved into key positions in organizations.

In an efficiency criterion, people again present the primary problem in the matrix—it is not possible to measure them, using one dimension, as it is with the other resources. People involve at least two efficiency factors: one is the amount of time they are working when they are employed for eight hours a day, and the other is how much of their total skill is required in performing their assigned duties. On both counts people are used much less efficiently than the other resources. In studies made of continuous production organizations, it is often concluded that if the work force is engaged in productive effort seventy percent of the time, a firm has an extremely efficient production function. Just considering rest periods, coffee breaks, and other approved company respites, it would be impossible to get above ninety percent, and in many organizations it is considerably less.

However, utilization of the time of people in organizations is creditable when compared with skill utilization. Many different studies have shown that organizations tend to be ineffective in using the reservoir of skill represented by the people in their organizations. It is, of course, impossible to be precise in this type of study, but generally it is shown that organizations utilize less then twenty-five percent of the skill and knowledge represented in the work force. It would, of course, be impossible to design every job in an organization so that one hundred percent of the skill of the incumbent is used. However, behavioral scientists are generally critical of the manner in which organizations, especially governments and businesses, utilize the skill of their membership. Too often jobs comprise simple, routine, easy-to-learn tasks that are far beneath the level of capability of the individuals employed to handle them. The claim is that routine tasks do not sufficiently tap human capability, resulting in disinterest and other psychological conditions affecting morale.

All of these considerations will receive in-depth coverage in later chapters. However, one point deserves emphasis at this time. The people dimensions of supervision are considered the great frontier of management, because manpower is the one resource that is currently being the least effectively used. A knowledgeable manager is already employing materials, machines, and money with a rather high degree of efficiency. It is the workforce that presents the greatest challenge in terms of utilization and where the major opportunity exists for improvement. With nonhuman resources, future improvements will primarily come through improved materials, better machines, and other contributions from chemists, engineers, and those responsible for technological upgrading. Psychologists and sociologists will provide a better understanding of people, but it is directly up to the manager to satisfy the goals of the individual and the organization through improved management concepts.

Value Considerations

The third column in the resource matrix in table 1-1 represents another characteristic of resource utilization. When the question of values is raised, people again turn out to be the most complex. Since materials, machines, and money are inanimate, economic values dictate their use, especially when the basic goals of the organization are economic (as in the business firm).

People are more complex to supervise, because the values in their utilization are broader than purely economic. People have inherent rights and values that laws force all organizations to respect. People cannot be mistreated, maligned, or physically punished. Laws exist relating to child labor, fair employment practices, nondiscrimination, and many other "value" aspects of the employment of people. Organizations also usually have goals relating to the social values and quality of life of people. Organizations exist for people—people do not exist for organizations.

Growth Features of Man

One final point is important in relating resource management to problems in supervision. Man is the main resource that experiences significant growth. The value of materials, an equipment inventory, or money may change with a change in the price index, but the quantity of materials or machines will not grow without an additional output of resources to purchase more units. True, money will bring a return over time if properly invested, but people are the main resource that will normally experience considerable growth with the passage of time.

A new employee is initially of limited value to the organization. As the individual receives training and becomes more knowledgeable of the processes, people, organization structure, objectives, and functioning of the company, he is much more able to positively contribute to what is done. A college graduate in accounting will initially come into an organization as a junior accountant. As he gains more knowledge and experience, he will be advanced to the position of an accountant, senior accountant, and eventually a supervisor, assuming he has the ability, interest, and opportunity to do so. Typically the learning curve is extremely rapid at first and gradually levels off over time. One of the major responsibilities of a supervisor in using resources is to establish an environment conducive to the growth potential of human beings. The supervisor also trains subordinates to increase their effectiveness.

The Significance of People in Management

The purpose of this analysis of resource utilization is to show why management literature and practice tend to focus on people. Labor is not only normally the most costly input on the basis of the average unit cost of an output, but people are also the most difficult element to manage. As stated, there are many more uncertainties and complexities associated with them than with material resources, and utilization of manpower is far less efficient. This is disturbing to both the individual and to the organization. In general, people want to contribute, they want to get a feeling of achievement from what they do, and they want to feel their skills are being used. Man can do what machines and other resources are incapable of doing: he has tremendous growth potential, and through his cognitive power and analytical skills he is the only resource capable of innovation, creativity, and nonprogrammed adaptation.

THE CONTINGENCY APPROACH TO MANAGEMENT

Evaluating the use of resources based on the matrix in table 1-1 highlights several of the problems that exist in the scientific advance of management as a body of knowledge. In evaluating the predictability of materials and the efficiency of their use, it is impossible to come up with a specific figure or percentage that is representative of all organizations. This is because the nature of the operations in each organization is different—as are the people performing these operations. It is difficult to generalize about any particular square in the matrix because no two organizations use materials, machines, money, or men in the same way. Each organization is unique when one considers its goals, the people involved, the tasks being performed, and the organization structure, to name only a few variables. Hence, it is extremely difficult to make broad generalizations or to identify management principles that have across-the-board application.

Not only is each situation different, but management is further complicated by the concept of *equifinality*. There is often not just one way to solve a management problem or one best course of action to achieve a desired condition; there are several and, of course, many inadequate ones. Just as many different people can successfully fill a position, so there are many different effective ways to manage a business. A manager's concern is selecting one of the desirable alternatives and avoiding one that is damaging.

These premises underlie the management theory and practice contained in this book. The *contingency approach* holds that there are few universal solutions to management problems. Managers must instead select techniques and make decisions consistent with the particular demands of the situations they face. Since these demands will differ, the solutions will differ. The use of any particular concept of management is dependent or contingent upon the conditions the manager experiences at any particular time. This approach emphasizes the uniqueness of organizations. However, as we shall see, similarities are often found in certain classifications or attributes of organizations, making some limited generalizations possible.

Other factors affecting variability are external considerations. Technological, political, and social forces, and conditions in a marketplace will have different meaning for different groups. Rarely is there just one solution to a management problem, especially one that applies to all organizations. Ultimates, universals, and absolutes find little place in the theory or practice of management.

For this reason this text emphasizes an adaptive approach to management, where concepts and techniques are of limited value outside of the context to which they relate. Management involves two aspects: knowing concepts and techniques and accurately diagnosing the situation so that the concepts and techniques can be properly applied. Concepts of management are considered more as guides to action than as principles containing broad truths that are applicable to the entire gamut of supervision encompassing all managers in all situations. This approach rejects the frequent assumption of traditional management that there is one best way to plan, organize, staff, or direct an organization. It instead postulates that there are many effective methods of planning, organizing, staffing, directing, or controlling, and that the central problem of management is to match particular concepts and techniques with the needs of particular situations.

IS MANAGEMENT A SCIENCE
OR AN ART?

One final subject deserves consideration in analyzing the nature of the management process. This relates to the current status of management knowledge and the means by which it can be acquired. Management theory is slowly evolving because it deals primarily with people, and our knowledge of human behavior is still in its formative stages. Furthermore, managers of organizations are required to evaluate a variety of conditions involving diverse causes, where managerial action is likely to have multiple consequences. Such analysis is hindered because management lacks a generally accepted body of knowledge encompassing all major variables and functions of management. Without such a body of knowledge, management remains primarily an art. Experience continues to be the best teacher, and it is only through experience that one comes to feel completely comfortable in applying different techniques and concepts.

Management as a Science

The current status of management as a science is a subject that is frequently discussed and evaluated. A *science* is a systematized body of knowledge. It is based upon information that has been empirically verified through the scientific method. (The scientific method involves identification of conditions or facts through observation, and verification of principles through experimentation. When certain facts and principles are interrelated into broader conclusions, they constitute the *theory* of a particular science or body of knowledge.) Verified principles of a science are useful for a practitioner or one applying the science, because it makes it possible to forecast or predict the outcome of specific actions.

Management as an Art

Application of the body of knowledge that constitutes the science is called an *art*. An art is often referred to as the systematic application of skill or knowledge in effecting a desired result. A science is something that is learned—an art something that is practiced. Stated another way, science is "to know" and art is "to do." Management is in essence an application of principles and concepts, and is therefore basically an art. The skill of a physician involves an understanding of the body of knowledge comprising medicine and the application of this body of knowledge through the art of treating patients. The skill of a manager involves understanding the body of knowledge comprising management and the application of that knowledge through leading and coordinating the activities of an organization.

Growth of Management Thought

As we shall see in the next chapter, the body of knowledge of management is rapidly expanding. However, as a science it is still one of the least developed and youngest of all sciences including those in the lesser-developed social sciences. The encouraging point is that this body of knowledge has recently expanded greatly. Prior to World War II there was a paucity of management literature. Now there is almost more management information being generated than managers can absorb. However, the extremely large number of variables in an organization, many of which are governed by the capriciousness of human behavior, make it unlikely that organizations and their management will comprise a highly predictable science in any known measurable period of time.

No one can read a text on management or learn the body of knowledge comprising management and from this alone be an effective manager. A manager's skills are developed and sharpened through practice in application. Knowing the body of knowledge of management will certainly speed up the learning of the art, and it will greatly assist the manager in making effective decisions and in developing a broad, analytical framework, but knowledge is not the only prerequisite to being a manager. The controlled environment of the knowledge-oriented physical sciences must be contrasted with the dynamic environment of the art-oriented social sciences, in which testing knowledge through practice in a variety of situations is an inevitable feature of extending the discipline.

A science and an art go hand in hand. They are not mutually exclusive. As the science of management increases, it will reduce the manager's reliance on those aspects of his art that are based largely on intuition, but it will never eliminate the need for this art. Management by definition is a process involving the application of principles and concepts relating to planning, organizing, staffing, directing, and controlling people engaged in group activities. Since neither the variables in the situation nor the management concepts and functions represent controlled constants, management action will necessarily involve some uncertainties where skill in application is significant.

SUMMARY

Organizations dominate human existence and are involved in essentially everything an individual does, and they are the vehicle that man has used to achieve his dominance on this planet. Organizations are made effective through management. Management is defined as the process by which the elements of a group are integrated, coordinated, and/or utilized to effectively and efficiently achieve organizational objectives. Accordingly, management is a process that concentrates on achieving common goals through the effective and efficient use of resources.

Five functions constitute the management process: planning, organizing, staffing, directing, and controlling. All management activities fit within these functions, and management skill is tied to being effective in applying their associated concepts. The functions are applied through decision making and communication, which are the two linking processes of management. Coordination and adaptation are the two conditions managers attempt to achieve through the use of proper management methods.

Traditionally the resources managers employ have been identified as men, materials, machinery, and money. Man is the most intricate resource to manage because he is more difficult to predict, more values are involved in his use, and his complexity makes it awkward to design jobs so that his skills are used and he obtains satisfaction from what he does. In a sense it is belittling to consider people as a resource, but since they are the primary movers in organizations and since they benefit from the output of the organization, it is generally in their interest to make organizations as effective and efficient as possible.

Management is difficult because organizations do not have constant, identical characteristics. Organizations and situations tend to vary, making the concepts and techniques managers use dependent on the situation. This is known as the contingency approach to management. Management is also a mixture of an art and a science. It is a science in that a body of knowledge does exist relating to management practice, but it is an art in that management skill is developed and honed through actual experience and on-the-job application.

QUESTIONS FOR STUDY
AND DISCUSSION

1. What activities do you engage in that are not affected by organizations?
2. Why is management called the *activating element*?
3. What are the five basic premises underlying the definition of *management* presented in the text?
4. What is the difference between the terms *effectiveness* and *efficiency* as they relate to management?
5. "Organizations exist only because the people in them have a common set of goals." Discuss.

6. Assume that you are establishing a small business such as a travel agency. What activities would you engage in to get this business into operation? Which of these would be technical and which would be managerial?
7. What is the difference between organizing and staffing?
8. Why are communication and decision making not considered primary functions of management?
9. In the economic model of the firm, what is the function of management?
10. What are the various reasons why management theory and practice tend to concentrate on people rather than other resources?
11. Contrast an airline, retail department store, and a furniture manufacturer in terms of problems in resource utilization.
12. How does the contingency approach to management differ from traditional ones?
13. Why is management considered to be primarily an art?
14. Can the art of management be learned in a classroom?

Case Study
CENTRAL VALLEY BANK

Clarence Johnson is Vice President of Operations for Central Valley Bank. The Bank has been concerned about their staffing so they hired a consultant to review their management structure. The consultant had each officer keep a daily log of his or her activities. Clarence's log for May 18 read as follows:

Prepared report for Board of Directors meeting—45 minutes.

Interviewed two applicants for secretarial position—50 minutes.

Established teller schedule for the week of May 20—30 minutes.

Met with the president to review the six-month performance evaluations made on all loan officers—35 minutes.

Held a meeting with all tellers to explain the revised procedures to be used for cashing out-of-state checks—25 minutes.

Wrote a memorandum to the president proposing that a separate supervisor be assigned to the tellers in the drive-in windows—15 minutes.

Attended a luncheon meeting of the Chamber of Commerce—1 hour and 15 minutes.

Discussed arrangements for maternity leave of a loan officer—15 minutes.

Reviewed and acted on proposed loans over $50,000—90 minutes.

Reviewed construction drawings to add 300 safety deposit boxes—45 minutes.

Discussion of problem of continual lateness with James Fornoff—15 minutes.

Telephone calls, chatting with customers, miscellaneous—60 minutes.

Which of these tasks or activities are managerial and which are technical?
Identify the management functions involved in each task or activity.
Which activities contribute to efficiency? To effectiveness?
Which tasks involve a science and which involve an art?

Case Study
TRAINING FOR POSITIONS

On the same day in two different newspapers the following excerpts were found relating to training for different positions:

May 8, 1975, *The Wall Street Journal,* page 1.

"As long as anyone can remember, riverboat pilots have 'learned the river' exactly as Mark Twain did more than a century ago, picking up the secrets of the profession slowly over four or five years from experienced pilots. But faced with a shortage of pilots in the rapidly expanding industry, towing companies are turning to formal, faster training for pilots. Five years ago, a group of 14 companies involved in the river industry founded the nonprofit National River Academy, the first and only of its kind. The cadet program began two years ago.

"'The old way of learning by doing is not good anymore,' says Pierre R. Becker, a retired U.S. Navy captain who is superintendent of the academy. One development that hastened this conclusion was passage of a 1972 federal law requiring licensing of towboat operators on the nation's 23,000 miles of inland waterways.

"The new academy, located on the banks of the Mississippi 10 miles downstream from Helena, Arkansas, offers prospective riverboat pilots a 22-month course consisting of 2-month sessions studying at the academy alternating with equal stints working on some of the nation's 4000 towboats." . . .

. . . "While the new school has won praise from cadets and towboat companies, some veteran rivermen remain skeptical. 'You can't make a pilot at a school,' one old hand says with a snort."

May 8, 1975, *The Salt Lake Tribune*, p. A17.

Jerry V. Wilson, former chief of police for Washington D.C. and a writer of criminal-justice textbooks states:

. . . "I have repeatedly urged against the popular notion, which incidentally is supported by recommendations from two prestigious national commissions on criminal justice, that only college-educated persons are qualified to be police officers. Simultaneously, though, I have maintained that we should encourage college graduates to enter police work and that we must stimulate those incumbent police officers with academic aptitudes to pursue further education.

"I oppose requirements of a college degree for police work because I reject the concept that either academic skills or a college education are magic measures of the worth of a person. My observation has been that many persons who do not hold college degrees prove to be superb police officers, detectives, and officials. Some of those individuals are fully capable of performing and profiting from college work. Others do not possess the aptitudes and skills, principally reading and writing skills, needed to benefit from typical college courses; still, with proper training, they make competent and sometimes outstanding police officers. . . ."

. . . "The police occupation, which has been a stepping-stone to the middle class for upward strivers of several generations, would be closed to many persons who are capable of doing the job. Those excluded would be both whites and blacks. But, for reasons—some obvious, some not fully understood—a disproportionate ratio of those excluded would be blacks."

Are these two articles conflicting? Why or why not?
Do you agree with the conclusions of the two writers? Discuss.
Should a manager be required to have academic training? Explain.
Should a manager be required to have management training? Explain.
What do the two writers each imply about their positions as far as management being a science or an art?

The Development of Management Thought

How did management develop as a discipline?

What groups have influenced the development of management thought?

Why has no single theory of management evolved?

What are the various schools or approaches to management?

What are the limitations of traditional theory?

What improvements are offered by systems theory?

What improvements are offered by contingency theory?

As part of one college's "Business Week," three distinguished businessmen were invited to serve on a panel and respond to student questions
regarding careers in business. One of the questions asked was, "What
skills are most important in being successful managers?" The first
executive to respond was the president of an insurance company. He
emphasized skills in persuasion and the ability to influence others.
"Management is getting work done through others. A manager must
understand people and be effective in interpersonal relations if he is to
be successful."

The second visitor was operations vice president of a public utility.
He felt that administrative skills were the most significant factor in being
a successful manager. "The manager needs to be a strong organizer and
planner. Running an organization is like fitting the parts of a puzzle
together. The proper location has to be found for each part, and when all
of the parts are properly placed, the organization will function smoothly.
Resources can be used efficiently only when everyone fulfills a particular
role and knows what he is doing. Organization is the name of the game."

The third executive was head of a consulting firm that specialized in
engineering work. "In my experience," he stated, "the skilled manager is
the adroit decision maker. If managers make good decisions they will
obviously be successful. Teaching people how to be effective decision
makers is the way to develop them into successful managers."

THE NATURE OF
MANAGEMENT THEORY

Management is one of the most eclectic of all disciplines. And like the
medical and engineering professions, it relies on other more narrow,
knowledge-oriented disciplines for its basic scientific foundation. The
rise of management as a field of study occurred within this century. Due
to its broad nature, it is dependent on other more specialized disciplines
for much of its theoretical thrust. The management process by definition
deals with people, which means that the advance of knowledge in this
respect is tied to improvements in fields such as sociology, psychology,
and anthropology. Management also involves decision making regarding
resource allocation, where vital concepts have been contributed from
fields such as economics, mathematics, and statistics. Many other disciplines are also involved.

Carving out a distinct body of theory and practice called management has been an erratic, often controversial process. Even today after
nearly a century of development, there is still disagreement over fundamentals like the scope of the discipline and the basic foundation of
principles and concepts. However, even though management is a relative

newcomer on the academic scene, the advances have been dramatic. What was a trickle of management literature in the early quarter of this century has now turned into a deluge.

Rather than chronologically tracing the development of management thought from its inception to the current time, an analysis will be made of the three primary sources that have contributed to the flow and content of management theory. The current status of management thought is easier to comprehend using this approach than sequentially identifying each individual who has had significant influence on management theory or practice. Management is a composite of many influences and events and can rarely be attributed to the brilliant achievements of a few men. Certain individuals will be covered in this analysis, but it should be kept in mind that they are selected primarily because they represent the knowledge and thought patterns that evolved during their period.

The three sources of management thought are known as the *classical, behavioral,* and *management science* schools. The classical school evolved around the turn of the century, based on contributions primarily from practitioners. Other names for this school are *traditional, process,* or *operational.* The behavioral school started in the 1920's as the *human relations* movement and gradually broadened through the contributions of sociologists, psychologists, and cultural anthropologists. The management science movement can be traced to early practitioners, but it is normally associated with the use of quantitative methods during World War II, when it became known as *operations research.* It has been expanded into the *management science* approach resulting from contributions by individuals trained in mathematics, statistics, economics, and engineering.

THE BEGINNING OF
TRADITIONAL THEORY

Management as a science stretches back less than a century, but management as an art reverts to the beginning of human existence. As an art, management was practiced with the first human group—the family unit. Many major accomplishments involving organized effort stand out in the history of each civilization. The Egyptians built massive pyramids, the Chinese a wall that stretched for 1500 miles, and the Aztecs elaborate temples. The Great Wall of China, started around the 4th century B.C., is considered the greatest building enterprise ever undertaken. These accomplishments involved the organized effort of thousands of individuals and the movement of tons of materials over a period of many years. Certainly this could not have been done without considerable skill in planning, organizing, staffing, directing, and controlling—even though

little formalized administrative knowledge is recorded in the writings
of the times.

Contributions from Military and Religious Groups

Organizations involving thousands of participants also existed at the time
of the Holy Roman Empire and in the centuries following. The most
important of these in terms of handing down management concepts were
religious groups such as the Roman Catholic church and military organizations. Organizational structures based on a hierarchy of authority,
specialization, and line and staff concepts existed in the churches and
armies of the middle ages.

The dominant organizations of any period of history are the crucibles
in which management practice finds its form. Thus religious and military
organizations predominated during the middle ages, and business and
governmental organizations have tended to be the central source of
management practice following the start of the industrial revolution.
Surprisingly, one of the astonishing features of the rise of the factory
system is that no systematic body of management knowledge developed
with it. In fact, little is known about management techniques of the era.

Influence of Economics and Mathematics

Early theoretical contributions were by economists like Adam Smith,
who emphasized the importance of the division of labor in his classic
The Wealth of Nations[1], written in 1776. Also, in 1832 the mathematician
Charles Babbage urged that scientific methods be used in managing an
enterprise. (Babbage proposed relatively modern concepts, including
giving a bonus for efficiency and using time study methods.[2]) However,
the world at that time was not ripe for the widespread acceptance of
these approaches, and it took another half-century before an American
engineer, Frederick Taylor, attracted widespread interest in scientific
methods of management.

FREDERICK TAYLOR AND SCIENTIFIC MANAGEMENT

Frederick Winslow Taylor was a practitioner who enjoyed a successful
career as an engineer with the iron and steel industry in the United States.
Beginning as an apprentice machinist in the 1870's, he completed an
engineering degree at night and at the age of 28 became chief engineer
of the Midvale Steel Company. In this capacity he observed that workers

were left to perform their physical tasks in essentially any manner they desired as long as they kept busy. Taylor was a keen observer, and he often noticed that workers used wasted motions and inefficient methods in their operations. He also spoke out against "soldiering," created by informal groups deliberately working beneath their capacities, contrary to the wishes of management.

Taylor's Concern for Efficiency

Resulting from his concern over inefficiency in the shop areas, Taylor had many studies performed, aimed at developing a means for organizations to maximize their productivity. He felt that this could best be done through observing and studying in minute detail the methods and timing required in performing the sequence of tasks involved in a particular job. After the job was studied and the methods requiring the fewest motions and least effort were established, this "one best way" should be standardized and imposed on the workers involved. Taylor felt the rewards of this improvement should go to both the firm and the worker. The firm would benefit by lower costs and more profit, and the individual would benefit by receiving a higher wage for his productivity. Taylor viewed man primarily in economic terms. With higher wages, employees would be more satisfied, eliminating the primary source of conflict between the management and workers.

Studies Conducted by Taylor

Taylor put everything that he preached into practice. His conclusions were frequently documented by extensive experiments that were intended to substantiate the validity of scientific management. Most notable are his studies on the hauling of pig iron, techniques of metal cutting, and the motions and tools involved in shoveling. These studies were conducted over a period of years, with investigators examining workers who performed the particular tasks. In each instance a series of motions that constituted the one best way to perform the physical task was established. Also, methods or tools were designed to optimize the operations.

In the example of shoveling, it was determined that twenty-one pounds per shovel was the optimum for an average worker engaged full-time in this operation. First the motions in shoveling were established, after which eight to ten different shovels were designated for the worker to use, depending on the weight of the material involved. The worker would select the shovel that would average twenty-one pounds when fully loaded. In relation to the experiment involving the loading of pig iron into railroad cars, the average amount per day hauled by the average worker was said to increase from twelve and one-half to forty-seven tons per man per day using Taylor's methodology.

Taylor's Contributions

Taylor became an effective spokesman for his "scientific management" principles. He stated that "management is a true science, resting upon clearly defined laws, rules, and principles. . . ."[3] In some respects the selection of the term *scientific management* was unfortunate. On the one hand he made a significant contribution by emphasizing that physical tasks could be made more efficient through study and analysis. However, he had at the time a narrow view of the term *management,* considering it to encompass the supervision of people engaged in physical tasks.

Taylor is frequently referred to as the father of modern management, but more appropriately he should be considered the father of industrial engineering, or shop management. He popularized the rationale behind time and motion studies and focused management's attention on detailed efficiency factors involved in performing physical tasks. He acknowledged the importance of the planning responsibilities of the supervisor, but he viewed the problem almost entirely from that of first-line supervision. Broader organizational considerations relating to planning, leadership, goal formulation, and organization structure were given limited attention. Taylor's philosophy is evident from his classic entitled *The Principles of Scientific Management* published in 1911:

> Now, among the various methods and implements used in each element of each trade there is always one method and one implement which is quicker and better than any of the rest. And this one best method and best implement can only be discovered or developed through a scientific study and analysis of all of the methods and implements in use, together with accurate, minute, motion and time study. This involves the gradual substitution of science for rule of thumb throughout the mechanic arts.[4]

Expansion of Scientific Management

After 1900, Taylor's concepts and those of his colleagues rapidly spread in the United States, followed by an expansion onto the international scene. Studies conducted simultaneously or after his death by such contemporaries as Frank and Lillian Gilbreth, Henry L. Gantt, Carl G. Barth, and Morris L. Cooke added to this interest and rapidly developed the "science" of time and motion study. Frank Gilbreth in his famous bricklaying experiments reduced the motions of a bricklayer from eighteen to five per brick. Studies were developed establishing data in tabular form for micromotions involved in minute movements of the arms and hands. The scientific management movement in the United States was almost too successful, since for several decades it concentrated the attention of management analysts and practitioners on physical tasks.

Taylor, as the pioneer in management theory in this country, actually made major contributions to two schools of thought. His emphasis on scientific investigation clearly establishes him as a forerunner of the management science school that developed a half century later. His emphasis on economy and efficiency and the timing of his contributions also place him in the traditional school, sometimes called the *productivity* school of management. Under any circumstances, he left an indelible mark on the scientific development of management theory and practice.

THE CONTRIBUTIONS OF HENRI FAYOL

The title, "the father of management," more appropriately applies to a Frenchman by the name of Henri Fayol, because he provided the philosophy that still serves as the basic framework for management theory. Fayol, like Taylor, was an engineer in the manufacturing and mining industries in France. Unlike Taylor, he did little formal experimentation in management. Instead, after the age of sixty, he wrote about his philosophy of management and identified what he considered to be sound management practice based on a process approach.

Fayol's most important work, a book entitled *General and Industrial Management,* was first published in French in 1916. The first edition in English was in 1929, but only limited copies were published. It was not released in the United States until 1949. However, the date of this latter printing is deceptive, because portions of his writings were available in the United States earlier, and his concepts had an influence on other writers who were developing their own theories during the formative period of management thought in the 1930's and 1940's.*

Fayol's Process Approach

Perhaps Fayol's major contribution was to identify management as a separate set of skills, or functions, performed by supervisors in organizations. He clearly delineated the difference between technical and managerial skills and noted that a supervisor must be proficient in both to be

---

*Any philosophical movement cannot be attributed to one man, and many writers in the United States were developing concepts similar to Fayol's during this time period. Notable among these were Henry Dennison,[5] Mooney and Reiley,[6] Luther Gulick,[7] and Alvin Brown.[8] Two British consultants, Oliver Sheldon[9] and Lyndall Urwick,[10] also deserve mention with this group. Each of these writers developed concepts of management similar to Fayol's, although most of them concentrated on concepts of formal organization, and none of them displayed the broad vision of management found in Fayol's writings.

successful. Fayol identified the following six functions in industrial activities:

1. Technical   production and manufacturing
2. Commercial   buying, selling, and exchange (Today commercial functions are more appropriately referred to as *marketing* activities.)
3. Financial   search for and optimal use of capital
4. Security   protection of property and persons
5. Accounting   stocktaking, balance sheet, costs, and statistics
6. Managerial   planning, organization, command, coordination, and control

Fayol considered management a process consisting of the five primary functions as indicated in six above. He defined management using these terms: "To manage is to forecast and plan, to organize, to command, to coordinate and to control."[11] (Note the similarity between these functions and the ones contained in chapter 1 of this book.) The functions of organizing, planning, and control are identical in both lists. Fayol's concept of command is similar to the directing function. The only basic difference is the addition of staffing as a function, and the viewing of coordination and adaptation as conditions resulting from the application of the five functions. The significance of Fayol's work is that he established a framework for explaining and dissecting the field of management which has withstood nearly six decades of challenge! This is especially unusual when you consider that Fayol's efforts represent one of the first attempts to identify the elements in the then uncharted field of management. The validity of his basic approach has been sanctioned by its continued use and acceptance by both practitioners and academicians.

Fayol's Emphasis on Universal Principles

Two other features of Fayol's theories have tended to constitute some of the basic tenets of the traditional (process) school of management. These are his concern for "principles" of management and his emphasis on the universal nature of management, as seen in his address to the Second International Congress of Administrative Science:

> The meaning which I have given to the word *administration* and which has been generally adopted, broadens considerably the field of administrative science. It embraces not only the public service but enterprises of every size and description, of every form and every purpose. All undertakings require planning, organization, command, coordination, and control, and in order to function properly, all must observe the same general principles.

> We are no longer confronted with several administrative sciences, but with one which can be applied equally well to public and to private affairs.[12]

The followers of Fayol and the prominent theoreticians of the process school during the 1950's and 1960's proclaimed the importance of the universal nature of management. They typically entitled their books *Principles of Management*[13], representing their approach to conceptualizing management thought. For these reasons it is essential to understand what Fayol had in mind when he presented his list of fourteen management principles.

Fayol's Principles

Fayol defined principles as "acknowledged truths regarded as proven on which to rely."[14] However, he used the term *principle* in a broad sense:

> I shall adopt the term principle whilst dissociating it from any suggestions of rigidity, for there is nothing rigid or absolute in management affairs, it is all a question of proportion. Seldom do we have to apply the same principle twice in identical conditions; allowance must be made for different changing circumstances, for men just as different and changing, and for many other variable elements.[15]

Fayol proclaimed universalism on the one hand, but he severely restricted it on the other.

Fayol's fourteen principles are abridged below. The principles are both broad and prescriptive in nature. Many are still widely used in management, and they have served as the foundation upon which the process school of management has been built. The principles concentrate on formal organization, but they also relate to concepts integrating the entire organization. Taylor was concerned with how individual workers performed operations. Fayol viewed an organization from the top or from the position of the general manager. His principles are important at all levels of supervision, but as he himself points out, they take on more significance as one climbs the hierarchy.

FAYOL'S FOURTEEN GENERAL PRINCIPLES OF MANAGEMENT

1. *Division of Work.* Specialization belongs to the natural order of things. The object of division of work is to produce more and better work with the same effort. It is accomplished through reduction in the number of objects to which attention and effort must be directed.

2. *Authority and Responsibility.* Authority is the right to give orders and responsibility is its essential counterpart. Wherever authority is exercised responsibility arises.
3. *Discipline.* Discipline implies obedience and respect for the agreements between the firm and its employees. The establishing of these agreements binding a firm and its employees from which disciplinary formalities emanate, should remain one of the chief preoccupations of industrial heads. Discipline also involves sanctions judiciously applied.
4. *Unity of Command.* An employee should receive orders from one superior only.
5. *Unity of Direction.* Each group of activities having one objective should be unified by having one plan and one head.
6. *Subordination of Individual Interest to General Interest.* The interest of one employee or group of employees should not prevail over that of the company or broader organization.
7. *Remuneration of Personnel.* To maintain the loyalty and support of workers, they must receive a fair wage for services rendered.
8. *Centralization.* Like division of work, centralization belongs to the natural order of things. However, the appropriate degree of centralization will vary with a particular concern, so it becomes a question of the proper proportion. It is a problem of finding the measure that will give the best overall yield.
9. *Scalar Chain.* The scalar chain is the chain of superiors ranging from the ultimate authority to the lowest ranks. It is an error to depart needlessly from the line of authority, but it is an even greater one to keep it when detriment to the business ensues.
10. *Order.* A place for everything and everything in its place
11. *Equity.* Equity is a combination of kindliness and justice.
12. *Stability of Tenure of Personnel.* High turnover increases inefficiency. A mediocre manager who stays is infinitely preferable to an outstanding manager who comes and goes.
13. *Initiative.* Initiative involves thinking out a plan and ensuring its success. This gives zeal and energy to an organization.
14. *Esprit de Corps.* Union is strength, and it comes from the harmony of the personnel.

Abridged from Henri Fayol, *General and Industrial Management* (New York: Sir Isaac Pitman & Sons Ltd., 1949), pp. 20–41.

LIMITATIONS OF THE
CLASSICAL SCHOOL

Fayol's approach emphasizing processes, principles, and universalism dominated the development of management theory from the 1930's to the 1960's. However, beginning as a discordant note in the late 1940's[16] and increasing to a major revisionary wave by the 1960's, has been a trend that has challenged some of the basic principles and sought to expand others. The tide of new thought has not constituted a total rejection of traditional theory. It has challenged some of the basic tenets of the school, but primarily it has evidenced the disenchantment with the direction in which the classical school is leading management theory and practice. Few would scrap or completely reject the contributions of the traditionalists. Generally it is acknowledged that management theory and practice are indebted to the process school for the initial giant strides already made in management as a discipline. The question now is more what modifications are needed to provide an improved base for the future development of management thought. The major limitations of the process approach are:

1. Many of the early concepts of the school were based on reason or logic and thus deductive in nature. They are not based on concepts verified through empirical research. Therefore, traditional principles are often considered more as truisms than principles.

2. The principles of the school are broad and general. Therefore, they are difficult to apply in a meaningful fashion by practitioners. As one writer stated, "a principle broad enough to cover all types of situations is necessarily so broad as to tell us little we did not know before."[17]

3. Closely related is the charge that traditional theory overemphasizes the universalism concept. The universalism postulate of traditional theory is based upon two assumptions. One is that management is the same process in all organizations and is composed of planning, organizing, staffing, directing, and controlling functions. The second is that management theory is equally applicable to business firms, social groups, governmental organizations, and any other activity involving joint human endeavor. The second assumption is much more tenous. The criticism as expressed by one writer is that "propositions which hold for such diverse phenomena as an army, a trade union, and a university must necessarily be either trivial or so abstract as to tell hardly anything of interest about concrete reality."[18] Supervisors managing different activities face different situations that call for the selection of concepts appropriate to that situation, not the reliance on principles to be applied universally.

4. Traditional management tends to concentrate on internally managing an organization under conditions assumed to be relatively static, rather than viewing an organization as a dynamic entity that requires skillful leadership to adapt to external organizations and forces. This internal focus has tended to be too devoted to structure (static in nature) instead of processes (dynamic in nature).

5. Basically the charge is that traditional theory has been too simplified. It was previously stated that people were left out of the early theories of the traditionalists. It was too mechanistic in viewing man in economic terms and ignoring behavioral influences such as informal organization, motivation, and supervisor-subordinate relations. Also, it emphasized the commonalities rather than the differences in situations. The logical consistency of traditional thought often glossed over the reality of complex situations.

THE BEHAVIORAL SCHOOL

The behavioral school of management was initially referred to as the *human relations,* or the *neoclassical* school. The reasons for it being called the former are self-explanatory; it was called the neoclassical school because it was initially a reaction to the shortcomings of the classical (or traditional) approaches of early management. It thus constitutes a revised, classical approach with more emphasis on human factors. This dimension of management thought became recognized in the 1920's, when the Hawthorne studies by Elton Mayo and associates were undertaken.

The Hawthorne Studies

In studies sponsored in the early 1920's by the National Research Council, a group of scientists were attempting to determine how illumination affected productivity. Elton Mayo, a Harvard University psychologist, was asked to head a research group and participate in these efforts. Beginning in 1924 the team under Mayo started a series of studies at the Hawthorne Plant of Western Electric near Chicago that continued for almost a ten-year period. These seminal studies are a landmark in management and the behavioral sciences, and are still widely discussed and debated. They are known as either the Hawthorne or the Mayo studies. Many have said the Mayo group received undue credit, since several other researchers were involved, and the most widely used chronicle of the studies is one written by two other participants, Fritz Roethlisberger and William Dickson.[19]

The Hawthorne studies actually consist of four different, though interrelated, experiments conducted at the Hawthorne plant. The first of these were the illumination studies, followed by the relay-room experiments, then an interview program, and finally the bank-wiring room study.

THE ILLUMINATION STUDIES.   The illumination studies, following the assumptions of scientific management, were conducted to determine how illumination (a physical factor) would effect worker productivity. Using a typical research design, the scientists attempted to hold all factors constant but two. Their objective was to determine how the independent variable (illumination) would affect the dependent variable (productivity). Two groups of workers were established, one in which the illumination remained constant and one where illumination varied. The results of the study were surprising to the researchers. The productivity in both groups went up, even when the candlepower was reduced in the work area of the experimental group. Some factor or factors other than illumination were obviously affecting productivity.

RELAY-ROOM EXPERIMENTS.   In 1929 they extended their research through the relay-room experiments. These studies were also conducted based on the assumption that physical factors dominate a worker's productivity. In these studies the researchers manipulated many variables in the physical environment to determine the effect on productivity of six female employees assembling telephones. These employees were entirely segregated from the rest of the plant in their work in order for the researchers to exert more control over the experiment. The workers had no regular supervisor, being subject only to the observation of the researchers. The physical factors manipulated during the experiments were the frequency and length of rest periods, the length of the working day, the temperature, and the method of payment in terms of a special group incentive. The results turned out similar to those of the first study. There appeared to be no strong correlation between any of these variables and productivity. Also, the productivity tended to constantly increase—even when they returned to conditions that existed at the beginning of the experiments.

INTERVIEW PROGRAM.   In the third phase of the study conducted between 1928 and 1930, it was decided to search for other variables through interviewing methods. Some 20,000 interviews were conducted. When the researchers switched to a nondirective interviewing technique, they came to conclude that the "soldiering" that Taylor had referred to was a productivity norm established and enforced by the informal group. Productivity was not regulated by the physical capacity of individuals *but by the informal group's concept of a "fair day's work."* The "fair day's work" norm involved a floor as well as a ceiling on output.

BANK-WIRING ROOM.   To verify the conclusion arrived at through inter-viewing, a final experiment known as the bank-wiring room study was conducted. In order to observe the informal group, fourteen operators, accompanied by their regular supervisor, were placed in a separate room where they performed their work assembling terminal banks for tele-phone exchanges. Under these circumstances, productivity did not in-crease as it did in the other experiments. The observers concluded that a strong informal group existed. Output was limited in accordance with what the group considered to be a "proper" day's work. The group used social ostracism as a means of getting individuals to comply with their work standards.

THE SIGNIFICANCE OF THE HAWTHORNE STUDIES.   The conclusions of the Hawthorne studies, even though often criticized because of the experi-mental design, provided the central thesis of the behavioral school of management. Productivity of the worker is not controlled by physical factors but is more strongly affected by psychological considerations. Motivating a person to be productive is not simply a matter of providing economic rewards but is also psychological in nature.

Mayo was personally convinced that group relationships were dom-inant. Establishing small compatible social groups where people are ac-cepted was considered the key to favorable work relationships and productivity. From the studies it was also apparent that when the em-ployees were given more freedom in the work situation and not subjected to directive supervision, they were more productive. The employees in the experimental groups were more satisfied with their jobs and had reduced absenteeism. (Also, they enjoyed being the center of attention.) Less strict supervision, higher recognition, and informal group ties re-lating to the concept of a fair day's work were much more influential in productivity than any physical factors involved in the experiments. Whatever the outcome, the one thing the Hawthorne Studies did accom-plish was to draw national and even international attention to human problems in organizations.

THE AFTERMATH OF THE HAWTHORNE STUDIES.   Both Taylor and Mayo were fortunate in their timing. Taylor was preaching the virtues of scien-tific management when the United States was rising to world power, boosted by its tremendous productive capacity. Mayo completed his Hawthorne studies in the 1930's, when there was a major shift in public attitudes, favoring labor and industrial humanism, as evidenced by the National Labor Relations Act of 1935.

During the late 1930's, interest in human relations in business orga-nizations rose, but the real explosion was to occur after World War II. In the late 1940's and the decade of the 1950's, business problems were seen more as people problems. The complex nature of man in organizations came under broad analysis. Up to that time, many academic disciplines refused to deal with the practical, applied, profit-oriented problems of business organizations. However, with many fields of study (such as the behavioral sciences), one of the main thrusts became oriented toward industrial problems. What was once a smattering of isolated studies became broad fields of concentration for an army of researchers. The rather sterile functions of the traditional school of management became examined in terms of the vagaries of the focal element in organizations—people. Management became popularly defined as "getting work accomplished through others," and chapters on motivation, leadership styles, informal groups, job enlargement, communication, conflict, and change began creeping into management textbooks.

By 1960 the behavioral school had almost taken over the field of management, but it was still common to present behavioral considerations in the traditional framework of Fayol. Management continued to be considered as the supervisory tasks of planning, organizing, staffing, directing, and controlling, but it was the behavioral aspects of these functions that received the most consideration. Since the establishment of the discipline of management by practitioners in the early 1900's, unquestionably the single most important influence on the discipline to date has been the behavioral sciences. (Recent developments of the behavioral sciences will be explored later in this text.)

QUANTITATIVE APPROACHES

The other major influence on management thought has been the quantitative approaches represented by contributions from mathematics, statistics, engineering, and other related fields. The emphasis on scientific analysis and investigation in management study was generated by Frederick Taylor at the turn of the century, but other than the time and motion studies associated with physical tasks, it lay essentially dormant until World War II.

During the war many problems existed with the optimum use of scarce resources to handle battle and supply conditions. Great Britain faced the problem of using limited fighter aircraft and antiaircraft defenses to protect itself during the heavy German air raids. Later, when the second front opened in Europe, the problem was to maximize the effectiveness of military supply lines. The United States used quantitative techniques in mining Japanese harbors and conducting submarine warfare. The term *operations research* (O.R.) came out of the war and signified all of the concepts used. If the words are considered in reverse order, the proper connotation is developed: operations research involves the application of *research* principles (or the scientific method) to *operational* problems.

The same emphasis on scientific investigation displayed by Taylor typified the movement, but forty years later more sophisticated tools were available. Application of linear equations, probability and game theories, and a host of statistical techniques to operational problems was now possible because of advances in these fields. (Chapters 6 and 7 explore the concepts in considerable detail.)

Methodology of Operations Research

The methodology of O.R. is similar to that of the physical sciences. Once a problem is identified, a model simulating the situation is developed. The model represents a simplification of reality in that it contains fewer variables, and this simplification enhances the feasibility of manipulating them. Once the model is established the variables are quantified and alternatives to the problem can be considered. O.R., or management science, is, in essence, an attempt to provide more exact methods of decision making through quantitatively evaluating decision models. It attempts to replace verbal, descriptive analyses of problems with models, symbols, and quantification. Management science places essentially its entire focus on decision making. In fact, some O.R. experts define management as being synonymous with decision making.

The Influence of Operations Research

O.R. concepts moved ahead rapidly, as evidenced by the formation of the Operations Research Society of America in 1952 and the Institute of Management Science in 1953. Here again, certain simultaneous, propitious events made this advancement possible. The most important of these was the computer and electronic data processing. In the late 1940's the computer was applied to business problems introducing a means of processing thousands of calculations quickly and inexpensively.

But management science has not yet become a force equivalent to that of the human relations movement. All managers experience human relations problems, so behavioral concepts have immediate application. However, few managers in the 1950's had mathematical backgrounds sufficient to cope with the quantitative techniques of O.R. Naturally, managers were reluctant to put their confidence in a decision when they did not understand the basis for arriving at it. Also, granted that almost every major decision a manager faces has human factors involved, it is these same human factors that will not readily submit to model building and quantification. Accordingly, operations research experienced rapid development primarily in relation to production problems, where non-human resources were involved, or in finance problems, when the variables could be converted to the common denominator of dollars. To date, management science has assisted managers in making far fewer decisions than have the contributions of the behavioral sciences.

Evaluating the Impact of Operations Research

The management science impact was felt more strongly during the 1960's. Business schools started teaching quantitative methods, and business students who were normally saddled only with accounting in the quantitative area were now required to take a series of courses in mathematics and statistics. Most major corporations set up operations-research groups as a staff unit to study and research business problems. Management science became the third major force in management theory, along with the behavioral sciences and the original traditional school. Currently it has had the least impact of the three, but then it also was the latest to arrive on the scene. Since it is considered to have the soundest scientific base, many writers predict that at some date in the future it will predominate, as management moves more in the direction of becoming a science.*

MANAGEMENT THOUGHT IN THE 1960's

By 1960 management theory consisted of a blend of these three influences: traditional thought, based on functions, provided the basic framework; behavioral sciences made man, interpersonal relations, and group dynamics the central issues in relation to each of these functions; and, somewhat belatedly, the quantitative tools of management science provided an emphasis on precision, scientific approaches, and eliminating intuition from decision making. However, a *general* theory of management still did not exist. There was no generally accepted body of knowledge that all management theorists agreed constituted the field of management. Each of the three schools emphasized its domain and was quick to point out the limitations of the other approaches. In Harold Koontz's well-known article[20], he pointed out this dilemma and called for an end of the "management-theory jungle."

---

*Many would object to considering management science as a *school* of management. With sound reasoning they argue that it consists of a set of tools which are available to the manager. It does not provide a framework for visualizing management other than the fairly narrow perspective of decision theory. Quite rightly it should be considered a thrust within the field of management rather than a separate alternative to the other approaches.

General Systems Theory

Two developments in the 1960's gave some promise of providing further integration and an improved framework for the study of management. One of these was the application of general systems theory to management theory. (Chapter 4 will explore systems theory and management.) In essence, systems theory emphasizes the importance of whole units, the relationship of the parts, or components, to this whole, and the relationship of the system to different systems or wholes. For example, a flashlight can be looked at and studied as a system, made up of different parts or subsystems or components (a bulb, dry cells, a casing, and so on). By the same token, the cells or bulb can also be studied as systems. Elements of this theory have existed as basic elements of many general philosophies, including epistemology (the study of knowledge itself). However, in the 1950's, systems theory was revived and expanded as a way of thinking and a method of structuring the knowledge about any topic or discipline. In the early 1950's the biologist Ludwig von Bertalanffy[21] and economist Kenneth Boulding[22] provided this renewed interest in systems theory, which brought it to the attention of theorists in many disciplines. In an article, Boulding attempted to structure all knowledge of the universe into a hierarchy of systems. Engineering disciplines applied systems theory to their fields of knowledge in the 1950's. In the early 1960's, general systems theory swept into all of the social sciences, including that of management. By the 1970's, systems theory had made its niche within management, and most writers devoted attention to its concepts.

The value of systems theory to a field such as management is that it provides a framework for integrating much, if not all, of the knowledge of management thought. Systems theory is not merely a new segment or appendage of knowledge attached onto a discipline—it is a way of thinking or restructuring the existing knowledge of a discipline. Thus it provides the potential for redirecting and resynthesizing management thought. Its influence is still too recent to accurately assess, but its value has obviously extended beyond that of a temporary fad.

CONTINGENCY APPROACHES TO MANAGEMENT

An even later influence on management thought has been the *contingency,* or situational, approach that developed in the latter part of the 1960's and is the approach used in this text. It evolved as a reaction to the limitations found in the universalism and principles doctrines of traditional management. Mary Parker Follett, a social worker and philosopher, recognized in the 1920's the "law of the situation." She noted that "there are different types of leadership" and that "different situations require different kinds of knowledge, and the man possessing the knowledge demanded by a certain situation tends in the best managed businesses, other things being equal, to become the leader of the moment."[23]

Miss Follett was far ahead of her time, but the same theme was picked up soon after World War II by other researchers on leadership. The traitist approach dominated leadership studies before 1945. These studies were directed at finding the universal set of traits that constituted leadership. By 1948, however, Ralph Stogdill[24], after reviewing leadership studies, concluded that the traits and skills required in leadership are determined to a large extent by the situation in which an individual is exercising this leadership. Since that time the situational explanation of leadership has been one of the most common theories. However surprising, this same theory was not broadened to encompass functions of management other than leadership until the 1960's. And little research was done to determine the primary variables in a situation that affect the success of different leadership styles.

In the 1960's the search began for a construct to integrate the three management schools. Coupled with this was a search for a construct that was an advance over the general approaches represented by traditional management. The field of management, including all support disciplines, had advanced to the point where it was now possible to cope with the complexity of multivariate analysis of causal factors in different situations.

Fred Fiedler, an organizational psychologist, demonstrated in his studies on leadership in 1967[25] that a contingency approach to leadership, emphasizing the factors that make it effective or not, was superior to the generalized approaches of the past. (In later chapters studies by Paul Lawrence and Jay Lorsch, Joan Woodward, James D. Thompson, and many others, expanding contingency theory to organization structure, the environment, and other factors, will be reviewed.)

Contingency View of the Management Process

The key to effective supervision in traditional management is to learn the principles of management associated with the five functions of planning, organizing, staffing, directing, and controlling. The science of management is considered to be this body of knowledge covering supervision. Applying these principles is considered the art of management and is learned through experience, since no specialized body of knowledge relating to application exists. The contingency approach to management challenges this latter assumption. It replaces it with a four-step methodology that extends the science of management into the gray area of application. The steps underlying contingency methodology are as follow:

1. To be effective a manager needs to be familiar with the various management concepts, tools, and techniques that are available to him. The manager's bag of tools consists of organization concepts, planning systems, operations-research techniques, and other similar "principles."

2. The manager needs to be knowledgeable of the advantages and disadvantages (trade-offs) that occur with the use of any particular concept or technique. The need is not just to know the existence of a management tool, but to be able to predict what will result—both favorably and unfavorably—from its application.

3. The manager needs to be able to decipher the situation he is facing. If he can map a situation so that he properly interprets the variables that are primary in that particular instance, he is in a position to determine which concepts or techniques will be effective. Application of management concepts does not have to be a hit-or-miss, intuitive guess. Situational variables can be classified and analyzed just like any other phenomena or set of related data.

4. The final step in contingency methodology is to match particular concepts or techniques with the needs of specific situations resulting in successful management.

The contingency approach to management, being the most recent on the horizon of management theory, is still lacking comprehensive, proven guidelines covering all classes of situations relating to step three of the methodology. Steps one and two have been the primary contributions of traditional, behavioral, and O.R. schools to date. Step four cannot be successfully accomplished without an understanding of step three, which places an even greater priority on developing a theoretical framework and body of knowledge to accommodate this phase of contingency analysis. (Chapter 3 addresses itself to such a framework.)

SUMMARY

Management theory has evolved based on three influences: classical management from practitioners, behavioral approaches, and quantitative methods. Initially practitioners such as Fayol and Taylor identified what they considered to be the responsibilities and functions of management. The theories of the early writers took many different forms, depending on their viewpoint. By the 1940's it was generally accepted that management consisted of a process involving planning, organizing, staffing, directing, and controlling. These were considered to be common to all organizations, and the future development of management as a science depended on the establishment of supporting universal principles.

Beginning in the late 1920's, the behavioral school of management, emphasizing the human aspects of administration, came into existence. This school grew in importance until, following World War II, it came to dominate management theory. In the 1940's another major dimension evolved through the contributions of the quantitative sciences. This management science, or operations-research approach, has provided many useful tools that can be applied primarily to nonhuman resource problems. These three influences constitute the bulk of management thought, but their supporters often disagree over fundamentals, and their theory is not integrated into one common body of knowledge.

In the past fifteen years, two broad relationships-oriented approaches have developed: the systems and the contingency theories of management. Both have not only added to our understanding of management theory and practice, but they offer a broad framework and methodology that give promise of eventually unifying and integrating management thought.

In this brief summary of the theoretical approaches to management, it is impossible to do justice to all those who have contributed to the development of management as a discipline. To ignore individuals such as Barnard,[26] Drucker,[27] and Simon[28] is indeed to shortchange the reader. However, our concern has been with the central themes that constitute these movements, not the contributions of individuals.

QUESTIONS FOR STUDY AND DISCUSSION

1. Why is management called an eclectic discipline?
2. What are the primary streams of thought that consitute management?
3. Why is the process school of management also called the traditional school? The operational school? The productivity school?
4. What contributions have practitioners made to management theory?
5. What management skills and knowledge existed at the time of the rise of the factory system?
6. What were Frederick Taylor's contributions to management?
7. Why is Fayol called the father of management? How did he define management? How valid are his principles of management?
8. What are the major criticisms of the classical school of management?
9. How did the behavioral school develop?
10. Why were the results of the Hawthorne studies surprising?
11. How did operations research originate?

12. Compare the behavioral sciences and the quantitative sciences in terms of their impact on management.
13. Should operations research be considered a separate school of management? Support your view.
14. What is a *general* theory of management? Why don't we have a general theory?
15. What improvements are offered by the systems theory?
16. What is the contingency theory of management?
17. Does contingency theory represent a rejection of the traditional school? Why?

Case Study:
SLATE BROTHERS PAINT COMPANY

The Slate Brothers Paint Company was formed in 1920. It was started by two brothers who gradually expanded the operations until by 1930 there were 65 employees with annual sales of over $1 million. The depression years saw little growth, but following the war the company was involved in a major successful expansion program. By 1960 when the two owners retired, sales exceeded $12 million annually. Upon retirement the owners turned the business over to their five children, three by one owner and two by the other. Initially the business went well, but by the 1970's there was considerable dissention among the five owners and also productivity problems within the plant. Many of the problems related to efficiency measures and the budget system. Within the past two or three years, some departments had exceeded their budgets by 25 percent. The company was also having trouble keeping up a favorable profit picture. Profits as a percentage of sales had actually decreased over the past three years.

To overcome the problem, a team of consultants recommended that lower-level supervisors be more involved in the budget process. Accordingly three years ago they followed this suggestion. However, the budget soon became a source of contention. Lower-level managers, not trusting management, tended to overstate their estimates, knowing that they would be cut in top-level reviews. Bargaining, gamesmanship, and politicking featured the process. Reports and figures were often distorted, and the company continued to experience low-profit returns.

How would Frederick Taylor, Henri Fayol, Elton Mayo, and current operations-research analysts view this case differently? What features would each emphasize? How would they solve the problem?
Does contingency theory add anything to the anaysis of this case? Does systems theory? Explain.

Case Study:
JIM PRESTON

Jim Preston is an accountant with a major public accounting firm. He is 38, married, and has two children. His typical daily routine is as follows: He gets up at 6:30 A.M. and has breakfast with his wife before the children arise. While the children are eating, he is getting ready to leave for work. He leaves with his carpool at 7:20 each morning and gets into the office at approximately 8:00. He performs audit work, so he travels frequently to different clients to audit their accounting records. He is known as an efficient employee and has a good record of advancement. He is frequently assigned to jobs with two other employees, Dan Carlson and Mike Isom. He belongs to a bowling league and to a social club, which takes him away two evenings during the week. He also is on the board of a local church.

How many different organizations is Jim identified with in the example given?

Which of these organizations would Frederick Taylor be concerned with? Henri Fayol? Elton Mayo? What operating aspects of the organizations would each be concerned with? How would they view the organizations differently?

Would the various management functions (planning, organization, staffing, directing, and controlling) be involved in each organization? Would these functions be the same in each? Would the application of concepts be the same?

Footnotes

1. Adam Smith, *The Wealth of Nations* (New York: Modern Library, originally published in 1776).
2. Charles Babbage, *On the Economy of Machinery and Manufactures* (London: Charles Knight, 1832).
3. Frederick Winslow Taylor, *The Principles of Scientific Management* (New York: Harper & Brothers Publishers, 1916), p. 7.
4. *Ibid.,* p. 25.
5. H. S. Dennison, *Organization Engineering* (New York: McGraw-Hill Book Company, 1931).
6. J. D. Mooney and A. C. Reiley, *Onward Industry!* (New York: Harper & Brothers, 1931). With some modifications appeared as *The Principles of Organization* (New York: Harper & Brothers, 1939).
7. L. Gulick and L. Urwick (eds.), *Papers on the Science of Administration* (New York: Institute of Public Administration, 1937).

8. Alvin Brown, *Organization of Industry* (Englewood Cliffs, New Jersey: Prentice-Hall, Inc., 1947).

9. Oliver Sheldon. *The Philosophy of Management* (London: Sir Isaac Pitman & Sons, Ltd., 1923).

10. See footnote 7.

11. Henri Fayol, *General and Industrial Management* (London: Sir Isaac Pitman & Sons. Ltd., 1949), pp. 5–6.

12. *Ibid.,* p. xv.

13. See Harold Koontz and Cyril O'Donnell *Principles of Management* (New York: McGraw-Hill Book Company, 1955). Also George R. Terry, *Principles of Management* (Homewood, Illinois: Richard D. Irwin, Inc., 1953).

14. Fayol, *op. cit.,* p. 42.

15. *Ibid.,* p. 19.

16. Herbert Simon, *Administrative Behavior* (New York: The Macmillan Company, 1947), p. 240.

17. Ernest Dale, "Some Foundations of Organization Theory," *California Management Review,* Fall 1959, p. 84.

18. Renate Mayntz, "The Study of Organizations: A Trend Report and Bibliography, *Current Sociology,* Vol. XII, 1965, p. 113.

19. Fritz J. Roethlisberger and William J. Dickson, *Management and the Worker,* (Cambridge, Mass.: Harvard University Press, 1939).

20. Harold Koontz, "The Management Theory Jungle," *Academy of Management Journal,* December, 1961, pp. 174–188.

21. Ludwig von Bertalanffy, "The Theory of Open Systems in Physics and Biology," *Science,* Vol. III, 1950, pp. 23–29.

22. Kenneth Boulding, "General Systems Theory—The Skeleton of Science," *Management Science,* April, 1956, pp. 197–208.

23. Henry C. Metcalf and L. Urwick, (eds.), *Dynamic Administration, The Collected Papers of Mary Parker Follett* (London: Harper & Brothers Publishers, 1942), p. 277.

24. Ralph M. Stogdill, "Personal Factors Associated with Leadership, A Survey of Literature," *Journal of Psychology,* January, 1948, p. 63.

25. Fred E. Fiedler, *A Theory of Leadership Effectiveness* (New York: McGraw-Hill Book Company, 1967).

26. Chester I. Barnard, an executive of Bell Telephone Company wrote an outstanding book viewing management and organization as a social system. See *The Functions of the Executive* (Cambridge, Mass: Harvard University Press, 1938).

27. Peter F. Drucker has been a prolific writer who has an unusual capability to view management in broad macro terms. His most famous work is *The Practice of Management* (New York: Harper & Row, Publishers, Inc., 1954).

28. Herbert A. Simon has also been a prolific researcher whose knowledge sweeps across several fields. His initial work of importance was *Administrative Behavior* (New York: The Macmillan Company, 1947), although he has written many important works on organization theory and decision theory since that time.

PART II

Management Using a Contingency Framework

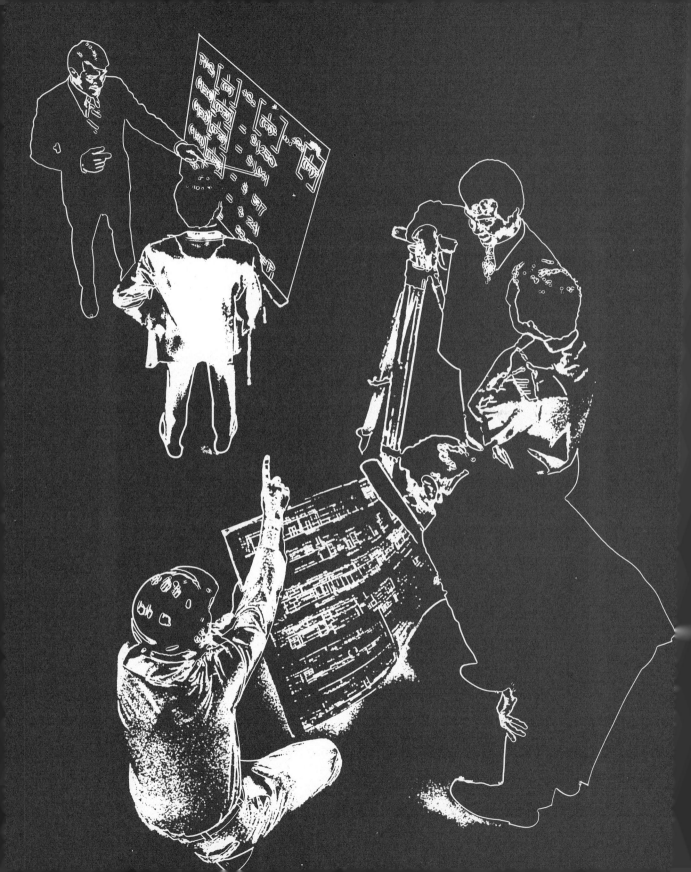

3

Management:
A Contingency Model*

Is the application of management concepts similar in all organizations?

Of the many variables that exist in management situations, which tend to be dominant?

How can a manager identify and evaluate the variables in a situation?

Can a common model be established incorporating these variables?

Should factors external to the organization be included in the model?

Can a framework for decision making be established based on contingency theory?

*The original basic model contained in this chapter was initially presented by the author in *Situational Management: A Contingency Approach to Leadership,* (New York: American Management Associations, 1973). Used by permission.

IDENTIFYING SITUATIONAL VARIABLES

Management based on a contingency approach is concerned with the differences and commonalities in organizations and situations. As an illustration of some of these factors, three different organizations, representing a retail outlet, a research laboratory, and a production plant will be examined. A summary of the differences is contained in table 3-1.

Retail Drugstore.   The store is situated in a new shopping center located in the suburbs of a community of over 200,000 people. It is a single proprietorship and there are fifteen full- and part-time employees. There is only one other drug store in the shopping center, and in the community there are over one hundred stores that compete in approximately the same product line.

Research Laboratory.   The Electrodynamics Laboratory is a research unit established under the College of Engineering of a major university. There are forty people employed in the laboratory: twenty are scientists, thirteen are engineering aids or part-time students, and seven are secretaries and administrative support. They are engaged in both pure and applied research, most of which is funded under contracts with the federal government.

Automotive Assembly Plant.   This assembly plant is operated by one of the "big three" automotive producers. Four thousand employees are engaged in the assembly of an economy-line car. No parts are fabricated at the plant, and it handles only final assembly operations. The plant is unionized and is located in a metropolitan area of over one million people.

Major Differences in the Three Organizations

Many of the differences among the organizations are readily apparent. Their size varies, the products are distinct, the skills of the work force are generally different, and the technical activities central to the functioning of each organization are dissimilar. However, these differences have little meaning in management if they do not influence decision making or the management process. The basic question is what implications these differences have for a manager in handling his planning, organizing, staffing, directing, and control functions. In these three organizations it would be possible to identify hundreds of differences, but only the few that tend to be dominant will be enumerated.

Table 3-1 Functional Differences in Three Organizations

	Drugstore	Research Laboratory	Assembly Plant
Planning and Control:			
Complexity of planning systems	minimal	general	elaborate
Nature of control system	informal	general	detailed
Specialized planning and control staff	none	limited	many
Uncertainty of planning	varies	uncertain	quite certain
Organizing:			
Formalization of structure	unwritten	limited	detailed
Centralization of authority	centralized	decentralized	centralized
Dominant organization feature	selling	research	production
Stability of structure	stable	unstable	stable
Levels in hierarchy	few	few	many
Staffing:			
Specialization of staff	limited	extensive	extensive
Skill required in basic operations	limited	extensive	limited
Performance evaluation	informal	mixed	formal
Directing:			
Supervisory control	centralized	decentralized	centralized
Independence for individual	limited	considerable	limited
Communication channels	few	few	many
Problems in motivation	varies	few	many

DIFFERENCES RELATING TO PLANNING AND CONTROL

Drugstore: Planning and control systems are typically limited and handled on primarily an informal basis. The manager or owner will perform most planning. Formal control will relate to minimal measures such as profit, cash flow, time cards, daily sales, and so on. There will be no specialized staff to collect and analyze data. Control will be maintained through personal interaction with the employees.

Research Laboratory: Some formalized planning and control systems will be maintained to meet the requirements of the contractor (federal government) and the university. A high degree of flexibility will exist internally within the laboratory. The uncertainties associated with research will make planning difficult, with reliance on techniques based on estimating and tracking cost, schedule, and technical performance. Lack of relevant historical experience will make any estimates of limited reliability.

Assembly Plant: Planning and control systems will be specific and detailed. The "knowns" of routine production will make cost, time, and performance estimates extremely reliable. Sophisticated cost and budget systems will be used. Output and productivity measurements will exist for each unit—enhancing effective control. Production planning to regulate the flow of the assembly line will be detailed and accurate.

DIFFERENCES RELATING TO ORGANIZING

Drugstore: Being small in size, the organization structure will most likely be much less formal. Job descriptions and written procedures will be few in number. In a single proprietorship with one store manager, authority will tend to be centralized. The organization will not have staff experts and will be relatively static in structure. The dominant function leading to success will be marketing or selling activities.

Research Laboratory: The small size of this unit will also contribute to informality, as will the open atmosphere normally found in a university. It will most likely be organized on a project basis, with considerable authority delegated to the project leader. The organization will be dynamic—resulting from the problem-solving nature of research activity, the instability of government contracting, and rapid scientific advance. The dominant function involving success will be capability in research.

Assembly Plant: The organization of the automotive assembly plant will be much more formalized and centralized. Detailed job descriptions, rules, and procedures will exist. There will be many levels in the organizational hierarchy, a well-defined chain of command, and large staff groups. The dominant function in this organization will be production.

DIFFERENCES RELATING TO STAFFING

Drugstore: With the limited work force and relatively few tasks to be performed, there will be little specialization. The relatively low-skill level of selling activities will minimize the need for training and for personnel with extensive experience or education. Performance evaluation techniques will surely be informal.

Research Laboratory: More complex research tasks will require people with specific education and training. Matching jobs and skills of individuals will be more difficult. Performance evaluation will be somewhat formalized, with greater reliance on peer evaluation.

Assembly Plant: The basic operations will require semiskilled employees. The size of the plant will necessitate considerable staff support, resulting in a variety of jobs. Performance evaluation will be highly formalized and handled by supervision.

DIFFERENCES RELATING TO DIRECTING

Drugstore: Under a centralized organization, it can be assumed that the manager will retain all authority to make managerial decisions. The owner-manager will likely be profit oriented and concerned with using his help efficiently. Due to the small size of the organization, communicating with employees will be relatively easy. Motivation procedures will vary, but it will often be difficult, because the tasks performed by subordinates are not necessarily very stimulating.

Research Laboratory: The professional scientists will be given a comparatively free rein in what they do. An open, creative atmosphere will likely exist. Motivation will be high because of the challenging, stimulating nature of the projects. Communication will be effective internally among the scientists, but difficult with outside groups unfamiliar with the scientific tasks. There will be little pressure from management.

Assembly Plant: The assembly tasks requiring integration of men and machines will emphasize conformity and coordination. Leadership styles will be directive and pressure oriented. The routine, physical nature of the work will tend to make task performance of secondary interest to the worker and not intrinsically motivational. Communication will be difficult because of the many employees, the long chain of command, and the diverse work groups. Strong informal groups will exist.

SITUATIONAL VARIABLES
AND A CONTINGENCY MODEL

Even though only a few of the more obvious differences among these three organizations are emphasized, the reader will probably still have had experiences or be familiar with situations that are not consistent with the generalizations made. Perhaps in a research laboratory the project leader is extremely autocratic, or in a small retail organization the owner is permissive with his employees. This again verifies the contingency nature of managing organizations. Even limited generalizations may be misleading. Each situation should be analyzed based on the blend of the status of the key variables involved. Small organizations with unskilled employees may tend to call for a directive leader, but if the manager is committed to a permissive leadership style, this variable naturally will predominate.

From a broad perspective, there are some common generalizations that can be made about the management of the three organizations. Even though the goals of the organizations are different, the supervisors have the common responsibility for achieving them. Also, as supervisors they are all engaged in the management functions of planning, organizing, staffing, directing, and controlling. They also perceive their role as being responsible for allocating and using resources in an efficient manner. The *process* is common, but the *means* the manager or organization uses to achieve its goals or attain efficiency is different. Even though all managers make decisions and perform management functions, the specific decisions they make and the concepts and techniques they use are dependent on variables peculiar to their situation.

Variables Common to Most Organizations

Certain variables stand out as being significant in essentially every management situation. If one were to attempt to account for the differences in the three organizations presented in the example, it would be possible to attribute the primary differences to less than a dozen factors. It is these factors that a manager needs to be concerned with, and which therefore are the factors constituting the basic contingency model as a framework for analyzing management. In our particular model, nine variables are involved, five internal and four external to the firm.

INTERNAL VARIABLES   The five factors comprising the internal contingency variables of organizations are as follows:

- The *purpose* of the organization

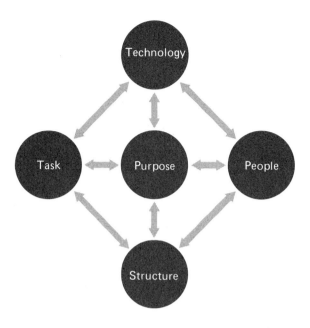

Fig. 3-1. Situational variables internal to the organization

- The *tasks* involved in performing the operations required to attain the purpose of the organization
- The technical content or *technology* of the tasks and operations
- The nature of the *people* who perform the tasks.
- The *structure* of the organization.

Figure 3-1 is a schematic presentation of these variables.[1] Central to everything taking place in an organization is the purpose for which it exists. Thus the basic purpose of the organization is shown in the center of the figure. The interdependent variables that are primary to accomplishing the purpose and goals of the organization are the people in the organization, the tasks they are engaged in, the technology of these tasks (including tools they use), and the organizational structure that facilitates and regulates their actions.

EXTERNAL VARIABLES: An organization's existence and effectiveness depend on its ability to adjust to external conditions or forces. A firm may have efficient internal operations, but if a competitor is more efficient and can undersell the firm in the marketplace, it will fail in attempting to accomplish its profit objectives. External variables can be summarized into four major categories:

> Time and again, managers who are outstandingly successful in one situation perform abysmally in another. Administrators, guided by the good results of, say, sharing responsibility with a group of subordinates are frustrated by their failure to replicate those results with another group of associates. What is lacking is a way of making the specifics of each situation reveal the clues upon which appropriate management action can be based. It is not enough to deduce from "currently useful generalizations" what will work. An inductive search for the meaning behind existing behavior is a prerequisite. But the inductive process needs a methodology, some kind of structure which is relevant to any type of organizational setting, yet practical and tangible enough to put into everyday use.

Quotation from John A. Seiler, *Systems Analysis in Organizational Behavior.* (Homewood, Illinois: Richard D. Irwin, Inc., 1967), p. x.

- *Political* and *legal* forces and institutions
- *Technological* forces and institutions
- *Sociocultural* forces and institutions
- *Economic* forces and institutions

Each of these is made up of many organizations and activities, and together they constitute the basic forces that are at work in any society or marketplace. They underlie the trends that dominate an era and are the forces that require organizations to assume adaptive modes in their operations. The significance of external variables is determined by the level in the organization at which a decision is made. A first-line supervisor, because of his scope of responsibility, is not as concerned with external factors as the chief executive officer, but he is concerned with the impact of his decision on higher-level internal organizational units.

The Comprehensive Contingency Paradigm

For our purposes the contingency model of management consists of these two sets of variables, constituting nine separate factors as reflected in figure 3-2.* The internal variables are represented in the inner circle (identified as the organization), and the four external variables are shown

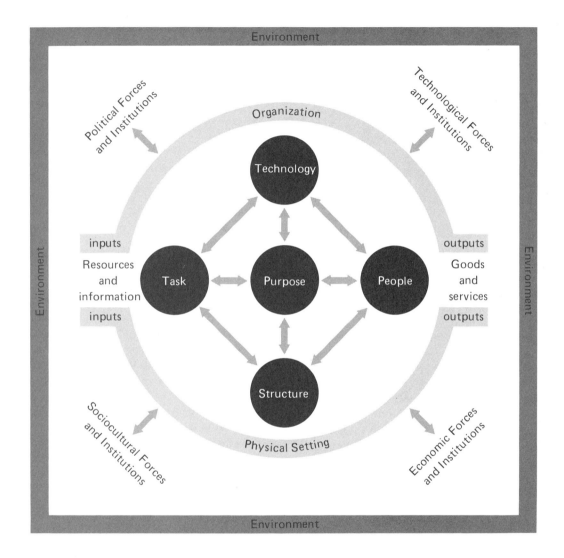

Fig. 3-2.　Internal and external variables in the contingency
model of a firm

---

*Figures 3-1 and 3-2 are adapted from *Situational Management,* Howard M. Carlisle. (New York: American Management Associations, 1973, pp. 20 and 29, respectively.)

outside it (constituting the environment). It will also be noted that the input-output model is shown with resources and information coming *from* the environment, with goods and services being provided *to* the environment. This model is specifically identified as one relating to a business firm. For a prison or school, the input would be people; the output would be changing behavior or providing skills. For a governmental agency, the primary input may be problems, which the agency attempts to resolve through enforcing regulations or some other activities. The varied purposes of organizations will be reflected in different outputs consistent with the purpose, and different outputs will often dictate the need for diverse inputs.

Two other features of the model should be noted. Organizational activities take place in a physical setting, and sometimes this physical setting can be a major variable in affecting organization functioning and the behavior of people. A plush office on Madison Avenue is a vastly different work environment than a tent for a field crew on a plateau in New Mexico. Laboring in a hot foundry is obviously different from working in an air-conditioned office. For these reasons, the physical setting is shown in figure 3-2 on the lower portion of the organization circle, even though the physical setting is only occasionally referred to in later chapters, since the implications tend to be obvious.

Another factor vital to organizations is the resources available for utilization or consumption. Devoting five percent of operating funds to advertising in a small firm will make it difficult to compete with a large company that uses five percent of *its* operating funds for the same purpose. Many small firms cannot take advantage of opportunities because funds are not available. Important as capital and the flow of funds are to an organization, they will receive limited attention here. (Financial management is a special field of study that is outside the scope of this text except for the budgeting and control section in Part VIII.)

One final point is important in relation to the model. Any graphic paradigm similar to figure 3-2 tends to reflect a static situation. However, organizations are dynamic processors that are constantly changing as a part of their adaption and transformation activities. Thus time is one of the most important elements in managing organizations. All activity takes place in a time frame. Perhaps the central variable in decision making is timing—relating to both the time available to make the decision and the timing of the decision in terms of when certain actions are planned to occur. The timing of a new product innovation is often as important as the innovation itself.

A final word of caution is appropriate. In some situations the enumerated variables may be of little significance. Making decisions regarding the redesign of a product may have little relationship to the people of the organization. On the other hand, weather (a variable not included in the model) will be one of the primary considerations for airlines, ski resorts, and construction firms. The significance of the variables will obviously vary with the situation.

Interdependent Relationships of the Variables

Before proceeding with an analysis of the variables, the interdependency assumptions involved in the contingency model need to be further highlighted. No variable exists in isolation, and variables cannot properly be comprehended if they are considered apart from the basic model. The contingency approach to management focuses on the interrelationships among variables. If a manager is to influence a situation, he needs to understand the forces at work. He will be more effective if he can modify the dominant controlling variables or if he can determine their influence before he takes some action, rather than merely reacting to a variety of conditions that represent little more than symptoms of underlying forces or problems.

Determining the relationship among variables is a complex undertaking, because their intensity and interdependency vary from situation to situation. In one instance a dominant personality (people variable) may be the most important factor in explaining the functioning of a work group. In another instance (a painter using a spray gun), the task and technology variables may be the most important factors in management and motivation.

Many questions arise in attempting to identify dependent and independent variables. The conditions of a dependent variable are determined by other variables. Independent variables are not reliant on other ones for their status or condition. When one variable influences another, the first is the independent one, the second dependent. Is motivation determined by the nature of tasks or by the interests and characteristics of people? In an electronics firm is structure determined by the nature of the tasks, the knowledge of top management, or external competitive pressures? Is the style of leadership determined by the knowledge, experience, and traits of the leader or by pressures evolving from the group? Are the management systems in a branch office selected because of task requirements, the whims of people, or the organization structure (dictated by home-office corporate procedures)? Clear answers are rarely available to questions such as these, but a manager will be better equipped to deal with reality and have more insight using this line of inquiry.

The relationship between variables is not only complicated because of multiple causation, but it is not necessarily consistent or linear. The relationship may change under certain conditions and be curvilinear or assume many different forms, which again cautions the analyst to carefully evaluate *all* of the conditions present in a situation.

ANALYSIS OF THE VARIABLES

In examining each variable in the contingency model of management, three factors become important. First, an analyst is concerned with the specific *features* or *attributes* of variables. When the same variable differs in two situations, it requires an analysis of the specific characteristics of each. The term *dimension* will be used to represent the specific features of variables. For instance, size is a feature (or dimension) of structure. In addition to knowing the dimensions of each variable, the other two concerns are the *relationship* between a variable and other primary ones, and the relative strength or *intensity* of each variable in a particular situation. The relationship among variables and the intensity of one particular variable can be evaluated only when all primary variables are considered together. This is the methodology to be followed in this chapter.

The Purpose Variable

The primary variable in organizational analysis is the purpose for which an organization is established—and the ends which the owners or membership of the organization currently seek through their participation in it. In a business firm, economic goals are predominant. The management of a company is measured by its ability to achieve these goals. The economic nature of the firm is the overriding consideration in planning, organizing, staffing, directing, and controlling. In a voluntary social organization, the leaders handle their management responsibilities in a considerably different fashion as a result of the unique nature of the group's purpose.

The basic institutional purpose of an organization has a deterministic effect on the other primary variables in the contingency model of management. Two examples will demonstrate this. A building contractor who owns and operates a construction firm is locked in to certain other variables. The nature of the firm dictates that individuals with skills and training in the construction trades will constitute the bulk of the work force. The nature of the tasks performed by the employees will involve the construction crafts consistent with the purpose of the organization. The leadership of the organization will be guided by criteria relating to keeping costs at a minimum and the efficient use of resources. Many of the dimensions of the other variables in the contingency model will be predetermined by the nature of the purpose of the organization.

The second example relates to government administration. In government, economic goals are normally secondary; social or political goals are primary. Resources and economic considerations serve more as constraints on what is done rather than as the purpose for the existence of the agency. The adoption center in a welfare department is concerned with locating adequate foster homes for children referred to the agency. The goals of the agency are essentially social, based on stringent value considerations. The basic tasks of the organization are determined by these goals, and the qualifications of the people employed by the agency are also established consistent with the goals. The technology involved relates to the level of knowledge about social work required to function in such a position. Accordingly, the basic purpose of the adoption center tends to determine the people, task, and technology variables of the organization.

The purpose of an organization is reflected in its goals. This again makes contingency analysis complex, because individuals and organizations have multiple goals. In the example of the construction firm, the owner could perhaps satisfy his economic goals more easily through selling the firm and investing the proceeds in some other endeavor. However, he likely obtains satisfaction from running his own business, being the executive officer of a company, and being responsible for constructing attractive or utilitarian buildings and structures. This would have to be at least partially sacrificed if he sells the company. In operating the business, he will also most likely have goals or values beyond those that are purely economic: he may be concerned with the esthetics of construction, the welfare of his employees, the effect of his construction activities on the environment, or other factors. Examples of different types of goals relating to institutional purpose are shown in table 3-2.*

The Task Variable

Tasks are the activities or assigned functions that people are engaged in when they belong to an organization. A *task is defined as an assigned piece of work to be finished within a certain time. An activity involves the tasks performed by people and the operations or processes performed by machines.*

Next to the purpose variable, task stands out as one of the most differentiating variables in organizations. Hospitals are basically different from retail department stores, because people are engaged in different tasks. The primary difference between the research and development, production, and accounting departments of an industrial firm are the tasks the individuals are engaged in.

TASK DIMENSIONS.   Figure 3-3 presents some of the common dimensions of the task variable. (These will be further expanded in chapter 12.) Traditionally, tasks have been differentiated into three categories, depending on whether they involve working with people, working with things (ma-

Table 3-2 Institutional Purpose

Common Dimensions	Means of Classification and Evaluation
Economic Goals	Traditional measures such as profit, return on investment, assets, liabilities
Social Goals	Provide particular services, attain specific need satisfaction, contribute to welfare of groups or individuals
Operational Goals	Achieve certain production levels, accomplish specific projects, handle certain maintenance functions
Utility Goals	Descriptive measures of benefits desired, efficiencies achieved, or satisfaction provided
Ethical Goals	Attainment of specific standards, achieving specific behavior, protection of a set of values
Political Goals	Power, control, modification of political institutions, regulation of specific activities
Ownership	Public, private, governmental

terials, machines, etc.), or working with information. The Bureau of Employment Security of the federal government has developed a *Dictionary of Occupational Titles* covering over 35,000 separate job titles based on these three dimensions.

Other important dimensions of tasks involve the repetition and time range of the job cycle. If an individual is tightening a torque wrench involving five different bolts as part of an assembly operation, he might repeat this task 25,000 times in one day. A sales clerk may make 100 sales during a day, and a research physicist may never repeat the same job cycle during eight hours. The boredom of the assembly line is associated with the repetitive continuity of the job cycle where little autonomy is permitted. Less-structured tasks, permitting a greater degree of independence are typically more challenging and interesting to individuals.

It will be noticed in figure 3-3 that most of the dimensions are shown as scales, with the low range represented on the left of the continuum and the high range on the right. This approach emphasizes the relative nature

*Table 3-2 is based on table 1, "Analysis of Organizational Purpose," contained in *Situational Management*, Howard M. Carlisle. (New York: American Management Associations, 1973, p. 22.)

Common Dimensions	Task Continuum	
People oriented		
	1 (low)	(high) 10
Things oriented		
	1 (low)	(high)10
Information (data oriented)		
	1 (low)	(high) 10
Repetition (job cycle)		
	1 (low)	(high) 10
Sequential interdependence		
	1 (little required)	(high) 10
Functional nature of task	Descriptive (no scales involved). Marketing, production, engineering, research, maintenance, education, regulation, health care, and so on.	

Fig. 3-3. Task variable

of variables in a situation. Perceiving the dimensions of variables, such as tasks, in this fashion is more realistic than perceiving them in black and white terms. Turning the torque wrench 25,000 times is obviously much more repetitive than making 100 sales during a day. The saleslady may consider her work to be extremely repetitive, but on a comparative basis this may not be the case.

Reflecting the dimensions as a scale is not based on the assumption that they can always be precisely measured or that there is a standard set of scales that interrelates all of the different dimensions of variables in the contingency model. Rather, it is based on the premise that there are significant relative differences in the attributes of variables. Precision is not implied, but relative status is. Using this technique, two situations can be compared by contrasting the status of different variables.

THE DETERMINISTIC NATURE OF TASKS.   Tasks constitute one of the strongest variables in a situation because they have a causal impact on other variables. The influence of tasks on the people variable can be clearly seen. Engineering tasks require people with engineering skills, whereas accounting tasks require employees with a background in accounting. The knowledge, training, and experience requirements of the people in an organization are a result of the complexity of the tasks they are hired to perform. Tasks are also the building blocks of structure. Most companies organize their subgroups around the tasks being performed. An oil refinery will be structured one way, given the tasks involved, while a hospital will be formally organized on a different basis.

The Technology Variable

There is a close relationship between task and technology variables. In many disciplines, such as sociology, little attempt is made to differentiate one from the other. However, when this practice is followed, it is easy to lose sight of the tremendous changes science and technology have generated in our society—including the management of organizations. Tasks involve the work-oriented activity in an organization, and *technology* is considered as the *scientific or mechanical content of tasks and operations*. Technology is one of the important features of a task or a series of tasks, but the influence of technology is sufficiently pervasive and deterministic to require separate identification.

Technology is not only found in the knowledge required to perform certain tasks, but it is also existent in tools, techniques, and machine processes. All of these extend human capability, which is the key to establishing the relative nature of technology. Tools or techniques that greatly extend human capability, such as a computer, are considered to be of high technology. As a tool a shovel has low technology. A physicist using a multimillion dollar ion accelerator involves a high technology level; a mechanic using a screw driver represents a lower one.

A few of the important dimensions of technology are shown in figure 3-4. (These are amplified in chapter 12.) Technology dimensions involve the scientific content of methodologies, operations, and machinery. In manufacturing, the simplest form of technology is considered to be *unit* production. The middle ground is producing items on a *batch* (or group) basis, and the highest level is represented by automation (or *continuous*) production.

Technology has a strong influence on the other internal variables of a firm. If there is a high scientific content in the tasks being performed, individuals with considerable education, training, and knowledge relating to these tasks are required. This results in an organization structure that is largely staffed by professionals. This, in turn, affects leadership types, decentralization, and other dimensions of the structure and people variables.

The deterministic influence of technology on other variables can be demonstrated through a change cycle that occasionally disrupts a company.

Common Dimensions	Technology Continuum
Sophistication of methods	
	1 (low) (high) 10
Knowledge	
	1 (low) (high) 10
Complexity of machinery	
	1 (low) (high) 10
Methodology and function	Describe the types involved, such as production (unit, batch, continuous process), research (basic, applied), etc.

Fig. 3-4. Technology variable

If a firm decides to automate its warehousing operations, it completely changes the skills required of its employees. Material handlers are replaced by maintenance personnel who are employed to monitor the automated equipment and by analysts who are trained to keep track of inventory levels through scanning computer printouts. These changes will also have an influence on worker morale because of the feelings of insecurity and social dislocation that are generated. Advancing technology can create upheaval in an organization, because social change is slower and more difficult to inaugurate than technical change.

The People Variable

Management theory is built around the study of people functioning in groups, which makes people central to any model of management. The people variable encompasses both the characteristics of the leader in a group and the individual characteristics of the membership. The relationship between the leader or supervisor and his subordinates is a feature of the functioning of organizations, and therefore part of the structure variable. The people variable relates specifically to the attributes and skills of individuals. Accordingly, dimensions in figure 3-5 include age, physical dexterity, mental capacity involving reasoning skills, language skills, and so on. (These are elaborated on in chapter 10.) One of the most important dimensions of people is their training and education. This qualifies them for certain positions or to handle specific responsibilities. Training and education are relatively easy to evaluate, in contrast to psychological dimensions such as personal needs, expectations, temperament, attitudes, interests, and value systems.

Common Dimensions	People Continuum	
Age	18	70
Physical dexterity	1 (slow)	(agile) 10
Reasoning skills	1 (low)	(high) 10
Language skills	1 (low)	(high) 10
Interpersonal skills	1 (low)	(high) 10
Degree of training	1 (little training)	(highly trained) 10
Other psychological factors	Describe and evaluate needs, expectations, attitudes, goals, values, emotional makeup, group identifications, temperament, interests, etc.	

Fig. 3-5.   The people variable

It is clear that a manager needs to temper any decisions relating to application of management concepts and techniques depending on an anticipation of how the people involved will react psychologically. Sound decisions that cannot be sold to the work group will receive half-hearted implementation. A manager must be armed with a fairly thorough comprehension of the people variable if he or she is to effectively lead them in achieving organizational objectives.

Structure as a Variable

Structure consists of the relationships developed in an organization that determine how it functions. Some of these relationships are formal, representing the intentional assignment of tasks, grouping of activities, and establishment of ties among the subunits. Other relationships are informal and emerge from the social interaction that takes place in the organization.

Skill in organizing has long been considered one of the most significant strengths of a manager. Organizing concepts have received primary—almost disproportionate—attention in management literature. The manner in which a group is organized is certainly one of the most critical factors in determining its functioning. However, organization structure often results from other conditions (and is primarily a dependent variable). Untrained, uncommitted employees will necessitate a more explicit, control-oriented structure; trained, committed employees permit a more open, flexible one. Repetitive tasks and continuous production operations will encourage a more detailed, rigid structure, while groups involved in

Dimensions	Structure Continuum	
Scale (size)	(1) few employees	many (25,000)
Hierarchy	(1) few levels	many (15)
Authority delegation	(1) decentralized	centralized (10)
Geographical dispersion	(1) one location	many locations (20)
Formalization	(1) few rules and procedures	many rules (10) and procedures
Informal structure	Involves the nature of the social structure including roles, communication channels, group norms, power structure, patterns of interaction, etc.	

Fig. 3-6. The structure variable

problem solving (research and development) will function better with a loose one. Structure is often also an independent variable as it relates to conditions in an organization. Low morale and disgruntled employees can result from a structure that is too rigid and does not permit the worker any freedom of action.

Certain selected dimensions of structure are shown in figure 3-6. (Chapters 12 through 16 contain an extensive review of the structure dimensions.) Some of the most significant attributes of structure are size, the number of vertical levels in the hierarchy, the degree to which authority is delegated downward, the geographical dispersion of the organization, and its formalization (represented by the number of rules and procedures that exist governing activities).

Variables of the External Environment

The four variables of the external environment are shown in table 3-3,* along with representative dimensions. These variables constitute the external factors that are typically of most concern to major organizations like business firms. The assessment of these variables is an important prerequisite to decision making by top management. Such decisions are aimed at adapting the organization to changes in the marketplace, consumer tastes, or the advance of technology. Focusing on the managerial responsibility for adapting the organization to external conditions is one of the important developments associated with the contingency and systems theories of management.

Table 3-3. The External Environment

Variables	Dimensions and Means of Evaluation
Economic	Measurements of economics as a force: gross national product, personal income, unemployment, sales, profits, size of markets, number of competitors, differentiation of products, etc.
	Economic institutions: competitors, suppliers, customers, labor unions, business associations etc.
Political and legal	Political forces: attitudes of public servants, attitudes of major groups and vested interests, public opinion, reactions to events, actions of foreign powers, laws of federal, state,

*Based on table 2, "Environmental Factors," *Situational Management,* Howard M. Carlisle. (New York: American Management Associations, 1973, p. 28.)

Table 3-3.   (cont'd.)

	and local governments, decisions of courts and quasi-judicial agencies, etc.
	Political institutions: federal, state, local and foreign governmental bodies and agencies.
Sociocultural	Sociocultural forces: cultural norms, values of society and subcultures within society, public attitudes, social groups and practices, etc.
Technological	Technology as a force is evaluated and measured by norms associated with each scientific discipline. Evaluation is in terms of the current state-of-the-art. It is reflected in knowledge and in improvements in machinery, automation, data processing, etc.

Economic Variables

The economic environment is more accurately considered when divided into two levels. The intermediate level for the firm is the marketplace. (For universities it would be other universities; for hospitals it would be other hospitals and health care centers.) In the examples given at the beginning of the chapter, the owner of the drug store is concerned with the actions of other competitive drug stores in the region. The prices they charge for their products, the services they offer (e.g., home delivery), and their plans for modernizing or expanding facilities all affect the decisions the manager will make. Of most immediate concern to managers are the actions of competitors relating to product lines, product differentiation, product pricing, and plant or store location. Under a free-enterprise system, competition dominates the marketplace. Conversely, in the case of governments or hospitals, the interorganizational climate may be one of cooperation.

At the second or outer economic level are the composite forces resulting from the functioning of national and international economies. Economic productivity for a country is measured on the basis of gross national product, comprising the total production of goods and services. Economic conditions determine what a firm must pay for its inputs (or factors of production) like its materials, machinery, energy sources, and manpower. It is these same conditions that affect the ability of the firm's customers to purchase its goods and use its services. Even though our knowledge of economics has increased significantly in recent years, economic changes are difficult to predict, and they require the careful consideration of management.

Political and Legal Considerations

All organizations are influenced by political considerations and the laws of governments. As legal entities business firms are subject to hundreds of different laws and government regulations. Governments play many different roles in relation to the firm and are the largest *consumer* of the goods and services provided by industry, amounting to twenty-five percent of GNP. Governments are also the primary *regulator* of business, as can be seen by agencies such as the Federal Trade Commission, the Interstate Commerce Commission, the Antitrust Division of the Justice Department, and the Environmental Protection Agency. Government is also a *promoter* of business, represented by the Small Business Administration, the broad sponsorship of research and development, commodity price supports, and other such activities. Finally, the government is also a *producer* of goods and services in competition with business, as one finds in electrical power generation, credit programs, railroads, and the use of public lands. Unquestionably, governments are the suprasystems of society. They have the means to impose their will on business firms, with the result that government trends are of critical significance to the manager.

Sociocultural Considerations

Organizations take on the characteristics of the society from which they are derived. The values, mores, and behavior patterns of a particular culture are evidenced in all of the institutions comprising it. As cultures change, their subsidiary organizations will also change. Customs affect the behavior patterns of individuals, and thus, indirectly, the demand for particular products. The youth culture of the United States is reflected in automobiles, clothing styles, and essentially all consumer goods. In analyzing change in the external environment of organizations, sociocultural considerations are primary.

Technology as an External Variable

Technology is both an internal and external variable in the contingency model of management. Internally, technology constitutes the technical level of the tasks and processes carried on within the firm. Companies with unusual research and development capability may have some capacity to scientifically update their total operational technology, but generally a firm must rely on external organizations, such as universities, for scientific advance and on suppliers for technological improvements that culminate in the technology of their machinery and operations. Competition in many markets is as much technological as economic. Staying competitive in industries such as electronics, aerospace, and medical equipment is dependent on keeping up with the forefront of technological change.

Technology has been described as "probably the most powerful force in today's business environment."[2] The deterministic influence of technology is undoubtedly pervasive. The mobility of society represented by steam generation, the gasoline engine, jet aircraft, and rocket propulsion are all offsprings of technology. Technology is not just an energy multiplier—it affects political events (through atomic weapons), education and social practices (through television), and merchandising (through the development of synthetic materials). In the contingency model of management, technology is one of the most difficult variables for a manager to assess, and it is also one of the most vital in terms of its importance in determining situations—especially in the long run.

USING THE CONTINGENCY MODEL

Several examples will be presented to clarify the use of the contingency approach in managerial decision making. These examples will relate to each management function and will introduce the profile approach to comparing situations.

Staffing

Assuming that a manager is to be given the responsibility for staffing a new branch of an organization, how should he go about deciding what skills and attributes are needed in the personnel? It is primarily a problem of determining which tasks are to be performed by the new group. The information he needs to make the staffing decision is dependent on the dimensions of the tasks to be performed, calling for a profile of these tasks. *A profile is a graphic representation of the measurements, or ratings, of the dimensions of a variable.* If a task profile is developed similar to the one in the top half of figure 3-7, it would serve as a basis for making the staffing decision. Two types of tasks are contrasted in the figure. Production tasks are shown as the solid line. Production involves primarily working with things, resulting in a high rating for this dimension. Working with people and with data are given low ratings. In production there is also normally significant sequential interdependence resulting from the task specialization of the assembly line, which also contributes to a short job cycle and little autonomy for the worker.

Research and development tasks of scientists (dotted line on figure 3-7) tend to be just the opposite. Scientists work much more with data,

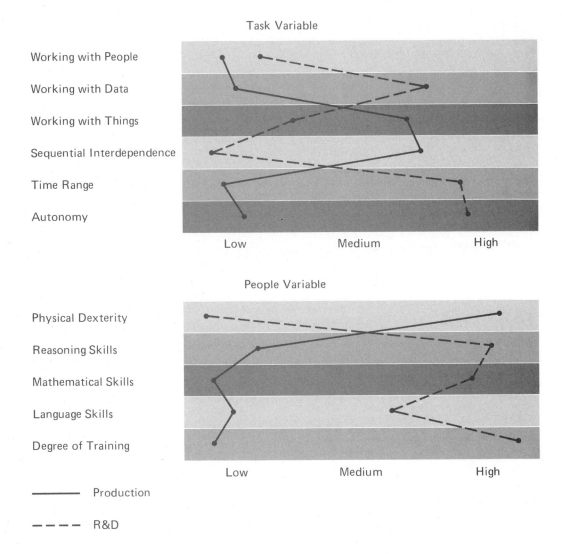

Fig. 3-7. Profiles for production and R and D operations of a firm

there is limited sequential independence among the tasks of different people, the time range for development work is typically very long, and they have a high degree of autonomy.

These two different sets of tasks tend to dictate the people requirements reflected in the bottom portion of figure 3-7. The production tasks require people with physical dexterity, whereas the other dimensions of reasoning skills, mathematical skills, language skills, and degree of training are relatively low. The skills of scientists are just the opposite, with physical dexterity being low and all of the other dimensions requiring high ratings.

> Management is a highly individualized art. What style works well for one management in a particular situation may not produce the desired results for another manager in a similar situation, or even for the same manager in a different situation. There is no one best way for all managers to manage in all situations. Every manager must discover for himself, therefore, what works and what does not work for him. . . . He cannot become effective merely by adopting the practices or the managerial style of someone else. He must develop his own natural style and follow practices that are consistent with his own personality.

Quotation from J. Sterling Livingston, "Myth of the Well-educated Manager," *Harvard Business Review,* January-February 1971, p. 84.

Leading

Leadership should be evaluated on the same basis. If one were attempting to determine what leader or what leadership style would be effective in a particular situation, he would first need to analyze the primary variables in the situation. This analysis can be either purely mental or formal through the development of a profile. As has been emphasized, there is no one leadership style that is appropriate for all situations. For example, if the task profile indicated nonrepetitive research tasks, the technology profile complex scientific operations, the people profile highly trained professionals, and the structure profile a decentralized, nonbureaucratic organization, all indications would then point toward the need for a more open, permissive style of leadership. Opposite profiles would most likely call for more directive leadership.

Organizing

Proper handling of the organization function requires a broad consideration of all major variables, starting with the purpose and objectives of the organization. A manager also needs to understand the tasks to be performed, the nature of the people in the organization, the influence of technology, and the interfaces with external organizations and forces before he can make sound decisions on structuring an organization. It is further complicated because each variable may influence different dimensions of the structure. As examples, tasks tend to dictate the basis on which subgroups are established, while people and task variables determine how much authority can be delegated.

Planning and Control

Planning and control concepts are many and varied. More exact methods are available when experience and repetition create many knowns relating to cost, scheduling, and performance (cost standards, unit-production standards, incentive pay systems, and so on). Different techniques will be used, however, when there is little repetition or when constantly changing activities are involved, relegating historical information concerning costs and scheduling to limited value. The profile on tasks presented in the upper half of figure 3-7 represents this situation. Continuous production operations would lend themselves to considerably different management planning and control techniques than would the erratic search process involved in research and development. Again, there is no one best way to plan and control—all planning and control systems must be adapted to the situation.

The Analytical Process Associated with the Model

In actual practice a manager would rarely need to collect data and develop profiles on major management variables before he made a decision. Most of his decisions are essentially automatic, resulting from facing the same variables and making the same types of decisions on a day-to-day basis. However, as the dimensions of the variables change, or as he moves to new situations where the outcomes are not as predictable, he needs to follow the methodology of evaluating variables, exploring relationships, and making decisions consistent with that changing environment. It is this analytical process based on a contingency framework that provides the key to situational analysis. It avoids absolutes, rejects pat answers, and concentrates on matching techniques with the unique features of each situation. It is basically an if—then analysis: *if* certain conditions exist, it *then* calls for the application of certain techniques or concepts. Concepts and techniques cannot be successfully applied without first determining situational conditions resulting from the status of variables.

Advantages of the Model

The four primary advantages of the contingency approach are as follows:

1. The contingency model is an improved representation of the true nature of management. It avoids the generalizations and simplifications that characterized the early development of management thought by providing a more complex, relationships-oriented model. It emphasizes the multivariate approach to causation, the primacy of certain variables, and the interrelationships that exist among these variables. Through considering the variables to be dynamic in nature and of varying importance in different situations, it is a more accurate depiction of the management process.

2. The model serves as a useful means to collect, integrate, and assess management knowledge. By establishing dimensions relating to the primary variables in a management situation and by linking the usefulness of different management concepts and techniques to different profiles of these dimensions, it provides a broad, balanced framework for management theory and practice. Management thought in the past has tended to be too narrow, as a result of concentration on principles associated with certain functions like formal organization. Accordingly, variables such as tasks and technology have been slighted, with the result that knowledge in these areas has tended to lag.

3. The model provides a better means of evaluating management situations and of applying management concepts, because it emphasizes the *relative* nature of these factors, rather than emphasizing absolutes and universals. Rarely if ever are the primary variables in two situations the same, so managers should be trained to deal with differences in situations and understand how these differences affect decision making. The dimension approach to measuring and evaluating variables is a means of overcoming the vagueness that has hindered the development of management theory and practice.

4. The model is a useful means of evaluating managerial action and approaching managerial decisions. It provides a basis for assessing the conditions in a situation and then selecting appropriate concepts and techniques given these circumstances. The model is an aid to the manager in understanding the forces at work in a situation, and it provides a better means of evaluating the relative advantages offered by specific management concepts and techniques. Ultimately, the primary value of the approach is to the practitioner by way of improved managerial action.

SUMMARY

All organizations display differences in their functioning. Some of the differences are significant in dictating the planning, organizing, staffing, directing, and controlling concepts that are appropriate to that organiza-tion. The contingency approach to management uses a model, consisting of nine variables, that takes these differences into consideration. The five internal variables are the purpose, people, tasks, technology, and structure of the organization. The four external variables include eco-nomic, political, sociocultural, and technological institutions and forces.

Situations involve different conditions, calling for the application of different management concepts, because of the varying status of the nine contingency variables. Situations can be diagnosed based on an evalua-tion of these variables. The primary attributes of variables that signify these differences are called dimensions. As an example, some of the com-mon dimensions or characteristics of people in a work group are their age, training, knowledge, commitment to the organization, interests, attitudes, and value systems.

The importance, or intensity, of these variables will differ from situa-tion to situation. The conditions in a situation are determined by the composite interplay of these variables and are rarely dominated by one factor. Situational analysis is, therefore, often complicated and uncertain, but it provides the insight essential to effective management.

QUESTIONS FOR STUDY AND DISCUSSION

1. Contrast the primary differences between a hospital, a university, and a bank.
2. For a hospital, a university, and a bank, indicate how the purpose vari-able influences the task, technology, people, and structure variables.
3. What are the important organizations, institutions, and forces in the external environment of the hospital? The bank? The university?
4. Explain how structure is both a dependent and an independent variable.
5. What are the variety of tasks performed in a supermarket? How do these tasks influence staffing requirements? How do they influence the technology of the operations? The structure of the store?
6. What differences would most likely be found in the organization of a large supermarket as opposed to a small corner grocery store?
7. Of what value are the dimensions of variables?
8. Suggest some people dimensions in addition to those given in this chapter.
9. How do technology and tasks differ as variables?
10. How do external economic variables influence government agencies? How do sociocultural variables?
11. Is the contingency model of management appropriate to a voluntary organization such as the Lion's Club? To a church? Why?
12. Develop comparative profiles for the following:

A. Tasks for a secretary, for a professor
B. Technology for a doctor, for a salesclerk
C. Structure for a gasoline station, for a university
D. People who are employees in a cafeteria, employees in a barbershop

13. Based on the profiles established in response to question 12, indicate how planning, organizing, staffing, directing, and controlling might vary.

Case Study
COMPARISON OF THREE ORGANIZATIONS

Central Valley Hospital. Central Valley Hospital is in a community of approximately 25,000. John Cortland, hospital administrator, reports that there are ninety beds and two hundred full and part-time employees. The hospital does not have a house staff of doctors—local doctors are on emergency-call rotation. Approximately forty-five local doctors have rights to admit patients to the hospital. The hospital is nonprofit and associated with a religious organization. In only one of the last five years has the hospital lost money.

Central Valley Brokerage Firm. Central Valley Brokerage is a firm that sells investment securities to customers in the local community. The firm does not have a seat on the New York or the American Stock Exchange. Central Valley specializes in the sale of mutual funds and in the stock of smaller local corporations that are sold over-the-counter. There are five salesmen, one accountant, and two secretaries in the office. The firm has been relatively successful: it has doubled its earnings every three years.

Central Valley Stud Mill. Central Valley Stud Mill produces two-by-four-inch lumber for use in the construction industry. Logs are obtained from rights purchased on U.S. Forest Service land that is located in mountains forty-five miles to the North. The logs are hauled by truck to the mill where they are cut, kiln dried, and then shipped by railroad car to locations throughout the western United States. One major lumber company purchases most of the studs, although over the past three years as many as six different distributors have purchased from them. There are forty-five year-round employees, with employment jumping to over one hundred during the summer months when the logging takes place. Operations have been very profitable except during the construction depression in the early 1970's.

How would the external environment of the three organizations differ?
How would the internal operations of the organizations differ?
What is the dominant competitive issue in the marketplace of each organization?
How will the marketing, finance, production, and personnel functions of the organizations differ?
How will each of the following differ?
   A. Employees
   B. Organization structure
   C. Planning and control
   D. Decision making
   E. Leadership

Case Study:
AMBER COPPER CORPORATION
AND HARCOURT AEROSPACE, INC.

Amber Copper. Amber Copper has been active in the mining industry since 1885. Their operations, primarily open pit, are concentrated in two different locations where they mine and process copper. The ore is first loaded into gigantic earth-moving trucks for transportation to large concentrators, where it is refined through a series of processes, and ultimately becomes nearly pure copper. Other precious metals also are removed from the ore, but their quantity is sufficiently small to classify them as by-products. Once the copper is in finished form, it is sold to a large number of industrial users for making wire and other products. There are only three or four major producers of copper in the country. Most of the jobs in the plant are associated with running the machinery to transport and process the copper. The operations are highly mechanized. Most of the work is associated with maintenance trades and machine operations. The plants are unionized, and pay and fringe benefits are high for the semiskilled type of work involved.

Harcourt Aerospace, Inc.; Henderson Plant. Harcourt Aerospace was originally a chemical firm, but when solid-propellant missiles were developed in the 1950's, they moved into rocketry, since some of their chemicals were those used in propellants. They established separate plants to handle their aerospace work in the late 1950's, when solid propellants demand grew because of their use in missiles like Polaris and Minuteman. Harcourt emerged as one of the leaders in the field. The Henderson plant employs just over 2000. Approximately half of these are scientists and engineers engaged in research and development of solid-propellant missiles. The other half are production workers and those providing support services. Over eighty percent of their work is performed under government contract. The balance is indirectly government work, since they serve as subcontractors to other firms with government contracts. The plant is nonunionized, and there is a broad range in wages and salaries representing the wide variety of skills involved. There are approximately six other firms that compete in the industry. The demand tends to be rather erratic, since year to year the government varies its procurement of missiles. Currently the plant is working on four different missile contracts, and their work force is organized around these projects.

What are the major differences between the plants?
How will the importance of the external variables vary?
What are the differences in the internal variables?
What functions are the most critical in the success of each plant?
What differences would exist in relation to the following:
  A. Marketing activities
  B. Financial activities
  C. Personnel activities
  D. Processing or operations activities
How will each of the following vary?
  A. Organization structures
  B. Planning and control
  C. Cost data and information systems
In what other respects will the plants most likely function differently?
Can leadership styles be expected to differ?

Footnotes

1. Variables similar to these are used in many different management models. One of the closely related, widely publicized models was developed by Harold Leavitt in the early 1960's. He used structure, task, technology and people as the four variables. See W. W. Cooper, H. J. Leavitt, and M. W. Shelly, II (eds.), *New Perspectives in Organization Research*, (New York: John Wiley & Sons, Inc., 1964).

2. James D. Bright, *Research, Development and Technological Innovation* (Homewood, Illinois: Richard D. Irwin, Inc., 1964), p. vi.

Systems Theory and the Contingency Model

What is systems theory?

Why are organizations considered systems?

What implications does systems theory have for management?

What are the features of open systems?

What are the subsystems and suprasystems of organizations?

What is the relationship between systems theory and contingency theory?

To view an organization from the perspective of systems theory introduced in chapter 2, it is useful to engage in a bit of fantasy. Assume that you are a giant and could carefully pry off the roof of first a factory and then a department store. What would you see and hear? In the factory people moving in many directions, the whine and commotion of processing machinery, the rumble of overhead cranes, forklifts scooting up and down marked aisles, and possible smoke and/or fumes would give an overall impression of concentrated confusion.

At first all of the activity would appear to represent complete disorder, but more careful observation would reveal a continuity in the operations taking place. Raw materials or components are taken from supply areas and proceed through a series of human and machine operations involving identical, sequential changes. Items would be processed the same way, stored in similar locations, and look the same after the processing was finished. The completed items would be transported to a warehouse or else packaged and placed in railroad cars for distribution. Some individuals in offices on the periphery of the assembly line might appear to be engaged in unrelated tasks, but in general the activity would be patterned, sequential, and interdependent.

In a department store, the activity might seem even more disjointed. Few machines would be involved, and there would be no obvious flow pattern in the processing or movement of materials. The activities of people would also appear to be random. Some would enter the building, wander from counter to counter, and leave without taking anything or affecting in any way the items on display. Others would take goods from the store after an exchange of money. Some would try on apparel, smell the fragrance of a perfume, feel the texture of material, or eat at a lunch counter.

Prolonged observation in the department store would disclose certain common patterns of activity. Goods would be taken from warehouses, stored in specific sections of the store, and exchanged with the more transient populace in the building. The activity would start and stop at specific times each day, and certain people would perform the same tasks daily—but not in the fixed routine of the production plant.

If you (as the giant) could stand back and take an even broader view of the operation of these organizations, you would find that other firms were supplying goods to them in a consistent and predictable fashion. You would also observe that the rate of flow of activity in the two companies is dependent on how rapidly customers purchased their output or products. You would soon conclude that the activity within the walls of the buildings is not self-contained. Instead, it is almost entirely dependent on outside organizations, such as suppliers, customers, investors, labor unions, competitors, and governments.

IMPLICATIONS DERIVED
FROM THIS ANALOGY

This explanation of the functioning of organizations supports many of the contentions contained in previous chapters: individuals functioning in groups are engaged in deliberate, purposeful activities; the primary activity in organizations consists of people interactions centering around the tasks they are engaged in; the activities of the organizations are structured but in different ways, depending on the purpose of the organization, the people involved, and the tasks being performed; the success of the organization is dependent on maintaining favorable relationships with outside groups such as suppliers and customers. The primary variables of purpose, task, technology, people, and structure combine with external relationships to predominate in organizations.

However, it is not merely the existence of certain key variables that is of interest in these examples. There is a patterned relationship among the variables that dominates the functioning of the organizations. The activities of each of the parts (or elements) is to contribute to the functioning of the whole unit. It is not possible for an individual to understand why any particular element of the plant or store exists without first comprehending the total sequence of operations. Isolated actions of a welder or saleslady are incomprehensible without knowing the total purpose of the organization. (By the same token, to understand the organizations one must perceive processes and activities, because these are what constitute their functioning.) If the observations were made at night when the store was closed or the plant not in operation, only dormant physical facilities could be observed—mere appurtenances of organizations, not the controlling elements.

THE NATURE OF SYSTEMS THEORY

And that's what systems theory is all about. Systems theory is concerned with these integrative relationships. It is a theoretical approach to analyzing a state of nature and focuses on the centralized entities around which physical matter and biological and human activity tend to concentrate. It involves studying relationships that exist among matter and among functioning, nonstatic structures. Systems theorists search for three things in the states of nature: a set of common elements; the whole that is represented by these elements; and the existing relationships among the elements that account for the characteristics or existence of the whole.

In the example of the giant, assume that you have the physical power to shake the buildings, moving the elements into disarray. Even though the same elements exist (assuming none was destroyed), the department store or plant could not function (the system would experience disruption), because the relationship among the elements changed. If the people and machines involved in final assembly operations were moved to the beginning of the production line, the functioning of the total system would be hampered—or even negated!

Definitions of Systems

Systems theory has been applied to every branch of knowledge. It tends to take on a different meaning and significance depending on whether it is applied to physical, mechanical, biological, or open systems (like organizations). Systems theory was applied in the physical science and engineering disciplines before it was introduced in management or organization theory, so engineering definitions and physical models have tended to dominate. Engineering definitions highlight the physical positioning and mechanical functioning of parts, whereas in human organizations physical patterns are of relatively minor consideration. Hence the definitions used here will be those appropriate to social systems.

In one of the early books on systems and management, written by Richard A. Johnson, Fremont E. Kast, and James E. Rosenzweig in 1963, a system is defined as "an organized or complex whole; an assemblage or combination of things or parts forming a complex or unitary whole."[1] R. L. Ackoff writing from a management science standpoint defines a system as "any entity, conceptual or physical, which consists of interdependent parts."[2] In both instances the three system's ingredients of parts, wholes, and relationships are present. For the purposes of this book *a system is defined as an entity consisting of a composite whole that is formed of interdependent parts or elements involving relationships, which contribute to the unique characteristics of the whole.* This latter definition is used because it emphasizes the particular characteristics of the whole resulting from the relationships of the parts.

Open and Closed Systems

Closed systems tend to be physical in nature and highlight the patterning of parts as the most significant systems relationship. A closed system has little interchange of energy or materials with the environment outside of the system. A watch is an example of a closed system in which the attributes and positioning of the physical parts constitute the system. (The only energy interchange with the environment is by man who—sometimes —must wind the spring or replace the battery that provides the energy to make the system function.)

In an open system, there is an exchange of materials or energies with outside systems and with the environment, which means that the boundaries of the system are permeable. Also, the open system has the capacity to adapt to changes in the environment. The input-output model of the firm is an excellent example of an open system. What is significant in an open system is not the positioning of physical parts but the processing of the system represented by the set of flows and exchanges that take place. In open systems, this exchange process typifies the growth, decay, and adaptation challenges of these systems.

Open systems represented by the firm are complex, because, as indicated in the example of the production plant, they are a combination of both physical and social systems. The social system is represented by the people and group processes of the organization, and the physical system is represented by the machines, materials, and technology involved in the tasks of the organization. In systems terminology this is referred to as the *sociotechnical subsystem* of the organization and encompasses the combining of social and technical processes. Sociotechnical considerations highlight relationships such as the interface between man and machines and the social interaction and task-oriented activities of human beings.

Why Systems Theory Is Important to the Manager

Of what real significance is systems theory to the manager? Well, for one thing if a manager concentrates on the relationships that constitute the functioning of organizations, he has a greater chance of being able to influence these relationships and hence the organization. Mere pronouncements by a manager that change is to take place will not often achieve the desired results. An understanding of the sets of relationships constituting the system is necessary—just as a mechanic must understand all of the apparatus and parts that make up a car.

In identifying systems, the most important point is the relative discreteness and independence of the system. A university is a relatively discrete and independent system, because it can provide a useful output in terms of discovering knowledge and educating students without direct, functional reliance on other groups. True, a university is obviously dependent on outside systems (funds are obtained from legislatures, endowments, investments, and tuition. Also, the services provided by the university must satisfy the needs of society). However, the output of a university is a relatively independent, usable one. The Admissions and Records Office or the Computer Center is obviously a part or subsystem of the larger university system. The Admissions and Records Office can serve no useful purpose or provide no useful product without the balance of the university. The same is also true of the Computer Center. These are parts of a larger, more discrete, independent suprasystem. Neither the university nor the Admissions and Records Office nor the Computer Center is independent, but it is the relative difference that is of concern in the analysis of systems.

Many different examples are appropriate relating to the coherence of systems. A golfer functions as a relative coherent system because he acts essentially alone in competing against the course. However, the offensive tackle of a football team is a definite part of a larger system. If he blocks left when the play goes right, the system will not function properly and it (the team) will not achieve its objective. The marketing function in a firm is definitely a part of a larger system. If a salesman guarantees delivery of a product on July 1 but production does not follow through in a coordinated fashion and delivery is not made, the system (the firm) will not function properly in achieving its goal.

System relationships become more difficult to evaluate and control as organizations grow in size. Size results in specialization and differentiation of parts. This increases the problems of coordinating the parts to achieve broader objectives. Systems integration is relatively simple in a five-employee automotive-repair garage but complex in a 10,000 employee production plant comprising multiple product lines.

General Systems Theory

General systems theory consists of a philosophical set of concepts that can be applied to any discipline. In recent years it has been common to apply general systems theory in fields such as engineering, sociology, and psychology. When this is done it results in a re-examination and re-evaluation of all existing knowledge using a systems framework. Systems theory is not intended to be a separate appendage attached onto an existing body of knowledge. Rather it is a means of reintegrating and re-explaining existing knowledge based on systems relationships.

In understanding systems theory, the important point stressed by its advocates is that it is "a way of thinking," rather than a specific set of principles, postulates, or propositions. It involves a specific mental approach to viewing knowledge or situations. Just as the scientific method is considered to be "a general method of thinking about and investigating problems," the same can be said for systems theory. However, the emphasis is different. The scientific method concentrates on subdividing research and analysis into smaller and smaller areas of investigation. General system theory is concerned with broader relationships, often extending *across* fields of knowledge. Total knowledge needs to be compartmentalized and segregated so it is manageable, but in doing so some aspects are distorted and artificial barriers created. As R. L. Ackoff states,

"We must stop acting as though nature were organized into disciplines in the same way that universities are."[3]

Systems theory holds that detailed information relating to a part is significant, but its import can be appreciated only through comprehending how it relates to the larger system. Systems theorists contend that too much of our current analysis is parts, rather than whole, oriented. Decisions cannot be made in isolation and information compartmentalized, because all matter and information are linked in some fashion with other matter and information through dependent relationships. It is these relationships that are of primary concern to the systems theorist.

Systems Theory versus Systems Analysis

The term *systems* is used in a variety of contexts. This has created considerable confusion. An example is the difference between systems theory and systems analysis. Systems analysis became a popular term in the early 1960's when Robert McNamara became Secretary of Defense. McNamara wanted an independent, civilian group to analyze defense problems. Accordingly, he established the Systems Analysis Office as part of the Office of the Secretary of Defense. The office was staffed by economists who were well trained in the newer quantitative methods. The publicity given to their efforts in analyzing weapon systems and defense strategies created considerable interest in system analysis and the associated techniques.

The primary difference between systems theory and systems analysis is that systems *theory* is a broad theoretical framework, and systems *analysis* consists mainly of methods or techniques of analysis, such as cost-benefit studies, decision theory, or linear programming. Systems analysis is similar to operations research—techniques that can be used to help solve specific problems. However, there is a definite relationship between the two terms, since systems analysis emphasizes that every decision should be considered in as broad a context as is practical. Therefore, to avoid the resultant confusion, as the original economists who started the Systems Analysis Office later stated, either the term *systematic analysis* or *quantitative common sense* probably should have been used.[4]

FEATURES OF OPEN SYSTEMS

From a management standpoint, our concern is with open systems, represented by organizations. The organization as an open system is both a contrived and a natural system. It is contrived because organizations are deliberately established by man, in order to achieve some common purpose. Organizations are also natural systems because many of the relationships are naturally developed because of the informal interaction of people and because the organization naturally evolves as it faces the adaptation challenge of its environment.

Organizations demonstrate a complexity that makes it difficult to comprehend them from a systems standpoint—especially when systems theory itself involves a new way of thinking which is often contrary to existing stereotyped thought processes. An understanding of open systems is centered about seven concepts that comprise a useful means of analyzing social systems:

1. There is an interdependence of all parts or elements in a system.
2. The whole is more than a summation of these individual parts.
3. The individual parts cannot properly be comprehended without understanding the whole also.
4. The boundary relationships, or interfaces, with other systems have special significance.
5. Social systems are made up of hierarchies of systems, so that supra and subordinate systems exist for any specific system.
6. Open systems are changing, adaptive entities.
7. Open systems experience growth and decay processes.

These principles are the essence of open systems theory and therefore will be elaborated in more detail.

Dependency of Parts

This first characteristic of open systems is the dependent relationship between the parts and the whole—this is the single most important way to identify a system. Elements are clustered around systems based on their relationship to the whole. If an element is changed and it has no impact on the whole, it is not a part of the system. The more reliant a system is on particular parts or elements for its functioning, the more coherent it is. (In the example given at the beginning of the chapter, if the lunch counter is removed from the department store, the store can still function —even though its profits and sales may be affected by the loss of that part.) The production line is a much more coherent system, because it cannot continue to function or produce its intended output if the final assembly section is removed.

The contingency model of management is based on this same premise. People, tasks, technology, structure, and purpose are the primary internal elements of an organization. A change in the attributes or functioning of any one of these parts will affect the whole. If the leadership (people variable) changes, it affects the whole; if the tasks and technology are modified, it alters the functioning of the organization; if the structure is redesigned, it will also transform the organization. The relationship of parts determines the functioning of social systems.

Another example of this concept comes from systems engineering. In recent years, as engineering projects have become larger and more complex, it has been increasingly difficult to ensure that the many parts being developed will mesh in the optimal functioning of the whole. An example is the weapons systems of the Department of Defense. Components are subcontracted to many suppliers because of the size and complexity of the weapon system. The job of the systems engineer is to make sure all parts of the system integrate so as to maximize the functioning of the total system. During the development stage, a contractor cannot add weight or length to a component without affecting other parts of the system. Accordingly, the system engineer does little design work, but he monitors the development of all parts to ensure their integration. For example, the relevant parts of a missile system are not just the hardware items that propel it. In addition to the hardware, the missile includes handling harnesses and transporters to move it, silos or launching platforms for firing it, and even the manuals used to train the personnel who will operate the missile complex. Unless the systems engineer makes sure that every part integrates with the balance of the system, there is a chance that the system will not function.

Synergy and the Functioning of the Whole

The second important feature of a system is that through the proper functioning and interrelationship of the parts, a total effect (synergy) is achieved that is greater than the sum of the effects of the individual parts functioning in an unrelated or independent fashion. This is the feature that really distinguishes a system. Elements and functions are combined in a way to achieve a purpose or an output that cannot be gained by those elements or functions acting independently. For instance, if a physical system like a watch or a motor is disassembled, it cannot function and cannot fulfill its intended purpose. The parts are still in existence, but they are not positioned so that they can function. This is a key distinction in evaluating systems. Wholes are not simply an aggregate or a summation of parts. The *number* of parts in an assembled versus a disassembled watch is the same. It is the *positioning* and *functioning* of parts that determine the system and allows synergy to take place.

The same is true of open systems. If five people constitute a group but they refuse to work together in coordinating their activities, they will have no greater output than the summation of what they do individually. However, if they coordinate their activities they can achieve an output greater than what they accomplish on an individual basis. Starting again with a physical example, five persons cannot individually lift a five-hundred-pound object. However, if all five lift the object at one time, it is easily accomplished. In a business example, if all five individuals attempt to perform the accounting, marketing, production, procurement, and finance functions of their organization, little will be accomplished; if they specialize and coordinate their activities so that each individual handles one of these functions, they will accomplish much more. The ultimate task of the manager is to achieve synergy for his organization. He must interrelate the parts and functioning of his organization so the output of the whole is maximized.

Understanding Parts

The holism concept of synergy is reversed in applying the third concept of systems theory. Rather than concentrating on the whole, the emphasis is on the part. The principle is that a part cannot properly be understood unless one comprehends how it contributes to the whole. If an individual has no understanding of a total activity and is merely acquainted with a part or subelement, it is not possible to really know this part. Knowing a part depends on gaining an understanding of how it contributes to the whole, because this is its primary function in a cohesive system.

Examples are plentiful. It is not possible to understand the advertising program of a firm unless one understands other parts, such as the products, and image and goals of the firm; if one understands only the functions of a nurse without comprehending the total activities of a hospital, it represents only partial knowledge; knowing the activities of a security officer in a department store is not meaningful without understanding the total activities of the store itself. This, again, is one of the basic tenets of the contingency theory and systems theory. To study phenomena in isolation is too restrictive to be meaningful. Complete understanding comes only from a knowledge of relationships involving the parts and functioning of broader systems.

Boundary Relationships and Interfaces

In comprehending systems, one needs to be aware of their boundary limits and relationships. The boundary of a system is that point at which it comes into contact with other systems. Some of the most significant relationships of systems are at these boundaries or interfaces. Again, the physical model is easier to visualize. Physical boundaries are discrete and easily identifiable—as evidenced by the human body or by a growing plant. Their boundaries are easily seen. However, the boundaries of open social systems are considerably harder to delineate. Furthermore, by definition they are permeable, as energy, materials, and information are exchanged with other systems and with the environment. The permeability of the boundaries is one of the ways of differentiating types of social systems. For instance, medical schools are relatively closed systems as far as obtaining membership is concerned; based on this criterion junior colleges are relatively open.

The value of this concept of systems theory is that it cautions the manager to be concerned with the boundary conditions of his organization. Boundary conditions help determine the quantity and quality of inputs and outputs. Typically groups like procurement, personnel, and admissions officers are responsible for obtaining organizational inputs. The quality of these inputs will be a significant factor in determining the quality of the output. (In future periods, as the energy crisis heightens and high-quality raw materials become scarcer, these input functions of firms will undoubtedly take on an added significance.)

The interfaces that a firm has with external systems involving its outputs include customers, governments, professional organizations, investors, and labor unions. The parts of the firm responsible for these interfaces include marketing, public relations, and general management. Traditional management theorists paid little attention to the management of these external relationships, viewing the organization more as a closed system. Systems theory provides a more balanced perspective.

Hierarchy of Systems

The fifth concept of open-systems theory relates to the hierarchical structure of systems. There are both external and internal systems when the organization is considered to be the *focal* system. These systems vary in size, scope, and function, which makes it useful to identify hierarchies of complexity. General systems theory holds that all matter and all activity are structured on this basis. Nature consists of a vast fabric of related and unrelated systems with all of the elements of nature contained within. Related systems exist in hierarchies, with the more elementary systems serving as the subsystems of more complex ones. V. I. Kremyanskiy states that "the organic system of each succeeding order contains the systems of the preceding order as its basic components; not directly, however, but mainly as a part of the subsystem."[5]

The hierarchy concept is significant, because it emphasizes that interaction not only takes place within a system, but with other systems on the same level and at higher levels of complexity. The firm deals with local competitors, but it is also influenced by governments and by national and international market forces. Depending on the level in the hierarchy that is selected for analytical purposes, there are subsystems and subsubsystems of the focal system—as well as supra and suprasuprasystems. This is not a one-on-one relationship, since many systems may exist at any particular level of the hierarchy. The importance of the hierarchy for the manager is that subsystems contribute to the functioning of any particular system, and suprasystems serve to subordinate, constrain, or enhance the focal system.

Systems theorists have provided little elaboration of the hierarchies relating to open social systems. The hierarchy concept internal to the organization is well established, with the primary work unit being the lowest level in the formal hierarchy, and several middle-management levels existing up through top management (the apex of the organization). Thomas A. Petit has gone beyond this to designate a four-step hierarchy consisting of the technical core, the organizational level, the institutional level, and the environment of the firm.[6] Depending on the orientation selected, the levels in the hierarchy relating to the firm can be represented in many ways.

BOULDING'S HIERARCHY OF SYSTEMS

One of the landmarks of general systems theory is an article written in 1956 by Kenneth E. Boulding, a noted economist. He felt there was a need for a theoretical construct that would incorporate the general relationships of the empirical world. Accdingly, he proposed a nine-level hierarchy "on which to hang the flesh and blood of particular disciplines and particular subject matters in an orderly and coherent corpus of knowledge." The nine levels are as follows:*

1. Static structures such as geography and the anatomy of the universe
2. Clockwork systems with predetermined, necessary motions such as the solar system
3. Systems where the transmission of information becomes important similar to the thermostat
4. Open systems involving a self-maintaining structure, the example being the cell
5. Genetic-societal systems such as the plant
6. Systems with mobility and self-awareness represented by animals

7. Systems characterized by human beings which display self-consciousness and the capacity to speak and interpret symbols
8. Social systems involving organizations, in which norms are established, messages are exchanged, and human interaction takes place
9. Transcendental systems involving the ultimates, absolutes, inescapables, and unknowables

*Abridged from Kenneth E. Boulding, "General Systems Theory—The Skeleton of Science," *Management Science*, April, 1956, pp. 197–208.

LEVELS IN THE HIERARCHY. A meaningful approach to considering the levels in the hierarchy, when the focal system is the firm, is represented in figure 4-1. The various levels are:

Level 1 The individual.   Performs operating functions

Level 2 Primary work groups.   Perform technical and social functions (The primary work group is used here in the broad sense to cover both formal and informal relationships.)

Level 3 Middle management.   Fulfills a coordination and integration function

Level 4 Institutional.   Integrates subfunctions and adapts the total organization to forces represented by higher-level systems

Level 5 Interorganizational.   For the firm this is the competitive level represented by the marketplace.

Level 6 Environmental.   Includes economic, political, technical, and sociocultural forces and institutions

The basic element of any social system is, of course, the individual, since organizations are contrived by, and exist for, people. The basic attachments an individual develops in the firm are usually with the primary work group. These relations are both formal and informal in nature. The primary work group is formally established to directly perform the technical tasks of the organization, but *informally the group serves as a center of social interaction.*

Because these first two levels of the hierarchy are so intrinsic to accomplishing the technical operations of the firm, supervisory qualifications at the levels are closely related to technical expertise. Also, because

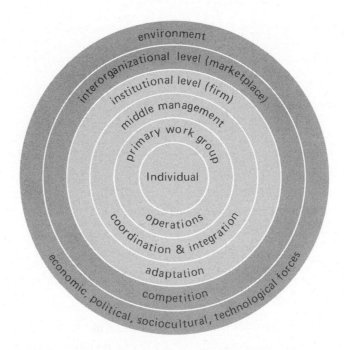

Fig. 4-1. Levels in the systems hierarchy of the firm

these technical operations are relatively self-contained, they are more controllable and predictable. Once inputs are obtained, the technical level operates internally as a relatively closed system. Short-run efficiency tends to be emphasized, based on precise standards and measurements.

Level three represents the integrative level, where the activities performed by the technical subsystems are coordinated to meet the intermediate goals of the firm. Little direct technical work is performed at this level, and the structure for integration takes many forms. It may be centered around functions (engineering, production, and so on), products (floor tile, paint, ceiling tile), processes (fabrication, assembly, spray paint, packaging), or many other alternatives. Middle managers at this level do not direct activity that is as predictable or controllable as that at the operations level. This level operates more as an open system, where judgment becomes important because fewer knowns make it more difficult to use precise, quantitative techniques in decision making.

The fourth level is the institutional level and in our example represents the firm. This is the focal level constituting the system from the standpoint of management theory. The primary concern of management at this level is to adapt the organization to the environment and to integrate all internal parts so the firm functions as one unit. To do this the firm needs strategies that will make it successful in competing with others in the next higher system: the marketplace. At this level management's concerns broaden to encompass the efficiency of competitors and the specifications of their products, as well as a firm's own efficiency and product specifications.

Compared with other sublevels in the hierarchy, activities at this level are much less controllable. Managers cannot regulate these, because dynamic forces in the environment require the firm to react rather than dictate changes. With the system being more open and less predictable, most decisions are based on judgment. The perspective is a broad one, where long-run considerations are most important. Internally the problem is one of balancing all the subsystems so synergy takes place; externally the problem is adapting to conditions in the marketplace and those emanating from the sixth level, the broader environment.

For the firm level five is the economic marketplace. It consists of buyers, suppliers, investors, competitors, and all of the organizations that a firm deals with or is affected by as it obtains its inputs and supplies its outputs in the dynamics of the marketplace. All of the organizations, individuals, or components of the marketplace are in turn affected by the sixth-level suprasystems and forces, represented by governments, customs, scientific advances, and conditions of the national and international economic markets.

ADVANTAGES OF THE HIERARCHY APPROACH. Many benefits are gained from analyzing the firm on the basis of a hierarchy of systems. By doing so, the uniqueness of the environment and the problems confronting management at the various levels of the organization are emphasized. Traditionalists were inclined to perceive management as the same process—regardless of the organization or the level in the organization. Systems theory makes clear the contingency assumption that the respective situations managers face are significantly different, depending on the level in the organization where a manager is located. For instance at the lower level involving more certainty, different methods in planning, control, communication, and decision making can be used than in the more uncontrolled and unpredictable environment existing at higher levels. The concerns and techniques of long-range strategy planning are considerably different from those used in short-run operations planning. (This will be treated in detail in part VIII.)

Another value of the hierarchy approach is that it clarifies many of the problems and barriers that exist in attempting to coordinate and integrate the various subsystems. At each level of the organization individ-

uals have a different perspective—they have unique goals and are striving
for different outcomes. The individual at the first level has specific personal goals that may not be compatible with the goals of the fourth level
or those of the firm. The primary work groups, especially informal
groups, will also have some norms that are divergent from those of the
firm. For middle managers to coordinate the activities of the lower subsystems, it is not simply a matter of establishing procedures or designating how integration should take place. The desire to cooperate is affected
by the perceived reward system and by the degree to which such cooperation will accomplish the goals sought by the individuals or work units at
that level.

Middle managers suffer from the "man-in-the-middle" syndrome.
The expectations of management (the fourth level in the hierarchy) and
the expectations of lower levels are often conflicting and divergent. Middle managers must reconcile these and retain the support of both groups.
Depending on where a manager is in the hierarchy, he should at least
understand the subsystem below him and the suprasystem above him,
because these levels will function differently from his level (and yet the
functioning of his level is highly dependent on relationships maintained
with the immediate interfacing supra and subsystems).

The hierarchy concept of systems is useful, but it can also be deceptive. All social systems do not fit into a known orderly table or matrix
that ties them neatly together. Often social systems exist in considerable
disarray, with little evidence of finite hierarchies. And they are not necessarily horizontally layered. Management subsystems are intended to cut
vertically through the hierarchy. Planning, control, and communication
subsystems of a firm extend vertically from the fourth level down through
the first, with the intent of tying together the various levels of the structure.

The important point is that at different levels of an organization,
people are identified with groups that function as systems. They have
separate goals, separate relationships, and an internal existence that is
somewhat self-contained and integrated. Their uniqueness is not duplicated at any other level in the organization. Accordingly, the levels are
dissimilar—even though they experience strong dependent ties—since
they serve as subsystems of higher-level systems and since lower-level
systems serve as their subsystems.

Social Systems as Organic Systems

One of the features of social systems that has been emphasized in several
different contexts is their constantly changing structure. Systems theory
adopts an "organic" view of organization structure as opposed to the

mechanistic one of traditional management. As organic systems, they are open ones comprised of a series of processes or a pattern of flows (such as was evident in the factory example at the beginning of the chapter).

The mechanistic view assumes that the processing of an organization is a fixed arrangement—like the parts of a machine. The organic view is that the organization is flexible and adaptive. To represent this, another biological analogy is frequently used in systems theory: *homeostasis.* Homeostasis is the condition of external equilibrium maintained through dynamic internal processes. The human body manages to maintain a relatively steady state, even though it experiences temperature extremes and variability in terms of physical and emotional activity. The internal systems of the body adjust to these changes to maintain a relatively constant overall temperature. Firms also often maintain a relatively steady state (trend lines in sales, units produced, etc.), which is achieved through consistent internal processes.

Considering organizations to be dynamic entities is not new in management. Philip Selznick, a sociologist, emphasized the organic, adaptive nature of organizations over a quarter of a century ago. Organizations are not only dependent on inputs for their existence, but they are in a constant state of redefinition from both internal and external forces associated with the primary variables in the contingency model of management. The nature of the work force is constantly changing, new machines are always being introduced, the technology of tasks experiences updating, governmental regulations are modified, economic conditions change, and essentially every element of the organization goes through a constant evolution involving processes that are adaptive in nature.

The Growth and Decay of Organizations

The seventh and last characteristic of open systems is closely associated with the sixth. Organizations not only change, but they exhibit the same growth and decay processes that typify organic systems. Closed systems are characterized by *entropy.* Because they cannot replenish their energy they experience decay and destruction. It is a law of nature that all systems move toward disorder, lack of resource transformation, and eventually death. Living systems have the ability to import materials and energy from their environment so they can at least temporarily avoid the decay process. This arresting of entropy is called *negative entropy.* Plant and animal systems tend to have relatively fixed spans of life during which they arrest entropy. However, organizations have no such common spans. Many firms, especially small businesses, experience a short period of successful existence. Approximately eighty percent of the newly created business firms exist five years or less! Other, larger firms have sufficient resources, energy, materials, and information to experience indeterminate periods of negative entropy.

Organizations also tend to exhibit growth characteristics, including an elaboration of their structure through differentiation or specialization. As organizations continue to evolve, tasks tend to be divided and differentiated, special units are created, and subsystems expand their activities and resources. Organizations display an innate, almost irrational urge to grow, which is primarily cultural in nature. Unless the aggregate of sales, membership, or capital increases, managers are dissatisfied and employees become apprehensive. Some studies have shown that organizations, such as manufacturing plants or universities, attain an optimal size for ease of management when they reach approximately 5000 employees or students. However, when organizations become that size, they are rarely satisfied. Cultural norms value growth as a goal of organizations. It will be interesting to see if governments and individuals can adopt new no-growth norms such as zero-population increase implies.

SYSTEMS METHODOLOGY FOR
VIEWING ORGANIZATIONS

In order to represent the organization as a set of flows and in order to interrelate the various subsystems, an organization is frequently shown, as in figure 4-2, in schematic form. The right half of the schematic is the typical input-output model. Inputs flow in from the environment, are transformed by the processor, and return as goods and services to the environment. The processor consists of a set of operations centered around the contingency variables of people, the tasks they are engaged in, the technology of the machinery and tasks, and the structure of the work groups.

The subsystems dealing with the managing of the organization are shown on the left half of the schematic. In order for management to take action and to make decisions, they need feedback on the status of each of the various flows and operations contained in the input-output model. Accordingly, feedback regarding the status of inputs, processing activities, and outputs is obtained by the sensory devices. When this information is obtained, it activates two different cycles. In the closed-loop cycle represented by the flow of information to the analyzer, actual performance is compared with expected performance or standards. This involves factors such as the status of inventories, the specification of the inputs, and the conditions of the output at various stages of the processsing, which are measured against the standards in the memory or data bank. If inventories are low or if the processing is not meeting these standards, a programmed decision, which automatically makes the necessary adjustments, is carried out by the effector. The plans of this pro-

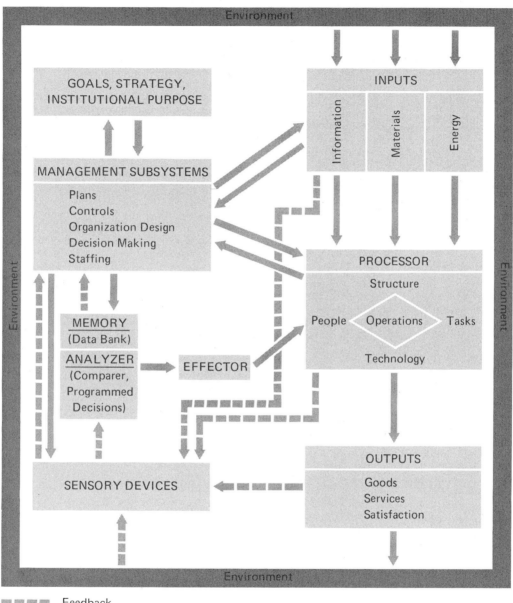

Fig. 4-2. Systems view of an organization—the political,
social, technological, and economic milieu

grammed loop are the performance standards. Control is accomplished by obtaining feedback on performance, comparing this with the standards, and automatically making adjustments when performance deviates from the established norms.

The second loop is a more open one, in which sensory devices inform management of the status of operations and of major deviations that are occurring. It will be noticed in the schematic that the sensory devices receive information from the environment also. This information is provided to management, who uses it to accomplish the nonprogrammed adaptation of the organization. A change in economic conditions of the marketplace or in technology will cause management to revise its plans, modify its processing, or make a number of other decisions that are not predictable—and therefore nonprogrammable.

The dominant element in the entire schematic consists of the institutional purpose and the goals and strategy of the organization. As reflected in the schematic, all management activities are governed by these considerations. However, as is shown, these can be adjusted. All other activities of the organization are regulated to accomplish these goals. Given the goals, it is management's responsibility to establish plans to control subsystems, and to staff and design the organization to optimize goal accomplishment.

SYSTEMS THEORY AND MANAGEMENT FUNCTIONS

The value of using a systems framework to analyze management problems can be seen in the following examples relating to primary management functions:

Problems in Organizing

In recent years, as organizations have tended to grow in size and complexity, some of the weaknesses of functional departments have become more evident. In functional structures, departments are set up based on common-skill specializations, so that engineering units report up through an engineering chain of command, production personnel are formed into production units, and research projects are grouped under research departments. The problem that frequently occurs in large organizations is that an integration of all functions of the organization, or system, does not occur in the hierarchy until the general manager's office at the apex of the organization is reached.

Most management decisions in an organization are made by middle managers, not by the chief executive officer. The result is often *suboptimization* (optimizing a part but less than the optimum for the whole), because a functional expert whose training and advancement in an organization have been entirely related to *his* function will have excellent knowledge and understanding of his part but will lack this same knowledge and understanding of other parts of the system. Decisions he makes will obviously be parts oriented or biased toward his function. Yet few middle-management decisions have repercussions that relate only to that function. When an engineer designs a product, there are manufacturing implications (relating to how it will be produced), cost implications (relating to the financial aspects of the organization), and marketing implications (relating to its reception in the marketplace). Balancing the various parts of an organization to maximize the functioning of the system and avoid suboptimization is difficult in this type of organization, and "empire building" by a function or a part is a frequent problem facing a general manager.

Problems in Staffing

The functional organization creates staffing problems also. When a general management position is vacated, where can a qualified replacement be found? If all the division managers have advanced up a function chain of the organization, after years of this narrow "parts" experience they are not usually prepared to suddenly start making decisions that must balance all of the subsystems of the organization. Training managers to have a broad systems perspective is difficult in rigid, functional structures.

Problems in Communication

Most of the reporting (electronic data processing and otherwise) in organizations is established to meet the special needs of specific parts. Financial reports go to the controller, production reports to manufacturing, and manpower reports to personnel department. The purpose of management information systems is to provide upper-level managers with integrated reports covering the total system, but success has been limited because of the complexities involved. When decisions of managers have implications outside of their function, they need integrated reports consistent with this decision making. Reports developed—based on a systems perspective—should highlight relationships, not just accumulate data.

Problems in Planning and Control

Planning and control systems follow the structure of the organization. In a functional organization, planning will start at the top and proceed down through the functional chain. Control involves the exercise of authority, so control systems normally rely on the chain of command. With planning and control systems dominated by functional organizations, they will tend to be parts oriented. From a systems standpoint, planning and control systems should integrate all of the parts to meet total systems objectives. If the inputs to these systems are generated and controlled by the parts, suboptimization is likely to occur.

SYSTEMS THEORY AND
CONTINGENCY THEORY

The close ties between systems theory and contingency theory should be evident. Both have features that tend to overcome some of the limitations of traditional management theory. To describe what a manager does or to describe broad principles he can use is not enough. These two approaches to management attempt to avoid descriptive analysis and focus on the relationships of organizations and situations. Identifying the systems involved in organizations and their management—and understanding the primary variables and the multivariate relationships among them —is the key to comprehending how organizations function. It is also the key to knowing what actions of a manager will be effective in influencing this functioning. Systems theory provides the theoretical emphasis on wholes, parts, and relationships. Contingency theory implements systems theory by identifying the specific key parts (variables) and their attributes that are significant in managing organizations (people, tasks, structure, technology, and so on) and relating these to the need for particular concepts and techniques.

Because of the changing, adaptive nature of organizations, the systems and contingency theories emphasize that even though organizations have similarities in functioning as systems, they are in a different state of growth, or entropy. They are also distinct because the relative status and importance of the primary subsystems or variables differs from organization to organization. Accordingly, managers cannot apply common principles or techniques and get uniform results. The techniques and concepts used must be selected and applied consistent with the needs of the situation.

SUMMARY

Systems theory is concerned with a set of common elements, the whole represented by these elements, and the existing relationships among them that account for the characteristics, or existence, of the whole. Systems theory involves a broad perspective that integrates parts and elements with subsystems and systems. A system is defined as an entity, consisting of a composite whole, which is formed of interdependent parts or elements involving relationships that contribute to the unique characteristics of the whole. Closed systems have little interchange with their environment. Open systems adjust to environmental changes and actively interact with the environment.

Systems theory is not a separate branch of knowledge but a framework for restructuring existing knowledge. However, certain principles of systems theory exist. The primary principles relating to open systems are as follows:

- All parts in a system are interdependent
- The whole is more than a summation of the individual parts (synergy)
- Parts can only be understood when the whole is comprehended
- Boundary relationships with other systems constitute important interfaces
- All systems exist in a hierarchy of systems
- Open systems are changing and adaptive
- Open systems experience growth and decay processes (entropy).

The failure to think in systems terms is evident in many problems of organizations. Functional department heads tend to make decisions that optimize their own function but that are harmful to the total organization. Middle managers are rarely trained to develop the broad perspective required by a general manager. Reporting in organizations tends to center around functions or parts rather than the whole. Planning and control functions also tend to be dominated by interests that are narrow and self-serving. Needless to say, thinking in systems terms is valuable to the rising manager in an organization.

QUESTIONS FOR STUDY AND DISCUSSION

1. What is a system? How can it be identified? Of what significance is this identification?
2. How do the concepts of systems theory differ when related to physical systems versus social systems?
3. Why are organizations open systems?
4. How does systems theory differ from systems analysis?
5. Column A represents five different organizations, Column B five different features of systems. For each organization, separately identify these five systems' features.

A. 1. An insurance company   B. 1. Interdependence of parts

2. A municipal government   2. Synergy

3. The personnel office of a department store   3. Boundaries

4. The National Football League   4. Supra and subordinate systems

5. An airport control-tower team   5. Differences in the individuals' goals and the organization units at each level

6. Are open systems governed by parts or processes? Explain.

7. Based on the dependency of each of the following parts, explain how coherent a system the university is—how vital each part is to the system:

   A. Library
   B. Physics department
   C. The people who maintain the buildings and grounds
   D. Student government

8. Why are large firms generally able to resist entropy better than small ones?

9. Provide examples, in addition to those in the latter part of the chapter, of how organizing, staffing, communication, planning, and control functions can be analyzed from a systems standpoint. (For example, why are university academic departments frequently parts oriented? Is suboptimization a frequent occurrence in organizations you are familiar with?)

10. What are the differences and similarities between the systems and contingency theories?

Case Study:
THE OPPORTUNIST

Merrill Williams accepted employment as a contract administrator with a growing missile contractor in 1958. Previously he had acquired excellent experience in this rapidly expanding industry. He had been employed for three years with the Department of Defense as a contracting officer and had been with a defense contractor for another three years.

The new company Merrill joined obtained several major missile contracts, tripling in size within five years. This provided many opportunities for advancement, and Merrill was careful to put himself in line for these promotions. He soon became Head of Contract Administration, and—after some strategic maneuvering—budgeting and marketing were assigned to him. He was an efficient administrator and developed intense loyalty from the members of his department. No one doubted his basic competence.

Merrill often experienced conflict with other departments and was branded as an "empire builder" and opportunist. However, he developed the most effective division in the entire company. Because of his favorable relations with top management, he was able to obtain ample resources, and management frequently assigned him special projects because he had sufficient manpower to do the job. He also perceived these assignments as new opportunities and attacked each with unusual flare and enthusiasm. However, his success and "fat" department caused resentment among his peers. Often other departments went out of their way to undercut him or his operations.

Analyze this situation from a systems theory standpoint.
How do the seven principles of system theory apply?
How does figure 4-2 apply?
Was Merrill efficient as well as effective? Explain your answer.

Case Study:
FORMING A FURNITURE COMPANY

As part of a management class, students were assigned a term project to do all of the planning necessary to start a company engaged in making metal patio furniture. Four students were assigned to each team that was given responsibility for one of the following sets of tasks: production processing, facilities, product design, manpower, raw materials and inventory, marketing, finance, and production scheduling and control. The students were to establish their own top management organization structure and assign officers.

At the first planning session following the election of officers, considerable controversy arose over what phase of the planning should be accomplished first. Remarks such as the following were made:

"First we've got to have a sales forecast. We just can't start manufacturing a product. Unless we know what the sales potential is, we can't make any plans."

Another student was quick to retort, "No, finances are the real limitation. If we can't raise the funds to produce the product, a sales forecast is meaningless."

"Yes," another student replied, "but how can you determine your finances unless you establish your processing and find out what it's going to cost to produce the product? Until we have a production plan we can't establish manpower needs, a bill of materials, or any of our resource requirements."

One member of the facilities team responded, "I agree with that. We can't determine manufacturing or warehouse space until somebody makes up the production schedule. I'm for doing that first."

As the debate continued, the student who had been elected president stopped the discussion. "We're not getting anywhere. We've got to establish some goals and develop an overall plan. This is confusing. Maybe we should go back to the instructor and get more guidelines."

Discuss the case from a systems standpoint.

What special problems in integration are involved in running a company?

If you were president, how would you settle the issue?

Footnotes

1. Richard Johnson, Fremont E. Kast, and James E. Rosenzweig, *The Theory and Management of Systems* (New York: McGraw-Hill Book Company, 1963), p. 4.
2. R. L. Ackoff, "Systems, Organizations, and Interdisciplinary Research," F. E. Emery (Ed.) *Systems Thinking* (Middlesex, England: Penquin Books Ltd., 1969), p. 332.
3. *Ibid.*, p. 342
4. Alain C. Enthoven and K. Wayne Smith, *How Much is Enough? Shaping the Defense Program 1961–1969* (New York: Harper and Row, Publishers, Inc., 1970), p. 62.
5. V. I. Kremyanskiy, "Certain Peculiarities of Organisms as a 'System' from the Point of View of Physics, Cybernetics, and Biology," R. E. Emery (Ed.), *Systems Thinking, op. cit.*, p. 130.
6. Thomas A. Petit. "A Behavioral Theory of Management," *Academy of Management Journal,* December, 1967, pp. 341–350.

Manager Profile

Ted D. Simmons
Vice President Operations
Real Estate and Construction Division
International Business Machines Corporation
White Plains, New York

Background and Experience

Ted graduated from Utah State University in 1953 with a bachelor's degree in business. He completed an M.B.A. in 1955 at the Harvard Graduate School of Business Administration. He was on active duty with the U.S. Air Force from 1955 to 1957, after which he joined IBM in the Kingston plant as a technical assistant in organization planning. He has held eight different positions with IBM, primarily in the planning and control areas. His last three positions were as Planning Manager, Director of Planning, and ultimately Vice President of Operations for the Real Estate and Construction Division.

Primary Responsibilities

1. As operations vice-president for the Real Estate and Construction Division, he is responsible to the president of the division for operations relating to the providing of all housing for IBM. This includes office buildings, plants, laboratories, and headquarters facilities for all divisions in the United States. (The group acts in a staff capacity to foreign subsidiaries, which function as independent corporations.)

2. His organization evaluates users' needs, establishes design criteria, employs outside architects to develop the design, and issues contracts to builders to construct facilities consistent with the design.
3. He is responsible for all energy and environmental programs, including pollution control.

Insights

"Aside from the traditional role of management in assuring the success of the business enterprise through creative thinking, orderly administration, and good follow-up, I believe the management role is to provide an avenue through which people in the organization can succeed in their individual jobs. Thus it is not management's responsibility to merely hire and fire, but to see that the employee is given every opportunity to succeed in his or her responsibilities. At the same time, it is very important that the opportunity is also there to fail. If he can't fail, it is fairly obvious that sufficient responsibility has not been delegated to him.'

"I am particularly conscious in this day for the need of top management to exhibit strong moral leadership if the business enterprise and the environment system in which it hopes to prosper are to succeed. Management must be committed to a set of beliefs that are moral in their derivation and stringently adhered to in administration. These beliefs must permeate every facet of the business enterprise. They cannot be abrogated for convenience, expedience, or short-range benefit."

Manager Profile

Bill Terrell
State Manager
Meadow Gold Dairies
Salt Lake City, Utah

Background and Experience

Bill has been with Meadow Gold Dairies, a division of Beatrice Foods Company (headquartered in Chicago), for thirty years. He joined the company in Boise, Idaho. In working up "through the ranks," he served in many different capacities including processing, product delivery, and supervisory. After five years he was appointed branch manager in Pocatello; for the past eleven years he has been state manager in Utah.

Primary Responsibilities

1. He is responsible for the production and sale of all Meadow Gold products in the state of Utah. This includes dairy products like milk, cheese, and ice cream, as well as certain institutional frozen foods.
2. He is responsible for 225 employees who are engaged in the production and sale of these products.
3. There are approximately eighteen branch managers and supervisors of production centers within the region who are responsible to Bill.

Insights

"Beatrice Foods is a very decentralized company. Within their guidelines and policies they let you run your own show. This provides considerable incentive and is one of the major keys to success of the organization.

"I work through an operating group of eight people. In my type of work, it is impossible to effectively supervise more. We meet monthly to review progress and take appropriate action. These eight individuals then communicate down through the next level on much the same basis. This provides sufficient structure within the broad delegation of authority we provide.

"I have respect from my subordinates, because I came up through the ranks and I have performed every job I ask them to do. This has caused me to be very employee oriented.

"Our company feels that bonus and recognition programs are very important in motivation. We have an honors club, and we annually give many prizes and awards. This involves money, trips, and other recognitions—such as trophies and awards."

PART III

Decision Making in Management

The Nature of Decision Making

How does a manager make decisions?

Why is decision making considered a process?

What procedure and steps are involved in rational problem solving?

What limitations are there in a manager using rational problem-solving methods?

What forces influence a manager in the decision-making process?

Why is decision making situational?

The nature of managerial decision making can be explored by analyzing the daily log of the chief executive of a medium-sized furniture company:

8:00   Reviews correspondence and dictates replies to secretary

8:45   Meets with the industrial-relations staff to develop strategy for upcoming labor negotiations

9:30   Meets with the production manager and his staff to review plans for accelerating the production schedule based on an increased sales forecast

11:00   Reads the report of the site-selection committee regarding possible location of regional warehouse facilities; asks for more information

12:00   Lunch with two visiting members of the Board of Directors

1:00   Tour of production facilities with visitors

2:00   Reviews files of top three applicants for position of plant security officer; conducts final interview with top applicant and offers him the position

3:15   Reviews the monthly management report; calls sales manager to find out why product C is lagging 20 percent behind forecast

4:00   Meets with the controller and other members of his staff to consider alternatives for financing construction of regional warehouse facilities

One of the primary conclusions that can be made from this log is that all management activity involves decision making. Essentially every entry reflects a phase in the process of arriving at fairly major organizational decisions. As one of the intervening or linking functions of management, decision making is the means by which managers plan, organize, staff, direct, and control. For this reason, some writers consider decision making to be synonymous with management.

Based on the assumption that organizations operate through people making decisions, the next question is, what determines the choices they make? Choices are influenced by the desire to achieve certain ends or goals. The plan to accelerate production is directed toward the ultimate goal of increasing output and profits. Regional warehouses are required to improve distribution, also leading to increased profits. Thus decisions are future oriented. Certain results are sought based on anticipated conditions, which forces decisions to be predictive in nature. The individual makes a decision to move from an existing state of affairs to new conditions or the desired state of affairs. Often this involves the selection of certain means (accelerated production) to get to the desired end (increased profits). When such events are linked in sequential fashion, they are referred to as a *means-ends chain.*

It is also evident from the log that decision making is a process and not a discrete event. In each instance the executive is engaged in one phase of that process. In the log above, the only instance in which a specific choice was made is during the 2:00 P.M. session when an individual was selected as the plant security officer. Otherwise the manager was engaged in considering alternatives, evaluating information relative to these alternatives, and appraising recommendations submitted by lower-level executives. The preliminary conclusions that can be derived from the above incident are important observations relating to the nature of decision making. These are:

1. Organizations operate through people making decisions.
2. Decision making is goal oriented.
3. Decision making is a process, not a discrete event.

For the purposes of this chapter, certain aspects of conclusions 1 and 3 need to be examined in more detail. (Conclusion 2, relating to decision making being goal oriented is elaborated on in chapter 22.)

THREE BASES FOR MAKING DECISIONS

Human behavior consists of people taking actions and making decisions. Some individual behavior is relatively automatic and not a result of logical thought processes—such as habits and conditioned response to stimuli. However, the more deliberate type of managerial behavior is punctuated by a series of decisions that are normally interrelated and rationally conceived. The decisions of managers are made in three different ways: they are intuitive, based on judgment, or else involve a detailed analytical process, such as one would expect to find in problem solving.

Intuitive Decisions

Intuitive decisions are made when an individual has no knowledge of the factors underlying a problem or is unfamiliar with workable solutions, so he or she merely has a hunch or "feel" for what action should be taken. This ready insight into solutions cannot be completely dispelled in explaining the success of certain managers, but since it represents little more than guessing it is hardly acceptable as a basis for directing organizations.

Judgmental Decisions

Decisions based on *judgment* are actually the type that consume most of the typical manager's time. His knowledge and experience gained through tenure in a particular position help him to be accurate in making routine decisions regarding the operations of the organization. Through his experience, he learns to depend on a set of decision rules or rules of thumb that guide his decision making. Through this common-sense approach, he often makes dozens of decisions during a day when there is no need to investigate the circumstances thoroughly because he is familiar enough with the activities to predict the outcome accurately. In the example at the beginning of the chapter, much of the correspondence dictated to the secretary would involve relatively routine matters where experience would determine the nature of the reply. Deciding which facilities to visit on the plant tour would also comprise a series of straightforward decisions with little cause for mental reflection.

Problem Solving as a Type of Decision

The third type of decision, that involving *problem solving,* is demonstrated in the log by the pending action on the location of the warehouse facilities. The plant manager would not have the necessary knowledge of each possible site in order to make a judgmental decision. In giving consideration to the criteria for site selection, the manager would need to have data collected on each criterion as it relates to each site. The same situation would prevail regarding the decisions covering strategy for the labor negotiations, revised plans for accelerating production, and finding sources for financing the warehouses. Problem solving involves a much more complex analytical process than decisions based on judgment. Facts must be gathered, trade-offs evaluated, and possible outcomes analyzed.

This latter type of decision making is the prime concern of this chapter. Decision making relying solely on judgment tends to be an art in which learning is gained from experience. However, problem solving is an analytical process using a method like that involved in scientific inquiry. The normal distinction between programmed and nonprogrammed decisions is similar to the differences between decision making and problem solving. Programmed decisions have relatively known consequences or outcomes, so they can often be handled electronically. Nonprogrammed decisions compare with problem solving in which outcomes are uncertain, and rational evaluation of the circumstances is required. Most managerial decisions are adequately made merely by using judgment based on a ready familiarity with the circumstances relating to the dominant variables in a known situation. Nevertheless, the success of an organization is ultimately dependent on how it identifies and resolves major difficulties where the causal factors are not obvious and decisions not automatic. A manager needs to master the method of problem solving, because this is one factor that distinguishes the effective manager from a clerk, who simply maintains ongoing activities.

THE DECISION-MAKING PROCESS
IN PROBLEM SOLVING

As indicated earlier, decision making is a process. It is not simply making a choice to proceed with a course of action—it is the development of alternatives, the collection of information to evaluate them, and the whole sequence of events that occurs, starting with when a problem is identified until that point at which it is effectively resolved. Nine steps can be identified in the problem-solving process:

1. Be aware of undesirable current conditions or desired future ones.
2. Collect and analyze information pertinent to the difficulty or goal.
3. Identify the underlying problem(s) or barrier(s).
4. Establish criteria and identify constraints relating to the decision.
5. Establish alternatives for solving the problem(s).
6. Collect data and evaluate alternatives.
7. Make a choice.
8. Gain acceptance for the decision and implement it.
9. Obtain feedback to determine if the decision is achieving the results desired.

The number of steps in problem solving is, of course, arbitrary. Also, some information is collected in every phase of the process, not just in steps two and six. In addition, in many situations all nine steps may not be necessary, depending on the circumstances. Accordingly it is the overall methodology of problem solving that deserves recognition, but it is convenient for analytical purposes to segregate the method into individual steps or phases. Each step will be examined by exploring the methodology involved in an example of a furniture manufacturer selecting a site for a regional warehouse.

STEP ONE: BE AWARE OF UNDESIRABLE CONDITIONS.   Many conditions can exist in an organization that make it apparent to a manager that things are not going as anticipated. These are referred to as *symptoms*. The term is used the same as in medicine, when a temperature and a headache tell the doctor that something is wrong, but he must search deeper to find the cause before prescribing a medicine. In a business, low morale, tension in the organization, high cost of production, and low profits are symptoms. They tell the manager that something is wrong, but from this information alone it is not possible to prescribe a solution. He must first identify the problem or problems that have created the conditions or symptoms. Symptoms relating to the example of our furniture manufacturer might consist of complaints coming from retail outlets that delivery of ordered furniture was slow or that ordering of special items was delayed to the point where the firm was losing customers. Also, freight costs might be excessive if individual items were shipped ignoring the advantages of bulk rates or carload lots. Step one might also have started by a desire for future conditions resulting from dissatisfaction with current profit levels.

STEP TWO: COLLECT AND ANALYZE INFORMATION PERTINENT TO THE ISSUE(S). The methods selected to identify problems are a function of the symptoms under study. If profits are low, a cost study could be undertaken to identify the cost elements that are excessive. It would then have to be determined why they are excessive. If low morale exists or tensions signal dissatisfaction in the organization, interviews could be conducted, attitude surveys could be undertaken, and many other means used to determine why the employees are dissatisfied. In the example of the regional warehouse, a study of time delays and costs associated with the transportation of the furniture could be conducted that compare their operations with those of competitors. The retail managers who purchase the furniture might be interviewed to obtain their perspective of the problem.

STEP THREE: IDENTIFY THE PROBLEM.   This is one of the most critical steps in problem solving. If a problem is inadequately identified, the solution cannot be effective. The adage that a well-defined problem is half solved holds much truth. Too frequently symptoms and problems persist in an organization because in the rush to resolve the issue the problem is never accurately identified. The manager attempts to remove symptoms without getting at their underlying causes. Psychological barriers make problem identification extremely difficult. A problem a manager is responsible for solving by definition implies an interrelationship between the problem and the solver. This personal involvement makes objective evaluation difficult.

Problem solving is complex also because there is often not just one but multiple causes contributing to the conditions. For this reason, if an individual comes up with a quick solution to a difficult problem, he or she normally has not identified the problem adequately. In the site-location example, the study undertaken in step two would most likely show that delay times and transportation costs were higher than those of competitors who have shorter distances to transport their furniture.

It would, therefore, indicate a need for storage facilities closer to retailers in the region.

STEP FOUR: ESTABLISH CRITERIA AND IDENTIFY CONSTRAINTS.   Normally before a manager can proceed with the solution to a problem, he needs to identify the constraints that will influence the methods he intends to use in the steps that follow (five through seven). If a firm has extremely limited resources, it will obviously eliminate any alternatives established under step five that call for a large commitment of such resources. Other constraints are the goals of the organization, company policies, the time frame within which the decision should be made, cultural constraints relating to values, the aspiration level of the individual, and many other factors representing situational differences. Step four may also include measures of effectiveness in relation to the goal desired. These measures and constraints are established based on the nature of the problem identified. An example of constraints in relation to the warehouse site is that construction or investment costs could not exceed $300,000; deliveries must be made to 80 percent of the retailers in the area within 4 days; and annual operating costs of the facility must be less than 5 percent of the value of the average inventory.

STEP FIVE: ESTABLISH ALTERNATIVES.   Establishing a set of logical alternatives ensures breadth of analysis. A common weakness in problem solving is moving too hastily in reaching a solution. In the rush to get the symptoms removed, managers are often inclined to select the first solution that comes to their minds or solutions that they have relied on previously. However, objective analysis of logical alternatives can often reveal a solution far preferable to the first hunch. Also, problems are often stated in a "yes—no", "go—no go" fashion. If this is done, the question is restricted to, Should we or should we not pursue a particular course of action? In reality this means that only one alternative is considered. If a regional warehouse goes on the market in a suitable city and the manager decides to purchase that warehouse without comparing it to other alternatives in other locations, he faces the possibility of making a poor decision.

Appropriate methodology has been developed for selecting alternatives. Alternatives should be restricted to those that appear to meet the criteria and those that are logical, based on information developed to this point in the decision process. It is desirable to restrict them in number so that this phase of problem solving does not get out of hand. Alternatives to locating the warehouse should normally be limited to ten sites and preferably less. With ten possible sites, differences between these ten locations and those left out would obviously be minor. Attempting to evaluate two hundred alternative sites makes the analysis unmanageable, since marginal differences between many of the sites would be inconsequential.

STEP SIX: COLLECT DATA AND EVALUATE ALTERNATIVES. A framework should be used to collect data consistent with all alternatives. When the type of information needed for evaluating the alternatives is established, the data collection relating to comparative costs, resources, time factors, and other variables can be undertaken. Another useful approach to the analysis of alternatives is to list the disadvantages as well as the advantages of each, which forces a more balanced, objective analysis. This "T" chart approach is shown in figure 5-1, involving if a decision should be made based on judgment or problem-solving methodology.

Psychological barriers are also evident in this step. Too often an analyst searches for data to support a decision that he has already mentally accepted. Also, it is often difficult to get objective data if the source of the information has something to gain from the decision that is made (e.g., the manufacturers of a product submitting data on an item they produce). Another important factor in alternative evaluation is the likelihood or probability that the alternative will be successful. (Techniques for dealing with probabilities will be discussed in chapter 7.)

STEP SEVEN: MAKE A CHOICE. If the problems are accurately identified, logical alternatives established, and a thorough search made for evaluative data, the choice becomes relatively simple. With all of this laid out before the decision maker, he or she is then in a position to make a proper decision. At this point, judgment again strongly comes into play. The decision maker must evaluate the information and use his judgment to arrive at a decision. Few solutions to major problems are automatic in the sense that all information points overwhelmingly to one alternative. In solving management problems, frequently the principle of *equifinality* predominates. (As noted in chapter 1, equifinality assumes there are equal ways of getting to a final condition.) There might be several ways to organize a project in which the outcomes resulting from the organization would be approximately the same or equal. The manager's task normally is to find desirable alternatives and avoid poor ones, being sure to select one of the former and pass up the latter. Contingency management theory cautions the decision maker to avoid the "one best way" syndrome, especially if it is assumed that one successful solution can be applied to other problems even if the problems are similar. The emphasis is on finding *effective* decisions rather than *correct* decisions.

Herbert Simon also cautions that managers search for satisfactory goals rather than the theoretical maximum which is the assumption of

Alternative 1: Use Judgment Only		Alternative 2: Use Problem-Solving Methodology	
Advantages	*Disadvantages*	*Advantages*	*Disadvantages*
1. Quick	1. Possible sound alternatives ignored	1. Thorough—all alternatives considered	1. Time consuming
2. If situation is familiar and outcome is predictable, more information not required	2. Adequate data may not be available to make a sound decision	2. Analytical—data collected to aid in making the decision	2. Time may not permit detailed analysis
3. Cost of making decisions kept to a minimum	3. Experience of decision maker may not be sufficiently broad to cover key variables in the decision	3. More balanced—not based solely on experience	3. Costly—takes time and resources
	4. Too narrow an approach for complex problems	4. Better decisions normally made	4. Not necessary if judgment is adequate
			5. Contrary to behavior followed in making most decisions—not natural

Fig. 5-1. T-chart approach to analyzing alternatives

traditional economic theory.[1] This *satisficing* theory made popular by Simon holds that managers work for solutions that are satisfactory or consistent with what owners, managers, and other perceive as satisfactory. Business firms typically seek *satisfactory* levels of profit rather than undertaking steps to always *maximize* profit. This rationale can be applied to our example. A warehouse site will be satisfactory if it reduces the transportation time lag to four days which is satisfying to most customers rather than exerting maximum efforts to reduce the time lag to that which is the lowest possible to achieve. Achieving the maximum often results in added costs far in excess of the marginal benefits derived.

STEP EIGHT: GAIN ACCEPTANCE FOR THE DECISION AND IMPLEMENT IT.   In decision making there are two significant aspects: first, making a good technical decision and, second, gaining acceptance for that decision. Many individuals have useful ideas, but they are never adopted by an organization because the individuals are unable to sell them to others. Decisions must also be sold. A decision-making process that gives no consideration to how others will react to the decision ignores a fundamental concept.

This is the bugaboo of the fiscal policies of governments. Economists can tell the president and Congress when a theoretically correct time exists to institute a tax increase to fight inflation. However, these recommendations are tempered by politicians—based on how they think the electorate will react to such a proposal. Even in a business organization where employees are paid to carry out the tasks of the organization, a manager must be concerned with how his work group and how external groups will accept the decision. The manager will most likely get far better results if he compromises what he would do by considering the attitudes of the groups affected—will this win their support rather than alienate them? Obviously, there is much more to implementing a decision than gaining group acceptance. However, the other topics encompassing resource allocation, budgeting, etc. are more appropriately covered later in the planning and control section of this text.

STEP NINE: OBTAIN FEEDBACK TO MEASURE RESULTS.   The final step in decision making is to obtain feedback on what takes place during the implementation phase—to make sure the desired future conditions are in process of being achieved. Unless the results are consistent with the criteria and goals established in step four, an inadequate decision has been made, or conditions have sufficiently changed to force a re-examination of the actions taken. (This step is considered a part of the control function of management and will be covered in Part VIII.)

Limitations of the Problem-Solving Process

The above problem-solving process assumes an ideal situation, in which human rationality is maximized in making decisions. However, rarely does decision making proceed in the logical sequence presented. The person running a small business often lacks resources to be this thorough, and the busy executive, under pressure to maintain performance, lacks time. However, the simplified process of establishing goals, developing alternatives, evaluating alternatives, and making a choice is a vital framework for objective and effective decision making. It is one of the fundamentals that every manager should develop as a part of an executive repertoire.

One other feature of the process tends to be deceptive. Constraints exist in terms of what Simon refers to as the "bounded rationality" of the administrator.[2] Even though the problem-solving methodology would imply that a manager should know all possible alternatives, have complete, accurate facts in relation to these alternatives, and be able to anticipate all results, this is, of course, not consistent with the real world. Perfect information rarely (if ever) exists. Some information is always lacking, and no one has ever demonstrated unerring foresight. Furthermore, the personal objectives, feelings, and perceptions of the decision maker tend to interfere with an objective analysis of the limited information available. Thus. rationality is always limited, and uncertainty is a normal variable in the decision process.

CONCLUSIONS REGARDING THE DECISION-MAKING PROCESS

Two major conclusions are appropriate regarding the characteristics of the decision-making process. The first of these is that no decision stands alone. Decisions tend to be interrelated and sequential. One decision typically leads to the need for others, demonstrating systems-dependency relationships. If a high school graduate decides to enroll in a particular college, many other related decisions must follow. Where is housing to be obtained? What financial support is necessary and how will it be provided? What curriculum is to be pursued? What time commitment is required? The decision process typically involves the selection of certain means to achieve particular ends. Typically these ends are intermediate steps to broader ends relating to the major goals of the individual or organization. All major decisions of organizations involve many more minor implementing decisions relating to resources, schedules, and tasks to be performed.

The second conclusion is that all decisions involve trade-offs. Of the alternatives selected, each will typically have some feature or features that are superior in some respects to those of other alternatives. The advantages of one alternative are only gained through sacrificing the benefits of another. (The quality of a product can be improved by using better materials but higher costs will be incurred compared to the lower costs of an alternative involving no change in materials.) Thus, managerial decision making is not a question of black and white or right or wrong, but an exercise in evaluating trade-offs where choices typically involve some form of compromise.

CONTINGENCY CONSIDERATIONS IN DECISION MAKING

Many of the contingency aspects of decision making have already been examined. The basic contingency model in chapter 3 (figure 3-2) is a decision model as well as one representative of the management process. It contains the primary internal and external variables that a manager should be concerned with in decision making. Situational analysis has also been covered in previous chapters, emphasizing that a manager must be familiar with situational variables—as well as management concepts and techniques—because it is the matching of these with the demands of a situation that is the mark of a manager. Managerial decision making involves knowing what concepts and techniques should be used under different circumstances so that when a manager encounters certain conditions, he or she will know which concepts are appropriate. Decision making using a contingency perspective thus holds that "if" certain conditions exist, "then" certain actions appropriate to those conditions become necessary.

The Decision Maker as an Evaluator of Forces

One other major consideration becomes important in viewing decision making from a contingency standpoint. That is that a manager not only should be aware of, and trained in, rational problem-solving processes like the nine-step sequence proposed, but he also needs to be aware of the primary human forces that are dominant in the situation being faced. Power figures, pressure groups, and the expectations of others influence the decisions that managers make as well as acceptance of these decisions by others.

PITFALLS IN DECISION MAKING

A third pitfall is oversimplification. If my experience has taught me anything, it is that the "192 principles" of organization that can be extracted from the textbooks do not begin to answer even the *least* complex organization problems. Why? There are many reasons. Values differ, conditions change, all the facts are rarely (if ever) available, nonrational as well as rational factors influence the decisions made. But the most pervasive reason is that organizing involves people. And people react on the basis of an almost infinite number of stimuli. I have yet to participate in the discussion of a concrete organization problem in which we did not spend more time discussing how a key figure would react, and the abilities, prejudices, likes and dislikes, and strengths and weaknesses of the principal executives involved than all the time (if any) spent discussing "unity of command," "span of control," the "scalar principle," and the "general staff concept."

Quotation from Harvey Sherman, *It All Depends* (The University of Alabama Press, 1966), p. 104.

Figure 5-2 represents this relationship. Decision making is divided into two sets of factors: rational decision processes and methods of analysis, and the pressures that come to bear upon the decision maker resulting from the particular individuals and groups that he identifies or is involved with in an influence relationship. In making a decision, an individual first wants to please (and is rewarded for) pleasing his or her supervisor. There will be a reluctance to carry out some action that a supervisor will not agree with. On the other hand, the decision maker also wants to maintain the support and respect of subordinates, so there will be an inclination to make decisions that will not alienate them. Those who see themselves as losing through the decision will resist the proposed action, and those who perceive themselves as gaining will apply pressure to have the decision consummated.

In a sense a supervisor experiences to some degree the pressures of a Congressman. He is being bombarded from all sides by individuals or pressure groups who are attempting to "influence his vote" or affect his decisions. All of the individuals he works with (or in some instances is even remotely associated with) will have expectations that influence his actions. He may not personally know the stockholders of the company, but he is aware they expect him to be engaged in actions that will

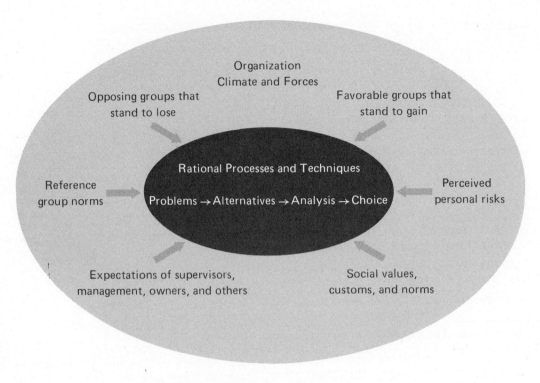

Fig. 5-2. Two aspects of decision making

promote efficiency and increase profits. Ultimately, the individual sensitive to group dynamics evaluates these forces and makes judgments about their potential influence on the projected outcome of a decision. Most individuals like to be on the "winning side," so that decisions will be modified as a result of evaluating the strength of the forces involved.

This is not to imply that a manager is always inclined to make the popular decision. Management is often a lonely position where friends must be rebuffed for the good of the organization. Discipline tends to be a distasteful but necessary part of a supervisor's job. Reductions in force, passing people over for promotion, and rewarding some while penalizing others is not normally a pleasant experience, but it is an inevitable feature of the types of decisions that supervisors are called on to make.

One of the most deceptive aspects of supervision and decision making involves an assumption frequently made by individuals unfamiliar with organizational processes: that the manager has a free hand to make unilateral decisions and move in any direction he desires. Managers are always subject to the forces and constraints shown in figure 5-2, and frequently their well-designed plans never see the light of day because the climate is not appropriate for gaining acceptance from the groups they rely on for their power base. In decisions directly influencing individuals and groups, power and personalities have more influence on the decision than do problem-solving processes emphasizing efficiency and economy. However, these factors will be reversed when the decision relates to material resources, such as would be involved in production. This once again demonstrates the situational nature of management.

Group Decision Making

A major contingency variable is the party or parties responsible for making the decision. Our assumption to this point in the chapter is that management decisions are always the responsibility of an *individual*. Often, however, decisions are the prerogative of a *group*, like the U.S. House of Representatives or a corporate committee set up to make recommendations on reorganization. Many of the decision processes relevant to individuals are also relevant to groups, but the shared authority and responsibility of the group tends to disperse power, placing a premium on bargaining, compromise, and group pressure tactics. Group decision making obviously complicates the decision process. No action can be taken until a coalition of individuals representing divergent viewpoints can come to some agreement. Typically group decision processes reward those effective in political behavior with some lessening of emphasis on the rational problem-solving process.

Other Behavioral Considerations

Before leaving the human factors in decision making, two other concepts should be introduced. One of the important abilities associated with leadership is that of maintaining an open climate in which subordinates feel free to state their opinion regarding a proposed course of action. Frequently a manager is inclined to collect around him individuals who will build up his ego and support him regardless of what he does. Such "yes men" (or women) have little effectiveness in injecting new ideas into the organization, and they normally fail to have their supervisor rethink alternatives that have been selected without proper analysis. Many of the industrial giants have experienced major setbacks because executives refused to listen to subordinates, and they eliminated those who told them things they did not want to hear. An open atmosphere conducive to the objective evaluation of proposed executive action is one of the most difficult—and one of the most important—conditions to establish in an organization.

Closely related to the above is the benefits that can come from participation. The more subordinates participate in the decisions that are made, the more they are likely to be open in evaluation and able to generate beneficial ideas. Also, this participation is the best means of gaining the commitment and acceptance of subordinates (in conjunction with step eight in problem solving). There are certain drawbacks to participation, as we shall see in chapter 18, but the cultural trend toward power equalization in organizations makes participation a more inevitable feature of decision making.

TIMING IN DECISION MAKING

The following quotation is reprinted from the July 7, 1975 issue of *The Wall Street Journal*, page 24. It is extracted from an article written by John R. Emshwiller, which explores the repercussions of the announcement by Lynn A. Townsend that he will retire as chairman and chief executive of Chrysler Corporation as of October 1, 1975.

"The charge of poor timing has haunted the company throughout the Townsend years. This fall, when its new compacts come out, they will compete head-on with Chrysler's aging but profitable Valiant and Dart compacts. Last fall, as the energy crisis loomed large and sent big-car sales plummeting, Chrysler had just introduced a restyled line of full-sized cars.

"Late last year, the company misread the growing weakness in the automotive market and continued to produce new cars. When sales collapsed in November, Chrysler was left with backbreaking inventories of unsold cars—a predicament similar to the one that plunged it deeply into the red during its previous major crisis in 1970.

"Chrysler officials have vigorously countered attacks on their management decisions. For example, they say they couldn't have foreseen the energy crisis when they planned their big cars. In addition, they note that the rest of the industry also was caught off guard by the size of the sales slump last winter. They say their decision to stay out of the subcompact market has been vindicated by sales successes in the compact field. And they add that other auto makers have frequently been buried under bulging inventories of unsold subcompacts."

IMPLICATIONS FOR THE DECISION MAKER

The complexity and situationality of the decision process have a variety of meanings for the decision maker. However, a few guides stand out as desirable attributes of those skilled in the decision process. The decision maker:

- is analytical in problem solving, being careful to make sure the problem has been properly identified, a wide range of alternatives has been considered, and information pertinent to both sides of the issue has been obtained.

- is sensitive to personalities and forces and effectively evaluates these in anticipating the problems in reaching and implementing a decision.

- is open to the opinion of others and creates an atmosphere in which those of lesser status in the organization feel they can express their views.

- has a feel for appropriate timing in making a choice and guides the decision process consistent with the time constraints.

- is enthusiastic once the analysis is complete, and decisive in making a choice. When a decision is made in a half-hearted fashion (or when a manager procrastinates in making a decision), this indecisiveness is felt by subordinates and implementation is characterized by the same lack of enthusiasm. It is often natural to second-guess oneself on major decisions, like the young man the morning after his marriage proposal. The manager should be alert for feedback that may lead him to think he made the wrong decision, but until problems are experienced in implementation, the decision should be vigorously pursued.

SUMMARY

Decision making is an act of choice, where an individual decides to pursue a course of action selected from a number of different alternatives. Decision making is the action or linking process of management, because it is the means by which the management functions of planning, organizing, staffing, directing, and controlling are carried out. Decision making is not a discrete event but a process. The process is simplified when the manager has little information and operates on a hunch or by intuition. Routine decisions are made on the basis of judgment, where repeated experience with the circumstances dictates what action will normally be successful.

Major difficulties characterized by many unknowns call for a more complex process known as problem solving. Problem solving involves nine steps:

- being aware of symptoms or undesirable conditions
- collecting information to better understand the issue at hand
- identification of the underlying problem
- establishing criteria to evaluate the decision
- establishing a set of logical alternatives
- collecting data to evaluate the alternatives
- making a choice
- gaining acceptance and implementing the decision
- obtaining feedback as the implementation takes place.

There are two aspects of the decision process. One is to use sound techniques and methods in arriving at a rational choice. The second is to evaluate the forces that come to play on the individual who is undertaking the decision. There is a political tinge to all decisions, since a technically sound one should be acceptable to the groups that are affected by it. Accordingly the manager needs to be a skilled evaluator of these forces.

The climate of the organization, relating to decision making, is an important factor in the decision process. Open organizations normally arrive at better decisions because of the broader, fewer one-sided analyses that take place.

QUESTIONS FOR STUDY AND DISCUSSION

1. Go through the log of the manager at the beginning of the chapter and identify the phase that each entry represents in the problem-solving process.
2. Distinguish between decisions made on the basis of intuition, judgment, and problem-solving methodology. Give examples of decisions you make on all three bases.
3. Illustrate the nine steps in problem solving by developing hypothetical examples relating to how each of the following should be handled:
   A. A student who enrolls at a university and has made no arrangements for housing

B. The owner of a restaurant where the turnover among his waitresses is 50 percent each month

C. A chief of police, when the accidents at an intersection tend to be 200 percent higher than any other intersection in the community

D. A manufacturing firm has experienced several wildcat strikes within the past ten months

4. How does the concept of bounded rationality relate to the four examples above?

5. Establish a set of alternatives that could be developed for each of the following problems:

A. A razor blade manufacturer who concludes that his advertising is less effective than competitors

B. A small businessman who needs additional funds to expand his operations

C. A history department that decides it needs to update its curriculum

6. "A decision maker is an evaluator of forces." Explain.

7. Planning and control functions are closely associated with the problem-solving process. Which steps are most closely associated with planning and which ones with control?

8. How does the contingency model of management relate to the problem-solving process?

9. In the latter part of the chapter, five major guides for decision making are provided. Can you identify any other significant ones?

Case Problem:
RALLISON SPORTING GOODS (PART I)

Gene Rallison owns and operates a sportings-goods store in a large metropolitan city. The store is located in a moderately fashionable part of the downtown area. He has operated the store in the same location for fifteen years and has had a very profitable business until the last three. Gene's sales started to drop off two years ago and were down twenty percent last year. He had assumed his sales dropped because other stores were often undercutting him on price. Starting last year, Gene reduced prices on many of his leading items. Sales during the year went up fifteen percent, but he still had a drop of five percent in profit over the previous year.

Is Gene dealing with symptoms or the problem?

How can Gene go about determining the cause(s) of his sales and profit decline?

How can he correct the situation?

RALLISON SPORTING GOODS (PART II)

Some months later, after studying the situation, Gene concludes that his store location is a disadvantage. Newer stores with more parking and higher volume seem to be doing better. Therefore he has set about the task of finding a new location. His friend has told him of a store that is for lease in a local suburb, and Gene is considering renting it.

Is Gene following the rational problem-solving process?

What constraints limit his choice?

How can he establish alternatives for site location?

What information should he use to evaluate these alternatives?

Who must he "sell" his decision to (step eight in the problem-solving process)?

Case Problem:
LAMBERT CLOTHIERS

Lambert Clothiers makes a complete line of clothing for skiing and other winter sports. At different plants they make pants, sweaters, jackets, and shirts. Most of the plants are located in small rural communities where there is a surplus of female labor, wage rates are low, and unions are virtually nonexistent. Ron Wicks manages a plant of 125 employees that makes jackets. Their recent output has been 600 jackets per day. However, for the past several months the vice president of production at the corporate office has expressed dissatisfaction with the plant's efficiency. He has stated several times that production should be higher, and in this morning's mail Ron received a curt letter stating that the corporate office expects him to increase production to 750 jackets per day within six months.

Ron felt considerable anxiety upon receiving the letter. Last year when he attempted to up production, he met considerable resistance from the work force, and he actually felt they deliberately engaged in a slowdown. The morale of the employees seems fairly good, but there are the usual complaints about wages, working conditions, and an inequitable vacation policy. Ron is also aware that some of the employees have talked with union organizers. In addition, he is concerned because he normally works ten hours a day including Saturdays in an effort to maintain high production. His wife has been quick to complain that he is not spending enough time with the family.

How should Ron handle the situation?

What are the sources of pressure that will influence him in the decisions he makes?

Is the rational problem-solving methodology of any assistance in making these decisions? In what ways?

Footnotes

1. Herbert A. Simon, *Administrative Behavior* (New York: The Macmillan Company, 1957). Second edition.
2. *Ibid.*, p. 52 ff.

The Role of Management Science

How can one account for the growth of management science?

What basic concepts characterize management science?

What advantages and limitations are associated with the use of management-science concepts?

What are some of the basic tools of management science?

Of what value are models to management?

How can linear programming assist a decision maker?

What variables are subject to quantification?

As indicated in chapter 2, the operations research, or management-science movement, began during World War II. It was founded on the use of mathematics, statistics, and physical-science research techniques in solving operational problems. The success of these techniques in military operations encouraged their adoption by business firms, initiating one of the major revolutions that has occurred in management theory and practice. The movement caught the interest of academicians, and soon a whole series of quantitative techniques was under study for business application.

This approach to solving business problems was initially referred to as *operations research* (O.R.), signifying the use of scientific-research methodology to solve operating problems. In later years as the movement has broadened, it has been also referred to as *management science*, conveying basically the same meaning of applying the scientific method to management problems. For our purposes the terms will be used interchangeably, although the latter term signifies a broader scope of associated methods and techniques. *Management science is defined as the use of the scientific method, models, and quantitative techniques to solve management problems and evaluate decision alternatives.* The main thrust of management science is to provide a scientific basis for decision making by developing models, analyzing relationships, and quantifying data so that tools such as mathematical equations and statistical probabilities can be used.

BASIC CONCEPTS OF MANAGEMENT SCIENCE

Even though there is a large number of quantitative tools comprising the bag of the management scientist, there is a limited number of concepts representative of this approach. Basically the movement has been built on five methodologies.

Use of the Scientific Method

The scientific method uses detailed analysis and experimentation to advance knowledge through verification of the existence of relationships or the uncovering of new data. The general methodology of scientific discovery is similar to the methodology of problem solving presented in the last chapter. It starts with the recognition of a problem or the need for new knowledge. This is followed by gaining a better understanding of the problem through observation or other methods of inquiry. From this a hypothesis is developed that is a tentative logical explanation of the problem or situation. Experiments are conducted and data gathered to test the hypothesis, which is often expressed in mathematical form. The hypothesis is either accepted or rejected based on this verification process. If the hypothesis is accepted, the problem is resolved and knowledge is increased. If the hypothesis is rejected, this information is often useful in developing other feasible hypotheses that are then pursued with this same methodology.

Establishing a Model

Management situations involve a blend of relationships and forces that frequently make it impossible for the human mind to deal with this complexity. Models are simplifications or abstractions of reality that are easier to comprehend. The model is developed based on those variables that are most important in representing reality or explaining the model's function. These are, therefore, the factors most deserving of consideration by the manager.

Deciding how detailed to develop a model is one of the primary questions for the operations-research analyst. Normally the more variables included, the more accurate the model. However, more variables add to the complexity of the relationships and the difficulty in comprehending the model. A road map is an example of a model that is fairly simple if the user's purpose is to drive to a certain location. With this objective he needs only to locate cities, distances, and the different type of roads. However if a company is using the map to lay a pipeline, contours, streams, and other geographical variables now become important. Organization charts, financial statements, position descriptions, flow charts, and explanations of the management process (such as figure 3-2) are all simplifications of reality—thus models. Models are usually classified into three types:

1. *Iconic* models are scaled reproductions that visually represent what is being duplicated. A mock up of an experimental product made to one-tenth the intended size and a road map are examples.

2. *Analogue* models use one set of properties to represent another in a way that facilitates understanding. The input and outflow of resources in a production plant are complex and therefore hard to comprehend. An analogue model based on the analogy of water flowing through pipes is often used to represent the appropriate flow and storage relationships.

3. *Symbolic* or *mathematical* models use symbols or mathematical representations of the variables in a problem. This is probably the most common and useful model for management scientists who rely on equations and quantitative methods to solve problems.

Quantification of Relationships

Unless a management scientist can quantify the relationships in a model or problem, he is extremely hampered in his analysis. The attempt is to substitute numbers for adjectives because of the imprecision of language. Also, quantification places all information in identical form, where it can be easily compared and rapidly manipulated. Problem solving through the use of models frequently involves experiments in which thousands of modifications to the data must be made—impractical in any way except through quantitative manipulation. For this reason it is much easier for the management scientist to work with "hard" data where specific measurements of physical phenomena are feasible, rather than with abstract information involving values, attitudes, or pecularities in behavior.

Use of the Systems Approach

The concepts of systems theory presented in chapter 4 are important elements of management science. Scientific approaches to decision making place emphasis on broad analysis, where all relevant variables are considered—not just those that are immediate and obvious. Operations-research methodology emphasizes the construction of elaborate models that identify the significant parts and the relationship among the elements of the system. Generally it is acknowledged that in the past, decisions involving organizations have been too narrow. By developing models that encompass more variables, better decisions will result. Decisions based on a narrow framework are frequently suboptimal. They may be optimal for the subunit or the individual but not for the broader system, in which the subunit or the individual serves as an interlinking part. Also, they are often optimal in the immediate future but suboptimal when related to long-range objectives. A methodology based on identifying systems and hierarchies of systems tends to avoid this.

Use of Interdisciplinary Teams

One of the concepts that developed out of the operations-research exercises conducted during World War II was that novel solutions to problems are more likely to be had if mixed, interdisciplinary teams are used. In attempting to solve persistent problems, such as those associated with the supply lines to the second front in Europe, it was found that often it was preferable to have scientists unfamiliar with the operations, but trained in the scientific method, work on the problem. Experts in logistics (supply) are trained to solve supply-type problems in particular ways, providing a stereotyped, although typically successful, approach. However, they found that when certain problems could not be resolved in this way, analysts using quantitative methods and the model approach of the scientific method were more likely to develop unique solutions. The more mixed the background of the team—as long as they are all trained in the scientific method—the more varied will be their interpretation of the situation and their alternatives for overcoming the difficulty.

Although the nature of the problem to some degree influences the makup of the team, it should normally include a physical scientist and an engineer. It is also recommended that mathematicians, economists, behavioral scientists, cost analysts, and groups like biologists be involved. Although the concept of the interdisciplinary team was initially one of the most touted concepts of O.R., in recent years it has frequently been ignored in practice, since colleges and universities have developed their own training programs in operations research, and the O.R. units of corporations are often comprised of younger analysts trained in these newer techniques, rather than a mixed, interdisciplinary team. Also, the expense and difficulty of maintaining O.R. units of mixed backgrounds tend to be prohibitive.

ADVANTAGES AND LIMITATIONS OF OPERATIONS RESEARCH

Advantages of Operations Research

The advantages of operations-research (management-science) methods in solving problems are obvious from the basic concepts discussed above. The proven means of developing other disciplines has been through the scientific method, and this same methodology will serve as the foundation of a science of management. Detailed observation, model building, experimentation, testing of hypotheses, quantification of variables, and manipulation of data through the use of the computer offer objective, systematized means for understanding relationships, discovering knowledge, and improving decision making. Operations research has broadened the range of decision making to include more variables, a wider variety of alternatives, a better understanding of the risks involved, and improved methods for evaluating trade-offs. Many of the techniques of operations research, especially those relating to physical variables, result in more accurate decisions where the guesswork is essentially eliminated. A summary of the advantages and limitations of O.R. is presented in figure 6-1.

Advantages	Limitations
1. Adds accuracy, precision, and factual data.	1. Often difficult to apply results of a model to the real world.
2. Tends to be thorough and analytical.	2. Executives are reluctant to accept recommendations if they do not understand the methods used.
3. Provides methods for evaluating risks and uncertainties.	3. Time will not permit model building.
4. Aids in developing unique approaches.	4. Assumptions used to develop models are generally judgmental.
5. Models make it easier to manipulate data and consider many different alternatives.	5. Models tend to concentrate on measurable data and play down that which is difficult to measure (values, human behavior, etc.).
6. Models aid in communication and understanding through providing a common framework for analysis and discussion.	6. Easy to become so enamored with the model or technique that the real world is modified to fit it.

Fig. 6-1. Operations-research trade-offs

Limitations of Operations Research

Even though operations-research methods are almost universally accepted as the means by which a science of management is to be developed, progress has frequently been slower than anticipated due to the difficulty of developing relevant models and quantifying behavioral relationships in the social sciences. Studies show that most major American corporations have established operations-research units using many of the techniques. However, the results have often been disappointing. Top managers, not familiar with the newer quantitative techniques, are often reluctant to accept the recommendations of their O.R. staff when they do not understand the basis for the recommendations. Often the models are too theoretical and call for optimal conditions that rarely exist. The language, methods, and decision-making environment of the O.R. expert is frequently too remote from that of the practicing manager.

An appropriate example is that of C. Jackson Grayson, Jr., Dean of the School of Business Administration at Southern Methodist University and a professor of operations research, who served as former President Nixon's Chairman of the Price Commission during Phase II of the Economic Stabilization Program during the early 1970's. Following that experience, he stated: "In the most challenging assignment of my life—putting together the Price Commission—I used absolutely *none* of the management-science tools explicitly."[1] Some of the reasons he was unable to do this, along with other current problems in using operations-research methods, are as follows:

- Model building is usually extremely time consuming and cannot be accomplished within the time constraints of the decision maker. Deadlines imposed by environmental constraints do not permit the time delay required to engage in extensive simulation exercises.

- Models are only as good as the assumptions underlying them, and these are often subjective and simplified. Before constructing a model, assumptions must be made regarding the primary variables, the environment, future conditions, goals, and a variety of other factors. Precise models based on erroneous assumptions can only provide misleading data. Thus the decision maker needs to carefully review these assumptions before placing credence in the results.

- Model building tends to focus on those variables that can be quantified and ignores the frequently predominant intangibles. The measurable, hard data is manipulated, and psychological data relating to factors such as the expectations of others, power considerations, personal interests, and group norms are ignored. (Relating to figure 5-2, the inner ring of rational considerations is incorporated, but the outer ring relating to the climate and forces affecting the decision maker are not evaluated because of their subjectivity.)

- Data tends to take on an aura of accuracy when presented in quantitative form. Information presented as a computer printout, chart, or statistical table gives an illusion of accuracy that tends to be deceptive. The users of such information should always check the assumptions, examine the rationale for the model, and consider its potential impact before implementing the recommendations.

- In some instances O.R. experts are too technique oriented instead of problem oriented. They are too concerned with optimizing the precision of a tool, rather than aiding a manager with his problems. Too frequently the attempt is to make the situation fit the technique rather than vice versa.

1. Jackson Grayson, Jr., "Management Science and Business Practice," *Harvard Business Review*, July–August, 1973, p. 43.

Placing O.R. in Perspective

Even though many problems are currently being experienced with management-science methodology, there is still no question but that it warrants enthusiasm regarding the future. Many of the current attempts are crude beginnings of what will eventually be very useful and sophisticated tools in aiding managers. As more information is uncovered regarding each dimension of the variables in the contingency model of management, simulation should become more realistic and model building more useful. However, it must be noted that the role of operations research is to narrow the judgment of the decision maker—not replace it. By making certain variables known to the decision maker, it eliminates evaluation based on judgment for certain aspects of the decision, but it will never eliminate all unknowns.

The discipline of management is gradually becoming more scientific and adopting the methods of operations research. Truisms and generalizations based on limited experience are now gradually being replaced by verifiable concepts and techniques. Broad models representative of the management process that tie together the different strands of the discipline are now in existence and make it possible to search for dependent relationships.

JUDGMENT IN DECISION MAKING

The following statement was made by two of the analysts who popularized operations-research techniques in the early 1960's when they were employed in the Department of Defense under Secretary Robert McNamara:

"In brief, the suggestion of a conflict between judgment and analysis is false. Ultimately, all defense policies are made and all weapon systems chosen on the basis of judgment. There is no other way. The real issue is whether judgments have to be made in a fog of inadequate and inaccurate data, unclear and undefined issues, conflicting personal opinions, and 'seat-of-the-pants' hunches, or whether they can be made in the clearer air of relevant analysis and experience, accurate information, and well-defined issues. The point is to render unto analysis the things that are analysis's and unto judgment the things that are judgment's."

Alain C. Enthoven and K. Wayne Smith, *How Much Is Enough? Shaping the Defense Program 1961–1969*, (New York: Harper and Row, Publishers, 1971), pp. 67–68.

TOOLS OF MANAGEMENT SCIENCE

The tools of operations research are many and varied. As indicated, their predominant use to date has been in instances where "hard" data is available as the result of measurable, physical properties of the variables in the decision process. Accordingly, problems relating to distribution, routing, replacement, scheduling, comparative costs, and waiting lines (queuing) of resource inputs, machines, and inventories have been those that are most conducive to resolution through operations-research techniques.

It is not possible to cover all of these techniques in detail in a general management text. This is typically reserved for courses dealing exclusively with production management or management science. Our purpose is to acquaint the reader in a primarily nonmathematical format with the basic tools of operations research. Some of the more predominant techniques, in terms of use, are:

Simulation

Simulation is a broad term indicating any type of activity in which the attempt is to imitate an existing system or situation in a simplified manner. Simulation is basically model building in which the simulator is attempting to gain understanding through replicating some phenomenon and then manipulating it by adjusting the variables. Simulation techniques like wind tunnels, scaled-down plant layouts, vacuum chambers for astronauts,, and other similar methods have been in existence for many years. The contribution of the management scientist to simulation has been to construct mathematical models that are easier to manipulate, especially through the use of the computer.

Simulation exercises are important to decision making in many respects. Rather than building expensive machinery or physical systems and testing the results, the same characteristics can be tested in smaller physical models or even in mathematical models. Also, because of the ease and low costs involved, the models can be tested under many conditions involving a multitude of variables and different decision alternatives. Simulation exercises force a consideration of the primary variables and their relationships in a situation. Consistent with the assumptions underlying the contingency model of management, this approach tends to maximize understanding.

Simulation has perhaps the greatest potential of all management-science techniques. In the problem-solving methodology outlined in chapter 5, step six involves the evaluation of alternatives. If alternatives could be simulated and the outcome of each alternative predicted at this point in the decision process, it would eliminate much of the guesswork from decision making. However, as noted earlier, many variables at this stage in the development of simulation are not subject to accurate quantification, and frequently time will not permit this depth of analysis.

SIMULATION OF CORPORATE OPERATIONS

An example of a major simulation model is one developed by Van den Berghs and Jurgens Ltd., a subsidiary of Unilever. The simulation consists of a set of fifteen interrelated computerized models that cover each of the major subsystems of the firm's operations. For instance, there is a separate model for raw materials, capacity, distribution, packaging, brands, and a generalized market model. In addition, there are models for expenses, fixed costs, total costs, and financial reporting. The model can accommodate up to five complete sets of data for different alternative strategies associated with each brand. These can be summarized on a division basis, and as many as five individually specified strategies can be handled for each division—representing an accumulation of many brands.

When different strategies are introduced into the total model, information on variables such as brand sales, raw-material requirements, refinery capacities, working-capital requirements, market share, fixed and variable costs, and financial reporting covering sales, profits, and the total company source and use of funds are obtained. In addition to the market variables, many other changes can be introduced into the model, such as raw-material prices, personnel costs, taxation rates, etc. Using this model, essentially the entire company's operations can be simulated. Each possible strategy the firm might pursue in relation to modifying brands or divisional operations can be examined. Five-year plans can be developed for each of the sets of strategies that the firm has under consideration. Assuming the total model is reasonably accurate, it can be a tremendous aid in both short-term and long-run decision making.

Abstracted from James B. Boulden, "A Systems Approach to Corporate Modeling," *Journal of Systems Management*, June 1973, pp. 14–20.

Linear Programming

Linear programming has probably been the most successful operations-research technique to date in terms of practical application. When a firm has a problem in allocating scarce resources, linear programming is often an aid in providing a precise, accurate method of arriving at an optimal solution. This technique is applicable whenever there is a straight line (or linear) relationship among the variables or resources in the problem. When such a situation exists, solutions can be developed through graphic methods or the use of algebraic linear equations. In the typical distribution problem where linear programming is appropriate, it can be applied if the following conditions are met: there is a clear statement of objectives; there are alternative demands for limited resources (raw materials, machines, etc.); the cost of the resources is the same on a unit basis and proportional to the number of units allocated; and there is a need for an optimal solution aimed at minimizing total costs. Examples of the application of linear programming are as follows:

- In the previously discussed example of locating a warehouse, the owners are concerned with minimizing transportation costs. When a company has several factories and warehouses, freight costs can be minimized by using linear programming to determine the storage locations to which they will ship the finished goods produced by the various factories.
- Linear programming is useful in mixing proportions of the ingredients in a final product. An example would be a dog food that has different resources (grains) serve as its inputs. The dog food has minimal levels of nutrients that must be met. Linear programming is used to determine the mix of inputs necessary to meet these minimum levels, based on the least cost of the mix given the current market price of each grain.

Linear programming can also be used to solve problems such as the allocation of salesmen to sales districts, the scheduling of machines, the production of different products from an oil refinery, and the re-allocation of empty railroad cars to distribution points. In each of these situations, there is a problem of minimizing costs in a decision relating to resource allocation.

Linear programming is an appropriate example of the use of situational analysis described in chapter 2. The four steps involved in situatonal analysis as they apply to linear programming are indicated below:

Step one   Knowing concepts and techniques: this involves an awareness of linear programming methodology using either graphic or computational approaches.

Step two   Understanding the advantages and limitations of the technique: the advantages relate to the accuracy and programmable approach this method offers for dealing with linear constraints and variables in decisions. The limitations are the appearance of mathematical complexity and the capacity to deal only with linear relationships in a problem.

Step three   Understanding the current situation: this involves being aware of the current situation well enough to know that the basic difficulty the decision maker faces is one of distribution in which the relationship among the variables and constraints are linear in nature.

Step four   Matching of the appropriate technique with the situation at hand: to complete this final phase, the manager must properly interpret the first three steps so that he appropriately selects linear-programming methodology to solve the distribution problem.

Linear programming is an extremely useful technique when conditions call for application of such a methodology. However, since most managerial decisions do not directly involve distribution problems with linear relationships, the technique has limited use, primarily being of value to those parts of the organization dealing with the production function.

Other Programming Methods

In addition to linear programming there are also methods, primarily algebraic, to solve problems involving nonlinear (quadratic) relationships, dynamic relationships (dynamic programming), heuristic sequences, and other issues when the variables are more inconsistent. All of these involve relating variables, normally resources, into multistage problems encompassing time sequences. Variables in resource problems are frequently nonlinear. Increasingly large orders of components can normally be purchased at lower unit cost because they are subject to quantity discounts. The result is that cost relationships are no longer linear. Transportation costs become significantly reduced when carload, rather than less-than-carload, lots are shipped. Accordingly, the nonlinear programming techniques have wide application, but they are also more difficult to model because the relationships are nonlinear in nature.

Waiting Line (Queuing) Theory

Queuing theory is a simulation technique that is useful in evaluating the relative costs incurred when irregular waiting lines exist. Waiting lines are common in situations such as customers waiting to be checked out at grocery counters, workers waiting to check out tools from a toolcrib attendant, trucks awaiting repair at a maintenance depot, or forklift trucks standing by to move supplies. Since the occurrence of waiting lines is often unpredictable, a simulation technique based on a table of random numbers is commonly used to replicate the likelihood of these waiting lines. Using this technique in the case of a repair station, the frequency and magnitude of the possible waiting lines can be determined, and this is surely an aid in establishing the number of repair units to be constructed at the maintenance station—as well as the appropriate staffing level. In other instances it makes it possible to evaluate the costs of workers waiting in line as opposed to the cost of adding another tool-crib attendant. Its basic usefulness is to determine the optimum cost of providing additional services versus the cost of having a nonfunctional waiting line.

Probability Theory

One of the most important factors in decision making is estimating the likelihood of events occurring in the future. Many events will occur in predictable patterns based on known circumstances or previous experience. These are referred to as *objective* probabilities. *Subjective* probabilities are less certain and are established through such techniques as accumulating the opinions of knowledgeable individuals regarding the events under consideration. Subjective probabilities are useful to decision makers even though they are not as accurate as objective ones. Probabilities are used in many decision-theory techniques, such as payoff matrices and decision trees. (Both of these are explained in the next chapter.)

Game Theory

Game theory was developed by mathematicians, economists, and others, based on conditions when a strategy is to be developed assuming the existence of a competitor or opponent. Military strategists have probably gone farther in developing game theory as a practical part of their training and decision making than any other group. However, game theory equally applies to firms in highly competitive markets. If a firm attempts to increase its share of the market by cutting prices, what will competitors do? If they also cut prices, it may result in a price war that will be disastrous to all firms in the industry. Competitive strategies in advertising, product innovation, and allocation of the sales force are subject to this sort of analysis. The simplest application is to two-party, zero-sum games, where if one party gains the other loses (for example, two firms bidding on a government contract). However, most actual situations are much more complex, with many competitors and nonzero sum situations the case, so that the gains of one party are not necessarily equal to the losses of another. Game theory has not had wide use in solving practical problems, but it has been of value in helping managers develop decision strategies.

Other Examples

The above examples of operations-research (management-science) techniques are but a few of those that can be found in the literature. Servo theory, symbolic logic, value theory, and broad fields such as information theory are also included as part of the O.R. repertoire. However, the examples given above are those most frequently associated with operations-research groups.

SUMMARY

Management science has injected a new emphasis in management theory and practice since World War II. It has developed a concern for undergirding management with a more scientific foundation through use of the scientific method, models, quantitative techniques, and other approaches that emphasize the development of hard data.

Models are simplification of reality, but they highlight significant relationships and make complex situations easier to understand. Through quantifying variables, models can be manipulated and data can be compared in a way that makes simulation both easier and more accurate.

Systems theory is an important element of management science, emphasizing the relationships among variables and the need to consider a broad range of variables in order to avoid narrow consideration of the factors involved.

Management science also encourages the use of mixed, interdisciplinary research teams for the purpose of bringing a variety of knowledge and problem-solving techniques to the solution of problems.

With all of its promise for the future, the inroads of management science in practice have been relatively slow. Practitioners are often reluctant to accept methodologies that they do not understand, and model building is frequently too slow and cumbersome for the impatient executive. Even though the techniques of operations research have been rapidly maturing, they are frequently difficult to apply in situations, since each carries its own brand of uniqueness. These techniques have proven to be valuable aids in narrowing the range of judgment, but the judgment of the decision maker remains the ultimate appeal.

QUESTIONS FOR STUDY AND DISCUSSION

1. What is the difference between the terms *management science* and *operations research*?
2. Why is so much emphasis placed on the scientific method by management-science enthusiasts?
3. Explain why the following are considered models.
   A. An organization chart
   B. The contingency model of management
   C. A financial statement like the balance sheet or income statement
4. If a department-store manager is attempting to determine how many toys to order for the Christmas season, what variables in this decision can be quantified? Which variables are difficult to quantify?
5. What major decisions do you make as a student in which operations-research techniques would be useful?
6. What aspects of your father's profession lend themselves to O.R.?
7. If a management-science staff makes a recommendation to the chief executive based on a model they have developed, what features of the model should the chief executive be concerned with? What questions should he ask about the model?
8. What are the major limitations to the use of management-science techniques?
9. In what type of situations is it appropriate to apply linear programming?
10. What is the difference between queuing theory and game theory?

Case Problem:
DISASTER PLANNING

Esther Gelt was the hospital administrator of the only hospital in a rural region that covered 75 square miles and contained a population of approximately 50,000. The hospital was located in a community of 25,000 that was near the center of the area. The closest major city of over 100,000 was 125 miles away.

Recently, at the insistence of several government agencies, the board of the hospital directed Esther to develop a disaster plan for the hospital. They had never had any major emergencies when more than a dozen people were attended to at any one time. However, the region was on a fault that made it vulnerable to earthquakes, and the population was becoming more concentrated, so multiple casualties from fire, plane crashes, and flooding were becoming more likely.

How should Esther go about developing this plan?
How can she simulate conditions that are likely during a disaster?
How can she train the staff of the hospital to prepare for such a disaster?
What are the most important variables in any simulation model that she will develop?

Case Problem:
RAILROAD-CAR DISTRIBUTION

Glen Schmidt had completed an MBA five years ago at a major Big-Ten school where he had specialized in operations research. He then went on to work for an automotive company in Detroit serving in a major operations-research unit. He conducted a variety of studies relating to capital investment, production-line simulations, inventory models, and equipment-replacement problems. Recently he accepted a position with a railroad that was setting up an operations-research staff unit for the first time. In fact, he was the first employee in the planning department with any major operations-research experience.

The first assignment Glen received was to develop a plan for returning empty railroad cars to those distribution points where demand was higher. Glen developed an elaborate linear-programming model that could be used to allocate empty railroad cars. He knew from previous experience that there would be some reluctance on the part of the executives of the railroad to accept his plan since it was based on a model they were not familiar with. He was, therefore, pondering how he should go about explaining the results of his study to top management.

What would you do if you were in Glen's position?

Quantitative Methods and Decision Theory

What costs are significant in evaluating alternatives?

What classifications of the environment are important in decision theory?

How are payoffs modified based on probabilities?

What guides are there for a decision maker under conditions of uncertainty?

How can *decision trees* aid in decision making?

What techniques can be used in large organizations to obtain individual opinions on proposed actions?

The purpose of this chapter is to introduce you to some of the quantitative methods and decision-theory techniques that have been developed to help in decision making. There is a wide variety of such techniques—far too many to survey here. For that reason only a few of the more common methods will be presented. These will include certain cost concepts, a classification of environments into four types (with appropriate methods for each), decision trees, and draft-position papers. (Methods such as network analysis used in planning will be presented in later chapters, where their coverage is more appropriate.) The aim in this chapter is to understand the workings and usefulness of a number of specific techniques, and not to become engrossed in the quantitative complexities.

Contributions to decision making have come from many fields, including psychology, philosophy, economics, and mathematics. These deal with considerations relating to the decision itself, the people making the decision, forces affecting the decision maker, and an analysis of the decision process. Our concern in this chapter is with the more narrow interpretation of *decision theory*, represented by theoretical economists who are concerned with resource-allocation methods that provide optimal results. The objective is to appreciate the quantitative and graphic methods used to evaluate the alternatives, the different states of nature, and the choices open to the decision maker.

COST ANALYSIS

Incremental Costs

One of the critical phases of decision making is accumulating and analyzing costs associated with each alternative (step six of the problem-solving process). Based on information available in accounting reports, it is common to reflect the total or average unit costs of each alternative. However, if certain costs are constant and identical for all alternatives under consideration, these can be ignored for the purposes of making the decision at hand. (Including them only confuses the analysis.) *Sunk costs* are those that are not recoverable and will be incurred regardless of the decision; for example, paying $50,000 for a consulting study or incurring $40,000 to get a medical degree. Once the study is completed or the degree has been attained, these costs are sunk, irrecoverable, and not part of future decisions. Therefore, making any decisions regarding implementing the recommendations of the consultant should have nothing to do with the fee paid.

When only the costs affected by the decision are included for analytical purposes, this methodology is referred to as *incremental analysis*. *Incremental costs* constitute the increment of total costs that will vary, based on the selection of different alternatives. This explanation appears simple, but in practice it is often difficult to apply. A few examples will demonstrate the usefulness of this concept in decision making:

- The total costs of driving an automobile may amount to approximately 16¢ per mile when the cost of the automobile is allocated over 100,000 miles, and license, insurance, gasoline, tires, and maintenance repairs are included. However, once an owner has a licensed, insured car, the incremental cost associated with the decision to take a 200-mile trip is only the gasoline, oil, and wear and tear on tires and other parts. The obsolescence cost on the automobile and the license and insurance cost are sunk. They remain the same whether the individual takes the trip or stays home. In this instance, the "out-of-pocket" costs are normally half as much as the total costs.

- The incremental costs of long-distance, station-to-station telephone calls at night are very small, because they involve the use of equipment that is essentially a sunk cost. The equipment is necessary to handle the heavy daytime load. These equipment costs will be incurred even if there is no nighttime use. Nighttime calls can be greatly reduced in cost and still be financially rewarding, since the additional (incremental) cost of handling them with no operators required is very small to the telephone company. The only precaution the company must make is to be sure that the lower charges at night will induce customers who would not ordinarily do so to use long-distance telephone services, rather than just diverting daytime customers to night calls because of the lower rates.

- A final example of incremental costs as they relate to pricing decisions is evidenced in airlines. If a plane with 80-passenger capacity is flying a route with only 50 passengers on board, the incremental costs of adding additional passengers is small. The plane, pilot, service personnel, and essentially all other costs are incurred whether 50 or 80 passengers fly. Food and only a few minor costs incrementally increase. If a ticket is priced at $100.00, less then 10 percent of this would cover the incremental costs of the added passenger. If the airline cut the price of the ticket in half for the added passengers, it would still be financially rewarding to the airline. Again, the airline has the problem of segmenting the market so that the 50 regular passengers will not qualify for lower-priced tickets. The lower-priced tickets should attract groups that would not normally fly (wives of business executives, students, military personnel and so on).

Opportunity Costs

Another important cost concept in decision making is *opportunity cost.* Opportunity cost is defined as the benefits of a rejected alternative that are sacrificed when another alternative is selected. In choosing an alternative, a manager will select the best one as he perceives it from his standpoint, but in doing so he sacrifices returns or benefits from the rejected alternatives. These lost benefits are referred to as *implicit,* or *imputed,* costs of the alternative. Since they are implied and not actual costs, they are not recorded as costs in the official accounting records of the organization. However, they are important costs or sacrifices in evaluating decisions. Again a few examples should make the meaning clearer:

- Going back to the example of an automobile, if an individual is deciding on whether to take $5000 out of his savings account to purchase a car, he is weighing the trade-off of its convenience against the opportunity costs of 6 percent annual interest on his $5000. If he buys the car, he sacrifices $300 in interest the first year, which is the first-year opportunity cost of the decision.

- The opportunity cost of owning a business is the return that could be attained by investing the same equity in other ventures.

- If a firm has a raw-materials inventory that is surplus to its needs, it has funds tied up that are not providing a return. If the surplus inventory amounts to an annual average of $100,000, the opportunity cost is the return that could be attained by investing this $100,000 in another alternative. Such a potential return should be considered as one of the costs of maintaining the inventory.

SITUATIONAL CLASSIFICATIONS
IN DECISION THEORY

In decision theory it is common to classify different situations based on the amount of information available to the decision maker. Given this criterion, four situational categories have been established to cover the four conditions of certainty, risk, uncertainty, and competition. This breakdown is important in contingency analysis, because specific problem-solving techniques are associated with each of the four classifications. The various decision-theory techniques have been developed to meet the unique characteristics of each of these environments. They are:

- *Certainty.* Complete assurance that a particular state of nature or set of conditions will exist (for example, the selection of a piece of machinery from four under consideration when the costs and performance specifications of each unit are known).

- *Risk.* Under conditions of risk, there are a number of sets of different conditions (states of nature) that can occur in the future, and the probability of each set occurring can be reasonably estimated (for example, the projected demand for a product that has been on the market for five years).

- *Uncertainty.* Under conditions of uncertainty, there is no information about the probability of the occurrence of any particular state of nature (for example, the development of a new product when there is no basis for estimating the likely demand for it).

- *Competition.* This situation assumes the existence of opponents or competitors. The strategies of these competitors constitute important variables in the states of nature.

Decisions under Certainty

Even though conditions are known or the state of nature is certain, decisions in this situation still can be complex. Various alternatives may be available involving several strategies. In theory this is relatively simple, since the alternative (decision theorists prefer the term *strategy*) with the largest payoff is accepted. However, as noted earlier, information is never complete, and collecting appropriate information for evaluating strategy trade-offs is often difficult and of limited reliability. Linear programming is a technique that has application to decisions under conditions of certainty. The costs and availability of resources are known, the constraints are also known, and the optimal goal (objective function) has been established. As a result the decision is made under conditions of certainty.

Going back to the example of regional warehouse facilities, assume that the company had determined that St. Louis, Chicago, and Omaha were essentially equally desirable sites, and the decision was to be made on the basis of the cost of constructing warehouses at each location. Estimated costs at the three sites are as follows:

	Land	*Buildings*	*Total Cost*
St. Louis	$25,000	$130,000	$155,000
Chicago	27,000	135,000	162,000
Omaha	19,000	130,000	149,000

Fig. 7-1. **Summary of construction costs**

Under this condition of certainty, the objective (*payoff* in decision theory terminology) is to attempt to minimize costs. Accordingly, Omaha would be selected as the site.

Decision Making under Risk

Decision making under conditions of risk occurs when several possible situations (states of nature) may exist, rather than one known environment. Since it cannot be determined which environment will exist, more risk is introduced into the decision process. However, there are quantitative techniques available to deal with this risk. The most useful one is to determine the likelihood (probability) of certain events occurring, based on other knowledge or previous experience.

For example, if a firm is negotiating a contract to complete a highway within a certain time span and the contract contains penalty clauses for late completion, the firm needs to evaluate the likelihood of two different environments: favorable or unfavorable weather. From past records the probability of different weather conditions can be derived. These probabilities can be used to evaluate the alternatives or the potential bids the firm is considering. The average weighted value of each strategy is developed based on the probability of future weather conditions. The weights used in arriving at the average weighted value (called *expected value* in decision theory) are the probability of different weather conditions. These weights are used to compensate for the random occurrence of the states of nature (weather in this instance).

The *expected value* of an event is defined as the value, if it occurs, multiplied by the probability of its occurrence. With no rain the firm would expect a profit of $80,000; 10–20 days rain $40,000; and 20–30 days rain a loss of $50,000. The probabilities of rain, based on historical records, are as follows: less than 10 days' rain, 0.7; 10–20 days' rain, 0.2; and 20–30 days' rain, 0.1. The expected value of the alternative of accepting a contract at that level would be as follows: EV $80,000 (0.7) + $40,000 (0.2) − $50,000 (0.1) = $59,000. The future condition that is most likely to occur receives the highest weighting; that least likely, the lowest. The expected value thus becomes a weighted average of these conditions and payoffs.

In an example to show different strategies, let's return to the firm selecting a warehouse site. Assume that the site-selection committee is now reviewing the annual operating costs of maintaining a warehouse facility at the St. Louis, Chicago, and Omaha locations. The operating costs (labor, taxes, insurance, etc.) would vary at each location, and they would also vary based on the average annual inventory maintained by location. This is a decision involving risk, since these are new districts being opened up. Future sales forecasts, with the resultant requirement for inventory, are not certain. Based on the best estimates available, it is determined that there is a 10 percent chance that a minimum inventory of $1 million will be required, a 70 percent chance that $2 million will be required, and a 20 percent chance that $3 million will be required.

Given the three alternatives (or strategies) of St. Louis, Chicago, and Omaha, the payoff matrix evaluating the alternatives would be as follows:

| Average Annual Inventory | $1 million | $2 million | $3 million |
| Probability | 0.10 | 0.70 | 0.20 |
Site	Operating Cost	Operating Cost	Operating Cost
S_1 St. Louis	$46,000	$96,000	$140,000
S_2 Chicago	57,000	97,000	145,000
S_3 Omaha	52,000	92,000	140,000

Ev (S_1) $46,000 (0.1) + $96,000 (0.7) + $140,000 (0.2) = $99,800

Ev (S_2) $57,000 (0.1) + $97,000 (0.7) + $145,000 (0.2) = $102,600

Ev (S_3) $52,000 (0.1) + $92,000 (0.7) + $140,000 (0.2) = $97,600

Fig. 7-2. Comparative annual operating costs of St. Louis, Chicago, and Omaha locations

Since the objective is to minimize costs, Omaha would be the preferable site because of the lower expected value of annual operating costs there. Thus probabilities are an extremely important factor in evaluating alternatives when different sets of conditions may exist in the future.

Decision Making under Uncertainty

When a manager is attempting to make a decision when certain significant variables relating to future conditions are totally unknown, he is making a difficult one, because of the uncertainty. With no information on future conditions, decision making comes close to being made on the basis of intuition. Alternatives can be developed and payoffs estimated, but since the payoffs are dependent on future conditions, it is difficult to determine which alternative (or strategy) should be accepted. However, certain decision-theory techniques have been developed to aid the decision maker under these conditions. These techniques are proposed acknowledging that such factors as the psychological predisposition of the decision maker (willingness to take risks), the quantity of resources available to the decision maker (his ability to take risks), company policies relating to risk, and other such factors will often predominate in the decision making.

Under the projected environmental situation of uncertainty, expected value concepts cannot be used because there is no basis for establishing probabilities. For this reason five separate criteria are established that take into consideration the attitudes and resources of the decision maker:

- Pessimism
- Optimism
- Coefficient of optimism
- Laplace
- Regret

PESSIMISM CRITERION. For the purpose of illustrating the five different techniques, assume that a situation exists in which a firm is setting up a new product line, and management is attempting to reach a decision of whether to make it initially machine intensive or labor intensive. If the demand turns out to be low, it would be less expensive to perform much of the work through human-operated, general-purpose machines. Under this alternative the investment in machinery is much less and greater flexibility is introduced, because the machinist can be put to work on many different jobs. However, if the demand is high, units could be produced on a mass basis at less cost through special-purpose automated equipment. This equipment would require a significant capital investment and would be of such a specialized nature that it would have little potential use other than to produce these items. A third alternative is to set up a production line that is a mixture of automated equipment and general-purpose machines.

The three strategies all involve known factors, because the costs associated with purchasing machinery and labor are available. Thus the payoff or return can be estimated accurately for any particular output of units. The only major unknown is the anticipated demand for this new product. For the purposes of this decision, it is estimated that sales could be as low as 100,000 and as high as 400,000 units annually, and there is no basis for calculating the likelihood of demand at any particular level. Based on these assumptions, the payoff matrix using the average unit cost of production is as follows:

	Future States of Nature			
	A (100,000 units)	B (200,000 units)	C (300,000 units)	D (400,000 units)
S_1 (Manpower Intensive)	$10	$ 8	$9	$11
S_2 (Mixture)	12	8	6	7
S_3 (Machine Intensive)	20	10	6	4

Fig. 7-3. Average unit costs of three different production strategies

Under strategy S_1, unit costs increase with demands of 300,000 and 400,000 units, since overtime must be used because of the limited capacity of this production arrangement. Under the mixed-production arrangement (S_2), costs are significantly less than strategy S_1 at 300,000 units, but these unit costs increase under the last condition of 400,000 units, when overtime is also required. Under strategy S_3, unit costs significantly decrease with each rise in demand, because the higher fixed costs of equipment are spread over more units.

The pessimism criterion is one that assumes the decision maker, due to certain factors (low capital, conservative company policies, personal dislike of risk), should be completely pessimistic. Thus he should assume the *worst* payoff for each strategy. Since the objective is to minimize unit costs, the worst (or pessimistic) situation is the one of highest unit costs. The pessimistic payoffs are identified by finding the highest cost in each row of figure 7-3 as follows:

Strategy	State of Nature	Minimum Payoff
S_1	D	11
S_2	A	12
S_3	A	20

Fig. 7-4. Payoffs of three strategies under pessimism criterion

From this matrix, the most desirable result is chosen—strategy S_1—or setting up a manpower-intensive production line. For the decision maker who is inclined to be pessimistic, this alternative will (if conditions turn out to be unfavorable) minimize costs compared with the other two alternatives.

OPTIMISM CRITERION. Under other conditions it may be desirable for the decision maker to assume the most favorable future conditions. This is, of course, just the opposite of the pessimism criterion. The decision maker determines which payoff is the maximum for each alternative and then selects the strategy (or alternative) that will provide the maximum gain. (In our example the minimal cost is the maximum gain, since lower costs will increase profits.) From the matrix (figure 7-3), it is easy to identify that the minimal unit cost for strategy S_1 is $8, for S_2 $6, and for S_3 $4. Given the guidelines for this decision technique, strategy S_3 will be selected, because this maximizes the return by providing the lowest unit cost.

COEFFICIENT OF OPTIMISM CRITERION. It is, of course, not necessary for the decision maker to be totally optimistic or pessimistic. Realistically he will be somewhere in between. Thus a coefficient of optimism can be developed to represent this composite. Assume that a decision maker feels he should be 60 percent pessimistic and 40 percent optimistic. Given this preference, the solution would be calculated as follows:

Strategy	Pessimism Criterion		Optimism Criterion		Payoff
S_1	(0.6) $11	+	(0.4) $8	=	$ 9.8
S_2	(0.6) 12	+	(0.4) 6	=	9.6
S_3	(0.6) 20	+	(0.4) 4	=	13.6

Fig. 7-5.   **Payoff of three strategies under coefficient of optimism criterion**

Given this decision rule, the second alternative (S_2) would be selected, because it provides the lowest unit costs.

LAPLACE CRITERION. Under the previous three methods, strategies are selected based on different approaches to evaluating payoffs, with little consideration for the likelihood of the different states of nature to occur. However, viewing these situations in terms of probabilities, in uncertain environments there is no basis for establishing the likelihood that one state of nature will occur any more frequently than another. By definition there is an equal chance that any particular state of nature will occur. In applying this logic to the production-line example, there would be a 0.25 probability that any one state of nature would exist. Therefore, the Laplace criterion is calculated as follows:

$$S_1 \ 0.25 \ (10 + 8 + 9 + 11) = \$ 9.5$$
$$S_2 \ 0.25 \ (12 + 8 + 6 + 7) = \$ 8.25$$
$$S_3 \ 0.25 \ (20 + 10 + 6 + 4) = \$ 10.0$$

Fig. 7-6. Payoff of three strategies under the Laplace criterion

Since our objective is to minimize costs, strategy S_2 would be selected.

REGRET CRITERION. The final method for dealing with decision alternatives under uncertainty involves a technique that is slightly more complicated than the others but encompasses some extremely useful strategy. The assumption behind this criterion is that, because of uncertainty, the decision maker should attempt to minimize the loss or the sacrifices of selecting the wrong alternative. This sacrifice has previously been identified as the opportunity cost of a decision. The decision maker in this instance is attempting to minimize his potential error, or regret, in selecting alternatives. The difference between the payoff of any particular strategy in a state of nature and the highest possible payoff under that particular state of nature is the decision maker's potential *regret*.

To arrive at a decision using this criterion, it is necessary to establish the opportunity cost of each alternative. For instance, if the demand turns out to be 100,000 units (the A state of nature) and the decision maker has adopted the machine-intensive alternative (strategy S_3), the opportunity cost would be $10 per unit. (The difference between the $20 per unit for strategy S_3 versus $10 per unit under the most desirable alternatives S_1.) To use the regret criterion in decision making, it is necessary to establish an opportunity-cost matrix reflecting the difference between the payoff of each strategy in a particular state of nature. Using this opportunity-cost (regret) approach, the payoff matrix for the equipment-utilization example is as follows:

	State of Nature				
	A	*B*	*C*	*D*	Maximum Regret
S_1	$ 0	$0	$3	$7	$ 7
S_2	$ 2	$0	$0	$3	$ 3
S_3	$10	$2	$0	$0	$10

Fig. 7-7. Payoff of three strategies under regret criterion

Since the decision maker under this criterion is trying to minimize his regret or potential error in selecting the wrong alternative, he would select the second strategy of setting up a production line that is a mixture of automated and general-purpose machinery. His maximum regret here is much smaller than the two other strategies (3 versus 7 and 10). At this point the criterion of pessimism is used, where the decision maker's goal is to minimize his regret.

As with any other technique of management, no one of these five methods for dealing with conditions of uncertainty is best. Also, they will not all provide the same answer. The pessimism criterion in this example favored strategy S_1, the optimism criterion S_3, and the coefficient of optimism, Laplace, and regret criteria S_2. The judgment of the decision maker is necessary in selecting the technique that is most consistent with his personal preferences, the policies of the organization, the resources of the organization, and other such factors. These are all situational variables of significance to the decision maker.

Decision Making under Competition

Decision making under conditions of competition (also called conflict) assumes the existence of a rational opponent. Accordingly, it takes into consideration the concept of strategy, since the decision maker is influenced by how an opponent will most likely respond to his actions. This type of decision making relies primarily on game-theory techniques that were discussed in the previous chapter. In realistic situations the techniques involving more than two competitors are too complex for discussion here. Also as indicated, even though these concepts are meaningful in theoretically developing and analyzing strategies, their practical usefulness is still limited at this point.

DECISION TREES

Another technique that is extremely helpful in certain decision situations is referred to as the *decision tree*. Decision trees use a method of graphically portraying sequential decisions in a way to highlight the decision points, alternatives, different possible future environmental conditions, and payoffs that are involved. Normally the payoffs are weighted, based on the likelihood of the environmental conditions. Decision trees involve an analytical method that forces the decision maker to be explicit in analyzing conditions associated with future decisions and in determining the outcome of different alternatives. They involve a sequential analysis of a series of decisions over time, where risks associated with the decision are taken into consideration. The term *decision tree* comes from the graphic appearance of the technique, which starts with the initial decision as a base with the various alternatives, states of nature, and subsequent decisions appearing like branches of the tree.

The decision tree is a flexible methodology that is applicable to a wide variety of situations in which emphasis can be placed on either sequential decisions, the probability of various conditions, or the highlighting of alternatives. Normally, decision trees are restricted to relatively short-term situations involving one or two years, but they can be applied to long-term investment decisions. (However, in the latter case they should be combined with other methods of decision analysis involving techniques that deal with the time value of money.) Generally decision trees are used to evaluate decisions under conditions of risk. Probabilities are established in relation to different future conditions, and results or payoffs are calculated based on these probabilities in the form of expected value.

The Methodology of Decision Trees

The methodology involved in establishing a decision tree is similar to that identified in relation to other decision processes. This methodology is as follows:

1. The need to make a decision is recognized. (This is called a *decision point*.)
2. Logical alternatives are identified (often referred to as *possible actions*).
3. The different possible future conditions or situations are identified (also called *states of nature*).
4. The likelihood of each state of nature is determined (*probabilities*).
5. The results of the alternatives are determined (*payoffs*).

6. The outcomes of the payoffs are calculated by multiplying the probabilities of the different states of nature by the payoff associated with each alternative and state of nature (*expected value*).
7. Finally, follow-on or sequential decisions are evaluated in the same fashion, involving the six previous steps.

Sequential decisions are obviously affected by the initial decision and by the states of nature associated with it. Thus if there is a one-in-three probability that an event will occur within a three-year time span, and it does not occur in the first year associated with the first decision, the probability then becomes 0.50, or 50 percent, that it will occur in the second year.

Steps one through six involve the same methodology as the payoff matrix discussed earlier. It is the graphic display and the effect of sequential decisions involved in step seven that make the decision tree unique.

Decision-Tree Example

As an example of decision trees, consider the problem faced by Norsk Recreation, Inc. in a site location. This firm is involved in the decision of where to locate a ski resort. They have narrowed their search to two locations. One is within 25 miles of a large metropolitan area. This accessibility makes it extremely attractive as a site, but it is located at an elevation 2000 feet lower than the second site, and the annual snow fall is less. The other location is 125 miles from the metropolitan area, but the higher elevation ensures better skiing conditions and a longer season.

Alternatives	Future Possible Conditions	Probability of The Conditions	Net Cash Flow (Payoff)		Expected Value
Close site	heavy winter	0.7	$60,000		$42,000
	light winter	0.3	−10,000		−3,000
				Total	$39,000
Remote site	heavy winter	0.7	40,000		28,000
	light winter	0.3	20,000		6,000
				Total	$34,000

Fig. 7-8. Expected value of two alternative ski resorts

During the first year at the close location, the firm would experience a favorable net cash flow of $60,000 if the weather is favorable, but it could result in a negative flow of $10,000 if snowfall is light. At the second location favorable weather conditions would result in a net cash flow of only $40,000, because the remote location would not attract as many skiers. However, if a mild winter is experienced they would still have a reasonably long season and experience a net cash flow of $20,000. Based on historical records, there is a 0.7 probability of favorable weather in terms of a relatively heavy snowfall and a 0.3 probability of a mild winter. Based on this information, figure 7-8 indicates a payoff matrix, followed by figure 7-9 that is a one-year decision tree based on it.

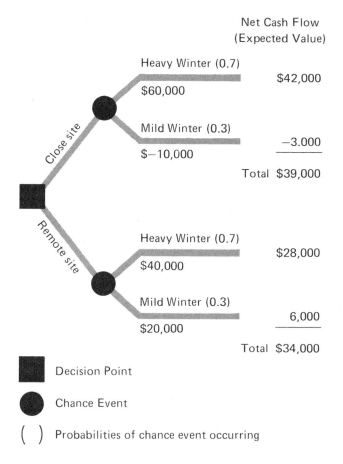

Net Cash Flow
(Expected Value)

Heavy Winter (0.7) $42,000
$60,000

Mild Winter (0.3)   −3.000
$−10,000

Total $39,000

Heavy Winter (0.7) $28,000
$40,000

Mild Winter (0.3)   6,000
$20,000

Total $34,000

Close site

Remote site

■   Decision Point

●   Chance Event

( )   Probabilities of chance event occurring

Fig. 7-9. **Decision tree of two alternative sites for a ski resort**

It appears obvious from the decision tree that the Norsk Company should select the site close to the metropolitan area, since it has a cash flow that is $5000 greater than the remote site ($39,000 minus $34,000). However, as indicated earlier, this decision is affected by many conditions relating to the willingness of the decision maker to accept a decrease of $10,000 in net cash flow—if a light winter does occur. The firm may not be in a financial condition where it could accept such a reduction, so it may select the lower but safer return of the remote site.

To illustrate the more complex form of decision trees associated with sequential decisions, assume that funds would permit the firm to construct only one ski lift at either site during the first year, they would have sufficient funds to add another lift the second year. If a mild winter was the case, they would be forced to continue through the second year with only the one lift. (This is true of both the close and remote site, because they calculate that a net cash flow of $35,000 is required to add another ski lift.) Based on this assumption, figure 7-10 illustrates the two-year decision tree.

Three decision points are identified in the decision tree (points A, B, and C). Both decisions B and C relate to the question of whether a new ski lift should be added at either site following the first-year experience of high cash flow resulting from a heavy snowfall. In both instances the decision from the information provided in the decision tree would be to add the second lift. (At the close site the net cash flow would be $67,500 with the second lift and $49,000 without it. At the remote site the net cash flow would be $51,000 with thee new lift and $38,250 without it.) Since the net cost flow in both instances is higher at the close site, this would again support the first-year decision of selecting it. In all instances net cash flow is expected to be higher the second year as the selected location becomes better known among skiing clientele.

Figure 7-10 illustrates why decision trees are usually restricted to three or four years or less. As more decision points are identified and states of nature considered, it results in extremely complex graphs. Also, the conditions actually experienced in the first year will modify significantly whatever occurs in later years. If decisions relating to the second year and beyond do not have to be made during the first year, the decision should then be delayed until knowledge gained from that first year is available to eliminate some of the uncertainty. However, beyond that time the decision tree is useful if it directly affects decisions made during the first year.

OTHER DECISION TECHNIQUES

In addition to the techniques presented (most of which had their origin in the operations-research movement), many other methods have been

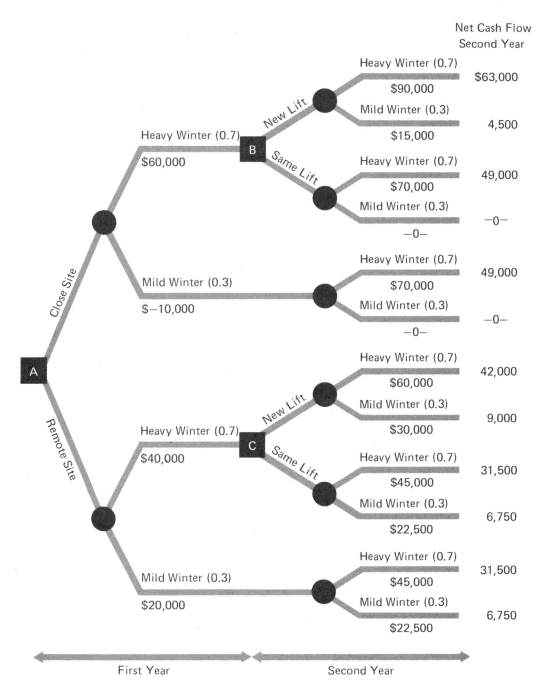

Net Cash Flow
Second Year

Heavy Winter (0.7) $63,000
$90,000

Mild Winter (0.3)   4,500
$15,000

Heavy Winter (0.7)   49,000
$70,000

Mild Winter (0.3)   —0—
—0—

Heavy Winter (0.7)   49,000
$70,000

Mild Winter (0.3)   —0—
—0—

Heavy Winter (0.7)   42,000
$60,000

Mild Winter (0.3)   9,000
$30,000

Heavy Winter (0.7)   31,500
$45,000

Mild Winter (0.3)   6,750
$22,500

Heavy Winter (0.7)   31,500
$45,000

Mild Winter (0.3)   6,750
$22,500

New Lift

Same Lift

Heavy Winter (0.7)
$60,000

Mild Winter (0.3)
$−10,000

New Lift

Same Lift

Heavy Winter (0.7)
$40,000

Mild Winter (0.3)
$20,000

A

B

C

Close Site

Remote Site

First Year   Second Year

Fig. 7-10. Two-year decision tree for site and equipment decisions

developed to aid managers in the decision process. Many of these are nonquantitative and little more than special guides resulting from approaches that experience has demonstrated to be useful. An example is a methodology we shall refer to as a *draft position paper*. One of the major difficulties in decision making in a large organization is getting the necessary input from subsidiary managers on a major policy decision. Major decisions frequently affect many groups, both internal and external to the organization. Also, there are often many different lower-level managers who have some specialized knowledge that is significant in relation to the proposed decision. These lower-level managers can usually evaluate the impact of a decision on their suborganization better than anyone else. The problem is getting all of the properly considered input in a decision before it is made.

The condition is all too frequent in organizations where the staff of the chief executive will recommend to him certain policy actions before they have properly done their homework in getting the policy evaluated by others who are more knowledgeable or more directly affected. To avoid such erroneous decisions, a useful technique is to have a draft position paper prepared by a staff expert or by some other qualified individual. This paper explains the action to be taken and substantiates why. It is then circulated for comment among the major suborganizations and among those who are knowledgeable of or directly affected. The comments are then submitted to the staff group, who reviews them with the chief executive to determine to what degree he wants the proposed policy modified.*

SUMMARY

Many different techniques are available to assist the manager in decision making. In evaluating alternatives, only the costs affected by the decision should be considered. These so-called incremental costs will increase or decrease if different alternatives are selected. Consideration should also be given to the benefits (opportunity costs) that are sacrificed when one alternative is selected over another.

---

*This technique was used effectively by the systems-analysis staff under Secretary of Defense MacNamara in the early 1960's. They referred to such documents as "draft presidential memorandums." When policy recommendations were developed for presidential consideration, they were submitted in draft form to such key personnel as the Secretaries of the Army, Navy, and Air Force for their evaluation. This procedure ensures thorough consideration of a policy decision before it is made. It is also motivational to lower level managers because it gives them a say in major actions being contemplated by the organization.

Decision theorists have divided decision environments into four types: decisions under certainty, risk, uncertainty, and competition. Under certain conditions the environment is a known factor, so it is not a variable in the decision process. Under decisions involving risk, environments are not known, but the likelihood of different ones can be estimated based on previous experience. Thus probabilities can be used to average the potential payoffs. Under uncertain conditions, there is no knowledge of potential environments.

Five techniques, the pessimism, optimism, coefficient of optimism, Laplace and regret criteria, have been established to aid in making decisions in uncertain environments.

Decision trees are also proposed as a graphic, analytical way to deal with decisions under conditions of risk. Decision trees reflect the strategies, states of nature, and probabilities of the payoff matrix, but they also reflect sequential decisions over time.

Finally, the draft position paper is proposed as a method of obtaining the input of many organizations and individuals before making major policy-type decisions.

QUESTIONS FOR STUDY AND DISCUSSION

1. Assume that the Mitchell Motel is generally full on weekends but operates at only fifty-percent occupancy during the week. What are the incremental costs of having additional occupants during the week? Is there any way that pricing can be changed during the week to take advantage of this situation? Explain.

2. In the above example, assume that the owner has $150,000 invested in the motel. What is the opportunity cost of this investment?

3. Modify the decision tree in figure 7-10 so that the probabilities in the second year will be 0.6 for another heavy winter and 0.4 for a mild winter, providing the first-year actual conditions turn out to be a heavy winter. If the first year turned out to be a mild winter, the second-year probabilities would be 0.8 for a heavy winter and 0.2 for a mild one the second year. How will this modify the net cash flow? Will it change decisions A, B, or C?

4. Many advantages of the draft position paper were stated in this chapter. What are some of its limitations?

5. Are conditions in relation to the states of nature ever completely certain or uncertain? If not, of what value are the techniques proposed for conditions of certainty and uncertainty in decision theory?

Case Problem:
PAYOFF MATRIX AND EXPECTED
VALUE IN FARMING

Bill MacDonald is a farmer in the northern part of Idaho. He is trying to determine which crops to plant. If the growing season is short, wheat is the best crop. However, if the growing season is longer, corn will provide a higher return per acre—and potatoes are even superior to corn. If the growing season is 100 days, wheat will provide a return of $100 per acre, corn $90, and potatoes $60.

Since wheat does not require a growing season of over 100 days, the maximum return for it is $100. However, if the growing season is 120 days, corn will return $100 per acre and potatoes $120. If the growing season is 140 days, the corn return will be $110 per acre and the potato return $130. Based on historical records, there is a 0.2 chance that the season will be 100 days, a 0.5 chance that it will be 120 days, and a 0.3 chance that it will be 140 days.

Develop a payoff matrix based on this information and calculate the expected values.

Case Problem:
DECISION MAKING IN
A STOCK PURCHASE

Three firms are in the running for a major aerospace contract. This contract will amount to billions of dollars and extend over ten years. An investor wants to place $100,000 in the stock of one of the three companies. He is operating under conditions of uncertainty because there is no basis for determining which firm has the best chance to receive the award. The payoff matrix for this situation (figures represent *percent return* on investment) is shown on page 177.
Based on this information, calculate the following:

  A. What decision would be made based on the pessimism criterion?
  B. The optimism criterion?
  C. The Laplace criterion?
  D. The regret criterion?

	States of Nature		
	Contract Award Made to Company		
	A	B	C
S1 (Buy stock in A)	12	8	8
S2 (Buy stock in B)	6	16	6
S3 (Buy stock in C)	7	7	14

Manager Profile

John Sipe
Operations Manager, J. C. Penney
Tucson, Arizona

Background and Experience

John first entered retailing with Montgomery Ward in Napa, California, where he soon became the sporting-goods department manager. He entered Ward's management-development training program and later became a merchandising trainee manager—then merchandising manager. He moved to the J. C. Penney store in Phoenix as operations control manager. He is now operations manager of the Penney's store in Tucson.

Primary Responsibilities

At the Tucson store, the basic organization chart is as follows:

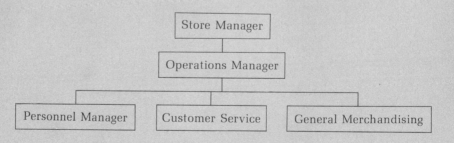

1. As manager of budget planning and expense control, he oversees all purchases, obtains funds, and approves all expenses.

2. John is ultimately responsible for all sales-support personnel, including office, warehouse, and service employees—about 150 people. Technically, he is their supervisor. John's job is to keep them busy, happy, and productive, as well as to resolve any disputes and problems that may arise. He oversees all of these functions through the personnel manager.
3. While the corporation determines and administers policies that pertain to all of its stores, each store has its own local policies that must be administered.

Insights

"Some managers try to do all of the work themselves. This becomes self-defeating, because they spread themselves too thin. A good manager must learn to delegate authority and assign responsibility effectively—there is no way that he can do it all himself.

"I like to think of myself as a 'peoples manager,' rather than a 'company manager.'

"When top management from Penney's comes to our store to consult with us, we feel that they are coming to aid and help us rather than to dominate us. The single best feature is that the instore managers have the authority—and the responsibility—to make local decisions, rather than someone outside of the store.

"The real art of management is to learn to work with and through people. Employees need to feel important, motivated, and—most of all—understood."

Manager Profile

Al Love
Owner-Manager, A-1 Gunnite Company
Houston, Texas

Background and Experience

Al went to work for a contractor in 1953 spraying gunnite for swimming pools. In 1960 he and two others bought a spraying machine and worked together in Phoenix. In 1969, he was able to purchase a huge gunnite spraying machine at a government sale from the U.S. Forest Service. This allowed him to really get a start in the gunnite business. He leased the big machine to various people until he had enough money to purchase necessary accessories and equipment. In 1970 he moved to Houston, where there is a great demand for swimming pools, and started his own business. His venture is very successful (he is now a partner of a company in Phoenix as well).

Primary Responsibilities

1. Maintaining adequate and efficient labor: Al does all scheduling—matching the necessary labor to the job. Weather and the great variance in his labor requirements are standard problems (He has a lot of job openings at good pay but has difficulty finding good employees willing to take on the necessary responsibility and work load.)
2. Acquiring the raw materials: A major problem in the past has been the availability of sand for the requirements of the job. He has recently leased rights to a sand bed with the right of way to the river bed. They now have enough sand available to meet all of their needs—present and future.

3. Promotion: Al has had no difficulty in getting the contracts for work to do. (There is a great demand for gunnite work in Houston, and he literally could get as much work as his business is able to handle.)
4. Records management. Al is responsible for all raw data; a local CPA is involved for the formal preparation of the books.
5. Purchasing of equipment and materials: There is an urgent need to maintain all of the supply inventories adequately. The most wasteful cost is having 12–15 employees sitting around waiting for supplies to arrive.
6. Collections: While the jobs are easy to get, collecting payment for doing work is difficult and time consuming. Bad debts are a major concern.

Insights

"I would consider myself a 'loose-knit' manager. I give my employees freedom and reward them for taking the initiative to do a job well.

"One of the big differences working in Houston (as opposed to Los Angeles) is that we do not work with the unions. There are both advantages and disadvantages that we are considering. I get a lot of pressure to go union—and may in the near future. Getting adequate, productive help has been my major problem since I came here.

"I have learned that I must control my temper in dealing with people. I must avoid losing it with people outside—as well as with the people within my organization. I expect the same from them."

PART IV

Macromanagement: The Environment

Interactions with External Forces and Institutions

What constitutes the external environment of an organization?

What is the relationship between an organization and its external environment?

Is an organization's role merely to react to external factors, or can it influence them?

How can a manager evaluate economic, technological, political, and sociocultural forces and institutions?

How do environmental factors influence planning, organizing, staffing, directing, and controlling?

Evaluating influences external to the organization has become an increasingly important responsibility of managers. This is because the trend is for these external factors to be characterized by greater complexity and change. These characteristics in turn, are reflected in the organizations existing in the environment. For example, governments tend to pass more laws and establish more regulations; technological improvements and product innovations occur more rapidly than ever before; society has modified its traditional value expectations of the firm in relation to environmental considerations and the quality of life; economic markets have become more sophisticated and complex. To be successful in today's environment, organizations need to become as skillful in managing their external relationships as they are in their internal.

But managing a firm's external relations is usually more difficult. Internal factors are more observable and controllable, and many can be regulated by the firm, whereas external variables consist of independent organizations or vague forces that are difficult to assess. This chapter is devoted to a better understanding of these external factors.

EXAMPLES OF ENVIRONMENTAL INFLUENCES

The interaction between different organizations and their environments can be demonstrated through several examples.

Selecting a Plant Location

When a firm conducts a site-location study, it is engaged in an exercise of evaluating its fit with the local environment. It is a two-way analysis involving the resources and services available in the community, but also an evaluation of how the firm will affect the local region. Site location decisions are normally made by a special committee which first develops a checklist of factors important to that organization. Each factor is weighted based on its relative significance. Common factors contained in site selection criteria are as follows:

1. Labor consideration
    A. Labor availability in terms of skills and quantity
    B. Wage rates in the region
    C. Strength of unions, existence of right-to-work laws, and so on
2. Support services
    A. Energy sources (electricity, natural gas, fuels)
    B. Air, rail, truck, and water transportation

C. Water supply and sewer disposal

D. Skilled support services involving construction, machining, legal services, financial institutions, etc.

3. Market location

A. Proximity to raw materials

B. Proximity to subcontractors and suppliers

C. Proximity to customers

D. Land availability and prices

4. Tax structure

A. Local property and community taxes

B. State income, sales, and other taxes

5. Climate

A. Temperature averages and extremes

B. Rainfall and humidity

C. Unusual conditions (fog, hurricanes, floods, etc.)

6. Community services

A. Schools, churches, and recreational facilities

B. Hospital and medical services

C. Hotels, motels, and convention centers

D. Roads and transportation systems

E. Housing availability and rental rates

F. City ordinances and zoning regulations

In evaluating each factor, the site-selection committee is assessing the fit between the firm and its environment. Is the labor supply adequate, both in quantity and training? Will excessive transportation costs place the firm at a disadvantage with its competitors? Will the community accept the congestion and industrial wastes created by the firm?

Besides being concerned with obtaining quality inputs at low cost, the firm is also concerned with the influence it will have on the community. Will it overextend community services? Will it become such a dominant employer in the region that the community will become overly reliant on it, making a reduction in the work force or a change in plant location difficult because of political pressures? (In order to avoid this, some national concerns have a policy that prohibits locating in a community where they employ over 25 percent of the work force.)

Public and Private Examples

The reciprocal relationship between a firm and its environment can be seen in many other examples. The western part of the United States is still dotted with ghost towns where mining operations or railroad construction once flourished. Often small communities grew in a few weeks to towns of 10,000 population and then rapidly subsided as a mineral vein ran out or the railroad moved on. Modern-day examples also are plentiful. The decision of the government to handle missile space launchings from Cape Canaveral in Florida and the decision of Walt Disney to place *Disneyland* south of Los Angeles had a major impact on these regions. An American oil company opening a subsidiary in an under-developed country will have many ramifications on that region. Even a small enterprise will exert some influence. The location of a gasoline station will to some degree affect land prices, local gasoline prices, the labor supply, and the adequacy of community services. The location of electronics firms around Massachusetts Institute of Technology and Stanford University are examples of educational institutions having a major influence on the local environment.

ANALYSIS OF ENVIRONMENTAL VARIABLES

Many different analytical approaches are used to evaluate the relationships between an organization and its environment. Traditionally, economists have followed the input-output model that focuses on resource utilization and profit maximization. Others view the environment as a network of constraints limiting what the organization can do. Laws, customs, and availability of resources restrict the firm in its operations. A third approach is to evaluate the environment on the basis of the claimants on the firm: stockholders are paid dividends, creditors receive payments, customers obtain warranties and service, and governments expect taxes and observance of the laws.

A more complex (but also more accurate) method is to examine the exchange between the organization and each of the institutions and forces that predominates in its environment. Under this method no one factor is considered primary. Instead the emphasis is on the variety of factors that tend to be interacting. All approaches will be considered, but the emphasis will be on the interaction model.

The Intermediate (or Task) Environment

The environment of an organization is multifarious. It consists of other organizations, the relationships among these, and a variety of trends, practices, and forces that combine in an institutional morass. For simplification purposes the environment of an organization can be divided into levels: the immediate organizations and claimants associated with a specific organization, and an outer level of macroforces and institutions. Consistent with figure 4-1, each of these constitutes a level in the systems hierarchy of a firm. The outer environmental level consists of economic, political, sociocultural, and technological forces and institutions. These are considered as the macroforces because a change in one variable will directly affect a firm, but it will also affect competing ones as well as the claimants of the firm, found in the intermediate level represented by the marketplace. Firms combine to help form a market, but it takes a combination of all markets to form an economy.

In viewing the relationships between a firm and the organizations and claimants in its intermediate environment, these ties can be examined individually, but (consistent with the real world) it is more realistic to look at composite relationships in decision making. A typical institutional set for a firm is reflected in figure 8-1. Stockholders, suppliers, customers, competitors, governments, labor unions, trade associations, and communities all interact with the firm. Many of these relationships, such as those with suppliers and customers, are deliberately established as the firm pursues its task-oriented activities. Other less obvious relationships also need to be monitored, because as a firm pursues its basic

Fig. 8-1.   The institutional set of a firm

goals, certain unintended side effects occur, influencing groups in the institutional set such as the local community.

The Claimants Theory

The claimants theory of the responsibility of the firm is based on a more extreme position. Financial ties result in stockholders and customers being obvious claimants. However, the claimant bond is more than economic. Many other groups have a stake in the firm's success, encompassing social as well as economic considerations. Employees are normally as reliant (or more so) on the firm for income than are the owners. Employees also seek a clean, safe place to work and an outlet for their skills.

Similarly, a supplier can be dependent on a firm. If one-third of a supplier's output is purchased by one buyer, loss of this account has major repercussions. The community is dependent on the firm for tax income and for outlets for employment. Many corporations pay out more to governments in taxes and to borrowers in the form of interest than they do in dividends or other returns to their owners. Since the future of each group is in some way tied to the firm, it results in an implied claim—with the firm's reciprocal obligation.

How the firm manages all of these relationships is the topic of the next chapter. At this point suffice it to say that maintaining favorable relationships with the groups in the intermediate environment is the special charge of top management and the specific units designed for external-coordination purposes.

Forces in the Macroenvironment

Typically the macroenvironmental variables covering political, sociocultural, technological, and economic influences have been viewed as constraints that restrict the operations or activities of an organization. While each of these factors serves as a constraint on an organization, each is also more than just a limit on what the organization does. Actually, each represents a fluctuating force whose ripple effect goes through all aspects of society. Because these factors constitute the outer level in the systems hierarchy of a firm, they have a more pervasive influence on it and its interconnecting systems than any other element or elements. When these variables are considered as forces, the manager's concern is with their present status and how they are likely to change. A meaningful framework for analyzing these relationships is shown in figure 8-2. The four variables in the macroenvironment are shown with the emphasis on the reciprocal relationships that exist between the firm and each factor. The nature of these relationships will be examined in detail.

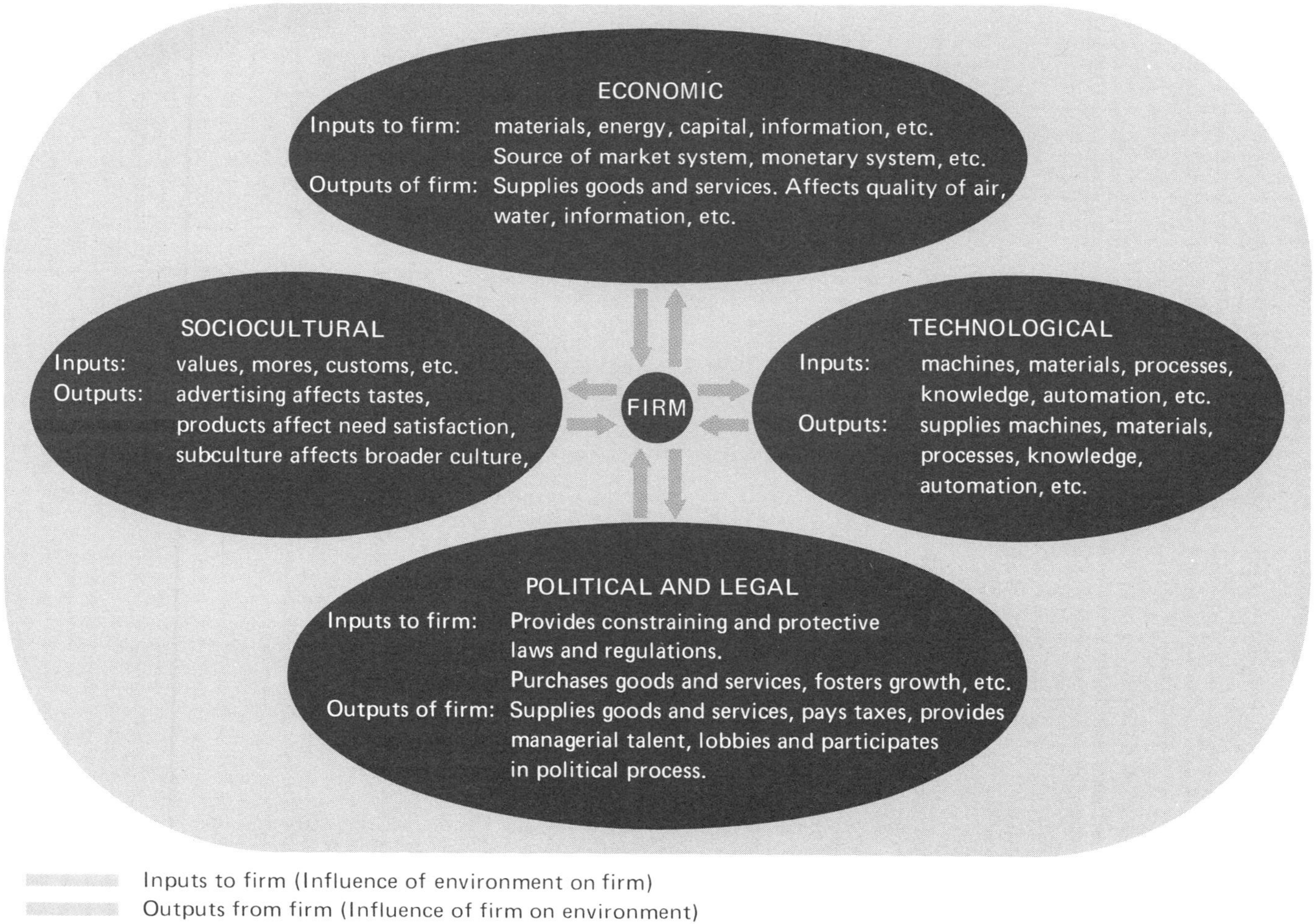

ECONOMIC

Inputs to firm: materials, energy, capital, information, etc. Source of market system, monetary system, etc.

Outputs of firm: Supplies goods and services. Affects quality of air, water, information, etc.

TECHNOLOGICAL

Inputs: machines, materials, processes, knowledge, automation, etc.

Outputs: supplies machines, materials, processes, knowledge, automation, etc.

SOCIOCULTURAL

Inputs: values, mores, customs, etc. advertising affects tastes, products affect need satisfaction, subculture affects broader culture,

Outputs:

POLITICAL AND LEGAL

Inputs to firm: Provides constraining and protective laws and regulations. Purchases goods and services, fosters growth, etc.

Outputs of firm: Supplies goods and services, pays taxes, provides managerial talent, lobbies and participates in political process.

FIRM

▓ Inputs to firm (Influence of environment on firm)

▓ Outputs from firm (Influence of firm on environment)

Fig. 8-2. Interaction between the firm and environmental variables

ECONOMIC FORCES AS A VARIABLE

The primal economic nature of the firm places this same primacy on the economic aspects of a firm's environment. A firm produces and sells its goods and services in competition with other firms, all of which are subject to international and national economic forces and conditions. Survival is dependent on being able to provide want-satisfying goods and services and being able to adjust to changes in these broader forces. A firm's financial success is dependent on the margin it can retain between what it costs to provide goods and services and what the public is willing to pay for them. All of the factors in this formula vary, depending on economic conditions.

Types of Markets

Economic markets are classified into five different types. It is common to refer to them as:

- perfect competition
- monopolistic competition
- pure oligopoly
- differentiated oligopoly
- monopoly

Two primary characteristics differentiate these markets. One is the number of buyers and sellers and the other is similarity or lack of similarity of the goods and services provided. Perfect competition and monopoly are the two extremes on the continuum. In perfect competition many sellers provide an identical product. No one seller can affect the price or the marketplace. Under a monopoly where there is only one seller, the firm has complete control over price and therefore dictates this aspect of the market. Monopolistic competition represents a large number of sellers, and both forms of oligopoly represent a limited number of sellers.

Although markets are separated on the basis of the number of buyers and sellers, they are also segmented on the basis of product differentiation. In monopolistic competition and differentiated oligopoly, the goods and services have different characteristics, or specifications, so that the buyer's choice is not solely on price but also on the nature of the goods purchased.

Many factors can upset the equilibrium of the marketplace. For example, more suppliers can enter the picture, the number of buyers can increase or decrease, technology can create product innovations, and goods may be produced more efficiently. Each individual market is also affected by national and international markets. On a national basis, gross national product (GNP) is one of the measures of the health of an economy. GNP represents the total goods and services provided by an economy during a certain time period. If all facets of the economy are favorable (low unemployment, improving productivity, high-capacity utilization, etc.) GNP will be moving upward. Generally this means that there is a greater demand for products and that purchasers have more income to buy them. Downturns or uptrends in GNP have ramifications that affect all markets—but some more than others. When economic trends are downward, wary consumers defer major purchases of durable goods like automobiles with the result that producers of these goods feel the pinch of a decline to a much greater degree. Since food purchases cannot be deferred, these will continue (with the less-expensive varieties likely to sell better).

Evaluating Economic Forces

Basic economic forces determine the value of all the property of a firm. They affect the price of corporate securities, the purchasing power of money, the resale value of machinery and buildings, and the price of finished-goods inventories. For these reasons one of the key factors influencing production, facility, and inventory decisions is anticipated future economic trends. Many firms, especially small ones, are initially very successful because they develop a unique product or approach to marketing one, but they soon experience failure because they do not keep attuned to economic changes. They build up inventories and add to their physical plant when economic trends indicate a need for less capacity rather than more, or else they market a product that is dependent on a large volume of consumer credit when the government is in the process of adopting tight money policies. Externally a firm is concerned with how it can remain competitive or keep ahead of other organizations supplying similar products, but it is also concerned with the general economic trends of the larger system. Since firms are subsystems of markets, and markets are subsystems of national economies, dependency ties exist through all three levels. However, the functioning of higher-level systems will dominate the functioning of the subparts.

POLITICAL AND LEGAL VARIABLES

Political forces are also composed of many elements. Their outward manifestation is found in the actions of governments and the establishment and enforcement of the legal system. In a narrow sense, the political variable is restricted to government institutions, but in the broad, pluralistic sense, they must include all participants in the political process. Since most groups have some role in political activities, it warrants a comprehensive analysis. However, for our purposes political forces will be restricted to the more direct influences relating to governmental actions and the legal systems. Even under this restrictive approach, governments fulfill four distinct roles in relation to business.

- *promote* business interests
- *regulate* business firms
- purchase or *buy* goods and services of business
- *manage* operations that provide goods and services to business, often in direct competition with business

Two observations are significant. First, governments are the suprasystems of society. Business certainly can influence governments, but governments have the legal right and the social power to dominate business organizations. Business in each country operates within the context of a climate dominated by laws and political power structures. The second point of significance is that there is no "normal" example of the various roles of government. Governments are evolving and changing. What was typical in the 1930's is not typical today. Furthermore, what exists today will not be typical in 2000. The evolving nature of political forces prohibits any analysis based on static conditions.

Government as a Promoter

Governments typically assume the role of encouraging economic development. As a means of doing this, they often attempt to foster the growth of business organizations. Massive grants of land and resources enticed railroad companies to open up the Western United States. Agriculture for nearly half a century has had the price of most commodities established and supported by the government. The Small Business Administration exists to foster small businesses. The federal government has also subsidized airlines, the development of atomic energy, and nearly every form of major technological advance. Across-the-board support is provided in the form of protective tariffs, taxation advantages, and maintenance of air traffic lanes and highway systems. In research and development alone, the federal government since 1950 has financed between 40 to 60 percent of our national efforts. Another broad means of support is educational, since governments educate and train the manpower hired by business firms.

Government as a Regulator

Government's most familiar role is that of a regulator. Every marketplace is subject to a myriad of laws instituted by all levels of government. The competition of the marketplace is under the stricture of laws and administrative rulings handed down by governmental units. Many of these are broad in nature, but many cover specific industries. The Sherman Antitrust Act of 1890 was one of the first of a series of laws aimed at promoting competition and preventing monopolies. Laws also relate to nondiscrimination in hiring, safety standards, pollution controls, procurement practices, financial reporting, and many other aspects of a firm's operations.

Certain industries, especially those determined to be "affected" with a public interest, such as public utilities, are subject to much closer controls. Independent regulatory commissions have authority to establish rates, approve entrance, extension, or abandonment of services, approve mergers, and, in general, to control the nature of competition. For instance, the transportation industry is regulated by the Interstate Commerce Commission, radio and television by the Federal Communications Commission, electrical utilities by the Federal Power Commission, and the securities market by the Securities and Exchange Commission. Most of these agencies were formed or strengthened in the 1930's, when the industries came into existence or when abuses brought demands for government control. It was during this same period (1935) when the National Labor Relations Act, which greatly strengthened the hand of labor unions, was passed. Another important regulatory agency is the Federal Trade Commission, which has broad responsibilities relating to deceptive advertising and unfair competitive practices such as price fixing.

In addition, local governments regulate zoning laws, state governments impose safety standards, and the federal government handles labeling laws. In fact, the regulations are so vast that large organizations need continual legal counsel to keep abreast of them. All of these external regulators are forces the firm continually must reckon with and be concerned about.

The greatest impact of the government as a regulator has not been through laws controlling the activities of business firms, but governmental policies aimed at influencing or regulating basic economic forces. After the crash of 1929, public pressure increased to find ways to eliminate boom-and-bust economic cycles. Fiscal (taxation and spending) policies and monetary (money supply) policies have been instituted to attempt to do this. Using fiscal policies such as "pump priming," governments attempt to stimulate the economy by purchasing more goods and services and increasing its budget, or by leaving more funds in the hands of consumers by taxing less. When the economy is to be cooled off, purchases are decreased as budgets are reduced, and taxes are increased to siphon off funds. Monetary policies affecting the total supply of money have much the same effect. These policies, although still somewhat controversial, are the everyday working tool of agencies like the Federal Reserve Board.

The Government as a Buyer

The largest single customer of the U.S. economy is represented by the U.S. government. Government agencies purchase nearly 25 percent of the gross national product. The federal government alone uses 25 percent of its budget to purchase goods and services from industry. In many markets, such as aerospace, the government is the largest single buyer and almost represents a *monosony* (opposite of a monopoly—only one buyer). Many individual firms sell most of their output to government agencies.

Similarly, state and local governments have increased their procurements from industry until they now rival the total purchases made by the federal government. Business provides most of the hardware items for defense arsenals, space work, atomic reactors, and construction projects. The government market tends to be controversial because of the controls and reduced-profit margins, but as long as one-fourth of our industrial output is absorbed by government, it will play a leading role in procurement practices and buying trends.

Government as a Manager

Industry builds highways, conducts research and development, and maintains equipment for governments, but governments in some instances carry on these same activities. Electric power is an example of where private and public producers exist side by side. However, the most prominent managerial role of the government is in land management. Approximately one-third of the United States is public domain, which means that it is controlled by agencies such as the Forest Service, Bureau of Land Management, and National Park Service.

The role of government as a manager is the least important of the four considered. However, two current trends could alter this. The government has a responsibility to ensure that a nation has adequate transportation and communication systems. As major elements of these systems have experienced financial failure (such as the railroads), it has become necessary for government to become more directly involved. Also, advanced technology has introduced massive, costly projects that often exceed the financial resources of private industry. Accordingly, government involvement has become more necessary as experienced with communication space satellites, the supersonic transport, atomic reactors, rapid-transit systems, and energy independence.

Growth of Government

All of the roles of government are constantly undergoing change. The one major direction of this change has been to increase the scope of government. In terms of regulation, as society has become more complex and interdependent, the need has increased for refereeing activities and setting standards. The growth of government in the United States has increased at a much faster pace than the production of business goods and services. Government purchases rose from 8.2 percent of GNP in 1929 to 22.6 percent in 1970. The not-for-profit section of the economy now employs over one-fourth of all workers. (In addition to government in the not-for-profit sector are hospitals, churches, social clubs, universities, and charitable groups.) What's more, international crises such as wars result in governments acquiring dictatorial powers. And after a major war the business community rarely emerges in the form it experienced before the military hostilities.

The Political Influence of Corporations

One of the most controversial political issues is the influence major corporations have on governments and on the political process. Some observers hold that our giant corporations are the prime institutions of power in our society, with their dominance resulting in a "corporate state."[1] Others hold that the relative political strength of business is not excessive, and that it has actually decreased in the past century.[2] In our pluralistic society, business corporations represent some of the major organizations involved in influencing public opinion and affecting the actions of legislators and public administrators. The financial power of the major corporation is far greater than most other organizations, but this is circumscribed by law. The Tillman Act, passed by Congress in 1907, prohibits corporate contributions to political parties and candidates in national elections. However, corporations influence legislation through lobbying activities, individual support of political candidates and parties, and maintaining close ties with government administrators —especially those influential in the purchase of their products. More than four hundred companies maintain full-time Washington representatives, with supporting staffs, to carry on these activities. They also join in major national organizations, such as the National Association of Manufacturers, founded in 1885, which is comprised of 14,000 corporate members.

ON THE DIFFERENCE BETWEEN THE ENVIRONMENTS
OF BUSINESS AND OF GOVERNMENT

A. J. Cervantes, twice elected as mayor of the City of St. Louis, was known as a "businessman's mayor." Several years later, in reflecting on this experience, he notes the following differences between business and government:

"Now that I have withdrawn from the clang and stress of public life and retired to the more placid tenor of the university lecturer and professor-student dialogue, I realize that the 'business' answer is not always the answer to the question of 'good government.' The good business executive is not necessarily a good government executive. On the contrary, the good business executive by the very fact may well be a poor government executive.

"Government is a business. The largest in our country. But government is more than a business. Government presides over a way of life. And if the government executive applies only the priorities and goals of business to the American government and to the American people, he will inevitably destroy the purpose of the American government."

Two of the several examples he uses follow:

"St. Louis has a large number of recreation programs operating in school playgrounds and parks. Some programs have many participants but others have few. An efficient businessman would say, 'Close those programs that have relatively few participants.' But this would mean that some neighborhoods would have no program for those who do use the facilities. Recreation centers must be reasonably close to everyone, so all of them stay open.

"On a larger scale, I wished to move the St. Louis area forward by building a modern airport suitable for the needs of the 21st Century. Federal officials and airlines agreed that the best location would be in Illinois, just across the river from St. Louis. Jobs would have been created, the area's economy given a boost, and the city's tax base improved. But Missouri interests—unions and business—wanted the contracts and jobs that would flow from the new airport. Even though Missouri did not have a site or funds for the land, they blocked the Illinois airport. Would a businessman have turned down an investment opportunity because one group of workers or subcontractors received the benefits rather than another? Not one who wanted to survive.

> Yet the political reality forced other government leaders to oppose the Illinois site."
>
> He summarizes his arguments as follows:
>
> "Business methods where possible, yes. Computerize your tax records. Use systems analysis to schedule your trash collections (but make sure everyone gets at least two pickups a week whether they need it or not!). Hire experts.
>
> "But if you want to be mayor, be prepared to drop that great gem of efficiency if it arouses the anger of the citizens or of any significant group of citizens. You may win the one victory—although you probably will not—but you won't win any more. The business of government is government, not business."

Quoted from *Business Week*, December 8, 1973, pp. 19–20.

SOCIOCULTURAL CONSIDERATIONS

Subsystems assume the characteristics of the larger system they are a part of. From a sociocultural standpoint, a firm is a subsystem of society. A firm established and developed within a particular culture will inevitably take on the social characteristics of that culture. Common value systems, mores, and behavior patterns will be evidenced in both individuals who are employees and customers of the firm.

Two societal trends have taken place in the United States that are now being mirrored in business firms: increased permissiveness and a decrease in the respect for authority. Open organizations characterized by a greater emphasis on equality of membership are evidenced in families, schools, and work groups. This has forced a change in the way that organizations are managed, since formal authority does not represent the force it once did. As a result, alternative methods of management based on more individual involvement have been developed.

Effect of Sociocultural Considerations on Management

The influence of sociocultural considerations on the firm has many implications for management. As cultures change, the tasks and life styles of consumers also change, resulting in a demand for new and different products. Firms again face the challenge of anticipating and adapting to this evolution. The clothing market is perhaps the prime example. Clothing styles change on a seasonal and annual basis. Shoes go from narrow high heels to low flat ones. Pants within a few years go from narrow "peg legs" to flares. A firm with a dated inventory of clothing will be fortunate to get a return of 50 cents on the dollar.

Another important sociocultural consideration relates to the management of multinational corporations. Often it is assumed that American managerial know-how can be moved across cultures and be equally effective. However, this is generally not the case. Managerial methods accepted and effective in the U.S. culture may be antithetical to the culture of a foreign country. As an example, in Japan and countries in Europe, employment with a country is considered more of a life-long contract. Employees do not change jobs, and they are not fired with the ease found in the United States. In this country, terminating a middle manager is still subject to few restrictions. In Europe a two-year notice is typically required, plus significant cash payments. Belgian courts have ruled that a fired employee should receive two-and-one-half years' pay.

Changing Value Systems

The value systems of a society are reflected in the behavior of people—including work situations. Individual, organizational, and professional norms are all shaped by the values of the broader society. They become engrained in leadership styles and are an important factor in decision making. Values are considered the desired state of affairs in a society. As such they serve as a standard for measuring behavior. They tend to restrict behavior, but they also serve as guides in establishing goals, determining priorities, and interacting with others.

Especially critical to managers are those values relating to the basic nature of man and his place in the work organization. Western society has been built on the capitalistic, or Protestant ethic. In the Middle Ages, commercial activities and profit making were considered crass and contrary to the standards of the religious orders that dominated society. However, in the 1600's the rise of protestantism brought with it an emphasis on physical work and frugality, and the resultant inevitable accumulation of capital. These values, known as the Protestant ethic, were closely associated with rugged individualism and a high regard for personal property, both of which contributed to the rise of capitalism in the following few centuries. The American economic system was derived and nurtured with these values as the touchstone.

Following the Great Depression in the 1930's and 1940's, the emphasis on self-reliance and survival of the fittest gave way to a concern for economic security, social justice, and eliminating the gross economic inequities existing in society. Government regulation of business increased with the aim of fostering full employment, ensuring minimum levels of personal income, and making the fruits of the economic system available on a more equitable basis to all citizens.

Changes in value systems inevitably introduce conflict. Individuals who benefit by the status quo typically are those who resist its change. However, with technology as a driving force, values have tended to change at a more rapid pace in recent years. This has been reflected in the corporation. The business firm was once evaluated almost strictly in economic terms, but as man's economic needs have been satisfied to a greater degree through productive economic systems, the emphasis has tended to switch to social justice. Thus the trend is to consider the firm as having social responsibilities in addition to its economic makeup. (The issue of the social responsibilities of the firm will be discussed in the next chapter.)

Demographic Changes

Business organizations compete in markets consisting of people purchasing and using goods and services. Therefore, any demographic change relating to the size, distribution, or age of the population will influence these same markets. This has been one of the major factors in the growth of the economy since World War II, estimated to account for one-third of the increase in GNP. The population boom following the war resulted in increased demand in essentially all markets. It took over a million years for the world to reach one billion people in 1830. The second billion came in the next one-hundred years and the third billion in thirty years, or by 1960. The fourth billion will again cut this time span in half to approximately fifteen years. The population increase, once a boon to the markets, is now considered a threat, since natural resources are not plentiful enough to match this rate of increase. Accordingly, the emphasis on zero growth in the birthrate is being more commonly adopted as appropriate national policy.

The other important feature of population is its distribution. With the rise in the birth rate, over half of our population is under twenty-four years of age. This has resulted in the youth culture, typified by products designed to appeal to this large market. Population distribution is also important in terms of geographics. The movement to the suburbs has left the crisis in the inner city. Business markets will inevitably follow population movements, since (as stated) markets consist of people.

TECHNOLOGY AS AN EXTERNAL VARIABLE

Of all environmental factors, none is more important in generating change than technology. Technology is a force that through scientific advance is continually taking on new characteristics. Technology, in turn, affects every feature of the external environment of a firm. The tentacles of technology are found in new product lines, economic productivity, political attitudes, and business strategies. The management challenge relating to technology is understanding this force for change—and developing strategies to cope with it.

Technology involves the application of science for practical or commercial purposes. Science consists of knowledge (including principles and laws), and technology is the application of this knowledge for practical purposes. Business is, therefore, the principal instrument in society for translating the output of science (knowledge) into goods and services for public consumption. It is the business firm that provides this vital link, resulting in the high standard of living enjoyed by current generations. Technology finds its expression in many forms. It is found in tools, materials, machinery, or the hardware aspects of production, but it is also found in processes, techniques, and skills: the "know-how" of production. Technology has been accurately assessed as comprising all of the techniques and processes that extend human capability.

The History of Technology

Before evaluating the total scope of technical change, a historical perspective is required. In the early 1970's a human skull and bones were discovered in Kenya below a layer of earth dated at 2.8 million years. In a cove in southern Africa a skeleton similar to modern man was uncovered and dated at 100,000 years. Man in a primitive form has existed for millions of years, in a more modern form for many thousands. For most of man's existence, he has lived in what is referred to as the handicraft stage of technology. He relied on hand tools, lacking the modern machines, energy sources, and sophisticated weapons that have ensured his dominance over other forms of life. Indeed, during this period man was just another species of life without the power of technology to gain his eventual superiority.

If one projects a linear timeline comparing the age of life on this planet with man's technical progress, all of the quantum advances would be shown on the current end of the time scale. The last one hundred years would show technical progress as a vertical line from the horizontal time axis. The printing press has been in existence for just over five hundred years; power stations for the generation of electricity, since the 1880's. The automobile and airplane have been in existence for less than one hundred years, and commercial television and electronic data processing for little more than thirty. Prior to 1850 most manufacturing in the United States was carried on in small shops or in households. Going from the tallow candle to the electric light, from the hand scythe to the reaper, and from the stagecoach to the space capsule has occurred within the past one hundred years.

Controlling Technology

Such rapid change is hard to comprehend—and even more difficult to evaluate. As any other change, it has its rewards but it also has its drawbacks. In accepting the benefits of a higher standard of living, man has sacrificed personal privacy, clean air, pure water, and open space. In this short time span, he has used up readily available fossil fuels to the point of an energy crisis. Trying to pinpoint the source of the advance and control its influences have proven difficult. The surging stream of science evolves from educational institutions, government laboratories, and, to a lesser degree, from business research efforts. As noted earlier, in recent years most of the research and development in the United States has been funded by the federal government, primarily for weapons and space efforts. Spinoffs have been applied to consumer-goods products, but the tie is often not deliberate or effective. Recognizing the need for better control and evaluation of the effects of technology, Congress passed an act in 1972 establishing an Office of Technology Assessment. Since technology is a mass infuser of change in our culture, we obviously need to channel it into output representing the best interests of society.

Interdependence of Technology

Attributing most of the dynamics of the environment to technology is also somewhat deceptive, because, as indicated, government has been one of the most important sources in fueling and directing technology. Other factors in the varying advance of technology are the cultural value systems and attitudes developed toward it and science. Also, technology is not a force unto itself but dependent on science, which is dependent on an educated populace and effective educational institutions. It is also dependent on resource availability and the accumulation of capital. The important thrust at this juncture of human existence is to harness and better control technology by directing it into outcomes more deliberately determined as being in man's overall interests.

Technology and Competition

The influence of technology in managing the internal aspects of a firm will be covered in chapter 12. The concern in this chapter is assessing how technology as an environmental variable affects—and is effected by—the firm. Technology and its turbulent influence on the environment is one of the primary forces making adaptation a central concern of top management. Unless a firm adapts and uses technological advance, it is difficult to maintain a favorable position with competitors: competition in many markets is as much technological as economic. The firm that quickly and effectively applies advancing technology finds itself at a competitive advantage. All of the recent scientific markets such as aerospace, electronics, optics, and medical technology attest to this observation. Japan's surge into the forefront as one of the international commercial powers was initially triggered by cheap labor, but in recent years it has been possible only through superior technology.

Management is concerned with keeping a company innovative so it can gain a competitive edge by developing technological improvements in products or processes. This is accomplished by staying on the forefront of scientific and technological advance. Small firms without large research capability hope to ride the shirt tails of the larger organizations when lack of patents will permit them to do so. (On the other hand, similar to marketing innovations, technology provides one of the few opportunities that small firms have to gain an advantage over the corporate giants. E. H. Land's developments with Polaroid cameras and film and the advances of Xerox in copy machines are two examples.)

It has been stated that science finds, industry applies, and man conforms. This has been probably most dramatic in relation to transportation systems. Nothing has modified human existence quite like the mobility provided by railroads, automobiles, and airplanes. The railroads provided the means for developing the West and were the key to industrial development in the last half of the nineteenth century. Automobiles further mobilized society. Television rapidly changed the leisure habits of individuals and created new industries (as it threatened others such as motion pictures). Just as surely as the rifle almost terminated the existence of the buffalo, changing technology terminates existing product lines as it opens up new opportunities.

The Pace of Technological Change

Perhaps the key point for the manager is that at one time these changes occurred so slowly it was possible for firms to react as they evolved. Now firms must anticipate and plan for change to avoid being left behind. Product lines, formerly lasting for ten to fifteen years, now experience a life cycle of five years or less. The time lag from scientific invention to the manufacture of a product was 112 years for photography. For the telephone it was less than half of this period. In recent years, the integrated circuit had a time lag of only three years. The accelerated pace of technology has shortened the reaction time of the firm, requiring an extremely keen sensitivity to external trends.

SUMMARY

The external environment of an organization exerts many pressures and establishes many conditions that influence a firm in its operations. Managers need to be aware of these and direct the activities of their organizations in such a way as to minimize the dangers or take advantage of the opportunities that are created. This is not strictly a one-way relationship, since organizations can also affect environmental forces, but usually the firm is only one small element acting on the environment.

   For analytical purposes, the environment of the firm is divided into an intermediate and a macroenvironment. The intermediate environment includes the groups that a firm interacts with as it functions in the marketplace. Thus it involves suppliers, competitors, customers, labor unions, and other organizations. The macroenvironment consists of major forces that influence the firm and other groups in the intermediate environment. Macrovariables include economic, political, sociocultural, and technological forces and institutions.

QUESTIONS FOR STUDY
AND DISCUSSION

1. Why is it easier for a firm to manage internal relationships than it is to manage external ones?
2. Give three examples you are familiar with where the action of an organization had a significant, observable impact on external factors.
3. What are the environmental consequences of establishing a community college in a city of 15,000 people?
4. What groups exist in the intermediate environment of a hospital? A labor union? A movie theater?
5. In your lifetime, what major changes have occurred in your environment? How have these influenced what you do?
6. Based on the claimant theory of the responsibility of the firm, what claims does each of the organizations in figure 8-1 have on a firm?
7. In what ways does a firm influence broader sociocultural forces?
8. What are the various roles government plays in our society? Which are the most important to the firm? How have these roles changed in recent years?
9. Give an example of an industry that is technology intensive and one that is not. How does technology affect each industry?

10. Give an example of several major technological advances you are familiar with. What was the source of these advances? What made them possible? How have these advances affected other environmental variables relating to sociocultural, political, or economic considerations?
11. As it relates to a firm, how does the environment and claimants theory differ if the focal organization is government?

Case Problem:
KAIPAROWITS POWER PROJECT

One of the world's largest power projects is currently scheduled for construction on the Kaiparowits Plateau in south central Utah. This is a sparsely populated area located some 29 miles from Lake Powell and the Colorado River. Plans are to construct a 3000 megawatt power plant fueled by coal. The power supply will be consumed by growing industrial and population needs in Arizona and Southern California. The first unit is to be completed in 1980 and the final units in 1982.

Four participating utility companies are to construct the plant under guidelines established by the Department of Interior. The plant will provide 28 percent of the increased power needs of the area over the next 10 years. If the plant was generated by crude oil, 33 million barrels would be required annually. There are an estimated 1.5 billion tons of coal (in place) on 47,000 acres of federal and state lands. The coal reserves are sufficient to fire the Kaiparowits project for approximately 70 years and is in seams 400 to 800 feet beneath the surface. All mining will be underground. The coal will be carried several miles to the plant by conveyors, where it will be pulverized and burned. The coal is a high-grade bituminous variety that has high heat output per pound and is low in sulfur, approximating less than one-half of 1 percent.

Over 45,000 acre-feet of water will be used in development of the plant, primarily for the cooling towers. The water, 4 percent of Utah's remaining allotment from the Colorado River, will be pumped from Lake Powell. Under the worst conditions, it is estimated that the project will contribute 1.7 percent of the annual allowable particulate standard and 11.0 percent of the 24-hour particulate standard based on Federal Government ambient air-quality regulations.

The project will develop 2500 jobs in permanent mining operations and 500 jobs in power plant operation. Another 2500 jobs will be involved in the peak of the construction period. When support services are added, over 8000 permanent jobs are projected. This will require a new community of from 15,000 to 20,000, which is ten times the size of any existing township in that area.

What are the major economic implications of this project?
What are the major social implications?
Are there any political or technological implications?
What alternatives are there for use of the water and coal resources?
How will it influence the local environment?
Should the project be approved?
Should Utah residents favor the project when most of the electricity will be exported to Arizona and California?

Case Study:
NORTHLAND TRUCK LINES AND
NORTHLAND COMMUNITY COLLEGE

Northland Truck Lines has been operating as in independent trucking firm since 1935. The firm, located in Colorado, contracts with a local meatpacking company to transport halves of beef to major population centers in Southern California. Since the trucks are refrigerated, the firm has obtained contracts to ship vegetables from southern and central California to Colorado on the return route. The firm has 20 trucks and approximately 50 employees. Business is fairly steady, and profits have increased an average of 10 percent annually.

Nearby, Northland Community College has been in operation since 1967. There are 6500 full- and part-time students. The college is located in downtown Northland and is financed by state and local funds. There are 170 instructors and over 500 employees. Tuition covers approximately 20 percent of the educational cost for each student.

Are there dependent ties between these two organizations?
How is the external environment of the two organizations different?
What difference is there in the relative significance of the economic, political, social, and technological variables?
How might the institutional *set* (see figure 8-1) of each organization differ?

How will decision making in the two organizations differ because of these factors?

What is the relative dependence of each organization on its environment?

How will changes in the environment affect the organizations?

Footnotes

1. Theodore J. Jacobs, "Pollution, Consumerism, Accountability," *Center Magazine,* Vol. 5 No. 1 (January/February, 1972).
2. See Neil H. Jacoby, *Corporate Power and Social Responsibility* (New York: Macmillan Publishing Company, Inc., 1973), chapter 7, Corporate Political Power: Involvement or Detachment?

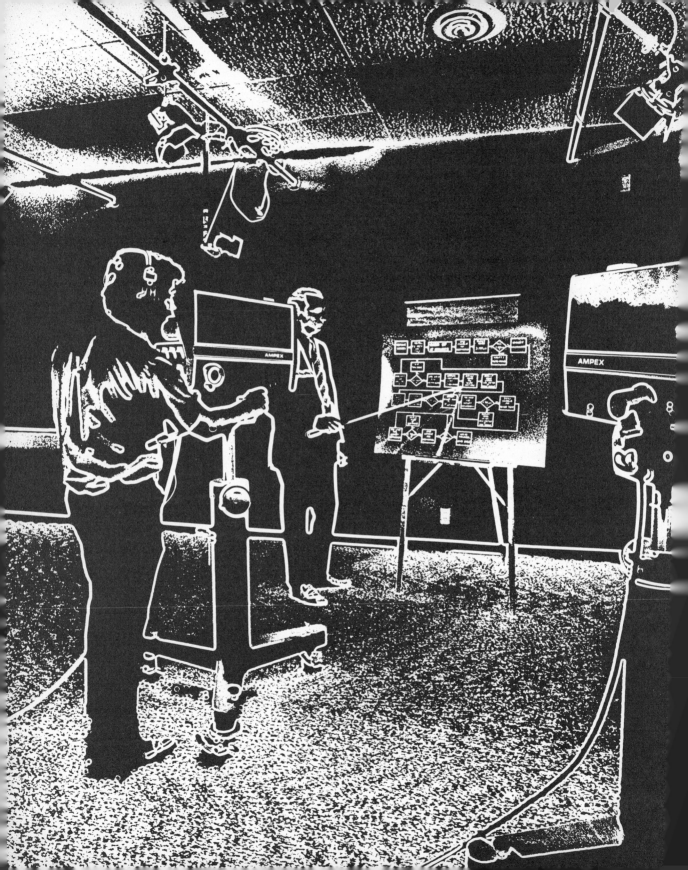

External Adaptation and Social Responsibility

What means can an organization use to adapt to external forces?

How should an organization be structured to maximize adaptation?

What organizational and competitive strategies should be adopted?

What are the social responsibilities of the firm?

Is a firm's adaptation primarily economic?

What is the environmental impact of the multinational corporation?

EARLY ADAPTATION OF
GENERAL MOTORS CORPORATION

An illustration of how a variety of external forces influences the status of a firm can be seen in the early history of General Motors. William C. Durant originally founded the company in the late 1880's. The product line consisted of two-wheel horse-drawn carts. With the invention of the internal-combustion engine (a technological development), Durant rapidly switched the company over to producing automobiles. Due in part to his marketing genius, the firm experienced substantial growth until a business recession in 1910 (an economic factor) found the company short of cash, and Durant was forced out. Within five years he was back at the helm, but then another external crisis occurred with the advent of World War I. At that time, the internal-combustion engine was not widely used for military purposes, but Durant continued the growth of the company by turning to the manufacture of tractors and refrigerators.

Following the war, the recession of 1920 (economic conditions) again caught Durant short, and he was ousted from the organization! In the 1920's General Motors began eyeing foreign markets. However, the high trade barriers existing at the time prohibited marketing large quantities of automobiles overseas. Therefore General Motors again adapted to a political situation and circumvented the tariffs by purchasing Vauxhall in Britain and Opel in Germany. The rise of General Motors as a multi-national corporation can also be associated with political events. As GM came to capture 50 percent of the automotive sales in the United States, management recognized that antitrust legislation would likely prohibit their increased dominance of the market. Therefore they placed more emphasis on foreign operations, with the result that on a world-wide basis they produce nearly 25 percent of all automobiles sold.

The success of General Motors, as with other firms, is a history of a series of adaptations to environmental factors. Adjusting to political and economic changes, product improvement of competitors, and social trends (such as concern for the environment) are the continual types of changes facing the modern manager.

METHODS OF ADAPTATION

Our concern in this chapter relates to the methods and strategies the organization uses in the adaptation process. In later chapters the internal-change process relating to modifying the organizational climate and the behavior of individuals will be considered. This chapter's focus will be on the systems challenge of how the organization regulates the exchanges that occur across its boundaries. Three different methods of adaptation will be considered:

- adjusting the organization structure
- developing organizational strategies
- developing competitive strategies

Assigning Responsibility to Suborganizations

The most common method for dealing with outside groups is to establish specialized units within the organization to maintain external relationships. The broad responsibility is normally given to a long-range planning staff that conducts long-range studies and forecasts environmental developments for the organization. However, there are also many specialized units dealing with groups in the intermediate environment of the firm. Purchasing or procurement units maintain relationships with suppliers; the labor relations department maintains contact with the appropriate labor unions; financial analysts keep in touch with the investment community; marketing representatives keep tab on competitors and on customers; research and development scientists stay current on scientific and technological advances; marketing research experts survey customers to determine their preferences and then join with research and development personnel to come up with marketable product innovations; and a public affairs or public relations staff typically exists to enhance community relations.

Such units are common to all major corporations. In a recent survey it was revealed that three-fourths of all large American corporations maintain a public affairs department to help shape public attitudes favorable to the firm. The danger in emphasizing specialized units is that their efforts must be integrated to mesh with what is desirable for the total organization. Obtaining this integration is often difficult in terms of providing a composite, favorable image or gaining the total adaptive posture that the system or organization desires.

Developing Organization Strategies

In addition to establishing specialized units to deal with outside groups, other methods involving modification of the organization structure can be used to cope with external groups and forces. Sociologists have identified strategies such as *cooptation*, which involve the absorption of protesting elements in order to eliminate them (permitting students to have a say in university affairs). *Reciprocity* is the process that different groups use to engage in cooperative arrangements beneficial to both parties (you scratch my back and I'll scratch yours). *Joint ventures* and *coalitions* are used to form an aggregate of organizational forces and resources that will be sufficient to compete with more powerful organizations. Effective organizational structure adds power to a group. Corporations, labor unions, and governments have considerable power in society primarily as a function of their size, internal support, and structural effectiveness. (Consumers have not had as much relative power because they have had no common, formalized organizational framework, but recently efforts by Ralph Nader and associates have helped make consumerism a public issue and supportive legislation has followed.)

As will be seen later, the nature of corporate structural arrangements is changing because of the more rapid rate of change in the environment. Highly structured, precisely designed organizations were once more efficient, but these are now often too cumbersome for the required adaptation to external forces. Accordingly, emphasis is switching to less formalized, more flexible ones.

Developing Competitive Strategies

The major methods selected and the broad approaches devised to achieve organizational goals in relation to external groups and forces constitute the strategy of the organization. *Organizational strategy* is defined as the methods or schemes developed, after consideration of environmental variables, that place the organization in the best position for goal accomplishment. Strategy is normally aimed at providing direction in the deployment of resources to achieve established goals. Strategy is not a decision, but it is the pattern developed in a stream of significant decisions. A firm has many separate strategies: it may have internal, external, marketing, financial, social, technical, and many other strategies.

A typical feature of a strategy that differentiates it from planning is the concept of an opponent. Strategies developed under this premise are referred to as *competitive* and are established based on the anticipated reaction of competitors. (This is the form of strategy implicit in the type of mental combat involved in military operations and game theory.) The goal is to win, and the strategies are the methods of outwitting the opponent in attaining this goal. Marketing strategies are an example of competitive strategies where a firm calculates how competitors will react to product innovations, more intensive advertising, changes in pricing, or other methods of promotion. All strategies do not directly involve an opponent. However, they normally include some obstacle, such as public opinion, where the strategy is to develop more favorable attitudes toward pending actions.

THE NATURE OF CORPORATE STRATEGY

Corporate strategy consists of a set of long-range decisions which establish objectives, policies, and plans to exploit opportunities or combat threats in response to environmental forces and developments. These decisions are the result of a complex decision-making process designed to establish organizational goals and long-range plans for resource allocation and action. . . .

. . . The decision process for strategy formulation consists of identifying and assessing the opportunities and threats posed by the competitive situation, deciding organizational goals in light of that assessment, and formulating broad strategies and plans for total corporate action. Those decisions should be based upon an analysis of the total situation within which the organization operates. That analysis entails determining what variables are to be considered in defining or evaluating directions for the enterprise, obtaining relevant information, and assessing it in terms of organizational competence, associated risks, and values of the executives.

Quotation from John W. Bonge and Bruce P. Coleman, *Concepts for Corporate Strategy* (New York: The Macmillan Company, 1972), p. 125.

CONTINGENCY APPROACH TO EXTERNAL STRATEGY FORMULATION.   Strategy is a part of planning and will therefore be considered in more detail in Part VIII relating to planning and control. At this point the broad methodology associated with strategies will be explored. The specific actions to be undertaken are contingent on many factors that relate primarily to external conditions. Strategy formulation is considered a process, and like the decision-making process it is based on a contingency framework and a sequence of related steps:

Step one   Evaluate the situation by analyzing the environment.
  A. This involves a continual process of scanning the environment. Relegating it to a once-a-year exercise in conjunction with planning cycles should be avoided.
  B. Information is collected and forecasts of relevant trends are made (economic, technological, political, social, etc.).

C. Surveys are undertaken to provide necessary information (market research on attitudes, pricing studies, wage rate studies, etc.).
D. An evaluation is conducted of the effects that the anticipated trends and future developments will have on the firm.
E. The opportunities created by these developments, as well as the constraints imposed, should be identified.

Step two Design proposed strategies.
A. This involves a broad consideration of a variety of approaches and alternatives.
B. Constraints identified in step one are used to establish appropriate strategy alternatives.

Step Three Evaluate the proposed strategies in light of situational variables.
A. Are the strategies consistent with the purpose, goals, and values of the organization?
B. Are the strategies consistent with the special competence of the organization—primarily in terms of manpower skills and facilities?
C. Are the strategies consistent with the resources available to the organization and to the priorities for these resources?
D. Are the strategies consistent with the justifiable risks that can be assumed and with the necessary time horizons?
E. How will outside groups (competitors, labor unions, community officials, etc.) respond to these strategies?

Step four Select appropriate strategies for implementation.
A. Which strategies best exploit the opportunities?
B. What are the comparative advantages and disadvantages of each strategy?
C. Which strategies best meet the requirements for success and have the best chance of achieving the objective sought?
D. What competition edge will be provided?
E. What contingency plans should be developed assuming conditions change or the selected strategy does not meet expectations?

Step five Make internal adjustments to execute the strategies selected.
A. Establish appropriate internal policies.
B. Make necessary adjustments in the organization structure.
C. Prepare plans, budgets, and programs.
D. Acquire and/or train necessary manpower.

APPLICATION OF CONTINGENCY STRATEGY METHODOLOGIES. Diversification is a strategy often adopted by a firm that is concerned because it has a narrow product line. The goal to expand its product line will result in a continual search for new product opportunities (step one). This requires an analysis of factors external to the firm such as changes in technology, the condition of competitors, firms representing potential merger opportunities, a forecast of future markets, and many other similar considerations. Once the organization identifies a strategy for adding to its product line (step two), it will then evaluate whether it has the capacity to pursue this opportunity (step three). This requires a careful analysis of financial resources, manpower, facilities, marketing capability, and managerial experience. It is, in effect, a resource audit that needs to be carefully conducted to avoid consequences that can be tragic. Once it decides to adopt the strategy (step four) the internal adjustments need to be made to take on the new product line (step five).

No one has developed any magic formulas for forecasting the future. Mistakes inevitably will be made. Following World War II, technology appeared to open up two vast new opportunities, projected as billion-dollar markets, that attracted many newcomers. Atomic explosives gave promise of peaceful application of atomic power for generation of electricity, and electronic data processing created the computer market. Many large firms jumped into these markets assuming that success was inevitable. However, the atomic reactor market, even with generous government subsidization, was extremely slow to develop, and firms decided they could not wait twenty years to break into the black. In the computer market the dominance of International Business Machines, the rapid turnover of equipment as new generations of computers were introduced, and the large number of companies attempting to compete made it a graveyard for many subsidiaries and product divisions. The uncertainties and dynamics of environmental factors continue to make external adaptation the most confusing and risky area of managerial decision making.

THE SOCIAL RESPONSIBILITIES
OF THE FIRM

Traditionally the firm has been considered an economic entity. Accordingly it has been analyzed and evaluated in economic terms. In classical economic theory the competition of the marketplace results in production of those goods that are most desired and least expensive. These goals are not only the most successful for the firm but also best for society. Classical economic models thoroughly consider the economic functioning of the marketplace, but they ignore external constraints and consider social values as extraneous. However, the more comprehensive systems approach to analyzing organizations views economic variables as only one aspect of the functioning of an organization. The firm is a social organization as well as an economic one, and so its actions have social as well as economic implications. In the interaction model, the firm interacts with many different external organizations and forces.

Definitive guidelines have been developed for the economic functioning of the firm, but until recent years there have been few guidelines for the social functioning. The social functioning is referred to as *social responsibility* of the firm, defined as the obligation that a firm has to foster the social as well as the economic ends and values of society. Even though society's basic expectations are for the firm to produce goods and services in an efficient and effective manner, the firm cannot ignore its social impact or social obligations. The economic marketplace effectively arbitrates the exchange of goods, but it is not an effective arbiter of social values and ethical standards. This is true even though it is impossible to realistically separate the economic and social consequences of a firm's actions. Unemployment is an economic and a social problem; misuse of resources is a social and an economic problem; and pollution of the environment also covers both dimensions. A manager is not only an economic decision maker but a social decision maker as well.

The difficulties the manager faces in giving consideration to social responsibilities are many: values are often vague, social implications are frequently disguised—because their impact is usually external to the firm—and measures do not currently exist for evaluating this impact. The accounting systems, financial statement, budgets, and formal reward systems in organizations are normally entirely economic or financial. Performance is measured on the basis of these, and social indicators to give the manager or others feedback on social dimensions are nonexistent. And, yet, society is changing its values and expectations of business to include a greater role in solving social problems. This again is imposing an adaptation challenge to the business firm.

THE SCOPE OF THE FIRM'S SOCIAL RESPONSIBILITIES

Some lip service has been paid to the social responsibilities of the firm for many years. However, it did not become a prominent theme in management literature until the 1960's, and it received only incidental attention by corporations prior to 1965. The scope of these social responsibilities and the barometers used for measurement are still in their evolutionary stage and the source of considerable controversy. Milton Friedman, the economist, leads a vocal group that is strongly opposed to the concept and considers it subversive to the nature of capitalism. In his words, "Few trends could so thoroughly undermine the very foundations of our free society as the acceptance by corporate officials of a social responsibility other than to make as much money for their stockholders as possible."[1]

However, proponents on the other side argue just as vociferously, and the passage of laws like the Civil Rights Act of 1964, corporate concern for the environment, and public opinion polls would indicate that Friedman's view is in the minority. (Both sets of arguments will be reviewed later in the chapter.)

Internal versus External Responsibilities

The internal responsibilities of the firm relate to a concern for, and protection of, human values—therefore primarily to the handling of employees. Due process, equality, and justice need to be ensured in employee selection, training, promotion, and termination processes. An employee has a vested interest in the firm, since much of his time and opportunities for self-fulfillment are job related. The work environment should be a clean, safe place to work, but it should also afford opportunities for upgrading and advancement, and it should contribute to the dignity of the individual. By contributing to the self-fulfillment of the individual, the firm is also contributing to a more skilled, motivated employee and to an improved society.

The external responsibilities of the firm follow the claimant theory discussed in chapter 8. According to this theory, all external groups (suppliers, governments, labor unions, customers) deserve to be treated with the same sense of justice and fair play. Each has a claim on the firm, and as a result the firm is obligated to respect this claim in a fair and ethical fashion. However, social responsibility is much more than an altruistic plea for ethical behavior. It is now interpreted to include positive programs to improve social ills or injustices. Programs included in this category are usually divided into three categories: urban, consumer, and environmental affairs.

URBAN (COMMUNITY) AFFAIRS Urban affairs include activities such as: providing equal employment opportunities, training and employing minorities and the disadvantaged; fostering economic development of urban areas (including minority-owned businesses), promoting physical development of housing, transportation, schools, and medical facilities, and supporting the arts and cultural improvements. Major strides have been made in recent years. In 1961 President Kennedy signed an executive order requiring nondiscrimination by government contractors. The Civil Rights Act of 1964 prohibits discrimination by race or sex in hiring. Numerous private programs have been started by businessmen like those of the National Alliance of Businessmen, formed in 1968 to train and provide job opportunities for the disadvantaged. Within two years under this program 23,500 companies joined in providing jobs for approximately

378,000 persons. Financial assistance has also been given to starting black businesses and to providing low-cost housing and cultural facilities in urban blight areas.

CONSUMER AFFAIRS   Consumer affairs includes providing safe, reliable products and services that perform as advertised; adequate information on goods and services to enable consumers to make comparisons before purchase; prompt, reasonably priced service; and products free from defects. Public concern over these issues is evidenced by passage of the Motor Vehicle Safety Standards Act of 1966, the Consumer Protection Credit Act of 1968, and other such legislation.

ENVIRONMENTAL AFFAIRS   Environmental affairs include protection from, and reduction of, environmental damage caused by air and water pollutants, solid wastes, pesticides, radiation, and noise. Business in the past has been one of the prime contributors to environmental pollution, and as the effects have become more pronounced, public attitudes have called for a halt to such activities. If a firm pollutes a stream, it is a cost to society—even though it is not a direct one to the firm. These are called *external costs,* because they are not directly assumed by the firm. However, the pollution standards now being established by government bureaus like the Environmental Protection Agency prohibit organizations from this action, forcing an internalization of the cost in the form of pollution-control devices.

CORPORATE ACTIONS IN SOCIAL RESPONSIBILITY

But behind the ballyhoo of antilittering campaigns, self-congratulatory advertisements and hot air from all sides, some major corporations are taking steps that they contend represent sincere efforts to gear social dimensions into their day-to-day operations. So far, the vast majority of these actions are in the realm of dealing with minorities. For example:

—Chase Manhattan Bank now demands that its young executives make special efforts to counsel minority-owned businesses and community groups on financial matters.
—General Electric plant managers are required to report regularly their percentage of nonwhite employees compared to the percentages of nonwhites in their areas. They also must submit five-year plans for increasing minority employment.

—Atlantic Richfield has instructed its managers to hire non-white job applicants ahead of equally qualified whites. "I still get a report on my desk every quarter indicating the minority balance in all parts of the company," says Thorton F. Bradshaw, president. "When an area is lagging, I do something about it."

—In Chicago, Standard Oil of Indiana recently announced it will insist on "an affirmative action program" to provide jobs for minority construction workers and contractors in building a $100 million, 80-story office building. The work force of the contractors must be 34% black, a rarity in the construction trades, and the company can cancel contracts if it isn't.

Reprinted with permission of the *Wall Street Journal*. © Dow Jones and Co., Inc. October 26, 1971, All Rights Reserved.

ARGUMENTS IN FAVOR OF
SOCIAL RESPONSIBILITY

There are many arguments given relating to the pros and cons of social responsibility. The case for social responsibility can be summarized using five basic themes:

1. Business, and any other institution, must meet the needs of society in order to survive. If business is not responsive to society's needs, it will lose the power it derives from public support. As social problems become of more concern, existing institutions must be effective in dealing with these problems—or they are replaced. Typically such forfeiture has resulted in the extension of the power of government. As one observer states, "Unless a much better balance is soon achieved between the social and economic power exerted by the private corporate sector and the social responsibilities it assumes, corporations stand an excellent chance of losing much of their existing power and independence."[2]

2. Not only is American society placing more attention on social problems, but society's expectations are that business will play a major role in solving these problems. This is reflected in the legislation referred to earlier and the changing stance found in recent years both in public attitudes and the response of businessmen. The economic needs of a society tend to predominate until the production of goods

and services results in a standard of living where basic economic wants are satisfied. At this point social needs become more dominant. Issues such as preserving our physical environment in its original status, the freedom to choose life styles, and a concern for clean air and water are tending to take precedence over unlimited economic growth.

The changes, highlighted by consumerism, racial demands, and concern for the environment, are not temporary. They represent a major shift in public expectations. This shift has far-reaching implications for the corporation. The social contract between business and society is changing. Society once looked to business for providing an abundance of products at low cost, but the competitive marketplace, with its emphasis on profit maximization, is not necessarily accompanied by social justice or by long-term considerations of world resource utilization. Society expects business to contribute to the quality of life in more ways than purely economic ones.

3. It is in the long-term self-interest of business to maintain a favorable environment, including social values and conditions. A firm relies on the environment for its existence. Without suppliers, customers, and favorable political, economic, and social conditions, business cannot function. With such total reliance on a hospitable environment, business cannot sit by and ignore the trends or developments taking place. This dependency on the environment implies that business should do what it can to mold an environment favorable to its future existence.

This, in turn, implies a concern for the developments evolving in society and government, as well as playing an active role in attempting to maintain institutions and values conducive to business. Business is one part of a dependent societal system where interrelationships among the parts determine how the system will function. Educated employees, prudent world resource utilization, a market economy, and limited central government are far preferable to an unskilled work force, exploitation of resources, and a strong central government under which the means of production are publicly owned. Such conditions cannot be left to chance.

4. Business is a major form of social power in society. Accordingly, it has social responsibilities commensurate with that power. Approximately seventy percent of the people who work in the United States are employed directly by business. A significant portion of their time is spent on the job. Furthermore, much of the productive capacity and managerial talent in the U.S. is under the control of business. All of this represents social as well as economic power,

making it impossible for business to ignore the social implications of its actions or existing social ills.

5. Not only because of its social power does business have the obligation to be concerned with social problems, it also has the know-how to assist in the solving of many of society's problems. Big business has capital resources, managerial talent, innovative skills, and a broad range of functional expertise that in many instances is unmatched by other institutions. Therefore, this capacity needs to be put to use in solving these problems. Business should be expected to take the lead in areas such as training and finding employment for the hard-core unemployed, reducing pollution, and renovating urban blight.

ARGUMENTS AGAINST SOCIAL RESPONSIBILITY

Five basic arguments are given for restricting business involvement in social affairs:

1. Business is basically an economic institution. Corporations exist to earn a return on the investment of stockholders. Social responsibility subverts the basic purpose of business and reduces its profit motive. This is the classic economic doctrine of restricting a firm to economic purposes based on economic values.

2. There are dangers in blending the roles of business and government. Accepting broad social responsibilities would move business into the traditional realm of government. No institution can possibly serve all of the needs of society. This is referred to as *functional analysis*. Under this concept the institutions most efficient in handling particular functions for society should be given the responsibility for these.

3. Even assuming business has social responsibilities, businessmen are not trained or qualified to make social decisions. The businessman's expertise is in economic affairs, and others are more qualified to solve social problems.

4. A business must maintain a profit to survive and incurring costs for social purposes will endanger the future of many firms. Business investments successfully applied are self-renewing, but social outputs do not provide a direct economic return. Furthermore, many marginal business firms will be forced into liquidation if they incur significant social costs. Already many firms have been forced to terminate their activities because they cannot afford the investment

necessary to reduce their external pollution to meet governmental standards. The higher cost of doing business will also weaken international balance of payments, because it will increase the costs of exports making them less attractive to foreign buyers.

5. One potential danger of social responsibility is that it will make business even more powerful and tip the balance now existing among the many institutions forming our pluralistic society. If business became dominant in economic and social affairs, it could result in a concentration of power unequalled by other organizations. This would endanger our society as we know it, and introduce another form of the monolithic state.

DETERMINING THE EXTENT OF SOCIAL INVOLVEMENT

The major question relating to social responsibility is what extent of social involvement is appropriate? The current trend is for business to assume greater involvement and for society to expect more. The answer again is situational. There is no formula appropriate for all firms. Major corporations with greater social power have the capacity and obligation to be more involved than small firms. Firms engaged in operations with high external pollution costs also have a greater obligation to society to reduce these harmful effects. The major constraints tend to be economic. A firm cannot weaken its financial structure to the point where it endangers its basic ability to compete. However, experience would tell us that the adaptive firm responding to these new expectations is the same firm that will be adaptive and successful in the economic sector of society. Also, costs are not always the limiting factor in social involvement. Many social actions (such as improved social justice in dealing with employees) have few, if any, economic costs associated with them.

EVALUATING THE SOCIAL ROLE OF BUSINESS

Even though the role of business in society is changing, business is still predominantly an economic institution. Ethical behavior should be paramount in the actions of managers, but their responsibility for social goods is definitely secondary to that for economic ones. As the social role of business increases, the relationship between business and government is moving toward one of greater cooperation. In this regard the recommendations of the Committee for Economic Development, a group of two-hundred socially minded businessmen and some educators, is interesting. They believe that the goals of American society can be realized only through a massive, cooperative effort of government, industry, labor, and education. In this cooperative endeavor government should determine the nation's goals and priorities, and business—with its managerial talents and resources—should be involved in the execution of social programs. Business involvement should be attracted by the incentive for profit. The result they see is as follows:

> The converging of two trends—the business thrust into social fields, and government's increasing use of market incentives to induce even greater business involvement—is gradually bringing these two powerful institutions into a constructive partnership for accelerating social progress . . . Fundamentally, it offers a new means for developing the innate capabilities of a political democracy and a private-enterprise economy into a new politico-economic system capable of managing social and technological change in the interest of a better social order.[3]

IMPLICATIONS OF SOCIAL RESPONSIBILITY FOR MANAGING

How does the doctrine of social responsibility affect the way a manager manages? What implications does social responsibility have for the functions of planning, organizing, staffing, directing, and controlling? Some of the more obvious ones are:

- *Organizing* Responsibility needs to be established within the company for defining its social responsibilities.
- *Organizing* Consideration should be given to including members on the Board of Directors who represent the elements of society affected by the firm's social actions.
- *Organizing* Consideration should also be given to establishing independent watchdogs who review the social actions of the firm. They could provide a social service similar to the financial service of public accounting firms.
- *Planning* Basic goals should be established relating to the firm's social actions. The policies and plans of the firm should also be sufficiently comprehensive to cover the social area.
- *Planning* Product development should include a search for products that are profitable and at the same time advance social interests.
- *Controlling* Provision should be made for social accounting and for a social audit. Methods and standards are required to measure

progress in social affairs, just as they are in financial ones. Until the social contributions of a firm can be measured, the tendency is to pay lip service to such values.

- *Staffing* As part of the performance appraisal of managers, consideration should be given to social contributions. The reward system should also be structured to compensate individuals for their part in successfully achieving social as well as financial goals.
- *Staffing* The staffing policies of the company should include active recruitment of the disadvantaged, advancement opportunities for minorities, training programs for underskilled and underutilized individuals, a system of social justice, and a respect for human values.
- *Overall business operations* Resources should be prudently used in the long-term interests of society, and industrial processes should be selected that minimize pollution and industrial wastes.

THE MULTINATIONAL CORPORATION

One of the most important recent developments in the environment of business has been the rise of the multinational corporation. Multinational corporations have emerged as some of the world's most powerful institutions. The multinational corporation is of interest in management theory because it represents a maximization of the interplay of environmental factors. Situational differences between plants or affiliates become extreme when the corporation is forced to operate across cultures.

Multinational firms are incorporated in one country, but they directly invest in plants or businesses in other countries. Merely owning the securities of another firm in a foreign country does not make a corporation multinational. To be considered multinational, a firm must own and *operate* foreign enterprises. In the true multinational, of which there are very few, the plant location, management, ownership, and company policies are not concentrated or identified with the home country but are global in nature. There are some limitations to this, since there is no international body that issues corporate charters, forcing a corporation to have legal national ties.

Rise of the Multinational

Multinationals started in the United States around 1900, when certain firms established manufacturing outlets in England. The first multinationals of size marketed raw materials, such as oil in the Middle East and copper in Chile. Growth was relatively slow, with only $11.8 billion in American direct foreign investment by 1950. The real period of growth was in the 20 years that followed. Direct foreign investment increased by a factor of 6 during this period, reaching $71 billion in 1969. This investment is held by 4500 firms that in 1970 produced an annual output of $200 billion. This makes multinationals the third largest economy in the world, ranking behind only the United States and Russia. This $200 billion industry was five times larger than American exports in 1970. The economic power of the multinational is displayed by the ten largest in 1971. Each produced more than the individual gross-national product of 80 of the smaller countries in the world.

Reasons for Growth

Two factors contributed to the growth of U.S.-based multinationals during this period. These were the lower costs of producing in a foreign country—primarily due to cheap labor—and export barriers that often tacked on as much as thirty percent to the price of the item. (To escape this products were produced and sold in foreign countries.) Only ten percent of the output of foreign subsidiaries is returned to the United States for consumption. Theoretically the multinational takes advantage of world economic conditions by obtaining funds in the countries with the lowest interest rates, producing in countries with the cheapest production costs, and declaring profits in countries with the minimal tax structure. This is, of course, difficult to achieve in practice, but many multinationals through this strategy earn a higher return on their foreign investments.

Other factors also contributed to the spurt in growth. The relative international tranquillity since World War II and the establishment of the Common Market in Europe have been two important developments. The elimination of trade barriers inside Europe has made this a natural market for American firms, with the result that two-thirds of American direct investment is in this area. Another factor has been the existence of anti-trust laws in the United States. These have forced some of the corporate giants to look at foreign markets, because their dominance of national markets approached legal limits. There are also advantages of geographical diversification, and often the competition is not as keen as in the U.S.

Problems with Multinationals

Multinationals also have their problems. The foreign firm always faces the specter of political and economic nationalism. The individual will normally support his country before his employer, and charges of American imperialism makes foreigners wary of the American intruder. If foreign governments decide to nationalize industries through expropriation, major investments may be totally lost, such as Anaconda and Kennecott experienced with copper mines in Chile. In 1959–1960 in Cuba alone, expropriation absorbed over $1.5 billion of foreign investments. Other problems are also experienced. Support services from other firms are often inadequate, and low educational standards can result in a workforce with limited skills.

Recent developments have minimized some of the advantages of foreign subsidiaries. The rising costs in foreign countries and devaluation of the dollar have resulted in greater equalization of investment opportunities. Wage rates in the more advanced foreign countries are coming closer to the United States, and former cost advantages are disappearing. Foreign investment, once proceeding at a rate of ten percent increase per year, is expected to slow to five or seven percent.

The Influence of the Multinational on the Environment

The multinational corporation is called a cultural catalyst. As a business firm stretches across its national boundaries, it carries with it the technology, culture, managerial practices, and operating philosophies of its home country. By introducing industry to underdeveloped countries, it tends to raise the standard of living and open up opportunities for employment. This mixing of cultures and economies tends to have an equalizing influence and to reflect the deficiency of the current nation-state structure. Neil Jacoby states that, "The multinational corporation is, beyond doubt, the most powerful agency for economic unity that our century has produced."[4]

Undoubtedly the multinational corporation faces the extremes in situational analysis. Moving across a national boundary is more than moving across a geographical line. It is a step into what is frequently a vastly different social, political, economic, and technological environment. Cultural shock is often experienced by managers when they assume positions overseas. Techniques and practices they relied on in the United States are inappropriate in the new cultural setting.

The political world is ill-equipped to cope with the multinational corporation. International legal systems do not exist that control and regulate global business activities. Nations attempt to do this individually, but the foreign holdings are justifiably not controllable on this basis. In 1973 the United Nations completed the first of a series of reports and studies dealing with international control of multinationals. Ideally this could lead to an international political structure that will bring more unity to the political disparities and legal jungle that currently exist.

Implications Multinationals Have
for Management Practices

The unique nature of the multinational creates special problems for the manager, since it is a central system that finds its extremities functioning in distinctly different social and economic environments. Some implications this has for handling management functions are:

Planning The greater uncertainty of the international environment makes planning both more difficult and more essential. It places increased emphasis on flexibility, and it restricts the use of extensive detailed, central policies because of the need to adjust to local cultures. Broad strategy is developed at the corporate level, but operations planning is decentralized.

Controlling Few across-the-board control systems can be established. Those that do exist will be primarily in the financial area, where dollars serve as the common denominator to equate operations. The complexity of varying exchange rates, national tax structures, and growth of inflation makes financial considerations difficult. Most control systems are established locally to meet specific needs.

Organizing Organization structures should be flexible and adaptive to match the local cultures. This places an emphasis on decentralization and heterogeneity in organization types.

Directing. Management philosophy will differ by culture—as will the response of individuals to different leadership styles. Leadership styles should be consistent with cultural norms, placing emphasis on the staffing of management positions from the local populace.

Staffing The strong class structure in many countries makes selection of personnel a sensitive issue. In many countries there is a large surplus of unskilled employees, many highly trained top managers, and a shortage of qualified middle managers. The total personnel subsystem relating to hiring, wage and salary structures, retention of employees, and retirement programs is governed by the local culture. As an example, layoffs typically are a more sensitive issue in foreign countries than they are in the United States.

SUMMARY

The adaptation of the organization to external factors takes many forms. One of the traditional methods has been to establish internal units to deal with each of the publics or external groups constituting the organizational set of the firm. As the environment has tended to change more rapidly, it has forced organizations away from rigid, bureaucratic structures to more flexible ones. The specific methods the organization selects for directing its external operations are called its strategies. Such strategies take many forms, but they primarily involve a planned use of resources to acquire new markets or profit milestones.

One of the most significant changes in the environment of business has been the one in public attitudes relating to the role of business and the nature of the services it provides. Originally business was evaluated on the basis of its ability to provide economic goods and services, resulting in a higher standard of living. As the standard of living has risen, the public has become more concerned with social problems and has looked to business to contribute to an improved social environment. Thus firms are now more concerned with solving social problems and with their own basic social responsibilities. Business and public attitudes are in a state of change regarding these issues, so generally accepted guidelines are lacking.

A final major environmental development of recent origin is the rise of the multinational corporation. The multinational is forcing a world-wide integration of cultures, technologies, and managerial know-how. The multinational also represents a supraorganization that surpasses national boundaries and therefore exists in a political "no-man's land." Consideration is now being given to international approaches to dealing with this international phenomenon.

QUESTIONS FOR STUDY AND DISCUSSION

1. In the example of General Motors, what adaptations would you say automotive companies have made to environmental variables in the last thirty years?
2. What organizational units are established by a university to deal with outside organizations? What units are established by a retail department store?
3. What organizational strategies have universities used to deal with antagonistic external groups? What strategies do smaller construction firms use to compete with large firms on major jobs?
4. Define the term *strategy* and explain what is meant by competitive strategies.
5. Using the strategy methodology developed in the chapter, explain what strategies a firm might consider if it decided to compete in the market with IBM. How would the firm decide which strategies to select? Do the same for a standard-brand gasoline station competing with a cut-rate station.
6. Why are economic goods also called social goods?

7. What social responsibilities does an airline have? An electric power company? A tire manufacturer?
8. Why should a firm assume social responsibilities? What are the drawbacks to doing this?
9. What evidence is there that firms are doing more than paying lip service to social responsibilities?
10. What are the differences between the internal and external social responsibilities of the firm?
11. How can the firm decide the appropriate extent of its social involvement?
12. What is distinctive about the multinational corporation? Why has it grown? What special problems in adaptation are introduced by the multinational corporation?
13. Why is the multinational corporation said to be contributing to economic unity at the same time it is challenging current political systems?

Case Problem:
SPEEDMASTER BOAT COMPANY (PART I)

Speedmaster Boat Company is a partnership formed by three individuals. In 1961, they began producing boats for sale in the recreation market. They initially started with 14- and 16-foot outboards, but in 1965 they expanded their line to include inboards and cabin cruisers up to lengths of 26 feet. The firm is known for its quality custom work and had considered going into sailboats, but no action was ever taken on this decision. The company had been extremely successful—see next page for gross sales and profit after taxes for the years 1965 through 1975.

The recession of 1974–75 was felt more severely in recreation industries than in most of the economy. Especially hard hit were high-cost, durable-goods industries like boat manufacturers. The firm is extremely concerned about its future and is pondering what to do. There are a large number of competitors that manufacture and sell boats. In fact, Speedmaster is one of the smaller firms in the industry. Water sports has been one of the fastest-growing markets in the recreation field, but the owners are worried about the impact of higher gasoline prices and potential fuel shortages.

Year	Sales*	Profit (after taxes)*
1966	$1,765	$186
1967	1,922	212
1968	2,615	284
1969	2,595	265
1970	3,895	404
1971	4,628	252
1972	5,742	675
1973	7,187	724
1974	6,954	514
1975	4,214	57

*figures in thousands

What strategies should the owners develop for their business?
What alternatives should they consider?
Should they expand their line to sailboats?

Case Problem:
SPEEDMASTER BOAT COMPANY (PART II)

In the late 1960's, the owners felt that perhaps they were not doing their part to hire minorities and afford equal opportunity in their organization. Two of the three owners had graduated from eastern universities and were committed to seeing that their organization contributed to making the community a better place to live. The plant was located in a midwestern metropolitan city of over one million people. Minorities represented approximately one-third of the community, but several years ago the owners on checking found that only 18 percent of their employees were minorities, and there was only one in a supervisory position. They immediately undertook a program to bring minority employment up to at least the 33 percent represented in the community. Many thousands of dollars were spent recruiting and training minorities, so that by 1974, 35 percent of the workforce consisted of minorities, and 26 percent of the supervisors were nonwhite or female.

With the downturn in business experienced in 1974 and 1975, it was necessary to layoff 75 employees. The company was not unionized, and it had few formal personnel policies. In handling the layoffs, they decided to make them on a seniority basis by job classification, which meant that 85 percent of those laid off were minorities. Total unemployment in the community had risen to 11 percent in 1975 with unemployment among young blacks over 30 percent. Because of the slow recovery of the firm in 1976, it became apparent that some permanent terminations would have to be made. The owners were undecided as to how many should be terminated and whether the seniority policy should be adhered to.

Should the firm incur extra costs by keeping on more manpower than they require in order to protect the jobs of some of their employees? Should the seniority policy be adhered to in terminations?

Case Problem:
BROKEN OPTICS

Lanie Parker was employed in the shipping department of a large industrial firm. Lanie's job was to open and inspect the incoming items at the receiving warehouse to ensure the proper units had been received and were undamaged. One day while unpackaging some very expensive optical equipment, she dropped and cracked one of the optics. Her supervisor noticed what had happened, walked over to Lanie, and said, "Put it back in the package. We'll return it to the freight company and report that it was damaged during shipment. Their insurance will cover it."

What should Lanie do?

Footnotes

1. Milton Friedman, *Capitalism and Freedom* (Chicago: University of Chicago Press, 1962), p. 133.
2. Barry Richman, "New Paths to Corporate Social Responsibility," *California Management Review,* Spring 1973, p. 36.
3. *Social Responsibilities of Business Corporations* (New York: Committee for Economic Development, 1971), p. 59. A Statement by the Research and Policy Committee.
4. Neil Jacoby, *Corporate Power and Social Responsibility* (New York: Macmillan Publishing Co., Inc. 1973), p. 122.

Manager Profile

Liz Heusman
Director of Personnel, Garcia Lange Company
Broomfield, Colorado

Background and Experience

Liz took several courses at the University of Colorado and then went to work for the university as a supervisor in the Dean's office. Later she left the university to become a client-relations supervisor for a group of attorneys. Shortly thereafter, she interviewed with Lange and became their personnel assistant. Within three months, she became director of personnel.

Primary Responsibilities

1. The administering and processing of all merit increases and performance evaluations.
2. The implementation of fringe benefits, policies, procedures and communications.
3. All personnel selection and placement.
4. The implementation of labor-relation laws relating to the state of Colorado.
5. The handling of all personnel complaints and problems.
6. Management of all union issues and labor relations (presently the company is nonunion, but they have had several union campaigns.)

Insights

"Companies are anxious to have effective, productive personnel. There are plenty of reward and promotion opportunities for those who are willing to exert themselves.

"As personnel manager, it is critical to make the employees aware that management cares about them and their problems. They need to feel that their work is important, and that they are making a contribution.

"I really do enjoy being the personnel director. At first, it required a lot of extra time to understand and become good at the job."

Manager Profile

Richard H. Headlee, President
Alexander Hamilton Life Insurance Company of America
Farmington Hills, Michigan

Background and Experience

Shortly after completing a bachelor's degree in 1953, Dick joined Burroughs Corporation. He progressed from senior systems consultant to special account representative for data processing systems. In 1963 he was elected president of the U.S. Junior Chamber of Commerce and took a one-year leave of absence to serve in that post. From 1966 to 1968 he acted as an advisor to Governor George Romney and on the "Romney for President" committee. In 1968 he became president and director of Morbark Industries, Inc.; in 1970, president of Hamilton International Development Company. In 1972 he became president and chief executive officer of Hamilton International Corporation and its major subsidiary, Alexander Hamilton Life Insurance Company of America. Assets of the company are over $170 million.

Primary Responsibilities

1. Serves as president and chief executive officer of Hamilton International Corporation and Alexander Hamilton Life Insurance Company of America.
2. Under the Board of Directors, he is responsible for all long-range planning and strategic development of Hamilton International Corporation and its subsidiaries.

3. He is responsible for the operating affairs of the corporate office and the Alexander Hamilton Life Insurance Company.
4. Subject to the approval of the Board of Directors, Dick establishes all internal and external operating policies.

Insights

"I have great confidence that any goal or objective can be achieved—and full knowledge that nothing can be achieved alone. Confidence coupled with team building is the best way to develop any successful organization. You must instill in each person the feeling that he or she is important and competent, and create an environment that encourages and provides for the development of the total person.

"Authority and information must be shared freely in order to optimize each person's potential. Openness and candor are essential in order to eliminate paranoia and corporate politics, which are expensive drains on an effective organization. The members of a management team should be selected carefully to assure that their personal philosophies blend into an effective corporate leadership group. A technical giant is of no value if he sours the management mix. Look for well-balanced, unselfish leaders, who are not only technically competent but socially complete.

"The complete individual is one who is able to establish a balanced relationship between family, religious, professional, and personal goals. When people are encouraged and supported in the achievement of their personal objectives—as well as their professional goals—they have a much more aggressive attitude toward the success of the corporation (or team). In every individual, and correspondingly in most organizations, there is a vast untapped potential measuring as much as forty percent. Maximizing success is dependent upon energizing this great unused resource, and the key to doing so is the display of corporate interest in the individual's goals, hopes, and aspirations."

PART V

Human Input:
Motivating People to
Perform Organizational
Tasks

Understanding the Individual

What accounts for the differences in human behavior?

What factors influence the development of personality?

Why do people interpret the world differently?

What factors affect how individuals learn?

How do the expectations of others affect behavior?

How do our assumptions about people affect our behavior toward them?

How do situational factors influence how an individual behaves?

What implications for management does a knowledge of human behavior have?

One of the most reliable conclusions that can be made regarding people is that they display individual differences in their behavior. Just as no two sets of fingerprints are the same so no two people have the same interests, aptitudes, ambitions, or physical features. Workers do not produce the same, analysts do not think the same, and individuals do not react the same way to rewards and punishment. This presents one of the greatest challenges for the manager, because, by definition, in managing an organization he or she is managing people.

As a prerequisite to understanding almost any facet of managing in organizations, it is first necessary to comprehend the basic nature of human behavior. Developing a plan, organizing an activity, or leading a project cannot be successful unless the manager understands how people will respond to this direction. Just as a chemist must understand the basic elements of chemistry before he can mix his compounds, so the manager cannot make organizational decisions without understanding the basic element of the organization—the individual.

Even though understanding people is central to being an effective manager, this is no easy task, because scientific knowledge of human behavior is still extremely limited. Basic questions as to whether abilities and personality characteristics are inherited or developed through experience are still subject to speculation. The difficulty is the same as that with our knowledge of management: many forces shape human behavior, with the result that it is difficult to isolate specific factors and determine their precise influence. Accordingly, behavioral analysis must take into consideration a wide variety of interacting variables. In order to remain within the confines of this chapter and yet provide a reasonably balanced presentation, we will consider the following: the nature of behavior, personality development, perception, learning processes, attitude formation, human needs, and the influence of certain situational factors such as peers and organizational ties.

THE NATURE OF BEHAVIOR

It is a central thesis of the contingency approach to management that the management process and organizations are best comprehended through visualizing the constant interaction between an organization and the variables and conditions existing in its internal and external environment. Human behavior can best be understood on the same basis. To know the attributes of an individual is not to understand his behavior, since behavior is triggered, hence a response to forces and conditions existing in his environment. It is an important proposition of psychology and also of management that all behavior is caused. An individual may be extremely security conscious. However, the degree to which his immediate behavior is influenced by this tendency is a function of the degree to which the factors in the situation he is facing are perceived as being either threatening or nonthreatening.*

Two Types of Behavior

Behavior is classified into two types: overt (or outward) and covert (or inward). Overt behavior involves acting or performing in a particular way. Covert behavior is internal and involves such actions as thinking or listening. Literally, behavior is anything that an individual does. Psychologists have classically viewed behavior in terms of the stimulus-response model, $S \rightarrow R$. A stimulus (sensory input) such as a bright light will cause a response (behavioral output): usually the individual will squint. In simple physiological actions like this, individuals will respond in very much the same way. However, to a stimulus like a bell starting classes, students and teachers will respond or behave in different ways. Thus a more complex model, $S \rightarrow O \rightarrow R$, was developed to bring in the organism as an intervening variable between stimulus and response. Different individuals with different attitudes, values, and knowledge will obviously respond to the same stimuli in different ways.

This identifies one of the primary differences between man and other animals. An animal's response is based primarily on instinct or innate behavioral predispositions, whereas people's are learned. This ability to think and learn from experience makes their behavior more variable and less predictive. Instinct tends to be "wired in," whereas human response is modified by each individual's unique experiences, knowledge, and desires. Human behavior is also characterized by a greater facility to adapt because of superior intelligence.

A more thorough view of human behavior is presented in figure 10-1. Stimuli from the environment are received by the individual who, based on a particular personality, responds in a particular way. As a result of this response, a new set of conditions comes into existence. Thus if someone is joking with another employee and the supervisor enters the workplace, upon seeing the supervisor the individual (stimulus) responds (usually returns to his job) and a new set of conditions now exists. We shall see in chapter 11 how the individual is again stimulated, depending on whether this new condition is perceived as satisfactory or unsatisfactory.) Figure 10-1 indicates only one response, whereas behavior consists of a stream of responses.

---

*Note: Some or all of the following material may already be familiar to you from previous courses. If so, skip ahead to the section, "Needs and Motivation."

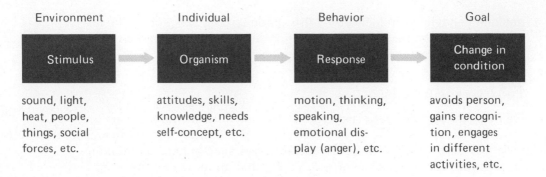

Fig. 10-1.   Stimulus and response behavior

Two Sets of Factors Influencing Behavior

Thus behavior is a function of two things: the nature of the individual and the social and physical context of the situation in which this behavior takes place. Individual behavior viewed as a reflection of stimulations received from the environment is schematically portrayed in figure 10-2. The individual represents a personality system that is an integrated combination of many factors, such as physical attributes, sensory capabilities, needs, interests, knowledge, values, feelings, and so on. His or her behavior results from the stimulus received from the environment, which consists of other individuals, groups, cultures, tasks, events, opportunities, reward systems, and a host of physical factors such as heat, light, sound, tools, equipment or what have you. Behavior is a composite of these two sets of factors. Common organizational problems like absenteeism, lateness, low morale, high turnover, and decreasing productivity require an understanding of the *total* situation—not just the person displaying this behavior.

PERSONALITY DEVELOPMENT

Personality represents the whole self. From a systems standpoint, it is the representation of the whole individual resulting from a composite of many factors like physical and mental ability, feelings, interests, attitudes, emotional makeup, etc. A simple definition of *personality* is to consider it the aggregate of all properties or qualities of an individual, both physical and psychological in nature. This definition is much broader than the popular one often accepted by most people, who normally relate it solely to the social skills of an individual. However, even this broader definition has some inadequacies, because personality is not just a composition of certain traits—it is how an individual perceives himself in terms of self-image, and also how others perceive and are influenced by him. Personality, as other human systems, represents a unique pattern of traits and conditions that are in constant interaction.

Physical attributes are included as a part of personality because they affect psychological traits. They also influence self-image and the impression one makes on others. The physical features of the attractive coed or the seven-foot basketball player certainly influence how they affect others and how they view themselves.

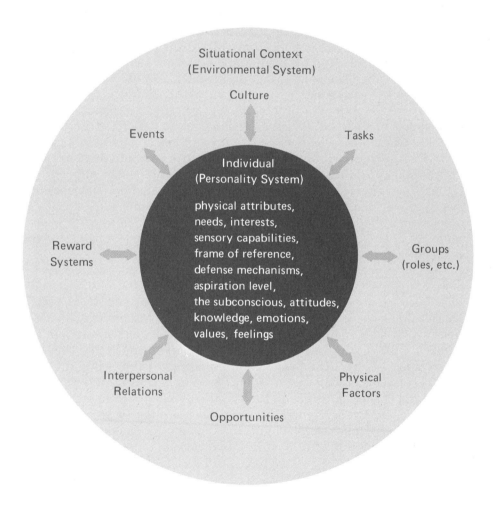

Fig. 10-2.   Two sets of factors affecting behavior

Determinants of Personality

The age-old argument of whether personality is inherited (called *constitutional factors*) or learned (*environmental factors*) has never been resolved. Personality traits are obviously a result of both factors, but the question is one of the relative importance of each. Physical traits are primarily inborn, but even if someone is naturally coordinated, practice can improve skill, as in swimming. Psychological traits are more controversial, as evidenced by the current debate over whether intelligence is basically a constitutional trait or environmentally developed.

Generally the trend has been to place greater importance on people being a product of their environment. There is no doubt that home life, educational institutions, peer groups, communities, and cultures tend to shape the evolving personality, especially during the early, formative years. Someone raised in the ghetto will obviously have different values and attitudes then someone raised on a rural farm; the perspective acquired through being a manual worker will also be at sharp contrast with that acquired in training to become a lawyer. The experiences one has throughout life will tend to develop confidence, emotional disturbances, a sense of acceptance or rejection, and hundreds of other feelings and behavioral patterns within individuals. Even if the inherited physical and mental capabilities of two individuals were identical, they would ultimately vary, because no two individuals come in contact with the same groups, face the same opportunities, adapt to the same forces, or otherwise have the same experiences. Inherited capabilities represent more the *potential* for development, and the environment serves as the regulator.

Personality development occurs in stages in a pattern somewhat parallel to physical development. An infant's behavior is obviously limited. Interests are shallow, perspective is short term, and awareness is restricted. As the personality is developed, behavior becomes varied, interests broaden, perspective becomes long range, and awareness expands to fuller horizons. Physical growth is rapid through maturity and then changes slowly. The personality also rapidly evolves and then experiences reduced modification as one becomes an adult. Attitudinal and behavioral changes are difficult to deliberately modify after adulthood—habits become strongly engrained, and people cling to life styles and beliefs. (This has many implications for attempts at behavioral modification by managers and will be covered later in more detail.)

Functions of Personality

Several behavioral phenomena are associated with the concept of personality. The first is what was previously referred to as adaptation. An individual's particular approach in adapting to the environment is a result of personality. In fact, some psychologists define personality in terms of the adjustment of the individual to his environment.[1] This process is again two-way. Adaptation is a reflection of the personality of the individual, but also one's personality evolves as a result of this adaptation.

The human personality is in a constant state of evolution, while at the same time the individual is seeking a steady state in terms of balance with his environment. This is called *dynamic equilibrium*. Erratic behavior does not typify the normal individual and tension reduction is the object of this behavior. However, the personality is constantly in a process of "becoming." Human behavior is typified by a striving for growth, improvement, and maturity. The human being's capacity to learn—and desire to learn—are unique characteristics.

PERCEPTION

Perception is the process through which individuals come to know the world around them. It is the exclusive means that an individual has of getting information from the environment. One must see, hear, taste, smell, or feel something to know of its existence. However, perception consists of more than just this input. Two aspects are involved: the first is the picking up of stimuli by the sense organs, and the second is an interpretation and organization of the raw sensory data by the mind. Both phases are subject to individual variation. However, the capability of people in terms of their ability to see, hear, taste, smell, and feel is relatively similar, while the interpretation of the sensations received through the sense organs often dramatically differs.

The image of the world that one develops is subject to many factors that create distortion or otherwise prevent one from knowing reality. The senses are bombarded with stimuli, far more than the perceptual processes of man are able to accommodate. Also, people are never aware of many stimuli because the energy levels are below the absolute thresholds of the sense organs. Thus a person is not able to perceive colors in dim light, hear extremely low- or high-pitched sounds, and still photographs become moving pictures when a 16 mm projector shows the frames in rapid succession.

Frame of Reference

The interpretation of raw sensory data takes place in terms of one's *frame of reference*. A child with no previous experience (knowledge) of a hot plate will see no reason not to place his hand on it, until touch sensations cause him to jerk his hand away. However, once the child gains the knowledge that a red-hot plate will burn, the sight of the red plate has meaning and he probably will never touch it again. An individual's interpretation of the world is based on prior experiences, because this is the only way raw sensory input becomes meaningful. Frame of reference is the experience repertory of the individual. Since this repertory obviously differs with individuals, they will perceive the world differently.

This also determines the meaningfulness of different sensory input to people. An American looking at a Japanese newspaper will see and perceive only unfamiliar characters. To someone who reads Japanese, these same characters will represent words and convey meaning. If two individuals attend a hockey game and one has been many times but the other is going for the first time, they will both have essentially the same sensory input. However, to one this input will have meaning and to the other it will represent little more than fascinating action. It is only natural that when a general manager presents a problem to his executive staff, the controller will see it as a cost problem, the head of manufacturing as a production problem, and the sales manager will see it in marketing terms. The uniqueness of the individual is created to a considerable extent by the fact that we interpret everything on the basis of our own experiences and background. We tenaciously hold on to this frame of reference because it is our interpretation of reality, and it provides the logic we use to justify our behavior.

PERCEPTION OF BUSINESS FUNCTIONS

One of the early well-known studies in selective perception by business executives was conducted by Dewitt C. Dearborn and Herbert A. Simon. In the study, twenty-three executives of a manufacturing firm were engaged in an executive training program. One of the exercises during the program was to analyze a complex case involving a steel company and then write a brief statement regarding the most important problem facing the company. The researchers then tested whether the most important problem in the case as identified by the manager corresponded with the departmental affiliation of the individual.

All of the twenty-three executives were middle managers. Six represented sales, five production, four accounting, and eight were classified as miscellaneous. Two of the latter were in the legal department, two in research, and one each from public relations, industrial relations, health services, and purchasing.

Five of the six sales executives identified sales as the most important problem. Of the remaining seventeen participants, only five others selected sales as the central issue and three of these were accountants who had close contact with product managers. Of the five product managers, four indicated that organizational problems were the primary issue and one specified a sales problem. In the miscellaneous category, three said the most significant problem was human relations, which would correspond to the public relations and industrial relations affiliations represented in that group.

Reprinted from Dewitt C. Dearborn and Herbert A. Simon, "Selective Perception," *Sociometry*, Vol. 21, 1958, pp. 140–143.

Selective Perception

The world, or reality, is formed of millions of information bits of which man's perceptual apparatus can pick up only a minute fraction. He therefore makes assumptions about reality when he has only a small sample of the information necessary to comprehend it. Unfortunately, there is no fixed correlation between data in the environment and data perceived, and since each individual will have different sensory input from which conclusions about reality are made, obviously people will interpret it in different ways. In actuality, we perceive the world not as it is, but in the image we have partially created.

An individual selects certain stimuli based on two different sets of factors. These are known as *stimulus selectivity* and *personal selectivity*. Stimulus selectivity involves that based on the external factors that are beyond our control and intrude in our perception. High-intensity sensations will crowd out low ones. (We all hear the sonic boom but perhaps ignore the whine of a high-flying jet. Bright lights, a sharp pain, and a strong odor will all catch our attention.) In addition to intensity, other factors such as size, contrast, repetition, and motion will capture our perceptual focus. Television advertisers capitalize on this knowledge by providing lively, colorful, repetitious advertisements.

Personal selectivity results from the frame of reference, motives, expectations, and needs of the individual. As stated, an individual perceives only a small portion of the bits of information that make up reality but makes organized wholes out of the scattered input received. Many perceptual visual tests are used to show our tendency for *closure*: finishing or completing diagrams or figures that are incomplete (drawing in the third side of a triangle or finishing a partially drawn circle).

The individual molds his collective experiences and knowledge into norms, attitudes, and values. We tend to distort data to fit our organized wholes, and we ignore data that conflicts with them. A primary principle of perception is that order is not in the physical stimulus but in the observer. The sensory input man receives is not complete and since the human mind is uncomfortable with this ambiguity—because it is contrary to the perceived world—the individual organizes the information to fit the world as he or she sees it.

Needs are also powerful factors in selective perception. The hungry individual walking through a supermarket will notice the food items and not the paper products. Those who have a desire for power will see opportunities for power that others will ignore. A man and a woman will perceive the attractive coed in different ways. A window display of fall fashions will catch the attention of some; others will quickly pass by it.

Perceptual Distortion

Certain sensory inputs are interpreted by the central nervous system with little distortion; other inputs become grossly distorted or even blocked in the process of interpretation. This is often referred to as the filtering process of the mind. If ten people are asked to write a paragraph describing a yellow pencil, all of the paragraphs will be approximately the same. However, if these same ten individuals are asked to describe a politician, a student activist, or a religious group, the descriptions will vary along a continuum ranging from highly favorable to highly unfavorable.

The causes of perceptual distortion become clearer by examining the differences between these two situations. In the first instance the object (pencil) has little social value, and people do not ordinarily have attitudes or values that either agree or conflict with the existence of it—no one becomes emotional or finds his self-interest threatened by a pencil. However, usually the opposite is true with objects related to political, social, or religious philosophy. To the degree that we select sensory input, we seek out those bits of information that substantiate or are consistent with our attitudes and personal interests; we cut out those that conflict. If the Republican hears a speech by the opposition, he listens for those things that confirm the Democrat is wrong, since that conclusion was reached before the speech began.

Many interesting experiments have been conducted to demonstrate perceptual distortion. In race relations, filmstrips are shown where parts of the film are projected at just below the threshold sensory level, so that one must "read in" what happened. In this test ninety percent of the individuals will reach conclusions consistent with their racial prejudices. One of the best experiments is for a college student when listening to a ball game, to switch back and forth between the broadcast stations representing the localities of the two teams. One wonders whether the two broadcasters are watching the same game!

The more anxiety an individual experiences, the less objective and rational he will be in his perceptual and thought processes. We tend to ignore data or input that conflicts with our attitudes or self-image, until this input represents danger; then we become emotional and defensive. Human beings tend to be extremely ego defending. This makes it difficult to be objective in relation to any events or sets of circumstances when the welfare of the self is at stake. We are inclined to protect, maintain, and enhance our well-being, and anything perceived as a threat will often bring on substitute perceptions and perhaps bizarre behavior.

Stereotyping

One of the common errors in perception is inaccurate *stereotyping*, the assumption that an individual has the same traits and attributes characteristic of a group or common classification to which he belongs. If we are informed that someone belongs to a certain social group, church, race, country, or sect, we assume that he has the characteristics we associate with that particular group. This error is common when it relates to different positions or roles in an organization. If we are told that someone is a worker, a foreman, or an engineer we immediately make certain conclusions about that person based on how we judge that particular category of people. Of course, all individuals have certain attributes different from their particular group identification, so all stereotyping is at least partially misleading. (However, it is a convenient shortcut that can be informative and useful.)

The Nature of Perception

The limits of man's perceptual apparatus result in the formation of bias and illusions. There are essentially no such things as *facts* in personal behavior—only filtered sensory perceptions. Attitudes, emotions, self-interest, and group identifications all rob us of our objectivity. We comprehend all things in terms of our own experiences and our rearranged recall of previous events. If we see the world in a distorted fashion, it is our experiences and our images that provide this distortion. Each person lives in a world of his or her own making, and it is only when one appreciates the elusive, emotional, frequently distorted nature of human perception that we fully appreciate individual differences and have a tolerance for the conflicting opinions and behavior of others.

THE LEARNING PROCESS

Learning is closely associated with concepts relating to perception and behavior. It is difficult to understand behavior without understanding learning, because it is through learning that behavioral change takes place. This knowledge is vital to the manager, since learning is essential in increasing productivity by using the potential of the organization's most costly resource: personnel.

To the psychologist, learning is more than knowledge or skill acquired by instruction or study. Learning is defined as *a relatively permanent change in behavior that results from practice or experience.* Unless a change in behavior is experienced, learning has not occurred. This change must be relatively permanent, since fatigue, growth, or sleep are not considered learning. The stimulus-response concept of behavior is fundamental to learning. A stimulus causes a response in the individual which, when tied to the person's thought processes, can result in relatively permanent behavioral change. Basically this is the process of adaptation. If a man is attracted by a certain girl and he responds by asking her for a date, if she continually refuses he changes his behavior by seeking out another female companion. A halfback soon learns that he makes more ground by following his blockers than by running away from them. Over a period of time the worker learns what behavior must be engaged in to please the boss. In all of these instances an individual learns by experience and adapts to environmental conditions. If conditions change (the girl accepts rather than refuses, the halfback is switched to end, or a new boss replaces the old one), different behavior is now required to achieve the individual's goals.

The Law of Effect

In general terms, a person will continue to respond to a stimulus in a certain way if he accepts the results of the response as rewarding. In the examples in the above paragraph, as soon as the results of behavior are not rewarding behavior will change. This tendency to repeat rewarded behavior or favorable experiences and avoid unrewarded ones is known as the *law of effect,* as designated by Edward Thorndike in the early 1900's. It is also known as *reinforcement* and is the most important concept developed to date to explain, predict, and control human behavior. If an individual's behavior is not rewarding, why should he repeat it? There is obviously little reason. However, the counterpoint is also significant. If someone wants to encourage certain behavior in someone else, this can best be done through rewarding the desired behavior when it occurs. This has many implications for the manager as the dispenser of many rewards in organizations (pay raises, promotions, job assignments, praise, assignment of equipment, and so on). It is therefore an important means the manager has to encourage people to contribute to the goals of the organization.

There are two aspects to the law of effect. The first is positive reinforcement or the rewarding of desired behavior, and the second is negative reinforcement or the removal of awards or punishment for behavior that is not desired.[2] Even though both are effective in changing behavior, they can have profoundly different implications. The individual's reaction to positive reinforcement is fairly obvious, because the inclination is to repeat that behavior which is rewarding. However, reaction to negative reinforcement can take several forms and is more complex.

The objective of negative reinforcement may be to stop current behavior (coming to work late), but it may also involve selection of an entirely new behavioral pattern, such as changing from an uncommitted to a committed student. People respond to punishment in many different ways. Often they are inclined to repeat only the externally desired behavior while the individual administering the punishment is present. Or they may be alienated, resulting in a desire to "get even" with the source of the punishment. Reaction to punishment is often defensive and emotional, which makes behavior more irrational and nonpredictive. Also, positive reinforcement tends to develop a favorable relationship between the individual and the source of the rewards (company, supervisor, etc.); negative reinforcement usually damages these relationships.

Other Learning Concepts

Learning encompasses too many concepts to be covered in detail for our purposes. However, a few additional concepts are especially significant to the manager. Feedback is a primary principle of learning. Individuals require a knowledge of results so they can be aware of their progress and modify their behavior if they are not satisfied with the outcomes. If they are accomplishing their goals, this is an important *intrinsic reinforcer* (self-satisfaction). It should also result in *extrinsic reinforcement* (praise, advancement, etc.). Such feedback is most effective if it is immediate.

Participation is also an important ingredient of learning. Operating a new piece of machinery is more effective than listening to someone explain the operation of it. Also, learning goals should be realistic and within the expectations of the individual. And if they involve new, challenging assignments, they will also generally be more stimulating.

A final concept in learning is that of *repetition*. An individual typically has to repeat an action up to five times before it becomes a relatively permanent part of his frame of reference. Learning occurs rapidly at first and then slackens as the activity is repeated. For instance the *learning curve* concept as it relates to assembly work shows that learning will be rapid during the first few times a motor is put together by a worker, but after he has assembled 500 motors, the time required to assemble another one will decrease only slightly, because he has learned all of the fundamentals in doing this work. (Mathematical approaches have been developed to predict this decrease in assembly time for cost-estimation purposes.)

ATTITUDE FORMATION

Some of the strongest determinants of behavior are personal attitudes. An *attitude* is an individual's feelings, thoughts, or predispositions to act toward an object or an element of the environment in a certain way. Attitudes are predispositions, because they are determined by activities, thoughts, and experiences that are antecedent to the present behavior. Since an attitude represents a readiness to respond, it becomes extremely important as a predictor of behavior. One of the primary values resulting from managers being aware of the attitudes of others is that this information is useful in predicting personal reactions to policies, decisions, or other such administrative actions.

Attitudes represent behavioral tendencies and are more emotionally charged than beliefs or opinions. An individual may have a *belief* that more women will enter the work force in the future, but an *attitude* is represented by the man who opposes women moving out of the home and into the workplace. Employee attitudes toward the company, its policies, reward systems, working conditions, fellow employees, supervision, assigned tasks, and other such variables are important factors in behavior and productivity. Furthermore, they are notoriously resistant to change. Attitudes tend to be enduring systems, because they are usually developed over long periods of time and have become a part of the personality of the individual. Some attitudes are relatively superficial, but most are locked into value systems and other components of personality so that altering them cannot be effected without altering personality. Basic attitudes relating to religious, social, political, and economic philosophy tend to be of that nature, as well as those closely related to the self-interest of the individual.

Attitudes serve an important function to the individual, because they provide the consistency and stability that the human personality requires. Furthermore, they have been reinforced by years of association with family, peers, and reference groups. Remolding these attitudes normally can come only through the same process where the norms of society, reference groups, or one's immediate associates also change. The simple guideline is obvious that attitudes based on limited experiences, peripheral interests, few group contacts, and superficial needs are subject to change. However, if they are based on a long history of experience, are given strong support by reference groups and individuals for whom an individual has high regard, and are consistent with personal needs, change becomes unlikely, or at least is a gradual, uncertain process.

NEEDS AND MOTIVATION

No discussion of human behavior is complete without introducing the basic concept of the needs and wants that motivate people. All behavior is motivated. People have reasons for doing what they do, and they have goals that are the object of their behavior. A *need* represents an internal state of an individual where deficiency exists, so he is energized and activated to reduce the tension associated with the need deprivation. Drive within individuals is set up to alleviate these needs. If an internal state like hunger exists, it results in the drive to initiate behavior to satisfy this need. Managers are inclined to consider behavior too exclusively in terms of the logical thought or cognitive processes rather than acknowledging behavior as a response to satisfying internal motives represented by needs. Quite literally, however, unless someone has the ability or power to satisfy someone else's needs, they cannot modify that person's behavior.

The needs of an individual are many. The physiological needs of food, clothing, and shelter are obvious. However, in recent years it has been recognized that psychological needs such as those relating to the desire for respect, acceptance by others, and a feeling of competence are powerful motivators that have been too long ignored by managers. An individual's commitment to an organization is a function of the degree to which the organization satisfies these needs. If an individual finds little reward (need satisfaction) in his association with the organization, he will have little commitment and likely not be positively motivated to perform assigned tasks. This has implications that thread their way through essentially all actions undertaken by a manager.

AFFECTING BEHAVIOR SITUATIONAL FACTORS

As indicated, human behavior is basically responsive behavior as individuals react to stimuli from the environment. Understanding perception, learning, attitude formation, and needs explains much of the inner self, but what takes place externally is equally important. A student's behavior in church on Sunday morning is different from what it is in class on Monday morning or at fraternity meeting Monday night. A boy will behave differently with a group of boys than with a group of girls. A worker will behave differently with his peers than he will when the supervisor is present or when the general manager happens to be in the work place. In each instance the personality of the individual is the same, but his behavior is different as he reacts to these different social conditions.

Two of the most powerful external factors are group identifications and the roles that an individual maintains in society. When an individual is a member of a group, other members have certain expectations of how the individual should behave, based on the norms of the organization. Roles in organizations primarily reflect the expectations of others regarding how someone should behave because of the position he holds. Social pressures for conformity represent powerful forces that few individuals are willing to ignore.

An individual's behavior can be seen as a reaction to many other environmental factors. One company experienced a fifty per cent weekly turnover of new forklift operators because they were required to work in cold-storage areas (a physical factor). Another individual's change in personality became evident when he started wearing side burns and long hair (a cultural factor); another demonstrated frustration in his behavior because the government placed a freeze on hiring and promotions as a result of defense cutbacks (a political and organizational factor); a student decided to drop a class because of what he perceives to be a personality conflict with the professor (a problem in interpersonal relations). Situational factors dominate the behavior of individuals just as they do organizations.

MATCHING PERSONALITY TO CONTINGENCY CONSIDERATIONS

Evidence is developing that for an effective organization there should be a match between the personality of its members and the internal and external environment. Jay W. Lorsch and John J. Morse conducted a study of ten organizational units in five different plants. One pair of units was selected from each, representing a low-performance and high-performance group. The conclusions of their study are as follows:

"The major question which this study sought to answer is whether a fit among the internal environment, the external environment, and the predisposition of members is related to effective unit performance, as well as to rewards for individual members in terms of their feelings of competence. When the total pattern of these data is viewed as a whole . . . the answer to this question clearly is in the affirmative.

"In the effective units within the two external environments studied, members experienced a strong sense of competence from very different kinds of work activities which, in turn, were supported by dissimilar kinds of internal environments. Likewise, the individuals working within the two external environments preferred different kinds of activities because of differences in their personal dispositions. When these three sets of variables—*the external environment, the internal environment, and members' personality dimensions*—were congruent with each other, units in both kinds of external environment were successful, and individuals were rewarded by stronger feelings of competence.

"On the other hand, in the less effective units within both external environments, members did not feel such a strong sense of competence. In their personality tendencies, however, they were quite similar to their counterparts in the successful sites within the same external environment. Even though a match existed between members' personalities and the external environment in all of the low performers, the important point is that the internal environments of the less effective units suited neither the requirements of the external environment nor members' dispositions. This incongruence in both kinds of external environment was associated with less successful unit operations and less reward for individuals from a sense of competence. All these data underscore that effective unit performance and members' individual feelings of competence are found only when a three-way match among member characteristics, the unit's internal environment, and its external environment is also present."

Quoted from Jay W. Lorsch and John J. Morse, *Organizations and Their Members: A Contingency Approach* (New York: Harper & Row Publishers, Inc., 1974), pp. 111–113.

McGREGOR'S THEORY X AND THEORY Y

No managerial discussion of basic human relations is complete without an analysis of the most well-known theory relating to managerial assumptions about human behavior in the work situation. This theory was developed by the late Douglas McGregor, a renowned psychologist, and is summarized in his classic on the subject, *The Human Side of Enterprise*. McGregor introduced his theory by stating, "Behind every managerial decision or action are assumptions about human nature and human behavior."[3] In other words, our attitudes toward others and the basic assumptions we make about the competence and desires of others affect how we behave toward them. People communicate and act differently toward children than they do toward adults because of assumptions made about the competency and ability of each group.

McGregor felt that the same type of assumptions affect the behavior of managers in their interactions with employees. Managers treat "poor" workers differently than they do "good" ones. In a broader framework he referred to the traditional view of man as constituting Theory X and the evolving modern theory of man as Theory Y. (He used these terms because he felt they were devoid of value connotations.) Theory X contained three postulates as follows:

1. The average human being has an inherent dislike of work and will avoid it if he can.
2. Because of this characteristic of dislike of work, most people must be coerced, controlled, directed, or threatened with punishment to get them to put forth adequate effort toward the achievement of organizational objectives.
3. The average human being prefers to be directed, wishes to avoid responsibility, has relatively little ambition, and wants security above all.

McGregor stated that Theory X was the dominant belief in a wide sector of American industry at the time the book was written in 1960. However, he felt this was based on outdated assumptions about people, and he proposed in its place Theory Y:

1. The expenditure of physical and mental effort in work is as natural as play or rest.
2. External control and the threat of punishment are not the only means of bringing about effort toward organizational objectives. Man will exercise self-direction and self-control in the service of objectives to which he is committed.
3. Commitment to objectives is a function of the rewards associated with their achievement. The most significant of such rewards; for example, the satisfaction of ego and self-actualization needs, can be direct products of effort directed toward organizational objectives.
4. Under proper conditions the average human being learns not only to accept but to seek responsibility. Avoidance of responsibility,

lack of ambition, and emphasis on security are generally consequences of experience, not inherent human characteristics.
5. The capacity to exercise a relatively high degree of imagination,
   ingenuity, and creativity in the solution of organizational problems
   is widely, not narrowly, distributed in the population.
6. Under the conditions of modern industrial life, the intellectual po-
   tentialities of the average human being are only partially used.

McGregor's theories contain many of the points that have been emphasized in this and earlier chapters: theories X and Y are based on attitudes that people hold, and attitudes are learned, not an inherent part of
man; some people avoid work and others like it, but again these are characteristics that are learned and not innate; needs are the source of motivation, and needs such as status and a feeling of competence are some of
the strongest determinants of behavior; behavior must be reinforced by
desirable rewards if it is to be maintained; the potentiality of individuals
is only partially used in organizations because job design and reward
structures are inadequate for higher levels of motivation. (Theory Y has
extremely important implications for managing that will be explored in
future chapters as we deal with topics such as motivation, organization
structure, and leadership styles.)

SOME PRELIMINARY CONCLUSIONS
REGARDING HUMAN BEHAVIOR

Human behavior within the social setting of the organization (chapter 16)
needs to be considered before comprehensive conclusions can be reached
regarding the implications human nature has for how a manager should
direct people. However, a few conclusions become evident at this time:

- In human behavior we tend to have overly simplified notions of
  causation. A human being's behavior represents a complex interplay
  between the individual and the environment.

- The factors that control the development of the human personality
  result in the formation of people who perceive the world differently,
  and who have attitudes, values, and habits that are at variance and
  often in conflict with others.

- We tend to be overly optimistic about the rationality of people—
  behavior is frequently dictated by predispositions or emotion, especially on major issues, and reason is of limited value in resolving
  attitudinal or emotional problems.

- Management methods should be directed at need satisfaction and reinforcing desired behavior to capitalize on developing human potential in the organization.
- Attitudes and behavior patterns become deeply engrained over time, and changing those that have become an integral part of the personality system is difficult and normally beyond the ability of the manager. (We can rarely change people to fit our desired patterns.)
- The expectations of others, especially those held in high regard or those with power, strongly influence the behavior of an individual.
- To understand others we should attempt to understand their background, how they see themselves, what needs they are currently trying to satisfy through their behavior, and the external factors that are significant in their environment (empathy).
- Generally we have a difficult time understanding others because we are too inclined to assume they have the same values, attitudes, and motives that we have. Also, we are inclined to believe that our logic is supreme.
- People's self-interest leads them to believe that their own spheres of action are more important than they really are, especially as these spheres relate to the total context of an organization.

SUMMARY

A knowledge of the individual has implications for essentially all managerial actions. However, understanding the individual is very difficult because human behavior is a composite of factors internal to the individual, but it is also influenced and sometimes dominated by external or environmental factors.

Behavior is a response to stimuli received from the environment. The nature of the response is determined by the personality of the organism. Personality represents the whole individual and encompasses physical as well as mental attributes. Personality is a function of inherited (constitutional) factors and learned (environmental) factors. At least in terms of attitudes and mental outlook, environmental factors are considered to be dominant.

Perception is the process through which an individual comes to know the world around him. Information about the world is processed through our sensory organs of sight, sound, taste, smell, and touch. The mind processes only a small part of the information that constitutes reality. Perception is also selective because previous experience, attitudes, and values influence the bits of information one selects, and they also distort the raw data received through the sensory system.

An attitude represents a predisposition to act toward an element of the environment in a predisposed way. Attitudes are slow to form and are also slow to change. The motivation of an individual is represented by a response to needs. Physical and psychological needs are some of the strongest determinants of behavior.

McGregor's Theory X and Theory Y represent important assumptions about the nature of people in the work situation. Theory Y provides many of the concepts underlying modern theories of management.

QUESTIONS FOR STUDY AND DISCUSSION

1. What personality differences would you expect to find among a foreign student from India, a retired military officer, and a 19-year-old woman from Chicago, all of whom are studying business administration at the same college?
2. How does a knowledge of human behavior affect how you organize a group, establish a plan, or supervise a project?
3. Using the stimulus-response model, explain the most likely behavior in response to the following events:
    A. Being informed that a close friend is being divorced
    B. Being told by a professor that you were receiving a C rather than the B you anticipated in a course
    C. Being informed that you were passed over for promotion
4. Define personality and explain how an individual's personality is formed.
5. What prevents everyone from perceiving things the same way? What factors limit and distort perception?
6. When a husband and wife walk through a department store, why will they notice different things? Why is it difficult to recall the color of paint, the pictures, or other features of buildings we are familiar with (churches, student center, dormitory, lobbies, etc.)?
7. What does it mean to be defensive? Give two examples of defensive behavior.
8. If you are introduced to someone who is a member of an organization that you belong to, what assumptions do you make about this person? What is this perceptual short cut called?
9. "In a very real sense we are the things we observe." "We see only what we are." Explain what these statements mean.
10. Why does negative reinforcement introduce more uncertainty than positive reinforcement?
11. Define *learning* and explain the law of effect.
12. Distinguish between an attitude and a belief. Why are attitudes difficult to change?

13. In terms of needs, explain why individuals respond to the expectations of others.

14. Why does McGregor reject Theory X? What do needs have to do with Theory Y? What determines whether an individual will accept responsibility?

15. How is it possible to manage a group of people when each individual in the group displays different tendencies?

Case Problem:
THE ASSEMBLY LINE

Many magazine articles have been written concerning the boredom of the assembly line. Several of the articles concentrated on issues involved in the strike at General Motors' Vega plant in Lordstown, Ohio. One article focused on the different views of Tom Orlosky (age 58 and a steelworker) and his son, Reese, who is 31 and employed in a truck-assembly division as a buffer and sealer. Tom, who is an inactive member of the steelworkers' union, cannot understand why the union Reese belongs to wants only a 40-hour week and no overtime. He shows his disdain for younger workers by comments like: "These kids who come up today want to sit on their fantails eight hours a day. They think the plant owes them a living. When I was young, you put in a day's work—no questions about it."

Reese is not so quick to concur with his father's nostalgia of the good old days. He dislikes working on the assembly line. He objects to the regimentation associated with assembly work and is actively engaged in union activities. He once held a teaching position (he studied part time for eleven years to get a degree in psychology) but later went back to assembly work because he could make $4.78 per hour, which was considerably more than his teaching job.

In 1972, Tom, who had been employed with his company for twenty-five years, operated a computer-programmed machine in a steel company on the night shift. His reasons for choosing to work on the night shift are that: "There's not as many of the higher brass around then. We have a "gentlemen's agreement" about the amount of work to be done, do it, and then read a book the rest of the night."

Regarding the labor problems in Reese's plant, Tom states that it results from "your younger generation of workers who just don't feel like working. Gee, I wish I had 24 minutes off twice a day!"

Why do you think Reese and his father have such different perceptions of the younger generation?

What does their different involvement in union activities indicate?

From an understanding of human behavior, how can it be explained that Reese gave up his teaching position?

On what basis can Tom justify his decision to work on the night shift and then criticize the younger generation for being lazy?

What can be done to make Reese and his father better understand the other's point of view?

What do values have to do with perceptions?

Case Problem:
THE RELUCTANT WORKER

The following comments were made by a supervisor as he discussed with his manager the problems he was having with one of his employees:

"John is a funny guy. I just can't figure him out. Of the eight draftsmen that I have, he is the slowest and does the sloppiest job. He has been working for us for three years and every year on his performance rating I note that he is functioning far beneath the level of the other draftsmen. Besides, at least every two or three months I bring him into my office and try to show him how his work is not satisfactory. I review his work very carefully and show him what is wrong, but he doesn't seem to listen to logic. I don't really know what to do other than reason with him. Each time I talk to him he doesn't say much. He just states that he will try to do better and sometimes acts a little irritated, but I'll be darned if it results in any improvement that I can notice."

Does John *want* to fail in his work?

What are some possible reasons why his work does not improve?

How can the supervisor be assured that he is perceiving the situation properly?

What suggestions would you give the supervisor for improving John's performance?

Footnotes

1. Gordon Allport's classic definition of personality is "dynamic organization within the individual of those psychophysical systems that determine his unique adjustments to his environment." Gordon W. Allport, *Personality* (New York: Henry Holt and Company, Inc., 1937), p. 48.

2. Some writers distinguish between negative reinforcement and punishment. Negative reinforcement involves doing something to avoid or diminish something undesirable (work harder to avoid complaints from a nagging boss). Punishment is when action is taken to decrease certain behavior. However, in our abbreviated discussion no distinction will be made between the two terms.

3. Douglas McGregor, *The Human Side of Enterprise* (New York: McGraw-Hill Book Company, 1960), p. 33.

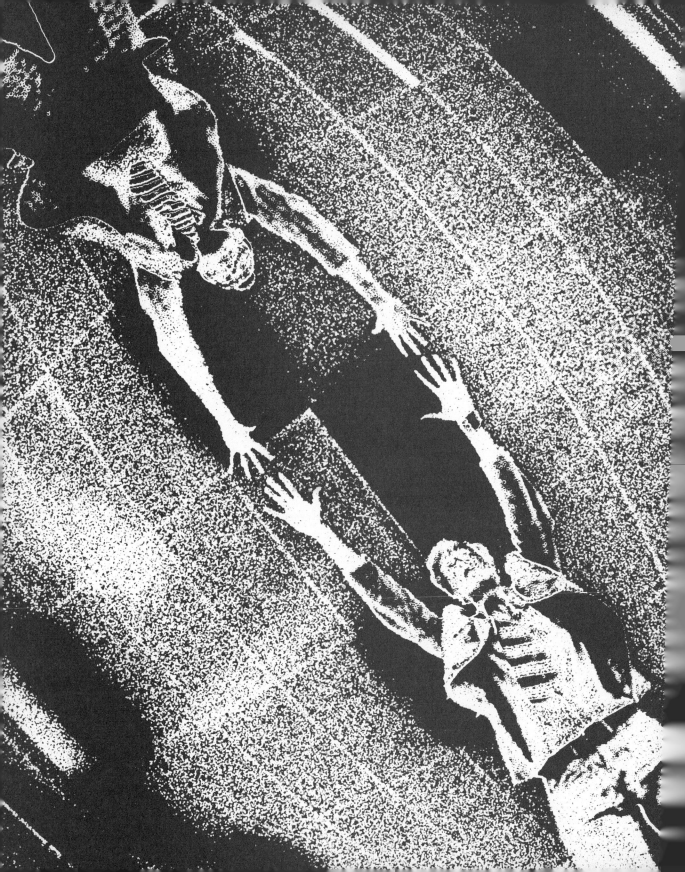

Motivation in the Work Situation

What accounts for the differences in the enthusiasm of individuals?

Is motivation learned?

What specific needs or motives direct behavior?

How do environmental variables affect motivation?

How significant is money as a motivator?

How do the expectations of individuals affect their motivation?

What can a manager do to influence the motivation of his work group?

Sam Garrett, director of sales for a medical supply company, had just completed the semiannual performance appraisals of his salesmen and was discussing the evaluations with a representative from the personnel department. "You know," he said, "I just don't understand the difference between people. Look at the ratings on Jack Lower and Hal Newsom. Both of these men have been with us for about a year. Jack has increased sales in his district by thirty-five percent. He's out hustling all of the time. He even asked me to increase the size of his district so he could have more customers. Only the other day he came in with a new sales approach that really seems to have promise. Then you've got Hal, who is almost the opposite. Sales have declined in his district, and some customers report he has not called on them for the past six months. He seems to have just as much ability as Jack, but even though I've spent a lot of time in his district to give him some help, I just can't seem to get him moving. How do you explain the differences between these guys?"

MOTIVATION

The answer to Sam's question is, of course, not simple. Human behavior represents a system of complex relationships. The aspect of personality that is associated with enthusiasm in carrying out different activities is called *motivation*. It is essential to recognize that all behavior is motivated. People do not act in a nondirective, random fashion but seek certain ends or rewards from what they do. Behavior is goal directed, and the intensity with which people engage in certain activities is a function of the benefits they expect to gain from them.

Motivation is another term that is subject to a variety of definitions. A common definition is that *motivation is what energizes, directs, maintains, and sustains behavior.* It is an urge to move in a specific direction—or more specifically, a response directed toward the reduction of a need. An individual has certain needs that create tensions and the individual behaves in specific ways to relieve these tensions. If a student is studying long hours for an examination or an engineer is still working on a design at midnight, they have certain goals that they are attempting to achieve through their behaviors. These goals will satisfy certain basic needs or wants that they have as individuals (a feeling of accomplishment, status, etc.). *Motives* are the goal-directed "whys" of behavior; *needs* are its initiating and sustaining forces. *Drive* is what moves an individual to satisfy his needs, and *goals* in this context are anything that will alleviate a need and hence reduce drive. When the student finishes studying and takes the test, his goal is achieved, and his drive to study temporarily subsides.

MASLOW'S NEED HIERARCHY

Needs are the key to understanding motivation. The most widely recognized, generalized approach to grouping and explaining needs is known as Maslow's Need Hierarchy. Maslow was an American psychologist who first published this theory in 1943.[1] His approach has been criticized for certain shortcomings, but it has almost universally served as the basis for more modern theories of motivation, and it has resulted in many innovations in management practice. Maslow grouped all needs into a five-step hierarchy as follows:

1. *Physiological*   These relate to physical well-being and include such needs as hunger, thirst, breathing, exercise, rest, and sex.
2. *Safety*   These involve physical safety such as being free from temperature extremes, assault, tyranny, fire, and other destructive forces. Maslow also implied that this category involved psychological factors, such as the desire for an orderly, predictable environment and being protected from threat and injustice.
3. *Social*   These are psychological needs and involve love, belongingness, a feeling of acceptance, and a desire for group involvement. The human being is a social animal and gregarious in nature.
4. *Esteem or ego*   People have a need for status, both in terms of self-respect and the esteem of others. Accordingly they seek feelings of achievement and competency. Men and women are striving animals who as they psychologically mature, attempt to attain higher levels of status and accomplishment.
5. *Self-actualization*   People have a restlessness for self-fulfillment. This involves a striving to realize the potential of the self, or as Maslow notes "to become everything that one is capable of becoming." It is this basic internal drive, largely unfilled, that characterizes them as wanting animals.

Significance and Source of the Needs

Several questions immediately arise. Which of the needs are most important? Are they innate or learned? Is behavior a conscious, rational response to needs, or are they part of the subconscious? In reply to these questions Maslow made his most important contributions. He first said that a satisfied need is *not* a motivator. Hunger is a motivating force when someone is hungry, but if an individual has this need temporarily satisfied, it is not a motivator. If someone is safe and free from threat, the safety needs are not motivators. Thus the potency of a need is a function of its current fulfillment.

Maslow also stated that the intensity of specific needs is related to the hierarchy he established. The physiological needs will be primary or dominate behavior until they are filled at a minimal level necessary for existence, and then the next-higher level, or safety needs, will become dominant. After safety needs are fulfilled at acceptable levels, social needs then predominate—and so on up the hierarchy. For this reason the psychological needs (social, esteem, and self-actualization) are also called secondary ones. However, in terms of potency they are not necessarily secondary, as most of the major accomplishments of human beings have been the result of the need for achievement and self-realization.

Maslow's hierarchy can be misleading, because he himself acknowledged that behavior is not a result of one need but relates to the composite interaction of all needs. Only the physiological needs function relatively independently (breathing air is independent from hunger or from status). Also, needs (even those that are physical) are never completely fulfilled, and psychological needs are always in a state of tension—reflecting a need for higher fulfillment. By his own estimate, Maslow felt that "the average citizen is satisfied perhaps 85 percent in physiological needs, 70 percent in safety needs, fifty percent in love needs, 40 percent in self-esteem needs, and ten percent in self-actualization needs."[2] A useful approach to visualizing needs is shown in figure 11-1. All needs are active in affecting behavior but the physiological needs are primary until a particular level of satisfaction is reached after which the needs at the next level become predominant. As the individual psychologically matures, the higher needs become more significant.

Are Needs Learned?

The questions of whether needs are learned or unlearned and whether they function as part of the conscious or unconscious are exceedingly significant ones. Obviously physiological needs are innate and unlearned. People do not learn to be hungry. However certain aspects of this behavior *are* learned. The choice to eat American rather than Chinese food is essentially learned. Whereas physiological needs are primarily an inherent part of people and part of their awareness when engaging in satisfying the need (eating), psychological needs (or at least the means of satisfying them) are primarily learned and unconscious. The human has an innate need for stimulation, understanding, affection, and curiosity, but the specific goals of individuals in obtaining gratification of these needs are learned, and the individual is not normally conscious that in behaving in particular ways to achieve them he is reacting to acknowledged, controllable needs.

For example, activities that gain recognition and a feeling of achievement differ by societies and cultures. Space exploration has provided

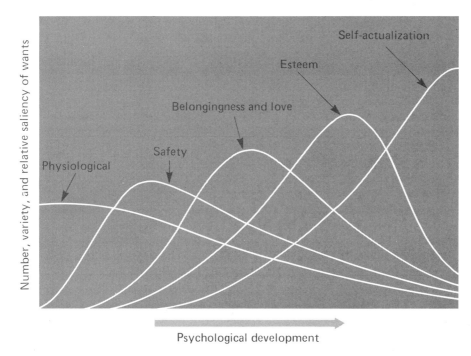

Fig. 11.1. **Relationship of needs to psychological development***

recognition and a feeling of achievement to scientists in American society, but in more primitive societies recognition came from killing game or raising sheep. The drive for power, security, and status are essentially unconscious ones and only understandable in a cultural context. Insecure individuals will not often acknowledge or give recognition to that insecurity, and reason alone is not often successful in eliminating the tensions associated with insecurity. Motives can operate and find expression entirely outside of awareness.

Probably the most important lesson to be gained by a manager from a knowledge of motivation and one of the most important guides relating to all human relations is that behavior can best be explained or modified through considering human response to needs. Since all behavior is motivated by needs, the manager should concentrate on how his or her actions affect the need satisfaction of others. The manager is not often successful in changing an individual's behavior by logical argument,

*As an individual psychologically matures more needs come into play in influencing behavior. Initially physiological needs are dominant, but psychological ones have higher intensity as the individual develops. The peak of one set of needs must be passed before the next higher need becomes dominant.

which is the first impulse. More likely success will come through modifying the reward system, changing the environment, or otherwise taking actions that appeal to the needs of the individual.

THE NATURE OF NEEDS

If all individuals had identical needs in terms of types and intensity, changing behavior through appealing to these static needs would be a relatively simple thing. However, even though all five sets of needs exist in individuals, they are often relatively dormant. This is because of three factors: they are either filled at temporarily satisfactory levels; the lower-level needs are not fulfilled so that the higher needs tend to be secondary; or reinforcement has taught people that certain behavior as a response to needs is not personally rewarding.

The uniqueness of the individual is reflected in needs as in other aspects of personality. Even though a person's needs will generally group consistent with Maslow's hierarchy, for many individuals this order is not appropriate. Some will ignore safety needs for status gratification by schussing down a ski run, jumping over barrels on a motorcycle, or scaling a rocky ledge. Some managers will step on friends and undercut associates in order to get ahead, while others will seek to maintain favorable relationships with their peers over opportunities for advancement.

Needs are constantly in a state of flux, depending on such conditions as how recently someone has eaten or on daily events that tend to threaten one's security or build up self-confidence. They are strongly conditioned by experience, which means they are continually being modified. Furthermore, needs are extremely difficult to assess, because any single act of behavior is likely the result of a response to several of them. (Buying a larger home can affect physical comfort, social relationships, and increase one's feeling of self-esteem.)

Cyclical Nature of Needs

The behavioral response to tension resulting from unsatisfied needs tends to occur in cycles. For physiological needs, the goal or level of satisfaction desired remains fairly constant. Thus in the morning after arising an individual is hungry and responds to this tension by eating breakfast. Once having eaten, the need is satisfied and the tension subsides. However, later in the day hunger again occurs, and the eating pattern is repeated.

The secondary or psychological needs also occur in cycles, but consistent with the psychological maturing of the individual, they increase in ascending cycles. Initially for the college graduate, obtaining an entry-

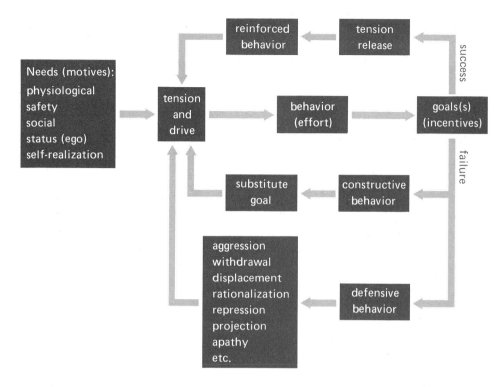

Fig. 11-2. Different behaviors associated with need cycles

level job in his profession is motivational on the basis of status and self-actualization needs. However, once that goal is achieved, a new higher-level goal will eventually replace it as the individual strives for greater accomplishment. If a man enters the organization as a junior accountant, he then seeks to become an accountant, senior accountant, and eventually perhaps a supervisor. If high levels of motivation are to be maintained, he must seek to use his skills in new, challenging ways. If after ten years in the company he is still a junior accountant, this position that once represented status and achievement now represents failure and lack of progress. In the constant state of maturing, as one skill is mastered or one goal is achieved, another takes its place. When individuals "peak out" and new goals do not replace the old ones, motivation tends to diminish.

This is reflected in the upper portion of figure 11-2. Unfulfilled needs result in tension, generating behavior to achieve a goal that will relieve the tension. If the individual is successful, drive is diminished, behavior is reinforced, and typically a new goal replaces the old one and the cycle is reactivated.

Behavior Related to Failure in Goal Accomplishment

In the examples presented so far, the assumption is that the individual is always successful in achieving goals. This is of course unrealistic, and when one is not able to achieve the level of accomplishment anticipated, two different types of behavior occur. Constructive behavior results when the individual, seeing that existing conditions prevent achieving an established goal, substitutes the previous goal with a new one that is more realistic given the conditions faced. If this results in eventual success rather than failure, the individual has made a desirable adjustment.

Occasionally a college graduate accepts employment with a company and has unrealistic aspirations of becoming a vice president within one or two years. Unless he adjusts his goals to something more realistic, he may experience the type of behavior associated with the lower cycle representing behavioral peculiarities resulting from the frustration of not being able to achieve what one desires. This defensive behavior takes many forms, but a few of the more common types are as follows:

Aggression	reacting by physically or symbolically attacking the barrier
Withdrawal	avoiding the barrier or situation either physically or psychologically
Displacement	taking the aggression out on another object or party other than the primary source
Rationalization	presenting an "excuse" for behavior or providing a reason other than the true one, usually because the erroneous reason is more socially acceptable and ego defending
Repression	excluding from consciousness experiences or feelings that cause or are associated with anxiety and frustration
Projection	attributing one's own feelings to someone else as a defense mechanism
Apathy	showing a lack of interest, concern, or personal involvement

These defensive behaviors are common with people in organizations, and all supervisors will at times face problems resulting from subordinates who display these or more neurotic tendencies.

Level of Aspiration

An important psychological concept closely associated with the intensity of needs is level of aspiration. *Level of aspiration* represents the long-run future goals and self-image of an individual. If an individual aspires to be a lawyer, it results in motivated behavior to achieve this long-term goal. Unless individuals aspire to do something, they do not try or put forth effort and thus will obviously not succeed in that endeavor. An individual is well-adjusted if abilities and opportunities are consistent with the level of aspiration. However, if this level of aspiration is lower than the abilities warrant, a person's potential will not be realized. Conversely, frustration can result if an individual has a level of aspiration that is beyond his capabilities and opportunities. Positive reinforcement is obviously a method of getting individuals to raise their aspiration levels, but adjusting any person's level of aspiration is subject to the same unknowns and uncertainties as attempting to adjust the intensity of needs.

IMPLICATIONS THAT PSYCHOLOGICAL NEEDS HAVE FOR MANAGING

The implications that physiological needs have for management are limited, because basically these needs are satisfied by most people in Western countries, and the means of obtaining need satisfaction are obvious. However, the fulfillment of psychological needs has many implications that deserve a manager's consideration. A few of these follow.

Social Needs

One of the main satisfactions that people gain from the work situation is developing friendships and being able to interact with others. Many individuals have promotional opportunities that would force them to relocate, but they do not accept them because they enjoy the community, like their fellow workers, and are comfortable in their current social situation. If a secretary is forced to type all day in seclusion, he or she normally finds the job disturbing, because one of the main sources of job satisfaction is interaction with others. Firms that have attempted to eliminate all nonessential conversation have usually found it creates such dissatisfaction that performance will go down rather than up. Too much socializing will obviously detract from productivity, but it can provide an escape from boring jobs. People generally do not like to work in isolation. They work better in small groups where they can develop affiliations rather than in large ones where they have little sense of identification.

MONOTONY IN THE WORK SITUATION

Mr. Trimarchi, age 32, is a tunnel patrolman in the Queens Midtown Tunnel in New York City, which goes under the East River and connects Queens with Manhattan. On a typical day, he spends four hours on "patrol"—sitting in a small booth inside the tunnel watching cars whiz by or overheat in traffic jams—two hours on duty outside the tunnel, one hour at lunch and one hour on rest break. Some days he gets a break—he gets toll booth duty all day.

"It's a lousy job," says Mr. Trimarchi. "Can you picture yourself just standing there for hours doing nothing? The monotony alone is enough to drive you out of your mind."

Inside the tunnel, Mr. Trimarchi, who is paid $10,300 a year, works in a glass booth about twenty feet long, three feet deep and seven feet high. Two ducts on the floor pump in air from just outside the tunnel; it is nearly as polluted with car exhausts as is the air inside the tunnel. There are two small heaters, a collapsible seat and a phone. During rush hours, Mr. Trimarchi stands, staring somewhat blankly, at the traffic pouring or creeping by. When traffic subsides, he sits, watching license plates or counting the tiles on the tunnel wall for the thousandth time. His job: to use the phone if there is an accident.

"It's not what you'd call creative work," says Mr. Trimarchi. "But it pays the rent. If not for the pay, they'd get nobody. Nobody would take this job." As it is, they are lined up to take that job. The Triborough Bridge and Tunnel Authority says there is a huge waiting list of candidates who want one of the 550 jobs as patrolmen on the seven bridges and two tunnels it controls.

Reprinted with permission of *The Wall Street Journal.* © Dow Jones and Co., Inc., July 22, 1971. All Rights Reserved.

Esteem and Ego Needs

Many of the routine, physical jobs in industry do little to satisfy one's need for recognition and achievement. Job design and organization structure often afford little freedom of action, so individuals feel confined rather than viewing their jobs as opportunities for creativity and self-expression. Reward systems should not just compensate the top few producers—improved performance by any employee should be reinforced. It is also important to self-esteem that the organization respect the dignity and worth of the individual and not regard employees as merely another resource or a cog in a machine. Unfortunately, the typical employee in most organizations is capable of doing more meaningful work than his job and work environment will permit.

Self-actualization Needs

Frequently the individual seeks outlets for self-fulfillment and creativity outside the organization (hobbies, membership in groups or clubs) when the work situation does not offer a feasible means of obtaining this satisfaction. Even though it is often difficult to establish self-fulfilling tasks in the work situation, more can usually be done to increase the incentive of employees by providing opportunities for personal growth (educational benefits, more complex assignments). Too often organizations are concerned with establishing policies that restrict people rather than expand them. McGregor's assumptions in Theory Y are that if the job provides recognition and self-actualization need satisfaction, supervision can be minimized, because the individual is highly motivated to achieve these personal objectives that are direct contributions to company goals.

THE CONTINGENCY APPROACH
TO MOTIVATION AND PERFORMANCE

Maslow's approach deals primarily with the intrinsic aspects of motivation or those involving the creation of tension and drive within the individual. More recent theories have emphasized the other major aspect of motivation, which is the environmental factors or external conditions. A systems approach to motivation broadly encompasses both the internal and external conditions that account for the drive of an individual in any particular situation.

A Model for Analyzing
Performance and Motivation

The motivation and performance of an individual in the organization are the result of two sets of factors. These are reflected in figure 11-3 in the form of questions one should ask if trying to find the answer to low motivation and inadequate performance. One set of factors relates to qualities the individual brings to the job in terms of personality, skills, and potential to perform. The other set of factors consists of tasks the individual is to perform and the variables of the work environment.

When an organization hires an employee, they bring on board a relatively mature personality who has a well-developed set of work habits, skills, attitudes, and emotions. He also has certain aspirations and goals related to his position in the organization. Inadequate performance on the job and lack of motivation can in many instances be tied to the personal attributes and aspiration of the worker. However, motivation is also a function of the opportunities for need satisfaction that exist in the work situation. Rather than asking what is wrong with the individual, we should often ask what is wrong with the work we ask him to do? Menial tasks are not motivational to individuals who have demonstrated their competence and who have high aspirations. Not many individuals display enthusiasm when given the task of washing dishes, digging trenches, or engaging in other activities that lower their self-esteem.

What the Individual Brings to the Job	*The Task and Job Environment*
What is wrong with the employee?	What is wrong with the work we ask him to do?
What is wrong with his training?	
What is wrong with his attitude?	What is wrong with the supervisor's relationship with the subordinate?
What is wrong with his work habits?	
What is wrong with his personality?	What is wrong with his relationships with other employees?
What is wrong with his physical energy?	What is wrong with the norms of the work group?
What is wrong with the intensity of his needs?	What is wrong with his pay? Fringe benefits?
What is wrong with his values?	
What is wrong with his skill?	What is wrong with the physical environment we ask him to work in?
What is wrong with his level of aspiration?	What is wrong with the future promotional opportunities?
	What is wrong with the psychological work environment?
	What is wrong with the rules, regulations, and policies of the organization?

Fig. 11-3.   Situational factors in motivation

As indicated in the contingency model in chapter 3, the primary internal variables in the situation are purpose, people, tasks, technology, and organizational structure. When individuals identify with the *purpose* of an organization (for instance, a nurse and a health care unit), they are much more likely to be committed to the organization than when one finds little personal identification with the tasks of his work unit (keypunch operator in an organization that sells computer services). If an individual finds his *tasks* interesting, challenging, and consistent with personal goals, this provides a motivational work environment. High-*technology* tasks are normally more psychologically rewarding than low technology ones, such as simple assembly work. Organization *structure* involves such important motivational factors as the amount of authority delegated to the individual, the rules and procedures that regulate his activity, the future promotional opportunities, and the freedom he has to perform his work.

An important consideration also is the *informal relationships* that are developed on the job. If an individual establishes favorable personal relationships with other employees, he achieves social need satisfaction and is less inclined to abuse sick leave or terminate employment. The norms of the informal group are also important in productivity, because the group is normally inclined to force its work standards on all its membership.

The relationship with the immediate supervisor is also a fundamental factor in motivation. If an individual perceives his or her supervisor to be arbitrary and unfair, he reacts by not contributing his best efforts to the organization. Also, the individual is highly concerned with the reward system of the organization. If the pay is considered inequitable, the fringe benefits inadequate, and recognition for his work unsatisfactory, the individual is not achieving his goals in the organization, and defensive behavior can result.

Implications the Model Has for Changing Behavior

It is again evident that behavioral change is related to many factors, both internal and external to the organization. It is also evident that motivation is situationally determined and influenced, which should encourage managers to use a situational framework for analyzing motivation and behavior. In addition, it should also be evident that the manager has much more control over the factors on the right side of figure 11-3 than those on the left. If an individual is untrained, increasing training opportunities should ultimately increase performance. However, as we have noted, changing well-developed personalities, attitudes, and work habits that an individual brings to the job is very difficult and subject to uncertainty. The manager has much more control over job design, reward systems, organizational policies, and the relationships within the organization. For this reason, most attempts to improve performance and increase motivation now concentrate on the task and job environment.

HERZBERG'S TWO-FACTOR THEORY

One of the most publicized theories of motivation was developed by Frederick Herzberg, an industrial psychologist, following original research he conducted with other associates in the late 1950's.[3] Based on their studies, Herzberg divided the environmental factors on the right side of figure 11-3 into two types. The first type, called *job content,* relates to the tasks the individual is performing and the work itself; the second type, called *job context,* relates to the conditions of employment like the pay, fringe benefits, and company policies as well as the interpersonal relations developed on the job. Herzberg's two-factor theory is based on the premise that only job-*content* factors are motivational. The significance of job-*context* factors in motivation is restricted to avoiding discontent or dissatisfaction.

Herzberg's Need Categories

The way in which needs are grouped by Maslow and Herzberg is similar. Maslow's esteem and self-actualization needs compare to the following six motivational factors listed by Herzberg: achievement, recognition, advancement, the work itself, the possibility of growth, and responsibility. Herzberg's ten maintenance factors (company policy and administration, technical supervision, interpersonal relations with supervisors, interpersonal relations with peers, interpersonal relations with subordinates, salary, job security, personal life, working conditions, and status) compare with the physiological, safety, and social needs of Maslow.

The primary difference between the two approaches is that Herzberg contends that his ten lower-level factors will not positively motivate people. If maintenance factors are not perceived as fair or adequate by employees, it will lead to dissatisfaction, and performance will be reduced. However, these factors do not *cause* individuals to work harder than they would under normal favorable conditions, and they do not cause people to be creative. Herzberg also referred to maintenance factors as *hygiene factors.* A company should keep its work environment healthy and hygienic so dissatisfaction will not result and decrease productivity. However, if people are paid a wage they perceive as fair, paying them more will not increase their productivity or creativity.

HYGIENE VS. MOTIVATORS

Let me rephrase the perennial question this way: How do you install a generator in an employee? A brief review of my movitation-hygiene theory of job attitudes is required before theoretical and practical suggestions can be offered. The theory was first drawn from an examination of events in the lives of engineers and accountants. At least sixteen other investigations, using a wide variety of populations (including some in the Communist countries), have since been completed, making the original research one of the most replicated studies in the field of job attitudes.

The findings of these studies, along with corroboration from many other investigations using different procedures, suggest that factors involved in producing job satisfaction (and motivation) are separate and distinct from the factors that lead to job dissatisfaction. Since separate factors need to be considered, depending on whether job satisfaction or job dissatisfaction is being examined, it follows that these two feelings are not opposites of each other. The opposite of job satisfaction is not job dissatisfaction, but, rather, no job satisfaction; and, similarly, the opposite of job dissatisfaction is not job satisfaction, but no job dissatisfaction.

The growth or motivator factors that are intrinsic to the job are: achievement, recognition for achievement, the work itself, responsibility, and growth or advancement. The dissatisfaction-avoidance or hygiene. . . factors that are intrinsic to the job include: company policy and administration, supervision, interpersonal relationships, working conditions, salary, status, and security.

Quotation from Frederick Herzberg, "One More Time: How Do You Motivate Employees?", *Harvard Business Review*, January-February 1968, pp. 56–57.

Job Enrichment

Herzberg's important contribution was in relating the significance of tasks and job design to motivation. Before this, motivation had concentrated on the hygiene factors. People will strive harder both in terms of effort and advancing their skills when they have jobs that provide them a sense of accomplishment and demand a high level of skill utilization. Herzberg's term for redesigning jobs to give the incumbent more freedom and to make them more psychologically rewarding is called *job enrichment*. The impact of his theory is such that hundreds of American firms have undertaken job-enrichment programs led by such industrial giants as American Telephone and Telegraph, American Airlines, and Texas Instruments.

Several other differences are noted in Herzberg's approach. His emphasis is on individual growth and psychology rather than group effectiveness and group psychology. Also, he considers interpersonal (or human) relations as merely a hygiene factor, when other behavioralists have stressed the importance of developing favorable group and supervisor-subordinate relationships to increase productivity. As with other theories of motivation, Herzberg's has its critics who claim that the research was method-bound and that its practical application is tied too much to one factor, but it constitutes one of the significant mileposts in the development of understanding motivation.

A CONTINGENCY MODEL OF MOTIVATION

Since Herzberg initially developed his theory in 1960, several more complex theories of motivation have been proposed. Those by Vroom[4] and Porter and Lawler[5] are probably the most significant. These theories include more variables and are more thorough than the earlier ones. They also use a contingency approach, based on the acknowledgment that there is "no one best way" to motivate; motivation is realistically a result of many factors that can vary from situation to situation. A contingency model that incorporates many of their considerations, but avoids some of the complexity, is contained in figure 11-4.

The model is divided into two parts: the motivational considerations relating to the individual and those relating to or resulting from the situation. The motivational considerations relating to the individual are the familiar ones proposed by Maslow, based on man's behavior being motivated by five sets of needs. Lack of need satisfaction results in tension, drive, and ultimately behavior. However behavior is also motivated by how the individual perceives his environment and the opportunities in the work situation. In terms of task goals the individual typically has several different options that will ultimately result in need satisfaction. (To get a feeling of achievement he can work in his garden, volunteer to head up the local heart drive, or attempt to take on a difficult project in the work situation). He might engage in all of these tasks, but the effort and creativity devoted to each is a function of the rewards (ultimately represented by need satisfaction) that come from his effort. Thus individuals select to engage in specific tasks because the ultimate outcome of

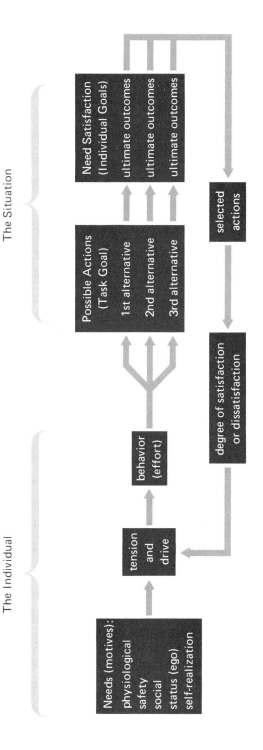

The Situation

The Individual

| Need Satisfaction (Individual Goals) |
| ultimate outcomes |
| ultimate outcomes |
| ultimate outcomes |

| Possible Actions (Task Goal) |
| 1st alternative |
| 2nd alternative |
| 3rd alternative |

selected actions

degree of satisfaction or dissatisfaction

behavior (effort)

tension and drive

Needs (motives): physiological safety social status (ego) self-realization

Selection of alternatives is a function of the:

1. intensity (valence) of the need set of an individual
2. alternatives available as perceived by the individual
3. rewards perceived to be associated with each alternative
4. expectancy the individual has of being successful in achieving the task goals and the ultimate outcomes (need satisfaction) associated with each alternative

Fig. 11-4. A contingency model of motivation

these are perceived as satisfying their individual goals, which ultimately are attached to personal need satisfaction.

Expectations and Motivation

One more important variable is implied in the action chain the individual selects and the effort that he puts into these pursuits. This variable consists, of the expectations he has that (1) his effort will result in successful accomplishment of the task goal, and (2) that he will be rewarded for his accomplishment. Such rewards are important to the degree they satisfy his individual goals (ultimately need satisfaction).

The expectations of an individual intervene to modify the logic of any simple model of behavior. Obviously an individual will not put much effort into an action, no matter how much he desires to be successful in that endeavor, if he thinks he will fail or if he expects to be inappropriately rewarded. An individual may refuse an opportunity for promotion if he does not expect to be able to successfully perform in the new position. He will also not attempt to increase his productivity if he perceives that this will not lead to greater rewards (increased pay, promotion, recognition, a greater feeling of achievement, etc.).

The return loop on the bottom part of the cycle indicates that an individual will experience certain satisfaction or dissatisfaction as a result of his activities that will affect the tension resulting from those needs. This also affects the degree of fulfillment and intensity of the needs. Furthermore, this experience will likely modify his expectations and perhaps even his individual goals. The cycle is dynamic consistent with an individual's behavior.

Value of the Model

This model is not complete, because it lacks many of the factors, covered in previous chapters, that influence how individuals make decisions regarding their behavior (especially group identifications and norms, role concepts, and interpersonal relations). However, its value is that it focuses on the prime determinants of motivation. Motivation is essentially a function of four factors:

1. *The intensity of the needs of the individual.* Intensity relates to the particular needs that are most significant to an individual, their degree of fulfillment, and so on. Also, intensity reflects the desire for a particular outcome (also called *valence*).
2. *The alternatives that are available.* These are options in terms of tasks or roles that the individual can engage in either outside or

within the organization. These opportunities (outlets for skill utilization or development) are determined by the conditions existing in the situation or total environment of the individual.

3. *The rewards that are associated with each of the alternatives.* Behavior and effort are a function of the anticipated and experienced rewards resulting from that behavior or effort. The magnitude of the rewards as they relate to the individual's goals will determine incentive. To the individual, rewards are goal accomplishment, such as increased pay, promotion, or greater productivity, but the ultimate reward is need satisfaction (status, achievement, etc.).

4. *The expectations (subjective probabilities) that each of these actions can result in the conditions desired.* If the individual expects to be successful in achieving the task goals and expects that this will bring the rewards he desires, he is strongly motivated to engage in the actions. However, if the probabilities are perceived as only slightly positive, his efforts will be much less intense, and if the probabilities are perceived as negative, he will reject the alternative altogether. Both of these sets of expectations (to be successful and to be rewarded for the success) are important. If the individual expects to be successful in trying to be more productive, but if he expects his supervisor not to recognize or reward this improvement, then efforts will not be directed to increasing productivity.

This is primarily a descriptive model of motivation. It does not prescribe what a manager should do to increase it. It does provide the guideline that motivation is a function of rewards, so an organization should structure its reward system to encourage the fulfillment of the tasks that are essential to its existence. It also implies that these rewards should appeal to the higher needs of individuals (recognition, achievement, etc.). Its prime value is that it is a more realistic, although more complex approach that directly relates individual motivation to organizational goals.

Application of the Model

One example will be given of the application of the model. Assume that you have just finished a degree in business administration and are contemplating what to do. You are considering taking a job or going on to law school. The decision you make will be a function of the four factors contained in figure 11-4. It will depend first on your personal individual motives relating to the need for status, self-actualization, affiliation, and so on. The intensity of these needs will create certain tension or drive to have them fulfilled. To satisfy the needs, you can accept one of the two job offers you have to work for a major retail organization, or you can go to law school. Your decision will be dependent on the rewards you perceive will flow from each of these opportunities and the expectations you have of being successful in following any one of these three pursuits.

If your grade-point average in college was below a three point and you are not too confident of your abilities as a student (in other words, you do not expect to be successful), you may reject going to law school—even though you feel that this would afford you the greatest satisfaction (prestige, pay, significant work, professional stature, etc.). The decision of which job to accept would also be dependent on the intensity of different needs and the rewards anticipated from being employed in either store. One may offer a higher commission and greater future opportunity, but if the other one is closer to home, social needs may sway the balance in dictating the choice. In any event, the ultimate choice is a function of individual needs, available alternatives, rewards associated with the alternatives, and expectations of being able to achieve the ultimate goals desired.

THE PSYCHOLOGICAL CONTRACT

One final model is appropriate in understanding motivation. This is referred to as *equity theory* or the *psychological contract*. Actually, it should more appropriately be considered a model of morale than motivation. *Motivation* is a propensity for particular behavior patterns to reduce a tension that results from needs. *Morale* is the current state of an individual's satisfaction with his membership in the organization. It reflects his attitudes and feelings toward his work, supervision, and the company.

Equity Theory

The balancing concept of the psychological contract is shown in figure 11–5. When an employee accepts a position with an organization, the company has certain expectations regarding how the individual will perform, and the worker has certain expectations regarding what should be received as fair compensation from the organization. The compensation is not limited to pay but involves working conditions, treatment by managers, opportunity for advancement, recognition for work, and interesting, rewarding job assignments. When the individual finds equity in the situation or feels that what he receives from the company in terms of treatment and compensation is fair in terms of the effort and skill he contributes to the organization, he is satisfied with the arrangement, and is normally committed to the company and its goals. However, when he feels that he is not being dealt with in a just manner, he tends to be dissatisfied. This has many implications, depending on how the individual

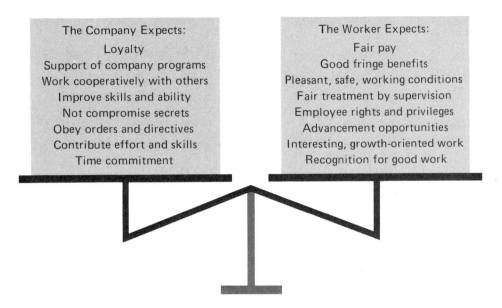

Fig. 11-5. Balancing the psychological contract

psychologically reacts to such dissatisfaction.

This model is called a psychological contract, because it consists of implied assumptions that each party has about the employment arrangement. In addition to the individual's expectations, the company also anticipates certain behavior from its employees. If the company does not feel that the individual contributes a fair share based on how the company rewards him or her, it is also dissatisfied with the individual and typically takes certain actions involving the use of authority that result in the application of pressure to force the individual to conform.

The psychological contract has many similarities to other approaches discussed in this chapter. Basically it is a model of satisfaction and dissatisfaction akin to Herzberg's maintenance factors. It is also a model of expectations similar to the contingency model of motivation. If both parties are satisfied, a healthy psychological climate predominates. However, if one party has unrealistic expectations (the college graduate who expects to be vice-president in three years), it is impossible to balance the model, resulting in low morale and dissatisfaction.

Imbalance in the Model

One of the most important concepts of the psychological contract is that of imbalance. The human mind does not gracefully tolerate deficiencies or imbalance. Imbalance, like tension, will force people to act to regain this balance. As in the model in figure 11-2, sometimes this reaction is rational and constructive in nature, but sometimes it is irrational. Since people will react differently, generalizations regarding behavior are impossible to make. However, the typical outcomes of behavior associated with dissatisfaction are absenteeism, high turnover, the support of a strike, and moderately productive, uncommitted workers. It should be noted, however, that studies on morale do not show that low morale always results in lower productivity. Many other variables tend to be involved.

Variations and Shortcomings of the Model

There are many variations of the psychological contract. One of the most important ones is how an individual feels the company treats him compared with how they treat other employees. The individual requires a feeling of fairness in such comparisons if he is to avoid dissatisfaction. The model does not reflect many other factors that determine satisfaction or dissatisfaction. It also ignores actions the individual will most likely take as a result of imbalance. A major shortcoming is the exclusion of external factors. The decision to leave the organization is strongly influenced by the status of the external labor market; fairness is not just a function of how an organization treats its employees but also of how similar organizations in the same industry or similar locality treat theirs. As a final point, it should be apparent that the psychological contract is unique for each employee. Each individual has distinct expectations that are influenced by others in the organization but are also a reflection of the personality of that individual.

FINANCIAL INCENTIVES AND MOTIVATION

Many of the management implications resulting from a knowledge of motivation have already been discussed. Primarily it is a question of what incentives a manager should use to increase the motivation of his work force. Too often in the past reliance has been on appealing to physiological needs—primarily through financial incentives. An analysis of money as a motivator is beneficial because it reveals many of the concepts that underlie our current understanding of motivation.

Money is an extremely significant incentive in the work situation. Its appeal as an incentive is much more varied and not nearly as direct as one would anticipate. It is an important means of satisfying physiological needs, but in a society where essentially everyone has these needs fulfilled at subsistence levels, its appeal in this regard is rather limited. In the depression of the 1930's, with twenty-five percent of the workforce unemployed, it was a different situation. However, as our society has become more affluent, the financial incentive has had its greatest appeal in satisfying higher needs. The nature of this appeal will differ by culture, since a person's desire for money and material things is learned, but in Western society money has generally been associated with achievement, status, and power. However, money is not always an *overriding* motive. A vice-president making $50,000 a year who is retained in his position but stripped of most of his responsibility and "put on the shelf" is a dissatisfied, disgruntled employee.

Money is obviously only one of many incentives in an organization. It is preferred by companies because it is relatively easy to manipulate (paying someone time-and-one-half to work overtime). Often it is the status aspects of money that are most significant. If one individual receives a ten-percent pay raise and another only five percent, it will quickly arouse defensive feelings. Furthermore, as Herzberg points out, additional money does not increase productivity unless low pay is currently a cause of worker dissatisfaction.

Probably the most important lesson associated with money as a motivator is the one emphasized throughout this chapter. Money as an incentive varies with how the recipient values it and with the degree to which it satisfies the needs of that individual. The school teacher and the priest typically have sacrificed money for other types of need satisfaction that they gain from those particular careers. As they move into the job market, many young adults select a lower-paying position in their home town rather than take a higher paying one in the big city. Individual variation—rather than fixed-preference hierarchies—typifies the motivation and behavior of human beings.

SUMMARY

Motivation is the force that energizes, directs, maintains, and sustains human behavior. Motivation is a response to the tension resulting from lack of need satisfaction. Maslow's need hierarchy is the best-known theory for explaining how different sets of needs, based on their current degree of satisfaction, affect behavior. In today's society the higher needs of affiliation, ego, and self-actualization tend to be the most important motivators.

Different behaviors result from attempts to achieve goals and gain need satisfaction. If one is successful, behavior is reinforced; otherwise, he either revises the goal or engages in one of many forms of defensive behavior.

Two sets of factors are involved in productivity and motivation. One is the personality and characteristics of the individual; the other is the tasks and factors of the job environment. Herzberg divides the job and its environment into two different sets of variables. The first is job content which controls motivation. The second, job context (pay, relationships with other workers, etc.), is more associated with satisfaction and dissatisfaction.

A more thorough contingency model of motivation holds that motivation is a function of the intensity of the needs of the individual, the alternatives or opportunities in the environment, the rewards associated with these alternatives, and the expectations of the individual regarding how successful he or she will be in achieving the task goals and obtaining the ultimate outcomes desired. The diverse nature of human motivation again supports the premise that man is a highly complex being interacting in an even more complex environment.

QUESTIONS FOR STUDY AND DISCUSSION

1. What relationship do needs have to motivation? What is unique about Maslow's approach to needs?
2. How do ego needs differ from self-actualization needs?
3. If needs are the source of motivation, what are the barriers to changing an individual's needs and thus changing his motivation?
4. Explain the following behaviors on the basis of needs:
    A. The college athlete playing football
    B. The actor in the school play
    C. The individual who refuses to accept the position as editor of the school paper
    D. The student who quits studying and goes to the movie at the urging of his roommates
5. What two types of behaviors result when an individual fails to achieve a desired goal? Give examples of five different forms of irrational behavior.
6. In what ways can a manager appeal to an individual's ego needs? To his social needs?
7. If the manager decides that the source of the motivational problem is not in the tasks the individual is performing or in the job environment, but in the individual, what can be done?
8. In Herzberg's two-factor theory, what influence do the maintenance factors have on motivation? On productivity?

9. In what ways do the expectations of an individual influence motivation?

10. In the contingency model of motivation, which variables are associated with the individual and which are associated with the situation?

11. Using the model in figure 11-4, explain the following:
   A. The college student who sacrifices study time to train for the track team
   B. The hourly employee who does only the minimal to retain his job
   C. The unemployable who refuses to apply for an open position
   D. The executive who works constantly and finds little time for his family
   E. The mother who hires a babysitter so she can pursue a work career

12. From previous job experiences, give an example of where the psychological contract was out of balance for you.

Case Problem:
THE RESIGNATION

Laura Simpson had just informed her supervisor in the payroll department that she was going to resign. The supervisor was dismayed at this disclosure and decided to pursue it further with her.

"I just can't understand this, Laura. You've been promoted twice within three years and we give you a very respectable salary. You know that you've been one of our top employees. I never dreamed you were dissatisfied with your job."

"I'm not dissatisfied with the job," Laura replied. "I just have this opportunity to work as a cost accountant with another firm, and I thought I could use my accounting experience and college degree better there. I've liked working here, but I feel the other is a better opportunity."

"It isn't for more money is it, Laura? If it is, maybe I can do something about it. I still don't understand it. You get along so well with everyone, and in time there'd be other opportunities here."

"I know that," she responded, "but I've thought it over carefully, and I believe it's in my best interest."

What needs are motivating Laura to make this decision?

Is the psychological contract in balance in her current job?

How is her decision explained in terms of figure 11-4, relating to the contingency model of motivation?

Is she currently *dissatisfied* with her work using Herzberg's definition?

Case Study:
INCENTIVES FOR EMPLOYMENT IN THE
MISSILE INDUSTRY

In the late 1950's, when the United States was in the thick of the missile race with Russia, many major research and development contracts were issued to firms for space work. The Department of Defense initially had plants built away from population centers because of their possible hazardous nature, and also it would better disperse them in case of attack. In one particular instance a plant that eventually came to employ over 6000 was built in the Western United States on the edge of a desert.

When the plant was initially constructed, it was felt the company might have trouble getting engineers to come to that part of the country, but since it involved the construction of the largest solid-propellant missile in the world and was considered a "glamour" project, engineers and scientists came from all over the nation. The test and development phase took approximately seven years, and then the project moved into large-scale production. The executives at the plant were concerned that when the interest and challenge of research and development were over, many of the top scientists and engineers would move on to companies that acquired some of the newer development contracts. However, some ten years later most of the scientific cadre that had been instrumental in the firm's success was still with the organization.

What needs were important to the scientists initially in accepting jobs with the company?

After 1965, why did most of the scientists refuse alternatives for employment with other companies? Is this consistent with Maslow's hierarchy? With Herzberg's two-factor theory?

Would you expect the turnover to be higher among the hourly employees?

What reasons do you think the scientists and engineers gave for remaining in the area?

Footnotes

1. A. Maslow, "A Theory of Human Motivation," *Psychological Review,* July 1943, pp. 370–396.
2. *Ibid.,* p. 389.
3. Frederick Herzberg, Bernard Mausner, and Barbara Snyderman, *The Motivation to Work,* (New York: John Wiley and Sons, Inc., 1959).
4. Victor H. Vroom, *Work and Motivation,* (New York: John Wiley and Sons, Inc., 1964).
5. Lyman W. Porter and Edward E. Lawler, III, *Managerial Attitudes and Performance,* (Homewood, Illinois: Richard D. Irwin, Inc., 1968).

Tasks, Technology, and Productivity

Why are the tasks of an organization significant
to managers?

What advantages accrue through task
specialization?

What are the psychological drawbacks of task
specialization?

How can a manager select those jobs that need
enrichment?

What impact does technology have on the internal
functioning of an organization?

Why are variables such as leadership styles,
organization structure, and people contingent
upon the tasks of the organization?

A management class was taken on a tour of a local firm that manufactures medical supplies. The class first visited the production facilities. The firm had several different production lines, and the students decided to inspect the one for surgical rubber gloves. The first phase of the production process was essentially entirely automated. Several hundred metal hand molds conveyed by overhead cranes were first dipped into a latex solution and then transported into heating ovens to be cured. In the next phase of the line, certain workers peeled the gloves from the molds, others inspected them, and other sanitized and packaged them for shipment. Each worker repeated the assigned task hundreds of times within one hour.

The tour next moved to the research and product engineering department. These operations were in sharp contrast to the order and routine of the production line. Clusters of engineers reviewed drawings, engaged in conversation as they pointed at models, or participated in group discussions. Other engineers sat alone at desks, some leaning back in deep thought, while others shuffled through papers. In the research laboratory, chemists were busily conducting a variety of tests and experiments.

The class briefly toured the accounting and marketing areas also. They observed the computer center, passed through an area where accountants—primarily working individually—were reviewing computer printouts, developing reports, and analyzing financial data. The marketing manager explained that his local staff was small because all of the salesmen were assigned to locations in the field. His primary tasks were to handle long-range planning, develop advertising campaigns, and coordinate field activity.

The next day in class after discussing the tour, the professor made the following comments: "As we proceeded through the different elements of the plant, we found people engaged in a wide variety of tasks. Some were fairly simple, some complex, some routine, and others lacked structure. What inferences are derived from the fact that people are engaged in different tasks? Does this affect the way the unit is organized? Does it affect the way in which a supervisor leads his group? Does it affect the way in which work is planned and controlled? Should a supervisor manage differently because of the specific tasks his work group is performing?" The answers to these questions are the basic issues to be dealt with in this chapter.

THE RELATIONSHIP OF TASKS
AND TECHNOLOGY

Taken together, tasks and technology comprise the work done, methods used, and operations performed in organizations. They represent the totality of methods—both human and mechanical—to achieve the practical purposes of the organization. Tasks are the more exclusive human element and are associated with the activities of individuals in the organization. Tasks literally are the assigned functions that an individual performs and are goal or "ends" oriented. Technology is "means" oriented, relating to the knowledge input of tasks and to techniques and methods of the workflow, including the mechanical aspects of the organization's operations.

Technology involves the use of scientific knowledge to perform practical purposes, whether this is by man or machine: technology consists of knowledge, techniques, or processes that extend human capability. Technology is generally related to the entire network of jobs and processes in an organization, but it can be related solely to the tasks of an individual. The knowledge required to function as a craftsman is higher than that of an unskilled worker, and thus the craftsman's tasks involve more advanced technology. Technology is an attribute or dimension of tasks, but it also encompasses the methods and mechanization involved in the total operations of the organization.

It is beneficial for the manager to distinguish between tasks and technology for two reasons: the human considerations associated with the tasks people perform have many implications for assigning work, identifying people to perform specific tasks, and leading people in organizations. The second reason is that technology acts as one of the primary (if not *the* primary) generators of change in society, and it is all too easy to blend technology into the other activities of an organization and lose sight of its role as one of the basic forces accounting for the conditions existing in a work group.

THE SIGNIFICANCE OF TASKS

In attempting to understand an organization as a system, one of the parts of the system that requires careful evaluation is the task or tasks being performed. This is because tasks have a strong, dependent effect on other organizational variables—especially people, organization structure, and leadership styles. Too frequently management research and writing have concentrated on what occurs at supervisory levels in organizations without giving due consideration to what occurs at the work level in terms of task performance. This is indeed unfortunate, since many of the problems managers deal with and many of the conditions existing at higher levels result from the basic tasks undertaken.

Leadership styles, organization design, staffing, and planning and control systems cannot be studied independently, because the methods and concepts used in each instance are to some degree dependent on the tasks of the work unit or organization. Reflecting the interdependency concepts underlying contingency and systems theories, the analysis of tasks in this chapter will be linked with concepts relating to variables covered in earlier chapters and will lay the groundwork for a more thorough analysis of concepts (such as organization design and leadership styles) to be studied in later chapters. To study tasks in a vacuum is to ignore the forces that dominate organizations. Tasks are of significance to the manager and to management theory for six basic reasons:

1. *Tasks are the basic building blocks of organization structure.* The purpose of structuring a group is to enhance the work carried on in the organization. The structure of an organization must be built around the basic tasks to be performed. There is considerable controversy regarding the issue of whether organization structure should be developed from the top down or from the bottom up. Regardless, the structure is centered around integrating, coordinating, and optimizing the flow of work in the organization, which therefore concentrates on individual tasks and the grouping of them to achieve organizational objectives.

2. *Tasks are the primary determinants of staffing, or people requirements.* People are selected to handle specific positions involving specific tasks in the organization. Personnel selection is basically a problem of matching people with particular skills who display specific temperaments with the demands of jobs involving designated tasks. Hospitals require individuals with nursing training because this type of organization is engaged in health-care tasks. Each organization selects, trains, and advances people in organizations based on the tasks to be performed. (As will be seen later, even the styles that leaders use in directing a work unit are appropriate based on the tasks of that unit.)

3. *Tasks are the basic building blocks of job design and personnel administration.* Job design consists of the clustering of specific tasks as they relate to a position in the organization. Jobs are then grouped and ranked into a hierarchical structure based on the complexity of the tasks and the specific responsibilities involved. All of the personnel functions including recruitment, performance evaluation, wage and salary administration, training, and manpower planning are derived from and dependent on this basic grouping of tasks and job design.

4. *Tasks and task specialization have been the traditional means used to maximize efficiency and productivity in organizations.* The factory system was developed with task specialization as the accepted standard for designing jobs and maximizing efficiency. Mass assem-

bly production results in greatly reduced unit labor cost. This efficiency is in part attributed to designing jobs so that each worker has a limited number of relatively simple tasks to perform.

5. *Tasks and task structure affect need satisfaction and thus the motivation and commitment of individuals.* The primary opportunity an individual has for psychological need satisfaction in an organization comes from the tasks he is assigned to perform. Changing tasks to make them more psychologically appealing has been one of the most active pursuits of behavioral scientists and is the aim of job-enrichment programs.

6. *Modifying tasks and job design constitute (in many instances) the most effective means that a manager has to generate change within an organization.* As indicated earlier, the manager's role is increasingly becoming one of accommodating the organization to change, especially that generated by the external environment. For many years it was felt that this could best be done through changing individuals using management development, sensitivity training, and other similar approaches. However, as we noted in chapter 10, changing mature individuals is a slow and uncertain process, so managers are again turning to the modification of tasks and jobs as a primary means of instituting change within organizations.

DIMENSIONS OF THE TASK VARIABLE

There are many bases on which the tasks of an organization or suborganization will differ. Eleven of those that are most significant to managers (as well as those representing standard terminology for classifying them) are presented in figure 12-1. The first three dimensions, relating to whether tasks are people, things, or information oriented, traditionally have been the three used by the Bureau of Employment Security of the Department of Labor to classify jobs in the United States. Based on the relative differences between tasks, as a result of these and other associated dimensions, the 1965 *Dictionary of Occupational Titles* classifies 21,741 separate occupations known by 13,809 additional titles—or a total of 35,550 job titles. These three dimensions are also critical in the staffing problem of relating the skills and interests of people to the tasks involved in a particular job.

Dimensions four through nine, relative to the physical and mental demands, repetition, standardization, autonomy, and sequential interdependence of the tasks, constitute those characteristics that are most significant in job enrichment, motivation, and leading people. They, therefore need to be highlighted in any model used by managers.

Common Dimensions	Task Continuum	
1. People oriented	(low)	(high)
2. Things oriented	(low)	(high)
3. Information oriented (data)	(low)	(high)
4. Skill required	(low)	(high)
5. Physical demands	(low)	(high)
6. Repetition (job cycle)	(low)	(high)
7. Standardization (structure)	(low)	(high)
8. Autonomy (independence)	(low)	(high)
9. Sequential interdependence	(low)	(high)
10. Organizational nature of task	Line, staff, operational, support, supervisory, etc.	
11. Functional nature of task	Marketing, production, engineering, research, maintenance, health care, welfare, protection, education, regulation, etc.	

Fig. 12-1.   Task variable

Dimensions ten and eleven relate to the standardized terminology used in organizations to distinguish different tasks. Chapters 13 and 14 interrelate tasks to particular types of organization structure. *Staff, line,* and *support* all represent types of organizational assignments that involve different tasks. The last dimension classifies tasks based on the functions performed in the organization. This covers the business functions of production, marketing, engineering, and research, and government functions like welfare, protection, education, and regulation.

TASK SPECIALIZATION AND PRODUCTIVITY

Underlying mass-production technology is the assumption that efficiency can be maximized through specialization of every link in the production chain. This has resulted in specialized equipment, facilities, and labor. Specialization is achieved through limiting the number of tasks handled by each worker. The entire job cycle for any one worker is typically three to four minutes or less. This involves attaching four bolts to a fender, spot welding seven locations on two pieces of adjoining metal, or soldering less than a dozen connections.

The rationale for specialization was expressed in 1776 by Adam Smith, one of the early economists. In explaining the advantages of the division of labor, he used workers making pins as an example. He noted that one individual making an entire pin could probably make only one in a day, certainly not more than twenty. However, when one man draws the wire, another straightens it, a third cuts it, a fourth points it, etc., ten persons can make upwards of 48,000 pins in a day, or 4,800 per person. There is obviously some exaggeration in this famous example, but there is little question regarding the tremendous increases in productivity that have resulted from the specialization of the assembly line.

Why Efficiency Results

The reasons for the increases in efficiency are many. The primary factor is that startup (or "make-ready") and cleanup times are experienced only once during the day. If an individual moves from task to task, there is generally some requirement involved in getting ready to perform these and in relocating equipment or tools once the task is completed. Also, if a variety of tasks is performed, frequently a disproportionate amount of time is spent in switching from task to task. If a service-station operator works alone, he intermittently pumps gas, repairs automobiles, answers the telephone, and maintains his accounts. In doing so, he spends so much time moving from one task to another that much of his efficiency is lost. Keeping a worker at one work station where he repetitively performs a job involving a limited number of tasks has proven to pay big dividends in mass production.

Other Arguments in Favor of Task Specialization

There are six other reasons favoring task specialization:

- Workers are easier to train, and it takes less time to train them. If an employee is restricted to performing a few simple tasks, he can be adequately trained in a day or less.
- Because the jobs involve less skill and less training time, workers are easier to replace.
- If the jobs involve less skill, the pay is generally lower.
- Because of the limited tasks a worker performs and the limited knowledge required to perform these, it typically results in less-difficult supervision, especially in the technical aspects of the job.
- With specialized tasks, specialized equipment can be developed and used, which also contributes to efficiency.
- There is normally less duplication of equipment because a worker does not perform a variety of tasks involving several pieces of equipment. He operates only one machine that is constantly in use.

JOB ENRICHMENT

The great paradox of task specialization is that it maximizes productivity, but it also maximizes boredom. In this century, division of labor has been attacked from many sources, especially psychologists, because it is dehumanizing—some would consider enslaving—and it alienates the worker. Repetitive, monotonous jobs requiring a shallow use of skills are said to result in worker dissatisfaction and are the main source of morale problems that tend to be experienced in mass production factories. The result has been a movement in the direction of job-enrichment programs (such as Herzberg's theory reviewed in chapter 11) or job-enlargement activities.

Attempts to eliminate the boredom and monotony of routine jobs have taken many forms. The simplest is *job rotation*. Using this concept a worker is moved from one job to another, each of which involves simple tasks. The change is intended to eliminate the boredom of continually repeating an identical set of physical motions. It also provides a broader perspective of the entire workflow, since a worker becomes acquainted with a larger segment of the total work sequence. However, the tasks are still menial and unrewarding, making it no less difficult to take pride in one's work.

Job enlargement involves expanding the job by requiring a worker to perform a larger segment of the work flow. This makes the work less repetitive, since the job cycle for an individual worker is lengthened. Since it involves more tasks, it also requires more knowledge. An example would be the assembly of office machines. One firm formerly had the tasks involved in assembling a mimeograph machine divided among five workers. Each assembled a portion of the unit, and the last worker connected the subassemblies to form a complete unit. When they introduced the job-enlargement program, one worker assembled the entire unit. In this particular instance the company experienced fewer assembly errors. Also, turnover and absenteeism were considerably reduced among the workers.

The arguments in favor of job enlargement are that the work is less repetitive (one-fifth in this instance), it requires more skill (because the entire unit is assembled by one individual), and the worker identifies more with the end item because he or she takes sole responsibility for assembling the entire unit. This form of job enlargement is called *horizontal* enlargement, since it involves broader groupings of tasks existing at the same level in the organization.

Job enrichment, as the term is used by Herzberg, must include more than just horizontal job enlargement. Herzberg argues that performing a wider variety of tasks—when they remain simple and far beneath the skill and psychological interest level of the individual—will do little to motivate the worker. Motivation must come through more challenging work, where the individual can get a greater feeling of recognition and accomplishment for the work performed. Thus he argues that to make work more motivating, it must involve *vertical* job enlargement or the term he prefers, job *enrichment.*

Job enrichment requires taking some of the tasks formerly handled by the supervisor and individuals at higher levels in the organization and combining these with the previous tasks to form a job where more responsibility, autonomy, and complexity in decision making are involved. In the example of the worker assembling office machines, some aspects of vertical job enlargement were incorporated. When customer complaints were received, they were sent to the worker who assembled the machine. The worker was to correspond with the customer, answer complaints, and make proper restitution when necessary under the warranty. This tended to reduce errors, since the employee became more totally responsible for the outcome of the work performed.

Psychological Basis of Job Enrichment

The basic arguments behind job enrichment are that people seek rewards in terms of psychological need satisfaction from their efforts in organizations. Performing menial, unskilled tasks makes it very difficult to get any sense of pride or feeling of competency from these efforts. When there is little psychological reward associated with tasks, there is little intrinsic motivation to perform them. Rewards must therefore be extrinsic (in the form of pay, fringe benefits, a friendly work group, etc.). More challenging and demanding tasks where the individual can identify with his output and performance can provide recognition and a feeling of accomplishment. This becomes motivational purely in terms of the tasks being performed. American Telephone and Telegraph is known for its highly successful job-enrichment program. Workers in groups examine jobs and attempt to determine how they can add more responsibility to the position and how the worker can get a more clearly defined sense of achievement. They also attempt to provide a system of immediate feedback so the worker can tell what he has accomplished. Such a climate tends to facilitate the change process.

Reaction to Unskilled, Repetitive Tasks

The key question is, how do workers react psychologically to jobs that are highly specialized and unskilled, a condition facing millions of workers throughout the world today? How do they compensate for work that is often mind-numbing and requires only surface attention? Generally, the conclusion is reached that it results in escape and alienation. Individuals escape by staying away from the job (absenteeism, stretching out breaks, etc.) or by engaging in fantasy, such as day dreaming. It is also possible to concentrate on minute differences like changes in the color of materials, the strands of thread, or the positioning of components. Sometimes it results in playing games and engaging in horseplay as a form of diversion. The alienated individual has little concern for his work, weak identification with the organization, and is not inclined to support management. (His behavior is similar to that portrayed in the lower cycle of figure 11-2.) Failure to achieve psychological need satisfaction results in frustration, displacement, and other peculiar behavior.

JOB ENRICHMENT IN SWEDEN

Now there are work-enrichment experiments all around Sweden. Best-known is the Volvo automobile plant at Kalmar, where the conventional assembly line has been scrapped for a number of computer-directed trolleys, each manned by a group of workers who together assemble an entire auto rather than repeat a single operation as an auto moves along a production line.

"This is a very tangible change—most people know what an assembly line is," Mr. Edgren says, but he points out that "the solutions to the problem are different in different companies, depending on technology." Some examples in various industries:

—Asea, the big manufacturer of electrical equipment for industry, has "moved the office onto the factory floor" at a plant in Vasteras that makes relays. Engineers, salesmen, product-design people and other white-collar workers share facilities with production workers. This helps lead to "product identification," Mr. Edgren says. And it gives the blue-collar men a sense of parity. Curt Nicolin, Asea president, notes the experiment has spurred efforts to reduce noise, improve lighting and correct other "evils which stem from the manufacturing process."

—At Hallstavik, just outside Stockholm, the Hollens Bruk Group has enlisted its workers to help design and build a big paper mill. The idea is to make the working environment as attractive as possible and shape it to the workers' needs.

—At Vasby foundry, a die-casting shop in the Granges group, the sixty production workers have been reorganized into eight semiautonomous groups sharing equally in production bonuses for work turned out by the foundry.

—The Orrefors glassworks, which was suffering from uneven work flow in the grinding and polishing department, turned the operation over to the workers, who reorganized it into three separate production groups. Jobs are rotated to make for variety and interest.

—At the rock-drilling machine assembly department of the Atlas Copco group, outside Stockholm, workers have replaced the assembly line with a round table for group work and a system of shared monetary rewards.

Evaluation of the Job-Enrichment Movement

The widespread support of job enrichment, primarily by psychologists and in management literature, has resulted in a tendency to overgeneralize and overstate the case for this program. Certainly the movement to enlarge routine jobs has been favorable, especially as the workforce has become better trained and educated. American industry is still handicapped by too many jobs that are simple and routine, being far beneath the skill level of the typical worker. Also, hourly employees generally should be given more independence and responsibility in their work.

However, there is little evidence that job dissatisfaction is widespread in all of American industry, and there is no evidence that all workers dislike routine jobs. For instance, in 1973 a Gallop Poll[1] indicated that only twenty percent of the respondents were dissatisfied with their job because it was boring. Another poll revealed that ninty-one percent of the men and eighty-four percent of the women liked their jobs, and only five percent of the men and twelve percent of the women disliked their work.[2] In the latter survey only three percent of the respondents indicated they would change their jobs to reduce the monotony.

Furthermore, "blue-collar blues" is not typical of all manual work. A skilled craftsman like a carpenter is usually given almost complete independence. He can identify with the work he performs and gains a sense of status and pride from applying his craft in a skillful manner. Alienation is more associated with machine-tending and assembly work where little skill is involved. In these instances, it is difficult to get achievement-need satisfaction because of the superficiality of what is done. Jobs of this sort are difficult, if not impossible, to enrich and can be eliminated only by replacing a person with a machine.

Also people do not abhor all routine. Day-to-day human behavior tends to be patterned, where an individual arises at the same time, has the same selection for breakfast, and continues his activities in a relatively repetitive cycle. This is an efficient way to conduct the "maintenance"-type activities of individuals as it is for organizations. Individual differences are also noted in people where some desire and are quite comfortable with routine work. Furthermore, what is a challenging task for an unskilled employee will likely not be challenging for the plant manager. One cafeteria operator noted that his most motivated worker, who also displayed the most pride in her work, was an individual of limited mental capacity who found this to be the first job she could successfully handle.

Basically an individual seeks tasks that are rewarding. Certainly jobs can be too large, and an individual cannot succeed because of the breadth of what is demanded. To ask a professor to teach economics and marketing as well as management will receive a quick rejection because it is not possible for an individual to acquire the knowledge to be an achiever simultaneously in all of these fields.

TASKS AND THEIR RELATIONSHIP TO OTHER CONTINGENCY VARIABLES

Recent research supports the contingency view that tasks represent one of the most significant variables accounting for conditions in organizations. The type and status of the tasks of an organization are one of the primal factors determining whether different concepts of management will be appropriate in specific situations. A brief review of some studies relating tasks to other contingency variables (figure 3-2) follows.

Task-to-People Relationships

Man's behavior is strongly affected by his environment, and one of the most significant factors in that environment is the tasks he performs. There is thus a direct relationship between tasks and people or the behavior of people in organizations. Frustration and apathy on the part of the worker can result from task performance just as can pride and a feeling of competence. These feelings cannot be understood apart from the joint people-task context.

Furthermore, it is obvious that people display individual differences, and that these must be taken into consideration in using management methods relating to tasks, such as job enrichment. Individuals who have different abilities and are characterized by needs of different intensity will display varying feelings of competency in relation to different tasks. Some individuals seek the safety and security of routine jobs. Researchers have concluded that "individuals with strong desires for higher-order need satisfaction respond much more positively to high-level jobs than do those who have weaker higher-order needs."[3] There is obviously no best way to design jobs, and people performing the tasks will react to them in different ways. Reif, through his extensive studies on job enrichment, concludes that the skill level, education, previous work experience, family background, and need priorities of individuals are all variables in matching people to tasks in programs like job enrichment.[4]

The tasks of the organization have two other significant influences on people. The basic tasks determine the skills required of people. Assembly-line tasks can best be met with people who are unskilled; engineering tasks require people trained in engineering; and marketing tasks require people with expertise in this area. Thus tasks act as a strong independent variable in determining people requirements. Tasks also have a major influence on the interaction of people within the organization because of the physical positioning required in many work situations. In work stations along an assembly line, the worker can easily talk only with the worker on his right or left. Work locations and the task assignments determine who individuals come in contact with, how often, and how long. This definitely influences interaction patterns and opportunities for social-need satisfaction.

Relationships of Task to Organization Structure

(Chapters 13 through 15 cover task concepts relating to organization structure, but it is important at this point to recognize that the tasks of an organization determine many of the features of the structure.) Organizations tend to be established consistent with the tasks performed. Since the tasks of organizations differ, there is obviously no one best approach to structure. As Lawrence and Lorsch note from their studies, we should "design organizations according to the tasks they [organizations] are trying to perform."[5]

The most obvious example is the way subunits of an organization are structured resulting from the work performed in these units. In an oil refinery or a mining operation, the entire organization is geared to process essentially one product. The subunits are normally designed to handle a separate phase of the processing. By contrast, an organization with a large number of separate projects tends to organize around these. If a firm has three separate contracts with the government, a team is set up to manage each project (the "project form" of organization structure). The basic work performed in a firm tends to dictate the appropriateness of certain types of structure, especially in grouping of tasks into subunits, called the *departmentation* process of organizing.

Burns and Stalker Studies

Another organizational feature of successful firms is that when tasks are finitely prescribed and structured (as with the assembly line), the organization is also finitely prescribed and structured. More open, flexible, problem-solving type tasks (management consulting) are most appropriately matched with an organization that is open, flexible, and adaptive. Tom Burns and G. M. Stalker referred to these two contrasting types of organizations as *mechanistic* and *organic*. In a study summarized in 1961, of twenty industrial firms in the United Kingdom, they concluded that structured tasks and mechanistic organizations are appropriate when conditions are stable; flexible tasks and organic, open structures are necessary when conditions are changing.[6]

Lawrence, Lorsch, and Associated Studies

In the United States the best-known studies relating tasks to organization structure are by Paul R. Lawrence, Jay W. Lorsch, and associates. They studied firms in the plastics, food, and container industries. They also found that more structured organizations functioned best in an environment that is structured, and less-formal structure is appropriate when uncertain, heterogeneous environmental conditions exist.[7] (Their studies are broad in magnitude and will be covered in more detail later.) In this context they concluded from their research that managers should tailor organizations to fit the task(s) and the people involved.

Jerald Hage and Michael Aiken came to similar conclusions in a study of sixteen health and welfare agencies. Organizations with routine work tended to concentrate more authority at the top of the organization and had more detailed, formal structures.[8]

Joan Woodward Studies

A final series of studies relating task and workflow technology to different types of organization structures resulted from the widely publicized research conducted by Joan Woodward and associates in Great Britain in the mid-1950's. The project involved the extensive study of over one-hundred British manufacturing companies. After searching for different variables that could be associated with similar types of organization structure, they concluded that the manufacturing processes of the firms provided the most direct relationship. They grouped the different tasks and manufacturing processes into three types: unit, mass (or batch), and process production. Unit production is the job-shop situation where each item is custom fabricated, usually to the specifications provided by the buyer. Mass or batch production involves situations where large numbers of similar items are produced by a firm to sell to customers, such as an automotive assembly line. Process production involves a continuous process to provide a product, the best example being a raw material like copper or oil.

When the firms in the study were grouped on this basis, the researchers found many similarities in the groupings that related to the features of the organizations. Firms using unit production had the fewest levels of management in their organization structure. The median was three versus four in mass production and six in process production. The median ratio of subordinates to supervisors was low in process manufacturing (1 to 15), high in mass production (1 to 48), and unit production was in-between (1 to 23). Management committees were much more common in process production than in either batch or unit. Many other differences were noted, such as the number of industrial workers to staff or support personnel, and the ratio of direct to indirect labor. However, for the concerns of this chapter, the most important conclusion of the study as stated by Woodward is that "the technology involved in carrying out the managerial function, is causally related to the structural . . . variations observed in manufacturing situations."[9] (The Lawrence and Lorsch, Burns and Stalker, and Joan Woodward studies will all be reviewed in more detail in chapter 15, on organization design.)

Relationships of Task to Leadership Style

The relationship of tasks to motivation was explored in chapter 11 and in earlier portions of this chapter: routine, repetitive tasks tend to be boring and have little intrinsic motivation. If there is little psychological reward in performing particular tasks, it generally means that leaders must be more forceful in getting work done. If tasks are interesting and challenging, they will willingly be performed by the worker because of the associated rewards, requiring a less-directive approach in supervision. In viewing organizations today, those with simple, routine tasks are generally typified by more directive, autocratic leaders, and those with more open, problem-solving tasks are typified by leaders who are less reliant on sanctions involving force and pressure.

Relationships of Task to Planning and Control System

Routine, standardized tasks are predictable because of their stability. They are associated with many knowns, such as the time of the job cycle, the costs involved in resources, and the specifications of the output that results (producing breakfast food). Nonroutine, problem-solving type tasks have few "knowns" in relation to costs, scheduling, or performance (for example, research involved in finding a cure for cancer). Detailed planning and control systems can be used with routine, standardized tasks because of the information available. More flexible, less-detailed systems must be used with uncertain tasks such as those involved in research and development. Thus the nature of the tasks dictates the need and feasibility of using different types of planning and control systems.

Relationships of Task to Internal and External Cultures

The influence of tasks in management is associated with two other considerations important in the functioning of organizations. These are the internal organization climate and the influence of broader environmental considerations associated with the culture of regions or nationalities. Structured tasks tend to generate structured organizations and a restrictive internal climate in which emphasis is placed on compliance. Less-structured tasks tend to be associated with a more open, permissive climate in which greater independence is encouraged.

The external culture seems to have a major influence in determining whether people will accept and tolerate routine tasks. Charles L. Hulin and Milton R. Blood conducted some extensive studies of job enlargement and found that different plants in different geographical locations tended to have workers who either liked or disliked routine tasks. In examining why different workers displayed these preferences, they found that in rural areas where the workers were more identified with traditional middle-class norms like the Puritan work ethic, they disliked routine tasks. In urban areas where the workers did not have the identification with the middle-class cultural norms evidenced in the United States, there was a far higher tolerance of routine tasks.[10]

SPECIAL CONSIDERATIONS RELATING TO TECHNOLOGY

Up to this point, our concern has been with how the tasks of an organization influence many other internal variables, such as motivation, structure, and leadership styles. In some instances these conclusions also relate to technology, because technology is one of the most important factors accounting for the condition of the tasks of an organization. This portion of the chapter is devoted to viewing technology as a separate variable in organizations. To do this it will be necessary to identify some of the dimensions of technology that tend to be most critical in the functioning of organizations. These dimensions are shown in figure 12-2.

Common Dimensions	Technology Continuum	
Scientific nature of operations	(elementary)	(pushing state of the art)
Knowledge required of people	(simple)	(high level)
Sophistication of methods	(low)	(high)
Complexity of machinery	(low)	(high)
Automation	(low)	(high)
Man-machine interface	(simple)	(complex)

Fig. 12-2. Technology variable

Technology is the application of science to practical purposes, and the most important dimension of technology is the degree to which the scientific aspect of the technological operations involves elementary concepts, as contrasted with those that are on the frontier of knowledge and thus pushing the state-of-the-art in that particular specialization (making routine laboratory tests versus developing new cancer experiments). Closely related to this is the second dimension, specifying the knowledge required of people who are involved in the operations. Where these knowledge requirements are minimal, technology may have little influence on the organization, but if these requirements involve advanced knowledge this will most likely have considerable influence on other organization characteristics—especially people requirements.

Dimensions three and four relate to the relative complexity and sophistication of the methods used in the workflow and the machinery that is part of it. The fifth dimension refers to the degree of automation in the workflow, which is a measure of the mechanization of the processes of the organization. From a sociotechnical standpoint, dimension six measures the complexity of the man-machine interfaces. Each of these dimensions is significant in identifying the nature of the technology of an organization which, in turn, is significant in accounting for the different conditions and processes that exist in a variety of work units.

Characteristics of
Advanced Technology

Technology is associated with three of the most critical features that differentiate modern organizations: the degree to which an organization experiences internal change; the predictability of internal operations and external environment; and the complexity of the overall organization. All three features are strongly influenced and frequently dominated by the technology associated with an organization and its processes. Chapter 8 linked technology to the change dynamics that occur in society. Technology is considered as generally the most dominant force in fostering environmental change. The rapidity of change within an organization is also closely associated with the technology involved in its tasks, operations, workflow, and products. The pace of technological change affects the degree of predictability and uncertainty associated with the functioning of an organization.

Under conditions of stable technology, the organization is more predictive and management is considerably simplified, because there are many knowns that aid in decision making. More uncertain, problem-solving technology, such as is evident in research and development or in industries where technology rapidly modifies operations, hinders the decision-making process. If it was possible to accurately predict when solar energy would be competitive from a cost standpoint, current power plants that dispense more pollutants could be constructed to phase out at that time. Sophisticated technology that is rapidly changing tends to maximize unknowns in a situation, and this introduces uncertainty into all phases of the management process—as evidenced by the difficulties in the 1960's and the 1970's of some of the nation's largest aerospace firms. Technology has also been associated with more mechanization, greater demands for capital, and more massive organizations, all of which contribute to this complexity.

THE AEROSPACE INDUSTRY AND TECHNOLOGY

On August 2, 1971, the Senate made the unprecedented move of lending Lockheed Corporation $250 million to keep it from bankruptcy. The next day, in an article entitled, "Lockheed May Survive, But Industry as Whole Faces Uncertain Future," *The Wall Street Journal* made the following observations:

"Aerospace executives, Defense Department officials, Wall Street analysts and bankers generally agree that the Lockheed debacle simply represents an extreme example of the sort of nightmares that already have afflicted other aerospace companies and that are likely to continue to afflict them in the future.

"Grumman Corp., for instance, has run into unforeseen technical and cost problems with its F14 Navy fighter plane; production costs of the combat jet threaten to exceed earlier estimates by some $2 billion, or $3 million a plane. General Dynamics lost $425 million on its disastrous venture into the commercial aircraft business some years back. Douglas Aircraft ran out of cash trying to build the DC9 passenger jet and had to be bailed out by a merger with McDonnell. Martin tried unsuccessfully to convert a World War II bomber into a line of commercial aircraft and finally wound up merging with a cement concern."

The article lists five factors that have placed the aerospace industry in such a "sorry state." The two relating to technology are as follows:

"——An unusually high dependency on evolving and often unknown technology, coupled with huge research and development outlays. This has the effect of increasing financial risk substantially, especially when a company is committed to a billion-dollar program (like the Lockheed L1011 trijet) that far exceeds its net worth.

"——A shrinking market for everything aerospace companies make: military, space and commercial aircraft systems. Not only will there be fewer major projects in years ahead, but those to come will be enormously more sophisticated and expensive and will likely be subject to more political pressures stemming from issues ranging from unhappiness with the Vietnam war to concern with the environment."

Reprinted with permission of *The Wall Street Journal.* © Dow Jones and Co., Inc., August 3, 1971. All Rights Reserved.

TECHNOLOGY AND ITS RELATIONSHIP TO OTHER CONTINGENCY VARIABLES

One should not lose sight of the point that it is the technology of the external environment that creates the technology internal to the firm. Advances are made in science, better materials are introduced, new machinery or machine processes are developed, and innovations like electronic data processing are discovered. These are then incorporated in the tasks, workflow, processing, or product improvements of the firm which, in turn, transfer the impact of technology to other variables, such as people and the structure of the organization.

Technology-to-People Relationships

Changes in technology affecting the methods, machinery, and processes of an organization may require people with different skills. Improved methodologies normally require more specialization and greater knowledge on the part of the worker (going from manual to automated material handling). As technology has increased so has the requirement for professional, scientific and white-collar workers. Supervisors need more scientific knowledge to supervise the technological tasks in their organization, with the result that people with scientific backgrounds (technocrats) have become more in demand in higher-level positions. The technology within an organization, more than any other factor, determines the organization's need for people of particular skill and training, although people and their knowledge can also be a source of technology.

Technology-to-Structure Relationships

Technology affects structure in a variety of ways. The most significant influence is in increasing the need for flexible, temporary organizations.

As noted earlier, more-stable organizations have more-formalized structures, while changing technology calls for a more adaptive structure. Alvin Toffler in his best seller, *Future Shock,* predicts that because of technology (which he calls the "growling engine of change"), we will see a collapse of rigid structures and a move to ad hoc or temporary structures, a form of organization he calls "Ad-hocracy."[11] Technology has also tended to increase the size of organizations. Advanced technology involved in communication satellites, jumbo jets, and mass transit has pushed the capital and resource requirements beyond the capacity of any individual firm. The imprint of technology is seen essentially in every organization structure. One invention alone, the computer, has altered in twenty-five years the structure of every major American corporation.

Relationships of Technology to Planning and Control

Complex, changing technology creates uncertainty in operations which reduces the number of "knowns" available to a manager. This makes planning and control more difficult. Detailed, specific systems give way to more flexible, results-oriented systems. Changing technology has established an environment that has tended to make traditional planning and control concepts outmoded. It has forced a search for new concepts and systems that has resulted in some of the major innovations in this respect. (See discussion of network analysis in chapter 24.) Differences in planning and control systems are primarily related to the certainty of the scheduling, cost, and performance information that is available to the organization.

IMPLICATIONS TASK AND TECHNOLOGY VARIABLES HAVE FOR MANAGING

The implications a knowledge of task and technology variables has for managing are fairly obvious in theory but difficult to apply. It is evident that task and technology variables are two of the most independent variables in organization behavior. A manager cannot effectively plan, organize, staff, direct, or control without considering the nature of the task and technology of an organization, because these variables strongly influence and often dictate the appropriateness of different concepts. A manager should be aware of the tasks and technology involved in the work of his organization and of other organizations so he will be effective in making decisions regarding the use of concepts and will appreciate why different concepts and techniques are desirable in different elements of the organization (such as production, marketing, and research and development).

As an example, the profile technique will again be used. One of the most common themes in organization theory since the Burns and Stalker studies referred to earlier is that more-formalized, stable organization structures are appropriate when tasks and the work environment are predictable and stable, whereas organic, less-formalized structures are more effective when tasks and the work environment are unstable and less predictive. This is shown in figure 12-3. The contrasting profiles are of an automotive assembly line and a marketing organization in a high-technology industry like copy machines.

On the assembly line, tasks are highly repetitive, standardized, with low autonomy and high sequential interdependence. The technology of operations is moderately complicated, primarily because of the automation involved. The knowledge required of the production worker is relatively simple. All of these characteristics are on the lower end of the scale for each dimension, which when projected up to the organization structure continuum (dashed arrow) calls for a mechanistic, stable structure.

Marketing and selling tasks in a high-technology industry have low repetition, standardization, and task interdependence. The autonomy of the salesman is high, and the technology of operations is complex and changing. Because of this, the knowledge required of personnel in marketing is also quite high. All of these ratings are on the righthand side of the dimension scales, which indicates a need for an organic, flexible structure. The marketing organization needs to be flexible to adjust to changing technology and to permit the freedom of action required to pursue selling and marketing activities.

SUMMARY

Tasks and technology include the processes and operations involved in the workflow of the organization. Tasks are the activities that people engage in as they contribute to this workflow. Technology is represented in the scientific complexity of the tasks but also in the machine processes, production methods, resource inputs, and other factors involved in the workflow of the organization. Technology is the application of scientific knowledge to practical purposes. Thus it is involved in marketing, finance, and other aspects of an organization and is not exclusively related to production.

Historically, task specialization through the division of labor has been one of the guiding principles leading to the efficiency of mass production. Assigning workers a limited number of simple tasks tends to maximize productivity and leads to physical efficiency, but it also results in psychological boredom. The assembly line is typified by the drudgery of workers repeating thousands of simple operations in a day.

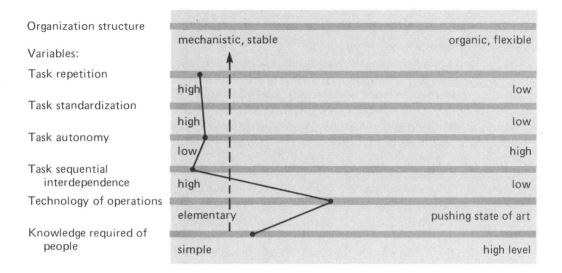

Production Assembly Line (Automotive)

Organization structure		
Variables:	mechanistic, stable	organic, flexible
Task repetition	high	low
Task standardization	high	low
Task autonomy	low	high
Task sequential interdependence	high	low
Technology of operations	elementary	pushing state of art
Knowledge required of people	simple	high level

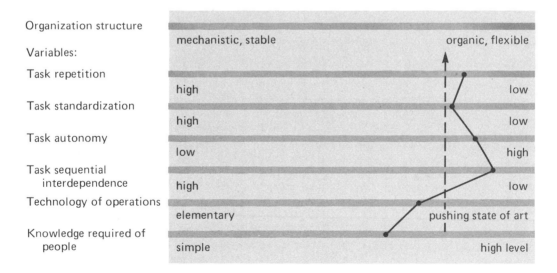

Marketing in a High-Technology Industry (Copy Machines)

Organization structure		
Variables:	mechanistic, stable	organic, flexible
Task repetition	high	low
Task standardization	high	low
Task autonomy	low	high
Task sequential interdependence	high	low
Technology of operations	elementary	pushing state of art
Knowledge required of people	simple	high level

Fig. 12-3. Profiles of two situations relating task and technology variables to the need for stable or flexible
organization structures

Job enrichment has been introduced to broaden jobs and make them psychologically more satisfying. Job-enrichment programs have caught hold with American industry, and they now involve well-established practices that are considered to be beneficial, even though research results are conflicting.

The tasks of an organization from a contingency standpoint deserve careful consideration by management, since they strongly influence the condition of the other variables that predominate in organizations. The nature of the tasks performed in an organization determines the skills required and even the psychological orientation of people necessary to perform them.

Tasks determine the appropriateness of different types of organization structure, as well as the concepts and systems that are applicable in the establishing of planning and control systems. Tasks have been too long ignored in management studies, because they comprise the basic element that influences the entire management superstructure of an organization.

Technology is important primarily because the condition of the technology associated with the operations of an organization establishes such characteristics as the rate of change, predictability, and complexity of the organizational environment.

QUESTIONS FOR STUDY
AND DISCUSSION

1. Explain the difference between tasks and the technology of an organization. How are they related?
2. What impact do tasks and technology have on the organization and on other variables such as structure, people, and organizational climate? How do they differ in their influence?
3. Using the dimensions of tasks contained in figure 12-1, indicate where the tasks involved in the following jobs would fall on each of the dimension continuums:
     A. dishwasher in a restaurant
     B. life-insurance salesman
     C. a computer programmer
     D. nurse
     E. college president
     F. aircraft assembler
     G. long-distance operator
4. For each of the positions contained in question 3, to what degree is division of labor involved in this job? If you were assigned to study each job in terms of enriching it, how would you change the jobs?

5. Do all people want enriched jobs? Justify your answer.
6. Explain how each of the following sets of tasks influences the people requirements, organization structure, and planning and control concepts used in that organization:
    A. instruction of college classes
    B. operating a local bakery with ten employees
    C. a work unit assigned to assemble radios
    D. the research group for a pharmaceutical company
    E. a city fire department
    F. a work unit tying flies to sell to fishermen
7. Explain how technology has influenced the following industries:
    A. automotive   E. certified public accounting (CPA).
    B. restaurant   F. advertising
    C. farming   G. insurance
    D. skiing

Case Problem:

REPORTING REQUIREMENTS IN SOCIAL WORK

In the following case, Bill is a regional welfare supervisor, and Diane is one of his professional social workers. Diane's work is average or better, but Bill is experiencing certain problems with her performance and in their relationship. One afternoon as it approaches 5:00 P.M., the following conversation takes place between the two of them.

Bill: Diane, I've been checking the files and I notice that you still have not finished last month's reports, which were due ten days ago. Also, on the portion you did complete, you were very sketchy in your descriptions—and some of those figures don't look quite right.

Diane: You know I have been spending many hours in the past two weeks with the Wilkinson and Johnston families. What's more important, anyway? Having food on their tables or those darned reports?

Bill: Diane, you know we've discussed that before. Sure these reports are drudgery, but it's a part of your job. You realized that when you transferred into this office.

Diane: Are you implying that I'm not doing my job? I stayed three nights last week and haven't restricted myself to a 40-hour

> week since I began. I don't think anyone could say I'm not giving the State their money's worth.

Bill: I'm not criticizing you, Diane, but one of our responsibilities is those reports, and we've got to arrange your workload so that you can work them in.

Diane: That's easy to say, but a little help from on top would help. I spent at least four or five hours this week trying to research our policy on aid for inadequate housing. That Wilkinson house is a disaster. The roof leaks, and the front porch is about to fall off. Even after I took action I'm not sure I did the right thing—our policies are so vague. I'll probably get in trouble for that too. They want you to do a job around here, but they sure don't want to give you any help doing it.

Bill: I know you work long hours and at times things do get pretty fuzzy, but your job description clearly gives you the responsibility to complete the necessary reports accurately and on time. Either you figure out how to get them done that way, or I'm going to have to note this discrepancy on your next performance rating.

How do you explain the behavior of these two people?
Why doesn't Diane do the reports?
How does she establish the priorities in her work?
How would you handle the situation if you were Bill?
Would job enrichment help?

Case Study:
TECHNOLOGICAL CHANGE IN THE CALCULATOR INDUSTRY

One of the markets that has experienced the most dramatic change in the past fifteen years has been business machines and, more specifically, calculators. The original mechanical calculators were bulky, slow to operate, and would normally perform only addition, subtraction, multiplication, and division. The electronics industry created electronic calculators that are small enough to fit in one's hand, will perform many more operations, and are only a fraction of the unit cost.

These electronic calculators have an electronic brain (called the chip) the size of a fingernail that performs the calculations. The development and mass production of the chip (called MOS-LSI for metal-oxide semiconductor—large-scale integration) have driven prices down and made the industry highly competitive. In the January 14, 1975 issue of *The Wall Street Journal* (page 30), it was reported that in 1972 there were 40 companies producing minicalculators; 3 years later fewer than 20 existed —with less than a dozen firms expected to remain in competition in the next 6 months. The chip cost $20.00 in 1970 and by 1975 it had dropped to $3.00. Time to assemble a calculator in 1972 was 25 to 30 minutes; 3 years later it took less than 10. All of this created a chaotic market in which industry sales increased 400 percent in 3 years, prices plummeted, and technical and price competition left more than half of the competing firms by the wayside.

How do you think this technology has affected *internal* conditions of the calculator firms?

How has it probably affected the firm's business functions like marketing, production, research and development, and finance?

How has it probably affected the management functions of planning, organizing, staffing, directing, and controlling?

How might it have affected the contingency variables of purpose and goals, people, structure, and tasks?

Footnotes

1. *Salt Lake Tribune*, April 1, 1973, p. 10A.
2. Parade Poll, *Parade Magazine*, June 3, 1973, pp. 17–18.
3. J. Richard Hackman and Edward E. Lawler III, "Employee Reactions to Job Characteristics," *Journal of Applied Psychology Monograph*, Vol. 55, No. 3 (June 1971), contained in W. E. Scott and L. L. Cummings, *Readings in Organizational Behavior and Human Performance* (Homewood, Ill: Richard D. Irwin, Inc., 1973), p. 229.
4. William E. Reif, "A Method of Selecting Jobs with the Greatest Potentiality for Enrichment," mimeograph of speech presented at Mountain-Plains Management Conference, Park City, Utah, October 11, 1973.
5. Paul R. Lawrence and J. W. Lorsch, *Organization and Environment* (Homewood, Illinois: Richard D. Irwin, Inc., 1969), p. 158.
6. Tom Burns and G. M. Stalker, *The Management of Innovation* (London: Tavistock Publications, 1961).
7. Paul R. Lawrence and Jay W. Lorsch, *op. cit.*, p. 182.

8. Jerald Hage and Michael Aiken, "Routine Technology, Social Structure, and Organization Goals," *Administrative Science Quarterly*, September, 1969, pp. 366–76.

9. Joan Woodward, *Industrial Organization: Theory and Practice* (London: Oxford University Press, 1965), p. 248.

10. Charles L. Hulin and Milton R. Blood, "Job Enlargement, Individual Differences, and Worker Responses," *Psychological Bulletin*, Vol. 69, No. 1 (1968), pp. 41–55.

11. Alvin Toffler, *Future Shock* (New York: Bantam Books, 1970). See Chapter 7, "Organization: The Coming Ad-Hocracy."

Manager Profile

Adolph M. Quilici
Ordnance Engineering Division
FMC Corporation
San Jose, California

Background and Experience

Adolph completed a bachelor's degree in mechanical engineering from the University of Santa Clara in 1953. He subsequently became employed with the Ordnance Engineering Division of FMC Corporation in San Jose, California. While employed there, he completed graduate management courses at the University of Santa Clara and the Advanced Management Program at the Harvard Graduate School of Business.

FMC, headquartered in Chicago, is an over two-billion dollar corporation in terms of annual sales and has 143 plants. Adolph is currently manager of the Ordnance Engineering Plant in San Jose. This division specializes in research, development, and design of armored personnel carriers for the Department of the Army, track landing vehicles for the Marine Corps, and high-mobility wheel vehicles for commercial use in the timber and other industries.

Primary Responsibilities

1. He is totally responsible for all business and engineering functions related to the Ordnance Engineering Division. This involves marketing, accounting,

personnel, design engineering, manufacturing engineering, an experimental shop, and other related functions.

2. The Ordnance Engineering Division is a decentralized profit center that is expected to generate profits and a favorable cash flow for the corporation. Annual sales amount to $25 million.

3. There are 1200 employees in his division, of whom 400 are engineers. The division is expected to provide work for the manufacturing divisions of the company through designing ground transportation vehicles they can bid on.

Insights

"Our industry operates in a volatile environment caused by sophisticated technology and changing Department of Defense requirements. We must be flexible, both in organization structure and in the methods we use. Since we have many ongoing projects, we use a matrix form of organization structure with functional departments established vertically and program responsibilities extending horizontally. This structure meets our needs, because it is both efficient and adaptive.

"We find long-range planning to be one of our most significant management processes. We have a formal planning procedure where we forecast five years into the future. I review this annually on a personal basis with the president of the company. It involves considerable negotiation. Our plans include objectives, strategies, contingency plans, and financial projections.

"Success in our organization is dependent on a willingness to work, being able to get along with peers, a commitment to the organization, and above all, a positive attitude. We attempt to identify early in an individual's career whether they have management potential. If they do, we put them on a 'nuggets list' and develop a program to deliberately build and broaden them through work experiences."

PART VI

The Structure and Functioning of Organizations

Establishing an Organization Structure

How does organizing relate to the other management processes?

What steps are involved in setting up an organization structure?

On what basis can different subunits be organized?

How are horizontal and vertical integration achieved?

How are individuals tied in to an organization structure?

When are committees appropriate?

Two engineers in an aerospace company were discussing the recent appointment of Mark Bowen as manager of the new space-development contract the company had been awarded by NASA. One said, "You know, the reason Mark got that job is because he's such a good organizer. When he's in charge of a project, everyone knows what he's supposed to do. Bowen assigns specific tasks to each unit, makes sure everybody gets detailed job assignments, and provides a central plan for everyone to follow. If some job isn't handled right, you can immediately pinpoint the responsibility because of the way everything has been spelled out. You should attend his Monday morning staff meetings! Each organization head reports in detail on how his phase of the project is going. It's just like clockwork. There aren't any loose ends when Mark heads up a project."

The other engineer thought for a minute and then responded, "Yeah, that's right, but I worked on a project Mark was in charge of, and all those requirements and procedures drove me crazy. You're supposed to do your job the exact way outlined—and nothing else. It seems like you don't have the freedom and flexibility to really exert yourself. Talk about red tape! Everything has to be checked and doublechecked. If you ever mess up, there's always someone assigned to follow your tracks so it'll be corrected. He runs a tight ship, but it sure takes a lot of manpower to get the coordination and follow-up he demands."

DEFINING ORGANIZATION STRUCTURE

In chapter 1 it was noted that the purpose of management is to efficiently and effectively achieve organizational objectives. Organizing is one of the primary processes a manager engages in to achieve the ends of an enterprise. Organizations become effective through managers coordinating and integrating manpower and resources. However, as indicated in the above incident, there is considerable controversy over the nature and use of organization concepts. Contrary to the desires of traditional writers, no one best way to organize has yet evolved, just as there is no one best way to motivate or to design jobs.

Organization, organizing, and *organization structure* are terms often used interchangeably but require more precise definition as one moves into organization theory. In considering General Electric or the city government of San Francisco as an organization, the term can encompass all of the people, resources, facilities, policies, regulations, methods, tasks, and many other factors that comprise these separate entities. However, in a narrower sense, the organization of General Electric or the City of San Francisco consists of designated authority relationships and duties that govern the official activities of individuals employed by these organizations. *Organizing* is more properly defined as a three-phase process of: (1) designating tasks and activities, (2) grouping these into subunits and positions, and (3) establishing relationships among the resultant elements for the purpose of achieving common objectives.

Organization *structure* or organization design results from the organizing process and *is the system of relationships, formally prescribed and informally developed, that governs the activities of people who are dependent upon each other for the accomplishment of common objectives.* The organization structure should coordinate and integrate the use of resources and the activity of people so that synergy results. Organizing as a process is closely interwoven (from a systems standpoint, it displays many interdependent relationships) with the other management processes. A sound structure facilitates planning and control, since it is established to marshall resources to carry out a plan. It is an aid in decision making, because authority is given to certain individuals to make specific decisions. It improves communication by identifying who is to be contacted in regards to particular problems and by providing channels of communication. It results in efficiency as a result of the division of labor and task specialization. Historically organizing has been central to the study of management. Classical writers provided more guidelines and principles in relation to organizing than in any other management process.

BENEFITS OF GOOD ORGANIZATION

When Director of Personnel Administration for the National Industrial Conference Board, S. Avery Raube concluded from studying member organizations that the following benefits accrue from sound organizational planning:

—Disposes of conflicts between individuals over jurisdiction
—Prevents duplication of work
—Decreases likelihood of "run-arounds"
—Makes communication easier through keeping the channels clear
—Shows promotional possibilities useful in executive development
—Provides a sound basis for appraisal and rating of individual performance
—Aids in wage and salary administration

—Permits expansion on the basis of manageable units without killing off executives through giving each too heavy a load
—Through sound planning you can provide for future expansion and new opportunities
—Increases cooperation when each person knows what he is responsible for and to whom he is responsible

Taken from S. Avery Raube, *Company Organization Charts* (New York: National Industrial Conference Board, 1954), pp. 7–13.

DIFFERENT TYPES OF ORGANIZATIONS

There are many different methods for classifying organizations, but two general distinctions are critical for the discussions contained in chapters 13 through 17. These are the differences between formal and informal organizations and between bureaucratic and adaptive structures.

Formal and Informal Organizations

Formal organization is that which is legally constituted or decreed by those in authority. It represents how an organization is "supposed" to function based on the deliberate assignment of tasks, functions, and authority relationships. Formal structures are actually fiction, because organizations do not operate as prescribed. *Informal* organization represents "reality," how the organization actually functions. After a formal structure is established, the informal organization emerges naturally within its framework. It results from continued social interaction, and modifies, confirms, or expands the formal structure. For example, the formal structure may designate that all personnel problems be taken directly to the Head of Personnel, but if individuals find they can get more help by going to the Associate Director of Personnel, they will be inclined to do so.

One of the important distinctions between formal and informal organizations is the impersonal nature of the former versus the personal nature of informal. Organizing on a formal basis is restricted to establishing positions—the staffing process involves selecting particular individuals to fill these. *Informal* organization results when the incumbent of a certain position develops social relationships with others in the organization. Establishing a position as Assistant to the Director of Personnel is a formal organization action. To assign Sue Johnson to handle this position is part of the staffing process. But informal structure comes into existence when Sue assumes the position, and through social interaction develops continuing relationships with the Director of Personnel and other individuals throughout the company.

Both formal and informal relationships affect the organizational role of an individual. Either may predominate, but managers are often inclined to underestimate the significance of these informal ties. (Formal structure is the topic covered in this chapter and chapter 14. Chapter 16 includes an analysis of informal organization in social systems.)

Bureaucratic versus Adaptive Organizations

Classical organization theory called for a high degree of structure. Taylor, Fayol, and others urged that tasks be specifically designated and that a precisely defined network of functional assignments and authority relationships be established. Fayol emphasized that sound organization principles bring the coordination, order, and structure necessary to integrate group activity. He felt that there should "be an appointed place for every employee and every employee in his appointed place."[1]

Max Weber, a German-born sociologist and a contemporary of Fayol, was a powerful proponent of structured formal organizations, or of *bureaucracy* as he called it. Bureaucracy involves specialization, adherence to fixed rules, and a sharply defined authority hierarchy. Bureaucracy in recent years has taken on the negative connotation of red tape, cumbersome structures, and over-organization. However, as the term is used in organization theory, it represents the detailed elaboration of formal organization structure in the form of position descriptions, authority delegations, procedures, rules, and designated functional relationships.

In recent years modern organization theorists have questioned the value of bureaucratic structures—especially as a more dynamic environment has forced organizations to be more adaptive. Thus there has been a movement toward less-rigid structures with less reliance on formally prescribed organization relationships. (Chapters 15 and 16 will cover this trend.) Classical theory is based on applying principles developed through reason to get a predictable response, which we have referred to as the rational (or *mechanistic*) approach to organizing. Modern organic views call for less structure, primarily because the participants are better educated and seek greater freedom in their work, but also because a more dynamic environment requires a more flexible, adaptive structure.

---

1. Henry Fayol, *General and Industrial Management* (London: Sir Isaac Pitman and Sons, Ltd., 1949, p. 35).

STEPS IN THE FORMAL ORGANIZATION PROCESS

Classical theory assumed that failure to specify and designate organizational relationships would result in confusion, conflict, and inefficiency. Therefore, the more that activities of individuals and subgroups could be prescribed, the more efficiently and smoothly the organization would function. Based on this premise, organization theory was divided into specific phases, accompanied by principles not nearly so precise, which were to serve as the guides for establishing an organization structure. These phases can be summarized in four steps, outlined in figure 13-1. Some of the terminology is of more recent vintage, but the principles are classic in nature. A controversy exists regarding whether organizations are established from the bottom up or top down. However, classical theory tends to support the top down approach.

1. Subdividing the total organization into subgroups—horizontal differentiation.
    A. Functionalization
    B. Departmentation
    C. Establishing support units
2. Establishing authority relationships—vertical differentiation.
    A. The scalar chain, or hierarchy
    B. Span of control
    C. Unity of command
    D. Supervisor-subordinate relationships
    E. Determining the type and scope of authority
    F. Line and staff relationships
    G. Centralization and decentralization
3. Interrelating the hierarchy—horizontal integration.
    A. Organizational manuals
    B. Functional specification
    C. Procedures
    D. Committees
    E. Task forces and temporary structures
4. Fitting in the individual—job definition.
    A. Division of work
    B. Position descriptions
    C. Operations sheets and job specifications
    D. Rules and regulations

Fig. 13-1. Formal steps in establishing an organization structure

Horizontal and Vertical Differentiation (Steps 1 and 2)

Differentiation, as it relates to organizing, involves the differences in the form and nature of the formal structure. As organizations grow in size, jobs become more specialized, and more subunits are established so that the organization becomes more fractured or differentiated. Step 1 deals with the various methods and organizational forms that are available to the organizer to implement this differentiation process. Functionalization involves subdividing the functions of the organization. Departmentation encompasses the optional forms available for establishing subunits or departments.

Step 2 comprises vertical differentiation. Different levels in the structure are established through assigning certain individuals and groups to report to other groups and individuals at higher levels in the organization. This establishing of an authority hierarchy involves some of the most important decisions a manager makes. (Because of the many concepts relating to step 2, chapter 14 will be devoted entirely to this topic.)

Horizontal Integration and Job Definition (Steps 3 and 4)

Steps 1 and 2 involve splitting the organization and subdividing it into smaller and smaller pieces. This increases in step 3 the need for mechanisms that will integrate the parts for the good of the whole. These include accomplishing integration through the use of procedures, committees, clear functional statements, and other similar approaches. Lawrence and Lorsch have developed the position that organizational processes consist of two vital but opposing forces. Differentiation is splintering the organization into more specialized groups and tasks, resulting in the need for countering integrative mechanisms to obtain synergy.

Steps 1 through 3 all deal with the total organization and its subunits. However, organizing is not complete until the individual is tied into the structure. Unless each individual knows what to do and how to do it, the full benefits of organization principles cannot be achieved. This is accomplished in step 4, through the previously discussed concept of division of labor and establishment of position descriptions, operations sheets, and rules and regulations.

(The balance of this chapter will be devoted to the concepts and classifications associated with steps one, three, and four in the formal organization process. The discussion of the concepts will be sequenced in accordance with the outline in figure 13-1.)

FUNCTIONALIZATION

Functionalization is the division of the total work and activity of the organization into separate functions. The whole is broken into parts (or the functions to be performed). If an organization decides to produce and sell a product, the functions established would be production, marketing, finance, and so on. When functionalization involves dividing up functions into individual tasks for workers to perform, it is a form of division of labor. To a large degree, the basic purpose of the organization determines the functions required to fulfill this purpose. Functionalization is important when a new organization structure is being initiated or when reorganization is under consideration; but since it is infrequent and largely determined by the technology associated with the purpose and product lines or services of an organization, it is not one of the central concepts of organization design.

DEPARTMENTATION

Departmentation is the process of establishing subunits like departments, sections, or divisions in an organization. It is a method of horizontal differentiation that becomes necessary as organizations grow in size or increase in their activity. The subunits developed through the process of departmentation are categorized in different ways, depending on whether the classifier is a sociologist, anthropologist, public administrator, or business analyst. For our purposes, the classical business nomenclature will be used. Following this approach, five different forms of departmentation are identified: *functional, product* (or program), *process, geographical* (or territorial), and *customer* (or clientele).

Functional Departmentation

This form of departmentization is associated with functionalization. Subunits are established based on the functions performed in the organization. Therefore, people involved in engineering are grouped into a common organization, and separate units are formed in marketing, production, and so on. Historically, this has been the most common type of departmentation and still tends to predominate in organizations—especially at the operations level. However, rarely will an organization follow the same form of departmentation through all levels. All organizations tend to be mixtures of different forms of departmentation, but functional departmentation is in the aggregate and, considering all levels and all organizations, the most common type. Figure 13-2 is a simplified

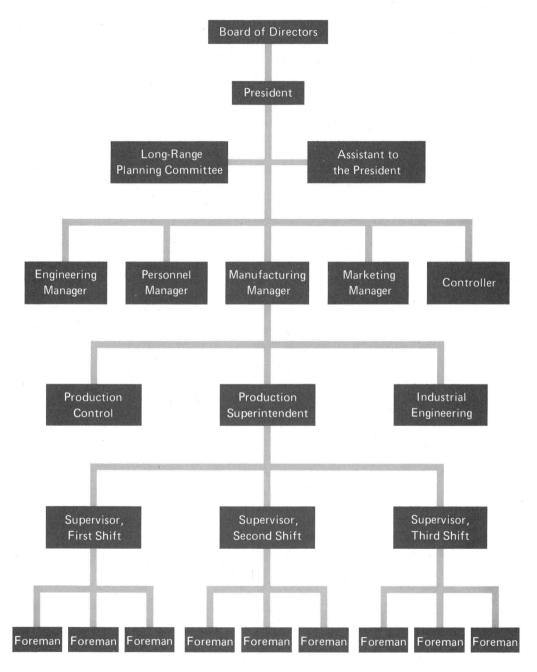

Fig. 13-2. Abbreviated organization chart for a manufacturing plant

organization chart for a manufacturing plant. The managers directly under the president head up functional departments.

Functional departmentation offers many advantages. It provides functional specialization based on division of labor, which is heralded to be the source of efficiency in production-type organizations. In practice, functional departmentation has proven to be highly pragmatic and adaptable in a variety of situations. To a considerable extent, this is derived from the ease it provides in supervision. It is obviously simpler for a supervisor like an engineer to direct people trained in the same expertise than it is for someone to supervise individuals performing a variety of tasks involving diverse fields of specialization.

The disadvantages of functional specialization involve the difficulties in integrating the functions to meet the needs of the total organization. Suboptimization frequently takes place because managers in the functions tend to make decisions that optimize their function but may be suboptimal for the total organization. Functional organizations are harder to control, because no unit individually produces an end item or independently accomplishes organization objectives. Profit centers are difficult to establish, and integration at the top of the organization becomes more critical. Also, people tend to be trained more narrowly as a result of the high degree of specialization.

Product Departmentation

Under product departmentation, subunits are organized about products—as opposed to functions. (General Motors has the Chevrolet, Oldsmobile, Pontiac, Buick, and Cadillac divisions representing this form of departmentation.) Since the 1950's, aerospace organizations have developed a more extreme form of product departmentation known as *project* (or *program*) *management*. Several varieties of program management exist, but basically it is a form of organization in which the total company is split up into smaller, independent groups based on different product lines. Thus if an aerospace firm is working on two different missile projects and producing two different planes, they would have four program organizations. Each would have its own engineering, marketing, production, and administrative departments. (See figure 13-3.) Product organizations make it easier to control products, but they also create integration problems in interrelating the multiproject activities of the entire organization, and it is more difficult for one individual to direct the heterogeneous tasks of a project. Since there is an "end item" produced by a division (missile or airplane), it is easier to monitor performance and maintain accountability. (The success of this form of departmentation in aerospace has resulted in its increased use in other industries.)

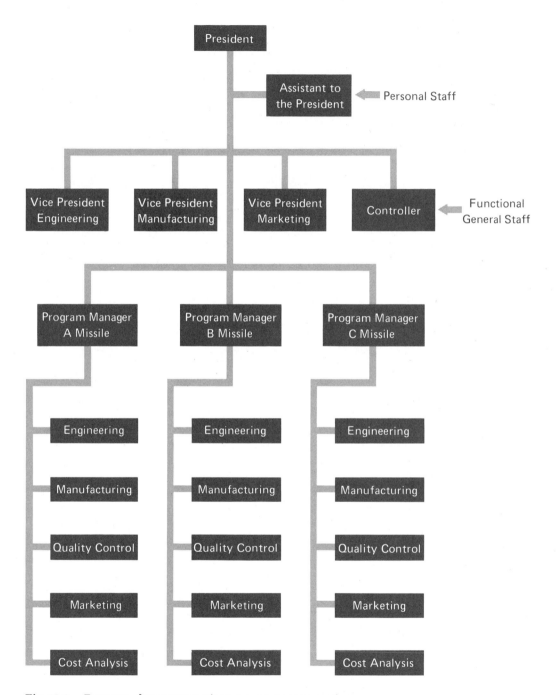

Fig. 13-3.   Program departmentation: an aerospace-project
management organization

WHAT'S NOT ON THE ORGANIZATION CHART

What it shows

1. Division of work into components. These components may be divisions or departments or they may be individuals. (Boxes on the conventional chart represent these units of work.)
2. Who is (supposed to be) whose boss—the solid lines on the chart show this superior-subordinate relationship, with its implied flow of delegated responsibility, authority, and attendant accountability.
3. Nature of work performed by the component
4. Grouping of components on a functional, regional, or product basis
5. Levels of management in terms of successive layers of superiors and subordinates

What the chart doesn't show

1. It does not show the degree of responsibility and authority exercised by positions on the same management level.
2. Distinguishing between line and staff is arduous, hazardous, and often inconsistent between companies.
3. Size and position of boxes do not necessarily reflect importance or status.
4. It does not show *all* the channels of contact or communication.
5. Shows only a few of the key links or relationships in the total organizational network
6. It does not show the informal organization that is a logical and necessary extension of the formal structure.

The essential value of the chart is the fact that it does strip the organization to the skeletal framework. For more complete documentation of what this chart means, companies rely on position guides, linear responsibility charts, statements of general responsibilities and relationships; indeed, the whole organization manual.

Abstracted from Harold Stieglitz, "What's Not on the Organization Chart," *The Conference Board RECORD* (November 1964), pp. 7–10.

Process Departmentation

In process departmentation, subunits are established based on the sequential phases of the production or refining process. It is most useful in companies with one basic product, where all operations relate to the processing of this product. (Oil refineries, mining operations, and some assembly lines are examples.) In a mining operation, the work units are established based on the sequential operations of extracting and refining the ore. In a factory making shirts, units are set up to sequentially receive the material, cut the patterns, distribute them to operators, sew the various seams, add the buttons, and button holes, and process the finished goods all the way through final inspection. For this type of manufacturing operation, process departmentation has proven to be the most efficient.

Geographical Departmentation

By the nature of the operations involved, many activities are most efficiently handled when units are established to cover specific territories. Post offices, sales territories, and Internal Revenue Service districts are set up on this basis to reduce costs and effort. It involves a method of covering broad-based operations by dividing them into smaller geographical units.

Customer Departmentation

In retail operations, satisfying customers is the dominant issue in being successful. Organizing to accommodate the customer is the most desirable thrust for this type of organization; therefore, department stores are set up with men's wear, women's wear, hardware, and such other departments to appeal directly to a specific type of customer. Banks use tellers, loan officers, and savings clerks to capitalize on customer departmentation. This is common also in wholesale activities, where sales units are designed to accommodate or appeal to specific categories of customers, like Westinghouse having a separate sales division to market appliances.

Critique of the Business
Departmentation Concept

The five-category basis of departmentation developed in classical theory has been subjected to considerable criticism by modern analysts. This method of classification is said to be primarily descriptive and to provide few prescriptive guidelines. Also, sociologists are concerned, since the nomenclature tells little about what actually happens in organizations. Others have said that distinctions such as "controlled operations" (production) versus problem-solving organizations (research and development) are much more important, because they have direct implications for the type of management concepts that are appropriate. It is also argued that most organizations involve such a hodgepodge of the various forms of departmentation that the traditional classifications are of limited value. There is some validity to all of these arguments, and ideally organization theorists will develop a more useful taxonomy in the future.

The one factor that is evident in these classifications is the value of making the dominant issue relating to competition in a particular industry central. In retailing—where marketing is predominant—the customer form of departmentation prevails; in aerospace—where performance on government contracts is critical—the product form is most common; and in mining—where massive extractive processes are existent—the process form is most successful. Certain types persist in different industries, in which they obviously fit the circumstances involved.

THE GROWING MANAGEMENT GAP

Allan Harvey, President, Dasol Corp.: Fifty years ago, most of our companies were small enough so that one chief executive had a pretty good idea of what was going on throughout the business. He could make decisions that took into account the business as a whole, including its suppliers, customers, and competitors, as an organic entity.

Then something called "scientific management" came into existence, and it led to breaking down the work of the business into separate and distinct parts. This took place first in the factory, but then it led to the functional organization of the enterprise, which assigned manufacturing to one executive, sales to another, and so forth, each with clearly defined authority and responsibility. Then as businesses grew still larger, there came the gospel of decentralization and the concept of the profit center, which dictated the breaking up of the business into units by geography or by product or by both.

And so what I think we have today is a business organized along nineteenth-century lines trying to do business in a twentieth-century environment. Our science and our technology view things as a whole. But our businesses are organized into bits and pieces, with an executive whose authority or responsibility is limited to one bit or one piece.

Functional Compared with
Product Organizations

The traditional departmentation classifications contain few primary issues in organization theory—with one exception. Functional departmentation works effectively in small organizations, but as they increase in size the integration problems become such that this form tends to be cumbersome and leads to empire building. In a plant of 1,000 employees it can be relatively easy for top management to coordinate operations when only ten to fifteen functionally specialized subunits are involved. However, when the organization has 50,000 employees and handles diverse product lines with geographically separated plants, integration borders on being impossible.

As organizations have become more differentiated, integration has become the central organizational problem in multicompany, multiproduct operations. (Problems in the past decade with big governments, conglomerates, and multinationals all attest to this.) To offset this, many have argued for semiautonomous units that can be more independently operated. However, it is not possible to make functional units semiautonomous, because each vertical channel (production, marketing, etc.) in the chain of command provides only one specialized part—or functional segment—of a total product or service. Thus many have argued for a move to product divisions and project management.

Systems theory is applicable in this argument. A company is a system in which efficient operation of parts is necessary to achieve high output (ultimately, profits). There is extremely strong interdependence among the parts in a functional organization, because if any part fails (marketing, production, etc.), the whole fails. Integration can only take place at the top in the organization. However, it can occur at lower levels in a product, or program, organization, because a project directly contributes to the good of the whole without this integration at higher levels.

If a division is successful in providing a missile under a government contract, it generates a profit for the company, and little integration is required with other divisions. There is some interdependence among the divisions, but it is a small fraction compared with a functional organization. Also, if one division fails (building airplanes), it will not cause the entire company to fail (unless it is such a large segment of the total business that it bankrupts the firm). However, if one department in a functional division fails (marketing), production cannot be successful on its own. The finest product in an industry cannot be profitable without a sales and distribution organization. Obviously program (product) organizations do not provide the one best way to organize, but they are appropriate for the large, diversified firm that is coming to dominate the American scene.

A further point to note is that of the thousands of managerial decisions made in an organization, only a small portion are made by top management, even though they are normally the most significant. The majority is made by middle managers, who, resulting from their long reign in a functional organization, inevitably make biased decisions that favor their specialization. Stated more simply, in functional organizations participants focus on functional goals. This creates special problems magnifying the need for integration, and for check and balance systems within highly specialized companies. Looking to the general manager as the sole source of integration in an organization and the one to emphasize product goals is unrealistic and has led to many problems. It also points to integration as one of the central organizational problems in the massive structures common in modern society.

Support and Auxiliary Units

Another type of horizontal differentiation is that related to the administrative functions of an organization. The need for specialized administrative units results from primarily two factors: as organizations grow in size, division of labor occurs in the support areas, just as it does in operating divisions. Also, as technology relating to administration has become more complex, experts are required to interpret laws, handle labor relations, conduct marketing research, and provide other administrative support. The difference between operating and support units is that *operating units* directly contribute to the objectives of the organization (a production unit working on the end product), whereas *support units* indirectly contribute to the accomplishment of objectives, by *assisting* the operating organizations.

Other terms such as *staff* and *auxiliary* are used in place of *support,* but they all have essentially the same meaning. They are units or positions that are more concerned with maintaining the organization (janitorial services, printing shops, personnel relations) or assisting those directly engaged in achieving the objectives of the organization (preparing studies, analyzing reports, developing recommendations, etc.). Supervisors knowledgeable in technological operations want to apply their energies and time in those activities related to their specialization. Administrative chores and followup activities involving support functions such as budgeting, personnel, and procurement are normally left to staff assistants. Types of staff units are as follows:

PERSONAL STAFF. Personal staff is composed of individual positions or units designed to personally assist an executive. Titles such as "assistant to" or "administrative assistant" are frequently used. The busy executive is likely to give any type of assignment to such assistants, although they normally serve in an information gathering, troubleshooting, or analytical capacity. Many times they will prepare correspondence, review reports, and even deal with lower-level managers in the name of the executive.

SPECIALIZED STAFF. This is a specialized form of departmentation relating to administrative functions. Accounting, personnel, purchasing, and computer operations are examples. A firm producing electronic gear does not exist to maintain accounts, hire and evaluate personnel, or purchase raw materials and components. These are purely support functions, which when grouped into separate departments provide a concentration of resources resulting in better equipment, more expertise in the staff personnel, and greater efficiency.

GENERAL STAFF. This is a carry-over military term from early management history. General staff units are not narrow like other support groups but are geared to provide assistance to top management that is broad in nature and cuts across departmental lines. There are two types of general staff—personal and functional. Personal involves a position such as "assistant to the president" where an individual serves as an extension of the president's eyes and ears. Functional general staff is most appropriately exemplified by vice presidents at a corporate office handling functions like marketing, industrial relations, engineering, and so on. They oversee the appropriate parallel functions at each plant on the basis of total company interest and objectives. Personal and functional general staff are shown in figure 13-3.

VERTICAL DIFFERENTIATION

In order to provide coordination and control in an organization it is necessary that there be a link between the executive at the top and lower level employees. This vertical series of interconnecting links representing levels in an organization is called the *chain of command*. This chain serves as a vehicle for decision making, communication, authority delegation, and for conducting in general the affairs of the organization. Just as an engineer designs a bridge in a certain way, so traditional writers felt that an organization had to be pieced together on a certain basis. Clear lines of authority should run from the top to the bottom. A supervisor should have just the right number of people reporting to him so that he can effectively direct and control their activities (*span of control, or span of management*).

In order to have the clarity and unity required in an organization, no subordinate should report to more than one supervisor (*unity of com-*

mand). The responsibility and authority of each supervisor should be clearly delineated in writing, and authority should be commensurate with the responsibility imposed. The extent and type of authority delegated should be clearly identified so that people in support activities are not given control over operations (line versus staff). The levels of authority should be kept to the minimum necessary to ensure control and unity in the organization. Traditional theory placed primary reliance on vertical differentiation in an organization, because it was intended that management control over the organization be exerted in this perpendicular fashion. (All of these concepts will be examined in the next chapter.)

HORIZONTAL INTEGRATION

The hierarchy establishes vertical channels of authority and communication flow within organizations. However, most activities and operations of an organization flow on a horizontal rather than vertical plane. At the working level, production and processing operations flow from workgroup to workgroup. Accordingly, there exists a major organizational problem of horizontal integration. Traditionally the concern has been with specifically identifying the functions and responsibilities of each unit and position. The various methods of achieving horizontal integration follow:

Organizational Manuals

The most common method for formalizing the functions and responsibilities of each unit (*functional specification*) is through establishing an organizational manual. This is made up of primary and subsidiary charts showing the formal organization as established, with functional statements specifying the activities that are to be conducted in each unit. Formal authority relationships are specified, and descriptions of the primary management positions are included. Manuals also occasionally contain statements of management philosophy, company objectives, and the principles that comprise the organization "creed." The functional statements in the manual are designed to ensure that all work is being covered, and that the segregation of functions and duties will obtain the mix and balance necessary to achieve organizational objectives.

Organizational Procedures

The primary processes of the organization characterized by horizontal flow require some regulation and direction if coordination is to be achieved. *Procedures* are established to assign appropriate responsibility to each organizational unit involved and to sequence the activities contained in the process. Each major function of an organization, such as marketing, finance, and production, normally has its own procedures. These are often vertical in functional departmentation, because essentially they exist within the chain of command. However, most of the procedures involving support functions such as planning, budgeting, personnel, and procurement cut horizontally or diagonally across the organization structure. For instance, the major steps in a budgeting procedure would most likely contain the following:

1. Establishment of the critical dates for submission of budgets and review by the budgeting department
2. Specification of the budget formats by the budget department
3. Preparation of estimates by the operating departments
4. Review of budget estimates by the central budget committee or by top management
5. Approval of the budget by top management

A budget procedure would, of course, be much more detailed. Its purpose is to assign responsibility and dictate the flow of the budget process both horizontally and vertically within the organization. Procedures are included here as a part of the organizing process, but it should be recognized that they are equally important to the management processes of planning and control.

Committees

One of the most common methods for achieving horizontal integration is through the use of committees. When an organizational process exists that cuts across departments, so that it is not within the domain of any one chain of command, a committee is often established, consisting of representatives from all of the involved units. (There are other uses of committees in organizations, but since the predominant objective is to attain "interest representation," our analysis of committees will be restricted to this usage.)

Committees are widely used in most organizations. In firms of over 10,000 employees, more than ninety-four percent use committees. Their use is primarily contingent on how essential an interest representation is to the organization. In a small business they find little use, but in governments or organizations like universities, committed to values that are democratic in nature, committees are at the heart of the administrative structure.

ADVANTAGES OF COMMITTEES.   Five advantages are associated with the use of committees:

1. They are an excellent device for obtaining group judgment and deliberation. They provide a means of bringing a wide variety of experience and knowledge to bear on a problem.
2. They ensure that the groups affected by a decision are involved in making the decision.
3. They are an excellent means of obtaining commitment to policies and decisions. This is especially important for voluntary organizations where commitment can be achieved through participation.
4. They are often important in developing managerial talent. The opportunity to participate in policy formulation is vital for aspiring managers.
5. They are a useful means of avoiding action and reducing pressure when an executive desires time and more information before moving ahead, an occurrence often seen in government.

DISADVANTAGES OF COMMITTEES.   Committees are frequently maligned by administrators. Six factors are associated with this dissatisfaction:

1. High cost is involved in committee action, especially in the time required of participants. One individual obviously can make a decision quicker, with fewer manhours involved, than can a committee.
2. Committees tend to be very slow to act.
3. Committees result in compromise decisions that therefore often represent only minor change from the status quo. Interest representation on a committee encourages decisions that at least partially pacify all major interests.
4. Under committee action no one individual is responsible. Furthermore, since committee work is normally an added assignment to an individual's normal job, vital matters are likely to drift from lack of attention and the splintering of responsibility.
5. Committees are of limited value in implementing policies or carrying out executive action. They are useful advisory groups but not action groups.
6. The interest representation concept of committees can encourage narrow, provincial views on the part of the participants charged with defending their particular interest. Another systems analogy is relevant here. If each member of the committee represents an interest (part), who is there to speak for or represent the total organization (the whole)?

CONTINGENCY CONSIDERATIONS IN USE OF COMMITTEES.   As in the application of other management concepts, contingency considerations are primary. The conditions in organizations that call for the use of committees tend to be the following: when interest representation is vital to the organization's purpose and values; when time permits deliberation and broad input such as in the formulation of objectives; when broad consensus is needed, such as in a voluntary organization; when strong leadership and quick executive action are not essential; during the formulation or policy development phase of a project but not during the policy implementation or execution phase.

MAKING COMMITTEES EFFECTIVE.   Since committees are an integral part of most organizations and since they are also commonly mismanaged, several pragmatic guides are proposed even though they represent oversimplifications. Committees should be kept small. The larger the committee, the more difficult it is to coordinate activities and reach decisions. Studies show that five people tend to be the preferred number, but when interest representation predominates the number is determined by the major interests involved.

Because of their tendency to move slowly and involve discussions tangential to their purposes, committees require strong but impartial chairpersons. The purpose and authority of the committee should be clearly defined. Before taking any action, goals should be established and a plan—including a timetable for completing segments of the work—developed. Before each meeting an agenda should be distributed, including copies of proposals or reports to be discussed. Where considerable information needs to be collected, a full-time staff should be assigned to expedite matters.

The above implies that the chairperson should be continually pressing for action. This is not always the case. At least initially, when committee members are not familiar with each other, time should be allowed for these interpersonal relations to develop before pressing for decisions. Another primary skill of a chairperson is knowing how long debates should continue, which will vary depending on the circumstances.

Using Temporary Structures: The Task Force

In recent years there has been greater reliance on temporary structures like the task force to obtain horizontal integration in organizations. A task force is similar to ad hoc committees, except the assignment is full-time rather than part-time. An ad hoc committee is set up for a specific purpose and terminates once its task is completed. A task force functions the same way, except the individuals are temporarily loaned to the task force on a full-time basis for the duration of the assignment, after which they return to their permanent organizations. It is common to use such a group to handle current problems or special projects within the broader organization. If the company is undertaking a special project (evaluating a potential merger) that requires representatives from marketing, engineering, production, and finance, using a task force to obtain integrated coordination may be beneficial.

INTEGRATING THE INDIVIDUAL INTO THE ORGANIZATION STRUCTURE

The fourth step in organizing involves fitting the individual into the organization structure through job design and task specialization. In management terminology this involves both a staffing and an organizing function, but no formal structure is effective until the role of each individual is defined. The four aspects of formal job definition follow.*

Position Description

A *position* (also job) *description* details the duties of any individual worker and defines the scope of authority associated with that position. Figure 13-4 is an example of a typical position description. Position descriptions are not intended to include all activities an individual is to undertake, and they do not specify how to perform them. The purpose of the position description is to ensure that the individual understands the basic duties he or she is assigned in the organization, and it is a method for the organization to ensure that all functions are ultimately tied to individual jobs.

Operations Sheets and Job Specifications

The position description defines the duties of an individual, and operations sheets specify how these duties are to be performed. Such methods do not normally apply to management positions but are primarily used to describe physical tasks involving a sequence of motions or operations to assemble a unit or machine a part. An *operations sheet* (also called operator's chart) in assembly work shows the sequential motions of the right and left hands in completing an assembly operation. *Job specifications* are the human requirements for an individual filling a specific position. Job specifications normally involve (1) education and skill re-

---

*Division of labor, involving the differentiation of functions into fewer and more specialized tasks, was explored in chapter 12. The advantages of specialization in terms of efficiency versus the disadvantages, in terms of boredom, were also discussed there.

POSITION DESCRIPTION	Division: OPERATIONS:	Date: 1/20/76
	Department: INDUSTRIAL ENGINEERING	Grade: 09

Position Title:

ANALYST, WORK MEASUREMENT

SUMMARY

Under guidance of the Supervisor of Methods and Standards or an industrial engineer, conducts work-measurement studies related to all aspects of product manufacturing.

DUTIES

1. Develops work-measurement procedures and conducts time-and-motion studies to promote efficient and economical utilization of personnel and facilities.

2. Reviews, evaluates, and consolidates standard time summaries.

3. Reviews and evaluates work performance and recommends alternate methods for more efficient work accomplishment.

4. Analyzes work study data and equipment specifications to establish time and production standards.

5. Performs other duties as assigned.

EDUCATION AND EXPERIENCE/KNOWLEDGE (ABILITY REQUIREMENT)

1. Normally, must be a high school graduate with two years of specialized training or equivalent in experience.

2. Requires a minimum of one year of related, progressively responsible experience, enabling incumbent to review and evaluate current work procedures and recommend improved and alternate methods.

Fig. 13-4. A typical position description

quirements, (2) problem-solving difficulties associated with the job, and (3) physical factors and working conditions.

Rules and Regulations

Procedures are required to control activities of individuals holding positions, just as they are required to integrate the activities of groups within organizations. However, a distinction in terminology must be made: management dictates aimed specifically at regulating the behavior of individuals are called *rules*. A rule is a precise restriction on individual action, such as a "no smoking in warehouses" or "no gambling on premises." As another example, a regulation like "no discounts on accounts over 30 days old" also controls to an extent what an individual does in an organization.

DIMENSIONS OF ORGANIZATION STRUCTURE

As with the other variables constituting the contingency model of management, the different attributes of structure can most accurately be portrayed as a series of continuums. These attributes are shown in figure 13-5. Based on the descriptions contained in this chapter, the terms are self-explanatory. Under contingency assumptions, interpreting attributes as a continuum is essential, because in comparing organizations it is the relative differences among these attributes that is so important in understanding organization structure and in making decisions.

IMPLICATIONS OF FORMAL ORGANIZATION CONCEPTS FOR THE MANAGER

Knowing how far to go in formally establishing an organization structure is another of those "fine lines" that a manager must discover, based on the particular situation at hand. All structures should not be formalized to the same degree. A formal structure should theoretically provide order, ensure coordination, and make it possible for each unit and each individual to know what is to be done in the context of the broader organization. It is also a tool the manager uses to emphasize the function that is most critical to the success of the firm, based on the competition of the marketplace. In addition, it provides the means the manager has of balancing the functions in the organization so as to attain the desired synergy.

However, in many respects formal organization concepts are deceptive in their simplicity. Changing functional assignments and a position

Formal Dimensions	_Continuum_	
Scale (size)	(1) few employees	many (25,000)
Hierarchy	(1) few levels	many (15)
Authority delegation	centralized	decentralized
Span of control	(1) few subordinates	many subordinates (40)
Integration of activities	low requirement	high
Geographical dispersion	(1) one location	many locations (20)
Job specifications	general	detailed
Formalization	few rules and procedures	many rules and procedures
Departmentation	Type: functional, program, territorial, process, customer	
Special structures	Classify and describe service, staff, committee, task force, etc.	

Fig. 13-5   Structure variable

description from "agricultural county agent" to the broader role of "community facilitator" has little influence on the behavior of individuals if they still give priority to pursuing agricultural interests. (As we shall see in later chapters, people and power factions within organizations are frequently more predominant in how the organization functions than are organization charts and manuals.) Concepts of formal organization are tools the manager has to _influence_ the behavior of individuals and of the organization, but they do not _determine_ the behavior of individuals or the organization.

SUMMARY

An organization structure is the system of relationships, formally prescribed and informally developed, that governs the activities of people
who are dependent on each other for the accomplishment of common
objectives. Formal organizations are prescribed by those in authority.
Informal relationships emerge from social interaction. Highly organized
structures are bureaucratic in nature, whereas modern theory calls for
adaptive organizations that are less formalized.

Four steps are specified in the formal organization process:

- Horizontal differentiation involves establishing subsidiary units
  through the departmentation process.
- Vertical differentiation is the establishment of hierarchical layers
  in the organization based on authority delegation and a chain of
  command.
- Horizontal integration is achieved through procedures and integrative means like committees and task forces.
- The individual is brought into the formal structure through division of labor, position descriptions, operations sheets, and rules and
  regulations.

Committees are essential administrative units for gaining interest
representation in administration. They get people involved and bring a
wide range of experience into problem solving. However, they are frequently mismanaged and misused, resulting in delayed, compromise
decisions that thwart administrative action.

QUESTIONS FOR STUDY AND DISCUSSION

1. Explain the difference between *organizing, organization,* and *organization structure.*
2. How does formal differ from informal organization? In organizations
   you are familiar with, give examples of relationships that are formal
   and those that are informal.
3. Identify the four steps in establishing a formal organization structure
   and relate the organization processes of differentiation and integration
   to these steps.
4. What are the five forms of departmentation? Explain which form the
   following organizations use:
   - A. Fire department   C. Chain variety store
   - B. Football team   D. Airlines

5. Why does product departmentation tend to replace functional departmentation in large organizations?
6. In the four organizations in question 4, what support or auxiliary units would most likely be associated with each?
7. Give examples of the three different types of staff units or positions.
8. Describe the degree to which committees are used in the following organizations and explain why this is the case:
   A. United States Congress   C. University
   B. Local department store   D. Hospital
9. Based on a knowledge of formal organization concepts, can a manager control the structure of an organization? Can he determine how it will operate? Why?

Case Problem:
LITTONE SCALE COMPANY

The Littone Scale Company has been in the business of manufacturing and selling industrial scales since 1926. It was a family corporation until 1964 when a public offering was made of the stock. It produces a large variety of scales for industrial users. Scales range in size from the smaller ones used in grocery stores to large ones for weighing trucks and their loads. The company currently has sixteen standard varieties of the scales, but they also produce special ones on a custom basis. Recently the company has decided to enter the retail market. They have developed a bathroom scale which they intend to mass distribute in two years.

Currently the Littone Company is organized on a functional basis. They have separate Engineering and Product Development, Production, Marketing, Finance, and Administration divisions. With this expansion into the retail market, the vice president for administration has suggested that they switch to the product form of departmentation.

What changes will be necessary if the switch is made?
What are the advantages of the current functional organization, or departmentation, compared with those of product departmentation?
Should the entire company be organized on one basis or the other, or can just one division be organized different from the others?
Assuming that a mixture of departmentation types is feasible, which divisions should most likely be organized on a product basis? Why?

Case Problem:
CENTRALIZATION OF COPY MACHINES

The vice president of Business of Northern State College was holding a meeting with the members of his business staff and representatives of each of the academic colleges on campus. The business staff had undertaken a study which revealed that it would be less expensive to centralize all of the copy machines on campus in one location. In support of such a plan, the vice president of Business made the following comments:

"There are several advantages to assigning all copy machines to the Printing Services Department and locating them at one center in the basement of the Administration building. First, we find that the current machines, now spread all around campus, are used thirty-five percent of the time or less. If we have them in one location, we could up this to approximately seventy percent, which means we would not need as many machines. Also, for those machines that are leased, the charge per copy decreases with volume, so rather than costing five cents per page as we now experience with some machines, this could be reduced to three cents or even lower in some instances. Also, with all machines in one location we can acquire many different models, so we can provide a variety of services. We can acquire some of the more expensive models that rapidly produce multicopies, we would have automatic collators, multisize reproduction, and other facilities and services. This is far preferable to the standard equipment located in most buildings."

"Do you intend to centralize all machines currently found in other locations?" asked the representative from the Arts and Letters College.

"We will leave several machines in the library, and off-campus buildings will have their own machines, but for the seventeen buildings located on our approximately one-mile-square central campus, we intend to have only the one copy center," the vice president replied.

With this statement, many protests were made by representatives of the colleges, such as the following: "Why the inconvenience? Now I just have to walk down the hall to copy a document and you want me to walk half a mile for the same service."

"Sure it might be cheaper in terms of renting or buying machines, but think of all the time we lose. Has anyone ever calculated that cost?"

"What's a few hundred dollars a month in equipment leases if it saves us all of that inconvenience?"

"We would just as soon keep responsibility for our own machines. Let us worry abut our own costs. We can handle it."

What are the advantages of centralizing this service?
What are the advantages of keeping it decentralized?
What should the college do?
Should a centralized staff group, such as Printing Services, have responsibility for all copy services?
What other alternatives are there?

Designating Authority Relationships

How do *authority*, *power*, and *influence* differ?

Does authority always result in someone having power?

What formal authority structure should a manager attempt to establish?

Are *line* and *staff* designations realistic?

Why do managers often violate the chain of command?

What authority relationships are involved in a matrix organization?

Carl Sorenson was a shift supervisor of the Newbury Paper Products Corporation. He had sixty hourly workers under his direction. One worker named Nick had been employed with the company for thirty years and was the acknowledged informal leader, who had almost complete support of the workgroup. If they were dissatisfied with company operations, they looked to Nick to call for a deliberate slowdown. If new procedures were introduced or new machinery installed, they again waited for Nick's reaction before showing compliance. Carl had the authority to direct the workgroup, but everyone recognized that Nick had the real control over the crew. Carl was also aware that if he wanted to make any changes, he had to sell them to Nick first.

The above example is a fairly common occurrence in organizations. Certain individuals are given the authority to direct an organization, but getting people to obey involves more than merely having authority. Authority is only one source of influence over the behavior of others, and as the preceding paragraph indicates, often other factors predominate.

AUTHORITY, POWER, AND INFLUENCE

Before exploring the nature of authority, three related terms—*authority, power,* and *influence*—need to be clarified. Unfortunately, there are no universally accepted definitions, and the terms tend to carry different connotations in the various social science disciplines. The one characteristic all three terms have in common is that they describe *relationships* between and among people and groups. Using the systems approach of concentrating on relationships, it is possible to make discrete distinctions. *Authority* describes a relationship between persons A and B where A receives from the formal organization the right to direct or command B. In the business firm this authority is derived historically from the legal rights of property owners. The owners have the total rights, but they delegate certain duties, decision-making authority, and control over resources to others in the organization.

Power is evident in a situation when A has *control* over B or can get B to do something he would not do otherwise. Power is derived from many sources, including authority. However, in defining *power,* the source is not significant, but the relationship is—the ability of one individual to control another.

Influence is normally considered a more moderate form of power. It exists when A can modify or affect B's behavior, but it does not imply complete control. Friends tend to influence other friends, but they do not usually control them. *Influence* is any behavior on the part of one individual that modifies the behavior of someone else. Influence takes place in all interpersonal relationships, whereas power in the extreme sense is not common. Following the contingency approach, the relationships between and among individuals and groups can most appropriately be viewed as an influence continuum, in accordance with figure 14-1.

Little control   Moderate control   Major control
                                                      (power)

Fig. 14-1.   Influence continuum

When A has little influence over B, the relationship is designated on the lower end of the continuum. If A has strong control over B, it is represented on the upper, or power end. The significant point is that interpersonal and interorganizational relations constitute a web of influence (or power) relationships. The functioning of organizations and societies can be explained only on the basis of these highly significant and constantly shifting dependent ties. Power is ultimately the underlying force that structures relationships among individuals and organizations.

Concepts of Power

It is common to view power in terms of its latent, rather than actual, use. Nuclear weapons represent power in international relations, even though they are not used; the authority of a supervisor to terminate a subordinate represents power in a business firm, even though this rarely occurs. Power implies a fear of punishment, harm, or loss of status.

Power is also associated with need satisfaction. If an individual seeks certain goals and there is only one source of satisfaction available, that source has potential power over the individual. The thief has power over those he holds a gun on because of their need for safety. The supervisor has influence over subordinates because he has authority to use the reward and punishment systems of the organization. Being able to influence someone else is a function of the degree to which one can provide or thwart their need satisfaction.

Sources of Influence

In viewing sources of influence, the following distinctions are important: *Influence* is the general term used to describe relative differences in interdependent relationships that exist between and among people and groups. *Power* is a form (the extreme form) of influence, and *authority* is a source of influence and hence a potential source of power. As indicated in the

Newbury Paper Co. example at the beginning of the chapter, Carl as supervisor had the authority or the right to direct the workgroup. This authority was certainly a means he had of influencing the group's behavior. However, Nick had no formally designated authority over the crew and yet his influence was stronger than Carl's.

Authority could more properly be described as *position*-based influence. Because of his position in the organization a supervisor will influence the behavior of subordinates. If individuals let others affect their behavior because they assume they have superior knowledge, it is referred to as *knowledge*-based influence. A doctor modifies patient behavior because of knowledge-based influence.

Influence is derived from many other sources, although authority and knowledge are the most important forms. Money or wealth is *property*-based influence. Certain strong personal characteristics (dynamism, honesty, self-confidence, appearance) resulting in power over others (like Nick obviously possessed) is considered in the general category of *charisma*-based influence. (In certain countries still under a caste system, *class*-based influence exists.) There are many other forms of influence, such as love and affection, physical force, and various sources of esteem. Information is a source of influence, because individuals cannot function in an organization unless they have access to the plan of what is to be done. Furthermore, influence is also possessed by groups. *Group*-based influence results from an individual's strong identification with an organization. When he takes certain actions as a result of group norms or group policies (a democrat contributing to his party or voting for another democrat), group-based influence is evident.

TRADITIONAL APPROACHES TO AUTHORITY

As a form of institutionalized influence, authority is influence derived from a position—not from an individual. Traditionally the tendency was to place emphasis on the "legitimacy" aspects of authority, especially the legal right associated with its delegation. Accordingly, classical organization theory developed a large number of principles directed at the specific rights and obligations associated with authority delegation. A few of the more significant concepts that continue to be a part of organization theory follow.

Authority Delegation and Responsibility

If authority is the legal right to command, *responsibility* is the corollary of authority, or the *obligation* to act in response to an order. Some prefer the term *accountability* rather than obligation, emphasizing that when authority is delegated, the individual becomes accountable for the duties and responsibilities assigned. An important distinction between authority and responsibility is that the supervisor *delegates* authority, but responsibility is *shared*. Delegation of authority gives a subordinate the right to make commitments, use resources, and take actions in relation to duties assigned. However, in making this delegation, the obligation created and the accountability for these actions are *not* shifted from the supervisor to the subordinate—they are shared. Once duties are assigned to a unit or individual, these cannot be completely divested by assigning authority for them to a lower-level unit. A supervisor always retains some responsibility for work performed by lower-level units or individuals.

The traditional emphasis on the legal nature of authority residing with owners places emphasis on how this authority is delegated. Authority is first delegated to the Board of Directors, then to the President, and on down through the levels of the organization. The result is a *chain of command,* with authority directly traceable to every individual employed in the organization. The assumption is that supreme authority exists at the apex of the organization, and that all subsidiary elements are dependent on, and represent a fraction of, the total duties and authority initially residing at the top.

Making Authority Commensurate with Responsibility

Classical writers emphasized that when an individual or unit is assigned certain duties and given specific responsibilities, the equivalent authority necessary to successfully accomplish these tasks should also be delegated. If one assumes that authority is the prime factor in accomplishing coordinative tasks in organizations, that conclusion naturally follows. This principle is aimed at a common weakness in supervision. Frequently individuals are assigned specific projects or tasks, but they are not delegated authority, so they do not have the position-based influence to gain the necessary cooperation from others, especially those at their same level in the organization. Some supervisors are reluctant to delegate authority for fear of weakening their own position, and they feel it might result in a loss of control in those aspects of their operations.

Unity of Command

Unity of command (having a subordinate report to only one supervisor) is necessary to maintain the integrity of the chain of command. If a clear chain is to exist from the top to the bottom of the organization, each individual is responsible to only one supervisor. Unity of command avoids conflicting instructions and makes an individual more totally responsible for the duties he is assigned. (However, there are cases when it should be ignored.)

Span of Control

One of the favorite concepts of early writers was span of control, or the number of subordinates that one manager can effectively supervise. Many studies have been conducted and theories developed attempting to determine whether this ratio should be ten to one, eight to one, or perhaps even lower. It is largely a question of the capacity of a supervisor to direct and monitor the activities of subordinates performing work in the organization. Even though it is basically a monitoring or control concept, writers in recent years have preferred the broader terminology of *span of management,* or *span of supervision.*

As early as 1933, a French management consultant, V. A. Graicunas, was searching for a mathematical formula to determine the span of management.[1] Even though his efforts were of limited success, Graicunas did perform an important service in indicating that as subordinates are added, supervisory complications due to multiple relationships tend to rapidly increase. Soon subgroups form, and the complexity of interpersonal relations increases faster than pure arithmetic progression.

It did not take many years for writers to adopt a contingency approach in relation to span of control. No universal ratio could be established, and conditions such as the nature of the tasks being performed, the training and ability of subordinates, the complexity of the mandatory formal ties with other organizations, the commitment of the organization to decentralization, and other such factors determined the appropriateness of any specific span.

Perhaps the major fallacy of span of control has been the tendency to treat it as an independent rather than a dependent variable. The assumption has been that in organizing, a supervisor deliberately establishes subunits that have the optimal span of control. Actually, span of control normally results from other overriding considerations. Frequently it is determined by the number of subordinates necessary to handle an organizational function. If a corporation requires four lawyers, the span of control will be three to one; if a college needs seven history professors and thirty English instructors, the ratios will be six to one and twenty-nine to one, respectively. Also, people considerations, such as finding supervisory slots for favored individuals, the competence of current supervisors, and other related factors will dictate the units established and the resulting spans.

CONTINGENCY CONSIDERATIONS IN SPAN OF CONTROL

Robert J. House and John B. Miner undertook an extensive study of the writings and research of management theorists and behavioral scientists relating to the relationship of group size and span of control. From this study they made the following conclusions regarding span of control:

"The implications for the span of control seem to be that (1) under most circumstances the optimal span is likely to be in the range five through ten; (2) the larger spans, say eight through ten, are most often appropriate at the highest, policy-making levels of an organization, where greater resources for diversified problem-solving appear to be needed (although diversified problem-solving without larger spans may well be possible); (3) the breadth of effective spans of first-line supervisors is contingent on the technology of the organization; and (4) in prescribing the span of control for specific situations, consideration must be given to a host of local factors, such as the desirability of high group cohesiveness, the performance demands of the task, the degree of stress in the environment, task interdependencies, the need for member satisfaction, and the leadership skills available to the organization. In particular, the degrees of stability, diversity, and uncertainty in both the environment of the unit and of the organization appear to be important considerations."

Robert J. House and John B. Miner, "Merging Management and Behavioral Theory: The Interaction Between Span of Control and Group Size," *Administrative Science Quarterly*, September, 1969, pp. 461–62.

Many times other organization concepts tend to take precedent over span of control. A commitment to centralization or decentralization will either narrow or broaden the span. Decisions emphasizing certain functions throughout the organization structure will also affect it. In addition, the number of levels desired in the hierarchy will modify the spans. A company committed to a flat organization with few levels will require broader spans. The assumption that an organization has broad discretionary freedom in establishing spans of control is basically an illusion.

Line and Staff

Line and staff as part of departmentation were identified in the last chapter. However, these concepts basically constitute an authority relationship. Line units, associated with the primary purpose of the organization, directly contribute to the objectives of the enterprise. A line supervisor has total authority over those in the chain of command beneath him or her. Staff units support the line and are advisory in nature, because their activities only relate indirectly to the end objectives of the organization. Line authority does, however, exist within staff organizations. A controller has line authority over all accountants and accounting units reporting to him, but his organization exists as a support or in a staff capacity to the basic line organizations (such as in a manufacturing plant).

Even though theory provides clear distinctions between line and staff, the authority relationships in organizations frequently are blurred. In a production organization, all units engaged in the manufacture of the product are line, and organizations such as personnel, finance, plant maintenance, computer operations, and printing services are support. However, the nature of the authority in groups like research and development, marketing, and long-range planning is fuzzy, especially if one considers power relationships in the organization. In nonmanufacturing organizations, distinctions are even more difficult to make.

Line and staff designations tend to be a source of continual conflict. Designating staff personnel as *support* or *advisory* has tended to make them "second-class citizens," creating status differentials that arouse feelings of hostility. Line personnel are inclined to perceive staff as drones who create paper work and fail to contribute to profit. Staff often finds line groups unwilling to cooperate and inclined to "put down" troublesome staff members, especially if they are auditing or checking on line activities. Unfortunately, it is often true that staff individuals, strongly committed to their functions, do suboptimize by pursuing their relationships with the line without due regard to their effect on efficiency and achievement of organizational objectives.

Line, Functional, and Concurring Authority

Closely associated with the line-staff concept is the notion of three types of authority: *line, functional,* and *concurring.* Line authority is held by individuals in a line capacity and implies unlimited authority as it relates to assigned duties. Functional and concurring authority are the types normally restricted to staff officials (except within their own functional chain of command). Functional authority is the right to command those outside the functional organization in regard to the specific function involved. Budgeting is an example. As noted earlier, the Director of Budgeting may be given the authority to assign specific due dates in getting budget data from line organizations, and he may have the authority to specify the formats the information is to be submitted in. In these two respects he has the right to command line organizations but cannot exert control over their basic functions or duties (such as telling an engineer how to design a product or allocating resources to a production foreman).

Concurring authority is the authority a staff individual has to approve the decision of a line manager before it is valid. Again, this approval is restricted to those aspects of the decision that relate to the functional assignment of the staff representative. For instance, if a marketing manager intends to make a job offer to a salesman, he proposes to the Personnel Department that John Elton be given the job offer at some figure such as $1000 per month. However, before the job offer is made, the Personnel Department has to concur that John Elton meets the minimum requirements of the position, and that the $1000 job offer is consistent with the wage and salary structure of the firm.

In traditional management writing, the advice to keep functional authority delegation to a minimum is always given. Too much functional authority in the hands of staff personnel creates conflict with line organizations and violates unity of command. Even though this has been an accepted principle, the tendency in organizations has been for staff and functional authority to proliferate. As indicated earlier, this is primarily because of the growth in size of organizations and the increased complexity of activities, such as labor relations, that require technical experts. There is no doubt that functional authority does complicate the chain of command and authority relationships. Functional authority is frequently shown as a dotted or dashed line on an organization chart. When functional designations are shown in this manner a chart for a large organization is a maze of criss-crossing dotted lines and almost incomprehensible. However, the major contributions that staff groups make to organizations and the value of retaining experts in the support-type activities make the growth of staff consistent with the growth of organizations inevitable.

Centralization and Decentralization

Centralization and decentralization represent different conditions in organizations, depending on the degree to which authority has been delegated to lower-level units. If most of the significant decision making is retained at the top or if decisions must be referred to the top for approval, the organization is considered centralized. If considerable freedom of action is permitted at lower levels (or by subordinates within an organization), the organization is considered decentralized. Delegation of authority is the *process* managers use to decentralize an organization. Decentralization is not a process but a relative *condition* resulting from delegation.

The concept of the hierarchy, chain of command, and all authority initially being concentrated at the top implies a bias toward centralization in classical writings. Fayol cited, as noted earlier, that centralization was the "natural order" of things. However as industrialization resulted in larger organizations, writers and practitioners soon came to recognize that businesses must further decentralize to maintain efficiency. No set of top-level executives has the time or the capacity to make all managerial decisions for an organization. Thus in the 1950's one of the major themes in management literature became that of increased decentralization. The principle was adopted that the authority to make a decision should be delegated to the lowest level in the organization where the individuals have the appropriate information and competence to make a sound decision.

Centralization and decentralization constitute some of the most important considerations in organization structure. There are many different forms and advantages and disadvantages associated with each type. However, determining whether to centralize or decentralize is entirely contingent on the nature of the organization and its environment. (Accordingly, the discussion of types and approaches will be reserved for the next chapter, where they will be treated based on contingency theory.)

LIMITATIONS OF CLASSIC APPROACHES AND MODERN VARIATIONS

The role of authority in the American culture and in business organizations has experienced considerable change in the past fifty years. There has come to be less reliance on formal authority and a greater movement towards power equalization. The need for modification of the classical approach to authority has been manifest in many quarters, but it has been especially strong with behavioralists. A few of the major criticisms and new directions for change, especially those involving an expansion of traditional theories, will be reviewed.

The "Acceptance" Theory of Authority

The acceptance theory of authority holds that authority has no influence or force unless it is accepted by subordinates. Authority is the right to command, but the influence of authority is a function of the subordinate's willingness to accept the command. In this sense authority is considered as derived from the group. Many groups have revolted against the authority of the leader and shown that it can be overridden. A young supervisor with experienced subordinates will not usually have the knowledge-based influence to back up his position-based influence, resulting in a workgroup that might thwart his authority. As indicated earlier, authority is just one factor influencing behavior, and the strength of supervisory authority is a function of how willing subordinates are to obey. This is not to say that position-based influence is a weak force in organizations, but rather to note that a supervisor who is considered to be lacking in knowledge by his workgroup and who has no other source of influence than authority is often dealing from a position of weakness.

The implication should not be drawn that the individual who refuses to obey an order is devoid of risk. However, in terms of power tactics in organizations, frequently a group can thwart the authority of a supervisor through slowdowns, ignoring procedures, or other combined actions. Groups can also outwardly show compliance but covertly thwart the dictates of supervision. The effectiveness of the authority of the supervisor is directly related to the degree the workgroup is willing to accept his direction. The important point is not that authority is ineffective, but that other factors in addition to authority determine the willingness of people to accept direction. Two shift supervisors will have identical authority over their workgroups, but one will undoubtedly be able to influence his group more than the other, resulting from knowledge-based influence and other factors. (This encompasses the broader concept of *leadership;* but authority is meaningful only in this broader context.)

Fallacies Associated with Line and Staff

Much of the criticism of traditional authority is based on the conclusion that the principles are often misleading and do not represent reality. They imply static, clear-cut relationships, when in fact organizations are dynamic, and the relationships are a blend of many variations. Line and staff principles are indicative of this paradox. Line is supposed to have full authority, and staff is intended to be in a more secondary, advisory role. However, in recent years power has tended to shift from line to staff. In many organizations staff units reporting to a president have as much influence over policy matters and the direction of the organization as line, which obviously is not the intent behind the original distinctions. The reason for the rise in influence of staff is associated with four factors:

1. As organizations have grown in size, many of the most significant responsibilities of line managers have been given to or shared with staff units. Examples are planning (long-range planning units), setting of work standards (industrial engineering), training (training departments in personnel), and resource allocation (budgeting). Control over these activities represents a major source of power in organizations.

2. Staff units are supposed to merely recommend, but since they are considered technical experts their knowledge-based is often stronger than the position-based influence of the line representative. A staff man in charge of coordinating long-range planning spends all of his time on planning problems and is technically trained in this area. The line middle manager in manufacturing will spend less than ten percent of his time on planning and has little, if any, formal training as a planner. He will be more knowledgeable of his operations, but the staff planner, placed at a high level in the organization, will more likely have the ear of the president on planning matters.

    The concept of *completed staff work* is relative to this issue. The classic concept of completed staff work is that the effective staff member not only studies a problem and makes a recommendation to his chief, but also prepares all implementing procedures and memoranda that are included with the final report. All the executive needs to do if he approves the recommendation is sign the documents attached. Obviously executives accept a significant portion of the recommendations of their personal staff, or they would replace them with more competent individuals. If 80 percent of the time an executive accepts the recommendations of staff, it is obvious this is where much of the influence in organizations resides.

3. It is apparent from some studies that in many instances line and staff considerations receive little attention in organizations. Former President Nixon's staff associates, R. Haldeman and John Ehrlichman, obviously had more power (if not authority) in the federal government than members of the cabinet. In a study conducted by Wendell French and Dale A. Henning of twenty-five firms, they found that many decisions normally considered of a line nature were jointly made by representatives of the personnel department and line officials. Joint participation was attributed to the following decisions (percentages indicate respondents agreeing that the decision was joint): approving individual job specifications (65%); promotions within a department (50%); approving transfers (49%); approving employee discharge (50%); type of wage incentive plan (60%); and establishing output standards (75%).[2] As Douglas McGregor states in his book, *The Human Side of Enterprise,* "Every member of lower- and middle-line management is subject to influences from staff groups which are psychologically indistinguishable from the authority exercised by his line superiors."[3]

4. It is also argued that staff has gained more influence in organizations because they have time to innovate. Line personnel supposedly do not have this luxury, because they are continually faced with getting

out the product or providing the service. This argument, although rather weak, has some merit.

Staff and line, like other management concepts, are not distinguishable in black and white. All units contribute to the goals of an enterprise, although some units do so more directly than others. Relative differences are the only demarcations. Overlap also hides certain differences so that distinctions become quite meaningless. The supervisor is considered responsible for the training and development of his subordinates, but the training division in a personnel department is also charged with this responsibility.

While having certain valuable aspects, line and staff concepts are nevertheless a source of conflict, friction, and misunderstanding in organizations. Some have said that they are obsolete and should be discarded. However, they are a common element of the vocabulary of practitioners and writers so that any treatise on authority requires their inclusion.

McGREGOR ON LINE AND STAFF

Douglas McGregor, the noted psychologist who originated Theory X and Theory Y as contrasting assumptions about people and work, made the following observations about line and staff concepts:

"The final irony of this whole situation is that it is the staff and not the line which is beginning to represent the real power in the modern industrial corporation. Quite apart from their inheritance of the control function, staff groups are the ones who make it possible for management to solve the ever more intricate problems of today's world—in the financial, technical, scientific, legislative, economic, and human fields. Their knowledge and training in their specialties, their techniques for analyzing and solving problems are absolutely essential to the success of the modern enterprise.

"Consequently, we have an odd reversal of conventional organization theory: The line—the central and fundamental authoritative chain of command—is becoming increasingly dependent upon a considerable number of specialized staff groups. Simultaneously the staff groups—the advisory and service groups who "cannot exercise authority" because of the logical necessity for unity of command—are becoming, both by virtue of the

> importance of their knowledge and skill and because of management's delegation to them of control and coordinative functions, the dominant, influential core of the organization. In one very large company, 70 percent of the personnel above the second level of supervision are staff, and the proportion is growing."

Quotation from Douglas McGregor, *The Human Side of Enterprise* (New York: McGraw-Hill Book Company, 1960), p. 155.

Violation of the Chain of Command

The chain-of-command concept assumes that each link will give direction to the next lower one and that there will be no "leapfrogging" or bypassing of links in the chain. However, in numerous seminars with practitioners I have found that one of the most common complaints is supervisors who violate the chain of command. Unquestionably this short-circuiting does present problems: the individual bypassed is not informed of what direction is given by someone higher in the hierarchy, and the individual who is the object of the bypass is receiving dual direction and is caught in a bind resulting from lack of unity of command. It represents a failure of supervisors to appreciate the psychological impact they have on others, especially the ego deflation of the individual bypassed. However, it is obviously an accepted expediency, or it would not be so common in organizations.

It is an indication that executives desire more of a free-form organization than traditional approaches would permit. It again typifies the fallacy of management absolutes. Maintaining the chain of command is a concept that is generally appropriate; however, there are situations when bypass has more benefits than it does limitations. The problem for the manager is to recognize this and minimize the limitations by practices like simultaneously communicating with the individual bypassed so that he or she is informed of the actions taken and the reasons for them.

Overreliance on Authority

Undoubtedly the major limitation of traditional approaches to authority is overreliance on it as the means of establishing a structure to control the behavior of people in organizations. Authority is without question the glue that holds an organization like a business firm together, but as we have noted knowledge-based influence, peer-group pressure, assigned tasks, and many other factors affect behavior too. In fact, too much reliance on authority in an organization can develop counter forces, especially among younger members, that may be detrimental to the organization. (In later discussions of leadership, we will find that it is normally preferable to "sell" people ideas than to force compliance through the use of authority.)

Matrix Organization Structure

There have been few major innovations in formal organization structure since 1945. However, one significant advance has been the establishment of the *matrix* structure, which is a combination of functional and program forms of departmentation. The matrix structure is of interest because it establishes a peculiar set of authority relationships that combines some of the desirable features of both functional and program departmentation. Even though it violates many traditional authority principles and is a more complex form of structure, it offers certain advantages, which indicates that it may be a forerunner of organizations of the future.

COMBINING ADVANTAGES OF FUNCTIONAL AND PROGRAM DEPARTMENTATION. As indicated in chapter 13, the major problem with functional departmentation (figure 13-2) is that integration of the functions contributing to the basic product or service of the organization does not occur until the apex of the organization is reached. Program departmentation (figure 13-3) achieves product integration at lower levels. However, it can be inefficient in smaller organizations, because the functional departments (engineering, production, marketing, etc.) must be duplicated under each program organization. With this arrangement, flexibility is lost—compared to having one combined department in relation to each function.

In order to overcome these deficiencies, medium-sized aerospace firms in the 1950's and 1960's experimented with organization structures that constituted an overlay of the two forms of departmentation (hence the name matrix.) Functional departments continued to exist in the traditional vertical hierarchy, and program departmentation was established as a horizontal overlay, as illustrated in figure 14-2.

RESPONSIBILITIES OF FUNCTIONAL AND PROGRAM MANAGERS. Under this form of organization structure, the functional manager remains in charge of all technical operations relating to his function. However, in establishing subunits rather than continuing with a functional breakdown, program departmentation is now used. Under the Director of Engineering, if five products are involved (A through E), there would be five divisions,

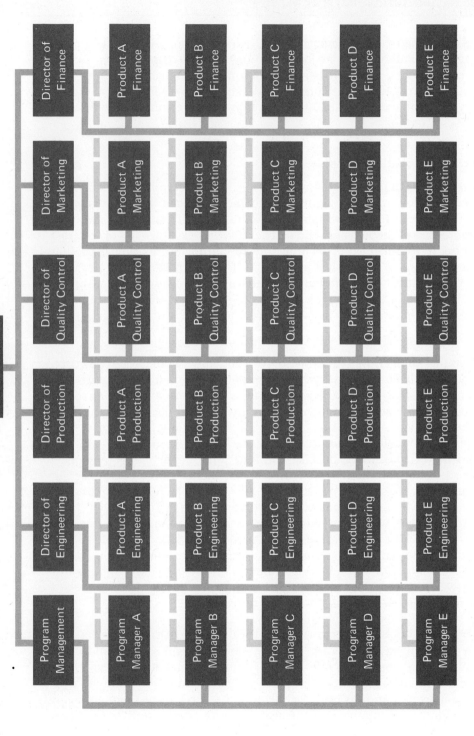

Fig. 14-2. Authority in a matrix organization

each associated with one of the products. The dotted line on the chart connecting Program Manager "A" with the "A" division of engineering, production, quality control, marketing, and finance indicates that these subunits all work with the program manager to successfully develop and fabricate product A.

This horizontal organization structure is a form of task-force management. These functional subunits associated with a product exist as long as the product continues. When the contract is terminated or product is dropped, the subunits are dissolved and become a part of the functional organization. The program manager coordinates the combined efforts of the product departmentation division heads working on his product in providing a finished one. The heads of the functional departments work with individual functional managers to optimize the activities of the subgroup as it relates to that function. The program manager's concern is interdependence—integrating the efforts of the groups to maximize product efficiency; the functional manager attempts to maximize the utility of the functional processes and methodologies employed.

Matrix structure is an obvious violation of unity of command. The head of product "A" engineering reports both to the Director of Engineering and the Manager of Program "A." Since traditional classifications of authority (line, functional, concurring) do not fit this situation, new distinctions are necessary. Functional managers retain the more traditional functional authority. They supervise lower level units in relation to the technical aspects of their functions. They determine *how* work is to be done, *where* it will be accomplished, and *who* will do it. However, the production manager does not have the total line authority he has in functional departmentation. For instance, he does not allocate resources to his subgroups because this is the responsibility of the program manager. He also does not do the overall planning and scheduling. He does assign the manpower to the project, but in practice assignment of manpower and budgets is often negotiated between the functional chief and the program manager.

If the operating or "how" decisions are the functional managers this leaves the program manager the *what* and *when* or *management* decisions. These managerial responsibilities are as follows:

- *Scope*   total responsibility to horizontally integrate all activities and subgroup effort to maximize product performance.
- *Resource allocation*   total responsibility for all resources used on the program. He allocates resources to the functional subunits based on the work they are to perform.

- *Planning*   conducts master project scheduling and planning activity, and issues work releases to the functional subunits.
- *Controlling*   monitors the activity of all functional subunits to ensure they are meeting program goals.

The program manager lacks line authority because he should not direct the functional units in how they *operationally* perform their work. His concern is meeting goals within time, resource, and performance constraints.

This peculiar combination of authority relationships offers considerable promise, especially in organizations with many different products and goals. Even though it violates classic bureaucratic concepts of the hierarchy, unit of command, and direct, complete control over subordinates, it provides a flexible, adaptive structure that is consistent with the more dynamic environment of modern organizations.

Contingency Considerations

The authority concepts analyzed in this chapter and the steps in formal organization reviewed in chapter 13 are based primarily on the classic approach to organization design. Experience has proven the value of many of these concepts, and they have strongly contributed to the American manager's reputation as being an excellent, almost unexcelled organizer. However, these concepts are not the absolutes or the universal principles they are often purported to be. Under proper conditions, each concept can contribute to a sound structure and a more efficient, effective organization, but the concept is valid only if the appropriate conditions exist.

Contingency considerations are involved in each instance. Unity of command is frequently desirable, but there are circumstances, such as the matrix structure, when off-setting benefits make it wise to violate this concept; staff personnel always experience variations of authority and power, and no universal example exists; bureaucracy can be effective in some organizations, but it can all but strangle others; the authority delegated to a subordinate supervisor should not be determined solely on the functions to be performed but should also be influenced by factors such as the personality of the individual, his relationship with the work group and other work units, his abilities and commitment to the organization, and the status of departmental plans. Furthermore, the use of committees, decentralization, and span of control are all obviously dependent on a multitude of conditions that exist in the organization and its environment. (The next chapter will delve into these intricacies of understanding the forces in an organization that make different types of structures and organization concepts appropriate in different situations.)

SUMMARY

Authority is the right to direct or command others in an organization. It is an institutionalized right that in capitalistic systems is derived from ownership. However, the right to command does not always mean that people will obey. It is a form of influence over behavior, but other factors such as expertise (knowledge-based influence) and personality factors (charisma) are also effective. Power is considered the extreme form of influence, where an individual or group controls the behavior of another.

Classic management theory resulted in many concepts relating to authority:

- When responsibility is assigned, an equal amount of authority should be delegated.
- A subordinate should report to only one supervisor.
- The number of subordinates reporting to one supervisor should be limited, so that he or she can control their activities.
- Line personnel handling functions that relate to the objectives of the organization should have unlimited authority in relation to their assigned duties, and staff personnel serving in a support capacity should be restricted to an advisory role.
- Staff personnel can be given functional or concurring authority, but it should be restricted and related only to the technical aspects of their duties.

In more recent years various modifications of the classic approach to authority have been proposed. The acceptance theory of authority was developed under the assumption that the authority of the supervisor comes from the group in terms of their acceptance of his direction. Line and staff concepts have been challenged, because staff units have tended to gain tremendous influence in organizations—resulting from their role in activities like planning, budgeting, and measuring performance.

In general, traditional principles placed an overreliance on the importance of authority. The matrix form of organization structure was proposed as more of a free-form type that overcomes some of the limitations of both functional and product departmentation.

QUESTIONS FOR STUDY AND DISCUSSION

1. Why is power called a *form* of influence, and authority is said to be a *source* of influence?
2. Explain the authority, power, and influence of a:
   - A. Professor
   - B. Senator
   - C. Policeman
   - D. Safety inspector
3. Why is power considered a latent force? How is it related to need satisfaction?
4. What is the difference between delegated authority and shared responsibility?
5. Is it realistic to assume that authority can be commensurate with responsibility?
6. Why cannot a universal span of 5 to 1 or 8 to 1 be established? Why is span of control considered a dependent variable?
7. Identify typical line and staff units in the following organizations:
   - A. University
   - B. City government
   - C. Department store
   - D. Hospital
8. What are the sources of line-staff conflict?
9. What are the differences between delegation of authority and decentralization?
10. How valid is the acceptance theory of authority?
11. Why has staff grown in importance in organizations?
12. What role should authority play in organizations and in organization structure?
13. In the matrix organization, what authority does the program manager have? How does this relate to the authority of the functional manager?
14. What weaknesses of functional departmentation does the matrix structure overcome? What problems does the matrix structure create?
15. How could the matrix structure be used in a university?

Case Problem:
THE AUTHORIZED BYPASS

An employee of the government agency reports the following situation.

This is the formal organization of my office:

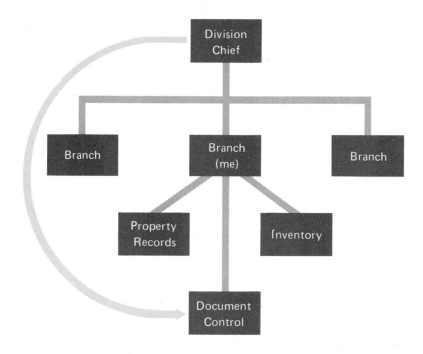

I am at the branch level. When I joined this branch, my division chief
told me in no uncertain terms that the section chief of document control
has complete authority to report to the division, and that she can bypass
the branch. The division chief claims that she is outstanding on the job
(which she is), and that he gets an honest answer from her. Also, the
division chief has given her authority to spy on everyone else in the division. She is a very honest and smart person but is blunt and tactless.
Needless to say, her authority to report directly to division level causes
a lack of respect for my position and creates a tremendous morale problem in the whole division. The division chief claims that he may or may
not get honest answers from his branch chiefs.

Why has the division chief authorized the Head of Document Control
to violate the chain of command?
How has the individual at the branch level who is being bypassed
psychologically responding to the situation?
What advantages and limitations are there in not following the chain
of command?
If you were the individual writing the case, what would you attempt
to do about this situation?

Case Study:
"THE NINETY-DAY WONDER"

In a certain mining company that has been in existence for many years, it is common for the miners to "test" new supervisors, especially when they are younger in age and not very familiar with mining operations. The miners are rough and hardy, and their average age is between forty-five and fifty. The company has high pay rates for these semiskilled workers and an excellent fringe-benefit package. Also, there are few other opportunities for employment in the area. Because of these factors, the average miner has fifteen or more years with the company.

In most instances the mining supervisors are promoted up through the ranks, but occasionally they hire younger individuals with more education and technical training. As indicated, the miners will frequently engage in a game of trying these supervisors' patience. They will ask a new foreman to solve technical problems when they think he lacks the appropriate knowledge, push company rules as far as they can, appear to not understand when they actually comprehend, deliberately engage in slowdowns, ignore or only partially respond to direction, challenge authority (based on the union contract), and send the young foreman on "wild-goose hunts" pertaining to trumped-up situations or problems.

Those new supervisors who cannot take the pressure are known as "ninety-day wonders," because they generally last for ninety days or less. Other young foremen who stick it out and effectively respond to the challenges win the esteem of the workgroup and continue on as respected supervisors.

How do the terms *authority, power,* and *influence* relate to this case?
How does the acceptance theory of authority relate?
Why do the miners test the young foremen?
What actions can a new foreman take that will win the favor of the miners?
How should a young foreman use his authority during this probation period?

Footnotes

1. V. A. Graicunas, "Relationship in Organization," *Bulletin of the International Management Institute* (Geneva: International Labor Office, 1933), in L. Gulick and L. Urwick (eds.), *Papers on the Science of Administration* (New York: Institute of Public Administration, 1937), pp. 181–187.

2. Wendell French and Dale A. Henning, "The Authority-Influence Role of the Functional Specialist in Management," *Academy of Management Journal,* September 1966, pp. 187–203.
3. Douglas McGregor, *op. cit.,* p. 146.

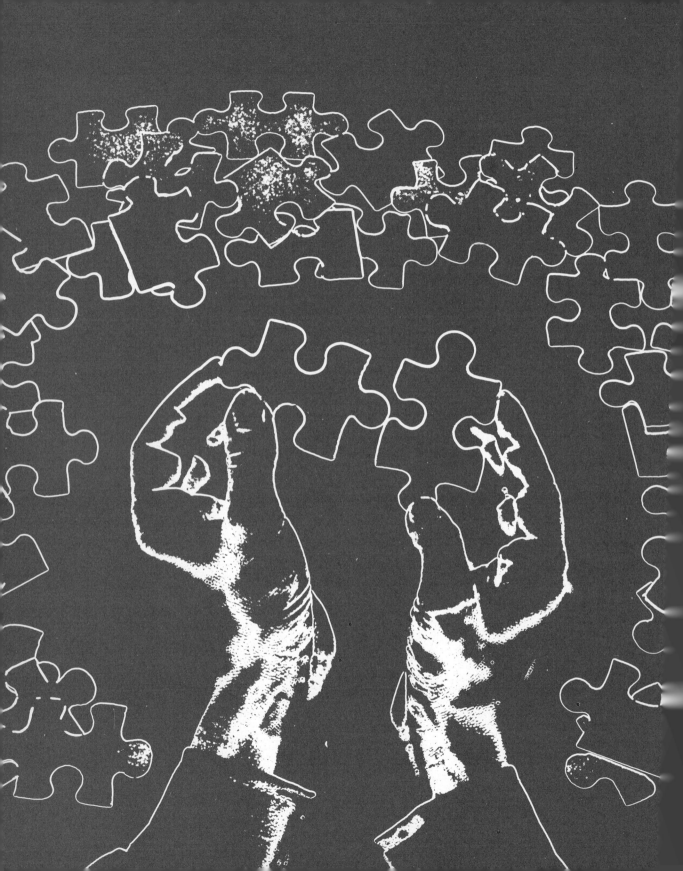

Contingency Considerations in Organization Design

What limitations are inherent in bureaucratic structures?

How does the external environment affect organization structure?

What internal factors of the organization affect structure?

Why is there no one best way to organize?

Under what conditions are more open, adaptive structures appropriate?

What considerations are important in determining whether to decentralize?

CONTINGENCY THEORY
AND BUREAUCRACY

The primary difference between classic approaches to design and the contingency approach concerns how we account for the existence of an organization structure. Classical theory emphasizes that design results from the application of abstract principles, but contingency approaches view design as resulting from a variety of variables existing in both the internal and external environment of an organization. One perceives abstract principles as constituting discrete, rational concepts, which when properly applied will establish an orderly structure. The other theory views structure as a dependent variable resulting from an adaptation to internal conditions and environmental forces.

Classic bureaucratic theory is concerned with how to maximize efficiency through task specialization, a hierarchy of supervisory-subordinate relationships, and procedures and rules to control activities. But contingency theory introduces an intervening step. Before organization principles can be selected and applied, the manager needs to be familiar with the internal and external conditions and forces relevant to the organization, because different principles and designs are appropriate under different circumstances. Efficiency in design does not result from use of bureaucratic principles—it results from matching appropriate principles with the particular set of conditions associated with an organization. Under certain conditions, classical principles may be appropriate; under other circumstances they may not.

LIMITATIONS OF CLASSICAL PRINCIPLES

Classical principles of organization have been, and still are, extremely significant factors in organization design. They have provided the rational basis for the early development of organization theory, and they are the pillars upon which current practice has been developed. As the work force has become more educated and as technology has forced increased change, these principles have become increasingly outdated, but they still constitute the everyday working tools of practitioners. Therefore these five limitations should be considered more as directions for change in organization theory, rather than a discarding of obsolete concepts.

1. *Classical principles are too general to be meaningful in application.* The attempt to provide universal principles resulted in broad generalizations with limited meaning for an individual who is faced with a specific organizational design problem. Principles so broad that they fit all organizations prove to be of limited prescriptive value.

2. *Formal principles is only one factor among many that determines the structure and functioning of organizations.* Classical theory assumed too simplistically that formal principles could be used to determine the structure and functioning of organizations when, in fact they are often of secondary importance. The web of relationships that constitute structure is derived from a variety of sources.

3. *Bureaucracy results in structures that are often too rigid and static.* The classical emphasis on the internal structuring of all activities and authority relationships was intended to provide a predictable, controllable structure. The open-systems concept states that organizations constitute a set of flows involving input from the environment and output in the form of goods and services. Adaptation is the relevant issue for most organizations—not maintaining the status quo.

4. *Classical principles relate to internal structure when many factors affecting structure are external.* Traditional principles are essentially devoted to internal aspects of organization design. However, more recent researchers have discovered that the stability or uncertainty of the environment caused by factors such as markets, competitors, technology, cultural norms, and political forces create conditions that firms must adapt to if they are to be effective.

5. *Bureaucracy tends to be impersonal and create conditions that are not conducive to motivation or organizational commitment.* Bureaucracy tends to make a fetish out of rules in the search for control, order, simplicity, and routine. Bureaucracy places a premium on conformance and discourages the freedom of action that can be a benefit in some situations but is generally contrary to the needs of individuals who are seeking an outlet for self-expression. Probably the greatest dysfunction of bureaucracy is that it alienates its own membership by restricting freedom of action.

THE DEVELOPMENT OF CONTINGENCY THEORIES

Contingency theories of organization evolved in the fifties and sixties. A number of studies was conducted almost simultaneously and came to the conclusion that there is no one best way to organize.

Burns and Stalker Studies

Tom Burns and G. M. Stalker conducted an intensive study of twenty firms in England and Scotland. Through interviews with the personnel of the organizations, they became familiar with the methods of operation, structure of subgroups, informal relationships, and so on. As the study developed, they attempted to relate the different conditions in these organizations to different management systems. The elements of the organization associated with different technologies (such as production and research and development) tended to operate more effectively with different types of structures. The external environment and the status of subgroups within the firm created certain conditions that were also matched by differences in organization structure. The external environment, as defined in their study, was limited to the market of the firm, or subgroup. They were concerned with the rate of change of both internal technologies and external markets which, in turn, would thrust uncertainty upon the organization.

For classification purposes they used the two extremes of organic and mechanistic structures, although they acknowledged that the continuum concept is more realistic. Mechanistic structure is characterized by differentiation of tasks, a hierarchy, vertical interaction of participants, and reliance on rules and instructions. Organic forms are characterized by reliance on knowledge-based influence, individuals who are committed to their professional tasks and the goals of the organization, lateral interaction, and communication based on advice rather than instruction. They associated mechanistic structures with production-type units and organic ones with high-technology organizations containing a large number of professionals, as in research and development.

Burns and Stalker concluded from their studies that no one organization type fits all conditions. With stable technology and a stable market environment, mechanistic forms are appropriate. When the environment is unstable and internal technology is also constantly changing, organic structures become mandatory. As they stated:

> We have endeavored to stress the appropriateness of each system to its own specific set of conditions. Equally, we desire to avoid the suggestion that either system is superior under all circumstances to the other. In particular, nothing in our experience justified the assumption that mechanistic systems should be superseded by organic in conditions of stability. The beginning of administrative wisdom is the awareness that there is no one optimum type of management system.[1]

Joan Woodward Studies

You will recall from chapter 12 that Joan Woodward and associates conducted a ten-year study of one hundred English firms in which they attempted to identify any similarities that could be associated with a firm's financial success. In terms of research methods they used surveys, case studies, and longitudinal and historical analyses. They analyzed the history, objectives, manufacturing processes, organization structure, cost factors, labor differences, and profitability of each firm.

They met with little success until they divided the firms into three groups, based on unit, batch or mass, and long-run process production*. Once they made this division, a strong relationship between success and organization structure became apparent. Successful firms in each of the three categories displayed common organizational characteristics. The two types on the extremes—unit and continuous production—tended to have more open, adaptive structures, and the middle range or mass production was characterized by the more traditional bureaucracy. The structure of firms that were engaged in batch (mass production) had more clear-cut definition of duties, less delegation of authority, more specialists, and a higher reliance on line-staff structure. Unit and process production placed more emphasis on technical knowledge and were characterized by less structure and greater delegation of authority. (These features, along with others, can be noted in table 15-1.)

Table 15-1. Relation of Certain Organizational Characteristics to Type of Production Technology

Organizational Characteristics	Unit	Mass	Process
Median levels of management	3	4	6
Median span of control (foremen)	23	48	15
Median direct to indirect worker	9:1	4:1	1:1
Median production to staff worker	8:1	5½:1	2:1
Line-staff structure	weak	strong	weak
Formalization of structure	flexible	detailed	flexible
Delegation of authority	high	low	high
Specialists	few	many	few
Communication	verbal	written	verbal

Source: Adapted from pp. 52–69 of Joan Woodward, *Industrial Organization: Theory and Practice* (London: Oxford University Press, 1965).

The assumption of Woodward was that as you move from unit to mass and to process production, the technology is more advanced. This higher technology is associated with more levels of management, a lower

*See chapter 12 for an explanation of the differences between these three types of production technology.

ratio of indirect to direct workers, more staff personnel, and lower spans of control. However, the tying link between organization structure and technology came when the features of the organizations were related to success. The more financially successful firms in each category were those that were close to the median of the category. If firms deviated significantly from the median characteristics (for unit production three levels of management, a span of control of 23, and so on), they tended not to be successful. Since each category had different organizational characteristics, this further verified that companies with diverse technologies required different types of organization structures in order to be effective.

Woodward was careful to qualify the technology relationships established in the studies, stating that they should be considered as associative rather than causal. Others have pointed out that the relationship is also somewhat environmental, because the technologies of different production systems are related to their products that have different market environments.* The studies developed strong support for the concept that organization structure must be linked to technology and environmental differences. As Woodward concluded, "Different technologies imposed different kinds of demands on individuals and organizations, and these demands had to be met through an appropriate structure."[2]

Lawrence and Lorsch Studies

The Lawrence and Lorsch studies began in the United States a few years after the Burns and Stalker and Woodward studies. They initially examined ten organizations in three different industries—plastics, consumer foods, and standardized containers. The three industries were selected because of their different environments. The researchers were concerned with the question of whether different structural designs are appropriate for different industries having distinct environments.

They recognized that different internal elements of a company may not have the same external environment, and therefore subunits should not necessarily be organized the same. They divided the external environment into three subenvironments representing marketing, production (technical-economic in their terminology), and research (or science as they referred to it). Each of these three functional areas involves different tasks and different subenvironments, resulting in varying needs for dif-

---

*The Woodward studies have been criticized on several bases. Some have said the results were more a function of size than technology. However, the studies generated a conviction and tremendous interest in the tie between technology and structure.

ferentiation and integration. As noted earlier, Lawrence and Lorsch consider differentiation and integration as the two fundamental processes associated with organization design. *Differentiation* is defined as "the differences in cognitive and emotional orientations among managers in different functional departments, and the differences in formal structure among these departments." *Integration* is "the quality of the state of collaboration that exists among departments that are required to achieve unity of effort by the environment."[3]

In their studies, the extent of differentiation was found to depend on the certainty or uncertainty of the environment and its diversity or homogeneity. If the marketing, production, and research subenvironments are similar in an industry (as they are in the standardized container industry), the environment was characterized as homogeneous. If the three subenvironments differed, the industry environment was considered diverse. Firms in the container industry, with the more homogeneous environment, had less differentiation than firms in the plastics industry which are characterized by a diverse environment.

The firms were also studied in terms of financial success. Successful firms followed the pattern described above; unsuccessful ones tended to deviate and therefore did not meet the environmental demand for differentiation. On the basis of structure, production units in all three industries were most formalized, research units were the least.

Integration needs existed in all three types of industries. Generally the greater the differentiation, the higher the need for integration. Also, the methods and sources of integration varied, depending on the "dominant competitive issue" in the industry. In plastics and foods, where innovative (research) issues are dominant, the research organization provided the internal integration. In the container industry, integration revolved around production, which is the dominant issue. This again supports the concept that the structure of an organization is influenced by its tasks and environment.

The Lawrence and Lorsch studies covered integrative mechanisms, conflict management, and many other factors that space will not allow us to review. Significant for our purposes are their contingency conclusions:

> . . . the internal functioning of organizations must be consistent with the demands of the organization task, technology, or external environment, and the needs of its members if the organization is to be effective.[4]

In general, the Lawrence and Lorsch studies supported the conclusions of Burns and Stalker and of Joan Woodward. In predictable environments, more bureaucratic structures are appropriate; in uncertain environments, a more open, participate structure becomes the most effective.

A TOTAL CONTINGENCY MODEL OF
ORGANIZATION DESIGN

In addition to the referenced studies, others have been conducted that relate some facet of the internal or external environment to organization design (some of which will be reviewed later in this chapter). However, few of these are multivariate studies interrelating a combination of many factors to structure. William B. Wolf identifies twenty-two strategic factors as important in management and organization design. These are the organization charter, location, physical facilities, size, ownership and control, labor force, history, competing organizations, leadership, labor market, supplies market, public image, technology, formal structure, status systems, cliques and interpersonal interactions, communications systems, finances, formal systems of controls, supervisors, job design, and strategic policy.[5] However, he provides little guidance in causally relating the factors to different types of organization structure.

A more complete model of contingency factors in organization design is provided by using the basic management model presented in chapter 3. The primary factors affecting organization tend to be the internal variables of purpose, task, technology, and people. Environmental factors affecting design are social, political, technical, and economic forces. Figure 15-1 displays how structure results from the interaction of internal and external forces. Total organization design is a composite of these factors, although—as Lawrence and Lorsch noted—different elements of the organization (marketing, research, etc.) will be associated with different markets or immediate environments. The effects of these variables on organization structure and design are summarized below.

Purpose (Goals) and Organization Structure

Goals are established that are consistent with the purpose of an organization. In pursuing certain goals, organizations are forced to engage in particular operations and function in specific environments. If an organization's goals are primarily economic, generally it is structured to maximize efficiency. Organizations with political goals (like governments) are less concerned with efficiency and more concerned with social, cultural, and political values, so that (in a democratic society) one finds participative structures, wider use of committees, and groups established to deal with special interests. Universities are also less formalized, with a greater emphasis on participation because of their commitment to democratic institutions and the open society. The economic, social, political, or utilitarian orientation of an organization permeates every aspect of its functioning—including structural relationships.

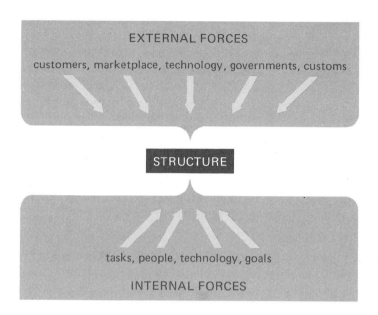

Fig. 15-1. Factors affecting the structure of an organization

Task and Technology Variables and Their Effect on Structure

Many of the studies referred to earlier in this chapter linked task and internal technology with organization design. Routine, standardized production tasks are facilitated by formalized, bureaucratic organizations. The more varied, problem-solving tasks of research require organic, adaptive structures. The routine tasks of production tend to be appropriate for functional or process departmentation, but problem-solving tasks can usually best be handled by product departmentation involving study teams or research groups.[6] People-oriented tasks (like selling) are also associated with less-rigid structure, while tasks that are "things oriented" (like inventory management) are more bureaucratic in nature. Routine tasks also permit a broader span of control than diverse ones.

The pervasive influence of tasks on management was summarized in chapter twelve. Division of labor, position descriptions, and job specifications are all modified by the nature of the tasks involved. Complex tasks call for professional people, who expect to operate with considerable freedom as long as they adhere to the norms of their profession. The Woodward studies noted that production technologies affect span of control, levels of management, line-staff structures, and many other variables.

People and Organization Structure

When the people in an organization are highly skilled and well trained, little control has to be exerted through structure. The result is less formalization, fewer levels, broader spans of control, greater flexibility, and less reliance on rules and procedures. People in jobs requiring limited skills tend to function better in bureaucratic atmospheres. Also, as indicated, professional people in applying their expertise tend to demand more freedom with fewer restrictions. Medical doctors, lawyers, or professional scientists will not tolerate the restrictiveness of overly bureaucratic structures.

If people display little commitment to organization goals or high conflict in interpersonal or intergroup relations, one would expect to find management exerting more control through a definitized structure and the imposition of rules and regulations. The absence of these conditions would barter for greater freedom. As we shall see in the next chapter, expectations determine the roles of individuals in organizations, so ultimately people are at the source of any organization structure.

John J. Morse and Jay W. Lorsch conducted a study of four organizations, two involving standardized duties of manufacturing and two the less routine tasks of research and development. Their basic assumption was that people require a feeling of competence in their work in order to be motivated and be high performers. In the successful production firms structured tasks and organizations were associated with motivation, while in research and development greater flexibility in tasks and organization design contributed to motivation. Thus they concluded, "Although this interrelationship is complex, the best possibility for managerial action probably is in tailoring the organization to fit the task and the people."[7]

The Interaction of Structure Dimensions

It has already been noted that if a manager opts for few levels in a hierarchy, broader spans of control will result; if the desire is for more decentralization, there is typically less emphasis on the hierarchy and fewer regulations affecting freedom of action. Broad differentiation results in a need for integrative mechanisms, and geographical dispersion contributes to decentralization. The features of structure tend to be highly interdependent so that changing one will affect the condition of others.

Scale or size is an example of one organization feature affecting other dimensions of structure. (This dimension is selected because there is an extensive body of research associated with it.) Increasing size tends to be correlated with the following dimensions: more levels in the hierarchy, greater formalization, increased need for decentralization and integration, greater differentiation, and use of the product form of departmentation. Smaller organizations can be successfully managed through personal contact, so there is less need for an elaborate structure featuring a multiplicity of staff units, procedures, and position descriptions. Large organizations are impersonal and require detailed structures to achieve coordination and keep people and work units apprised of how they fit into what is being done. Stanley H. Udy, Jr., a noted sociologist, reached the following conclusion from his studies: "The larger the size of the organization, the greater the number of subgroups in it; hence, the greater the overall emphasis on formal and impersonal rules and specificity of roles."[8]

Some studies do not support the contention that size always results in complex, formalized structures. Organizations like the Democratic party or the alumni association of a large university are examples. Size alone is not necessarily overpowering in demanding a complex structure, but when combined with other variables like sophisticated technology or multiple services and goals (such as the federal government), it tends to move in that direction.

The External Environment and Organization Structure

The various studies referred to in this chapter point out the overriding influence of the external environment on internal structure. The central theme of organizational contingency theory is that changing dynamic environments require organic, adaptive structures for firms to be successful. Stable, more predictive environments call for formalized, bureaucratic structures. However, each internal element of an organization that has the responsibility for obtaining input to the firm or distributing output from it is organized to effectively interface with the portion of the environment that is appropriate. The personnel and procurement departments of an organization are structured to relate to sources of labor and material input. If a firm purchases raw materials, components, and energy sources as inputs, there will be buyers who are specialists in each of these areas. A labor-relations division will be established to deal with unions, and recruiters will be set up as specialists in the categories of manpower that the firm requires.

Output subunits are influenced by external groups in the same way. The marketing department of an organization that sells exclusively to the government will be organized considerably different from one that sells to a variety of commercial outlets. Also, as indicated, the customer form of departmentation will predominate in retailing organizations in order to meet these environmental demands.

Many other elements of the organization are structured by the environment. Various recent studies have shown that the composition of Boards of Directors is influenced by environmental pressures. As another example, firms will switch to franchising when competitors prove that this method of expansion is successful. A firm must adapt to the conditions of the marketplace, and when product lines are modified or customer tastes change, internal structural adjustments are often required.

TECHNOLOGY AND CHANGE.   The question is often asked, what makes some environments volatile, while others are stable? As indicated in chapter 12, the rate of scientific and technological innovation is one of the most important factors. If continual improvements are being made in products and processes, uncertainty is introduced in the marketplace. For instance, since 1950 the introduction of the computer has altered the internal structure of every major corporation in the United States today. In the Lawrence and Lorsch studies, uncertainty of the environment was measured by (1) rate of change of conditions over a period of time, (2) the certainty of information about conditions at any particular time, and (3) the timespan of feedback on decisions. (Quick feedback provides certainty; slow feedback does not.) All three of these factors are strongly influenced by technology.

SOCIAL AND POLITICAL FACTORS AND STRUCTURE.   Many indications have been given of the influence of societal attitudes on organizations. As society has placed less emphasis on authority and stressed the quality of living, organizations have reflected these in their internal functioning. Political actions modify structure in a more obvious way. As governments pass laws relating to equal opportunity employment or environmental protection, organizations respond by appointing affirmative-action officers and setting up pollution-control units. In the accounting, safety, and quality-control aspects of a firm's operations, many activities are designed to monitor and enforce government regulations.

CONTINGENCY ANALYSIS AND DECENTRALIZATION[9]

As a means of representing a total contingency approach to organization structure, the example of decentralization will be used, involving the application of the four-step contingency methodology; (1) Knowing concepts and techniques; (2) Being aware of the trade-offs or the advantages and disadvantages associated with these techniques; (3) Understanding the context of the situation faced; and (4) Matching the trade-offs of the concepts with the needs of the particular situation. Decentralization is selected because interest in the concept has developed an abundance of

information that fits rather easily into the methodology. Another reason for using decentralization is that when the concept became popular in the 1950's and 1960's, many errors were made by firms who adopted it without regard for how it applied to their situation.

CENTRALIZATION OR DECENTRALIZATION

In favor of the decentralizers, it can certainly be said that excessive centralization is a common error which can do extreme damage to an organization. Most people are familiar with the pattern: the ever-lengthening delays while head office makes up its mind, the futile attempts to lay down universal laws and procedures however inappropriate to the special circumstances of those affected, the top people growing more and more out of touch with the day-to-day realities, the men who work close to the products or customers having to refer decisions which they have the knowledge and experience to make correctly up to people who have neither, the stillbirth of enterprising ideas because of the frustration of waiting for the go ahead until it's too late, or getting it in time but hedged in with reservations and modifications which make success almost impossible. But, of course, the dangers of excessive decentralization are just as damaging: production schedules being drawn up without consulting a sales forecast, two representatives—one from the region and one from the product division—trying to sell the same product to the same customer while telling him conflicting facts about it, sales drives aimed at a volume of orders which the factories cannot in fact meet, good young managers bottled up in inadequate jobs because their bosses will not release them for promotion in other departments and have no vacancies in their own, and the general state of affairs where the planning department is an expensive joke and the firm has as many policies as managers.

Quoted from Antony Jay, *Management and Machiavelli* (New York: Holt, Rinehart and Winston, Inc., 1967), pp. 58–59.

The Trade-offs of Centralization and Decentralization

Certain advantages are associated with decentralization that are the corresponding limitations of centralization, with the reverse also being true. The advantages of centralization are as follows:

- The most common argument in favor of centralization is that it is a means of achieving conformity and coordination. If all major decisions emerge from one point, it is simpler to integrate the activities of units or individuals, the example being an airport control-tower operator.
- Top managers are generally the most experienced and proven executives. Accordingly, they should be better equipped to make decisions.
- Top-level managers have a broader perspective of the total organization because of their training and the level at which they function. Accordingly, they are more likely to make broader decisions and avoid suboptimization.
- Centralized decision making will ensure better balance in the organization. In functional organizations or in those with competing subdivisions (such as the athletic program of a university), this balancing of organizational interests cannot occur except at the top (by the Director of Athletics).
- Centralized control tends to avoid the duplication of resources, equipment, and personnel that can occur when operations are decentralized.
- Centralization at the top permits the pooling of sufficient resources to employ staff experts when this is desirable. Planning, personnel, and procurement are examples.
- Centralization tends to be consistent with the need for strong leadership. Centralization adds power and prestige to the executive, which may be critical in time of crisis or when momentum is needed to exert an all-out effort to accomplish a particular objective. In this respect, it is consistent with the ego needs of executives who seek status and power in organizations.

The seven advantages of centralization are countered by seven advantages of decentralization:

- Decentralization reduces the workload on overburdened executives. The typical American executive works fifty-five to sixty hours per week, and yet organizations suffer from delays in getting top management to act on backlogged issues. Decentralization is set up to relieve the executive from operating problems so he can spend more time on policy matters.
- Decentralization is strongly supported by behavioralists as a means of improving motivation at lower levels of the organization. It en-

hances recognition, status, and feelings of accomplishment. The opportunity to make decisions and function independently activates strong drives within individuals. This can result in greater commitment to the organization and improved productivity.

- Decentralization is said to be more democratic and consistent with the rights of people in organizations. The individual does have greater say, and position-based influence is more equally divided.

- Decentralization gives individuals an opportunity to learn by doing. It is difficult to develop managerial talent if upcoming supervisors are not permitted to make decisions and participate in the management process.

- Decentralization leads to quicker decisions at lower levels, since decisions do not have to be referred up through the hierarchy.

- The individual immediately associated with a problem will normally be more aware of local conditions than the higher-level executive.

- Decentralization often results in improved controls and performance measurements. When relatively independent units are established, the managers can be held responsible for costs and productivity. Profit decentralization (such as that made popular by General Motors) provides considerable freedom of action on the part of plant managers as long as they achieve profit objectives.

Situational Variables in Decentralizing

Research studies and management practice point to thirteen situational variables that determine the appropriate relative organizational mix of centralization and decentralization:

1. The purpose and goals of an organization
2. The knowledge and experience of executives
3. The skill, knowledge, and attitudes of subordinates
4. The scale or size of the structure
5. Geographical dispersion of the structure
6. The level of technology in the tasks
7. The time frame of the decisions
8. The significance of the decisions
9. Whether subordinates will accept and be motivated by the decision
10. The status of the planning and control systems
11. The status of the information systems
12. The degree of conformity and coordination required in the tasks and flow of work
13. The status of environmental factors (governments, markets, etc.)

PURPOSE AND GOALS. As indicated earlier, organizations committed to open, democratic relationships, such as universities, will need to be decentralized—a clothing store that is a sole proprietorship will not. On the other hand, a diversified corporation like a conglomerate will be forced to decentralize because of the varied product lines.

KNOWLEDGE AND EXPERIENCE OF EXECUTIVES. If top managers are considerably more knowledgeable and experienced than lower-level subordinates, it creates conditions conducive to centralization.

SKILL, KNOWLEDGE, AND ATTITUDES OF SUBORDINATES. One of the obvious prerequisites for decentralization is skilled, trained, and committed subordinates. When these conditions exist in the workforce, it greatly reduces the risks of decentralization.

ORGANIZATON SIZE. In large organizations, top executives do not have the time or knowledge to make all managerial decisions. They are forced to decentralize in order to keep the organization functioning.

GEOGRAPHICAL DISPERSION. The more dispersed plants and offices are, the more difficult it is for a central individual to have the knowledge of local conditions that is a prerequisite for decision making.

TECHNICAL COMPLEXITY OF TASKS. Technology has increased the complexity of tasks and placed greater reliance on knowledge-based influence. The hierarchy of a firm today represents much less a knowledge hierarchy than it did fifty years ago. No one is more familiar with the technical details of a project than the responsible research scientist, and frequently higher-level managers are ill-equipped to make this sort of technical decision. Increased expertise in all organizational activities has forced a funneling of authority to these centers of knowledge.

THE TIME FRAME OF DECISIONS. A quarterback, sergeant, or control-tower dispatcher makes decisions under different time constraints than a committee considering policy changes. When quick on-the-spot decisions are to be made, the authority to make them should be delegated.

THE SIGNIFICANCE OF THE DECISION. Historically the standard criterion for delegating authority has been the significance of the decision. High-cost decisions are retained; decisions with a minimal cost impact are delegated. Position descriptions often define authority to make decisions on a cost basis. A junior buyer can sign contracts up to $5000, a buyer $25,000, and a senior buyer $100,000.

WILLINGNESS OF SUBORDINATES TO ACCEPT AND BE MOTIVATED BY THE DECISION. Subordinates are more likely to accept and be motivated by a decision if they participate in making it. When acceptance of the decision by subordinates is important (such as in a voluntary organization), and especially when the subordinates are to function independently in implementing the decision, decentralization is advisable.

STATUS OF THE PLANNING AND CONTROL SYSTEMS.   If a company has clear goals and a plan for achieving them, a supervisor is more willing to let subordinates make decisions. If a subordinate is aware of plans and procedures, the supervisor feels more assured that the right decisions will be made—consistent with organizational objectives.

STATUS OF INFORMATION SYSTEMS.   In decision making it is emphasized that the individual with the most complete, accurate information should make the decision. Many management experts predicted a return to centralization in the 1960's and 1970's because the computer would place current, comprehensive information in the hands of the executive. However, such recentralization has not occurred, although realtime (instantaneous) management-information systems do place the top executives in a better position to make more decisions.

CONFORMITY AND COORDINATION REQUIRED IN THE WORKFLOW.   When the workflow requires the coordination and integration of a large number of units, this can most effectively be achieved through central control. Such orchestration is accomplished in production through a central planning and control unit. In more independent tasks like selling, there is little need for centralization.

ENVIRONMENTAL FACTORS.   As an organization interfaces with outside groups, it is usually desirable to internally centralize these points of contact in order to maintain continuity and achieve more expertise. (Dealing with labor unions, customers, suppliers, and communities are examples.) Also, decentralized structures are normally more adaptive and resilient and therefore more appropriate in firms with unstable environments.

MATCHING THE TRADE-OFFS WITH THE DEMANDS OF SITUATIONS.   The problem for the organizer is to diagnose his or her own situation well enough to know how far to go in decentralizing. He or she must evaluate the significance of the thirteen situation variables (and others that may be appropriate,) and match these with conditions desired in the organization, based on the benefits of centralization or decentralization. All thirteen factors will not apply in all situations, and the significance of each will be weighted differently, based on conditions unique to each organization. Many of the variables will also likely be conflicting, in that some will point to centralization, others to decentralization. However, it is on the basis of this broad analysis that a sound decision can be made and a long period of trial and error avoided.

Many of the current practices in American industry support the methodology proposed. Organizations with products and tasks requiring coordination and tight control are centralized. Companies with dispersed plants, scientific operations, and unstable environments are more decentralized. Major corporations such as General Motors, General Electric, and Esmark are known for their decentralized structures. (Esmark started a decentralization process in the late 1960's that took six years to accomplish and resulted in the establishment of one thousand profit centers.[10]) Others, notably in chemicals, transportation, and banking and finance, have remained more centralized.

There are many variations within a corporation. Manufacturing operations tend to be decentralized, because a local knowledge of operating conditions is required and production lines cannot be shut down while decisions are referred to higher levels. Financial management is usually the most centralized of all internal functions because of the cost consequences, the centralized processing of most financial data, and the tendency for the basic controls of a company to rely on financial measures. Marketing is typically a mixture. Sales is decentralized because of geographical dispersion and because different approaches and methods must be used with different customers. However, advertising is centralized in order to pool resources and gain conformity in projecting company image. Computer operations are normally centralized because of the major capital investment required. Personnel functions are usually centralized to gain conformity in wage and salary administration and to control top-level staffing, but dealing with morale problems is typically a local condition and therefore decentralized.

Decentralization is also standard in organizations comprised of professionals. Also, decentralization is more common when things are going well and a firm is meeting its profit objectives, but centralization occurs when times are difficult and top management feels that they need to exert more control. There is obviously no answer to the question of whether centralization or decentralization is preferable except as it applies situationally.

CONTINGENCY THEORY AND ORGANIZATION DESIGN

Contingency theory as it relates to organization design holds that structure results from a set of interacting internal and external forces. Since these forces are often changing, it argues for flexibility in structure and a capacity to adapt. It calls for managers who are sensitive to organization variables and who are capable of evaluating a broad set of conditions. It also expresses a need for a high tolerance of ambiguity, because in analyzing forces and conditions in organizations no clear signals will point to the requirement for any pure form of design. The blend of mixed forces will normally result in a blend of organization concepts. Searching for pure organization forms becomes as fruitless as the search for the one best way to organize.

In viewing structure, the methodology of contingency approaches is again best shown through the use of profiles. The major theme in contingency design, based on the Burns and Stalker and Lawrence and Lorsch studies, is that firms with stable environments are most effective with mechanistic, stable structures, while organizations with unstable, dynamic environments generally require organic, flexible structures to be effective. Figure 15-2 represents profiles of two firms that are characterized by these different environments.

The top profile is of an electric power company. The assumption is that the firm currently relies on hydroelectric power, where technology is stable. Sales are also quite stable resulting from a known group of users and available forecasts on the population and industrial growth of the region. The product—electric power—stays the same, and competitors are also fixed—with often no major direct competitor in the market region. Government regulation of utilities is known and relatively static, although social values in relation to power companies are changing—especially if their processes emit pollutants. All of these conditions call for a mechanistic, stable structure for the power company.

The lower portion of figure 15-2 is a firm that develops and produces pollution-control devices, many of which are sold to electric power companies. Products would include cooling towers, fabric filters, mechanical collectors, precipitators, scrubber systems, and other devices. In this industry, the technology is rapidly changing, product innovation is common, competitors are entering and leaving the market, government regulations are increasing, and social values have experienced considerable modification in recent years. All of these contribute to instability of sales and the need for an organic, flexible structure to match the uncertain environment.

SUMMARY

Classic theory viewed organizing as a problem in applying abstract principles. The contingency approach to organizing emphasizes that structure results from the interaction of a set of forces internal and external to the firm. The limitation of classical principles is that they result in a

Electric Power Company

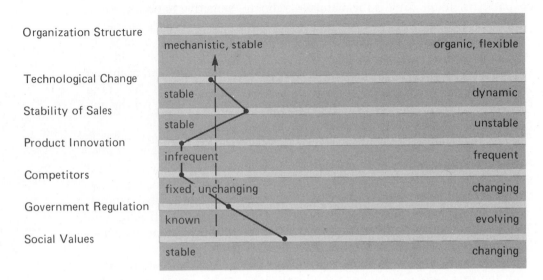

Firm That Develops and Produces Pollution Control Devices

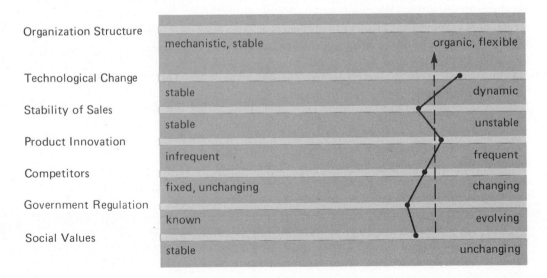

Fig. 15-2. Contingency considerations in an organization design

bureaucratic structure that tends to be rigid, and they often deceive the practitioner into assuming that structure is determined by application of a limited number of rational concepts. Also, classical principles tend to ignore factors external to the organization and are often contrary to modern concepts of motivation.

Studies conducted by Burns and Stalker, Joan Woodward, and Lawrence and Lorsch all indicated that different conditions call for the application of different organizing concepts, and that there is no one best form of organization design. Their studies point to technology and the forces creating either stability or uncertainty in the external environment as the most significant factors.

A total method for interrelating the primary factors affecting structure is provided by the contingency model of management. The purpose, task, technology, and people involved in an organization all provide certain types of pressures for structural design. External factors like the marketplace, political and social forces, and technology also place demands on structure, meaning that a given design results from many forces and conditions.

Decentralization provides a comprehensive example of contingency theory. The many different advantages and limitations of both centralization and decentralization were presented, and thirteen variables were proposed as those that are the most significant in determining the degree of decentralization that is desirable.

QUESTIONS FOR STUDY AND DISCUSSION

1. In what respects is the contingency approach to organization structure different from classic approaches?
2. Why have bureaucratic approaches to structure been criticized?
3. In the following studies, explain the variables that the researchers concluded affect structure:
   A. Burns and Stalker
   B. Joan Woodward
   C. Lawrence and Lorsch
4. Explain how the following affect structure:
   A. Organizational purpose   C. Tasks
   B. People   D. The marketplace
5. Explain how different internal and external variables affect the structure of the following organizations:
   A. Movie theater   C. Student ROTC unit
   B. Church   D. School board

6. To what degree should the total organization and its subunits be decentralized in the following examples:
   A. Post office   C. Life insurance company
   B. Hospital   D. Local chain drug store
7. How can a manager determine whether to use a bureaucratic or organic structure in his particular organization?
8. Develop profiles similar to figure 15-2 for a bank and a clothing store.

Case Problem:
COMPARATIVE DIFFERENCES
IN ORGANIZATION STRUCTURE

Case One:
The firm involved makes frozen pastries for sale in retail grocery stores
and supermarkets. It makes a variety of frozen cakes, pies, and cookies.
There are over 600 employees in the plant working on a three-shift basis.
Over 500 of the employees are unskilled and performing the various
machine, baking, and packaging operations necessary to produce the 40
different varieties of pastries. Because of sanitation considerations and
the timed-sequence involved in baking, tasks are specifically defined and
restricted by many rules and regulations. The firm has three other production plants and a separate marketing division.

Case Two:
The university in the same community has a special education project.
The division, operating under the College of Education, has its own
laboratory and classroom for children between the ages of five and fifteen
who are mentally handicapped or have special learning problems. The
school is dependent primarily on federal funds and is experimental in
nature. There is a staff of over forty psychologists, teachers, and educators
who are specialists in working with children displaying these problems.
The division has a variety of programs ranging all the way from regular
classes of up to fifteen students to working with one individually.

How would you expect the structure of the two organizations to differ?
Why?
How would the environments of the two organizations differ? Would
this affect internal structure?

How would the tasks and people of the two organizations differ and how would these affect structure?

Case Problem:
HOW MUCH DECENTRALIZATION?

There are three buildings located in a shopping center in a community next to each other. One is a chain grocery store with thirty-five employees. It has a store manager, three department managers, and thirty-one checkers, baggers, and stock clerks. The headquarters for the store is in Chicago, and there are over 200 outlets in the United States.

The second building houses the branch office of a life insurance company. The branch has one division manager, fourteen salesmen, and three secretaries. The company sells only life insurance, although it has a wide variety of policies.

The third building contains a travel agency. The agency is locally owned and operated. The agency acquires tickets on all major airlines and is tied in with a group that arranges tours and excursions. The owner has six employees who make travel arrangements and deal with the public in ticket sales.

Would the degree of centralization or decentralization differ in these companies? Why?

In the example of the first two organizations, which aspects of their operations are decentralized? Which aspects would be controlled by the home offices? Would pricing be decentralized? Advertising? Could either change product lines? Could they build new buildings without home office approval?

How much authority would each of the local managers delegate to their subordinates? Would it differ in the three companies?

What major difference in decentralization would you expect to find comparing the branches to the home offices of the first two organizations assuming each headquarters had over 1000 employees?

Footnotes

1. Tom Burns and G. M. Stalker, *The Management of Innovation* (London: Tavistock Publications Limited, 1966), p. 125.
2. Joan Woodward, *op. cit.*, p. vi.

3. Jay W. Lorsch, "Introduction to the Structural Design of Organizations," contained in Gene W. Dalton, Paul R. Lawrence, and Jay W. Lorsch, *Organizational Structure and Design*, (Homewood, Illinois: Richard D. Irwin, Inc., 1970), p. 5.

4. Jay W. Lorsch and Paul R. Lawrence, *Studies in Organization Design* (Homewood, Illinois: Richard D. Irwin, Inc., 1970), p. 1.

5. William B. Wolf, *Management: Readings Towards a General Theory*, (Belmont, Calif: Wadsworth Publishing Company, Inc., 1964), p. 325.

6. For a verification study supporting this concept see Arthur H. Walker and Jay W. Lorsch, "Organizational Choice: Product versus Function," contained in *Studies in Organization Design, op. cit.*, pp. 36–53.

7. John J. Morse and Jay W. Lorsch, "Beyond Theory Y," *Harvard Business Review*, May–June, 1970, p. 68.

8. Stanley H. Udy, Jr., "The Comparative Analysis of Organizations," in James G. March (Ed.), *Handbook of Organizations* (Chicago: Rand McNally and Company, 1965), p. 693.

9. This section is adapted from chapter 4 of the author's book *Situational Management* (New York: American Management Associations, 1973), and from "A Contingency Approach to Decentralization," *S.A.M. Advanced Management Journal*, July 1974, pp. 9–18.

10. *Business Week*, August 3, 1974, p. 48.

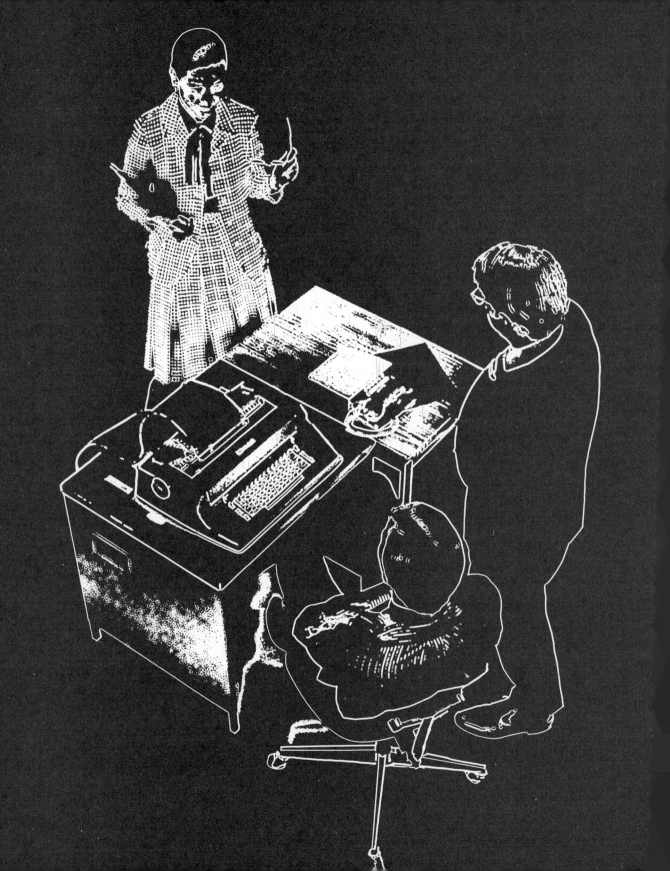

The Organization as a Social System

What relationships exist in a social system?

What structure exists in an informal organization?

What characterizes a group?

What determines how a group functions?

How do roles influence an individual's behavior?

What determines the status relationships within a group?

SYSTEM RELATIONSHIPS
WITHIN AN ORGANIZATION

When a formal organization is established and people are brought into close physical proximity for long periods of time, they are forced to continually relate with each other. Even though they must interact to accomplish their assigned duties, they also seek to interact in order to satisfy social needs. Out of this interaction, social relationships and patterns of behavior that tend to be perpetuated are developed. Some of these relationships are formally prescribed in procedures, job descriptions, and other guides, but a significant number evolves merely from the interaction process itself. Status differences develop, communication channels are established, and a set of practices and techniques unique to that organization becomes accepted. Each organization has its own internal life that tends toward a closed system: it condones the behavior of members adhering to the subculture and rejects outsiders who are not part of the group.

Natural System Relationships

Group behavior is dynamic as people come and go, duties are modified, external environmental factors fluctuate, and other elements of the organization experience forced or voluntary changes. This is referred to as the *natural-systems* approach to organizations, which places emphasis on the *functioning* as opposed to the *structure* of groups. Organizations composed of people display many of the growth, decay, and maturation processes of other living systems. Adaptation and the evolution of unique patterns of interaction characterize the existence of an organization more than the static organization charts.

Organizations display basic systems relationships and thus cannot be understood by studying the acts of any single member—just as a system cannot be understood by studying individual parts. Through interaction, joint goals are established, codes of conduct developed, and communication channels that characterize group behavior perpetuated. The social interaction that constitutes the functioning of a group is, by definition, a set of dependent relationships. When individuals interact, they are engaged in a mutual set of influence relationships. Interaction tends to develop into repetitive accommodation patterns as individuals find rewards from the reciprocal ties established and seek stability in their interpersonal relations.

The Organization as an Open System

The other dimension of an organization as a social system is tied to open-system concepts. A firm constitutes an open system as it obtains input in the form of manpower, materials, and energy from the environment, processes these, and distributes goods and services to its membership or consumers in the environment. Using this as a point of departure, many different subsystems can be established relating to production, communication, distribution, and finance, as well as the social structure involving people.

INFORMAL ORGANIZATIONS AND GROUPS

The differences between formal and informal structure have already been enumerated. Another significant distinction is between an informal organization and a group. Informal organization will be examined in detail, followed by a comparative analysis exploring the nature of groups.

Informal (Emergent) Organization

After a formal organization is established, the informal structure evolves naturally through the interaction of the participants. The informal structure is also called the *emergent* structure, because it arises naturally within the formally established organization. It is impossible to formally prescribe everything that is to take place in an organization. The gaps are unofficially filled in by individuals as they go about their prescribed duties. Certain procedures will be established for a retail-sales position, but the individual will also have to develop methods for handling relationships with groups like buyers, customers, and the credit office. A repairman will be given responsibility for maintaining copying machines, but he may have to develop his own work sequence, points of contact within departments, and a system of priorities. The elaboration of the formal structure through informal action is essential if the organization is to function.

Informal organization is spontaneous and dynamic. It changes a static structure into a functioning organization. Informal organization provides the social grease that lubricates the formal apparatus. Duties, procedures, and functional statements are converted from vague guides into specific actions. Where the formal structure is ill-conceived, means are developed to bypass it in the effort to "get things done." The emergent organization is best represented by the influence structure rather than the authority hierarchy of an organization. The authority structure may point to the new second lieutenant as being in charge, but the informal structure may look to the experienced sergeant for direction. Informal organization provides the flesh around the bony superstructure that converts an organization into a living, functioning, goal-directed group.

The Nature of Groups

The primary difference between a *group* and an *organization* is that in a group people are psychologically aware of each other as they interact to achieve common objectives. (To avoid confusion in terminology, such a unit should be referred to as a *psychological group* rather than just a *group* as the term has been more loosely used so far in this text.) If MacDonald's builds a new restaurant, hires a manager and other workers, and gives each employee prescribed duties, they have established an organization. However, as the business comes into operation and individuals start to attribute certain status, knowledge, and ability to others, they tend to behave differently because of this knowledge.

This awareness of others that influences interaction patterns signals the formation of a psychological group. Since such awareness can normally be attained only through face-to-face contact, it means that psychological groups are small in size, usually numbering twenty or less. Being small, they offer unusual opportunities for status and belonging need satisfaction, which means they hold strong appeal for the participants. Small groups enhance participation and understanding, which result in more internal cohesion and commitment to the group.

Groups also differ from organizations in that not only are common goals shared, but member values, sentiments, and frames of reference are generally more compatible. Groups develop a subculture of their own that is constantly monitored in the intimate contact of face-to-face relationships. A final distinction between informal organization and groups is that groups can be deliberately established (formation of a poker club) as well as arise spontaneously (individuals who tend to go to coffee together). Informal organization, on the other hand, always evolves spontaneously from within the formal structure.

The Formation of Groups

(In the examples provided in the balance of this chapter, spontaneous groups will be utilized rather than groups deliberately established. Formal group formation has already been explored in detail, and spontaneous group characteristics apply to informal organization also.)

Since groups arise from the interaction of people, it means that physical proximity is a primary cause. When workers are forced into a common location—such as on an assembly line—spontaneous groups soon develop. However, there are many other factors that contribute to group formation. Common values, interests, occupations, and age are conducive to this process. Similar backgrounds and organization ties, such as going to the same college or belonging to the same church, initiate the evolution of groups. Many form as chance groups (a carpool), but normally a shared interest such as sports, politics, or cooperating to undercut a supervisor will spark the initiation of a group. In the work situation, status groups resulting from similar job titles at different levels in the hierarchy are a primary contributor to group formation. Hourly employees tend to go to lunch together, converse on coffee breaks, and participate in football pools. Individuals who are middle managers, engineers, full professors, or members of the basketball team tend to do the same.

The underlying reason people belong to groups (as indicated in our discussions on motivation in chapter 11) is because of the rewards or need satisfaction gained from this behavior. Groups are the most significant source of need satisfaction open to individuals. Security, status, and affiliation needs are all satisfied through groups. An individual feels more secure in a group than facing the world alone. When threatened by a supervisor, individuals tend to strengthen their ties with other group members ("The supervisor is unfair, isn't he!") as a means of offsetting this insecurity. Studies show that soldiers in battle are braver with comrades than they are fighting alone. Also, acceptance needs are best achieved in the intimacy of the small group. Status, or recognition by others, results from interpersonal relations. Self-actualization is achieved through groups providing appropriate outlets, such as are found in professional organizations and groups engaged in sporting activities, hobbies, etc. In the aggregate, an individual's identification with a group resulting in group cohesion is a function of the degree of need satisfaction obtained through membership.

The Structure and Functioning of Groups

Because groups are formed from the interaction of members and consist of shifting alliances that are modified by daily events, the primary concern of organization analysts is the process underlying what happens in groups. Even though this tends to be varied, groups develop patterns of interaction and behavior that tend to be repetitive and hence constitute structure. This social structure forming the organizational fabric of the group consists of the following nine features:

1. common goals
2. group norms
3. reward and punishment systems
4. informal leadership
5. expectations and roles
6. status relationships

7. communication networks
8. decision-making processes
9. organizational climate

1. COMMON GOALS.   Common goals are the hub around which all of the activity in an organization is centered. People have influence in an organization if the balance of the group perceives them as capable of making major contributions to goal accomplishment. Clearly defined goals tend to facilitate group performance and contribute to group cohesiveness. The goals of the group are established so as to suit a majority of the membership or those with the most influence. The individual's commitment to the group is primarily a function of the consistency between his goals and those of the group.

2. GROUP NORMS.   Norms are commonly held ideas among group members, regarding how categories of persons (usually group members) should behave under specific circumstances. As a group develops, members tend to establish guides constituting acceptable behavior on the part of those persons identified with the group. Norms relate to specific acts, such as attendance at meetings, support of group activities, acceptable levels of production, and so on. *Values* are commonly held beliefs that are broader and more universal than norms. They relate to what is right and wrong or proper and improper—such as honesty, frugality, and so forth.

The most commonly discussed informal group norm in management literature is the concept of the *fair day's work*. A company will typically establish a formal production standard for an individual or a work group such as daily assembling 500 radios or processing 150,000 cartons of frozen peas. However, it is inevitable within each informal group that an informal norm be established regarding the level of production that the group deems acceptable. If the group feels that 450 radios or 140,000 cartons of peas is "fair," this usually regulates the pace at which the group produces. The fair day's work concept results from the process identified in chapter 11 as the psychological contract. Based on how fair they perceive the company treats them in terms of pay, working conditions, nature of supervision, etc., the group evolves a standard or level of production they feel the company deserves in return.

Groups offer extremely strong forms of social control. Studies show that typically ninety percent of a group will stay within the range established by the group norm, and only ten percent will reject the norm or be "rate busters." Individuals coming into work groups bring with them specific work habits, aspirations for "getting ahead in the organization," and feelings of commitment toward their employer. However, the opportunities for security, affiliation, and status need satisfaction offered by the group motivates most individuals to adhere to group norms and adjust their work habits, aspirations, and loyalties accordingly. Norms like the fair day's work concept tend to be extremely strong at lower organizational levels, where many of the opportunities for need satisfaction are derived from group activities. As one moves higher in the organization, the norms of the group tend to be more closely tied to formal organization norms because of the rewards involved. Also, individuals at higher levels find more opportunities for status and achievement from their assigned duties.

Group norms, as other features of groups, can work both for and against the formal organization. If the individual norm as established by the group is to machine fifty to sixty parts an hour, the group will apply pressure on the individual producing seventy-five parts to get him to reduce his effort, but members will also pressure the individual producing thirty-five parts to carry his fair share of the load. A forester tells the story of how among twenty-five summer hires there was one individual whose personal habits of cleanliness were objectional to the others on the crew. The forester wondered whether to personally bring this to the worker's attention at the possible risk of the individual gaining the sympathy of the informal group. However, the supervisor wisely knew from previous experience that as the individuals interacted the group would take care of the problem. Within a short time several members of the group, were throwing the person in the shower nightly, and soon his behavior changed to that more consistent with the group norm.

An important lesson that every supervisor comes to learn, whether he is directing key-punch operators, carpenters, secretaries, or accounting clerks, is that the problem of raising productivity is not merely working with individuals to get them to increase their output, but attempting to adjust the informal group's productivity norm. Success is a function of many things, but it relates primarily to the strength of the group's ties, the relationship between the supervisor and the group, and the group's identification with secondary organizations, such as labor unions.

3. REWARD AND PUNISHMENT SYSTEMS. Groups establish reward and punishment systems as a means of getting individuals to conform to group norms and support group goals. These are all tied to the rewards (need satisfaction) an individual gains from group identification. Individuals who will not conform are typically isolated (deprived of social need satisfaction). Those who conform or lead out in providing support gain status in terms of respect and leadership positions. Initially punish-

ORGANIZATIONAL SOCIALIZATION

Organizational socialization is the process by which a new member learns the value system, norms, and required behavior patterns of a group. Edgar H. Schein explains the concept as follows:

"Organizational socialization is the process of 'learning the ropes,' the process of being indoctrinated and trained, the process of being taught what is important in an organization or some subunit thereof. This process occurs in school. It occurs again, and perhaps most dramatically, when the graduate enters an organization on his first job. It occurs again when he switches within the organization from one department to another, or from one rank level to another. It occurs all over again if he leaves one organization and enters another.

"The new member must learn not to drive Chevrolets if he is working for Ford, not to criticize the organization in public, not to wear the wrong kind of clothes or be seen in the wrong kind of places. If the organization is a school, beyond learning the content of what is taught, the student must accept the value of education, he must try to learn without cheating, he must accept the authority of the faculty and behave appropriately to the student role. He must not be rude in the classroom or openly disrespectful to the professor."

Quoted from Edgar H. Schein, "Organizational Socialization and the Profession of Management," *Industrial Management Review*, Winter 1968, pp. 2–3.

ment involves kidding or some verbal goading, but it then moves to ostracism and can lead to physical force (as in the example of the forestry crew).

These steps are illustrated in an incident involving skilled workers who made sand molds in a metal-refining operation. The informal norm had been for each worker to make twelve in the morning and twelve in the afternoon. A skilled worker was hired who initially made the molds at approximately double the pace of the average worker. He was informed by several of the workers that he had better slow his pace and produce along with the rest of the group. Initially he ignored their warnings and continued at his established pace. After several days, when going to the morning break, the other members of the group walked through his molds and ruined his work. Soon his output came in line with that of the group's.

Students find group pressure in their activities. If the rest of the group decides to go to a movie rather than study, there is pressure on the "bookworm" to go along. If a student's associates want to study together for examinations, pressure is applied to the person who may prefer to study alone. Research studies demonstrate that people are inclined to conform to the group and accept group perceptions. In a series of studies, six individuals were asked to guess the length of a line or to tell if a spotlight moved in a dark room. The first five individuals were instructed to give erroneous answers (the line being much longer than it actually was or the light moving when it did not). Under these conditions, the sixth individual typically modified his answer to more nearly conform to group perceptions.

4. INFORMAL LEADERSHIP. A feature of all groups is that informal leaders emerge who influence group activity and are looked to by other members in time of crisis or at key decision points. Informal leaders gain and lose influence with the tide of events and the constant shifting of group ties. The same leader is normally not the leader in all situations. If aggressive action is required, the members may look to one individual, but if negotiation and reconciliation are necessary, they may look to another. Leaders arise for a variety of reasons. Age, seniority, knowledge, personality characteristics, work location, and many other factors can be significant. Basically, as noted, the group looks to the individual as leader who is perceived to be most influential in achieving the group's goals. The leader's values, objectives, and behavior are usually congruent with the group's.

The existence of informal leaders provides relatively clear implications for the formal manager. The manager must be aware of the group processes and of informal leaders, because if he is attempting to introduce change—such as new methods or production standards—he needs to develop a strategy for gaining acceptance of the informal leader or leaders. Taking actions that will alienate group leaders will almost surely result in failure. When a manager purposely engages in a power struggle with the informal leader, he is creating tensions that can solidify the group against the formal organization. This does not imply that the manager should "give in" to the informal leader. The objective should be to win the support of the leader through effective interpersonal relations, thus gaining a valuable ally instead of creating an enemy.

5. EXPECTATIONS AND ROLES. The expectations that individuals develop concerning their own activities and the actions of others in a group are strong determinants of behavior. (A more thorough discussion of these concepts is reserved for a later section in this chapter.)

6. STATUS RELATIONSHIPS.   As individuals become psychologically aware of each other through group processes, they attribute certain competence to their associates. These subtle differences eventually result in a status structure within the group. The development of status differences in informal groups is as inevitable as the hierarchy in formal structures. (The complexity of status considerations necessitates that it also be covered in more detail later in the chapter.)

7. COMMUNICATION NETWORKS.   The intimacy of the small groups makes communication both open and rapid. Referred to as the *grapevine*, the informal communication channels established in small groups spread both fact and rumor at a wildfire pace that normally exceeds that of information processed through official channels. The knowledge of who communicates with whom, how frequently, and over what subjects tells much about what happens in groups. Communication deserves its recognition as one of the most important processes relating to group activity.

8. DECISION-MAKING PROCESSES.   Closely associated with communication channels is the decision-making process. In order to function and carry on its activities, a group must engage in decision making. Groups develop methods for making decisions that are consistent with their other internal processes. Strong informal leaders will tend to dominate the processes in some groups, while a more analytical approach will be characteristic of groups containing members who are trained accordingly. In some groups, broad participation will characterize the process; in others it will be controlled by the power faction.

9. ORGANIZATIONAL CLIMATE.   Organizational climate represents a synthesis of many of the first eight factors covered. Organizational climate consists of members' perceptions of the prevailing attitudes, modes of behavior, constraints, and other properties that relate to the internal setting of an organization. Climate results from the existence of group norms, expectations, prevailing leadership styles, reward and punishment systems, and group goals. The composite influence of these factors, along with those involving formal structure, is to create a psychological atmosphere which the individual perceives as "open," "closed," "encouraging innovation," "demanding conformity," "dominated by fear," "aloof," "considerate," or having many other such dimensions. Climate is to a degree the shared frames of reference that individuals come to experience in cohesive groups. Their values, attitudes, and feelings about things both external and internal take on a group orientation.

Group versus Individual Characteristics

Groups have many of the characteristics of individuals and other living organisms. They are adaptive and experience stages of growth. However, as is frequently pointed out, a group does not have a will of its own; group action is directed by the concensus of the dominating element of the group and consists of individuals interacting in a common social context. However, individual perceptions are not the same as group perceptions, and the individual's norms and values are rarely identical with those of the group.

When people perceive themselves as a group, a set of composite needs evolve which typifies group behavior. These needs are only motivational, because they meet the needs of the individual members, but they result in group reaction to factors such as external threats. For instance, a group has needs relating to internal consistency, continuity, security, and quite often growth. An administrator who attempts to eliminate a group or formal organizational unit soon learns that he is inviting the wrath of the individuals involved. Even when the initial purpose and goals of a formal group may have been achieved or are superseded, the group responds to its composite needs by attempting to extend group goals and find other reasons for continuing its existence. The Brotherhood of Locomotive Firemen, the March of Dimes (converting from infantile paralysis to birth defects), the Census Bureau (expanding from the conducting of a census every ten years to a major statistics-gathering agency of the federal government) are all examples.

Individuals function in groups by combining to thwart external threats, acting to maintain consistency, and attempting to expand group power. The latter growth incentive possibly represents a value of the larger American culture. There is even a phenomena such as a group-aspiration level that rises when the group is successful and falls when it experiences failure.[1] However, even though cohesive groups have an internal life of their own that strongly modifies the behavior of members, this internal life is created, modified, and subject to destruction by individuals.

ROLES AND THE SOCIAL SYSTEM

Role is defined as the behavior expected of someone who occupies a particular position within a group. Two points are significant in this definition. One is that role relates to a position, not an individual. It relates to the position of "foreman," not to expectations regarding Bill Jeffries, who happens to be the foreman. The prescriptions for Bill's behavior result from his holding the position of foreman, not from his personality or individual characteristics. Personality influences how Bill will fulfill the role, but the basic role pattern derives from the position. Also, role represents the set of expectations that all members of a group have for an individual who holds a particular position within the group. It is not solely management's or Bill's expectations, but the composite of all expectations.

The feature of group activity that is probably the most influential in determining individual behavior is the role one assumes. In fact, role is of such significance in structuring organizations that two leading social psychologists define an organization simply as an "open system of roles."[2] They also call role the "building block of social systems and the summation of the requirements with which the system confronts the individual member."[3]

Role is determined by the social system. Three sources are normally involved. In a formal group, a role is partially determined by management. The individual is given a specific job description that depicts duties and responsibilities and hence partially defines what management expects of the incumbent of a position. Role is also determined by the incumbent's perceptions and expectations. The individual has certain values, attitudes, and knowledge that he brings to the position which influence his interpretation of how he is supposed to behave. The third source of role is the expectations of peers and others that one works with in the organization. These expectations are projected through interpersonal relations, and are strongly influenced by the social setting of the group.

Role Set and Multiple Roles

Role is a common phenomena of all groups. Women have had a traditional role in society, which has recently undergone significant modification; a father has a particular role in the family; the company president is subject to a set of expectations that represents his role in the firm; and individuals perceive that custodians are to do certain things and behave in a certain way. When an individual assumes any of these positions, his or her behavior becomes structured by the expectations of others. The more varied the duties and activities of the position, the more varied the role, resulting in many different role patterns.

A *role set* is composed of the different orientations that are expected of an individual who occupies a position. These different orientations result from the varying expectations of individuals who interact with the person functioning in the position. The classic example is the foreman as the "man-in-the-middle." Management has certain expectations of an individual who occupies this position. He is to achieve company goals, be loyal to the company, maintain high levels of productivity, be intolerant of inefficiency, and what have you. However, the workers under the foreman also have certain expectations regarding his behavior. They frequently look to him for protection from unreasonable demands of management, to ignore minor indiscretions, and to be an advocate in obtaining new equipment and better working conditions. Other individuals also have expectations that will influence the foreman. As he deals with union representatives, industrial engineers, cost analysts, and other foremen, he will experience different projected orientations. The role-set concept is shown in figure 16-1. The position is shown in the center, with individuals involved in a typical role set shown in a concentric pattern.

Multiple roles result from the orientations of individuals holding different positions in a variety of organizations. A foreman may be a father, member of a bowling team, Rotarian, Presbyterian, director of the credit union, republican, and member of a carpool as well. Each of these positions involves a set of expectations that obviously will differ. Thus an individual faces multiple sets of expectations relating to his or her behavior. Some roles are more latent than others, depending on the setting the individual finds himself in at any particular time, but behavioral cues associated with roles are never as solitary or unitary as one would prefer.

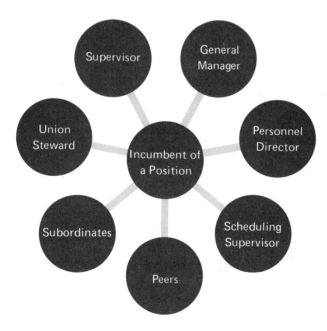

Fig. 16-1. Sample role set for an individual
holding a position

Role Transmission

The expectations associated with a particular position are communicated in many ways. If the role sender is the supervisor using formal organization channels, it is typically written in the form of a job description or transmitted through verbal instruction. The expectations conveyed (called *role sent*) by subordinates are typically through verbal communication and body actions (gestures, speeding up or slowing down the pace of work, displays of enthusiasm or rejection, etc.).

The interpretation of the role sent (called *received role*) by the incumbent of a position is dependent on the individual's perception and cognition of the verbal messages and influence actions. The more biased and prejudicial the person is toward the role sender, the less objective will be the interpretation of the role sent.

Role Conflict

As a result of the roles people assume in organizations, the potential for conflict is extremely high. This conflict consists of three types:

PERSON-ROLE CONFLICT.   The individual brings to a position certain personal needs, values, and abilities. Often these are inconsistent with the expectations others have for how the individual fulfills a position. The supervisor may expect him to deal harshly with low-level performers, when the individual may prefer to use a softer approach. He also may be instructed to take actions that are antithetical to his personal values, such as engaging in misleading advertising. Another type of person-role conflict is *role overload,* the term used to describe a situation when the expectations of others are greater than what can be accomplished given the abilities of the individual and the time and resources available. Expecting a new program manager to finish a project within an unrealistic schedule or expecting him to be an expert in the engineering, production, quality control, cost, and marketing aspects of a project are examples.

INTRA-ROLE CONFLICT.   Intra-role conflict results from people in the role set having differing expectations regarding the position. The foreman as the man-in-the-middle is an example, where the subordinates and supervision expect the foreman to take actions that are contradictory. The President of the United States is subject to different pressures from a wide variety of groups—as is the president of a university. Intra-role conflict can also occur when the source of the expectations is inconsistent. The supervisor may criticize the foreman for poor quality one day and for too much attention to detail the next.

INTER-ROLE CONFLICT.   Inter-role conflict results from individuals fulfilling many roles in society. An example of inter-role conflict experienced by individuals relates to use of spare time. On a Saturday a person is often pressured by group members to devote time to their activities. The work supervisor expects him to come into the plant and help catch up if they are behind; he has promised his wife for several weeks that he will paint the kitchen; the Lion's Club is going to sell brooms for the blind; his golfing partners expect him to fill out the foursome; and the church is conducting a clothing drive.

Under situations of inter-role conflict, how does the individual make a decision? Earlier we emphasized that it is a function of rewards, in terms of need satisfaction associated with the activities of each group. The expectations of his supervisor are usually stronger than those of subordinates, because the supervisor distributes the basic rewards he is interested in. If the individual has weak identification with an organization, there is obviously limited reward in his ties with that group, so their expectations will be of low priority.

Individual actions cannot simply be attributed to potential rewards. The social setting at the time a decision is made also has significance. In the social setting of the church on Sunday morning, when a request is made for volunteers the answer is more likely to be positive because of the immediate identification with the organization and group pressure for conformance. The carpool members may get a commitment from him to play golf on Saturday when returning from work on Friday night. However, if they call on Saturday as his wife stands close by with paint bucket in hand, the decision is more difficult.

Resolving role conflict is a daily part of individual behavior. However, major conflicts that bring into question the advisability of continuing in a position or involve rebuffing influential role senders creates stress, personal strain, and indecision. Managers should be keenly aware of the position they place others in when they make demands that may be at variance with significant expectations derived from other individuals and other roles.

STATUS STRUCTURES WITHIN GROUPS

Status is an individual's social rank in a social system. Status hierarchies are an inevitable result of group dynamics. Individuals are given certain roles and granted certain esteem because of their knowledge or other attributes. They also tend to group with other individuals granted similar esteem, which accentuates subgroup formation along status lines. The social-system components of an organization, such as group norms, informal leadership, roles, communication networks, and decision-making processes are all influenced and partially structured by status differences.

Sources of Status

To a significant degree the sources of status and the relative emphasis on it are culturally determined. Western culture has honored the rugged individualist and the self-made man, while some American Indian cultures look down on those who attempt to distinguish themselves on an individual basis. Status is also closely associated with the subculture of a group. Groups tend to attribute status to individuals who display the values, norms, and expectations of the group. They also lend status to individuals who are considered achievers in relation to group goals. In some student groups, the diligent student who receives high grades is attributed status, while in other groups more committed to extraneous or extracurricular activities, this may not be the case.

It was noted in the discussions on authority that influence over others is associated with position, knowledge, wealth, personality (charisma), sex, and social class. These are all sources of status, as well as influence. In addition, age, associates, group membership, seniority, and personal achievements are considered sources of status. Therefore status is associated with both a role (position status) and with characteristics of the individual (personal status).

Status Symbols

Status symbols within organizations are many and varied. They often occur in the title of positions (junior as compared to senior engineer). They are also associated with the location and size of offices or work space. Being on "mahogany row" is a sure sign of status, as is a large office or private secretary. Office furnishings, especially such trappings as draperies or carpeting, are telling signs of prestige. Pay is obviously a significant status symbol, but many individuals would be willing to forfeit minor pay increases for the carpeted office or even moving in next to the boss. Other common symbols are location of parking stalls, uniforms, and privileges, such as not punching a time clock.

Benefits and Limitations of
Status and Status Symbols

It should be recognized that status differences are inevitable in groups, and no executive can stamp them out. They are dysfunctional to equality, and yet they are natural and not to be denied. Status is an extremely strong source of motivation, and individuals will strive to be rewarded with the power symbols of their organization. On the other hand, excessive preoccupation with status can create friction and be damaging to internal relations. Status or lack of it enhances or restricts what one can do in the eyes of associates. Some sort of a pecking order is required in organizations to provide the structure necessary for the system to function. Leaders must be chosen, positions assigned, roles established, communication systems developed, and decision-making processes instituted. Status helps provide the structure necessary for this functioning, but an overemphasis on it can also damage the desire to cooperate, restrict communication, and subdivide groups into warring factions.

STATUS AND THE THWARTING OF TECHNOLOGICAL CHANGE

The experience of McGraw-Hill, Inc., was typical of what happens when a company goes to WP (word processing) without adequate planning and when the vendor is selling hardware rather than a solution to a problem. In 1967, IBM convinced the big publisher that it should install 22 editing typewriters in a WP center at its New York Headquarters. McGraw-Hill's goal was to reduce the number of its secretaries. What went wrong was quite simple: Nobody used the center. Says the project manager: "Without the secretary outside their door, managers felt they were downgraded." The system was costing McGraw-Hill $80,000 annually, so in 1970 it called it quits.

Quoted from "The Office of the Future," *Business Week,* June 30, 1975, p. 61.

MANAGEMENT IMPLICATIONS OF GROUP DYNAMICS

An awareness of groups has many implications for the manager. A few of the more significant ones are as follows:

- Groups are strong determinants of individual behavior, so understanding the individual is dependent on understanding the groups that the person is identified with—especially the immediate work group. Developing teamwork is also dependent on understanding group dynamics.

- Groups are important sources of security, social, status, and self-actualization need satisfaction and are therefore extremely significant in motivation. People normally attain higher need satisfaction in smaller groups, because they know others more intimately, they get to participate in the group to a greater extent, and it is easier to arrive at a concensus or maintain compatible relationships. Small groups are generally more cohesive, and there is a greater personal commitment to the group. This therefore alerts the manager that when the workflow involves tasks in which group cohesion and supportive social interaction are primary to success, small groups should be established. The same is true when the manager seeks anxiety reduction in the workforce.

- Large organizations will inevitably split up into small informal groups. Large organizations have the advantage of greater resources, but they are more difficult to lead because of the complex social structure resulting from many informal groups. However, large organizations generally will tolerate more structure and directive leadership than small groups.

- The behavior of individuals in organizations is strongly influenced by their roles. Assigning tasks to an individual, which is a partial determinant of role, is one of the significant management functions and deserves considerable care. Where possible, formal role assignments should be consistent with and reinforce informal roles. Since role and performance are influenced by the expectations of others, it is advantageous for the manager to hold realistic but high expectations of his associates.

- Role conflict is inevitable because of the different expectations various people have for an individual who holds a position and because of the diverse positions that an individual assumes in his or her many group attachments. Managers should be aware of these conflicting pressures, since unnecessarily increasing them can result in anxiety, which is often detrimental to performance.

- Change in organizations can rarely be accomplished by attempting to change individuals. Individuals cannot be isolated from the social context in which they function, and it is their roles and the group norms in this social context that guide their behavior. Generating change is therefore more effective through attempting to modify group norms rather than modifying individuals.

- Organizations are major stabilizing factors, and they assist the manager by discouraging deviations from common behavior patterns. The limitation of organizations is that they resist change. Informal group norms provide a strong structure that tends to be impervious to modification by outsiders. When the informal group norm is consistent with management goals, supervision is relatively easy. However, if the norms contradict those of management's, it presents an extremely difficult situation. Changing the norm involves many considerations, such as the equity of the psychological contract and the rewards involved in performing the work, but major modification is frequently beyond the control of the immediate supervisor.

- Strong group ties can be established by selecting individuals who have similar skills, personalities, interests, status, and so forth. Such groups are more compatible with a greater commitment to the group norms, but they are also more difficult to externally change.

SUMMARY

When people interact over periods of time, they develop relationships that take on systems characteristics. They establish norms of behavior, develop channels of communication, and become dependent on each other for acceptance and goal accomplishment. Informal organization fills in the voids of the formal structure. Though interaction, people develop methods and techniques for getting work accomplished.

Groups differ from organizations because in the former people are psychologically aware of each other. Their knowledge and awareness of others affect what they do and how they function. Group characteristics consist of common goals, norms, reward and punishment systems, informal leaders, roles, status relationships, communication networks, decision processes, and a unique organizational climate.

The roles and norms of the group strongly influence an individual's actions. Role is the behavior that group members expect of a person who holds a particular position. Norms are the common understandings that group participants maintain about how members should behave under specific circumstances.

The individual's willingness to conform to roles and norms is based on the rewards he perceives that he receives from the position and group identification. These rewards are primarily need satisfaction relating to security, acceptance, and status.

All groups segregate positions and people into different status levels. This aids in the functioning of the group, but it can also be detrimental to group cohesiveness.

QUESTIONS FOR STUDY AND DISCUSSION

1. Why is an organization called a social system? What dependencies are developed? What are the parts of the system? What are the supra-systems and subsystems of the focal system?
2. How does an informal organization differ from a group? Is an informal organization always a group? Is a group always an informal organization?
3. Is a college class a group? Is there an informal organization in a class? At what point and under what circumstances might a class be considered a group?

4. Why do groups form? Identify some groups you are associated with and explain what caused the formation of each one. Why do you maintain membership in the groups?

5. What are the nine features of groups that constitute structure? In the groups enumerated in question 4, identify each of the nine features.

6. How do group norms differ from group goals? What norms exist in the family unit or among roommates you are currently living with regarding:

   A. Studying   C. Use of items owned in common (car,
   B. Eating habits   stereo, television)
                            D. Housecleaning

7. In organizations you have worked in, give examples of the fair day's work norm. What reward and punishment systems were used to enforce the norm? Who was the informal leader? Why was that person the leader?

8. What is a *role*? Why is it called the "building block of social systems"? What are the three major sources of role?

9. Explain your role set as a student. Identify your multiple roles. Give some examples of role conflict that you face.

10. What is the role set for each of the following and how will the expectations of the role senders differ:

    A. Professor   C. Dean of Students
    B. Policeman   D. Person in charge of office-space allocation

11. What are the three types of role conflict? Give examples of each.

12. If you were instructed by your supervisor to violate company regulations and make a direct (sole source) procurement by purchasing some equipment from one of the supervisor's friends, what would you do? If you are instructed by your supervisor to doctor some production figures, how would you respond? What role conflict do you find in these examples?

13. Should a university play up status differences (for example, the classifications of sophomore, junior, senior; honorary societies for the students with high gradepoints; honors programs)?

Case Study:
THE NEW DIRECTOR OF
INTERNAL AUDIT

The Oxford Plant of ABC Corporation provides a variety of metal parts to firms in the automotive industry. The Oxford plant has over 15,000 employees and is located in a large metropolitan city in the Midwest. The plant has a staff of seven internal auditors plus the Director of Internal Audit. The auditors conduct a variety of studies relating to compliance with company procedures, effectiveness of financial operations, and general management problems. These studies are often handled independently by one auditor although frequently they work in pairs.

Of the seven auditors, two have been with the company for more than twenty years, and only one has been with the firm for less than three. They have all worked together for a long period of time and have developed a favorable group rapport. The Director of Internal Audit recently retired, and Larry Baugh, one of the auditors with twenty years' experience, has been appointed in his place.

Do you think Larry's behavior will change when he assumes the new position? Why?

What will influence how Larry behaves in his new role?

How should he handle his relationships with the other members of the internal audit group?

In what respects is Larry going to be a "man-in-the-middle"?

Case Study:
THE NEW EMPLOYEE

Brent Jacobsen recently completed trade school as an apprentice plumber. He had also worked several summers in this capacity. Recently he received full-time employment in the maintenance section of a major chemical processing plant. The first day on the job, the foreman assigned him to work with Scott Bryce, who had been working in the section for over ten years.

The pair was assigned to do some repair work on a storage tank that was located two miles to the north of the maintenance station. As they drove to the area in a pickup truck, Scott stopped by a pump house to collect a bet over a baseball game the night before. Brent was eager to get to work his first day, and as he showed his impatience while Scott chatted with his friends, he received only glares of disapproval.

Once on the job, Brent quickly climbed into the truck to get the tools, and this time Scott remarked, "What's your hurry? That job isn't going to run away."

Several times throughout the morning, Scott put Brent down for his enthusiasm. As he got up to go back to work after the morning break, Scott again asked him what his hurry was. When he sped back in the truck to get some materials from the warehouse, Scott remarked that he acted like he was being paid doubletime. When they had to wait forty-five minutes for an electrician to change some electrical connections, Brent wanted to start on other work, but Scott told him to "hold tight and handle one job at a time."

At lunch, Scott ate in the cafeteria with three other buddies and played cards. As Brent looked around the cafeteria for someone to eat with, he noticed that all of the guys were bunched in small "groups" eating together, so he ate alone.

The afternoon went pretty much like the morning. Scott worked at a fairly steady pace all day as he kidded around with the same group of friends, griped about the same service groups, commented about the "stupid people upstairs", and "horsed around" occasionally with the gang. Brent quickly learned that if he went along and followed Scott, there was no trouble, but as soon as he attempted to go it alone, he was sure to get a put-down or smart-aleck crack from Scott.

What group processes are taking place in this case?
If Brent conforms, why will he do so?
What risks are there in his not conforming?
Is it possible for Brent to change the fair day's work norm?
Is there anything the foreman can do to take advantage of Brent's enthusiasm and avoid his following the group's established work patterns? Should he?

Footnotes

1. Alvin Zander and Herman Medow, "Individual and Group Levels of Aspiration." *Human Relations,* 1963, pp. 89–105.
2. Daniel Katz and Robert L. Kahn, *The Social Psychology of Organizations* (New York: John Wiley & Sons, Inc., 1966), p. 172.
3. *Ibid.,* p. 171.

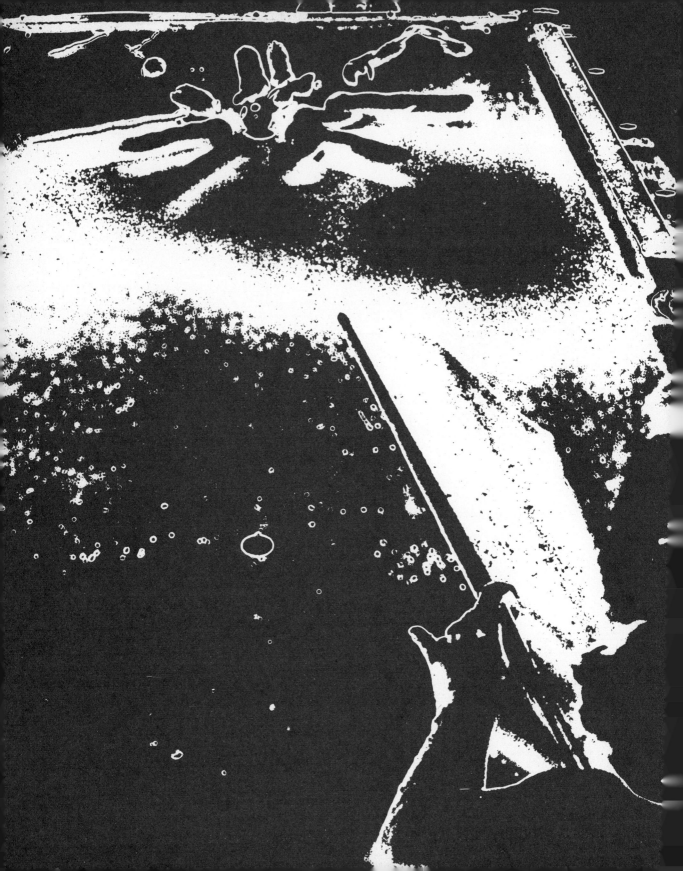

Organization Behavior: Conflict and Change

How does conflict affect an organization?

What are the sources of conflict, and how should this conflict be managed?

What factors determine whether conflict is desirable?

What is the relationship between conflict and change?

What are the methods a manager can use to gain acceptance of a change?

How can the culture of an organization be changed?

Cliff Nielsen, Assistant to the President, was chatting with Ernie Hanline, Director of Quality Control, following the weekly executive staff meeting. "You know, we just can't seem to make any progress on establishing new profit centers. That's the third straight meeting that has ended in a stalemate," he noted.

"We've discussed those issues time and again, but the Controller and the Director of Budgeting won't agree," Ernie replied. "It seems to me the president needs to do a little head knocking."

"That's right," Cliff added. "But have you noticed how the budget director seems to oppose whatever the Controller presents at meetings— whether it's on profit centers, overhead rates, or any other matter? The issue between them is much deeper than merely a difference over what profit centers to set up in manufacturing."

"Yeh, I've noticed that too," Ernie responded. "I think that goes back to the reorganization two years ago, when budgeting was removed from under the Controller and assigned to the Director of Administration."

"I think you're right. They've been at each other's throats ever since. I don't think we're going to make one bit of progress on any problems involving those two departments until that basic source of conflict is eliminated. They just won't cooperate."

"But how do you do that?" Ernie countered. "Do you remember how that battle between marketing and manufacturing went on for years? It never *was* resolved until some of the key figures retired."

"True," Cliff agreed. "But to tell you the truth, I kind of enjoyed the tiffs those groups got into. They provided a little spark in every staff meeting."

THE NATURE OF CONFLICT

Conflict, such as that described in the preceding incident, is common in most organizations. Indeed, interpersonal or intergroup conflict of one form or another is an inevitable feature of any group activity. Accordingly, supervisors need to know how to successfully manage it. Modern views of the value and management of conflict attack some of the sacred traditions of management, resulting in novel approaches to directing groups.

From a management standpoint, *conflict is defined as disagreement between two or more parties resulting from an incompatibility of goals, interests, perceptions, or values.* Basically it is a situation where, in their relationships with others, individuals or units seek the advancement of their interests or the predominance of their views. When defined in this sense, conflict involves either individuals and/or organizations. Even though conflict *within* the individual (over values, multiple roles or so forth) is a form of conflict, it is purposely excluded from this definition.

(Also, since the more overt aspects of role conflict were covered in chapter 16, they will receive only minor consideration in this chapter.)

Traditional Approaches to Conflict

Traditional administrative theory views the smoothly operating organization—characterized by unity, coordination, order, and machinelike efficiency—as the epitome of management practice. Harmony, consensus, and cooperation are the virtues of organizational life. Conflict is disruptive and something to be stamped out. (It will be recalled that Fayol stressed unity and structural integration, and Mayo concluded that compatible, happy work groups are productive ones, initiating a strong behavioral science bias for congenial interpersonal relations.)

There is also a strong cultural bias for the avoidance of conflict. Values taught in the home, school, and church tend to view conflict as degrading and contrary to the common interest. Furthermore, psychologically the individual is not normally comfortable with conflict. People tend to psychologically ignore discordant elements and avoid where possible the anxiety associated with intense conflict. This tends to be the case even though democratic political institutions are structured to encourage institutionalized conflict, and change in society is to some degree dependent on conflict.

Modern Contingency Views

More recent views of conflict consider it a neutral term: it can certainly be damaging to organizations but can also be of benefit. If a group is lethargic and in a drift condition, generating conflict over goals, means, or performance may be energizing and provide the necessary stimulus to change. This value-laden term is the same as most other nonethical management concepts—inherently, each is neither good nor bad. Its usefulness can be assessed only as it relates to different situations.

Conflict, as other contingency concepts, is most appropriately conceived as a continuum as illustrated in figure 17-1. There are many different modes of conflict, not one universal absolute. As the intensity of conflict increases, different conditions come into existence (as depicted by the descriptive terminology used in figure 17-1). In low-level conflict, there is some rivalry between the parties, but it is friendly in nature and the common good of the parties predominates. In situations where the intensity of conflict is higher, a clash of interests and a struggle for dominance start to appear. The common good is still primary, but the other party is more distinctly perceived as an opponent. In conflict of high intensity, there is a complete severance of relationships, a win-or-lose situation prevails, and hostility, even accompanied by violence, is in-

volved. Some would question whether this extreme form is ever of benefit. Society has often resorted to war, strikes, and forms of violence to
solve its problems. (However, even though violence cannot be condoned,
there is no doubt that the racial and student demonstrations of the 1960's
brought needed reforms.)

Low	Medium	High
Mild disagreement.	Significant disagreement.	Complete breakdown in relationships.
Rivalry over goals or interests.	Clash of interests and ideas.	Primary goal is to defeat enemy.
Common goals predominate.	Common goals predominate.	Common goals ignored.
Opponent is a friend.	Opponent is part friend, part foe.	Hostility leading to violence.

Fig. 17-1.   Conflict continuum

ADVANTAGES AND LIMITATIONS OF CONFLICT

Before exploring contingency considerations in more detail, the benefits
as well as the drawbacks of conflict need to be examined. Five advantages
are evident.

Advantages of Conflict

1. CONFLICT SERVES AS ONE OF THE PREREQUISITES TO CHANGE.   A simple
model representing the deliberate change process in organizations is as
follows:

dissatisfaction ———→ conflict ———→ change ———→ adaptation

People become discontent in organizations because they find problems
with existing procedures, reject current methods, perceive that others are
unfairly rewarded, or are in some way in opposition with what is taking

place. Because of this, they initiate overt conflict by challenging the methods or procedures and by repudiating the actions they oppose. This challenge can lead to a re-evaluation of the policies or actions and, ultimately, the change desired.

Change comes from a basic dissatisfaction with the status quo. When a firm is dissatisfied with its profits, it takes steps to be more competitive; when a young man experiences some disagreement with his girl friend, he asks someone else for a date; when the mayor receives numerous complaints from citizens regarding the frequency of garbage collection, he changes the schedule. Conflict is important in overcoming the apathy necessary to generate change. In public affairs there is little consensus as to what action should be taken in relation to welfare, the defense budget, or decentralization of the federal government. However, out of the debate and conflict over these issues evolves public policy that determines the direction of social and political change.

2. CONFLICT GENERATES ENERGY AND ACTIVITY.   When two individuals or organizations experience mutual disagreement, each attempts to strengthen its position and "win out" over the other. This generates renewed effort, where individuals typically strive harder in order to predominate. Competition, a form of conflict, is well known as a motivator, not only on the athletic field but in instances such as individuals vying for a position, or manufacturing shifts attempting to outproduce each other. Also, many individuals work better under the pressure of a deadline or in a conflictful situation where tension is present. Conflict is of value when people are too content, and mediocrity is the accepted norm.

3. CONFLICT STIMULATES INTEREST, CURIOSITY, AND IDEAS.   No situation is more detrimental to an organization than to let poor decisions go unchallenged. Challenging the proposals or plans of others forces them to defend and think through these actions. It normally results in a broader consideration of alternatives and associated trade-offs. It has been demonstrated through research studies that three times as much probing occurs in an organization with an open atmosphere where differing views are invited compared with a closed environment where the norm is to accept managerial decisions without question. Re-evaluation of goals and policies is the sign of a healthy organization. In a competitive market, one finds much more innovation than in a market where no competition or a monopoly exists. In the budgeting process where units compete for scarce resources, they are forced to clarify their goals, defend their performance, and think through future actions and resource requirements. Under such circumstances, each unit attempts to put its best foot forward in influencing the resource allocation decision.

4. EXTERNAL CONFLICT RESULTS IN INTERNAL GROUP COHESION.   It has been long recognized in group dynamics and international affairs that a common external threat or enemy will internally consolidate a group. Individuals will be more committed to an organization and its goals when conflict is experienced with other organizations.

5. CONFLICT CAN RESULT IN A REDUCTION OF TENSION.   Latent conflict converted to manifest conflict may serve as a catharsis that clears the air and leads to improved relationships. Bringing irritants into the open makes it more possible for differences to be minimized so that improved interaction takes place. It can also lead to the institutionalization of conflict, where it can be contained within desirable limits.

Disadvantages of Conflict

The harmful effects of conflict tend to be associated with the more extreme forms: those high on the intensity continuum. The damage resulting from conflict can be separated into three types, although they are all closely interrelated:

1. EXTREME CONFLICT CAN RESULT IN INSTABILITY AND CHAOS.   The debilitating influence of conflict results primarily from the hostility that develops between the parties. It often polarizes thought and action and cooperation comes to a standstill.

2. CONFLICT DISRUPTS THE FLOW OF ACTIVITY AND MODIFIES ORGANIZATION PROCESSES.   Conflict tends to destroy cooperation and is therefore damaging since continuity is basic to a firm's operations. Warring factions within an organization tend to focus attention on the dispute rather than on the tasks necessary to achieve the organizational purpose. When conflict degenerates to a win-or-lose situation, the goal is to beat the opponent even if superordinate goals and personal or group values are sacrificed.

3. EXTREME CONFLICT REDUCES RELIANCE ON REASON AND EVOKES EMOTIONAL BEHAVIOR.   The low trust and suspicion associated with conflict causes individuals to reduce interaction with the opposition, conceal activities, restrict communication, and take untenable positions. Perception is distorted, making reconciliation difficult. Few things tend to stand in the way of tearing down the opposition.

Assessing Optimal Levels of Conflict

Evaluating the advantages and limitations of conflict involves assessing the trade-offs of collaboration versus dissention. If an individual is unwilling to challenge a proposed course of action because it will upset the harmony of the group, there is obviously too much emphasis on internal compatibility. On the other hand, if dissent results in chaos, it is usually to be avoided. Conflict over ideas, policies, and plans is typically desirable in the proposal stage. However, once a decision is made, those in opposition should support the action taken.

An example of an actual experience where conflict would have been beneficial is drawn from a firm bidding on a major government contract. The president in a meeting with his top staff stated that the primary weakness of the firm's proposal was a current lack of plant capacity to handle the new work. He felt the answer to this problem was to spend several million dollars to purchase an old naval gun plant that was for sale in a nearby city. He dutifully asked for the opinion of his staff, at the same time expressing his own enthusiasm. All staff members nodded their approval, leaving the impression he had their whole-hearted support. The president left the meeting early to catch an airplane. As soon as he left the room, staff members began chattering about the foolishness of this decision. The plant was outdated with machinery that was of little value other than as scrap. Since it was a government plant, the agency reviewing the proposals was obviously aware of its limited utility. However, no one felt secure enough to speak out against the decision, and a costly mistake was made.

TYPES AND SOURCES OF CONFLICT

The antecedents as well as the various forms of conflict are far too numerous to cover here. The most common organizational forms relating to line and staff, functional departments, vested interests, and interpersonal rivalries have been analyzed earlier. Basically, conflict is of two types. The first, *interest conflict,* is when the individuals or organizations involved seek to personally gain either materially and/or in terms of power and status from the encounter. The second type, *affective conflict,* results from parties with different opinions, values, and norms. The clash in this instance is not over resources or power but is philosophical and attitudinal, involving basic personality differences. A third type, not normally a part of conflict literature, is that relating from mismanagement.

Interest Conflict

Individuals and organizations (since they serve as a power base for individuals) are motivated by self-interest and by the need for status and recognition. Individuals and organizations are inclined to pursue their own interests, resulting in conflict when these interests are at cross purposes with those of others. All organizations experience resource scarcity,

resulting in competition among the departments and units for the resources of the larger organization. In the competition of the marketplace,
firms attempt to make their products more attractive than others. Groups
representing different vested interests in the political process struggle to
gain power and exploit the opportunities that come from this dominance.
Labor seeks higher wages, suppliers higher prices, and management reduced costs. As long as scarcity exists, conflict is inevitable.

Affective Conflict

When two individuals argue over political, religious, aesthetic, or philosophical differences, there is typically no interest to be gained other than
the satisfaction of one's ego and the unlikely predominance of one's
views. Basic personality differences relating to diverse frames of reference, biases, attitudes, and values will inevitably spawn disagreement
when people interact. The more dogmatic the individual, the more likely
conflict will occur. Group identification contributes to this perceptional
distortion. Group members normally rate their group as better than average. Their performance and their norms are considered superior—again
inviting a clash with units who do not perceive the focal group in this
same light.

Conflict Resulting from Mismanagement

Many of the sources of conflict in organizations result from mismanagement. Undesirable situations and inequities in organizations will cause
dissatisfaction and ultimately conflict. If an organization has low wages,
unrealistic production standards, a poorly designed structure, unfair
supervisors, or an inequitable reward system, conflict is sure to result. In
these instances, conflict is desirable if the consequence is a change that
eliminates the inequities.

Forms of Conflict

Most disputes involve a blend of interest and affective conflict. Labor
management negotiations involve bargaining over resources and power,
but they are also complicated by philosophical differences. Line and staff
personnel are often involved in a struggle for power (interest conflict),
but their relationships are also hindered by perceptual differences. When
the Economics and Marketing Departments at a university compete for a
large piece of the budget pie, they are engaged in interest conflict, but
basic perceptual and professional (value) differences contribute to the
controversy. Personality clashes between individuals may be more purely

in the affective realm, although rarely can conflict be attributed to one source.

THE MANAGEMENT OF CONFLICT

The primary fear associated with conflict is that it will become over-heated or mismanaged. One of the obvious responsibilities of a manager is to be aware of the level and sources of conflict and to be prepared to either lessen or encourage it. There are various techniques for doing this.

Methods for Encouraging Conflict

There are five general methods for stimulating conflict. The first four are commonly used. The fifth category is less frequent, because it has other ramifications that tend to be self-defeating.

1. CONFLICT CAN BE STIMULATED BY ENCOURAGING COMPETITION.   This is done by establishing relatively equal units and then generating competition between them. Profit centers, similar forms of departmentations such as in chain stores, sales territories, and school districts are examples of equivalent units. Rewards to encourage competition include renumeration (a bonus), the best "won-lost" record, incentive pay systems, citations such as "salesman-of-the-month," and praising or reprimanding individuals or units that meet or fail to achieve quotas and goals.

2. AN OPEN ORGANIZATION CLIMATE ENCOURAGES CONFLICT.   In open organizations where individuals feel free to challenge existing methods and proposed actions, manifest conflict is more common. With little fear of reprisal, an individual will be more likely to express himself when he disagrees with others.

3. TASK AND STRUCTURE DIFFERENTIATION LEADS TO CONFLICT.   When tasks, positions, and the structure of an organization are subdivided and further specialized, distinct elements representing diverse interests are created. This subdivision of tasks and workgroups tends to destroy unity and encourage conflict.

4. THE MANAGER CAN SERVE AS A CHANGE AGENT IN STIMULATING CONFLICT. As a change agent, a manager can engage in activities like preparing proposals to revise current operations, rewarding innovation, assisting the group in assessing its strengths and weaknesses, constantly re-evaluating goals, or sending up trial balloons representing new directions the organization might take. The resulting change will most likely benefit some

individuals or groups at the expense of others, making conflict a natural concomitant of change.

5. POTENTIALLY DAMAGING FORMS OF STIMULATING CONFLICT SUCH AS CREATING UNCERTAINTY, ATTACKING OTHERS, DEMONSTRATING INCONSISTENCY, ETC. CAN BE USED.   Leaders who restrict communication, criticize and belittle others, and leave groups unsettled and insecure create inevitable conflict. However, usually the deleterious effects of these actions offset any benefits derived from such conflict.

Methods for Resolving Conflict

There are many different methods for resolving conflict. Those most commonly used ones follow.

1. USE OF A THIRD PARTY.   When two parties are unable to work out their differences, a third party such as an arbitrator, umpire, mediator, judge, or higher-level administrator is often used. If two individuals disagree over which procedure is applicable, the supervisor will settle the issue. As another example, arbitration is the accepted method for resolving labor disputes.

2. CONFRONTATION BETWEEN THE PARTIES.   When two parties are forced to interact and discuss their differences in an open climate (commonly referred to as *encounter groups* or a *confrontation meeting*), they may clear up misunderstandings and show greater empathy, so conflict is reduced. Behavioralists have developed many techniques (to be discussed later in this chapter) for developing this openness and trust.

3. SETTLEMENT THROUGH NEGOTIATION. One of the most common methods of settling conflict is through bargaining and compromise. Organizations engaged in power plays normally compromise their activities rather than accept a situation that involves complete isolation or chaos. They typically seek workable solutions rather than destruction of the larger system. The entire political process in a democracy is built on compromise and negotiation. In fact, all social groups interact in essentially the same manner.

4. REDESIGNING THE STRUCTURE TO MINIMIZE CONFLICT. A variety of adjustments can be made in the structure of an organization to reduce conflict. This can be done through giving one unit dominance (assigning them total responsibility for an overlapping function), separating the

parties (assigning one unit to a different division), establishing a buffer (making newsmen deal with the press secretary rather than directly with a police commissioner), or other similar modifications.

5. ESTABLISH SUPERORDINATE GOALS. When two lower-level units are engaged in an intense rivalry, the higher-level supervisor can attempt to establish superordinate goals that will tend to cause the units to switch their concentration from the immediate dispute to the broader objectives of the organization.

6. CO-OPTATION AS A METHOD OF CONFLICT RESOLUTION. Co-optation (see chapter 9) is a strategy designed to absorb discordant individuals or groups into the organization. Critics are put on advisory councils, given committee membership, or merged with existing units.

7. SMOOTHING OVER DIFFERENCES. One of the most common methods for playing down conflict is for the two parties or an interested third party to attempt to smooth over the differences. However, this is often only cosmetic in nature, because the source of the conflict is left unresolved.

8. REMOVE THE ISSUE OR CONDITION THAT IS GENERATING THE CONFLICT. In many instances conflict exists because people lack knowledge, communication is inadequate, treatment of employees is unfair, standards are unreasonable, the reward system is biased, or methods for resource allocation are arbitrary. Under these and similar circumstances, management action improving the situation usually reduces the conflict.

Application of Conflict Resolution Techniques

The methods used to resolve conflict depend on the type involved. Table 17-1 relates the various resolution techniques to the different types of conflict. When there is mismanagement resulting in major inequities in the structure and functioning of the organization, conflict is overcome by taking action to eliminate these inequities. Interest conflict, such as labor-management differences, are typically resolved through collective bargaining, compromise, third-party intervention, or action by a group representing all parties (like a committee). Affective conflict can sometimes be lessened or resolved through confrontation of the parties in an encounter group. Superordinate goals can also be used to bring the parties together. More temporary solutions are the dominance by one group (or the withdrawl of the other), and smoothing over differences.

Table 17-1. Methods for Resolving Conflict

Type of Conflict	Examples	Resolution Techniques
Inequities in the system (mismanagement)	Unfair standards, weak communication, poorly designed structure, inequitable reward system, etc.	Take managerial action to modify the system. Improve standards, communication, structure, and reward system.
Interest conflict	Competition for scarce resources and for power. Competing departments, labor-management relations, etc.	Compromise, bargaining, third-party intervention, committee action.
Affective conflict	Emotional, perceptual, and value differences. (Liberal versus conservative, marketing versus production, school bussing, etc.)	Confrontation, use of superordinate goals, dominance of one party—withdrawl of other, smooth over differences.

CONTINGENCY APPROACHES TO CONFLICT

Variables Requiring Consideration

The level of intensity of conflict desired in an organization is a function of many different factors. In general, these are the same factors that predominate in other situations, such as the interdependence of the tasks, problem-solving technology, stability of the environment, and maturity of the people involved. Using the contingency model of management as a framework, the desirability of conflict is related to the following variables.

PURPOSE AND CONFLICT.   The purpose and goals of an organization, when matched with its environment, will determine how significant conflict is to goal accomplishment. Political parties and interest groups in a pluralistic society represent factions seeking power in relation to other parties or interests, with the result that conflict is inevitable. Any group promoting a narrow interest that is bucking the status quo or the tide of majority opinion, such as the Sierra Club or John Birch Society, can reach its ends only by taking issue with the current predominant practices. Organizations that benefit from existing conditions will likely react to suppress the conflict.

TASKS AND CONFLICT.   When tasks are interdependent and cooperation is required, conflict should be avoided (for example, in the cases of nurses and doctors or cooks and waitresses); when tasks are relatively independent, conflict may be desirable (salesmen, candidates for political office, etc.). Incentive pay systems tend to be effective when tasks are independent, but group incentives are more effective when cooperative effort is involved.

TECHNOLOGY AND CONFLICT. Work situations with highly structured, routine tasks and technology, involving little opportunity for creativity, find little benefit from conflict. Where a diversity of ideas is desirable—as in problem-solving tasks—disagreement and differences of opinion are conducive to innovation.

PEOPLE AND CONFLICT.   The level of conflict generated and tolerated in a group depends on the personalities of the individuals involved. Authoritarian, dogmatic, individuals tend to be sources of conflict. Also, some individuals can perform effectively under tension while others cannot. Professions trained to deal with differences of opinion (lawyers, consultants, etc.) are better able to cope with, and gain from, conflict. The capacity of leadership to deal with conflict is also a key variable.

STRUCTURE AND CONFLICT.   If an organization is characterized by interdependent tasks linking different groups, intense conflict will most likely be damaging. Independent units (parallel departmentation, profit centers, separate projects) typically benefit from conflict. Also, it is often desirable in bureaucratic structures where more change is necessary. However, structures needing more formalization can benefit, because conflict resolution is usually accompanied by more specific rules and regulations, clarification of authority delegation, and so on. In close-knit groups, where individuals have developed an open relationship, there will be a greater tolerance of conflict than in larger ones where individuals lack this familiarity. In general, conflict is more desirable in organic structures involved in problem-solving tasks, such as research and development, where diverse opinions are helpful in aiding the search process.[1]

ENVIRONMENTAL FACTORS AND CONFLICT.   Since conflict is a predecessor to change, it is generally more a part of organizations existing in uncertain, dynamic environments in which the challenge to the organization is to be adaptive. Conflict is of less value and more disruptive to firms with mechanistic structures involving stable environments.

TIME AND CONFLICT.   In urgent situations where quick, coordinated action is required, conflict is normally detrimental. However, for a committee that is thoroughly evaluating policy changes, taking time to get a diversity of views is desirable.

Management Guides for Monitoring Conflict

An organization cannot effectively use the full capacity of its membership without diversity and conflict. People have differing knowledge and opinions, but unless there is an outlet for these, the organization is not capitalizing on the use of its human resources. Open environments conducive to debate over policy-type actions tend to be stimulating and innovative. As long as conflict is kept within bounds, it is productive. The manager needs to be on guard for signs which tell him that conflict is becoming damaging. Typically this is when the combatants start to shun their common goals and concentrate on win-or-lose tactics. It is also when an open discussion of issues starts to be replaced by distorted communication and a reduction of interaction, reflecting increased hostility and lack of trust.

CHANGE IN ORGANIZATIONS

Change is as inevitable a feature of organizational life as conflict. Organizations as open systems represent a flow process involving resource exchange and a constant adaptation to fluctuating forces and conditions. Organizations, like people, experience growth, decay, and maturation processes, so that no "normal" condition for an organization exists; any current condition is only a temporary snapshot analysis of what is in reality a motion picture of constant evolution. The manager's responsibility in relation to change is twofold:

- He needs to be concerned with the organization's adaptation to forces that are beyond its control, and he needs to be an effective agent when deliberate change is required. The first responsibility is a major one, as interpreted by Alvin Toffler and others.[2] Toffler feels change is becoming so rampant in our society that it is pushing at the extremes of man's physical and psychological capacity to adapt. He proposes that "future-shock absorbers" be built into every fabric of society. Since successful firms are often those that accommodate to new conditions, it places organizational adaptation high on the list of the responsibilities of top management.

- The second responsibility involving the generation of change is also important. A manager is not just responsible for maintaining the system (organization), but also for improving it. He therefore needs to know how to be a facilitator in the change process. Even though people accept many of the change dynamics of their environment, overcoming resistance to change is a persistent management problem.

RESISTANCE TO CHANGE

Often managers feel that subordinates tend to resist all change because of difficulties experienced in implementing new methods and procedures. However, there is little resistance to anticipated change when previous outcomes have been positive. The housewife likes changes in clothing fabrics; the public looks forward to improvements in automobiles; and the teenager eagerly awaits being sixteen, when he can drive the family car. Electronics alone has resulted in hundreds of improvements that benefit the public at large. Change is primarily resisted when the outcome is perceived as negative or when it is uncertain, imposing feelings of insecurity. Even though the public has benefited from electronics, the individual employed in a plant currently making mechanical calculators would likely resist industry changes associated with the introduction of the electronic calculator.

Maintaining the Status Quo

Based on the fairly simple assumption that where change is perceived as beneficial and rewarding (need satisfying) it will be accepted, but where it is perceived as threatening or uncertain it will be resisted, it is obvious that those who benefit from current conditions (the status quo) will most likely resist change. If someone holds a poker hand with four aces, he does not want the deck reshuffled. Change often results in a redistribution of power (especially that deliberately instituted, such as a reorganization). Accordingly, individuals will resist such a reorganization if they expect to lose out.

Workers will thwart change on the same basis. If they expect unemployment, loss of pay, or loss of status through a change, they will resist it. If automation in the past has resulted in layoffs and less reliance on the worker, probably no amount of propaganda will convince the individual otherwise. Resistance to change is difficult to overcome, because insecurity brings on emotional reactions where logic and reason too often prove ineffective.

Other Factors Affecting Change

Sometimes management is reluctant to change because of the strong commitment they have to current activities. The sunk costs in current operations are often tremendous. If a firm has an automated production line involving equipment valued in the millions of dollars, any change that would make this system obsolete will require significant offsetting benefits. (Sunk costs in new-product development or in plant location are other examples.)

Probably the most significant structural factor resisting change in organizations is the social system. Roles, norms, and expectations are all sources of pressure for conformance to existing values and behavioral patterns. This therefore means that any change involving behavioral modification will have to delve deeply into the forces that govern interaction.

Finally it should be noted that external organizations can affect the change process. As an example, labor unions maintain as one of their roles the protector of the security of the union member, which therefore engenders a suspicion of all changes instituted by management.

Change Techniques

Based on the above analysis, several practical guides become evident:

- The reasons and benefits associated with proposed changes should be communicated to those involved as far in advance as possible. Rumor generated by the grapevine often tends to foster uncertainty and dwell on the negative. To offset this, management should communicate its intentions thoroughly. Sometimes this is difficult to do. Informing the work force of proposed changes in product design or product lines is often tantamount to placing confidential information in the hands of competitors. Public institutions are also restricted, because leaks to the public may be damaging (a presidential decision that may affect stock prices). However, no step is more important in gaining acceptance for change than to fully inform individuals so they can act on the basis of fact—not rumor.

- Protection should be provided for those who will potentially be harmed by the change. This involves simple rules like handling all reductions-in-force through attrition rather than by terminations; retraining for those displaced in their jobs; and voluntary rather than forced transfers.

- Those who go along with a change should be rewarded. Higher rates should be paid to those retrained for more demanding positions; all costs associated with a transfer need to be completely covered; important assignments should be given to those committed to the new activity.

- Change should be as gradual as conditions will permit. People tolerate evolution much more than revolution. Often trial balloons are used to see if the climate is appropriate for change (a technique often used in politics where a member of the President's staff deliberately leaks a proposed action). It should be recognized that structural changes normally require a minimum of one year to implement and test out, whereas major surgery on an organization can require three years or more to reap the full benefits.

- Where possible, those affected should participate in developing the change. If people participate, their interests will be considered, and they will be more committed to the actions taken. Sometimes participation may not be desirable (such as in a win-or-lose situation where two candidates are being considered for an important position), but when it is feasible it smooths the path and change will flow easier.

- The change agent should be familiar with the change process and with change techniques (to be elaborated in the next section).

Before examining change methods, let's look at an example of resistance to change. The particular plant involved served as a distribution center for all of the company's products in the Western United States and Asia. The company decided to investigate the automation of several of its warehouses. They put their design engineers to work on the project, and six months later it appeared sufficiently favorable to move ahead. After a few months, the Personnel Department noted that turnover in the warehouse division had increased 100 percent among workers and first-line supervisors. They also had several requests for transfer and for voluntary demotions. Following an investigation, they found that employees were concerned about potential reductions in force, and with jobs involving new skill requirements, such as reading computer print-outs. When the company thoroughly explained their plans for retraining employees and assured them there would be no reduction in force, worker morale improved significantly and turnover dropped to a more normal level. Management history is full of examples where farsighted planning is undertaken in relation to the technical aspects of change, but the social and human implications are poorly planned or totally ignored. Too often technical change is instituted, followed by a belated attempt to repair the social damage.

THE MANAGEMENT OF CHANGE

The direction and status of an organization is determined by existing internal and external forces. If one is to bring change about in relation to an organization, it can be accomplished only by modifying these forces. In evaluating the options open to a manager to instigate change, it is necessary to identify the primary forces and then relate the appropriate change methods to each. The forces with associated methods, using a contingency framework, are shown in table 17-2.

Table 17-2.   Forces and Methods Affecting Change

Variables or Forces	Change Methods
Purpose and goals	Redefine purpose or mission Modify goals Management-by-objectives
Tasks	Modify nature of tasks Modify sequencing of tasks Job enrichment
Technology	Modify methods Modify machinery Automation
People	On-the-job training Job rotation Sensitivity training Management development courses
Structure	Change position descriptions Modify departmentation Modify authority and responsibility Organization development programs
Environmental forces (political, sociocultural, economic, and technological)	Improve understanding of forces Develop an adversary or ally

Organizational Purpose and Change

Any modification of the basic purpose or mission of an organization will directly influence how it functions. Tampering with the purpose and goals involves intervening in the fundamental processes that characterize the organization. If a company seeks revitalization or redirection, formally modifying its goals is an essential method for doing this. The popularity of goal setting and management-by-objectives (MBO) programs (see chapter 22) has resulted from the effectiveness of these methods in fostering change.

Tasks and Change

Modifying tasks has come to the forefront as one of the most common change methods for two reasons. One is because it is often easier for a manager to change tasks than it is to change the people or the cultures of groups. Also, programs such as job enrichment (see chapter 12) have demonstrated that improved performance and job satisfaction (common goals of change) can result from combining tasks to make jobs more challenging.

Technology and Change

Technology, as the great engine of change, forces almost all other aspects of an organization into an adaptive posture. The devastating effects of new methods, new materials, and improved machinery causes an organization to be cautious in order to avoid completely unsettling the established structure. Since technical change typically proceeds at a quicker pace than social change, the problem for the manager is keeping these two aspects of change aligned.

People and Change

As has been indicated, changing the behavior of people is a slow and uncertain task. Where knowledge is instrumental in change, traditional techniques such as on-the-job training and job rotation have been used. In recent years, new methods like sensitivity training have been introduced to dig deeper in changing the perceptions and attitudes of people. (Sensitivity training, along with other methods for modifying individual and group behavior, will be examined in more detail later.)

Structure and Change

Managers have traditionally looked to adjusting the formal organization structure when improvements are desired. This involves modifying job content, revising functional assignments, reorganizing departments, and/or shifting authority delegations. Difficulties experienced in behavioral modification of people have revived interest in the efficacy of restructuring the formal organization for this purpose. However, even though changing the formal structure will alter roles and expectations, often it does not cut deep enough to affect individual attitudes and group norms. As noted earlier, changing the title and responsibilities of a position may not drastically influence behavior when the incumbent's knowledge, biases, and behavioral patterns are entrenched through years of reinforcement. For this reason, a group of methods referred to as *organization development* (O.D.) have been established to both more intensively and extensively transform the culture of an organization.

Environmental Forces and Change

As noted in chapters 8 and 9, organizations are constantly accommodating to political, sociocultural, economic, and technological forces. Effective managers attempt to better understand these forces and adapt the organization accordingly. In figure 8-2, exploring the interaction between a firm and these forces, it is noted that organizations can to some degree affect external conditions, but usually this is limited. The firm is clearly often reacting rather than proacting in this regard. Finally it should be noted that the deliberate cultivating of an external ally or adversary can serve to influence group cohesion and personal commitment, but this is not a common method for encouraging internal change.

MANAGEMENT DEVELOPMENT AND ORGANIZATION DEVELOPMENT

In recent years behavioralists have taken an intense interest in the methods associated with organization development as a means of improving and changing organizations. O.D. has moved center stage in behavioral literature. Many research studies have been conducted, a mass of supporting literature written, and several societies dealing with this methodology formed. To appreciate the full scope of O.D., it is first necessary to explore the shortcomings of more traditional management-development practices.

Management Development and the Change Process

Management development programs are designed to enhance supervisory and top management skills. The assumption is that to improve an organization you need to improve its leadership. Thus training programs devised to increase an individual's knowledge of management functions and practices have proliferated. These involve learning theoretical models and management concepts and techniques. They rely on pedagogical methods such as lecturing, case studies, role playing, and stimulation exercises. However, often these approaches do not necessarily change attitudes or perceptions that govern behavior, especially social interaction.

Sensitivity or *"T" training* (T standing for *training*) was introduced after World War II as an experiential method for gaining increased self-awareness, both of one's own feelings and the feelings of others. The assumption was that profit-minded managers are often not sufficiently conscious of the influence they have on others and of interpersonal relations in general. To sensitize managers to these relationships, training sessions involving ten to fifteen people were developed, with no agenda or chairperson to direct the discussion. In these sessions, usually lasting from one to two weeks, an unstructured group will structure itself, and in the process the group learns from its own experiences. Members are encouraged to concentrate on the "here-and-now" situation. It involves a frank sharing of reactions and feelings about each other and about what is happening in the group. Individuals normally receive open feedback regarding how others perceive them. These sessions are not only intended for greater self-awareness, but participants also learn to be open in their relationships with others and how to facilitate or inhibit group functioning. These sessions became widely used and publicized during the 1960's when their equivalent in sociology (encounter groups) also became widespread.

Individuals who participate in sensitivity training usually find it an exhilarating experience and one where they return to their organization eager to tackle their job in a different fashion. However, it was found that after a period of time the individual tends to function in the work situation fairly much the same way he did before the training experience. When placed in his old role, he will respond to existing group norms and to the expectations of others representing the status quo. Behavioralists therefore concluded that if change is to take place in an organization, it must involve the entire culture of the organization. The term *organization development* (O.D.) is used to represent this much broader and more time-consuming program for achieving change in an organization.

Concepts Involved in Organization Development

The goal of management development is to train the manager. The goal or organization development is to initiate a process that will change the organization culture. This involves modifying values, norms, attitudes, interaction, and effectiveness. It is a normative strategy that deliberately attempts to enhance group functioning in specific ways.

The typical O.D. goals are to make organizations more effective through improved problem-solving and renewal processes. Resulting from its origin in the behavioral sciences, the value assumption is that this involves organizations where there is: better understanding and agreement on goals; open communication; mutual trust; collaborative relationships: effective management of conflict; power equalization; fostering of human values; and an emphasis on achieving individual, as well as organizational, goals.

AN ORGANIZATION DEVELOPMENT INTERVENTION TECHNIQUE: THE CONFRONTATION MEETING

Many O.D. intervention techniques involve getting the group to generate information about its major problems, analyze underlying causes, and take steps to improve the situation. One of the most well-known interventions is the confrontation meeting popularized by Richard Beckhard. The six steps in the confrontation meeting according to Beckhard are as follows:

Step 1   Climate Setting (forty-five to sixty minutes): The Top manager states the goals for the meeting and emphasizes that a free, open discussion of issues and problems is encouraged. The consultant follows with an emphasis on the importance of problem solving and communication in organizations.

Step 2   Information Collecting (one hour): Small, heterogeneous groups of seven or eight members work in teams to identify problems in the organization such as burdensome procedures, unclear goals, an inadequate reward system, and other conditions contributing to poor attitudes or performance.

Step 3   Information Sharing (one hour): The findings of each small group are placed on newsprint on the walls. Usually the team leader categorizes these into common types of problems such as communication, evaluation systems, etc.

Step 4   Priority Setting and Group Action Planning (one hour and fifteen minutes): A list of the categorized items is given to everyone. Teams are formed similar to the regular formal organization structure so that a subordinate is working with his supervisor. These work groups then identify and discuss issues and action steps to remedy the situation. They also designate

> priority issues for top management, and decide how to communicate the results of the confrontation meeting to subordinates.
>
> *Step 5*   Immediate Follow-up by Top Team (one to three hours): After the others have left, the top management team meets to determine what follow-up action should be taken on the basis of what they have learned during day. These plans are communicated to the rest of management within the next few days.
>
> *Step 6*   Progress Review (two hours): Four to six weeks later a follow-up meeting of the total management group is held to report progress and review actions resulting from the meeting.

Abstracted from Richard Beckhard, "The Confrontation Meeting," *Harvard Business Review,* March–April 1967, pp. 149–155.

Organization development is normally undertaken by change agents who are external to the client system. Their role is not to identify and solve organization problems, but to institute a process by which the organization will do this for itself. Many of the techniques (called *interventions* by O.D. specialists) have been discussed previously. These involve knowledge transmission through lecture sessions, role playing, job enrichment, goal setting (management-by-objectives), sensitivity training, confrontation meetings, problem-solving techniques, team-building exercises, survey feedback, process consultation, and interviewing.

Grid Organization Development

One of the best known and thorough programs for organization development, developed by Robert R. Blake and Jane S. Mouton, is known as Grid Organization Development.[3] The term *grid* comes from a two dimensional scale used to relate an individual's "concern for people" compared with "concern for production." (The grid will be covered in more detail in the next chapter.) Blake's and Mouton's program for O.D. involves a series of sessions that extends over a number of years. The phases in the program are as follows:

Phase 1   This is typically a one-week session, in which initially each participant's behavior is assessed as it relates to concern for people or concern for production. Problem-solving exercises emphasizing face-to-face feedback are also used.

Phase 2   These exercises focus on team development via coordination and an improved organization culture. Feedback is again emphasized, relating to the individual's contribution to team effort.

Phase 3   This phase moves to the broader parameter of intergroup relations. Emphasis is on avoiding win-lose situations and fostering collaborative relations.

Phase 4   This involves the group's establishing an ideal strategic corporate model. It views management from the next higher level, relating to the broader perspective of planning corporate strategy.

Phase 5   Phase five incorporates methods for implementing the ideal corporate model.

Phase 6   The last phase evaluates what has been accomplished in the first five phases and takes corrective action as necessary to achieve the desired objective.

Organization Development in Perspective

O.D. has made significant strides in improving our understanding of organizational change. Its limitations are its often rather narrow focus on the people variable and its implicit value assumption that open, collaborative, mutual-influence organizations are always appropriate. A broader view is to recognize the multiple-causation nature of change, requiring a variety of interrelated change methods. It is also of importance to recognize that people may be the most difficult of all variables to modify. In many instances, it is easier to change tasks, jobs, work assignments, formal structures, or other variables in the work setting.

SUMMARY

Conflict, consisting of disagreement between two or more parties resulting from an incompatibility of goals, interests, perceptions, or values, is existent in all organizations. This conflict can be beneficial or detrimental, depending on conditions intrinsic to the organization. Some competition between groups or individuals may be stimulating as long as their common goals predominate. Conflict is also natural and beneficial when individuals express different views over policy issues and organization actions. When conflict turns into hostility, involving malicious actions against opponents, it is obviously damaging and needs to be reduced.

Typically, change is preceded by conflict. Different elements of the organization are not satisfied with the current situation, so steps are taken to modify the functioning of the system. Change is also an organization process that needs management support if the organization is to remain adaptive.

Members of an organization often resist change because the associated uncertainty threatens their current security, social, and status need satisfaction. In attempting to facilitate change in an organization, the manager needs to evaluate the field of forces that is represented in the organization. Instituting change requires a modification of these forces.

In recent years a broad methodology for changing organization culture, known as organization development, has been developed. It is an improvement over management development because it is not restricted to changing the knowledge, skills, and attitudes of individuals since it attempts to modify the entire context within which individuals function.

QUESTIONS FOR STUDY AND DISCUSSION

1. Why did traditional management theory oppose conflict?
2. In the following examples, analyze the benefits and limitations of conflict:
   - A. Labor-management relations
   - B. Line-staff differences
   - C. In the Department of Defense, differences among the Departments of the Army, Navy, and Air Force
   - D. Ralph Nader and his attacks on product safety and consumerism
   - E. Student protest over no-smoking regulations in classrooms
3. Give examples of interest and affective conflict.
4. Indicate the value of each of the following techniques in resolving (1) interest conflict and (2) affective conflict:
   - A. Compromise
   - B. Confrontation
   - C. Smooth over differences
   - D. Third-party intervention
5. Explain how the following affect the need for reduction or expansion of conflict:
   - A. Interdependent tasks
   - B. Problem-solving tasks
   - C. On-the-job trainees
   - D. Firm with a stable environment
6. What is the relationship between conflict and change?

7. Which of the following are most likely to resist change? Why?
    A. Clerk with no formal schooling
    B. Individual with a political appointment
    C. Hospital administrator
    D. Dean of Students
8. In the above examples, what are some methods that could be used to reduce the individual's resistance to change?
9. In attempting to institute change, indicate the benefits and limitations of using one technique versus the other as follows:
    A. Structural or behavioral change
    B. Changing tasks or changing goals
10. Explain the difference between management development and organization development. Why do organizations generally still rely more on management development?
11. Is a change in an individual's knowledge or attitudes the most difficult one to make? Why?

Case Problem:
THE RELUCTANT CONTROLLER

The preparation of the annual sales forecast for the Board of Directors and management of New Products Electronics, Inc. has always been a problem because of the rapid increase in sales and the cost uncertainties associated with their many volatile research and development projects. The controller has handled this function for the past two years, but the variance from the forecast each year has been over 15 percent which management did not find acceptable. Accordingly, the president took the prime responsibility for preparation of the sales forecast away from the controller and assigned it to the director of the Long-Range Planning Department. This department requires the support of the controller to prepare the forecast, since detailed historical cost information, a forecast of overhead, and other cost data are required. The controller is obviously resentful over the whole situation and has shown signs of being unwilling to cooperate.

Why is the controller unwilling to cooperate?
Does this case involve interest or affective conflict?
What action would you take to get the controller to cooperate if you were the director of the Long-Range Planning Department?

Would any organization-development techniques be useful in dealing with this problem?

Case Problem:
ALLGOOD MANUFACTURING, INCORPORATED

Allgood Manufacturing Incorporated is a medium-sized conglomerate that has followed a policy of growth through acquisition. Six years ago they took over StickWell Adhesives as a subsidiary. Previously, Stick-Well had been the second largest adhesive manufacturer in the United States, but at the time of the takeover by Allgood, the sales and profit position of StickWell had rapidly deteriorated. Allgood's management felt StickWell was a good buy in this depressed condition, and they were confident they could turn the company around.

The first new general manager Allgood assigned tried for five years to change the profit position, but he met little success. StickWell operates two plants, both in rural areas in the Midwest and the South. Each plant employs approximately 800 people. At both plants the employees and management are very set in their ways and are not receptive to new ideas. In fact, last year at one plant the work force almost rebelled against top management.

What are the barriers to change in this case?
If you were appointed as the new general manager, what would you do?
How can new ideas become accepted at the plants?
Are any of the organization-development techniques appropriate in this instance?

Footnotes

1. See William M. Evan, "Conflict and Performance in R & D Organizations," *Industrial Management Review,* 1965, pp. 37–45.
2. Alvin Toffler, *Future Shock* (New York: Bantam Books, Inc., 1970), p. 326.
3. R. Blake and J. S. Mouton, *The Managerial Grid* (Houston, Texas: Gulf Publishing Company, 1964).

Manager Profile

Georges Hanzi
Handy City, Inc.
San Antonio, Texas

Previous Experience and Background

Georges joined the world of retailing with Fed Mart, where he became an assistant manager of a store in Phoenix and then a store manager in San Antonio, Texas. He went on to become a member of the board for the Diana Stores Corporation.

Later he left Diana Stores Corporation to become the founder and president of Handy Dan retail stores. This chain now has fifty-seven stores. Georges serves as chairman of the board of the new Handy City stores. Sales are approximately $25 million per year.

Primary Responsibilities

Georges day-to-day responsibilities deal with finance, merchandising, operations, advertising and promotion, and research and development.

Of these activities, the market research associated with new store location is the most critical. A team will go into a new city, collect all of the research as to future growth, sales, competition, locations, etc. and then decide where to expand with another store. They do this without the use of consultants.

In the earlier stages of the company, finance, promotion, and operations were more important. Now that they are established and successful, expansion through venture analysis has become the most significant.

Insights

"What I have learned most as a manager is how to motivate people. If the employees are enthused, the venture will be successful. Incentives are critical for the employees. We pay them well and we expect a lot in return. We have excellent management bonuses that are paid on a quarterly basis.

"As a management team, we have been together so long that a shoulder or eye movement means something.

"The most important thing that I can do as I travel and work in the stores is to identify with the employees at their level. I work the cash register, clean the floors and windows, set up the displays, and answer customers complaints. I look at it as *my* job to make the employees realize how important their jobs really are.

"More than anything else, it is the employees that make the customer come back to the store."

Manager Profile

Lee C. Frischknecht
President, National Public Radio
Washington, D.C.

Background and Experience

After completing a bachelor's degree in radio and speech, Lee became a radio announcer with KID in Idaho Falls, Idaho. He later moved to Michigan State University where he obtained a master's degree and ultimately became manager of the school's television station. He then became associated with National Educational Television (now Public Broadcasting Service). For two years he was in charge of institutional relations for a university and then became employed with National Public Radio, where he has been president since 1974. National Public Radio, located in Washington, D.C., is a private, nonprofit corporation established in 1970 to provide a national program service for the nation's public radio stations. It does national programming and provides the electronic link among 175 stations located in 43 states, the District of Columbia, and Puerto Rico. Most of the funds are provided by the federal government through the Corporation for Public Broadcasting. The majority of the member stations are located at colleges and universities.

Primary Responsibilities

1. Acts as a member of the National Public Radio Board of Directors.
2. Acts as the chief executive officer of National Public Radio.
3. Directs the day-to-day affairs of the corporation in accordance with normal corporate practice and the policies of the board.
4. Appoints all staff, supervises general fiscal operations, and establishes corporate goals and objectives.

5. Exercises ultimate responsibility and authority for approval or disapproval of all programs produced or acquired for broadcast.

Insights

"Many staff members are led to organizations like NPR, not for monetary reasons, but because of the corporate goals and the individual freedom in helping attain those goals. Management must permit and encourage this highly motivated, creative staff to participate fully in the organization within an operating structure that retains controls for the sake of efficiency and direction.

"One of the most destructive elements in an organization is a fear of managers and supervisors to hire staff members who will challenge them.

"Communications organizations are as prone as others to suffer from a lack of internal communications. At NPR, staff meetings are impossible, due to schedules that run around the clock. Other mechanisms must be found to communicate the shared sense of mission and goals in order to experience a common motivation.

"Decentralization of authority is beneficial and can work wonders if the basic goals, policies, and procedures are well established, commonly agreed to, and fully understood."

PART VII

Leadership and Management

Leadership Styles
and Concepts

What is the difference between a *manager, leader,* and *bureaucrat?*

How significant is the leader to the success of an organization?

What means are there of categorizing different types of leaders?

Why is no one style of leadership always preferable?

What are the advantages and limitations associated with each style?

How can discipline successfully be accomplished?

THE NATURE OF LEADERSHIP

The leader is the individual with the most influence in a group, whose role is to get others to achieve organizational goals. Leadership is almost entirely explained on the basis of influence relationships and motivational considerations. For this reason, the following review will rely primarily on the authority, power, and influence principles discussed in chapter 14 and the motivational concepts enumerated in chapter 11.

Defining Leadership

Leadership, like other key concepts in management, tends to be viewed differently, depending on whether the orientation is behavioral, economic, or managerial. For our purposes, the most important distinction is that behaviorists tend to emphasize the influence or power aspects more, while management writers concentrate on the concept of goal achievement. However, even here the orientation will vary, depending on whether it is viewed from the level of the chief executive officer or the first-line supervisor. For our purposes leadership *is defined as the process of providing direction in group activities and influencing others to achieve group objectives.* The central concept of the definition is "influencing and stimulating" others to become followers. The leader is the individual who can persuade others to engage in certain behavior, or who has power in the group.

The second important aspect of leadership is that of being able to steer the organization so that successful goal accomplishment results. Strictly speaking, an individual who can get others to engage in certain actions detrimental to the organization (not expanding operations when it is appropriate) is a leader, because he is able to get others to follow, but since his leadership results in group failure, he cannot be considered an effective one from a managerial standpoint. Management theory is prescriptive in nature, so leadership success is dependent on the organization's also being successful (*success* being defined in terms of goal accomplishment).

Differences Associated with Leadership, Management, and Bureaucracy

There are distinct differences in meaning among the terms *management, leadership,* and *bureaucracy,* and these are summarized in table 18-1. As indicated in chapter 1, management is the process by which the elements of a group are integrated, coordinated, and/or utilized so as to effectively

Table 18-1. Management, Leadership, and Bureaucracy Comparisons

Management (Manager)	Leadership (Leader)	Bureaucracy (Bureaucrat)
Responsible for effectively and efficiently achieving organizational goals	Attempts to develop a clairvoyant grasp of the future so he can be effective in guiding the organization to high levels of accomplishment	Conducts daily operations relative to ongoing organizational affairs
Responsible for planning, organizing, directing, staffing, and controlling processes as they relate to the total organization or work unit	Influences group processes resulting in the establishment of goals that will contribute to a high level of group attainment and satisfaction	Precisely adheres to existing policies, procedures, and regulations, viewing them more as an end than a means of administration
Formulates broad policies to guide organizational operations	Shows the way through demonstrating enthusiasm and initiating activity that will contribute to goal accomplishment	Attempts to maintain and sustain current operations through elaborate rules and controls
Responsible for defining and reshaping institutional role and purpose and establishing objectives relating thereto	Stimulates individuals to contribute to group goals and/or follow his direction	Views the manager as a processor of materials, information, reports, etc
Responsible for adapting the organization to external forces	Has a major influence in establishing and modifying organizational climate	Orientation is toward activity, not results
Focuses on promoting the welfare of the entire organization by minimizing or balancing internal vested interests	Monitors, clarifies, and influences the roles and task performance of individuals so as to maximize their personal rewards as they simultaneously contribute to group goal attainment	Orientation is to the status quo—not the future

and efficiently achieve organizational objectives. Management implies total responsibility for the functioning of an organization and is viewed more in formal terms in the context of official duties and functions.

Leadership is a subset of management (one of the five management functions) dealing with the human aspect of how a manager relates to and influences the members of his organization. Leadership is not always associated with a formal position; it can also arise spontaneously. The leader *influences* people to effectively plan, organize, staff, and control, whereas management encompasses *all* concepts associated with these functions. Leadership involves the personal characteristics of the leader, his sources of power, and how he handles interpersonal relations. The responsibility of the manager and the leader is the same—that of successfully achieving organizational objectives. However, the basic difference is that the manager is concerned with all aspects of an organization's functioning which encompasses primarily the rational domain, and leadership is restricted to influencing and motivating others involves more the emotional. Leadership is also future oriented. Ideally the leader is the visionary who assists the organization in the development of goals and the commitment to a mission that result in unusual accomplishment.

For contrasting purposes, the term *bureaucrat* (for lack of more appropriate terminology) is used to represent the nonleader. Bureaucracy is normally associated with a highly formalized type of organization structure. As it relates to leadership, it involves individuals whose main concerns are the form and functioning of the organization. This emphasis on processing and efficiency contrasts with the leader's concern for accomplishment and effectiveness. The bureaucrat is the caretaker who maintains the organization; the leader is one who spurs the group on to greater accomplishment. One attempts to maintain the current system, while the other is concerned with its future. This is not to downplay the importance of efficiency-minded administrators. Every organization finds them of benefit; however, the greatness of an organization is more dependent on its leadership.

Significance of Leadership

The significance of the leader in organizations is somewhat controversial. Historically the leader has been considered paramount, but in recent years emphasis has switched to the productivity of the total group, represented by the combined contributions of individual members.

An illustration will highlight the arguments behind this controversy. When General Omar Bradley brought the 90th Infantry Division to Europe, during World War II, it had a commander who was new to the unit. After four days of floundering on the Normandy beachhead, it was decided that the division needed a new commander. The new appointee made many changes in the staffing, but he was no more successful. Bradley's subordinates recommended that the division be dissolved and the men transferred to other units. Bradley responded that man for man this particular division was on a par with any other: "they vary only in the skill and leadership of their commanders."[1] He then appointed another commander who made sixteen changes in the 16,000 man unit. Within only a few months it was considered one of the finest divisions on the allied front!

Similar examples can be found in business organizations. Companies in the same industry and location pay approximately the same wage rates and receive employees who have relatively equivalent skill and training, so that man for man there is little difference. Many factors may contribute to the differences of these organizations, but leadership is one of the most pronounced. On the other hand, examples like changing cabinet secretaries at the department level of the federal government or military leaders in a civilian-manned Department of Defense organizations often have no real impact on how these organizations will function. Political appointees and military officers come and go approximately every two years or less, but often the fundamental workings of the departments or units stay about the same.

Again the answer depends on the situation. Some organizations are highly dependent on the foresight of a few individuals, while others have developed that function essentially independent of top management. However, the author is inclined to agree with another management writer who states: "No one who has looked closely at even a small number of industrial corporations can fail to be impressed by the dependence of the entire enterprise on the vision and vitality of a relatively small group of highly placed managers."[2] Without question the major shortage of managers in the United States today is at the executive level. Executives who resist change and hinder progress can have a devastating impact on organization effectiveness, whereas a leader who responds to the change of events and the desires of the membership can be one of the most important factors in a group achieving its potential.

LEADERSHIP STUDIES AND CLASSIFICATIONS

The history of the study of leadership is marked by a variety of different approaches. Interest in leadership as a field of study began at approximately the same time as that of management—around 1900. Since then three different approaches have predominated. The first emphasized leadership *traits*, the second concentrated on leadership *behavior*, and the final, current approach considers leadership *situational*.

Traits Approach

Early writers, following the "great man" theory of leadership, searched for the set of traits that distinguished someone as a leader. They assumed that if one best set of traits could be identified, individuals could be trained to develop these, and leadership would flourish. Between 1930 and 1950 hundreds of different studies were conducted, attempting to link factors like intelligence, appearance, knowledge, judgment, initiative, integrity, self-confidence, social skills, age, socioeconomic background, and appearance to leadership.

However, reviewers analyzing these studies all tend to arrive at the same conclusion: there is no set of traits that isolates a leader from the balance of the group. Interpersonal skills, above-average intelligence, motivation, self-confidence, decision-making ability, and decisiveness surfaced often in these studies, but the conclusions of Ralph Stogdill are generally accepted. "A person does not become a leader by virtue of the possession of some combination of traits," even though "the pattern of personal characteristics of the leader must bear some relevant relationship to the characteristics, activities, and goals of the followers."[3]

Behavior Approach

Disenchantment with the traits approach led to a search for new means of analyzing and understanding leadership. One of the conclusions from traits research was that leadership behavior depends on more factors than just the traits of the individual. Thus the focus switched to the leadership process and concentrated on leadership behavior, especially the manner in which an individual relates to followers.

Two different methods of classifying leadership using leadership behavior as the central focus developed. The first assumed that the most important factor in the leader's relations with followers is how he uses his authority or position-based influence. The second approached leadership in terms of the concern of the leader for task accomplishment and productivity versus his concern for people and intragroup relations.

LEADERSHIP STYLES BASED ON USE OF AUTHORITY. Lewin, Lippitt, and White conducted leadership studies in 1939 based on three different styles—autocratic, democratic, and laissez faire.[4] The autocratic leader provides most direction, determines policy, seeks obedience, and relies on authority to force work to be done. The democratic leader gets members involved in determining policy, seeks ideas and suggestions from the group, and gives members a voice in how the group functions. The laissez-faire leader provides essentially no central direction and lets people function on their own. This terminology and these styles have become widely accepted as a means of classifying and analyzing leadership. (A later section in this chapter will be devoted to a more thorough explanation and evaluation of the styles approach.)

THE LEADER'S CONCERN FOR PEOPLE VERSUS CONCERN FOR PRODUCTION.   Another closely related method for analyzing leadership was developed at Ohio State University studies beginning in 1945. The two dimensions of leadership included in these studies were "consideration" and "initiating structure." *Consideration* is the extent to which job relationships are characterized by mutual trust, interpersonal warmth, and consideration for subordinates' ideas and feelings. *Initiating structure* is the extent to which the leader organizes and defines subordinates' activities and relationships. Many studies have been conducted examining these relationships, and some of the best-known leadership models use this approach. Other common terminology (which is more descriptive of the relationships involved) is whether the leader is "employee centered" or "job centered," displays a "concern for production" or a "concern for people," or is "relationship oriented" as opposed to "task oriented."[5]

Contrary to the three-style approach to leadership, using the two-dimensional approach involves characteristics that are not mutually exclusive, so methods for portraying different styles involve a mixture of these relationships. The Management Grid used by Mouton and Blake is a good example (see chapter 17). Figure 18-1 shows the grid with five styles identified, based on different blends of a leader's concern for people and concern for production. The lower-left corner (1,1) represents a minimum concern for people and production. The upper left (1,9) is a minimum concern for production and a maximum one for people. A 9,1 style is the opposite of this, and 9,9 is the maximum for both—which Blake and Mouton consider the ideal managerial style.

Situational Leadership

The inability to find any one set of traits that constitutes leadership or any one style that is appropriate under all conditions soon led researchers and others to conclude that leadership was situational. In 1948 Stogdill stated, "It becomes clear that an adequate analysis of leadership involves not only a study of leaders, but also of situations."[6] Just as the motivation of an individual cannot be understood when he is separated from his environment, so leadership cannot be understood by separating the leader from the social situation.

The leader's qualities and behavior are only two factors affecting leadership in an organization. The qualities and behavior of other group

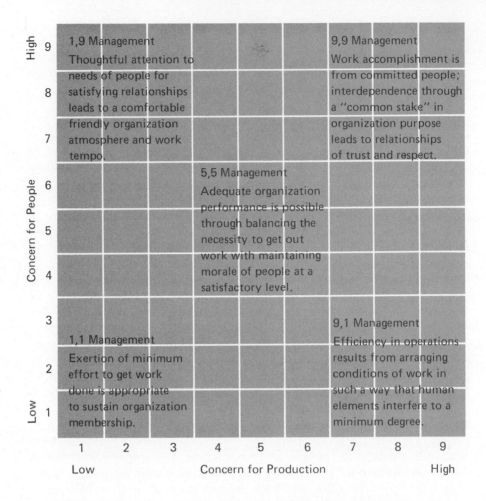

Concern for People (vertical axis: Low 1 to High 9)

9 1,9 Management Thoughtful attention to needs of people for satisfying relationships leads to a comfortable friendly organization atmosphere and work tempo.

9,9 Management Work accomplishment is from committed people; interdependence through a "common stake" in organization purpose leads to relationships of trust and respect.

5,5 Management Adequate organization performance is possible through balancing the necessity to get out work with maintaining morale of people at a satisfactory level.

1,1 Management Exertion of minimum effort to get work done is appropriate to sustain organization membership.

9,1 Management Efficiency in operations results from arranging conditions of work in such a way that human elements interfere to a minimum degree.

Concern for Production (horizontal axis: Low 1 to High 9)

Fig. 18-1. The managerial grid

members, the tasks being performed, the organization structure, and many other factors constituting the situation also affect the leadership process. Individuals will be leaders in some situations but not in others, and different styles of leadership will each be appropriate, depending on conditions in an organization. Even though situational theories of leadership have predominated since 1960, the theoretical development and research verification of these concepts have evolved slowly. (Chapter 19 will be devoted to this topic.)

LEADERSHIP STYLES

Before examining *autocratic, democratic,* and *laissez-faire* styles in more detail, a few words of caution are appropriate. There are not three discrete styles for a leader to choose from. These styles simply represent a range of behavior in which the now-familiar continuum concept is appropriate. For example, some analysts subdivide autocratic leadership into despotic, benevolent, and bureaucratic—depending on how a leader uses his authority. Also, even though an attempt will be made to examine the advantages and limitations of each style, the superiority of any one style will obviously vary with the situation. Any analysis of styles alone will always be tempered in application by situational differences.

> The maxims of leadership we shall state are . . . not to be taken as absolutes but only as convenient guides for the behavior of a leader. They apply only within limits determined by the situation that faces him, and there are situations in which the maxims will conflict with one another. What a leader needs to have is not a set of rules but a good method of analyzing the social situation in which he must act. If the analysis is adequate, a way of dealing with the situation will suggest itself. And if, as a working guide, the leader does have some simple rules in mind, analysis will show him where their limits lie.

Quotation from George C. Homans, *The Human Group* (New York: Harcourt, Brace, and Company, 1950).

Style Characteristics

The more modern terminology relating to the three styles of leadership will be used throughout the balance of the book. In recent years it has become common to substitute *directive styles* for autocratic, *participative* for democratic, and *free rein* for laissez faire. Not only are these more accurate terms, but they are also freer of value connotations: the original terms have political implications in Western culture that automatically introduce bias when they are used.

Table 18-2 summarizes the characteristics associated with each style. The most distinguishing characteristic is that directive styles are leader centered, participative styles are group centered, and free-rein styles are individual centered. In serving as the decision maker and center of activity, the directive leader typically seeks stable situations and rewards

Table 18-2. Comparison of Leadership Styles

Condition	Directive (Leader Centered)	Participative (Group Centered)	Free Rein (Individual Centered)
Decisions	Leader makes most decisions	Subordinates involved in decisions	Subordinates make decisions
Independence	Little freedom of action permitted	Fosters some independence	Almost complete independence
Use of power	Uses power and discipline	Tries to persuade, not force	Reliance on self-control
Communications	One-way communication	Two-way communication	Free, open communication
Leader involvement	Leader stays aloof from group	Leader involved in group	Leader not identifiable in group
Subordinates' feelings	Limited concern for subordinates' feelings	Considers subordinates' feelings	Subordinates' feelings predominate
Responsibility	Leader assumes responsibility	Leader shares responsibility but still is ultimately responsible	Individual is responsible
Leader's role	Provides direction	Group involvement	Provides support resources
Organization climate	Leader seeks stable, predictable climate	Flexible and adaptive	Flexibility related to individual performance
Employee orientation	Obedience	Cooperation	Individual performance
Psychological result	Dependency	Participation	Independence

Source: Adapted from table 4, page 130 of *Situational Management* (New York: AMACOM, 1973) by the author.

subordinates who are obedient, which results in subordinates being dependent on the leader. The participative leader seeks group involvement, forcing a more flexible, adaptive structure. Since the emphasis is on group relations and productivity, the norms of the group emphasize cooperation and participation. Free-rein leadership is almost an abdication of it. Individuals are essentially free to function on their own. The leader's role is more to provide the support resources necessary for people to handle their tasks. With few constraints, there is a high degree of flexibility, highlighted by the independence of the worker. (The psychological implications of these different styles are enumerated in characteristics nine through eleven.)

Benefits and Limitations of Directive Leadership

The primary advantages of directive leadership are as follows:

1. Functioning as a directive leader is motivating and rewarding to the individual who tends to be hard driving and egocentric. It maximizes the utilization of the leader's skills.
2. It results in central control and coordination, because all direction comes from one source.
3. It results in more consistent policies and direction, since decisions are made by one individual.
4. Quicker decisions are made, because others do not have to be consulted.
5. Directive leadership is typically strong leadership, which is useful in overcoming major obstacles, generating change, or handling crises.

The drawbacks associated with directive leadership are primarily behavioral in nature and can be summarized as follows:

1. It fosters a restrictive environment in which individuals are limited in what they can do. Hence they do not develop their potential as much as they would otherwise—or contribute to the maximum of their abilities.
2. It often results in low morale, because people generally do not like to be closely controlled, and they find limited opportunity for status or self-actualization need satisfaction. It is difficult to take pride in one's work when someone else provides all of the direction.
3. It tends to alienate workers so that they react by performing at the minimal level necessary to "get by." It is also associated with hos-

tility, retaliation, scapegoating, and other behavior associated with frustration.

4. Weak, one-way communication leads to misunderstanding and people who are not well informed.
5. Directive leadership is relatively inflexible and hard to reverse. When a leader uses another style, the followers question his motives and tend to maintain their "obedience" posture.

Evaluation of Participative Styles

Participative styles of leadership have been widely acclaimed in management literature since the human relations movement of the 1930's. The reasons for this acclaim are as follows:

1. Having the freedom to function independently and to contribute through participation is extremely motivational. Participation satisfies psychological needs, since one has the opportunity to contribute, use skills, and gain recognition from the results of independent effort.
2. It provides outlets for using the knowledge and potential of the entire group. Using the skills and knowledge of the group results in better, more creative decisions. Even though the leader may be the most knowledgeable individual in the group, the combined knowledge of all members will usually be superior to the leader's, especially when complementary skills are considered.
3. People are more committed to an organization when they have a say in what it does. These feelings of ownership result in more cohesive groups in which people are more cooperative and involved.
4. Giving people greater freedom and independence is consistent with the values of a democratic society. Participation is normally associated with a commitment to industrial humanism, which places emphasis on individual rights and the dignity and worth of the individual.
5. Effective two-way communication results in people who are better informed. They are also forced into the broader perspective of considering organizational issues instead of just those associated exclusively with their job.
6. Having an opportunity to participate is an important factor in developing managers. Management is still largely an art in which one learns by doing. Through participation, an individual can practice the art of management and gain this expertise.
7. In organizations where all people are involved, there is greater openness and trust. Working out policies and actions together forces greater tolerance and flexibility in the organization.

Despite the many virtues of participation, there are also some handicaps to this method of operation:

1. To keep people informed and get them involved in organizational actions takes time. Busy executives find difficulty squeezing in this time, and frequently the urgency of decisions will not permit participation.
2. With many people involved in making a decision, the tendency is to compromise and water-down proposed actions. If all issues are settled at the lowest common denominator, it can result in a protection of the status quo.
3. Based on two above, a commitment to participation may hold down the innovative, farsighted leader. Some argue that participation shackles the strong leader.
4. The diffused responsibility associated with participation can result in no one taking action. If responsibility is too diluted, no one feels a direct commitment to act.
5. Managing with a participative style is extremely difficult and often contrary to the ego drives of individuals. Unless there is a relatively equal degree of competence within the group, some people will tend to dominate, and participation may be a farce. Not all people in a group may be able to positively contribute, and yet the leader must use some ideas put forth or resentment and alienation can result. The hard-driving executive also finds that power equalization may be contrary to his own interests and internal drives.

Advantages and Weaknesses of Free-Rein Styles

Free-rein styles of leadership are not as common as the others. They are also more of an extension of participative styles, permitting this analysis to be abbreviated. Under certain conditions, free-rein styles are appropriate and provide the following benefits:

1. It can be extremely motivating to certain individuals to be given essentially complete freedom to function in their position. Some would even say that it is maximizing the "quality of life" in an organization.
2. The bureaucracy of most organizations tends to restrict creativity. The openness of free-rein styles encourages it, thus maximizing the potential of the individual.
3. It encourages a more "free-flowing" organization that is flexible and adaptive.

The drawbacks of free-rein styles are obvious to those with a strong management orientation:

1. Free-rein styles can result in chaos because of lack of central coordination and integration.
2. Emphasizing individual performance may result in suboptimization as far as the group is concerned. Individual rather than group goals are likely to predominate.
3. A lack of central control may result in things getting too far out of hand before corrective action is taken.

Productivity Associated with the Various Styles

Note that in no instance was it ever stated that one style is more productive than others. This is, of course, because different situations determine each style's appropriateness—in terms of productivity. Research studies support the conclusion that participative or free-rein styles are preferred because they are more satisfying to the individual. The individual generally enjoys the freedom and growth potential of these more open styles. However, research results are conflicting on the productivity of any particular style. In his comprehensive review of leadership studies, Stogdill concludes: "The above results clearly indicate that neither democratic nor autocratic supervision can be advocated as a method for increasing productivity, but member satisfaction is associated with a democratic style of supervision."[7]

USING PARTICIPATIVE STYLES

The widespread support for participative styles and the difficulty of using participation warrants an examination of methods the leader can use to implement this style. Basically there are two such methods. The first is referred to as the "how" approach and the second as the "managerial" approach.

Letting Subordinates Make "How" Decisions

The rationale for letting subordinates make the "how" decisions is based on the behavioral concepts already elaborated. People want a feeling of competency from their work, and they seek psychological need satisfaction in terms of recognition and independence. (However, in some instances their need for security may restrict yearnings for independence.) It is difficult to feel competent unless an individual independently makes some decisions. The obvious decisions that a subordinate can make without jeopardizing or assuming the responsibilities of the manager are the *how,* or operating decisions. A skilled individual in a profession or job should be able to make the technical decisions that relate to that job (for instance, an electrician when wiring a house or a secretary when typing a letter). When a supervisor tells a person like this how to perform the technical operations, he or she is in fact belittling the individual by displaying a lack of trust and respect.

Probably the most important methodology in supervision follows this reasoning. It starts with the assumption that the manager is ultimately responsible for results and he cannot forfeit or delegate this responsibility to a subordinate. To obtain results he should establish goals, provide plans and procedural guidelines, thoroughly train individuals, hold high expectations for their performance, and then let them gain motivation and self-actualization within this framework by functioning in a relatively independent fashion in performing their jobs or making the how decisions. It is often difficult for a manager to psychologically "let go" in this fashion, but why should he be concerned with the details of how work is done as long as he gets the desired results? Also if people require some independence to be motivated, it is generally the technical decisions that can become their responsibility. This is especially so in jobs of low technology. In high-technology jobs (designing a space craft), this may not be the case.

Participation in Managerial Decisions

Many people misunderstand democratic styles by assuming that decisions are made on a one-man, one-vote basis with the majority ruling. This is basically a method of organization structure and is not a leadership style. Participative styles assume that subordinates are involved and that the leader draws on their ideas and knowledge. He views subordinates more as social equals. However, the leader is held responsible for results and for the management processes of planning, organizing, staffing, and controlling. When participative styles are used in these management activities, subordinates participate through *recommending* alternatives or courses of action, but the manager makes and has sole responsibility for the final decision.

The following example may help illustrate how a supervisor uses participation in the managerial aspects of his work. Assume that you are in charge of a government bureau and the legislature has just passed a new appropriation providing $500,000 to start a new project in six months at the beginning of the next fiscal year. As manager, your job is to develop the plans, set up the organization structure, select staff members, and start the project. In your bureau you have three section heads who are all knowledgeable and can contribute to these activities. The participative leader would acquaint the section heads with the project and ask for their recommendations regarding how it should be planned, organized, and initiated. He might get them involved with him as he handled these activities or could give them two weeks to think this through separately before coming back with their recommendations. He would, of course, be formulating his own ideas during this period.

Upon receiving the input from subordinates, he would discuss it with them, obtain necessary clarifications, and then select any ideas or recommendations that he feels would be useful. However, participation does not stop here. If the supervisor does not use the ideas of subordinates, he should explain why. By doing this they will learn from experience, and they will also feel that their ideas were not ignored. A thoroughly participate leader would then have the subordinates critique the final plans before he began implementation. Such involvement makes people feel important, provides outlets for their ideas, and should result in better plans and actions. However, as valuable as participation is, it is not a panacea. It is only one facet of the successful functioning of a manager.

INFLUENCE SYSTEMS:
APPLYING REWARDS AND PUNISHMENT

Since leadership is an influence relationship, the sources and use of this influence become important. (The sources of influence were enumerated in chapter 14 and involve such factors as position, knowledge, personal characteristics, charisma, wealth, social class, physical power, and group norms.) Leadership style relates to how an individual uses this influence. Positive reinforcement methods more closely identified with participative and free-rein styles were identified in chapter 11, on motivation. They relate to providing challenging tasks, giving recognition for outstanding effort, and establishing a supportive relationship. Punishment involves depriving someone of the rewards of positive reinforcement, but it is also using sanctions to take action against an individual or group.

Discipline is one of the necessary but distasteful aspects of leadership. Typically the disciplinary approach associated with directive styles is considered a last resort. Under normal conditions a manager should attempt to provide some freedom and independence for the individual, but when these methods are not successful it frequently means that pressure must be applied and sanctions enforced. Overdoing discipline can certainly be harmful, but a supervisor can lose the respect of his subordinates if he permits lagging performance or antagonistic behavior to go unchecked.

Discipline is a delicate matter and requires careful consideration by the supervisor. The general guidelines for disciplining are as follows:

- Get the facts.
- Be fair and consistent.
- Forewarn—so the work force is aware of the rules and regulations.
- Discipline in private.
- Be prompt.
- Condemn the act, not the actor.
- Attempt to make the penalty a constructive learning experience.

Based on our previous analyses of behavioral concepts, the rationale behind these guides should be obvious to the reader. A supervisor is usually more effective if he supports the workgroup. Obviously he must enforce the rules of the organization, but he should do it in a way that does not destroy his relationship with the individual or individuals involved. Showing partiality, flaunting power, belittling the individual, and causing him to lose face in front of others can only generate resentment, rather than a desire not to engage in the behavior that brought on the disciplinary action.

One of the most important guides is that of promptly notifying an individual when his behavior is contrary to rules and regulations. Discipline has a much greater impression when closely associated with the act. Also, if not done promptly repeated violations may occur that will be harder to deal with. If a supervisor tolerates absenteeism or lateness when regulations specifically prohibit this, it soon becomes an accepted informal norm, and when the supervisor reverts to enforcing the formal norm, he or she is put in the position of taking away a privilege.

SUMMARY

Leadership is the process of providing direction in group activities and of influencing others to achieve group objectives. Leadership is one of the five functions that are part of the management process. Leadership involves the actuating, motivational, goal-directed aspects of planning, organizing, and controlling. Leadership is future oriented, whereas administration is concerned with efficiently handling current operations.

There are many methods of classifying leaders, but the most common relates to styles of leader behavior based primarily on how the leader uses his authority and influence. The three styles—more properly portrayed as a continuum—are directive, participative, and free rein. Other appropriate terminology is leader centered, group centered, or individual centered. Each style has certain advantages that makes it preferable, depending on the particular situation. Participative styles have received strong support in behavioral literature because they develop favorable intragroup relations and are satisfying to the individual, but productivity is dependent on the total situation.

QUESTIONS FOR STUDY AND DISCUSSION

1. Define leadership and explain how it relates to concepts of influence and motivation.
2. How does a leader differ from a manager or a bureaucrat? Is an informal leader a manager?
3. How significant do you think the following leaders are in the success of their organizations:
   A. College president   C. Apartment-house manager
   B. Hospital administrator   D. Chief Executive Officer of Sears
4. How does the two-factor approach (task versus relationship) differ from the style approach to leadership?
5. Is there any set of traits associated with leadership? Why has this approach been of limited success?
6. Why have situational approaches to leadership predominated?
7. Explain how the following differ when directive, participative, or free-rein styles of leadership predominate:
   A. Communication   D. Needs of subordinates
   B. The leader's role   E. Commitment of people
   C. Behavior developed   to the organization
      by subordinates   F. Productivity
8. Regarding the participative style, answer the following:
   A. What are the restrictions in using participative styles?
   B. Why is it difficult for a manager to develop expertise in participative styles?
   C. Under this style, are all decisions group decisions? Explain.
9. In your own personal experience, what leadership styles did the following people use? How successful were these styles?
   A. Your high school principal
   B. Your parents
   C. A company you had a summer or part-time job with
   D. A coach you had
10. Indicate how someone should handle the discipline of a person who was found:
    A. Smoking in a no-smoking area
    B. Cheating on travel-expense statements
    C. Sleeping on the job

Case Study:
DIRECTING SUBORDINATES

Alan Kerr is in charge of maintaining the machinery for an oil refinery. He has twenty-five subordinates in his group who are pipe fitters, machinists, and plumbers, among other tradesmen. Alan has two particular subordinates—with exactly opposite characteristics—who tend to be perpetual problems.

Jak Robinson is a pipe fitter who has been with the organization ten years. He has good skills and generally does his work at an acceptable quality level. However, he tends to resent any direction that Alan tries to provide. When Alan comes around to check on his work, he is rarely cordial. He wants to be left alone, and he resists even minor suggestions about how to do a job or how the work can be improved. When Alan assigns him maintenance projects, Jak hardly says a word and is inclined to rush off to the job before Alan can discuss it with him. Even if he runs into problems when he needs assistance from other tradesmen, he is inclined to go directly to them rather than through Alan.

Spence Green, on the other hand, is just as dependent as Jak is independent. He is a machinist who has been with the company for five years. Whenever Alan assigns him a job, he can expect Spence to bother him with dozens of questions. He will even ask Alan about the details of performing the job when Alan feels that he is thoroughly knowledgeable. Two or three times each morning and afternoon, Spence will hunt down Alan and ask him questions about the work he is doing. Alan gets a little mad sometimes and will tell Spence to quit bothering him, but the next day he is back at it again. Spence also is an average or better employee, so Alan sees little need to provide this continual direction.

Why do you think Jak and Spence react as they do?
How should Alan handle each of these situations?

Case Problem:
THE NEW CITY MANAGER

Marion Russell was recently appointed city manager of a community of 25,000 in central Wisconsin. Before he left, she had a long talk with the former city manager, who was leaving to take another similar post. One of the topics discussed was problems relating to the managing of certain departments.

The former city manager praised the streets department. Snow removal and street repair were both efficiently handled. The problem was with the department head. He has a good relationship with subordinates in the department, and the department maintains outstanding esprit de corps. However, as department head he tends to be highly critical of all other departments in the city. In staff meetings he continually gripes about coordination problems with the procurement and finance departments. He constantly complains about actions taken by the Council, the efficiency of other departments, and the burdens of working in city government. This tends to carry over to subordinates, who are then also critical of the activities of other units. The former city manager cautioned him several times about this attitude, but it seemed to do little good.

The other problem in administration is the water department. The department head is competent and aggressive. Detailed planning is carried out months in advance, and standards exist for all jobs within the unit. Everything is worked out in detail, so there is very little confusion over what is required. However, things are almost too structured. The attention he gives to scheduling, planning, and setting standards is not necessarily met with enthusiasm by his subordinates. Morale seems to be low even though pay and working conditions are on a par with other departments.

What should the new city manager do?

Footnotes

1. Omar N. Bradley, *A Soldier's Story* (New York: Henry Holt and Company, 1951), p. 297.
2. Richard F. Neuschel, "Management's Need for Theory and Research," contained in Harold Koontz, Ed., *Toward a Unified Theory of Management* (New York: McGraw-Hill Book Company, 1964), p. 182.
3. Ralph M. Stogdill, *Handbook of Leadership* (New York: The Free Press, 1974), pp. 63–64.
4. *Ibid.*, p. 365.
5. Major contributors to leadership theory such as Rensis Likert, R. R. Blake and Jane S. Mouton, and Fred Fiedler use these approaches.
6. Ralph M. Stogdill, "Personal Factors Associated with Leadership: A Survey of the Literature," *Journal of Psychology*, 1948, Vol. 25, p. 65.
7. Ralph M. Stogdill, *Handbook of Leadership, op. cit.*, p. 370.

Contingency Approaches to Leadership

What factors are important in determining the appropriateness of different leadership styles?

Can an individual "select" a leadership style?

What variables are involved in Fiedler's contingency model?

What factors are critical in the influence relationship between the leader and followers?

How do external factors affect the leader-follower relationship?

DOMINANCE OF SITUATIONAL THEORIES

As indicated in chapter 18, situational theories of leadership became dominant after the early failures associated with the traits approach. Typical of these theories is that presented by Douglas McGregor in his classic, written in 1960, *The Human Side of Enterprise*. McGregor stated that there are at least four variables involved in leadership:

1. The characteristics of the leader
2. The attitudes, needs, and other personal characteristics of the followers
3. The characteristics of the organization such as its purpose, its structure, and nature of the tasks to be performed
4. The social, economic, and political milieu

Furthermore, he noted that "leadership is not a property of the individual, but a complex relationship among these variables."[1]

Even though McGregor and others identified the key leadership variables and emphasized the interdependence among them, few attempts have been made to construct models that comprehensively examine these relationships. The purpose of this chapter is to review some of these models and to present a prescriptive methodology for examining and using situational approaches. Situational theories of leadership are especially important for our purpose because they are the forerunner of the broader contingency approach to management—which is, of course, the subject of this book.

THE CONTINUUM APPROACH TO LEADERSHIP STYLES

One of the most widely read articles on leadership was written in 1958 by Robert Tannenbaum and Warren H. Schmidt.[2] In this article, leadership is considered to represent a range of behavior and is shown as a continuum as indicated in figure 19-1. Their approach contrasts the use of authority by the boss versus the amount of freedom provided subordinates. Seven styles of leadership are presented, with the high use of authority by a manager represented on the extreme left of the continuum and almost complete freedom for subordinates represented on the right. The left side also represents boss-centered leadership; the right, subordinate centered. Areas in-between are blends of these factors.

The most significant aspect of Tannenbaum and Schmidt's model is not the continuum concept but the recognition that leadership consists of three sets of forces: those in the manager, in subordinates, and in the situation. Forces in the manager consist of factors like his value system,

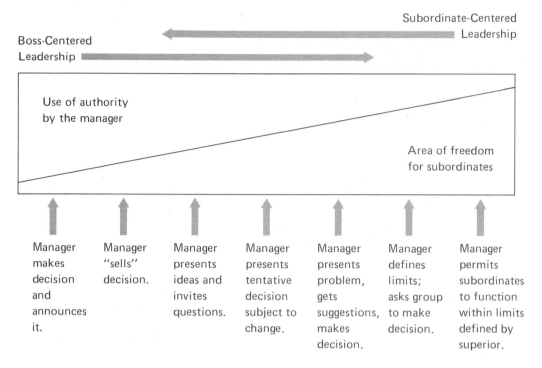

Boss-Centered Leadership

Subordinate-Centered Leadership

Use of authority by the manager

Area of freedom for subordinates

| Manager makes decision and announces it. | Manager "sells" decision. | Manager presents ideas and invites questions. | Manager presents tentative decision subject to change. | Manager presents problem, gets suggestions, makes decision. | Manager defines limits; asks group to make decision. | Manager permits subordinates to function within limits defined by superior. |

Fig. 19-1. Tannenbaum and Schmidt continuum of leadership behavior

confidence in subordinates, leadership inclinations, and feelings of security in an uncertain situation. Forces in subordinates consist of their needs for independence, readiness to assume responsibility, tolerance for ambiguity, knowledge, interest in the problem at hand, identification with the goals of the organization, and expectations of sharing in decision making. Forces in the situation include the type of organization (size, geographical dispersion, etc.), group effectiveness (cohesiveness, permissiveness, confidence, etc.), the problem itself (complexity, significance), and the pressure of time.

They concluded that the successful leader is one who can assess the forces and determine appropriate leadership action at any given time. Few guides are provided regarding how a manager makes this assessment. The "answer depends largely on what he wants to accomplish" in terms of employee motivation, acceptance of change, quality of decisions, and other such factors.[3]

In 1973, when this classic was reprinted in the *Harvard Business Review*, the authors were asked to make a retrospective commentary.[4] In updating their theory to include subsequent societal changes and new management concepts, they incorporated recent behavioral science findings and the contributions of open-systems theory. These are reflected in figure 19-2. Using open-systems theory, they emphasized more the interdependency of forces and the forces outside the organization, such as cultural changes, labor unions, and so forth. They also replaced the words *boss* and *subordinate* with *manager* and *nonmanager power*, because they view these as less demeaning and dependency laden. Finally, they recognized the strong relationship between how a manager is *inclined* to lead and his or her reliance on *group acceptance* for the influence possessed. Their approach has been extremely important in clarifying the forces involved in leadership and in emphasizing that no style can be labeled right or wrong but is appropriate or inappropriate based on the situational blend of forces.

FIEDLER'S CONTINGENCY THEORY

The situational approach to leadership found little more than practical experience to sustain it until Fred Fiedler came forth with his contingency model in 1967.[5] This model was a culmination of extensive psychological studies beginning in 1951. From these studies he concluded, "One style of leadership is not in itself better than the other, nor is one type of leadership behavior appropriate for all conditions."[6] Accordingly, he set about constructing a contingency model that would determine under what conditions different styles are appropriate.

Leadership effectiveness, as Fiedler defined it, is based on group performance—primarily in terms of output or how well it carries out its assigned functions. Group effectiveness is contingent upon the existing relationship between "leadership style" and the "group situation." Fiedler used the two-factor approach to leadership style, or the "relationship-oriented" versus the "task-oriented" leader. The group situation is dominated by three factors—listed in order of importance: leader-member relations, task structure, and leader position power. Thus Fiedler's leadership model relates the two different styles of leadership to situations that are differentiated on the basis of how favorable the leader-member relations are, the task structure of the group, and how much position power he maintains.

Favorable and Unfavorable Situations

Before exploring the relationships of the model, it is essential to understand the basis on which it is determined: whether a leader is task or relationships-oriented, and how mixtures of the three variables determine whether situations are "favorable" or "unfavorable" for the leader. The

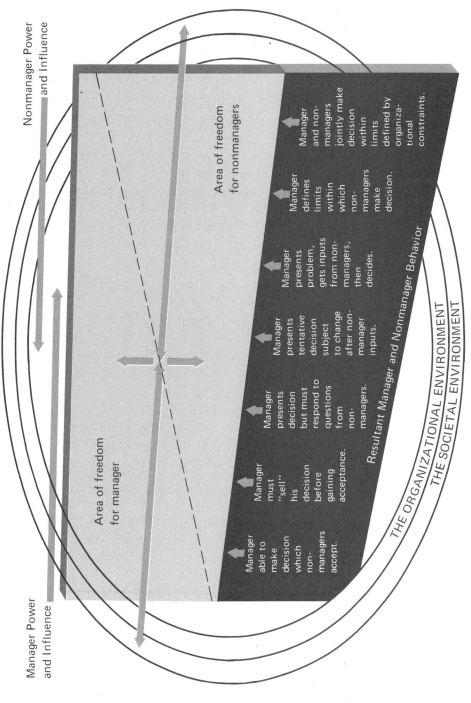

Continuum of Manager-nonmanager Behavior

Nonmanager Power and Influence

Manager Power and Influence

Area of freedom for manager

Area of freedom for nonmanagers

Manager able to make decision which non-managers accept.

Manager must "sell" his decision before gaining acceptance.

Manager presents decision but must respond to questions from non-managers.

Manager presents tentative decision subject to change after non-manager inputs.

Manager presents problem, gets inputs from non-managers, then decides.

Manager defines limits within which non-managers make decision.

Manager and non-managers jointly make decision within limits defined by organiza-tional constraints.

Resultant Manager and Nonmanager Behavior

THE ORGANIZATIONAL ENVIRONMENT
THE SOCIETAL ENVIRONMENT

Fig. 19-2. Revision of the Tannenbaum and Schmidt con-tinuum of leadership behavior

leadership orientation of an individual is determined by a questionnaire where the respondent is asked to think of all the people with whom he has ever worked and then describe his least preferred coworker (LPC). The favorableness in which he describes his coworker on seventeen bipolar scales determine whether he is task or relationship oriented. (Task-oriented people define the least preferred coworker very unfavorably and relationship-oriented personalities show them relatively more favorable.)

The three situational factors in terms of favorableness are determined as follows. When the leader is liked and has good leader-member relations, he has more influence, so the situation is favorable; when he is disliked, he has less support from the group, so the situation is unfavorable. The greater the structure found in tasks, the easier it is for a leader to tell subordinates what to do, so the situation is favorable; if tasks are ambiguous, it is more difficult to provide direction, so the situation is unfavorable. If the leader has high position power, he has more influence, so the situation is favorable; if he has little position power, it is more difficult to influence subordinates, making the situation unfavorable. When the three factors are shown in three-dimensional fashion, they provide eight classifications of group-task situations as shown in figure 19-3.

Contingency Leadership Model

The composite chart relating Fiedler's research results to the relationships between leadership styles and situations is shown in figure 19-4. Task-motivated leaders perform better in either highly favorable or unfavorable situations (below the mid-point line), and relationship-motivated leaders perform better in mixed situations (above the mid-point line). The line on the chart represents results of studies involving over 800 different groups. It reflects the correlation between leadership style and group performance. In summary, Fiedler's model holds that in very difficult (unfavorable) or very easy (favorable) situations, a strong task-oriented leader is needed to be effective, and in situations of moderate difficulty, a leader who emphasizes interpersonal relationships will be the most effective.

It is difficult to give examples involving the different situations represented by the octants, because the most important factor—leader-member relations—will differ with the personalities involved. Regarding the other two factors, a military combat group would represent the highly favorable situation, in terms of structured tasks and strong position power. A voluntary organization seeking new sources of funding would involve unfavorable conditions of unstructured tasks and weak position power. A leader liked by his research and development group who has

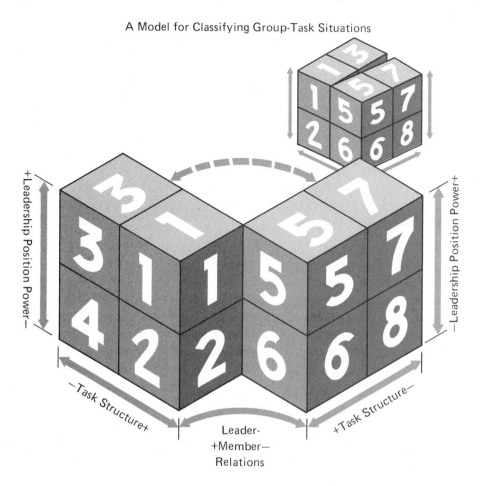

A Model for Classifying Group-Task Situations

Fig. 19-3. **Three situational variables representing eight cells in the Fiedler contingency model**

weak controls or sanctions (position power), such as at a university, would represent the fourth cell.

One of the interesting conclusions of Fiedler's studies is that rather than attempting to fit the leader to the job, we should fit the job to the leader. He is critical of training programs that attempt to change the leadership style of an individual. He views it generally easier to change a man's work environment than it is to change his personality (which we acknowledged in chapters 10 and 17). Changing a man's work environment involves redesigning jobs, developing more homogeneous groups, improving leader-member relations, providing more position power, and other similar actions.

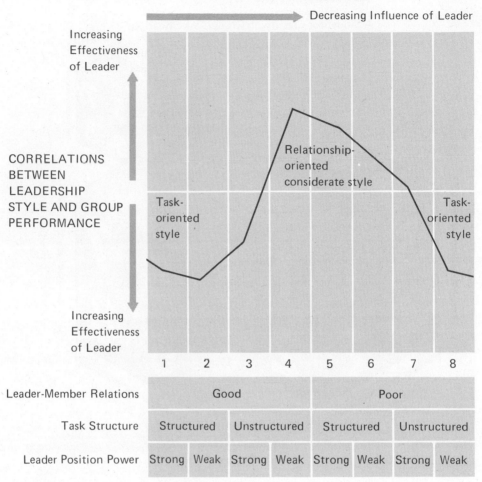

Fig. 19-4. Fiedler contingency model relating style of leadership to situational variables*

Limitations of the Contingency Model

There are several limitations of the Fiedler approach. Some researchers have questioned his methodology and conclusions.[7] Practitioners have also experienced some frustration in applying it to their own situations. However, probably the prime limitation is that it assumes situations are dominated by three factors—leader-member relations, task structure, and the leader's position power. These factors are undoubtedly important in determining the appropriateness of a particular leadership style, but many other factors are also involved, as we shall see in the next section. However, even with these limitations, Fiedler's contribution is the most significant to date in conceptualizing and integrating situational factors in relation to leadership.

OTHER CONTINGENCY MODELS

In addition to Fiedler's approach, other contingency models have been developed in recent years. (These tend to be somewhat more elaborate, which prohibits their full disclosure in this text.) A brief summary will be made of the two most important evolving contingency theories of leadership that are still in the developmental stage.

Path-Goal Theory of Leadership

One of the theories of leadership that has received major recent interest is an outgrowth of expectancy (contingency) theories of motivation (see chapter 11). Robert J. House and others[8] view the leader's primary role as attempting to have a favorable impact on subordinates' motivation. Since motivation is a function of the individual's (1) expectations that he will be successful in performing the tasks, (2) expected rewards or outcomes perceived from performing the tasks, and (3) value of these outcomes, anything the supervisor can do to improve these factors will increase motivation and, one hopes, performance. Appropriate actions for the leader are to clarify the path required to achieve desired goals, remove barriers in this path, increase the appropriate payoffs for performing the tasks, and similar actions. In doing this, four kinds of leadership behavior are identified: directive, supportive, participative, and achievement oriented. Contingency factors are considered to be variables like the nature of the task that moderate the relationship between leader behavior and subordinate satisfaction. The characteristics of subordinates and task environmental factors will influence the type of leadership style that should be used.

Leadership Using a Decision-Making Model

In 1973, Victor H. Vroom, one of the leaders in the development of expectancy theories of motivation, teamed with Philip W. Yetton to propose a theory of leadership postulating that properties of the problem to be solved determine the degree of participation or the leadership style necessary.[9] Problems are considered to be group or individual, with five methods existing for solving group problems, five for individual ones. These methods differ primarily in the amount of participation involved, ranging from making a decision yourself—based on available information —to delegating the problem to a subordinate or letting the group make the decision.

In making decisions and selecting the appropriated degree of participation, a decision-tree approach (see chapter 7) is used. Decisions rules are provided (such as the leader not making the decision when he lacks the information or expertise to make it, the leader making the decision when subordinates cannot be trusted to make it consistent with organizational goals, or employing a participative style if acceptance of the decision is critical). Because of the newness of the Vroom-Yetton model, it has received only limited application in theory and practice. Its primary value is that it shifts the study of leadership from directive or participative leaders to directive or participative situations.

SELECTING LEADERSHIP STYLES: A MOTIVATION APPROACH

Robert A. House and others have developed the "path-goal theory of leadership." This approach emphasizes the leader's role in maximizing motivation to achieve individual and group goals. Under this theory, the strategic functions of the leader are as follows:

1. Recognizing and/or arousing subordinates' needs for outcomes over which the leader has some control
2. Increasing personal payoffs to subordinates for work-goal attainment
3. Making the path to those payoffs easier to travel by coaching and direction
4. Helping subordinates clarify expectancies
5. Reducing frustrating barriers
6. Increasing the opportunities for personal satisfaction contingent on effective performance

Different contingency variables will determine which style of leadership will be most effective in performing these functions.

Reprinted from Robert J. House and Terence R. Mitchell, "Path-Goal Theory of Leadership," *Journal of Contemporary Business*, Autumn 1974, pp. 81–97.

SELECTING LEADERSHIP STYLES:
A DECISION-MAKING APPROACH

Victor H. Vroom and Philip W. Yetton have developed a recent approach to leadership that relates style to the particular problem to be solved. Their model assumes that the properties of the problem establish the "appropriate form or amount of participation." The variables that determine the desired degree of participation are as follows:

1. The importance of the quality of the decision
2. The extent to which the leader possesses sufficient information/expertise to make a high quality decision by himself
3. The extent to which subordinates, taken collectively, have the necessary information to generate a high quality decision
4. The extent to which the problem is structured
5. The extent to which acceptance or commitment on the part of subordinates is critical to the effective implementation of the decision
6. The prior probability that the leader's autocratic decision will receive acceptance by subordinates
7. The extent to which subordinates are motivated to attain the organizational goals as represented in the objectives explicit in the statement of the problem
8. The extent to which subordinates are likely to be in disagreement over preferred solutions

Reprinted from Victor H. Vroom and Philip W. Yetton, *Leadership and Decision-Making* (Pittsburgh: University of Pittsburgh Press, 1973).

A TOTAL CONTINGENCY MODEL
OF LEADERSHIP

The comprehensive model of leadership to be used for our purposes is shown in figure 19-5. It will be noted that there are many similarities between this model and the contingency model of management presented in chapter 3. The primary difference is that the people variable is divided into those who are leaders and those who are followers. This leader-follower relationship is the central focus of the model, which is natural because leadership is basically defined as a leader-follower influence

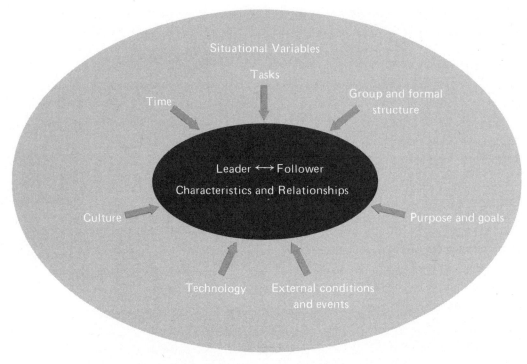

Inner circle: Basic influence relationship between leader and followers
Outer circle: Factors that influence the basic leader-follower relationship and
                    determine the appropriateness of different leadership styles

Fig. 19-5. Situational-leadership model

relationship. With this as the central issue, our primary concerns are the characteristics of the leader and followers and the relationships that develop between them as a result of their interaction.

One should not lose sight of the fact that leadership comprises much more than just the personality traits of the leader and followers. The context of any situation (outer circle in figure 19-5) is composed of the tasks individuals are engaged in, the technology associated with these tasks, the structure of the group and formal organization, the purpose and goals of the organization, and broader environmental factors (such as customs, the tide of economic, political, and societal events), and the time frame within which interaction and decision-making take place. Each of these affects the motivation, influence, and behavior of individuals. They therefore become variables in the leader-follower relationship.

Leadership-related conditions and events are a composite reflection of all of these variables and thrust the leader into dynamic situations in which different styles become appropriate. Typically, great leaders arise during periods of crisis—such as a war or a depression—or when the organization faces a major challenge requiring dramatic redirection. Such events involve situations in which there is a need for individuals with particular skills and traits. Leaders with other characteristics will prove to be more effective in tranquil or stable situations. However, it should not be assumed that the primary conditions determining the need for particular styles consist of the certainty or uncertainty of the environment. Normally, it is a more localized problem, like knowing when to be directive or participative with individuals, based on their knowledge, commitment, and the complexity of tasks involved.

Variables in the Leader-Follower Relationship

The relationship between the leader and followers is a function of the characteristics (personality, skills, attitudes, values, etc.) of the leader, those of followers, and the mutual ties developed. Some of the more common characteristics determining this relationship are shown in figure 19-6. The scales represent separately the characteristics of the leader and the followers. The conditions relating to these different characteristics influence the leader-follower interaction that takes place, and the mutual relationships (not shown in figure 19-6) that result, such as loyalty, warmth, rejection, acceptance, consideration, and trust or distrust.

These relationships are extremely important, because as noted earlier, the influence and power of the leader are a function of the degree to which the group accepts his leadership (see chapter 14). It should also be noted that the leader-follower relationship is not merely the result of the *status* of these two sets of characteristics, but it is how each party *perceives* the other, their joint expectations, and the situational context in which the interaction takes place. Leader-follower characteristics like those shown in figure 19-6 are instrumental in determining four of the important conditions tied to leadership:

1. Who is selected and maintained as leader
2. The sources of influence of leaders and members
3. The degree of participation and freedom the leader should encourage
4. The appropriateness of particular leadership styles, given the nature of leader and followers characteristics

Personality and Needs:	Leader		Followers	
1. Aggressiveness	timid	aggressive	timid	aggressive
2. Authoritarian	low	high	low	high
3. Dependency	dependent	independent	dependent	independent
4. Responsibility	avoids	accepts	avoids	accepts
5. Tolerance for ambiguity	low	high	low	high
6. Security needs	insecure	secure	insecure	secure
7. Acceptance needs	weak	strong	weak	strong
8. Status needs	weak	strong	weak	strong
9. Achievement needs	weak	strong	weak	strong
Skills and Abilities:				
10. Knowledge	low	high	low	high
11. Training and experience	limited	extensive	limited	extensive
12. Technical skills	low	high	low	high
13. Interpersonal skills	low	high	low	high

Fig. 19-6.   Matching leader-follower characteristics

Attitudes and Values:	Leader		Followers	
14. Commitment to group goals	low	high	low	high
15. Commitment to tasks	low	high	low	high
16. Commitment to human values	low	high	low	high
Other:				
17. Expected tenure with group	short time	long time	short time	long time
18. Position-based influence	low	high	low	high

Fig. 19-6. (cont'd.)

1. SELECTION OF LEADERS. As Stogdill notes, groups tend to choose leaders whose values, interests, and personalities are similar to their own.[10] The following relationships shown in figure 19-6 are evident in this regard: aggressive individuals will seek leaders who are aggressive, and authoritarian personalities those who are authoritarian. Individuals with high acceptance needs will support leaders who are relationship-oriented. Groups in which knowledge, training, technical skills, and/or interpersonal skills are important will look to individuals high in these characteristics for their leaders. In addition, the group will tend to select as leaders individuals who are strongly committed to the goals, tasks, and/or values of the group.

In some instances individuals will support those who have opposite traits. Examples are the timid selecting someone aggressive, the dependent personality selecting someone displaying independence, an individual who avoids responsibility supporting someone who accepts it, the insecure following the secure, and those with low knowledge having confidence in those with greater knowledge. The selection of opposites results from feelings of inadequacy and what is called referent power (identifying with others whom one admires).

2. SOURCES OF INFLUENCE.   Since leadership is basically an influence relationship, the characteristics of individuals that provide influence in the group are important in understanding the nature of leadership. As noted earlier, influence tends to come from knowledge and skill, position-based influence, motivation, and certain traits like aggressiveness and willingness to accept responsibility.

LEADER-FOLLOWER CHARACTERISTICS AND SUPERVISION

Supervision is . . . always a relative process. To be effective and to communicate as intended, a leader must always adapt his behavior to take into account the expectations, values, and interpersonal skills of those with whom he is interacting. . . . There can be no specific rules of supervision which will work well in all situations. Broad principles can be applied to the processes of supervision and furnish valuable guides to behavior. . . . These principles, however, must be applied always in a manner that takes fully into account the characteristics of the specific situation and of the people involved. Sensitivity to the values and expectations of others is an important dimension of effective supervision. Measurements of the intervening variables can be of great assistance. They can reveal the expectations, values, and perceptions of the persons with whom each supervisor interacts.

Quoted from Rensis Likert, *New Patterns of Management* (New York: McGraw-Hill Book Company, 1961), pp. 95–96.

3. DEGREE OF PARTICIPATION AND FREEDOM.   As indicated in the last chapter, the extent to which a manager should use participative leadership styles is related to characteristics of the individuals comprising the group. These include factors like their knowledge, training, technical skills, motivation, willingness to accept responsibility, tolerance for ambiguity, commitment to group goals, and expected tenure with the group. When all of these factors are high, a manager is inclined to use participative styles, because the individuals are knowledgeable enough to contribute, and they display the necessary commitment to the organization and its objectives. When the individuals in the group are rated low in relation to these characteristics, directive styles are usually more effective. When individuals perceive themselves as having the ability to meet their task demands, they prefer participative leadership, but they also like a leader who is task oriented.

4. THE APPROPRIATENESS OF PARTICULAR LEADERSHIP STYLES. The personality of a leader will dictate his preferences for particular leadership styles. Aggressive, authoritarian, highly knowledgeable individuals typically will be directive leaders. Individuals low in authoritarianism, with a strong commitment to human values will be more participative. This does not necessarily mean that they will be successful, because these traits must be appropriately linked with subordinate characteristics and situational factors. Leader and follower characteristics should be matched as follows: directive styles are necessitated when subordinates are dependent, avoid responsibility, have a low tolerance for ambiguity, are low in psychological need intensity, have a weak commitment to group goals, intend to be with the organization for a short period of time only, and are low in skills, abilities, and training. When the group displays traits that are on the opposite end of the continuum, participative or even free-rein styles are usually more effective. Directive styles are not just appropriate when the skills or attitudes of subordinates are negative. Directive styles are also often appropriate when the leader is very knowledgeable and the group is highly committed to group goals and to the tasks. In instances of this sort, they look to the competent leader to maximize their achievement as a group. Research also shows that when subordinates prefer autonomy and self-control, participative styles are more satisfying and effective.[11]

VARIABLES INFLUENCING THE LEADER-FOLLOWER RELATIONSHIP

The factors in the context of the situation that influence the leader-follower relationship are shown as the outer circle in figure 19-5. An enumeration of some of the most significant characteristics of each variable in terms of how they influence the leader-follower relationship is shown in figure 19-7 and elaborated below. (The scales are established so that situations with characteristics identified on the left-hand side call for directive styles of leadership; situations with characteristics on the right-hand side call for participative or free-rein styles.)

	Group Characteristics	
Existing leadership roles	directive	free rein
Existing member roles	obedience	independence

Fig. 19-7. **Situational variables in leadership (leader and follower characteristics excluded)**

	Group Characteristics	
Quantity of interaction	little	extensive
Group unity	conflict	cooperation
Trust	low	high
Membership	heterogeneous	homogeneous

	Formal Organization Characteristics	
Size	large	small
Authority delegation	centralized	decentralized
Formalization of structure	high	low
Geographical dispersion	one location	many locations
Departmentation	functional	program

	Task Characteristics	
Complexity	simple	complex
Repetition	repetitive	varies
Rewards for task performance	minor	major
Interdependence of tasks	high	low

Fig. 19-7. (cont'd.)

Task Characteristics

Autonomy permitted		
little		considerable

People oriented		
low		high

Things oriented		
high		low

Predictability		
certain		uncertain

Technology Characteristics

Knowledge required		
simple		complex

Sophistication of methods		
low		high

Safety hazards		
many		few

Purpose and Goal Characteristics

Economic goals		
major emphasis		minor emphasis

Social and human goals		
minor emphasis		major emphasis

Environmental Characteristics

Predictability of environment		
certain		uncertain

Time to make decisions		
little		considerable

	Environmental Characteristics	
Social customs	authoritarian	democratic
Human values of culture	de-emphasis	emphasis

Fig. 19-7. (cont'd.)

Structural Characteristics That Influence the Leader-Follower Relationship

The existing subculture and roles of a group will strongly influence the leadership style assumed by an individual. As indicated earlier, roles or the expectations of others toward the holder of a position are a major factor in determining behavior. The organization culture tends to perpetuate existing patterns of leadership. If previous leadership roles have been directive and the member role is one of obedience, this will influence the leader-follower relationship when a new manager takes over. Factors such as the quantity of interaction within the group, its unity, and the amount of trust existent in the group will also affect leadership styles. Cooperative groups displaying high interaction and trust in their relationships will favor participative and free-rein styles. Groups characterized by conflict, low interaction, and distrust will be more effective with directive styles.

At this point, cause-and-effect relationships again cloud the issue. Conflict, low trust, and reduced interaction can *result* from directive leadership so that one may be justifying a style of leadership based on conditions it creates. As indicated previously in several instances, our knowledge of the behavioral sciences is such that we can identify many associative relationships, but cause-and-effect determinants are often primarily speculative in nature. In each such situation, an analysis is necessary of why conflict exists, why there is low interaction, and why little trust is evidenced among the membership. If the style of leadership is causing these conditions, the style should be modified, but if the conditions are from another source, the style is most likely appropriate. The complex interplay of variables and attempting to account for the resultant conditions are the prime difficulty in situational assessment.

Another important factor in group characteristics is the degree to which the membership has common characteristics (is homogeneous) or has diverse characteristics (is heterogeneous). As indicated in the last chapter, homogeneous groups, in which people have relatively equivalent knowledge, skills, and values make participative management effective and beneficial. When groups are highly diverse, a more directive leadership style is necessary to integrate effort.

Several features of formal organization structure influence style. With small groups, it is much easier to be participative. In extremely large organizations, it is impossible, and some form of representation becomes necessary. Highly centralized, formalized structures are also more efficiently operated by directive leaders, but when structures are decentralized and dispersed, it is difficult for central direction to be effective. Also, in functional forms of departmentation, directive leadership is more common, because the technical knowledge of the leader is the same as the group's—e.g., an engineer over engineers—so the leader can be more directive in making technical decisions. In a program form of departmentation, this is not possible, because the program manager has a mixture of technical areas and skills represented in the people supervised.

Task Characteristics and
Leader-Follower Relationships

As indicated in chapter 12, one of the most important situational factors dictating the behavior of an individual is his assigned tasks. Simple, repetitive tasks with little autonomy and minor rewards provide very little intrinsic or extrinsic motivation. With few motives for engaging in specific behavior, it means that inducements such as more directive styles of leadership become mandatory. However, with simple tasks, subordinates are likely to reject a directive leader. When tasks are complex, varied, and rewarding, there is sufficient natural motivation, so the leader's role can essentially be supportive. But this depends on the competence of subordinates. If the tasks are too complex for them, the leader will assume more control. Because of the nature of the tasks performed, directive styles of leadership are more common in production organizations and at first-line supervisory levels; participative styles are more common in professional groups, research and development, universities, and at upper-management levels.

Other task characteristics affecting leadership are the interdependence of the tasks performed by individuals and work units (coordinating the work of many different groups normally requires central direction), whether the tasks are people oriented (salesman can often function free rein), things oriented (interpersonal relations are not as important), and the predictability of the tasks (if structured and certain, directive styles can be used; but if they are uncertain, more discretion must be left to the individual).

Technology Characteristics and
Leader-Follower Relationships

Technology affects the complexity of the tasks and the sophistication of the methods, which in turn influence the skills required of the work force. The impact of these factors on the leader-follower relationship has already been discussed. An important consideration in operations like mining involves the safety hazards of the technology used. When there are major safety hazards, procedures and enforcement that are directive in nature are called for. This again argues for flexibility in leadership behavior. A mining supervisor may be participative and even free rein in many aspects of his operations, but when it comes to activities involving safety hazards (wearing hard hats), he would be directive in his approach.

Goal Characteristics and
Leader-Follower Relationships

In organizations with essentially economic goals where efficiency is maximized through structured, confining operations (such as an assembly line), directive approaches to management become more appropriate. In organizations where social and human goals predominate (government agencies, universities, voluntary organizations), participative modes of leadership are more desirable.

Environmental Considerations and
Leader-Follower Relationships

A central theme of contingency theory is that in more certain and stable environments, there is an appropriate dominance of structured organizations and directive leadership styles, whereas in more unstable ones, the flexibility of open organization structures and greater freedom for the individual become mandatory. However, during crises or when there is little time to make a decision (military action, fire fighting, or so on), strong, directive leadership can best handle the situation. Situations requiring quick action simply do not allow time for participation.

A final important factor in leadership styles is the broader culture of a society. Leadership styles must conform to group norms to be effective, but they also must conform to societal ones. Leadership styles successful at a plant in the United States will more than likely not be as effective if that manager is transferred to a plant in a foreign country where he must develop relationships with people representing a different culture. In authoritarian cultures with little emphasis on human values, participative styles will not very likely be as useful. Western culture, with its

democratic tradition, lends credence to the arguments for more democratic styles—even in economic institutions.

APPLICATION OF THE SITUATIONAL
APPROACH TO LEADERSHIP

Many problems are involved in application of a leadership approach
which holds that styles should be modified based on the situation. Situations are fluid rather than static; cause-and-effect relationships lack distinction; the multiplicity of factors makes it difficult to strain out those
that are most significant; and there are limitations in the flexibility possessed by an individual in dealing with different situations. However,
there is frequently considerable interdependence among the variables,
resulting in common classes of situations. (Highly trained people tend
to be knowledgeable, committed to tasks, motivated, responsible, functioning in open structures, rewarded, etc.). Also, the characteristics of a
few dominant variables will be representative of the balance, so that
when they are accurately interpreted they properly designate the most
appropriate style of leadership.

An example of the application of situational methodology to the
effectiveness of leadership styles is shown in figures 19-8 and 19-9. Figure
19-8 represents a profile on group and situational characteristics of a
circumstance in which a supervisor is directing a summer workcrew
that is fighting fires, making trails, putting up fences, and maintaining
campgrounds. The supervisor is a permanent U.S. Forest Service employee, but all members of the crew are temporary summer hires who
generally have had little experience in any of the designated operations.
The profile in figure 19-9 represents a National Forest Supervisor who
directly under him has three district rangers, two range-management
specialists, and one engineer, all professionals in the organization.

In the profile involving the first situation, the members of the work
crew have limited knowledge of the operations, little training, no long-
range commitment to the tasks or organization, and are engaged in
relatively simple, physical tasks that require little skill. Because of the
fire-fighting responsibilities, the safety hazards are high, and there is little
time to make decisions. The crew is rather large (thirty members), and
they usually work together in one location.

All of these conditions point to the need for a directive leader. This
is reflected in figure 19-8, where a central line is drawn through the profile
to the upper scale representing the leadership continuum. Because the
workcrew is not trained or well informed, it will be necessary for the
leader to provide most of the direction. Also, because they do not have
much identification with the organization or the tasks, it will probably
be necessary to be more directive. The safety factors would best be

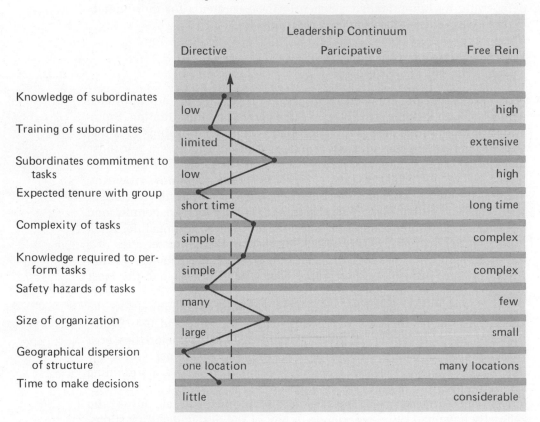

Fig. 19-8. Situation involving a supervisor of a temporary summer workcrew of foresters

handled with directive styles, and the size and location of the organization would certainly make directive styles feasible.

The National Forest Supervisor, even though he is identified with the same organization, finds situational variables that are generally the opposite of those of the crew supervisor—and therefore appropriately handled through more participative styles. The employees he deals with directly are all well trained, knowledgeable professionals who are strongly identified with the organization and its tasks. They do not need close supervision; in fact, close supervision would most likely be stifling and degrading. The forest districts are spread out over many miles, making it impossible for the supervisor to direct all operations in detail. The type of policymaking and planning handled at the National Forest Office also leaves considerable time for decisions (most planning is accomplished

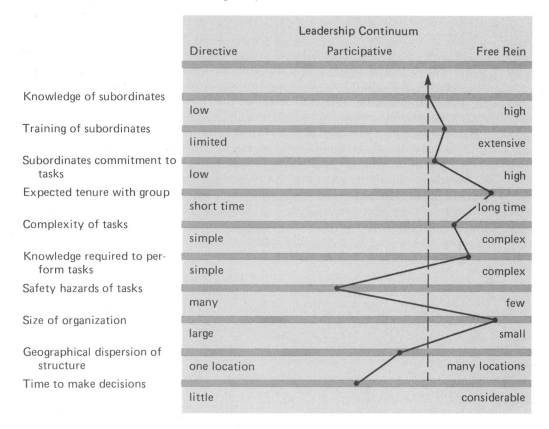

Fig. 19-9. **Situation involving a National Forest Supervisor of permanent professionals**

in the winter and implemented in the summer), and the small number of individuals reporting directly to the supervisor makes participation in the policymaking and planning much easier.

Profiles such as shown in figures 19-8 and 19-9 can be developed for all situations involving group activities. The significance of the different factors will vary from situation to situation, but generally the knowledge and other characteristics of the people in the group, the organization climate, and the tasks being performed tend to be predominant.

FLEXIBILITY OF LEADERSHIP STYLES

One of the primary arguments among the experts in leadership relates to the flexibility and adaptability of the individual in the role of a leader.

At this point a distinction between leadership *style* and leadership *behavior* is important. Leadership style is closely related to an individual's personality and involves a relatively enduring set of behaviors characteristic of an individual—regardless of situations. Thus subordinates can generally classify their supervisors as representing some point along the leadership continuum. However, the behavior of an individual will vary from situation to situation. An individual who is normally quite participative will become directive during an emergency, the first day a new subordinate is on the job, or during a situation involving discipline. Furthermore, individuals demonstrate flexibility by treating (relating to) children differently than they do adults, or handling low-performing workers differently than they do high ones. People have certain personality traits and needs that lend consistency to their behavior, but as conditions vary they respond by modifying this behavior.

Accordingly, to assign an authoritarian personality who displays directive styles to a position where the organization climate, subordinates, and tasks all call for participative leadership is a mismatch that will create anxiety and affect efficiency. However, it is logical to assume that the directive leader will give considerable freedom to the skilled subordinate who has a technical expertise that he is lacking. So although behavioral flexibility typifies humans, major changes in personality or motivation are highly unlikely.

IMPLICATIONS CONTINGENCY MODELS HAVE FOR LEADERSHIP

Contingency theory has certain implications for leadership that are often contrary to current practices in organizations:

- Organizations tend to restrict the criteria for selecting leaders to individuals who possess certain traits (aggressiveness, decisiveness, etc.) or who have demonstrated unusual technical expertise. However, these are only two factors that determine leadership effectiveness. This effectiveness is a function of many variables and conditions relating to the group and broader situational factors.

- No one leadership style should predominate throughout an organization. This sort of inbreeding is damaging, because different elements of the organization will display characteristics that call for different types of leaders. Organizations should seek to maintain a repertoire of leaders.

- There is no *one* training approach to leadership because there is no one best style. Furthermore, attempts to change basic styles are often hazardous and always difficult. Leadership training should emphasize flexibility in behavior and skill in diagnosing situations.

- Selecting and capitalizing on effective leaders involves matching the skills, attitudes, values, and personality traits of the leader with the characteristics of members, organizational climate, and other variables. If a mismatch exists or changes are desired, rather than concentrating on changing the leader, more success will usually be achieved by modifying factors in the situation such as tasks, position power, organization structure, and other such variables.

SUMMARY

Following the difficulties experienced by those using the traits approach, situational theories of leadership evolved. Most theories were speculative in nature until Fiedler developed his research-based contingency model in the early 1960's. This approach opened the way for many other theories leading to the dominance of situational constructs.

The basic relationship of leadership is the influence interaction between the leader and followers. Factors involved in this relationship are the personality traits, skills, knowledge, attitudes, values, and other similar variables associated with the leader, along with the same set of characteristics displayed by followers.

The basic leader-follower relationship is influenced by the variables forming the context of the organization and its environment. Primary factors affecting this relationship and the need for different leadership styles are the tasks the group is engaged in, the technology associated with their operations, the structure of the group and formal organization, the purpose of the organization, and broader environmental factors, such as economic and political conditions, customs, and the time available for analysis and decision making. It is the composite influence of all of these variables that determines the effectiveness of leaders and the styles they implement.

QUESTIONS FOR STUDY AND DISCUSSION

1. What did McGregor mean when he stated that "leadership is not a property of an individual but a complex relationship among variables?"
2. In the Tannenbaum-Schmidt model of situational leadership, what determines the difference between the seven different styles of leadership presented? How do the different "forces" in their model influence the need for different leadership styles? Why did they revise the model in 1973?

3. Regarding Fiedler's contingency model:
    A. What variables does Fiedler use to represent "the situation" and why does he select these?
    B. How is it determined whether a situation is favorable or unfavorable to the leader?
    C. How is it possible for task-oriented leaders to perform more effectively at the extremes or in both favorable and unfavorable situations?
    D. What limitations are there to Fiedler's approach?
4. How does the leadership contingency model presented in this chapter differ from the contingency management model in chapter 3?
5. Using figure 19-6, relating to leader-follower characteristics,
    A. How does a professor deal with class members (followers) based on how he perceives their characteristics?
    B. What leadership style is appropriate if the group is characterized by high aggressiveness, independence, and low commitment to group goals and tasks?
    C. What style is appropriate with group characteristics of high acceptance needs, medium knowledge and technical skills, and strong dependency?
6. How do the following factors influence the need for different leaders?
    A. Organization climate   D. Safety hazards
    B. Organization size   E. Organization goals
    C. Task complexity   F. Culture
7. Based on the knowledge you have of the situational variables involved, develop a situational profile similar to figure 19-8 for the following:
    A. A social studies teacher in a high school
    B. The head supervisor of nurses in a hospital
    C. Supervisor of laborers repairing railroad track
    D. Supervisor of engineers designing a bridge
    E. Supervisor of guards at a prison
8. What is the difference between leadership style and leadership behavior? What factors determine each?

Case Problem:
LEADERSHIP STYLES IN A LIBRARY

Carma Feldsted is assistant librarian at Winslow State University. In this capacity, she is in charge of all reference librarians and the part-time student help that handles the check-out desk and reshelves all books.

There are eight reference librarians who are assigned on a two-shift basis to the two reference desks in the library. All of the reference librarians have a masters degree in library science or a related field. Their length of employment with the university ranges from three to fifteen years, so they are well trained and knowledgeable in their work. Two are part-time employees and the other six are full-time.

Eight students are employed part-time in checking out and reshelving books and magazines. The students work approximately sixteen hours per week. The average length of employment is eighteen months, although some will be employed as long as five years. The students come from all colleges at the university, with humanity majors being the most common among the applicants and employees. Scheduling is a major problem because of the need to work around the students' classes.

What leadership styles should Carma use with these two groups?
Develop profiles on the groups similar to that in figure 19-8.
How would Fiedler's theory help determine which leadership style to use?
Would the path-goal theory help?
Would the Vroom and Yetton decision model help?

Case Problem:
MANPOWER PLANNING IN CROWN CORPORATION

Gil Clauson is in charge of manpower planning for Crown Corporation. Three young supervisors have been in their current positions for over two years, and Gil is attempting to determine where they should be reassigned. The three individuals involved are as follows:

Tim Smith: Very relationships oriented and nonauthoritarian. Strong interpersonal skills. Moderately aggressive. Average intensity of psychological needs. Business administration major with five years' experience in administering fringe-benefit programs.

Gerald Wilson: Highly aggressive and authoritarian. Strong achievement drive. Independent. Goal oriented with an unusual willingness to accept responsibility. Liberal arts major with five years' experience in shipping and receiving.

Jay Hammond: Personable and goal oriented. Works well with others and is known for cooperative, considerate attitude. Is aggressive and seeks responsibility but puts group relations as primary. Considered knowledgeable in engineering where he has been employed for five years.

What suggestions would you offer Gil regarding the types of future assignments these three individuals should be given and the types of groups they would be matched with as supervisors?

Footnotes

1. Douglas McGregor, *The Human Side of Enterprise* (New York: McGraw-Hill Book Company, 1960), p. 182.
2. Robert Tannenbaum and Warren H. Schmidt, "How to Choose a Leadership Pattern," *Harvard Business Review,* March–April 1958, pp. 95–101.
3. *Ibid.,* p. 100.
4. *Harvard Business Review,* May–June 1973, pp. 166–168.
5. Fred E. Fiedler, *A Theory of Leadership Effectiveness* (New York: McGraw-Hill Book Co., 1967).
6. *Ibid.,* p. 247.
7. See G. Graen, J. Orris, and K. Alvares, "Contingency Model of Leadership Effectiveness: Some Experimental Results," *Journal of Applied Psychology,* 1971, Vol. 55, pp. 196–202.
8. R. House, "A Path-Goal Theory of Leadership Effectiveness," *Administrative Science Quarterly,* 1971, Vol. 16, pp. 321–340.
9. V. H. Vroom and P. W. Yetton, *Leadership and Decision-Making,* (Pittsburgh: University of Pittsburgh Press, 1973).
10. Stogdill, *op. cit.,* p. 214.
11. A. S. Tannenbaum and F. H. Allport, "Personality Structure and Group Structure," *Journal of Abnormal and Social Psychology,* 1956, Vol. 53, pp. 272–280.

The Communication Process

Why is communication considered one of the
linking processes of management?

What is the relationship between communication
and behavior?

Why is communication one of the most persistent
problems in management?

What can be done to improve communication in
organizations?

What contingency factors are involved in
communication?

What is the relationship between leadership and
communication?

Bart Wilson, president of Garner Development Company, was meeting
with George Bryington, his adminstrative assistant, Jerry Bruner, director
of all development programs, and Sherman Lilly, program manager of a
development contract that had just been cancelled by a major corporation in the energy field.

Wilson was shaking a telegram in his hand as he spoke: "This can-
cellation notice says we're five months behind on the project, overrunning
by $50,000, and results to date have not been what we promised. Why
wasn't I told about this?"

Jerry looked at Sherman and then said, "We called attention in
the June monthly progress report that we were experiencing some difficulties in these areas and—"

The president interrupted him: "Those damned progress reports!
You know I have time to only skim them. Why wasn't I personally
informed?"

"I really didn't know things were as bad as they were," Jerry replied. "However, you'll remember that in a staff meeting last month
I did note that there were some problems on the project."

"What?" the president exploded again. "You weren't aware of the
magnitude of the problem either! Sherman, why didn't you inform him?
How long has this mess been going on, anyway?"

Sherman hesitated and then responded, "For about a year now, we've
been falling behind. I didn't want to alarm you, so I just kept working
hard to get the thing back on track. But things just keep getting worse
instead of better."

"I'm at fault too," Jerry cut in. "I kept thinking things would improve
also, so I delayed giving you my full assessment."

"Well, I guess we can't resurrect it at this point, but I want a full
report. Get it to me as soon as you can. That's all for now."

After Jerry and Sherman had left, the president turned to George
and said: "Just how do I go about getting accurate information? I can't
seem to get the straight scoop on any program. Everyone is crying for
more manpower, more space, or more budget, but every time I look into
it, they're overstating the situation. What burns me up is that two weeks
ago I even went into the plant area where Jerry has been running this
cancelled project, and everyone gave me the impression that things were
great. I'd sure like to know how to get people to communicate."

COMMUNICATION AND MANAGEMENT

*Communication is defined as the exchange of information conveying
meaning between two or more people.* Two points are important in
this definition. First, there must be a minimum of two parties involved

for communication to take place; and second, the exchange must be informative—or carry meaning. If someone is talking to himself in an empty office or shouting in the woods and no one is within hearing distance, that person is speaking, but no communication occurs. If an Italian is speaking to a Frenchman and they do not understand each other's language, no verbal communication takes place. (However, their facial expressions and body gestures will carry some meaning to the other party, so some communication actually might occur in this exchange.)

In fact, *any* means an individual uses to convey ideas, feelings, information, thoughts, or attitudes to others involves communication. We typically do this in symbolic fashion by one party speaking or writing and the other party listening or reading. However, as indicated, facial expressions like smiling or frowning are often a more accurate means of conveying feelings than what one writes or says. Hair styles, makeup, dress, and other means of expressing lifestyles are also a form of communication. The short skirt, long hair, or double-breasted suit sends a message to the culturally oriented observer.

Communication as an Integral Part of All Management Processes

Any discussion of communication from a managerial standpoint is necessarily broad and integrative, because it encompasses essentially everything that occurs in the management process. All individual behavior and managerial actions in organizations involve communication if others observe or interact with the focal person. In chapter 1, communication and decision making were identified as the two linking processes of management. All effective organizing, staffing, directing, planning, and controlling are dependent on communication. Group processes are totally dependent on communication, for without it no joint action or understanding can take place. Since the manager's role is to maximize the effectiveness of group activity, communication becomes one of the most vital aspects of the management process.

Another way to note the significance of communication is based on how much time individuals spend communicating. The typical office employee devotes 60 to 90 percent of his time on the job communicating. Normally, higher-level supervisors will spend more time than those at lower levels who are more directly involved in technical operations. In one study of white-collar workers, the average employee was communicating 70 percent of the time. The forms of communication involved were as follows: listening 45 percent, speaking 30 percent, reading 16 percent, and writing 9 percent.[1] Obviously, when this process dominates the activity of people to this degree, effective communication should be a primary goal of management.

Communication and Leadership

Most management studies of communication have been conducted in conjunction with leadership. Gaining the support of others is highly dependent on communication skills. In directing a group, communication serves as the vehicle. One of the few traits that tends to be common among leaders is their ability to communicate. The leader sets the stage for communication within the balance of the organization. If he is open, straightforward, information seeking, and encourages feedback, this will strongly influence the organization climate to take on these same characteristics. Leadership and communication are both forms of behavior. As outlets for behavior, they will be characterized by the same traits that are dominant in the individual's personality.

The Effectiveness of Communication

Communication is of primary concern in management, not solely because of its ubiquitousness, but because weak communication is one of the most common complaints relating to organization effectiveness. "The right hand doesn't seem to know what the left one is doing," "Do they expect us to believe that," "But they just don't understand," and "He's already made up his mind" are statements heard often in organizations. Trainers involved in conducting management seminars for practitioners soon become aware that supervisors are typically disgruntled because of communication breakdown within their organizations. In one study, managers were asked: "What causes you trouble in your job?" The most common response (80 percent) was *communication*.[2] In another cross-cultural study involving companies in Japan, Great Britain, and the United States, approximately 74 percent of the managers sampled cited communication breakdown as the single greatest barrier to corporate excellence.[3]

Dealing with communication breakdown is not a simple issue, because it is usually a symptom of more basic difficulties within the organization. Individuals restrict or distort communication because of distrust, fear, conflict, bias, or other such factors. Improved communication can be achieved only by eliminating or reducing this distrust, fear, conflict, or bias. Weak planning, control, and reporting systems will also result in a deficiency of information that can be overcome only by improving these systems. Some communication breakdown is directly attributable to skills, such as listening and speaking, but most is rooted deeper within an organization's existence. As a result, many of the solutions for improving communication rely on improving activities and systems relating to the other management processes covered elsewhere in this book.

THE COMMUNICATION PROCESS

Managerially there are two different ways of viewing communication. One is to consider it as behavior and hence an integral part of all interaction that occurs within a group. The other is to view communication as a subsystem of management similar to the presentation in chapter 4 (see figure 4-2). In the latter instance, the concern is developing a communication network that will provide accurate, comprehensive, and timely information on the status of an organization's operations. It is also a subsystem that integrates with the planning and control subsystems to help form the total management system. (This approach to communication will be further elaborated in chapter 23, on management information systems.) Accordingly, this chapter is restricted to viewing communication from the leader's position of keeping followers informed, being aware of their feelings, and coordinating group activities to achieve common objectives.

Communication as Behavior

Human behavior is typically social behavior, characterized by people interacting with others. This interaction is communication and is the outward manifestation of perceptions, attitudes, feelings, need drives, interests, emotions, and values. Through an individual's actions, these behavioral characteristics are communicated to others. Furthermore, the same external factors that affect behavior (peers, group norms, the expectations of others, opportunities, power figures) also affect how and what one will communicate. Since communication is behavior, evaluating the effectiveness of communication and the means for improving it are dependent on the behavioral concepts contained in chapters 10, 11, 16, and 17.

One last point is necessary in understanding the communication process. Because of the emphasis on "two-way communication," implying a vertical exchange between supervisor and subordinate, it's easy to make the false assumption that most communication goes up and down within the organizational hierarchy. But, communication follows interaction—and individuals interact laterally with peers and diagonally with others in the organization as much as they do vertically with supervisors and subordinates. In one study of ninety-one businessmen, the managerial communication flow was split almost evenly on a horizontal, vertical, and diagonal basis (30.2 percent, 32.8, and 36.9, respectively).[4]

Elements of the Communication Process

There are three basic elements in the communication process. These are: a *sender* who transmits a message through a *channel* to the *receiver* who interprets the message. This relationship is shown in figure 20-1:

Fig. 20-1.   The three basic elements of communication

By our definition, as long as information is transmitted from one party to another for whom it provides meaning, communication takes place.

A more elaborate model of communication is shown in figure 20-2. This model states that the sender has an idea that is developed in the form of a message (encodes is the terminology used in information theory). This message is transmitted as a signal through some media to the receiver who interprets (encodes) the message. Communication takes place through this half of the cycle if the message provides meaning to the recipient. Effective communication is normally dependent on providing feedback to the sender, which lets him know that the message was interpreted and the reactions of the receiver. In the feedback cycle, the process is now reversed, so that the receiver becomes the sender.

VARIABLES IN THE
COMMUNICATION PROCESS

The variables and problems involved in communication are most easily understood when they are grouped according to the three elements of the communication process (see figure 20-1). A summary of the associated sender, receiver, and transmission variables is shown in figure 20-3 and discussed here.

Sender-Receiver Variables

Eight variables influence communication effectiveness. These relate primarily to the personality, frame of reference, and values of the indi-

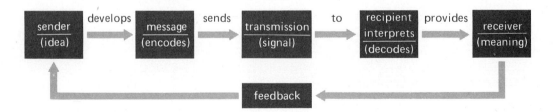

Fig. 20-2.   The communication process

viduals involved. These are shown separately for sender and receiver in figure 20-3. However, since the categories are the same for each, they will be combined for discussion purposes.

Sender Variables	Receiver Variables	Transmission Variables
1. Communication skills	1. Communication skills	1. Speak (words, numbers)
2. Frame of reference	2. Frame of reference	2. Write (words, pictures, numbers)
3. Needs	3. Needs	3. Gestures and actions
4. Personality and interests	4. Personality and interests	4. Electronic media
5. Attitudes, emotions, and self-interest	5. Attitudes, emotions, and self-interest	
6. Position and status	6. Position and status	
7. Assumptions about receiver(s)	7. Assumptions about sender	
8. Existing relationship with receiver(s)	8. Existing relationship with sender	

Fig. 20-3. **People and transmission variables in the communication process**

SENDER-RECEIVER COMMUNICATION SKILLS.   The communication skills of the sender are speaking and writing; for the receiver they are the senses involved in perception—especially that of hearing or listening. One of the most common causes of communication breakdown is the inability of individuals to express their thoughts clearly and succinctly. However, the reception by the receiver is considered an even greater obstacle. Some studies show that individuals hear and understand as little as 25 percent of the sound waves that are within their sensory threshold. Part of this is because individuals speak at 100 to 200 words per minute, but a listener's brain can process the words much faster. During this idle time, the person is anticipating what is to be said, concentrating on other matters of immediate concern, evaluating the source of the communication, or engaged in other distracting activity. We are also bombarded with sound from many sources, so that from a selective perception standpoint, a person must tune in on what is considered of most significance.

FRAME OF REFERENCE.   As indicated in chapter 10, each individual develops a unique frame of reference based on his or her particular experiences and knowledge. Symbols like language have meaning only if they relate to experiences or knowledge that are part of this frame of reference. No two people will apply the same meaning to these symbols, because their knowledge and experience will be different. *Semantics* is the study of the meaning carried by words or forms. The word *boat* may bring delight to the individual who likes sailing, but it can strike terror in the heart of someone who has experienced a near drowning: words carry multiple meanings to different individuals. The *Oxford Dictionary* records an average of twenty-eight separate meanings for each of the five-hundred most commonly used words in the English language.[5] Little wonder the initiator of a message often experiences difficulty in getting across his intended meaning.

NEEDS.   The intensity of the needs of an individual will strongly affect behavior and communication. The insecure person will restrict or distort communication more than a secure one will. (The individual seeking social acceptance will be less inclined to rebuff others and will often hide feelings that may hurt his relations with them. The status-conscious employee will be inclined to give favorable feedback to influential figures in the organization who can affect his future.)

PERSONALITY AND INTERESTS.   Individuals who tend to be introverted will obviously not communicate as frequently or as thoroughly as the extrovert. Some people communicate in a lively, exuberant fashion, while others are more matter-of-fact. The likes and dislikes of an individual will influence the effectiveness of communication. A person will listen carefully to things he is interested in but turn a deaf ear to topics that bore him. Television advertisements are designed to catch the attention of the viewer through lively activity, attractive people, pleasant experiences, or appealing life styles.

ATTITUDES, EMOTIONS, AND PREJUDICE.   The great distorters of communication are attitudes, emotions, and self-interest. As indicated in relation to perception, these factors serve as a filter to our senses and warp the data input. We are inclined to hear what we want to hear and ignore or reject that which conflicts with our values and biases. If someone makes favorable statements about something we are opposed to, we tend to immediately reject the communication. Nothing destroys the logic of thought and the resultant communication quicker than emotions like fear, love, or hate. When an individual is fearful, he will obviously be inclined to protect himself by slanting communication. Emotion robs the individual of reason and restricts the ability to comprehend.

Self-interest is just as debilitating. When a person is defensive, he or she wards off any sensory input that reduces status. Furthermore, when engaged in activities where personal gain or loss is involved, people are inclined to communicate so as to favorably affect the outcome. As Robert Heilbroner states, "Armies and corporations alike have ways of sweetening the news as it ascends the hierarchy of command."[6] One of the most difficult tasks for an executive in any organization is to get objective information. Individuals and organizations tend to perpetuate their own interests, making it difficult to obtain the facts to support major decisions. The situation is too often that expressed by two of the assistants to Robert McNamara when he was Secretary of Defense: "A more basic explanation of the poor quality of many defense analyses is the fact that their authors often begin with a predetermined conclusion—usually a service position—and make the analysis, in effect, a sophisticated sales pitch."[7]

THE COMPANY PRESIDENT AND COMMUNICATION

In one large multidivision company, the president was concerned over how the workers felt about their employer. All the reports he received from his top managers were that the people like their jobs, favored the company, and expressed no major dissatisfaction. However, records on productivity, absenteeism, and turnover led him to believe otherwise. In order to become more fully informed, he planned a tour of several of the plants. But in each instance, like most other official inspections, everything he saw and all of the feedback he received was favorable.

He then hired a consulting firm that specialized in communication to conduct worker attitude surveys. These surveys revealed that the employees were dissatisfied with some of their working conditions and company relations. However, he was still uncertain about what to do, so the communications consultant recommended that he could come face to face with the situation by anonymously working for a few days in one of the plants. He dressed up in overalls and worked as a laborer in one plant where no one knew him. After one week, he reported that it was the most revealing experience in his twenty-five years with the firm. Workers discussed company policies in a way that he had never heard before, and for once there was no hedging or union line in expressing their views. He came back with his ears burning and a little chagrined, but much better equipped to consider and handle problems on employee relations.

POSITION AND STATUS.   The relative position and status of the sender and receiver are powerful factors in altering communication. This phenomena is referred to as *status distance* (also administrative or organization distance). If individuals hold the same relative position and status (are peers), they communicate more openly, because they share greater familiarity and have little to fear from "leveling" with one another. But when the status distance is great (a first-line supervisor communicating with the company president), there is more to lose, and the individual cannot usually predict the other party's response. It is not easy to oppose the judgment of those with prestige—especially when their opinions affect one's future in an organization. Being "called on the carpet" by managers with superior position-based influence is a traumatic experience in which most people are hesitant to communicate any unfavorable information.

ASSUMPTIONS ABOUT OTHER PARTY(IES) INVOLVED.   The assumptions the sender has about the receiver and the receiver's assumptions about the sender determine what and how one communicates. If the receiver is assumed to be knowledgeable, loyal, and trustworthy, a person will communicate in one way, but if the traits are perceived as the opposite, he will restrict and distort communication accordingly. We tend to communicate to the extent that we feel is necessary and appropriate, and this is governed by the projected knowledge and prestige of the other party. As indicated previously, we communicate differently with a child, a novice, and an expert. We tend to prejudge messages and to infer meaning based on the source. If we are biased against the source, we make premature, negative evaluations of communication before it is received. People are obviously reluctant to communicate with a supervisor if they lack confidence in his integrity.

EXISTING INTERPERSONAL RELATIONSHIPS.   This factor is closely related to the one above. If mutual confidence and trust depict the current relationship between the communicators, they will be open and objective in their communication. However, if fear, rivalry, and a "win-or-lose" philosophy predominates, the communication will be impaired. If the individual concludes that communication with the other party has been of benefit in the past, he or she will be inclined to perpetuate the exchange.

Information is power in interpersonal relations. If an employee has little information to make a decision on, he becomes less effective. If a supervisor wants to make himself indispensable and force the group to rely upon him, he will spoonfeed subordinates the basic information needed to perform their jobs, such as assigning tasks, providing schedules, and making them aware of goals. When an individual is cut off from information flow, he is cut off from a major factor determining his effectiveness.

Transmission (Channel) Variables

The problem for the communicator is to select the media or method of message transmission that will be most effective. This, of course, depends on several factors, such as the location of the receiver, the number of people involved, and the purpose the sender has for delivering such a message. He must select an avenue that will reach the senses of the receiver, but he is also interested in factors like speed, cost, and impact. The methods he has to choose from follow.

SPOKEN COMMUNICATION.   Generally the most effective form of communication is that which is verbal and face-to-face. This is because an individual not only hears the words of the other party, but he can observe facial expressions and gestures that convey feelings and emotion. Also, it is possible to ask questions if there is misunderstanding and get immediate feedback. Although face-to-face communication tends to be both quick and accurate, there are several limitations. First of all, it may be inconsistent unless all parties hear the same message. If someone tells three different individuals the plans for developing a product, it is unlikely that the information provided will be the same to all of them. Also, the personal contact of the other party in face-to-face communication may cause the individual to modify what he would otherwise say. Spoken communication includes not only conversations between two individuals, but also group activities (such as staff meetings) that are an extremely important means of keeping others informed and solving joint problems.

WRITTEN COMMUNICATION.   The main advantage of written communication over verbal is that it provides a record for referral and follow-up. People tend to retain 50 percent of what they hear for one week, and only 25 percent after two weeks, so written records become very important. Also, the written record provides the same information to all receivers. Mass distribution of procedures or executive orders is an inexpensive means of providing an identical message to individuals. The problem with written communication is that people will not interpret this message the same way, and if they do not understand, there is no automatic means of obtaining clarification or providing feedback. Not knowing how the receiver accepts the message is the primary limitation of written communication. However, the paper mill of organizations represented by letters, memoranda, reports, official notices, company newspapers, and posters on bulletin boards attest to its importance in organizations.

ACTIONS AND GESTURES.   The common saying, "actions speak louder than words," has special significance for leadership. No matter how much a manager espouses verbal backing for a proposal, until he demonstrates support through action, subordinates will most likely consider his behavior only as "well meaning." The familiar "V" sign of the politician, and the smile of approval by a supervisor are both actions that stand little chance of misunderstanding.

ELECTRONIC MEDIA.   The telephone, television, computer, and other electronic gadgetry all have special uses in communication that provide advantages where instantaneous processing or broad coverage is desired. Television especially has revolutionized the means that companies use to advertise their products.

THE CONTINGENCY APPROACH TO COMMUNICATION

Communication is affected by many contingency variables. These are reflected in figure 20-4. Note that there is a close similarity between this model and the one relating to leadership (figure 19-5). Just as the central relationship in leadership is between the leader and followers, so in communication the central relationship is between the parties (sender and receiver) involved in the communication.

Situational Variables

The personalities and other variables that dominate this relationship have already been analyzed. The outer circle in figure 20-4 represents the situational factors that influence the basic sender-receiver communication relationship. These variables affect communication in the following ways:

DISTANCE.   As indicated, face-to-face communication is usually the most effective. However, when the parties in communication are separated so that communication cannot be handled on this personal basis, the selection of the medium for communication (letter, telephone call, etc.) becomes significant and will affect the outcome.

TIME.   Probably the most common cause of communication breakdown is because executives are too busy to keep others apprised of what policy decisions are taking place or what developments have transpired. The pressure of other duties makes it difficult to arrange all of the personal contacts necessary to keep others informed. Time is also important in terms of when communication occurs. If it is delayed or occurs prema-

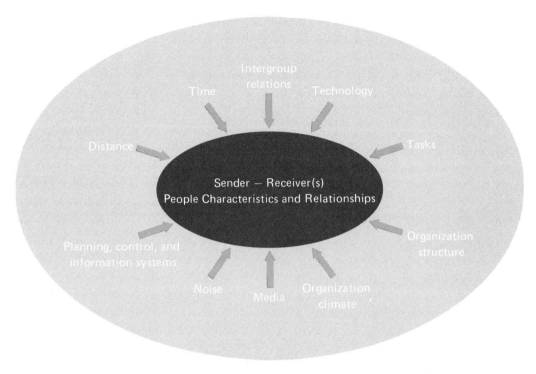

Inner circle: Characteristics and relationships of sender and receiver affecting communication

Outer circle: Contingency factors affecting communication of sender and receiver

Fig. 20-4. Contingency model of communication

turely before an individual has the facts, it can result in ineffectiveness and distortion.

NOISE. In communication theory, changes or distortion in the transmitted signal are called *noise*. In the broadest interpretation, it encompasses all distortion caused by behavioral factors such as those we have discussed, as well as interfering sounds (other people chatting in a crowded room).

PLANNING, CONTROL, AND INFORMATION SYSTEMS. The status of an organization's planning, control, and information systems affects the quantity and quality of information transmitted. These systems provide the vehicle for obtaining the basic information on how an organization is functioning as compared to how it is intended to function. This information is of little value unless it is communicated to the manager, who will then use it in making decisions.

TECHNOLOGY.   As noted earlier, advanced technology has introduced scientific terminology that is meaningful only to the individual trained in that discipline. This makes communication between line and administrative support groups much more difficult in organizations with highly technical tasks.

TASKS.   The manner in which tasks are grouped and jobs are structured determines who individuals will work with—and therefore how communication will flow. The truck driver will find little opportunity to communicate, whereas the sales clerk relies on communication to handle his or her job.

Organizational Variables

ORGANIZATION STRUCTURE.   There are many features of organization structure that influence the communication process. Size and geographical dispersion are two of the most important. If the organization is small and people are in one location, personal face-to-face communication will predominate. However, in large scattered organizations, communication will be more formalized and generally in written form. Departmentation affects communication in that an organization that is structured functionally combines into subunits individuals with the same technical background, while a program organization will mix occupational groups. A large span of control will restrict communication between the supervisor and subordinate; a small span will increase it. People in line capacities will be inclined to communicate with each other, but they will find less need to keep staff people informed.

Probably the most significant factor in organization structure affecting communication is the hierarchy and associated degree of centralization. Communication tends to lose approximately 30 percent of its effectiveness every time it is passed from one individual to another. When a large number of levels exist in the hierarchy of an organization, communication normally experiences major distortion. In one study of 100 business firms, the loss of information in communication going from the Board of Directors to the vice president was 37 percent. By the time it passed through three levels to the plant manager, it was only 40-percent effective. Through four levels it was reduced to 30-percent, and when it reached the worker (through the five-level average for the typical firm), it was only 20-percent effective.[8] Little wonder that the people at the top in large organizations rarely understand the attitudes and perspective of the work force.

In another study, foremen were asked how well they understood the problems of their workers. Approximately 95 percent said they understood them well, but only 34 percent of the workers felt this way.[9] Studies also show that individuals in organizations conduct approximately 90 percent of their face-to-face communication with people who are within two levels of them in the hierarchy. A top executive is communicating with people of the same mental set and with the same information that he has. Even when the executive does communicate beyond these two levels, getting accurate information is difficult because of the status distance of the people involved.

ORGANIZATION CLIMATE.   The openness of the climate within an organization is a strong determinant of the accuracy and extent of communication. If people feel free to communicate without harsh retaliation, they are inclined to be open. A threatening climate will force communication underground. The norms of the organization will also affect communication. Individuals are generally reluctant to speak out against accepted norms.

INTERGROUP RELATIONS.   The relationships between the groups the communicators are associated with can also affect communication. Group hostility will restrict and distort communication the same as interpersonal conflict will. People in competitive groups will communicate with each other differently than when the same groups are engaged in cooperative endeavors.

METHODS OF IMPROVING COMMUNICATION

Because of the perennial problem of inadequate communication in organizations, it is easy to point out weaknesses. The much harder task is to do something about them. Many suggestions have been provided in other chapters. To lighten the burden of an executive so he has more time to communicate, an organization can decentralize; positive reinforcement is more effective than punishment as a means of changing behavior and improving communication because of its nonthreatening aspects; participative, supportive leadership encourages two-way communication, while the directive approach is more restrictive and one-way; conflict over ideas may encourage communication, but interpersonal conflict of a win-or-lose nature will distort and restrict it; knowledge-based influence is a better means of getting people to obey than relying solely on authority.

Ultimately, all management actions tend to affect communication in one way or another. More specifically, there are seven areas of activity where potential exists for improvement of interpersonal communication:

Improving Communication Skills

The most obvious way to improve communication is to improve the communication skills of individuals. People can be taught to write and speak in a simple, direct fashion. Reducing the "fog index" of tedious reports and technical language can also be achieved through training and practice. Especially in verbal communication, there is a need to train individuals to come directly to the point rather than beating around the bush with the hope of making the message more palatable. Preparing for communication by getting the right information, selecting the right media, intentionally introducing some redundancy, and establishing a means of obtaining feedback to check accuracy are all important.

Probably the main skill that needs to be sharpened is that of listening. Dozens of guides have been developed for improving listening, but most of these are dependent on other factors, such as the interest of the individual in the subject under discussion, his ability to concentrate, confidence in the knowledge and integrity of the source, and intergroup relations. Four guides are critical for the manager who wants to know more about the feelings of subordinates:

1. Set aside sufficient time—without interruptions—to hear the problem out. Nothing is more distracting to communication than constant interruptions or the feeling that the listener wants to get on to other matters.
2. Avoid interrupting the communicator, especially with observations that are disquieting or emotional in tone.
3. Watch for the feelings expressed by the communicator or purposeful evasions of points that are obvious but sensitive.
4. Avoid putting people on the defensive by direct questions, value judgments, or insinuations. Defensive behavior is protective, restrictive, and makes people avoid open discussion and evaluation.

Learn to Communicate by Concentrating on the World of the Receiver

Empathy is a difficult skill to develop but vital to communication. If a communicator, uses terminology familiar only to him—in contexts that are of his own choosing, covering his beliefs, his values, his interests, and his role set—interpretation will obviously be difficult for others who act on a different set of experiences and value premises. The communicator should concentrate on choosing words and concepts that fit the listeners learning and field of experience. He should seek feedback to ensure that the other party interprets the message as intended. Much of this is dependent on the leader creating an open atmosphere in which individuals feel their ideas and evaluative input are sought.

Develop a Nonthreatening Work Environment

Open communication is considerably enhanced when individuals have no fear of reprisal. This is one of the primary arguments in favor of participative, supportive leadership styles. It cautions a manager to "cultivate" rather than "force" if he wants open communication. If a subordinate sees a supervisor as a source of help, he will bring his problems to him, but if he sees him as a source of criticism and punishment, he will avoid him. This means that the supervisor will get more accurate input when he is information-seeking instead of challenging, and when he recognizes difficulties as joint problems, rather than primarily the fault of the subordinate. The "we" rather than "you" orientation is entirely proper since the supervisor is responsible for the performance of his work group.

Overcoming communication barriers caused by status distance is based on the same principles. If individuals are more reluctant to openly communicate in the presence of managers representing higher status positions in the organization, it is a warning that those managers should play down the status symbols when seeking information from others. Calling an individual into the president's office to discuss a problem when he is confronted by the private secretary, a large-paneled office, and waiting room full of visitors is not going to encourage communication. The higher-level manager will get a better response by dropping in to chat with the person in his or her familiar work setting, getting others with less status to obtain the information, or even finding some occasion off of the work premises to discuss an issue.

Another useful but difficult technique is known as *nondirective counseling,* or interviewing. As human beings, we are inclined to want to present our views and let others know what we feel is right. (Since we are obviously correct, we feel the need to straighten out the thinking of others.) However, soon the individual is responding to our views rather than independently articulating his own. Nondirective interviewing is a technique in which the interviewer manages to conduct a conversation with someone he wants information from without interjecting his own bias until near the end of the conversation, after the other individual has fairly well exhausted his desire to communicate.

To maintain this innocuous position, the interviewer serves as a mirror by restating the other person's feelings, comments, or inquiries.

If he wants to know more about an issue, he restates the comment of the other person in the form of a question, rather than rewording and possibly distorting the original meaning of the inquiry. He rarely interjects his own comments except to keep the conversation going. His purpose is to gain information first and evaluate afterwards (or at the end of the discussion). Anyone's willingness to talk is dependent on how much confidence and trust the person has in the interviewer. The interviewer, therefore, needs to show that he is interested and understands. One of the primary goals of this type of interview is to get the individual to think through his own problem and arrive at his own solution. He will be committed to his own solution but may not inwardly accept one forced on him by others.

Use Independent Sources for Evaluation and Transmission of Information

Because of the natural bias inherent in information from people when their self-interest is involved, the manager needs to take special care in attempting to have this information evaluated independently. The first guide is to obtain information directly from the original source, because, as indicated, some distortion occurs each time it passes through a link in the communication network. It is also desirable (when the situation permits) to have sensors—staff assistants, liaison representatives, analytical groups—obtain and interpret such information. If they are a part of the office of the executive, they will have little reason to foster the interests of any particular group. Ombudsmen serve as a liaison between minority groups and the top officials in an organization. These are individuals who by experience are sensitive to the viewpoint of the minority group, and they also have an understanding of the broader interests of the entire organization.

It is also appropriate for managers to "test out" information or communication before it is finalized. Asking for its interpretation by individuals not connected with the issue is a means of getting objective evaluation. Another common technique is to circulate, for comment, policy statements or other significant proposals in draft form before implementation. Feedback received can often eliminate false assumptions and prevent poor decisions from being made.

Using the Grapevine

Another source of information that should not be overlooked is the *grapevine*. Informal communication is frequently based on rumor, but it also often accurately reflects the feelings of people because it usually involves peer communicating with peer or an individual communicating with others based on a trust relationship. Because of the manager's position in the organization, it is almost impossible for him to tap into the informal grapevine. He must often rely on his assistants to find out the latest rumor, gossip, and speculation that make up the scuttlebutt of informal communication. (Terminating one or two employees can often be expanded to a major layoff through grapevine distortion.) However, many employees will accept the news from the grapevine more than they will official company proclamations, if the integrity of management is suspect.

The grapevine is not only useful in obtaining information about the attitudes of employees; it can also be used to transmit information. Starting the rumor that the company is going to crack down on tardy employees can often solve the problem. The grapevine is an inevitable element of human interaction, so it cannot be squelched or eliminated. However, rumors can often be stopped by the company formally providing the facts to offset what is basically speculation.

Use Formal Reports and Management Information Systems

Executives are bombarded with communication in the form of information flowing in from many sources. This information must be refined and organized into a limited number of channels for a manager to have the time and capacity to absorb it. If every worker in an organization of five hundred employees tried to communicate directly with the president, the executive would have time for nothing else. The number of government regulations that relate to operating a business alone are more than one individual can comprehend.

Thus the organization must be structured and communication channeled to provide the manager the information he needs to make decisions—but not to overload him. Long reports are set aside for review when time permits (which means they rarely get more attention than being shuffled from pile to pile). If a manager does nothing but attend meetings, he will obviously be shunning other responsibilities. If a manager hears or reads similar information five or six times, the communication network is not very efficient. The movement in the past two decades to develop succinct reports that integrate information consistent with the way managers use it in making decisions has been a major step forward in eliminating communication overload. (Chapter 23 will deal with methods for providing reports that contain less information but result in better-informed managers because of the information's direct relevance in decision making.)

Consider Communication within
the Total Management Setting

Communication is more accurate and useful when the manager is sensitive to the many factors that influence and are influenced by it. As a linking process of management, communication touches on everything that takes place in an organization. Improvements in communication are achieved through improved organization structure, planning, job design, assignment of personnel, redefinition of procedures or goals, and many other factors. Understanding communication and attempting to modify it is meaningful only within this broader perspective. Communication is an accurate reflector of how an organization functions. The flow of it in an organization is one of the most revealing features of group dynamics. It discloses who has power, who is being ostracized, how decision making is handled, where conflict exists, the leadership styles employed, control mechanisms, and many other aspects of organizational behavior.

SUMMARY

Communication is the exchange between two or more people of information that conveys meaning. It includes speaking, writing, listening, reading, and nonverbal communication like body gestures. It is a linking process of management because it is involved in everything a manager does as he plans, leads, controls, organizes, and staffs group activity. Managers typically spend 60 to 90 percent of their time communicating.

There are three basic elements involved in communications: the sender, a form of transmission, and a receiver. There are many sources of communication breakdown associated with each of these factors. People are generally weak listeners, they interpret words and symbols differently, and their interests affect how they communicate to others and how they interpret what others say.

In the broader contingency framework, other communication variables are distance, time, intergroup relations, technology, tasks, organization structure and climate, media, noise, and the status of the planning, control, and information systems.

Communication can be improved in many ways but primarily through upgrading basic communication skills, bettering our relationships with others, and developing a more accurate, integrated means of formal input, such as management information systems.

QUESTIONS FOR STUDY AND DISCUSSION

1. What prevented the president from getting "the straight scoop" in the incident at the beginning of the chapter?

2. What are the various means that an individual has of communicating with someone else?
3. What do you assume from the following:
   A. Person who drives a Lincoln Continental
   B. Hitchhiker with his thumb out
   C. Muslim wearing a turban
   D. Young lady wearing a necklace with a cross
4. How is communication linked to the following:
   A. Goal setting   C. Organizing
   B. Controlling   D. Leadership
5. Provide some examples of communication breakdown in:
   A. School administration   C. International relations
   B. Municipal administration   D. Minority-group relations
6. Why is communication breakdown generally considered a symptom?
7. What behavior is *not* communication?
8. What are the three basic elements in the communication process and what distortion is associated with each of these elements?
9. What is involved in *encoding* and *decoding* in communication?
10. What various meanings are associated with the following words?
    A. Rip off   D. Joint
    B. Round   E. Range
    C. Function   F. Drag
11. Under what circumstances is written communication preferable to spoken? When is the reverse true?
12. How do the following situational factors affect communication:
    A. Time   C. Structural hierarchy
    B. Intergroup relations   D. Organizational climate
13. How can an organization improve its internal communication?
14. How can management use the grapevine?
15. What is nondirective counseling? When should it be used?
16. What distortions occur in communication when:
    A. The President of the United States holds a press conference.
    B. A student is engaged in a job interview.
    C. Your parents ask how school is going.

Case Study:
COMMUNICATION BARRIERS

Diane Abbott is an engineer with a large construction firm in Los Angeles. She has been employed with the company for five years. She has been particularly effective in estimating jobs that the company bids on, resulting in her being assigned full-time to the estimating department. Recently the company bid on a science building at Long Beach State

College. She prepared the bid for her company. When the bids were opened, the firm Diane worked for was the low bidder. However, the bid was half a million dollars lower than any other submitted—the bid she prepared was $3.5 million, but the other twelve bids ranged from $4.0 to $4.7 million. She has just received a call from the president of the company who wants her to come to his office.

What might be the barriers to communication in this instance?
Why will the sender and receiver communicate differently and perceive the communication of the other party differently? (See figure 20-1).
What methods can be used to minimize these barriers to communication?

Case Study:
THE LATE FRY COOK

Rex Swenson is a fry cook for a local drive-in restaurant. He has been employed in this position for three years while working his way through school. He is a dependable employee and well liked by the owner, Tim Wicks. However, something happened in late August that changed all that.

Rex was supposed to work the Sunday evening shift but his mother was sick in the hospital in Dallas, some twenty miles away, and he had gone to visit her during the afternoon. On the way back, he got caught in a traffic jam after a Dallas Cowboy football game and got to work an hour late. Tim was not at the drive-in at the time, but other employees told him that the fry cook on duty had to wait over an hour until Rex got there. On Monday, Rex also had the evening shift, but his car broke down on the way to work, and again he was delayed one hour.

When he walked into the kitchen, Tim glared at him and said, "Late again, eh? Two times in a row. You know I can't put up with this. When you hired on here, you knew how important it was to be on time. We can't expect everyone else to adjust their schedule to yours. I've had to pay overtime for the past two days 'cause you failed to get here. This is serious, Rex. What've you got to say for yourself?"

Rex was taken aback by Tim's abrupt approach, and he replied rather flippantly, "I had a few problems."

Before he could say another word, Tim shot back, "You had some problems! What do you think your absence gives me? I'm trying to run this operation with employees who ignore work schedules and you tell me you've got problems. Things better shape up, Rex. What's wrong, anyway?"

By now Rex was obviously irritated and a little embarrassed. He answered sullenly, "I just had some problems."

"Is that all you're going to say? I'm going to have to start looking for another fry cook if you can't do better than that."

"Then why don't you?" Rex countered and turned to leave.

What communication breakdowns occurred in this situation?
Why did they occur?
How could the situation have been avoided?

Footnotes

1. Ralph G. Nichols, "Listening Is Good Business," *Management of Personnel Quarterly,* Winter 1962, p. 2.
2. Homer L. Cox, "Opinions of Selected Business Managers about Some Aspects of Communications on the Job," *The Journal of Business Communication,* Fall, 1968, p. 7.
3. R. R. Blake, and Jane S. Mouton, *Corporate Excellence Through Grid Organization Development* (Houston, Texas: Gulf Publishing Co., 1968), p. 4.
4. A. K. Wickesberg, "Communications Networks in the Business Organization Structure," *Academy of Management Journal,* Vol. IX, 1968, p. 257.
5. William M. Sattler, "Talking Ourselves into Communication Crises," *Michigan Business Review,* July 1957, p. 30.
6. Robert Heilbroner, et. al., *In the Name of Profit* (Garden City, N.Y.: Doubleday & Company, 1972), p. 226.
7. Alain C. Enthoven and K. Wayne Smith, *How Much is Enough?* (New York: Harper & Row, Publishers, 1971), p. 321.
8. Nichols, *op. cit.,* p. 6.
9. Rensis Likert, "Motivational Approach to Management Development," *Harvard Business Review,* July–August, 1959, p. 78.

Manager Profile

Diane Campbell
Manager, Food Services, Harold's Club
Reno, Nevada

Background and Experience

Ms Campbell started as a waitress in 1956. One of the founders took an interest in her and encouraged her to go into management training. After hostessing for some time, she became the personnel manager of food services. She became assistant manager in 1962 and has been general manager since 1971.

Primary Responsibilities

1. She is completely responsible for the sales, service, and management of all food services. Sales are about $4 million per year.
2. Complete responsibility for all of the 300 employees.
3. She has four managers who report directly to her:

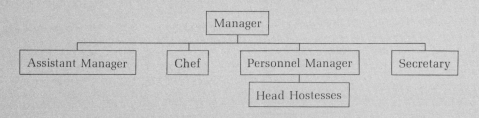

4. She is personally responsible for menus, selection, and prices of the food.
5. She has the ultimate responsibility for all preparation and service.

6. As a function of corporation management, she prepares short- and long-term projections of sales and profitability for purposes of corporate planning.

7. Profitability is her major concern. She constantly analyzes food, supply, labor, and maintenance costs in relation to planned and actual revenue. Maximizing the profitability of the operation is Diane's primary responsibility.

8. She does all of the purchasing, and must maintain adequate, least-expensive inventories.

Insights

"In our organization, no one is the 'big I.' We have all worked together for many years—and all work as a team. Those with the least authority are made to feel just as important as the managers.

"In management, the process of communication is the most important one. If you can be honest, open, and sincere with your employees, not only will they respect you, but they will be happier on their jobs.

"I relate personally to each of my people. They never feel that I am too important to be bothered by them or their problems.

"Accurate planning is critical in my job. We must try to keep inventories, supplies, and labor to a minimum, yet we must be prepared for the big rush. It has taken many years for me to learn to plan properly.

"Recently, we have been successful in cutting waste. Bonuses are paid to some of the managers when costs are significantly reduced."

Manager Profile

Gilbert A. Fuller
Christensen, Inc.
Salt Lake City, Utah

Background and Experience

Gil received a bachelor's degree in accounting from the University of Utah in 1966, followed by an M.B.A. degree in 1967. He later successfully completed the CPA examination. While attending school, he worked part-time for Kennecott Copper Corporation. Upon completing school, he became employed full-time with Kennecott in the Internal Audit Department. In 1970 he accepted a position as controller with Boyles Brothers Drilling Company, a division of Christensen, Inc. Two years later he was promoted to the central corporate office as assistant to the treasurer. He is now treasurer of Christensen, Inc., which specializes in the use of industrial diamonds for drilling bits, mining exploration, concrete blades, and other industrial applications.

Primary Responsibilities

1. He is in charge of all financial reporting for the corporation, which includes some forty entities with operations in sixteen countries.
2. He handles the allocation of financial resources to each of these entities. (The company has $100 million in sales and a $20-million credit line).
3. He is responsible for internal financial control and has the following managers reporting to him: Internal Auditor, Corporate Accountant, Financial Analyst and Foreign Exchange Currency Manager.

Insights

"I try to have people work for me who are capable of doing my job. This creates an atmosphere of competitiveness, stimulates creativity, and ensures that I have adequate back-up.

"I am careful to specifically define for each individual reporting directly to me what is expected to be accomplished. When individuals have definitive objectives and know what is expected of them, they are more satisfied and will accomplish more.

"It is extremely important to keep open channels of communication. Communication flow—both upward and downward—is vital in accomplishing the goals of the company. If a manager does not feed information downward, he soon finds that he does not get adequate information flowing back up. Communication flow is an exchange process."

PART VIII

Management Subsystems: Planning, Controlling, and Information

Planning and Control: Systems and Concepts

How significant are planning and control in the management process?

How does planning differ from control?

What benefits result from effective planning and control?

What types of plans and methods of control are available to the manager?

What organizational options are available to handle planning and control?

What are contingency plans?

PLANNING, CONTROL, AND
THE MANAGEMENT PROCESS

Large organizations represent or have access to masses of materials, machinery, manpower, and information. It is management's role to co-ordinate, integrate, and schedule these for the purpose of optimally contributing to the achievement of the organization's objectives. This is primarily accomplished through the planning and control subsystems established by management. Because management is defined as the ef-ficient and effective use of resources to achieve common objectives, these planning and control responsibilities are normally considered as some of the most important—if not the most important—in the entire management process.

The planning and control process represents the primary means available to managers to exert their influence in pursuing their basic duty of making organizations effective. Without effective planning and control, organizations tend to be in a drift condition. With them, an organization can be mobilized into an integrated, highly efficient system. In many in-stances, organizations can function with the handicap of some manage-ment process not being properly handled, but adequate planning and control systems, especially for business firms, are vital to the survival of the enterprise.

Planning and Control as a Process

In chapter 1, planning and control were identified as two of the five func-tions constituting the management process. However, it was noted that because of the interrelatedness of these two processes, they would be considered together for analytical purposes. Actually a three-step plan-ning, execution, and control process is involved, as is shown in figure 21-1. First, plans are established. These are then implemented through the leadership and direction provided by the manager (called execution or actuating), and once progress is made in relation to the plans, the control function comes into existence.

Planning as the first phase is basic to the entire management process. If the manager's responsibility is to efficiently and effectively achieve goals, it is through planning that these are established and means are developed to attain them. The execution phase is to bring life into the plans by initiating organizational activity to carry them out. To move a plan into action and make it a reality, the manager must provide direc-tion, motivate others, and be an effective leader. All of these execution functions have been covered in previous chapters.

The control phase begins once the execution phase is initiated, so that accomplishments or progress can be measured in relation to the

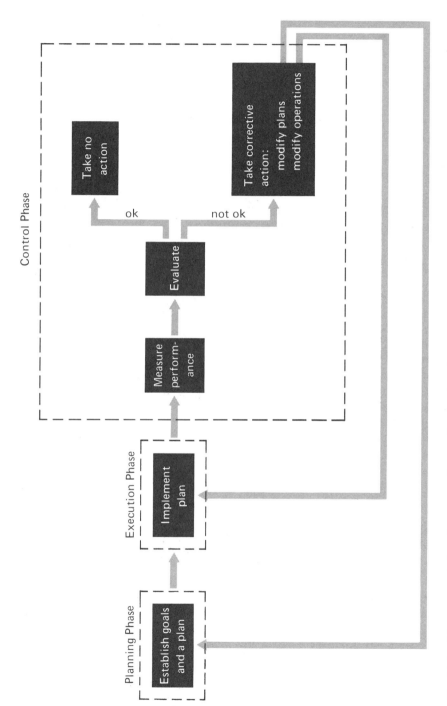

Fig. 21-1. Management planning, execution, and control cycle

plan. Control is dependent on being able to measure this performance, make an evaluation regarding whether progress is consistent with the plan, and take corrective action when exceptions to the plan are noted. Of course, if progress is in accordance with the plan, no action is required—as is reflected in figure 21-1. However, if progress is not consistent with the plan, two options are open to the manager. If the plan still appears to be valid, but something is wrong with the processing, he makes adjustments to bring the operations in line. However, if the operations appear to be functioning adequately and the original plan was ill-conceived or conditions have changed to invalidate it, the manager should make adjustments to the plan accordingly.

Because of the interdependence of this entire cycle, planning, execution, and control are considered as one continuous process. Planning and control are especially interrelated. Operational plans are established to acquire the control necessary in the organization to achieve long-term objectives. Also, control is impossible without a plan or standard to monitor performance against. Control systems are set up to achieve specific plans, but as indicated, the control process can also result in the modification of plans. One cannot function effectively without the other, and line managers are responsible for making the entire process effective. Concentrating on any one phase can result only in suboptimization.

One further point is important. Most of the systems used to plan and control incorporate both processes. A budget is not solely a plan or a method of control. Strategy in relation to attaining long-range objectives is obviously planning, but this strategy must be developed consistent with the control systems and capability of the organization. Planning and control constitute a dynamic, ongoing process. The feedback mechanisms of control are constantly modifying and adjusting plans so that any artificial separation of the processes is misleading.

The Difference Between Planning and Control

Planning is much less confusing than control because it is restricted primarily to the first phase in the combined process. In a general sense we considered planning as the establishing of objectives and a plan of action to accomplish them. More specifically *managerial planning is defined as determination of a desired set of future conditions, the strategies required to achieve these ends, and the formulation of the estimated means (activities and resources) necessary for goal accomplishment.* This definition identifies the three parts of managerial planning: the establishing of objectives, strategies to achieve those objectives, and a step-by-step determination of the activities and resources necessary to attain them. The planning process is similar to the decision-making process. Conditions are evaluated, desired improvements are established, alternatives are considered for achieving these ends, the alternatives are evaluated, and a decision regarding which course to pursue is made.

Control is much more confusing, because the term is used in diverse ways. Also, it incorporates other basic management processes—planning, reporting, decision making, and evaluation—as part of the control process. In fact, no part of the control process can be considered exclusively a control function as goal setting can be considered primarily as a planning function. In a loose sense, control is considered as the exercising of restraints and the influencing or regulating of others (or the processes of an organization). However, *managerial control*, like managerial planning, has a more restrictive meaning as it relates to the management process. *Managerial control is the monitoring and modification of organizational activity and resource utilization to ensure that predetermined standards are met and plans are carried out.*

This definition of control highlights three phases of the control process—just as there are three phases of the planning process. The control process first assumes the existence of a plan or a standard. An example of a standard in this context is a production standard for a worker to fabricate seventy-five parts during one hour. Once the plan is established or the standard is set by management, the control process involves:

- Measuring performance against the plan or standard
- Evaluating this performance
- Handling the exceptions or deviations from the plan or standard by taking appropriate corrective action

As noted, this can relate either to a change in operations or an adjustment in the plan. If a worker is producing fifty parts during an hour rather than the standard of seventy-five, it would involve determining why the performance is low and taking those actions that are necessary to bring it up to standard. If there is a deviation between performance and the plan because a planner underestimates the complexity of introducing some new manufacturing process, the plan would need modification.

DIFFERENT APPROACHES TO PLANNING AND CONTROL

Planning and control systems are established for a variety of purposes and can therefore be perceived in several different ways. A few of the more significant approaches are as follows:

- They are conceived as a means for the organization to adapt to external forces and conditions.
- They are viewed as a means of regulating the activity of people in organizations.
- They are considered as the primary means for obtaining, allocating, and using resources in organizations.
- They are regarded as either open or closed systems featuring the processes or operations being carried on by an organization.

The range is all the way from trying to estimate conditions twenty years in the future to means of currently protecting company assets. (Each of these approaches will be considered in this chapter and in chapters 22 through 24. At this point only the systems model requires further amplification.)

The Systems Approach to Planning and Control

Because of the inextricable manner in which planning and control are interwoven—both in relation to each other and the total management process—it is useful to view them in terms of systems theory. Figure 21-2 is a simplified systems model similar to the models presented in chapter 4. Systems theory assumes that an organization is an ongoing, functioning entity with input taken from the environment, the organization serving as the processor of the resources, and output being returned to the environment.

Planning is introduced by establishing goals and standards relating to processing activities and to the desired output of the system. Controlling includes the sensor and an analyzer that evaluates and regulates the input-processor-output flow. The sensors are set up to obtain feedback on these operations. The significant measurements are on the resource inputs, the processing activities, and the quantity and quality of the output. The analyzer (or comparer) takes this feedback information and determines if the system is functioning as intended by comparing it with the goals, plans, and standards established. If all measurements are consistent with these plans, no adjustments are necessary. However, if deviations occur, modifications are made to bring the system back to functioning as intended.

A *closed-loop* system, for example, is one in which an effector automatically regulates the system with no evaluation necessary. The thermostat of a furnace is a common example of a closed-loop system. Electricity, natural gas, or other energy serve as input to the furnace. The output is heat. The regulator is set by the dial of the thermostat. The

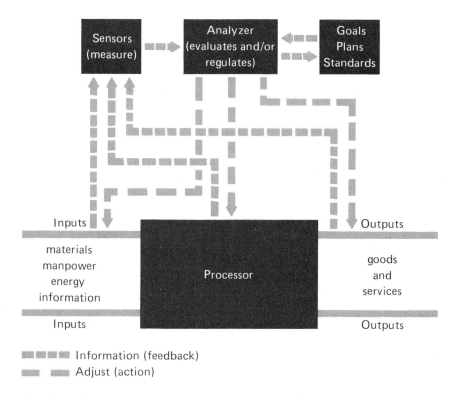

Fig. 21-2. Systems model of planning and control

bimetal sensor of the thermostat activates the electrical circuit and turns on the furnace when the temperature gets below the setting on the regulator. The regulator turns if off when the processor brings the temperature of the room back to the setting. An *open-loop* system is not automatic. When the daily labor-efficiency report indicates that a worker has fabricated only fifty parts instead of the standard seventy-five, it alerts the foreman that some action needs to be taken, but no automatic action is built into the system.

The advantage of using a systems model is that it forces managers to view the total organization in terms of its interdependent functioning and the need for comprehensive, integrated planning and control. It also emphasizes the importance of the total process, rather than the functioning of any one part. It further argues that systems must be balanced and integrated to function effectively. Relying on the budget to provide all planning and control is both too narrow and suboptimal. No single financial, operational, or behavioral control can meet the needs of complex organizations.

Organizations as Adaptive Systems

Even though parts of organizations will function as closed-loop systems (such as computer-controlled machines), the organic approach to viewing groups is more realistic. No one plan for an organization that will remain unchanged can be established and implemented. Dynamic organizations functioning in dynamic environments will necessarily force planning and control to be dynamic as well. Much of the literature on planning and control is deceptive in leading the reader to believe that a single plan is established, and then an organization forces all activities to conform to this plan. If planning and control were this simple, they would not present the enigma they do in organizations today.

Contingency considerations again become important. Certain organizations will have more established processes and a more stable environment, so that planning and control systems can be relatively detailed and precise. However, others will have variable processes and a volatile environment, making planning uncertain and erratic. Many organizations will be able to follow the rational approach to planning and control presented in this and the next three chapters, while others will experience frustration in attempting to use this logical sequence. Many stable business firms can follow these guides to the letter, but a governmental group might find it impossible because of the shifts in political power and public opinion.

The adaptive model of planning and control presented in figures 21-1 and 21-2 implies that plans and operations are continually being modified as conditions change. All plans will require some adjustment, because people will never be 100 percent accurate in predicting the future. This is the primary paradox in planning and control as shown in figure 21-3. Detailed planning establishes a step-by-step sequence for accomplishing

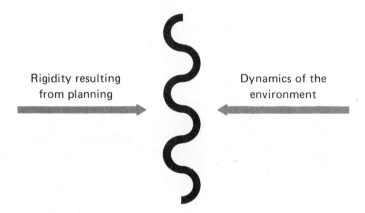

Fig. 21-3.   Two opposing forces

goals. This tends to generate rigidity, especially if managers are reluctant to deviate from established plans and if the reward system benefits those who do not deviate. However, the dynamics of the environment always make some aspects of planning inappropriate or outmoded. The greatest hurdle in establishing these systems is to obtain the control desired and yet maintain the flexibility required by an open system. The end result is that some organizations can plan on a more formal one-time basis, but for other organizations planning and the associated control are intermittent, intuitive, and sporadic. Here the development of a variety of contingency plans becomes appropriate.

CONTINGENCY PLANNING

. . . the very nature of corporate planning is undergoing a dramatic change, and the companies that fare best in coming years may well be the ones that adapt most quickly to the new styles in planning.

Instead of relying on a single corporate plan with perhaps one or two variations, top management at more and more companies is now getting a whole battery of contingency plans and alternate scenarios. "We shoot for alternative plans that can deal with "either-or" eventualities," say George J. Prendergast, in charge of planning at chemical giant E. I. du Pont de Nemours and Co.

Companies are reviewing and revising plans more frequently in line with changing conditions. Instead of the old five-year plan that might have been updated annually, plans are often updated quarterly, monthly, or even weekly. Arizona Public Service Co. last year adopted a 'dynamic' budget that looks ahead two years but is rolled over every month. At Ralston Purina Co., a 1 percent change in the price of a prime commodity kicks off a change in the company's cost models, and the whole corporate plan may change accordingly."

Quoted from "Corporate Planning: Piercing Future Fog in the Executive Suite," *Business Week*, April 28, 1975, p. 46.

ADVANTAGES OF PLANNING AND CONTROL

Although the primary benefits of having plans and controls in organizations are relatively obvious, some of the major advantages are often overlooked. For this reason they are enumerated below.

Advantages of Planning

There are eight reasons why planning is considered one of the primary management functions:

PROVIDES A SENSE OF DIRECTION IN AN ORGANIZATION.   The statement is often made that unless you know where you are going, any road will get you there. If individuals or organizations are drifting, it is obviously difficult for them to be effective. Planning directs effort into endeavors that contribute to goal accomplishment and harmonizes the use of facilities and resources. By providing a framework for what occurs in an organization, planning makes work meaningful and activities orderly.

FOCUSES ATTENTION ON OBJECTIVES AND RESULTS.   One of the themes presented through this text is that organizations exist because people have common objectives and managers are in charge of organizations for the purpose of attaining results. George Odiorne, one of the leaders in the management-by-objectives movement, and others have warned managers about getting caught in the activity trap. It is easy to get swallowed up in daily activity and lose sight of the objectives that are the purpose for the activity of organizations.

AN IMPORTANT INTEGRATING FORCE.   The purpose of planning is to interrelate the entire resources and activity of an organization so that common goals are attained. Planning must necessarily be comprehensive in considering all internal conditions and processes, and relating these to external events and forces. It stimulates a deeper understanding of the complexity of a business as it struggles to adapt to external forces.

HELPS ANTICIPATE PROBLEMS AND OFFSET UNCERTAINTY.   A significant aspect of planning is obtaining information to forecast conditions in the future. This involves "what if" situations, in terms of considering what should be done, given different sets of future conditions. Collecting such information provides a better understanding of what is likely to happen in the future and how an organization should react if different conditions occur. It also helps keep management alert to changing events.

PROVIDES GUIDELINES FOR DECISION MAKING.   Decisions are future oriented. When plans covering the future exist, managers will be inclined to make current decisions consistent with these plans. If plans are not in existence, there is no sound basis for making future-oriented decisions. Planning also reduces suboptimization, because without organizational plans individuals will obviously make decisions favorable to their unit or personal interests.

PROVIDES A BASIS FOR DECENTRALIZATION.   The benefits of decentralization were outlined in chapter 15. A manager is reluctant to delegate
authority to others unless he can predict how they will make decisions.
Without plans it is difficult to feel confident about how a subordinate will
use his authority. Well-established plans that are known and accepted
by subordinates greatly reduce these risks.

SERVES AS THE PREREQUISITE FOR ALL OTHER MANAGEMENT FUNCTIONS.   It
has already been noted that it is impossible to have a control system
without first having plans. Other management processes are dependent
on planning to essentially the same degree. Organizations are established
and structured to accomplish certain goals or plans; people are selected
to make the organizations function consistent with these plans; providing
leadership and direction are dependent on knowing what is to be accomplished.

MOTIVATIONAL BECAUSE BEHAVIOR IS DIRECTED TOWARD GOAL ACHIEVEMENT.
In chapter 11 on motivation, it was noted that individuals behave so as
to achieve goals or rewards from their behavior. All individuals have
certain images of what they want to achieve in the future, and behavior
is directed at achieving these. People give priority to activities based
upon deadlines or goals so that the goal setting process is an important
element in motivation. (For example, how do you make priorities when
the deadline for a term paper approaches?). Goal setting will be explored
further in the next chapter.

Advantages of Control

Most of the advantages of planning also relate to control since planning
is not effective without control. Control accentuates four features of
effective management.

GUIDES BEHAVIOR TOWARD USEFUL ORGANIZATIONAL ENDS.   Control monitors and directs the activities of people into channels that are beneficial
for the organization. Lack of control results in erratic behavior that may
be tangential to organizational goals.

ENSURES THAT RESOURCES ARE EFFICIENTLY UTILIZED.   One of the main
purposes of control is to monitor the allocation and use of resources, thus
seeking to avoid the waste of these in useless endeavors or inefficient
operations.

FOCUSES ATTENTION ON FACTORS ESSENTIAL IN ACHIEVING ORGANIZATIONAL
EFFECTIVENESS.   Measuring performance at the strategic points in a com-

pany's operations concentrates attention on the factors that are vital in an organization's success, such as meeting performance criteria, quality standards, and achieving goals.

ENCOURAGES THE ACTION NECESSARY TO MAINTAIN PERFORMANCE. Controls are generally considered to provide rigidity and restrict behavior. However, management control calls for adjusting plans or operations when exceptions occur. A key feature of control is determining when an organization is going astray so that corrections or adjustments can be made in a timely manner.

The benefits of control are summarized in a statement by a well-known management observer: "Effective controlling provides for adequate visibility in a timely fashion with the least expenditure of time and effort."[1]

APPROACHES TO PLANNING

Formal and Informal Plans

Plans are of two types—either formal or informal. Formal planning is comprehensive and rational. It will be considered in this and following chapters. Informal planning is conducted by many managers who develop plans for the future, but they never formally put them on paper and may not even communicate them to others. Few small businessmen ever formalize their strategy, but they maintain certain goals and images for their organization as it relates to the future. Peter Drucker, from his extensive study of business organizations, concludes, "Every one of the great business builders we know of—from Medici and the founders of the Bank of England down to IBM's Thomas Watson in our days—had a definite idea, indeed a clear 'theory of the business,' which informed his actions and decisions."[2] However, these were rarely formalized, since long-range planning is essentially a phenomena developed since the mid 1950's. Even though our emphasis is on formal planning, informal is as inevitable as informal organization. Likewise, informal plans are often more significant than formal.

Expediency or Contingency Plans

In addition to the two basic types of plans, there is an in-between mode referred to as *expediency* or *contingency* planning. It is a flexible type that is necessarily sporadic as conditions change and forecasts are altered.

New conditions, ideas, or attitudes will introduce opportunities that were not conceived in earlier planning, so that these guides need to be revised to take advantage of the new situation. Charles Lindblom is well known for this approach, which he refers to as successive limited comparisons, or "the science of muddling through."[3] His model is primarily derived from political situations where long-range planning is difficult because of the frequent changes in political parties in power, the shifting of public opinion, and the diffusion of power through many different administrative groups.

Expediency planning occurs in a staccato fashion. As more information becomes available on conditions relevant to the plan, and (in the political situation) as sufficient support is obtained to pursue an issue, decisions relating to the future are made. The expediency aspects of planning are illustrated by a man taking a fishing trip. He may plan the trip several weeks in advance so he can apply for leave from his job and make other necessary arrangements. However, he does not make advance decisions on which particular stream or what time of the day to fish, or what to use for bait until he gets there and checks on the weather, stream conditions, and feedback from the locals on what the fish are taking. On the same basis, if five acres of land adjacent to a firm's plantsite suddenly come up for sale, it may cause the company to revise its financial plans in order to make this unanticipated purchase. One time, formal planning is appropriate when conditions are known, such as developing the design for constructing a building, but expediency planning is common when conditions are erratic and contingencies are difficult to predict.

Strategic, Annual Operating, and Short-Range Plans

Formal planning is typically divided into two types: strategic (or long-range) and operational (or short-range). Short-range is also referred to as *tactical* planning. Writers and practitioners identify different time periods with long-range and short-range planning, depending on industry characteristics. In more stable industries, short-range can extend up to five years, but more typically it is defined as periods of less than a year. Long-range therefore becomes any planning that extends beyond a year.

A third category of planning becomes important because of its frequency. Annual planning or annual operating plans are used essentially by all organizations. Government bureaus receive appropriations on an annual basis and business firms submit financial reports annually. As a result, budgets are established and controlled on this annual cycle, so in many organizations (especially those that are service oriented) the annual plan predominates.

Characteristics of Formal Plans

The characteristics of the three types of formal plans—strategic, annual operating, and short-range—are shown in table 21-1. Strategy was considered in detail in chapter 9, relating to how an organization adapts to its environment. Strategic planning is the broadest type of planning conducted by an organization. It involves top management making decisions as to how an organization will compete in its marketplace and adapt to anticipated changes in the external environment. These are relatively enduring decisions affecting major strategic factors like product lines, diversification, meeting the challenges of competitors, expansion, product innovations, and other desired future conditions. Strategy is not solely these "ends." It also involves the broad deployment of resources or the "means" of goal attainment. Because of the difficulty of forecasting future conditions, long-range plans are formidable to develop and primarily judgmental in nature. These plans represent the general thrusts of the organization and are not usually backed up by extensive detail. Just as you would find it a worthless exercise to plan on a *daily* basis what you will be doing five years from now, so an organization finds little merit in planning when the unknowns make estimating sheer speculation.

Short-range planning is almost the opposite of long-range. The concerns are the internal environment, not the external; the purpose is not to set objectives but to implement strategic objectives; middle managers are normally responsible for developing the plans, not top management; known tasks and operations are being forecast, not relatively unknown future conditions; the decisions are of a tactical, short-term nature and will not carry forward long periods into the future; repetitive operations are involved, in which exact standards and data are available, contrasted with the limited data for strategic planning; controlling operations through detailing activity steps and allocating resources is the concern, rather than forecasting future conditions and determining what niche a company hopes to fulfill.

Annual operating plans are basically short-range and operational in nature, so they have the same features as short-range plans, although they tend to take on some vagueness. Short-range operating plans in manufacturing companies are generally three-month rolling plans (as one month is completed a new plan for a third month is added). Since short-range planning is three months versus the twelve months of annual plans, they will obviously be easier to forecast and more accurate. Annual operating plans and budgets are a necessary part of the functioning of all organizations, and since many organizations do little formal planning beyond this period, they take on special significance, because they force the organization to make critical decisions in resource allocation.

Table 21-1. Variables Associated with Different Types of Plans

Characteristic	Plans		
	Strategic (Long-Range)	Annual Operating	Operational (Short-Range)
Time horizon	over one year	one year	under one year
Purpose	establish objectives and future states	set and implement goals	implement goals
Organizational level involved	top management	top and middle management	middle and lower management
Systems level	external environment	primarily internal	internal environment
Activity controlled	total performance, systems relations	task and total performance	tasks, operations
Decision range	relatively enduring	primarily short-term	short-term
Basis for planning	primarily judgmental	exact data and judgmental	exact data and standards
Content	broad, general	specific, detailed	specific, detailed
Predictability	uncertain	quite certain	highly certain
Anticipated accuracy	within 25%	within 5%	within 2 or 3%
Management functions involved	planning dominant	planning and control	primarily control
Management control of variables	slight	significant	almost complete

Because of the certainties associated with internal operations, accuracy in the typical short-range production plan is within 2 to 3 percent. This assumes routine, continuous production, such as on an assembly line. In intermittent production (a job shop fabricating work to a customer's order) the accuracy would not be as high. The annual operating plan stretches out longer than the short-range plan, so accuracy now drops to 95 percent. Long-range planning of five years or more involves considerable speculation because of the difficulty of predicting future conditions, so that 75 percent accuracy is considered acceptable. These assumptions are important to convey to those engaged in planning operations. Individuals are often reluctant to participate in long-range projections because they know it is impossible to be accurate. However, if management recognizes the different degree of accuracy associated with each type of plan and makes this known to those involved, reluctance to participate is reduced.

In developing strategy, basic planning activities like forecasting and goal setting are dominant. However, operational planning is more the internal means of implementing long-range objectives, so control considerations dominate. In fact, some writers consider operational planning as part of the control process.[4]

The Commitment Principle of Planning

The period covered by long-range plans is normally determined by the *commitment principle* of planning. This principle states that an organization should plan in the future as far as it is committed by its current decisions. In other words, when an organization makes current decisions the impact should not extend beyond their current plans. Public utilities with major capital investments in power generators or pipe lines will plan for a minimum of 20 years because facility decisions normally encompass this time frame. Firms in the consumer products industry where fashions rapidly change will not carry product planning beyond three years at most. Five years is the common span for comprehensive planning, although facility planning will typically extend for ten. Most federal government agencies currently follow a five-year projection.

Sears Roebuck and Strategic Planning

One of the classic examples of strategy and its impact on the growth of firms is the Sears—Montgomery Ward story, following World War II. Both of these retail giants started as catalog stores, providing mail-order service to the American farmer. Both began adding retail stores in the 1920's, and by 1941, Sears had sales of $1 billion versus $667 million for Ward. Following World War II, they adopted divergent strategies. Ward, under Sewell Avery's leadership, was convinced that the depression would return, and they maintained a strong cash position, not building any new stores between 1946 and Sewell's demise in 1955. On the other hand, Sears followed an aggressive expansion policy by relocating old stores and building new ones, primarily in the rapidly growing suburbs. As a result, by 1960 Sears had sales of $4 billion dollars and Montgomery Ward had expanded only to $1 billion.

The dramatic growth of Sears is punctuated by a series of major strategy decisions. After Sears added retail stores in the 1920's, they turned to central merchandising in their headquarters in Chicago. They then decided to develop their own specifications for 95 percent of the goods sold in their stores. Next, they pursued the aggressive expansion policy started in the 1940's, which proved to be their most significant strategy decision. In the 1950's, they expanded sale of soft goods to support their primarily hardware line. Soon after, they decided to play up style and fashion in appealing to the middle- and higher-income bracket of buyers. This was followed by the decision to set up a service organization, expand into insurance and other financial services, and to invest in major suppliers to maintain their distribution strength.

These decisions all seemed to be correct until the recession of 1974–75. In 1964 Sears had 56 percent of the total sales of the big four in retailing (Sears, J.C. Penny, S.S. Kresge, and Montgomery Ward), but by 1974 this had dropped to 47 percent. Sears had been losing out primarily in terms of the low-income buyer. This again caused a change in their strategy as they cut prices and added some "budget" lines in an attempt to undersell the competition.[5]

Functional and Resource Plans

Following the establishing of broad strategy guidelines the types of subsidiary, lower-level plans developed in an organization will vary, depending on the nature of the organization structure. Plans are supposed to guide the activities of organizations, so they must be developed consistent with the structure. In companies organized on a project basis, *program* (also called *project*) *plans* will be developed. In firms with functional departmentation, each major function will develop a plan that incorporates its subgoals, operations, and required resources.

The derivative plans that a functional organization develops following the establishment of the general company strategy and objectives are shown in figure 21-4. Each major function such as marketing, engineering, production, quality control, and research and development establishes a separate plan, showing what activities it will undertake to ensure that the broad plans are implemented. The list of functional plans in figure 21-4 is not intended to be comprehensive but only representative of typical plans, based on the normal functions in a manufacturing organization.

Following the establishing of the functional plans, the staff units responsible for support activities will then combine all of the requirements contained in the functional plans into summary plans relating to each resource. The manpower requirements derived from the functional plans will be summarized into manning tables, showing the buildup of manpower by skill category required to support the general plans of the organization. Resource plans come last in the planning sequence, because, using manpower requirements as an example, they cannot be established until each functional organization develops its operational plan covering the activities and effort necessary to support its functions.

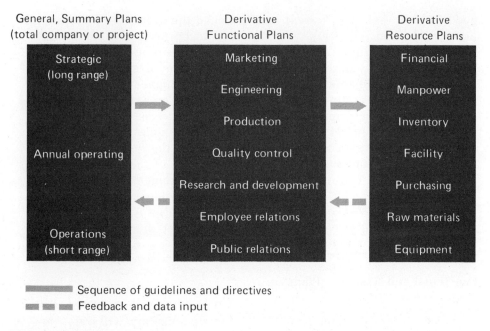

General, Summary Plans (total company or project)	Derivative Functional Plans	Derivative Resource Plans
Strategic (long range)	Marketing	Financial
	Engineering	Manpower
	Production	Inventory
Annual operating	Quality control	Facility
	Research and development	Purchasing
	Employee relations	Raw materials
Operations (short range)	Public relations	Equipment

▬▬▬ Sequence of guidelines and directives
▬ ▬ ▬ Feedback and data input

Fig. 21-4. Planning sequence

Thus planning is an iterative process, with the broad objectives first being established and then each organization developing subsidiary plans that relate its functions or support activities to the total company strategy. The total plan for a company may consist of as many as twenty or thirty separate plans. The broad strategy, annual, and short-term plans are summarized at the total organizational level, but each major subunit will have a separate subsidiary plan covering its activities.

An example of this sequence can be demonstrated by the plans associated with a company objective of increasing production and sales by 10 percent in the next year. Given this objective, marketing would develop a plan to show how they will generate a 10 percent increase in sales. Production would develop a plan for increasing its capacity, as would quality control and the other organizations. Following this, resource plans would be established to show the increase in dollars, manpower, inventory, facilities, raw materials, and equipment to support the 10 percent rise in production and sales. (Methods and sample formats relating to these different plans will be presented in chapter 24.)

Other Types of Plans

It is common in planning literature to consider policies, procedures, and rules as *standing plans*. Policies and procedures do provide guidelines for operations and for decision making, so they are in this respect plans. They are called standing plans because they are not frequently changed, and they cover repetitive action versus the one-time projects of single-use plans. (Procedures and operations sheets are included as part of organization structure in chapter 13 and therefore require no further explanation here.)

Policies are closely related to strategy. Policies constitute more the internal strategy of the firm. They are general guides to organizational behavior and provide operating parameters within which decisions should be made. Each major function of a company will have policies relating to that function. An example of a financial policy is "to not incur debt as a method of expansion." A marketing policy might be "to meet the lowest price of competitors." Policy making is the prerogative to top management. It constitutes one of the most significant responsibilities of management at this level.

In conclusion, it should be recognized that governments, hospitals, educational institutions, and businesses all carry on operations that display some special features, so the array of different types of plans is almost endless. All that can be done in this text is to indicate the types of plans that tend to predominate.

APPROACHES TO CONTROL

Every plan should be supported by a control system to monitor implementation and ensure that activity is conducted consistent with the plan. Thus the types and varieties of control systems tend to duplicate the types and varieties of plans. Furthermore, the control system must be integrated with the total management design, because it is the function of the control system to see that the organization operates in desired ways.

As noted earlier, in the broad sense *control* can be considered as any restraint, curb, or regulation on behavior or organizational processes; *management control* is more restrictive, relating to systematic measurement and revision of behavior or processes. Sociologists and psychologists quite naturally view control in terms of the influence processes affecting behavior, whereas management writers restrict it more to regulating operations and resource allocation within an organization. No matter which definition is accepted, there are still many different types of controls used by organizations. Some of the more common ones are identified below.

Control of Inputs, Processing, and Outputs

One of the useful ways to categorize controls is to relate them to the model contained in figure 21-2. Organizations provide standards and other controls relating to input, processing, and output. The manpower input is controlled through the selection process. People with particular skills and experience are hired to meet specific job specifications. Organizations have material, energy, and equipment specifications covering each input. Budgets serve as a restraint over input in terms of quantity. Processing is regulated by a large number of standards relating to performance, scheduling, procedures, resource utilization, and job specifications. Output controls are on quantity, quality, and measurement of results in relation to goals.

Specific Types of Controls

The most common controls in organizations are listed in table 21-2. These are forces, formal systems, or other limitations that influence the behavior of people or the internal processes of an organization. Each is a restraint or a check on what is done. The characteristics of each type of control are shown in table 21-2 and described below.

GOALS AND STRATEGY.   The strategy and goals established by organizations influence the motivation of people and the decisions they make. Goals channel behavior into activities perceived to be related to goal achievement. Goal accomplishment can often be measured quantitatively but is also highly judgmental.

STRUCTURAL CONTROLS.   One of the most important factors regulating and channeling behavior in organizations is their formal structure. Chapters 13 through 15 dealt with concepts of departmentation and the chain of command. All of these concepts restrict the activities of people in organizations. Other aspects of the formal structure, such as the appraisal system and existing policies, also influence behavior. Measurement of how well an individual conforms to these guidelines is primarily determined through observation by supervisors and others.

SOCIAL CONTROLS.   Chapters 14, 16, and 17 covered informal types of control that result from personal interaction and group processes. Major constraints on the behavior of an individual are caused by the expectations of others. Existing roles, customs, values, group norms, and predominant leadership styles all serve as regulators of behavior. The "fair-day's-work" group norm is often a stronger determinant of behavior than formally established production standards. Social (also called indirect) controls are intangible and monitored through observation. They typically constitute some of the strongest curbs on behavior, especially when the formal structure is loose and ill-defined.

Table 21-2. Characteristics Associated with the Different Types of Controls

Type of Control	Element Controlled	Nature of Control	Method of Measurement (Feedback)
Goals and strategy	manpower and total performance	anticipated future conditions, goal setting	some quantitative data; also judgmental
Organization structure	manpower	position descriptions, delegated authority, hierarchy, functional assignments, procedures, appraisal system, etc.	compare with guides; observation
Social control	manpower (behavior)	roles, expectations, group norms, customs, values, leadership styles	observation, interaction
Financial control	resources	dollar limits, ratios, cash flow, return on investment, etc.	quantitative data, reports
Budgets	resources	limits on quantity of manpower, materials, equipment, etc.	quantitative data, reports
Production control	manpower and resources	operation sheets, standard methods, routing, bill of materials, productivity standards, etc.	quantitative data, inspection, charts, observation
Quality control	output	specifications, standards, tests	quantitative data, charts, inspection, observation
Audits	resources and performance	inspect and evaluate reports and operations	inspect and test data; reports; observation

FINANCIAL CONTROLS.   Many standards have been developed to measure the financial health of an organization. These standards relate to ratios like return-on-investment, profit margin on sales, inventory turnover, current assets versus current liabilities, and others. (These will be considered in chapter 24.)

BUDGETS.   Budgets limit the quantity of resources like manpower, materials, and equipment that are used for specific operations. The budget is the best known, comprehensive device available to management to control internal operations. (For this reason budgeting is given thorough consideration in chapter 23.)

OPERATIONS OR PRODUCTION CONTROL.   The techniques used to route, schedule, dispatch, and follow up on production are numerous and well developed. They include Gantt charts (to be considered in chapter 24), operations sheets, productivity standards, bills of materials, and many other techniques. The production-control unit is the nerve system of a manufacturing organization. It provides master schedules for all operations, keeps tab on progress and resource utilization, and integrates all elements of the production process.

QUALITY CONTROL.   Techniques relating to quality control will also be explored in chapter 24. These include specifications, comparison of attributes, and tests to ensure that the output of the organization meets desired standards. As part of the control process, items are inspected as they are fabricated and when they are finished goods.

AUDITS.   Audits are one of the few devices that are used almost purely for control purposes. Audits ensure that reported information is properly prepared and accurately portrays what is intended. Traditionally the most common type has been the independent appraisal of a company's financial records by public accountants. However, large companies generally have *internal auditors,* who potentially can audit the quality of all internal reports and operations. An internal auditor is primarily concerned with making sure that the control system of an organization functions as intended.

Internal auditors should not report to managers who are responsible for functions they are checking on. It is desirable for them to be assigned directly to top management. *Management audits* have also been developed as a systematic approach to appraising the overall performance of management. The American Institute of Management has a comprehensive procedure for doing this, involving over three hundred questions that rate companies on the basis of corporate structure, earnings, fiscal policies, production efficiency, sales vigor, and other factors.[6]

Balance in Control Systems

The common feature in all of the controls enumerated is the intent to standardize performance. Controls are also designed to protect the assets of the organization—and in some instances to motivate—but basically they are to standardize the quality of inputs, the processing operations, and the quality of output. Primarily they control people, because manpower is the most important and costly resource input. Also, the decisions of managers determine how resources will be used and what eventual financial, production, and performance standards are attained. Many different types of controls are identified in table 21-2. Each should be an element in the broad control system designed by an organization. The control system should be established with two criteria as primary: it should be comprehensive, so that all facets of the organization are covered, and it should be balanced, so that certain controls do not receive undue emphasis while others go essentially unnoticed.

ORGANIZING FOR PLANNING
AND CONTROL

Companies will organize differently for planning and control, depending on whether they are a conglomerate, single-plant company, or small business. A small business will not have the resources to hire a full-time planner, so planning is completely handled by managers. Extremely large organizations will have full-time planning staffs that will prepare forecasts as sophisticated as those provided by the Council of Economic Advisors and other forecasting groups. Even with this wide variation, certain guidelines are available for organizing to effectively handle planning and control.

Organizing for Planning

Planning is a major part of the responsibility of all supervisors, although normally they do not have the background or time to do the analytical work and forecasting that modern planning requires. This is one of the major dilemmas of top management. They have no more major responsibility than determining the strategy of the organization, but as Senator Henry M. Jackson of Washington states, "I am convinced that we never will get the kind of policy planning we need if we expect the top-level officers to participate actively in the planning process. They simply do not have the time, and in any event they rarely have the outlook or the talents of the good planner."[7] Even though this is somewhat of an overstatement, it does express the reason why the way in which planning is organized is usually the cause for the downfall of planning within a company. Strategic planning is a key responsibility of top management, but to provide the emphasis needed to handle the function a separate staff (or an office such as the vice president for planning) is required. The first point crucial in organizing for planning is that the planning group should report to top management. If it is lost in the lower levels of the organization, planning will not receive the attention it deserves.

The second point of significance is that full-time planning groups should be considered as staff. Top management is responsible for making the planning decisions like those on strategy and objectives. The planning group's job is to aid management in doing this—through developing economic forecasts, projecting market demand, conducting market research, developing proposals for new ventures, providing planning formats, summarizing and evaluating divisional and functional plans, assisting in the development of objectives, and providing planning guidance to those seeking assistance. If top management forfeits their responsibility for making planning decisions by informally leaving these to the planning staff, they are sure to gain the resentment of line managers who are responsible for implementing the plans, and they will violate sound organization practice by letting the staff group make the decisions but not having the ultimate responsibility for results.

Participation is extremely important in developing plans. Management needs the commitment of line managers if they want the plans properly implemented. Normally this commitment is attained only by "having a say" through participation. For this reason many companies establish a long-range planning committee under the chief executive. Typically the chief executive officer is the chairman, and each major function is represented on the committee through their division manager. Using such a committee ensures a balanced input in planning and achieves the participation desired. When long-range planning committees are used, the planning staff reports to the committee through the chief executive officer. The planning staff collects and summarizes data for committee action.

There are many other alternatives for organizing planning besides using an executive committee and/or a planning department. Russell L. Ackoff favors General Electric's approach of using a temporary planning task force. He also encourages using planning review boards that vertically tie together a company's planning activities.[8] However, the two primary points in regard to organizing for planning are that top management should be involved and make the strategy decisions, and that sufficient planning data can be acquired only through a permanent planning staff responsible for obtaining and developing this information.

One last point is important to this topic. Generally today's problems have a way of demanding attention and taking precedence, so future planning is deferred. And planning requires uninterrupted attention for thinking through strategies and alternatives. For this reason, many companies annually or even quarterly take their planning committee and staff to a remote location away from telephones and visitors where this activity can go on for several days without distraction.

Organizing for Control

Formal strategic or operational planning does not necessarily involve all levels of an organization. A functional plan frequently can be made without including each first-line supervisor engaged in that function. The supervisor will have to carry on daily planning to handle his activities, but he may have little input to the formal company plan. The depth of planning involvement in an organization will depend on the knowledge and information lower-level managers can contribute. However, all managers are engaged in control or monitoring company plans, so the control system must necessarily directly involve them. A few of the more important guides in organizing for control follows.

THE CONTROL SYSTEM SHOULD SUPPORT THE AUTHORITY STRUCTURE OF THE FORMAL ORGANIZATION.   One of the purposes of the formal structure is to facilitate control. Control systems should follow the chain of command, authority delegation, and functional assignments as established. Staff groups can be used in the measurement phase of control (such as internal audit), but the decision-making or corrective-action phase is a line responsibility. One of the most deceptive terms used in industry today is that of *controller*. The controller is supposed to design and maintain financial and reporting systems, but he is not the one who allocates resources or controls operations.

IT IS DESIRABLE TO SEPARATE THE "MEASURER" FROM THE "DOER."   In chapter 10 (relating to perception) and chapter 20 (relating to communication), it was noted that individuals tend to maintain a favorable bias toward their activities, so it is unlikely they will be objective in evaluating their operations. In the tremendous cost increases experienced by Lockheed on the C-5A jumbo jet transport and General Dynamics on their 880 and 990 commercial jets in the early 1960's, there were no independent sources that had access to the appropriate information, so management was not adequately warned of the impending disasters. One of the difficulties in using "percent complete" as a control measure on the physical completion of projects is that normally those preparing the report must go to the project manager in charge to obtain this estimate.

OPERATIONS SHOULD BE ORGANIZED SO AS TO ESTABLISH CLEAR-CUT RESPONSIBILITY.   If responsibility can be identified for profit, productivity, and/

or performance, it enhances the control function. If separate profit or responsibility centers can be established by creating clean breaks between the various phases of a firm's operations, costs and performance can be isolated—so measurements are more meaningful and responsibility for taking corrective action is pinpointed.

DESIGNING AN EFFECTIVE CONTROL SYSTEM IS BASED ON SELECTING KEY STRATEGIC POINTS TO OBTAIN MEASUREMENT AND INSTITUTE CONTROLS.   An instructor in a class does not need to give an examination every day to determine whether or not students are learning the material. Examinations are conducted at significant points during the course when appropriate portions of the material have been covered and when more integrated feedback is necessary. An examination every day devotes far too much time and resources to the control function. However, if only one examination is given at the end of the course, there is no time left to take corrective action. An auditor does not examine every entry but has a system for checking certain vital information at designated points. State governments locate weighing stations for trucks at a limited number of sites where they intercept most of the traffic. Good control is certainly not maximum control; rather it is one where costs and benefits are balanced.

SUMMARY

Activities are carried out in organizations through a sequence of planning, execution, and control. Planning involves establishing of strategy and objectives and determining the activity sequence and resources necessary to attain them. Execution includes the conducting of operations under the plan. Controlling is the measuring of performance to ensure that results attained are consistent with the plan. When operations and results are consistent, no corrective action is required. However, when exceptions exist, either the plan must be changed or operations modified.

The nature of planning and control systems is dependent on the stability of an organization and its environment. Stable organizations provide opportunity for a mechanistic approach to planning and control, based on known standards and predictable operations. Firms functioning in dynamic environments require more flexible planning and controls.

Planning provides a sense of direction to an organization, is an important integrating force, and serves as the prerequisite to the effective handling of other management functions. Control guides behavior and organizational activity into useful channels, helps ensure resources are efficiently utilized, and keeps the organization functioning in a coordinated fashion.

Formal plans are of three basic types: strategic (or long-range), annual operating, and operations (or short-range). Strategic planning is the responsibility of top management and relates to broad goals and conditions, usually projected five to ten years in the future. Annual operating and short-range plans relate to the internal environment of the firm and involve more exact data covering the scheduling, cost, and performance standards of a company's operations. Functional and resource plans are highly specialized and are developed following the establishing of overall strategy and objectives.

There are many different types of controls in organizations. Some of the most common are goals and strategy, organization structure, social controls, financial controls, budgets, production control, quality control, and audits.

QUESTIONS FOR STUDY AND DISCUSSION

1. Identify the planning, execution, and control phases in the following activities:

    A. Constructing a building   C. Operating a restaurant

    B. Teaching a class   D. Managing an office for the FBI

2. What is the difference between *planning* and *managerial planning?* Between *control* and *managerial control?*

3. As a process, why is control more difficult to specifically tie down than planning?

4. Identify the sensors, analyzer, and plans in the following systems:

    A. Utility company providing services and billing customers

    B. Gasoline service-station operator

    C. Hospital

5. Why are the following considered as advantages of planning?

    A. Provides a basis for decentralization

    B. Is an important integrating force

    C. Is a prerequisite for other management functions

6. Under what circumstance is informal planning likely to predominate?

7. What circumstances are conducive to expediency or contingency planning?

8. What are the basic differences between a long-range and a shortrange plan?

9. Give examples of functional and resource derivative plans that would be developed with the following organizational goals:

    A. University expecting a 10 percent reduction in enrollment

    B. State park director expecting a 40 percent increase in visitors in the next two years

      C. Tire manufacturer expecting the energy crisis to reduce tire sales by 6 percent

10. List the types of controls that exist in the following situations:
    A. Student graduating from a university
    B. Student spending funds received from parents
    C. Controls influencing the behavior of a first-line supervisor in a meat-processing plant
    D. Controls over the chief executive officer of a corporation
    E. Controls over the performance of a secretary

11. What part does staff play in planning? What part do line managers play? Are the roles of each any different as they relate to control functions?

Case Problem:
PLANNING AT
WINSLOW STATE UNIVERSITY

Winslow State was started as a state college in 1960 when the World War II baby boom was just on the verge of rapidly increasing enrollments in higher education. The school is located in an area that was also experiencing population growth associated with industrial expansion. There are seven other institutions of higher learning in the state system.

Winslow grew from an enrollment of approximately 2000 in 1962 to over 13,000 by 1969. In the 1970's, the school experienced the "steady state" of higher education, and by 1976 there were 14,000 students. Planning is fragmented throughout the university. A separate engineering group is in charge of facilities planning, and financial planning is included in the budget process. In 1976 the central administration of the university decided that they needed a more comprehensive, formalized approach to institutional planning, and they appointed Allen Wilson to head up a newly created planning office. Allen has had 10 years' experience in industrial planning with two different firms, but he has had little experience in higher education. He is to present a report to the Faculty Senate indicating briefly what he intends to do in setting up an institutional plan and why he is pursuing the course he is proposing.

What should the major ingredients of a university institutional plan consist of?

What advantages of planning can he provide in his report to the Faculty Senate?

How can he convince the Faculty Senate that his office will do anything other than provide a little more bureaucracy?

Do you think Wilson will find planning in a university different from industry? Why?

Case Problem:
CONSTRUCTION FOREMAN
OF THE MINIDOME

Winslow State University is located in an area that frequently has inclement weather, so the school decided to construct an enclosed sports arena that will seat 22,000. The minidome will be used for football, basketball, and other school activities. Nine months ago the school awarded a contract for $25 million to Nielsen Construction Company to build the facility.

The company has experienced a variety of problems during construction. They were supposed to be 40 percent complete with construction as of December 1, but they are only 32 percent finished. They are also over-running their cost projection by 15 percent. Some of the increase has been due to the rise in prices of materials, but the company president is convinced that the construction superintendent has not adequately managed the job—especially in relation to the control functions. Recently he fired the foreman and replaced him with an experienced superintendent who has efficiently handled other jobs for the company. Most of the construction is by the company workforce, although they are subcontracting the electrical and mechanical utilities and the brickwork.

If you were the new foreman, what types of controls would you be most concerned with?
How would you go about controlling the costs and the work in progress?
How would you deal with the current work crews?

Footnotes

1. George L. Morrisey, "Without Control, MBO Is a Waste of Time," *Management Review*, February, 1975, p. 12.
2. Peter F. Drucker, "Entrepreneurship in the Business Enterprise," *Journal of Business Policy*, Vol. 1, 1970, p. 5.
3. Charles E. Lindblom, "The Science of 'Muddling Through,'" *Public Administration Review*, Spring 1959, pp. 79–88.
4. Robert Anthony, *Planning and Control Systems* (Boston: Harvard University, 1965), pp. 18–19.
5. See "Sears Makes it Look Easy," *Fortune Magazine*, May 1964, and "Recession Spurs Sears to Cut Prices, Return to Past Sales Strategy," *The Wall Street Journal*, February 10, 1975, p. 1 and 13.
6. Jackson Martindell, *The Scientific Appraisal of Management* (New York: Harper & Row Publishers, Inc., 1962).
7. Henry M. Jackson, "To Forge a Strategy for Survival," *Public Administration Review*, Summer 1959, p. 159.
8. R. L. Ackoff, *A Concept of Corporate Planning* (New York: John Wiley & Sons, 1970), see chapter 7, "Organizing the Planning Effort."

Establishing Goals and Plans

What steps are involved in formal planning?

How can a firm evaluate its current status before setting goals?

What information needs to be obtained on future conditions?

What various methods can be used to forecast future conditions?

How should goals be established?

What types of goals should be established?

What benefits are derived from a management by objectives programs?

Ronald Whitmier, chief executive officer of a conglomerate, annually discusses the performance of each division with its president. One particular problem this year is the office-furniture division headed by Earl Farnsworth.

"Your performance was way below the other divisions," Whitmier complained. "Your return on investment was only 5 percent, which was less than half of any other unit. Even sales on the major product lines aren't holding their own. We seem to be losing ground each year. What have you come up with to improve performance in the future?"

"You saw our goals for next year," Earl replied. "We want to increase profit and sales both by 20 percent. Didn't you get a chance to review the goal statement?"

"I received the statement all right, but goals mean nothing unless you have some plans to support them. How are you going to increase sales? What are you going to do next year that you failed to do this year? Planning involves a lot more than just setting a few goals, you know."

"I realize that," Earl replied. "But these things take time. We're so busy getting the bugs out of our production processes and straightening out our sales staff that we just haven't gotten around to it."

"That's what you told me last year, Earl. But your long-range plan contained nothing more than just a few goals. Johnson Company, your largest competitor, increased their sales by 28 percent, but your increase was less than what we can account for by inflation. You've got to have some action plan. How are you going to offset their grabbing a larger piece of the market?"

"We've given some thought to that, but until we improve our current operations I don't see much reason to worry about the future. If you do a good job today, tomorrow will take care of itself."

THE GROWTH OF PLANNING

Despite the many benefits derived from planning, it remains one of the least effectively handled management functions. Almost every company pays lip service to planning, but only a minority finds the time, resources, and talent to do it effectively. Furthermore, the theoretical aspects of planning are underdeveloped. However, major improvements have been made in recent years. The 1960's are referred to as the "decade of long-range planning." This is because only a limited number of corporations had significant capability in strategic planning at the beginning of the decade, but more than 75 percent of the major American corporations demonstrated this capability ten years later.

Historically, DuPont Company established a planning department in the early 1900's, but many major corporations, like General Electric and American Telephone & Telegraph, did not create such units until the

1950's. In a study in 1956 by the National Industrial Conference Board, they reported that only 8 percent of the companies surveyed had one or more persons engaged in full-time, long-range planning. By 1963 Stanford Research Institute concluded from a study that over 50 percent of the 500 largest industrial companies in the United States had formalized corporate plans. In a 1966 survey of 420 companies, the National Planning Association found that nearly 85 percent said they prepared long-term plans.[1]

The dramatic growth in long-range planning results from several trends that were discussed in earlier chapters. Firms are growing larger, resulting in a greater need for coordination and overall integration. Also, the pace of technological change has increased to the point that there is a continual squeeze on the lead time between developing a product and placing it on the market. The entire environment of business has become more complicated and demanding; this makes strategy formulation more difficult but even more essential. It is a situation in which the typical reaction times in today's markets and environment simply do not allow for playing "catch up" by those who straggle along without plans.

STEPS IN A TOTAL PLANNING PROCESS

The elements of planning are easier to conceptualize when they are divided into seven phases. This is also beneficial, because the first five parts represent the typical sections of a long-range plan. The seven steps constituting the rational, formal approach to planning are as follows:

Step one   Determine where you stand today: Unless an organization has a firm handle on where it stands today, it is difficult to project where it wants to be in the future. Financial, market, resource, and social measures of present status serve as a baseline for future comparisons. This step also includes an evaluation of the firm's strengths and weaknesses in relation to competitors and to achieving its current goals.

Step two   Develop planning premises relating to current trends and conditions likely to exist in the future: This step involves a forecast of environmental forces and likely conditions during the period covered by the plan. Goals can only realistically be developed for a firm after consideration of probably future conditions.

Step three   Establish strategies and objectives: Following the forecast of the environment, a firm is now in a position to make decisions regarding what strategies it wants to pursue and what objectives are likely attainable, given the aspirations the owners and top management have for the organization.

Step four   Program activities to achieve objectives: One of the major weaknesses in planning is that organizations establish lofty goals, but they do not ensure their implementation by determining in detail what steps must be taken and activities pursued to achieve these ends. Programming is tedious and time consuming, but in it lies the rewards of planning.

Step five   Determine the support resources required to conduct the prescribed activity: Step five involves estimating and scheduling the labor, materials, machinery, facilities, and other resources to carry out the activity specified in step four. Sometimes steps four and five are handled simultaneously, but technically cost estimates cannot be developed until it is determined what work and processing needs to take place.

Step six   Execute the plan: The execution phase, as shown in figure 21-1, includes the implementing action to initiate activity and make resource allocations consistent with the plan.

Step seven   Evaluate performance in relation to the plan and make adjustments as necessary (control phase): Control is identified as a separate step, although some aspects of the control system are involved in every phase. Control uses planning formats, data, and objectives as a base to evaluate what takes place in the organization.

Steps one, two, and three of the planning process will be intensively reviewed in this chapter. Steps four and five relating to programming will be covered in chapters 23 and 24. Step six was included in chapter 21 and earlier chapters. Step seven, on control, will be integrated with the planning discussions in chapters 23 and 24.

Step One: Data Base on Current Operations

An organization needs an accurate assessment of how successful it currently is—including the identification of existing difficulties—before it can realistically project what improvements it desires to make and where it wants to be in the future. Information is required in four areas, plus an overall assessment of strengths and weaknesses.

STANDING IN THE MARKET.   One of the most useful indicators for a business firm is the percent of sales that it captures in a particular market. A firm might delude itself into thinking it is doing well with an 8 percent increase in annual sales, but if industry sales are increasing 12 percent, the organization is relatively losing ground. To obtain this information a firm needs total sales by product line as well as industry sales for each product line.

FINANCIAL STATUS.   The best-known measurements of performance for a business are financial ones. Annual reports provide historical data revealing trends in profit, build-up of capital, debt structure, and other important information. Probably the most common ratio to evaluate overall success is the return on investment. This percentage is found by dividing net earnings for the year (profit) by the amount of the book value of the owner's share of assets (common stockholders' equity). The status of working capital, cash flow, and backlog (undelivered orders) affect credit ratings, the willingness of firms and investors to make capital available, and management's freedom to commit the organization.

COMPARATIVE ADVANTAGE.   Some of the most important factors in evaluating a firm are the attributes of the enterprise that constitute its uniqueness and provide it strength or weakness. Basically this is an evaluation of the special capabilities or advantages a firm has in relation to competitors, or else the reverse—the advantages competitors have. Factors to evaluate are: experience in producing and marketing a product, special competence or facilities in research and development, specialized production equipment, location advantages, protective patents, and the capacity to expand.

STATUS OF HUMAN RESOURCES.   The critical role of the work force in a firm's success necessitates an evaluation of organizational manpower before undertaking strategic planning. Questions to be asked are: How does the depth and talent of our management team stack up with competitors? What are prevailing employee attitudes? What skill shortages and surpluses exist? How efficient is the work force? What is the current status of union relations? Does the firm have sufficient creativity in areas where innovation is critical?

OVERALL ASSESSMENT.   The final phase of step one is to make an overall assessment of the firm. What is the image of the firm in the eyes of the public, customers, employees, and owners? What is the current growth rate? In what areas has the firm been effective in meeting goals, and where has it been deficient? Is the firm currently gaining ground or losing it in relation to competitors? Is it achieving anticipated improvements? Only after such questions are answered is an organization ready to tackle the problem of where it wants to be in the future, and what strategies it should use for getting there.

Step Two: Developing Planning Premises

Planning premises are the assumptions made about the conditions that will exist external to the firm during the period of the long-range plan. These assumptions are important for two reasons. First, if each unit developing a portion of the plan does not use the same assumptions, the operating, functional, and resources plans will be inconsistent. One unit may assume a plentiful labor supply, while others forecast a skill shortage. Second, it is the condition of these external forces that determines the constraints and opportunities for a firm. Establishing goals without taking these dominating external circumstances into consideration is like putting on a coat without first looking outside to see if it's clear or raining. These planning premises are made available to all participants in the planning process before the development of any comprehensive or subsidiary plans.

The external forces and conditions to be forecast are the economic, political, social, and technological variables in the contingency model. The effort devoted to data collection and forecasting of these variables will naturally depend on their significance to the organization. For a business, the financial and market forecasts will be primary; a university will be concerned with financial forecasts but also political trends (especially for public institutions), demographic trends (birth rate, teenagers in high schools, etc.), and social attitudes like the prestige of a technical education. Hospitals would be concerned with economic trends, political laws (Medicare), social attitudes (care for the elderly), and technological advances in medicine and health care. A more thorough enumeration of some of the more important measures associated with each variable follows.

FORECAST OF ECONOMIC CONDITIONS.   Three types of forecasts are necessary: the macro forecast relating to total economic conditions, a market forecast covering trends in the specific industry, and a factor forecast involving the future supply and prices of resource inputs.

The macro forecast includes familiar trends, such as the gross national product (GNP), disposable personal income, and interest rates. The sales of firms in durable-goods industries (automobiles, appliances, etc.) fluctuate with the trends in GNP and disposable personal income. A buyer's willingness to make major durable-goods purchases is a function of factors such as his current income and how confident he feels about the future. There are many economic forecasts for the planner. Government economists, private institutions, banks, universities, business magazines, and newspapers make forecasts or print those made by others. The problem is not in finding a forecast, but in selecting one that will provide sufficient accuracy to meet planning needs.

The forecast of trends within an industry is more difficult to obtain than is one of trends in the total economy. The first step involves determining how national and regional economic trends will affect a firm's particular market. As noted, in durable-goods industries it is direct. For a publishing firm selling college textbooks, the relationship would not be as direct, and other factors would be important (number of students attending college, effectiveness of the used-book market, etc.). Data and occasional forecasts of a market (aerospace, computers, copy machines, and so forth) are provided by trade associations and some government agencies—primarily the United States Bureau of the Census and the Department of Commerce. Larger businesses have economists who make forecasts for major markets estimating future demand. Also, market research personnel poll consumers to find their preferences, test products in limited markets, and use other techniques to forecast demand. For each relevant market, it is beneficial to know the supply-and-demand characteristics, problems of entry and exit, and the basis for competition (product differentiation, price differentiation, service, distribution, and so forth).

Forecasts of a firm's resource inputs are almost as important as sales forecasts of its product (or service) outputs. The availability and price of inputs obviously influence the quantity and affect the price of outputs. Potential energy shortages provide special problems for firms using large energy inputs. The scarcity and price of certain metals will force firms to use substitute materials, like plastics. If a firm is considering expansion, other factors of production—such as land, capital, manpower, construction costs, and equipment—must also come into consideration. The fertilizer industry would appear to be an attractive market to enter because of unmet demand and high prices; the problem, of course, is getting access to the raw material.

THE HAZARDS OF FORECASTING

Another reason for caution is, bluntly, that the performance of most forecasters has been far from perfect, particularly in recent years when worsening inflation has distorted some key economic guideposts. A case in point is a survey of about three dozen prominent forecasters, taken in late 1973, a time of worsening inflation. The great majority predicted that the economy would continue to expand in 1974. In fact, as we painfully know, economic activity contracted sharply last year.

In view of the hazardous nature of forecasting, the wisest attitude for a forecaster may be that of Gilbert Heebner, economist of Philadelphia National Bank. In a recent "midyear out-look" report, he begins: "Economists should approach the current midyear forecast with an extra measure of humility. For it was only a year ago that the profession erred so badly in failing to predict the sharp drop that began last fall." He goes on to suggest that economists should probably provide, along with a basic forecast, supplemental information that would indicate "in which direction it is likely to err."

Quoted from "The Outlook: Review of Current Trends in Business and Finance," *The Wall Street Journal*, August 18, 1975, p. 1.

TECHNOLOGICAL FORECASTING. Chapter 12 covered the importance of technology in forcing change within an industry. High-technology industries (such as medical instrumentation and aerospace) compete as much on technology as they do on price. The firm with the most advanced product is normally the most successful. Also, in industries where automation can provide major production efficiencies, technology is a factor that executives keep a wary eye on in order to avoid a situation where a competitor gains a major advantage.

Attempting to forecast technological improvements is no easy chore. It requires keeping up on advances in basic research and on major development projects. Some forecasts are found in trade and technical journals. Typically the scientist likes to participate in technological forecasts of markets relating to the firm's product lines. The Delphi technique (to be described later) is frequently used. The difficulty in technological forecasting is not necessarily predicting the breakthroughs, but determining when they will occur and trying to stay competitive from an economic standpoint. Landing on the moon and using atomic power for peaceful purposes were predicted long before they became realities. Currently the energy crisis is dependent on predicted advances like solar energy and peaceful application of thermonuclear power. Economic desalinization of sea water and undersea farming, which hold considerable promise, are advanced in other areas.

Technological forecasting is relatively undeveloped. Its significance is indicated by the fact that major companies now derive 50 percent or more of their current sales from products developed and introduced in the past ten years.[2] However, as one expert noted, "Technological forecasting is not yet a science but an art, and is characterized today by attitudes not tools; human judgment is enhanced, not substituted for it."[3]

FORECASTS OF THE POLITICAL AND LEGAL ENVIRONMENT.   Governments and laws restrict and enhance potential markets for a firm. Antitrust laws restrict the expansion of corporate giants like General Motors and International Business Machines. Technological breakthroughs, such as the supersonic transport, are rejected because of government's unwillingness to participate in the funding. However, the government is still the largest purchaser of research and development, defense systems, and sanitation equipment—and purchases approximately 25 percent of the gross national product. Of special importance are predictions relating to future government regulatory trends and taxation, such as depletion allowances for the oil industry.

Political forecasting is of special importance to multinationals who risk the loss of major investments through nationalization. Mergers and acquisitions, frequently a strategy in long-range planning, are all subject to governmental approval. Political forecasting is primarily qualitative in nature. It involves obtaining current information and likely developments from government agencies, legislatures, public officials, pressure groups, and analysts reporting on political activities. Judgment is then used to decide on likely future conditions.

SOCIAL FORECASTS.   Evolving customs, public attitudes, and the tastes of consumers affect the demand for products and trends in industries. Trying to get the American consumer to switch from automotive to public transportation is proving difficult. On the other hand, public attitudes toward pollution have drastically altered the production processes of many organizations.

An example of the problem presented by changeable consumer tastes is provided by the European subsidiary of Levi Strauss and Company in the early 1970's. Levi, the world's largest manufacturer of pants, had never experienced a quarterly loss since the Great Depression until the fourth quarter of 1973. In 1970, sales were booming as they turned over their inventory seven times, compared to the normal four for the apparel industry. However, in 1971 European tastes for jeans underwent a surprising change. Bright colors and far-out styles, using fabrics like "hosiery" and velvet became popular. Levi's inventory consisted of straight-legged blue jeans and corduroy pants. As the company attempted to switch to this market, patch-pocket jeans became popular. By the spring of 1972, flared jeans became the rage. Just as Levi's pants were reaching full production of flared cords, the market for corduroy pants shriveled, as customers switched to denim flares. In mid-1972, 65 percent of all pants sold in Europe were corduroys; a year later the figure dropped to 15 percent. Levi was caught with a large inventory of pants that ultimately was unloaded at one-fourth the original wholesale price.

ECONOMIC CONDITIONS AND A PLANNED COMMUNITY

Jonathan, Minnesota provides an example of how external conditions can raise havoc with a company's plans. Thorough architectural and environment planning preceded the development of Jonathan, a town 25 miles from downtown Minneapolis. It was one of the first start-from-scratch towns begun under the 1968 and 1970 clauses of the Federal Housing Acts. It provided a layout of 8,000 acres with over one-fifth set aside for lakes and parks anticipating a population of 50,000 in twenty years. However, in the early 1970's the inflation, high interest rates, energy shortage, and resultant depression in the housing industry left the project by 1975 $30 million in debt with 60 townhouses and condominiums and a dozen single dwellings finished but empty.

Reprinted from *Newsweek Magazine*, February 24, 1975, p. 10.

Sales Forecasts and Forecasting Methods

The prediction of future conditions associated with environmental variables is known as *external forecasting*. Once this is completed, the firm moves to the next step of predicting how successful it will be, given these external conditions. These forecasts are known as *internal forecasting*. The primary internal forecast is the sales projection by product and price for six months, a year, or even longer.

The difference between a forecast and a plan is extremely significant. A forecast provides a prediction of what results (in this instance, sales) will be attained—*assuming management makes no changes in the way things are being done.* Planning, on the other hand, involves the use of forecasts in making decisions regarding what an organization *wants to accomplish* in the future. Forecasting is part of step two, involving planning premises, because it is a projection, developed by or for planners, which explains what will happen, given a set of conditions. If management is satisfied with the future achievements associated with this forecast, they will continue operating as at the present time. If their objectives call for results different from the forecast, they are faced with modifying operations so as to attain the different results. If the forecast projects a 15 percent return on investment but top management develops a goal of 18 percent, planning is undertaken to achieve this higher objective.

The sales forecast is one of the most critical assumptions contained as a part of planning premises, because top management and the long-range planning committee (if one exists) use this as the standard for determining whether or not current operations are satisfactory or if major changes are necessary to obtain higher results.

GENERAL FORECASTING CONCEPTS.   All forecasting techniques use historical data as the basis for making future predictions. Obviously such predictions involve uncertainty. The uncertainty varies with the time horizon of the forecast, the stability of factors related to the forecast, and the information that is available to the planner. Forecasts are based on fact and judgment. Ideally, sufficient facts will be available so that judgment will be narrowed, but most forecasting today relies heavily on the judgment of experienced managers.

FORECASTING METHODS.   Six of the methods used in forecasting should be briefly described:

Survey of Executive Opinion   This technique attempts to take advantage of the knowledge and experience of qualified managers. Based on contacts with customers, knowledge of internal operations, and experience in the industry, a manager has a reasonably valid feel for what will happen to sales in the immediate future. Using this technique, estimates are obtained from the various functional managers, who are aware of market conditions. These are then averaged—sometimes on a weighted basis—by the planner. This is the oldest and simplest method of forecasting.

STEPS IN SALES FORECASTING

The National Industrial Conference Board recommends the following steps in forecasting sales:

1. Determine purposes for which forecasts are to be used.
2. Divide company products into homogeneous groups.
3. Determine factors affecting sales of each product group and their relative importance.
4. Choose a forecasting method or methods best suited to the job.
5. Gather all available data.
6. Analyze the data.
7. Check and cross-check deductions resulting from analysis.
8. Make assumptions regarding the effect of factors that cannot be measured or forecast.

9. Convert deductions and assumptions into specific product and territorial forecasts and quotas.
10. Apply these to company operations.
11. Review performance and revise forecasts periodically.

Reprinted from *Forecasting Sales* (New York: National Industrial Conference Board, Inc., 1964). p. 8.

Delphi Technique. The Delphi technique is used primarily in technological forecasting, rather than sales forecasting, but since it represents a refinement of the survey of executive opinion, it will be included at this point. The method was developed extensively by Olaf Helmer and others at the RAND Corporation in the mid-1960s.[4] It represents a method of refining the opinions of experts in a particular technical field regarding improvements likely to occur in the future. The experts are not brought together. Opinions are obtained through questionnaires to avoid social influence. The steps in the process are as follows:

1. The questionnaire is aimed at obtaining opinion on specific technological breakthroughs or market advances (e.g., desalinization of salt water). Experts are to specifically estimate dates, developments, and/or volumes.
2. The investigator summarizes the distribution of the results indicating median, mean, and quartile ranges.
3. This information is returned to each participant, asking if he desires to modify his original estimate. Also, those providing the extreme estimates from the mean are asked to justify their original answers. These are sent to all participants.
4. A new summary is prepared and the process of determining results and asking for justifications is repeated.
5. Steps one through four will normally result in a convergence of opinion. The Delphi technique is not to provide one answer. A range is acceptable. However, if further convergence is desired the iterative process can be repeated.

   The Delphi technique is based on opinion and qualitative in nature. However, the opinions of the experts in a field are often the best single source of information.

Sales-Force Composite. This is a bottoms-up approach that involves each salesman preparing a forecast for his district using a standard form. Results are accumulated at each level in the sales organization until one composite forecast is gathered for the total company. Typically, marketing personnel or planners at central headquarters make an independent estimate to use as a comparison. Bottoms-up estimates are often not overly accurate, since salesmen are noted for their optimism. However, it serves as a valuable tool to force sales personnel and district offices to evaluate customers, sales efforts, and prospects for the future.

User's Expectation Method. Often the customers can be an important source of information on future sales. This is especially the case when a firm sells most of its output to a few industrial users. If a firm provides parts to two or three automotive manufacturers, it can rely on these customers for estimates of future needs.

Time-Series Forecasts. Time-series forecasts involve the projection of historical sales trends into the future. It is a technique that can be applied through visual extrapolation or through the use of complicated mathematical methods. Sales forecasts usually contain three trends: long-range growth, shorter-term cyclical business fluctuations, and seasonal variations. A fourth factor in time-series forecasts is irregular or random occurrences. Retail sales forecasts for a department store will show all of these factors. Seasonal sales will always peak in December with the Christmas season; sales will rise and fall with increases or decreases in gross national product; longer trends will be apparent when monthly or annual sales are plotted on a graph; and an irregular drop will occur when a major competitor opens a department store close by.

Statistical Correlation Techniques. The most common statistical technique used to forecast sales is correlation analysis. Various methods are involved. In simple correlation with two factors, one is the dependent and the other is the independent variable. In sales forecasting this involves relating sales (the dependent variable) to some other index of activity—normally of an economic nature. Simple correlations are numerous. The amount of soft drinks and beer sold will tend to vary with the temperature. Income at ski resorts will vary with the amount and condition of new snow. Synchronous series are where events occur simultaneously (GNP and car sales). More useful are leading predictors, where the series of events associated with the independent variable occurs first. This would be the case in the number of housing starts versus the demand for plumbing supplies.

Statistical correlation techniques vary from simple scatter diagrams to the multiple correlation of many variables. Figure 22-1 is a simple scatter diagram relating the sales of Mason Power and Gas Company to population trends in Mason county. The trend line can be drawn in by sight, or else it can be statistically calculated with the least-squares

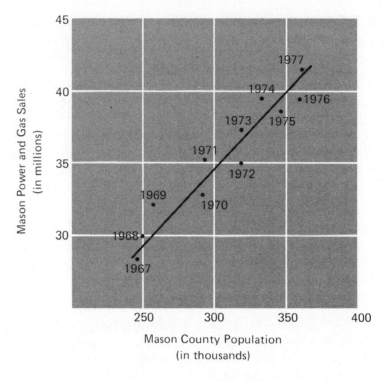

Fig. 22-1. Scatter diagram of Mason Power and Gas Co. sales and population trends in Mason County

method, a statistical technique that places the trend line where the squares of the deviations about the line are at a minimum. Multiple regression and correlation techniques relate several independent variables to the dependent variable (annual sales in this instance).

Other Forecasting Methods. In addition to the six methods enumerated, there are other techniques for forecasting sales. Computer simulation (see chapter 6) can be used. Other fairly common methods involve econometrics and mathematical programming.[5]

Step Three: Establishing Objectives and Strategy

After data is collected on the past and current status of the organization, and a forecast is made for future trends, the firm is finally in a position to establish its objectives and strategies for the planning period. These objectives should reflect the desires and aspirations of the organization as interpreted by the owners or top management, but they need to be developed in the light of what is feasible, given the conditions that are likely to exist.

The goal-setting process is an extremely important activity of organizations. It has been our contention since chapter 1 that organizations exist because people have common goals. Charles Perrow adds to this by stating, "Organizations are tools designed to achieve various goals. To understand them fully, one must understand the goals they pursue."[6] Organizations, being organic units, are continually engaged in a transformation process, but they are also continually engaged in goal-setting or goal-modification activities. Our approach here involves the more formal methods of sequentially establishing objectives and supporting strategies, but goals also become modified and superseded on an irregular, informal basis as people interact in carrying out prescribed duties.

DEFINITION OF TERMS.   To this point, a distinction has been made between *purpose* and *goal,* or *objective,* but the latter two terms have been used interchangeably. Other terms like *charter, mission, targets, quotas,* and *standards* also creep into the literature. The purpose of an organization represents the basic reasons for which it was established and the ends for which it exists. The purposes of a university are typically stated in general terms like *teaching, research,* and *public service.* The terms *charter* and *purpose* are essentially identical. *Mission* is a word used primarily in the military to represent a major program objective or one of the major thrusts of an organization.

An *objective* is a desired condition. Objectives represent general statements relating to future results or conditions an individual or organization desires to achieve. In relation to a university, an objective would be to "provide courses that are relevant to the concerns and interests of society." Targets, goals, quotas, and standards are all similar terms. They represent specific qualitative or quantitative aims that imply more exact actions or accomplishments. A goal for a university, however, might be "establishing five new courses within the next two years that would more specifically meet the general education objectives of the institution."

Figure 22-2 represents a hierarchy of organizational aims. *Purpose* is broad and general and relates to the economic, social, utilitarian, ethical, or political ends of the entire organization. Objectives are formed consistent with the purpose and represent more specifically desired results typically associated with designated time periods. *Strategies* are the methods or schemes assigned to achieve the objectives. *Goals* and *targets* relate to the operational activities required to attain the higher objectives. Goals are more concrete and short-range than objectives.

Fig. 22-2. **Hierarchy of organizational aims**

Organizational, subunit, and individual goals occur in descending sequence, because this is the order in which they should be established to ensure goal compatability.

Even though this terminology is useful, it is difficult to apply in practice, because popular usage does not include these distinctions. The popular "management by objectives" program would be more properly retitled as, "management by goals" if these definitions were sacrosanct. Fortunately, most of the concepts relating to goal setting are equally applicable to establishing objectives, so intermixing the terminology provides little distortion.

GUIDES TO ESTABLISHING GOALS.   Space will not be devoted to providing guides for developing statements of purpose and objectives. Primarily this is because they represent general statements often involving philosophy, ideals, or creeds, where personal or group interests and values predominate and "techniques" are of limited use. The major concern in purpose statements is to adequately represent what is actually intended ("providing information systems" not "fabricating computer hardware"). The more specific guides provided for goals encompass the full gamut of suggestions useful for establishing organizational aims.

Goals are usually established in relation to issues such as profitability, growth patterns, market position and penetration, market product mix, product leadership, productivity, human resource development, manager performance and development, employee attitudes, public image, and social objectives relating to the community, consumer, and environment. Eight guides apply to establishing these goals:

1. The more specific the goal, the more useful it is for management purposes.
2. Goals should be verifiable.
3. Goals should be action oriented and results centered.
4. Goals should encourage higher levels of attainment and yet be realistic.
5. Goals should highlight problem areas or areas requiring major improvement.
6. To provide a proper focus, goals should be limited in number.
7. The individual or individuals involved in accomplishing the goals should be involved in their establishment.
8. Goals should provide balance and integration in the organization.

1. *Making Goals Specific.* The most common weakness in goal setting is to state goals in general terms that actually are little more than platitudes. "Motherhood, flag, and country" statements may be acceptable at the objectives level, but they are self-defeating when they constitute goals. If goal statements are so general that they can be switched between similar organizations or individuals and no one can tell the difference, they obviously do not provide the direction and specificity required. Lower-level goal setting and programming cannot effectively be undertaken unless higher goals provide direction or imply specific actions. In some instances, vagueness is desired when information is lacking or conditions are uncertain, but these are merely concessions made to meet an unfavorable situation. In other instances, goals may be general to permit an individual to be innovative in developing his own role, but this again involves unusual circumstances. The freedom should be more in letting the individual set his own goals rather than in letting him establish fuzzy ones. Flexibility is required, but, in general the tendency toward vagueness means that the emphasis *must* be on specifics.

2. *Making Goals Verifiable.* If progress cannot be measured against goals, they lose their value from a control standpoint. A goal "to increase profits" is verifiable in a general sense, but increasing profits by 5 percent or 50 percent will both meet the goal. If it is set to "increase profits 10 percent," progress is measurable, it implies specific action to those involved, and variance analysis between performance and the goal becomes meaningful. Where time constraints are appropriate, they should also be stated. A more complete goal statement would be "to increase profits by 10 percent during the next fiscal year."

It often requires considerable mental exercise, but most goals, even those involving service functions, can be stated in quantitative terms that normally make them verifiable. As examples, plant morale can be related to figures on absenteeism and a service center can attempt to reduce the number of complaints per month from fifty to twenty-five. The one danger in attempting to make all goals quantitative is that qualitative goals relating to "how well" things are going will tend to be left out. However, care in establishing goals can avoid this. Several examples of improper versus properly stated goals are indicated below:

Poor Examples of Goals	Improved Goal Statements
improve product quality	reduce quality rejects to two percent
improve communications	hold weekly staff meetings and initiate a newsletter to improve communications
improve social responsibility	hire fifty hard-core unemployed each year
issue monthly accounting reports on a more timely basis	issue monthly accounting reports so they are received three days following the close of the accounting period

3. *Action-Oriented and Results-Centered Goals.* Goals should focus on results, not activity. Goals are supposed to achieve certain conditions (results) in the future. Activity is the means by which goals are accomplished, but more activity does not necessarily result in more favorable results. An improper goal based on activity would be "to issue ten new procedures each month." It is not the number of procedures but the result obtained from procedures that is important. A better goal would be "to obtain improved coordination in the procurement function by issuing appropriate procedures." Goals should be action oriented also. If a goal does not imply required action, it is not fulfilling its motivational purpose.

4. *High Performance, yet Realistic Goals.* No organization or individual functions perfectly, so improvement goals are always appropriate. In fact, developing and maintaining an "improvement orientation" is one of the primary advantages of goals. Some individuals have argued that goals should be set extremely high, forcing individuals to stretch way beyond their expectations. Some "reach" is desired, but as indicated in chapter 11, on motivation, if a person feels he cannot accomplish something, he will normally not put out the effort to try. The reinforcement concept also argues that people are more stimulated by success than failure.

5. *Highlighting Problems and Areas of Required Improvement.* In a sense, goal setting follows the exception principle. If three aspects of an organization's functioning are proceeding equal to or higher than expectations, and one area is hampering the entire organization because of low performance, goals should concentrate on the latter area. The areas going according to plan should not be ignored, but management should concentrate its efforts on bringing the lagging one up to standard. Sometimes it is desirable to rank order goals from most to least important. However, the interrelated nature of organizational activity often makes this unrealistic. Which should be given highest priority, production or quality control? Classes in marketing or classes in economics?

6. *Limit the Number of Goals.*   If goals are to provide a focus, they should be limited in number. One of the most common weaknesses in goal setting is to inundate the organization and individuals with goals that tend to confuse because they encompass so many different activities. One organization had a long-range plan with general company goals that numbered over five hundred. Lengthy goal statements are like lengthy reports—they will rarely be read or remembered. Rules-of-thumb are always necessarily violated because of numerous exceptions, but it is generally advisable to restrict each organizational unit to fifteen goals or less, and in personal goal setting, six or less are appropriate.

7. *Participation in Goal Setting.*   To make goals realistic and to obtain appropriate commitment, it is necessary to have the persons involved in implementing the goals participate in their formation. It is easy to reject a goal as unfair and unwarranted unless the individual provides input, especially if the goal covers activities in which that person is the most knowledgeable.

8. *Providing Balance and Integration.*   Since goal setting is an iterative process, starting at the top of the organization and moving downward, the goals of top management should be balanced by touching on each major function or activity. This provides a guide for establishing goals relating to the functions at the next lower level. This integrated framework will also tie together the aspirations and activities of the entire organization, and it will ensure consistency. Linking goals in this organizational way also identifies responsibility for their accomplishment.

KEEPING GOALS CURRENT.   Once goals are established, the next problem is keeping them contemporary, because new opportunities, unanticipated events, and other changes will occur that make further adherence to them undesirable. This can be done formally and informally. It is generally recommended that goal statements be reviewed quarterly and modified where appropriate. Also, when required, individuals should obtain approval to deviate from them or apprise others of reasons why a different course of action is being pursued.

STRATEGY IN SUPPORT OF OBJECTIVES. Numerous examples of strategy have been given in previous chapters. However, as a means of implementing objectives, one more example is appropriate. If an objective for a company is "to increase sales by 10 percent during the coming year," a problem is now presented in how this will be attained, given the conditions in the marketplace and the likely actions of competitors. Alternatives are to lower prices, increase advertising, add to the sales force, introduce a new product line, move into new territories, and other similar actions.

Deciding which strategy to pursue is dependent on many factors, relating to existing market conditions and assumptions about the actions of competitors. Will reducing prices cause a similar response from competitors and a price war in which nobody wins? Is advertising near the saturation point where declining marginal gains can be expected? Are current customers being ignored because of the lack of salesmen to make contacts? What costs and problems are involved in opening up new territories? Can present products be improved in sufficient time? Selecting the appropriate strategies is supported by some factual information, but it is also highly judgmental. It involves making assumptions about the trends in the marketplace, the action of competitors, and the firm's capacity to deliver. It is basically an evaluation of the risks management is willing to undertake.

"FILLING THE GAP" IN PLANNING. Some of the most important strategy decisions relate to deciding what should be done to "fill the gap" between the forecast for existing products as compared to the total growth in sales and profit contained in the objectives. Figure 22-3 shows these relationships. Current forecasts of products A, B, and C are plotted for a five-year period. The corporate goal of increasing sales 8 percent each year is shown as the cumulative top line on the graph. This leaves a gap between current forecasts and corporate objectives that needs to be given special attention in the planning process. Strategies include methods to increase the sales of current products, introduction of new products, acquisitions, and other such alternatives.

Contingency Plans

Since planning involves uncertainty and dealing with uncontrollable variables, deviations from plans will always exist. When these devia-

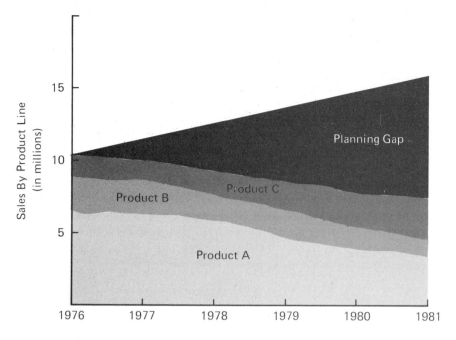

Fig. 22-3. Projected sales and planning gap for Acme Corporation

tions are such that the original plan is no longer workable, alternative plans must be pursued. Accordingly, contingency planning, well developed in the military, is now becoming popular. In planning an invasion, military strategists do not wait until they see what happens if the operations do not go as planned. Alternative courses of action are developed that can be immediately implemented if unanticipated difficulties are encountered or if greater advance is made because of weak enemy resistance. If a firm's accepted strategy is to increase sales by reducing prices assuming competitors will not reduce theirs, a contingency plan should be included as part of the strategy based on what will be done if competitors follow suit.

One of the frequent problems with budgets, plans, and appropriation requests to legislatures is that they give decision makers basically three choices: to accept the plan, reject it, or modify it. Actually, only one plan or alternative is involved. The decision-making methodology presented in chapter 5 emphasized that decision makers should evaluate a series of appropriate alternatives and select the one that is most desirable.

RESPONSIBILITY FOR PLANNING

A flowchart showing the sequencing of planning steps and the responsibilities of the planning staff, top management, and operating departments is shown in figure 22-4. Basically, it is the responsibility of the

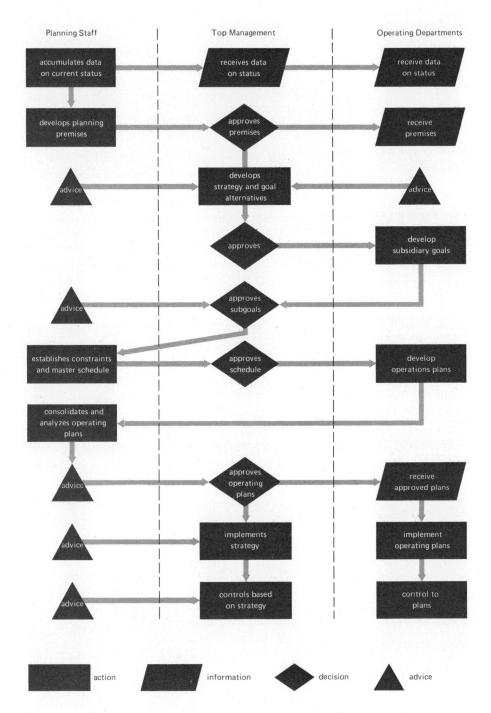

Planning Staff	Top Management	Operating Departments

accumulates data on current status → receives data on status → receive data on status

develops planning premises → approves premises → receive premises

advice → develops strategy and goal alternatives ← advice

approves → develop subsidiary goals

advice → approves subgoals ←

establishes constraints and master schedule → approves schedule → develop operations plans

consolidates and analyzes operating plans

advice → approves operating plans → receive approved plans

advice → implements strategy → implement operating plans

advice → controls based on strategy → control to plans

■ action   ▰ information   ◆ decision   ▲ advice

Fig. 22-4.   Planning cycle: sequencing and responsibilities

planning staff to develop the planning premises, advise top management on strategy and planning, accumulate and prepare analyses of division, functional, and resource plans, and assist the operating departments in the preparation of estimates. Top management makes all of the primary decisions, develops strategy and objectives, and implements the plans. The operating departments develop subsidiary goals and plans to carry out the broader company objectives and strategy.

MANAGEMENT BY OBJECTIVES

One of the management techniques that has received much publicity and broad adoption in the past fifteen years is management by objectives (MBO). MBO advocates usually look to Peter Drucker and his classic *The Practice of Management*[7], written in 1954, as being the start of this movement. Drucker emphasized the significance of goals and goal setting in the management of organizations. Writers like George Odiorne[8] and Edward Schleh[9] popularized the movement in the early 1960's. It is reasonable to assume that by 1970 every major American corporation had at least considered it as a method for improving productivity and as a system for managing.

MBO provides little that is new in organizational goal setting. Generally, proponents state that goal setting should start at the top and work down through the organization—as we have advocated. The innovative feature of MBO is that the individual sets goals in relation to his job. Often planning is not very effective because top management establishes plans, but the operations level, where the primary work tasks are performed, is never clearly aware of the plans and does not participate in developing them. MBO prevents a company's planning from being sterile by directly relating it to individual effort.

Use of MBO

One of the primary advantages of MBO is that it is a flexible system that can be used with an entire organization, a subunit, or only one subordinate. It is generally desirable to use it as a total management system involving the entire organization. However, MBO provides few advantages when current production measures are quantitative and easy to obtain, and where people are locked in to repetitive, mechanical tasks. However, MBO is a breakthrough in dealing with service-type activities, supervision, and professional positions where productivity standards either do not exist or are vague and unreliable. It provides a special boon to government agencies and higher education, where measures are lacking and professionals tend to dominate.

Management Concepts Involved in MBO

Management by objectives is a process by which the members of a work unit individually meet with their supervisor to establish performance-related goals. Each member, with the assistance and guidance of his supervisor, defines his area of responsibility, evaluates the current handling of these duties, sets objectives for improved results, develops a plan of action to achieve the objectives, implements this action plan, and periodically holds performance reviews.

In this mode, MBO takes advantage of many of the primary concepts of management. The primacy of planning and the value of objectives in motivation are foremost. However, concepts such as participative management, an open environment to encourage creativity and improve communication, and using self-evaluation to increase feelings of responsibility are inherent elements of the system.

An Example of MBO

MBO is like other management systems: there is no universal approach that can be adopted by all organizations. Each organization should specifically design a system to meet its particular needs and methods of operation. In the example provided below,[10] it is assumed that tasks are relatively ill-defined, and there is a low degree of task interdependence among coworkers, such as one might find in governmental or professional organizations.

In this abbreviated example, there are four stages in the MBO process, each involving a minimum of one meeting between the supervisor and subordinate (although more are likely required). The manager sets the stage for these sessions by thoroughly explaining what the program entails and emphasizing that it is to be of benefit to both the individual and the organization. Through a better-defined job, the employee gains an improved means of performance evaluation and more success in his work. The organization gains by a more satisfied worker, generally higher productivity, and improved planning and control. The four series of sessions proceed as follows.

PHASE ONE: DEFINING THE JOB.   The person is asked to define his or her job in two or three pages and rank order tasks on the basis of those that are most important and least important. The supervisor will independently do the same (so they don't influence each other). At the second session, the job descriptions, as defined by each party, are compared. If there are major discrepancies (there is normally 25 percent difference), this explains part of the misunderstanding that exists between the subordinate and supervisor. Different priority rankings obviously indicate different perceptions regarding how the job should be handled. Through joint discussion, this gap should be narrowed so that misunderstanding is reduced.

PHASE TWO: EVALUATING THE JOB. During this phase, both the subordinate and supervisor—again independently—indicate the aspects of the job that are going favorably and those needing improvement. This can be done by rank ordering the three strong points and three major problems associated with the job. In the follow-up session, the two evaluations are compared. The supervisor has the opportunity for praising the individual for things that are going well. In relation to problem areas, if the individual identifies significant problems, the supervisor does not need to make him defensive through criticism but can merely raise the question of where do we go from here in attacking the problems as outlined? This phase tends to be extremely informative to both parties, because frequently the strengths and weaknesses are perceived differently.

PHASE THREE: SETTING OBJECTIVES. Once the two parties agree on aspects of the job where improvements can be made, each develops suggestions concerning what goals should be set and action plans implemented. This encompasses determining what performance standards can be established for each of the major duties outlined in phase one. This is the point where the supervisor must assume his supportive role in asking, "What can I do to assist you in reaching these goals?" An important principle of MBO is that the program is not a one-way street in terms of commitment. The organization must also frequently make commitments involving resources for training, better machinery, establishing improved relations with other organizations, tolerating trial-and-error experimentation, and other such activities.

PHASE FOUR: IMPLEMENTING THE PROGRAM. Once the goals are agreed upon and support resources are obtained, frequent sessions should be held between the supervisor and subordinate to evaluate what is taking place and to make any necessary changes. Where adequate feedback is provided, MBO programs tend to be successful, but with little feedback, the system generally fails. Another caution is that like other management systems, supervisors are often impatient and scrap MBO before it has had time to prove effective. Frequently, it takes as long as two years for the system to function as intended.

Advantages of MBO

Where the system is appropriately adopted and properly implemented, MBO results in improved productivity because:

- The goal-setting process improves motivation.
- The role and tasks of the worker are clarified.
- Communication is more open and directed at the fundamentals of task performance.
- Peformance appraisal is improved because it is based on results, not traits or vague impressions.
- MBO develops an "improvement climate" and dissatisfaction with the status quo.
- Planning and coordination are improved.
- Better control standards exist, with more emphasis placed on self-control.
- Improved supervisor-subordinate relations result because of enhanced understanding and greater freedom for the individual.
- MBO contributes to personal development and to the commitment of the individual to organizational goals.

From the above it can be seen why MBO is considered a total management philosophy, not just a goal-setting process as part of the planning function.

Limitations of MBO

MBO is not an easy system to use. The complexity is often underestimated, especially the behavioral considerations. Organizations tend to rush into it without adequate preparation or understanding. It also has the same limitations as other planning systems. If goals are rigidly adhered to so that new opportunities are passed up, and if flexibility is not built into the system, it can hurt the organization. Also, the tendency is to set goals only on activities that are easily measurable. If the only purpose is to get more production out of the worker, it can also be scuttled in a wave of resentment. A final death knell is when over-enthusiastic promoters bury it in a flood of paper work and red tape. Simplified management systems are always preferable if they will do the job.[11]

SUMMARY

Seven steps are involved in planning: determining where you stand today; establishing premises for the future; determining strategies and objectives; establishing a program to achieve the objectives; determining the resources necessary to conduct the activity required; executing the established plan; and controlling operations to achieve the plan.

Step one, determining where you stand today, includes collecting data on market standing, financial status, special capabilities (such as human resource skills), and an assessment of the firm in relation to its competitors.

Step two, developing planning premises, involves a forecast of future economic, political, social, and technological conditions. It also necessitates a forecast of the firm's sales using techniques, such as surveying executive opinion, sales force composite, users' expectations, time series, and statistical correlation.

Step three, on goal setting, is an involved process that occurs at all organizational levels. Guides to establishing goals are designed to make them specific, verifiable, results centered, realistic, directly related to problem areas, and limited in number. They should be established using principles of participative management, and they should provide balance and integration in the organization.

Management by objectives (MBO) has become widely used in both public and private organizations. MBO is unique because it involves personal goal setting by the individual. These goals are established in conjunction with the supervisor, and if properly adopted, the system can result in improved motivation, communication, performance appraisal, planning, control, and supervisor-subordinate relations.

QUESTIONS FOR STUDY AND DISCUSSION

1. Why are the 1960's considered as the decade of long-range planning?
2. Why is the establishment of strategy and objectives not considered the first step in planning?
3. Explain some criteria that might be used by the following organizations to determine "where they stand today":
   A. Football team   C. Health maintenance organization
   B. University   D. Department store
4. How would the planning premises for the four organizations listed in question 3 vary?
5. Could Levi Strauss have prevented the near disaster it experienced with its European subsidiary in the early 1970's?
6. Are the same methods used in external and internal forecasting?
7. What is the difference between forecasting and planning? Give an example of each.
8. Why are forecasts other than statistical techniques used?
9. How can the organizations listed in question 3 forecast future sales or levels of activity?
10. Differentiate between the purpose, objectives, and goals of the organizations listed in question 3.
11. Using the guides for goals presented in this chapter, give three properly stated goals for each of the organizations in question 3.

12. Write five goals that relate to your activities during college or your job for the coming year. How can performance in relation to these goals be measured?

13. What management concepts are involved in management by objectives? What are the advantages and limitations of this approach?

Case Study:
CARLSON MANUFACTURING COMPANY

The Carlson manufacturing company is a family owned corporation that was formed in 1960 to produce off-road "track" vehicles. The company sells them to the U.S. Forest Service, telephone companies, ski resorts, oil companies, and other customers where they are used in their operations during the winter. The company has experienced a steady growth in sales until the last few years, when they have tended to level off. A summary of their net sales and profit history over the past six years is as follows:

Year	Sales	Profit
1970	$22,000,000	$2,100,000
1971	28,200,000	2,900,000
1972	32,500,000	3,300,000
1973	34,200,000	3,200,000
1974	34,500,000	3,250,000
1975	34,400,000	3,100,000
1976	34,300,000	3,050,000

They are the second largest producer of this type of vehicle in the country. They originally captured 40 percent of the market, but last year their position slipped to only capturing 34 percent.

Currently they have 540 employees. Their employees are all located in a company-owned plant that is used to capacity during the summer months when they build up their inventory for heavy sales in the fall. During the winter months when sales drop off, their employment decreases to approximately 300.

The owners are becoming concerned about the future of the company. They feel that something needs to be done to offset their deteriorating position. However, any major changes the company might consider would be difficult because they have limited funds for capital expansion.

The company has had little planning other than the traditional production planning. You have recently been hired by them to be in charge of long-range planning.

How would you determine where Carlson Manufacturing "stands today"?
How would you establish planning premises regarding the environment and market of the firm in the future?
What are some specific goals you would recommend be contained in a long-range plan to improve their position? (Write four or five primary goals.)
How would you go about forecasting sales for the firm?
To ensure that the goals will be carried out, indicate briefly how you would implement each one (in terms of derivitive or subsidiary plans or other follow-up action).

Case Study:
GOAL SETTING IN THE
PERSONNEL DIVISION

Fine Style Printing Company is one of the largest printers of business forms in the United States. They have eight plants located throughout the country and print business forms of every kind, based on orders received from customers. Typical orders involve thousands of copies of insurance reports, purchase orders, bank checks, and application forms.

The Washburn plant is located on the Northeastern sea coast. There are 600 employees engaged in all aspects of taking orders and printing the business forms. The printing portion of the plant works on a three-shift basis. The order-taking department and all of the work units involved in developing the formats and costing out the services work only one shift. In the plant, there are three individuals employed in the personnel department. They handle all of the recruitment, training, evaluation, employee relations, and union relations. The printers, constituting one-fourth of the employees, is the only unit unionized. The personnel department also administers the fringe-benefit program. Training tends to be a major problem, because essentially all employees are hired unskilled and then trained for their particular jobs. Turnover is 8 percent annually.

The manager of the personnel department is concerned about one of his employees, Gary Jensen. Gary has been working in personnel for two years where he was promoted from the photography department. Gary has been slow to adjust to the new position. Because of the limited staff, each member of the department participates in all of the personnel functions, although Gary's main job has been screening applicants for employment. He has been fairly successful in finding competent people, but the Director of Personnel feels that he is slow and not very aggressive. Positions have often stayed open for as long as six weeks because Gary didn't line up sufficient qualified applicants. His supervisor also feels that Gary is slow in picking up the details of the union contract and handling union relations. When the supervisor confronted him with this during his annual evaluation, Gary responded that he did not know he was expected to do that. The supervisor also feels that Gary has not done an adequate job in coordinating training programs. Too often training is entirely on the job, even when six or eight new employees are being trained in essentially the same work.

If you were the supervisor, how would you handle the situation with Gary?

How could a management by objectives program be incorporated?

What goals should be set for the personnel department?

What personal goals can be established for Gary? (List four goals for him. Also list what implementing actions will be undertaken to see that the goals are accomplished.)

By what process should Gary's goals be established? (What role should the supervisor have in establishing these goals?)

Footnotes

1. George Steiner, *Top Management Planning* (New York: The Macmillan Company, 1969), pp. 15–16.
2. *Management of New Products,* 4th ed. (New York: Booz, Allen and Hamilton, Inc., 1964), p. 6.
3. E. Jantsch, *Technological Forecasting in Perspective* (Paris: Organization for Economic Cooperation and Development, 1967), p. 15.
4. See A. R. Fusfeld and R. N. Foster, "The Delphi Technique: Survey and Comment," *Business Horizons,* June 1971, 14, pp. 63–74.
5. A useful explanation of forecasting techniques is found in Steven C. Wheelwright and Sypros Makridakis, *Forecasting Methods for Management* (New York: John Wiley & Sons, 1973). A contingency approach to the utilization of the various techniques is found on pages 198–201.
6. Charles Perrow, *Organizational Analysis: A Sociological View* (Belmont, Calif: Wadsworth Publishing Company, Inc., 1970), p. 180.
7. Peter F. Drucker, *The Practice of Management* (New York: Harper & Row, 1954).
8. George Odiorne, *Management by Objectives* (New York: Pitman Publishing Corporation, 1965).

9. Edward Schleh, *Management by Results* (New York: McGraw-Hill Book Company, 1961).

10. This example is based on an article the author wrote entitled "Management by Objectives: Making It Work," *Chemical Engineering*, October 28, 1974. pp. 124, 126, 128.

11. For further information on MBO, see Stephen J. Carroll, Jr. and Henry L. Tosi, Jr., *Management by Objectives, Applications and Research* (New York: The Macmillan Company, 1973).

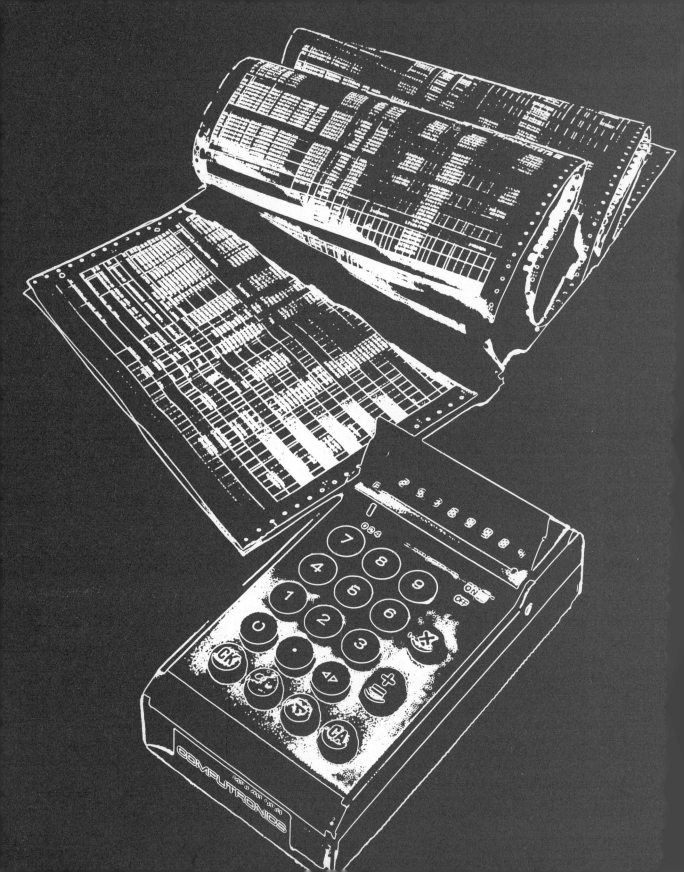

Budgeting and Reporting Systems

Why is budgeting one of the most essential
management functions?

What is the difference between fixed and variable
budgets?

What are some of the human problems in
budgeting?

What management concepts are involved in the
planning-programming-budgeting system (PPBS)?

What variables need to be considered in
management reporting?

What contingency concepts are involved in
management reporting?

BUDGETING AS A MANAGEMENT TOOL

One of the most important tools of management is the budget. It is the most widely used system for planning, coordinating, and controlling operations in organizations. A company can exist without formalized plans, but essentially all organizations require methods for allocating and using available resources. The unfortunate circumstance found all too often in organizations is that accounting and financial considerations dominate the budget process when managerial requirements should be primary. Since budgeting tends to be handled by individuals with an accounting or financial background, budget formats and methodologies reflect this orientation, rather than management's.

Organizational units and activities depend on resources for their level of functioning. Organizations have the opportunity to grow or flourish when backed by resources, but reducing resources results in retrenchment. The budget is the valve that management uses to let resources flow to functions or programs, depending on which ones they want to expand or restrict. No other tool is as effective in expressing the will of management. Resources represent power in organizations. With resources an organization can obtain the input it requires to perform its operations; without adequate resources, plans are not implemented and half-way efforts restrict effectiveness. It has long been recognized that those who control the purse strings of an organization wield considerable, if not omnipotent, power.

Budgeting in Business as Opposed to Public Institutions

In some respects budgeting is more vital to public than to business organizations. The only source of income for most government agencies is appropriated funds. Since the entire input to an agency comes through the appropriation process, the amount of this and its internal allocation through the budget process is a "life or death" proposition for subunits and activity centers. For this reason, budgeting in government agencies is given top priority in the management process.

The inputs of a business firm on the other hand, are regulated more by the revenue it receives for its outputs. Generating more sales or improving internal efficiency affects the amount available to purchase resource inputs. In a business firm the budget process is only one phase or aspect of an integrated system involved in obtaining, allocating, and consuming resources. However, even here programs and organizations are dependent on resources for their existence, so it behooves every supervisor to seek to acquire budgets consistent with the role and future expectations of the organization.

Definition of Budgeting

A budget is a plan expressed in quantitative (normally financial) terms. Organizations are not allocated resources arbitrarily. They are provided resources to carry on specific operations to achieve predetermined purposes or goals. These purposes, goals, and operations represent the plans of the organization. Plans are the *ends,* or dominating element, of budgets, and resources are the *means.* This is one of the primary reasons why budgeting is considered a management tool and not a financial technique. It is also the key criterion for evaluating a budget. If the budget represents resource allocation based on very little planning, it is an indication that the organization is perpetuating current operations, rather than steering resources into activities that are consistent with the changing needs and aspirations of the organization.

Following the guides presented in the last chapter, plans of both a strategic and operational nature should be developed. These plans will obviously be established within the constraint of the anticipated resources of the organization. Once plans are developed, resources can then be assigned to organizations. When the organizations start to use the resources, the control phase of budgeting is initiated, wherein activity is monitored and adjusted to see that the plans are accomplished.

The Significance of Budgeting

In summary, budgets comprise one of the primary arms of management for the following reasons:

- They constitute a uniform plan that encompasses the entire organization. They are established to correlate all effort and resource utilization.

- Budgets provide a comprehensive basis for integrating and comparing all operations since they are expressed in a common denominator—dollars. Activities conducted by different organizations are normally not comparable (number of radios assembled by production versus the number of invoices processed by accounting). Converting resources to dollars makes universal comparisons possible.

- For a business firm, the budget system is established to measure and emphasize the primary objective of the organization—profit. For all organizations, budgeting emphasizes one of management's foremost concerns—efficiency, and it helps channel capital into the most profitable endeavors.

- Budgeting involves resource allocation, which is one of the most significant responsibilities of management.

- Many of the most critical decisions that management makes are tied to the budget process. Decisions, such as adding facilities and capital equipment, starting new product lines, the magnitude of research and development, funds for advertising, the size of pay increases, and other resource-associated decisions, are normally consummated as part of the budgeting cycle.

- Meeting budgets represents efficiency and is rewarded as part of performance evaluation. Thus budgets affect motivation and are significant in the appraisal process, both for individuals and organizations.

As central as budgeting is to the management process, it is frequently downplayed in management literature, primarily because it is erroneously considered as a financial function. The significance of budgeting makes the reporting of cost information and budget comparisons a vital aspect of accounting and finance. However, this is essentially a reporting function, as compared to the planning and control implications that are managerial in nature.

Organizing for Budget

The organization for budgeting should be essentially identical to that for planning. In fact, in figure 22-4 the term *budgeting staff* could be substituted for *planning staff* with little distortion. Budgeting is a planning and control responsibility that rests with top management and line organizations. Budget personnel accumulate data for budgeting, develop budgeting premises, advise top management and line supervisors on budgeting, set up the budget cycle, consolidate and analyze estimates, and issue budget-status reports. However, they are not supposed to approve programs or make resource-allocation decisions in their capacity as staff representatives.

The other guides relating to organizing for planning are also appropriate for budgeting. It is often desirable to have a budget committee (chaired by the president) to make the budget decisions. This ensures the broad participation that is essential in this total organizational function. It also gives each major function a say in the vital decisions that are made. The budgeting staff is usually attached to the controller or accounting function, but there are valid reasons—especially in companies with complex technological operations—to establish the central budget staff as a subdivision of the planning organization (or as a part of program management if this type of departmentation is used).

Prerequisites of Budgeting

There are two prerequisites of a sound budgeting system. One is an effective accounting and reporting system; the other is a clear, relevant organization structure. Obviously the reporting system must contain cost categories that are meaningful, based on the organization's operations, if the reporting of results is to be useful for control purposes. Also, because budgeting is implemented through the organizational hierarchy, if the structure is ill-defined and fuzzy, the budget allocations will be imprecise, and accountability will be difficult.

TYPES OF BUDGETS

Budgets are established to support each of the plans contained in figure 21-4. The sales forecast, or strategic plan, is normally the basis for establishing subsidiary budgets. The sales forecast provides the ceiling for the development of lower-level budgets. In addition to the summary budgets (equivalent of summary plans), three types of budgets are typically established: organization, resource (cost element), and program (or product). These three types of budgets are shown in the three-dimensional cube contained in figure 23-1. The hypothetical example is of the U.S. Forest Service and is simplified for illustration purposes. Table 23-1 shows an organization budget by cost element and program, with an organizational summary.

Organization Budgets

To be effective as a control system, budgets should cover organizational units or cost centers where the responsibility for work can be identified. Thus each organization (or grouping or subdivision of units if cost centers are used) has a budget that provides resource limits for that organization —either for periods of time or as related to specific products or programs. These budgets are subdivided on the basis of resources, called *cost elements* in accounting and budgeting terminology. Standard cost elements are direct labor, direct materials, components, travel, tooling, the variable portion of factory overhead, and other controllable costs. For information purposes, the budget will also often contain certain costs that tend to be fixed and therefore not directly controllable, such as depreciation on buildings, insurance, property taxes, and business licenses.

Resource Budgets

Labor, materials, purchasing, and other resource budgets are developed summarizing the total manpower, materials, components, and other resource requirements contained in the operational plans. The organization and cost-element budgets thus comprise a two-dimensional matrix in which costs can be summarized in either direction. A key resource budget is the summary financial budget, showing total revenue and expenses. Cash budgets are also established based on disbursements and cash receipts.

Table 23-1. Types of Budgets for Grandview National Forest office (cost in thousands)

Organizational Budget by Cost Element

salaried labor	$1,325
temporary labor	200
indirect labor costs	175
materials	1,500
equipment	150
communications	30
travel	40
office supplies	20
total	$3,440

Organization Budget by Program

recreation	$540
camp ground maintenance	400
range management	700
fire fighting	600
timber management	200
roads and trails	1,000
total	$3,440

Organizational Summary

District A	$800
District B	900
District C	740
District D	1,000
total	$3,440

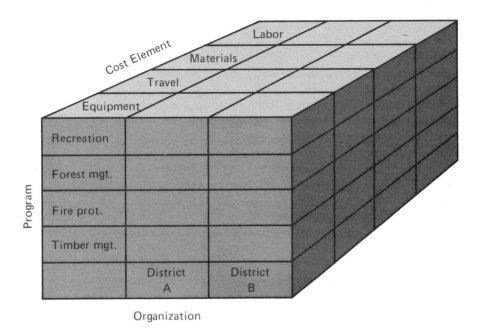

Fig. 23-1. Three types of budgets: organization, resource, and program

Program or Product Budgets

Until recent years, almost all government budgets were by organization, with costs subdivided into cost elements. The limitation of this approach is that a rational basis does not exist for increasing or decreasing budgets. An organization is provided either greater or fewer resources, but the basis for making this allocation is often vague. What services or programs is a legislator funding when he votes to increase an agency's budget by 15 percent? If a legislator approves more manpower and equipment for an agency—without specifically knowing what benefits will occur in terms of the agencies objectives and programs—it is obviously not a results-oriented process. If an organization has only one activity and provides only one function, then budgeting on an organizational basis is acceptable, but since most agencies provide a variety of services or products, the budget should be tied to the specific results of each program area.

Following the budget reform movements in the 1940's and 1950's, government agencies have turned to *program budgets*. Under a program budget, the focus is on budgeting programs, rather than organizations.

A *program* is a grouping of activities necessary to accomplish a major objective. As shown in table 23-1, budgeting by organization involves setting a budget for each district in the National Forest. Budgeting by program involves allocating funds for recreation, campground maintenance, range management, and so on, based on results to be obtained by engaging in these activities. Manufacturing organizations budget by product. A product budget for such an organization would include 100,000 manhours for fabricating desks, 25,000 for chairs, and 10,000 for typewriter stands, each of which constitutes a product line and marketing goal of the organization.

Even though program budgets have been widely acclaimed in administrative reform movements, their adoption has been rather slow. Medium and small businesses, as well as state and local governments (including colleges), typically struggle along without full-fledged program budgets. In some instances, because of the simplicity of the operations, an organization can get by without budgeting based on the major functions it performs. Generally such budgets are avoided because they considerably complicate the budget process. Rather than two dimensions (organization unit and cost element), it now becomes tridimensional.

If each program, product, or major activity is separately budgeted for each subunit, it means that many more estimates must be developed and cost categories established. If an engineering organization is doing design work on fifty different products or projects, several hundred cost codes will be involved when the costs are recorded by each subunit, cost element, and project. However, to maximize the rationality of decision making involved in budgeting, resource allocations should be based on goals, desired results, and the activities required to achieve these ends—rather than merely financing an organization.

Fixed and Flexible Budgets

Using budget methodologies as a basis for classification, there are two different types of budgets: *fixed* and *flexible*. Program, organization, and resource budgets are based on the *content* of the budget rather than *methodologies*. A flexible (or variable) budget automatically adjusts to different levels of activity or production and is normally not specifically related to any period of time. A fixed budget is not automatically adjusted if different levels of activity are experienced.

Fixed budgets are normally associated with specific time periods and are also called "forecast," "appropriation," and "managed" budgets. They are called *forecast* budgets, because estimates are forecast for time periods (such as months during a year), and actual costs or sales are compared against this forecast. This represents a fixed-budget situation, because the budget does not adjust as different levels of activity are experienced.

Government budgets are typically fixed. Appropriations constitute a fixed sum, normally on an annual basis. If a welfare department receives an annual appropriation of $1.5 million dollars, and a recession occurs doubling the number of individuals on welfare, the budget does not automatically adjust to this higher level of activity. Generally the legislature would have to pass a supplemental appropriation for more funds to be made available.

Managed budgets of a fixed nature are annual allocations for research and development or for advertising. If management makes the decision to spend $4 million dollars for advertising during the next fiscal year, this is a fixed sum available for this purpose, which is not subject to automatic revision based on the level of activity during the coming year. It is adjusted only at the discretion of management.

Flexible budgets, when they can be used, are preferable to fixed because they are more realistic. They will increase or decrease as activity goes up or down. If an individual plans to buy three quarts of milk but purchases only one, the expenditure will be one-third the amount originally anticipated. If the budget is fixed, high temporary savings are shown, but these savings are deceptive, because only one-third of the amount originally planned was received.

A common type of flexible budget is a *standard cost* or an *engineering standard.* In repetitive production situations, where costs become known through long experience or through measurement by an industrial engineer, these predetermined costs are used as the basis for recording costs. Actual costs are then compared with these standards to determine if operations are using the resources expected or are "performing according to standard." Standards represent "should be" costs, and when actual costs deviate, it normally indicates high or low performance.

An example of a standard-cost budget is the assembly of a radio. If industrial engineers using time-and-motion studies and historical costs substantiate that twenty minutes should be required to assemble a radio, this serves as the standard. If a worker assembles three radios in an hour, he is performing according to the standard. However, if it takes him an average of twenty-five minutes to complete an assembly, then he is higher than the standard and considered a slow worker.

With flexible budgets, the budget is set on a unit basis for a single product. If nine radios are assembled, the labor budget is three hours, but if only six are assembled, then the budget is two hours. The budget adjusts to this lower activity level. Assuming a condition where the plan was to assemble thirty radios with a budget of ten hours, and the plan was changed so that only twenty-four radios were assembled, the flexible budget would be eight hours. If the actual time for assembly was eight hours, a *fixed budget* would show an underrun (deviation from budget) of two hours (ten budgeted versus eight actual). The *flexible budget* would show no budget variance (eight budgeted and eight actual). Flexible budgets are called *earned budgets,* because the budget earned is based on the units completed (twenty-four units completed at twenty minutes per unit is an earned budget of eight hours).

Another example of the use of a flexible budget is in a foundry. If management anticipates that the foundry will operate at 75 percent capacity during the coming year, but business could drop to as low as 65 percent or as high as 90 percent, then estimates are prepared for all three levels. When actual experience shows that the foundry operated at 82 percent, the budget is adjusted to that level, based on the relative differences in the three estimates provided. Thus, again the budget is adjusted to the level of activity.

BUDGET VARIANCES.   One of the primary purposes of budgets is to evaluate efficiency. Under a standard-cost system, if the actual costs are lower than the standard, it indicates that the worker or work unit is efficient. If the actual hours or costs are higher, then it typically signifies a problem that needs supervisory attention. (Such budgets are widely used in the automotive industry and other industries involving continuous production.)

The advantages of a flexible over a fixed budget are apparent in variance analysis. Table 23-2 reflects this advantage. The example of radios is again used, with 20 minutes required to assemble a radio. In the month of March it was intended to assemble 9000 radios. A fixed budget based on this plan would amount to 3000 manhours at 20 minutes per assembly. However, during the month 8439 radios were assembled rather than the 9000 planned. Actual manhours to assemble these radios were 2813, leaving a budget variance of 187 hours less than the fixed budget. At first glance it would appear that the assembly operation was very efficient, because 187 fewer manhours were required than budgeted. However, since fewer units were assembled, the variable budget more properly reports the situation. The variable budget is 2813, so there is no budget deviation—and the group is producing according to standard.

In April, the plan remained at 9000 units, but only 8700 were produced (table 23-2). Under the fixed budget, the variance is 200 manhours, reflecting an efficient work group. However, this efficiency is overstated, because 100 of these 200 hours result from there being 300 fewer units assembled than originally planned. The variable budget again more properly represents the situation by showing that the 100-hour underrun is entirely attributable to efficiency.

The May figure is even a better example of the deceptiveness of a fixed budget. There were 10,500 units planned with an actual result of 10,200 units. At 20 minutes per unit, the fixed budget is 3500. Actual hours are 3450, showing a favorable underrun of 50 hours. However, the situation is not favorable considering that 300 fewer units than anticipated were assembled. Actually the situation is unfavorable, because the earned (variable) budget is 3400, and actual hours are 3450 or an overrun of 50 hours.

The desirability of flexible budgets is demonstrated by evaluating the causes of budget variances. Basically there are three: a change in plans (if a fixed budget is used), a poor estimate (inaccurate standard), or efficiency (inefficient if not able to produce to standard, efficient at standard or less). Flexible budgets eliminate the first cause of variance, a change in plans, because they adjust to the actual level of activity. The problem in variance analysis is that when accurate production counts are not available (which is representative of most work in organizations), it is difficult to determine what portion of the budget variance represents a change in plans or operating levels and what represents efficiency.

Table 23-2. Comparison of Budget Variances for Assembling Radios*

	March	April	May
Planned assembly of radios (units)	9000	9000	10,500
Actual units assembled	8439	8700	10,200
Fixed budget (hours)	3000	3000	3500
Actual hours	2813	2800	3450
Variance	−187	−200	−50
Flexible budget (hours)	2813	2900	3400
Actual hours	2813	2800	3450
Variance	-0-	−100	+50

*Based on a standard budget of 20 minutes to assemble one radio

CONTINGENCY CONSIDERATIONS IN BUDGET TYPES. One would wonder why fixed budgets are ever used, based on the advantages of flexible ones. It is, of course, because accurate production counts and standard costs are not available on all of the work done in organizations. Routine, repetitive production is common in manufacturing organizations, but it is unusual in service organizations, staff work, governmental operations, research and development, marketing functions, and other similar areas. Even in manufacturing, it is unusual when over 60 percent of the personnel are working under standards. Also where fixed sums are available, such as government appropriations, the level of activity is restricted to the fixed budget. Business organizations also need to make time-oriented forecasts like sales, profit, and cash projections. Accordingly, the type of budget system an organization uses is contingent on the nature of its tasks (primarily in terms of repetition), the availability of standards, the certainty of its environment (frequent change makes adjusting standards difficult), the organization climate relating to the acceptability of standards, and other such factors.

PROBLEMS IN BUDGETING

Budgets and Rigidity

One of the major problems associated with budgeting (similar to most planning and control systems) is that once an organization is set up and operating, it tends to perpetuate current operations or maintain the status quo. Ongoing operations are automatically funded with little question. However, since the increase in funds available through incoming revenue or appropriations is often little more than inflation (5 to 10 percent a year), there is a tendency to redistribute the budget the same as the previous year, by spreading the increase on this same percentage basis to all organizations and programs. There are two problems with this approach: it protects current programs that should be reduced or eliminated, and it makes it difficult to introduce deserving new programs or enlarge those that should be expanded. Such rigidity discourages innovation, and it robs an organization of the flexibility that is often necessary to adjust to its environment.

To overcome this problem, several techniques are used. These are known by such terms as "zero-base budgeting" or "90-percent base budgeting." The assumption behind zero-base budgets is that no permanent budget base should be accepted for an organization, but it should justify all of its programs and activities for the coming year or budget period. The 90-percent base assumes that 90 percent of last year's base is protected, but the organization must justify (on a competitive basis with proposed new programs) 10 percent of last year's base and any new increases for the upcoming budget period. Such budget techniques are especially appropriate for staff organizations, support groups, and service functions, where the contribution of each unit is difficult to evaluate because easily measurable results are not available. As the changing environment of organizations increases the pressure for adaptation, budget techniques of this sort will become more common.

Human Problems in Budgeting

It is inevitable that human problems will arise as part of the budget process. With any system of measurement and evaluation, some individuals will perform well and "look good," while others will not meet the standards or goals and be considered "failures." Budgeting is especially amenable to such problems, because the stakes are extremely high. Also, organizational reward and punishment systems are closely tied to the budget.

This has several implications for those who administer the budget process. Extreme care should be taken to ensure that the system is as equitable as possible and that individuals responsible for budgets be involved in developing them. Again, participation is a key to minimizing human problems. If supervisors and participants in the budget process feel it is *their* system and for *their* benefit, they will be inclined to cooperate and make it effective. However, if they view it as the "budget director's system" and something imposed upon them from an external source, that is not for their benefit, they will reluctantly participate and often effectively undermine it.

Budgets are sometimes perceived as unnecessary restraints—and budget analysts as individuals who attempt to reduce costs regardless of the consequences. When such attitudes develop, it is indeed unfortunate, because budgeting should be perceived by supervisors as one of the most useful, positive tools for managing and attaining organizational goals. Many of the guides provided in earlier chapters therefore become appropriate: budgeting should receive the support and involvement of top management; budgets and standards should be developed by those who are responsible for their implementation; care should be taken to not reward short-run budget performance at the expense of long-range goals; and the support personnel in charge of budgeting should play a low-key role consistent with that of staff functions.

A question that arises in budgeting, as with other control systems, is how much pressure to apply in attempting to gain conformance to budgets? Applying pressure conveys the expectations of management, and it will motivate some individuals who work better under these conditions. However, too much pressure can create anxiety, strife, resentment, and defensiveness. As noted in chapter 11 (see figure 11-2), defensiveness can result in a variety of behaviors like aggression, withdrawal, scapegoating, and apathy. It often also tends to consolidate informal groups against management, since individuals under attack feel more protected in a group. It is dangerous for management to turn budgets into "whipping posts," because this will tend to scuttle the entire budget system from the lack of ground-level support.

A final problem with budgets is "game playing." In developing budget estimates, supervisors will want to protect their share of the total budget, and if they feel it is management's practice to automatically cut estimates by 10 percent, they will provide a 10 percent padding. On the other hand, if management feels that estimates always contain this padding, they are inclined to reduce them to something realistic. Coping with this problem is almost universal in budgeting, and it is usually minimized only by basing estimates and decisions on information and facts rather than hunches.

PLANNING-PROGRAMMING-BUDGETING SYSTEM

One of the most important developments in the management of public institutions occurred in the 1960's, when the federal government adopted an approach known as planning-programming-budgeting system (PPBS). This system was initiated in 1961 in the Department of Defense when Robert McNamara became Secretary and brought with him a staff of economists and operations research-oriented professionals, such as Charles J. Hitch, Alain Enthoven, and K. Wayne Smith. Due to the success of the system in the Department of Defense, it was adopted on a national basis by the federal government in August 1965, when President Johnson instructed all agencies to use the program. Since then it has been introduced on a broad basis in state, county, and local governments also.

Antecedents of PPBS

PPBS is a system aimed at improving policymaking and management in public institutions through more effective planning, budgeting, and decision making. Sometimes PPBS is misinterpreted as being the same as program budgeting. However, budgeting is only one process of the several constituting this integrated approach to policy formulation and management. There is actually little new in the individual concepts of PPBS; it is the packaging of the concepts into a total system that has caught the attention of public officials and management analysts.

The roots of PPBS go back sixty years to Frederick Taylor and his emphasis in scientific decision making. Following the scientific-management movement, General Motors introduced planning and budgeting systems based on programs and objectives in 1915, and the War Production Board used such a system in 1942. However, the blossoming of the concept is associated with the development of operations research and systems theory following World War II. Increased impetus was also provided by the Hoover Commission studies of the federal government in 1949 and 1955. These studies emphasized the many shortcomings in current federal planning and budgeting and urged the adoption of performance or program budgets.

Federal Planning and Budgeting Before PPBS

To appreciate the changes associated with PPBS, it is necessary to consider the conditions that existed previously. Prior to 1960, agency planning was sporadic and lacking in uniformity. Financial systems were set up to hold public officials accountable—primarily in terms of checking on their honesty—rather than as an aid in management or decision making. Budgets were developed by organizations based on input or resources. Major program goals and objectives often were not identified, and then only in the written verbage to support budget requests. The budget covered a three-year period. The first year always involved historical costs, and by the time Congress acted on the agency budgets, two years were already historical. With the budget now representing only a one-year forecast, Congress was adopting multiyear programs by funding and analyzing the tip of the iceberg. Because uniform budget codes based on programs or major activities were not used by all agencies, it was difficult to make trade-offs between funding requests or to determine the cost of programs that cut across agency lines. Budgeting clearly tended to predominate, with prerequisite planning nonexistent or secondary. As former Deputy Secretary of Defense Roswell Gilpatric stated:

> In the past, the Defense Department has often developed its force structure by starting with a budget and sending it off in search of a program. Our new system of program packaging has reversed this procedure, by first determining our overall strategy, then fitting the hardware and manpower to these objectives.[1]

Changes Introduced by PPBS

PPBS was established to make the following improvements in the federal planning, budgeting, and decision-making processes:

- Planning was to become primary, with budgets a fallout of the planning process.
- Setting objectives and establishing plans based on the major missions and programs of the agency became the first step in the PPBS program.
- The time horizon for planning was extended for five years beyond the budget, or through the total life cycle of a program if it exceeded five years (such as the Apollo program to place a man on the moon).

- Common program categories were to be established so that total appropriations for a function of government, such as education, could be accumulated across agencies. (The Office of Education has only one-fifth of the total federal education budget.) The government-wide program structure should predominate—with agency considerations of secondary importance.

- Budgeting was to be on a program basis. The major line items were agency output or programs (activities related to major objectives) rather than input or resources (manpower, materials, equipment, and so on).

- Plans and budgets were to be established giving consideration to the alternatives available to achieve an objective. This contrasts with only one alternative being proposed that is scaled either up or down (funding a major hydroelectric power project).

- More sophisticated decision-making tools were emphasized for evaluating alternatives, such as the costs and benefits associated with each. (What are the relative costs of each weapon and how effective is each in destroying an enemy's industrial capacity?) Also used were investment techniques such as discounting future benefit streams associated with capital improvements, and operations research simulation and modeling concepts.

- Based on systems theory, the emphasis was now on making decisions in as broad a context as possible so that narrow, suboptimal decisions can be avoided. All pertinent costs were to be considered, including future-year implications and trade-offs encompassing social as well as economic costs.

As can be seen, PPBS includes many of the management concepts emphasized in this text. The primacy of planning is essential. Budgets are merely a phase of planning and are designed to emphasize program outputs as they relate to resource input. A comprehensive management information system is required to obtain data necessary for evaluating performance over time and for making comparisons between programs and agencies. Also, enlightened decision-making techniques like those considered in chapters 5 through 7 are necessary. Adoption of these planning, budgeting, management information system, and decision-making concepts represents a major step forward in government administration.

Implementing PPBS

In the decade since former President Johnson's executive order requiring PPBS, progress has been slow in achieving the results anticipated. In a sense, long-range planning is not consistent with a democratic form of government, and it is idealistic to assume that governmentwide trade-offs can be conducted in an institution as complex and confusing as the federal government. In the political arena, characterized by frequent shifting of public opinion, by strong pressure groups, and where major elections change the political structure at least every two years, it is obvious that short-run contingencies will often predominate over long-run plans developed by career public officials or political predecessors. However, PPBS has performed a major service by providing more usable, broad-based information to the decision makers and influence components of public policy—and by providing a more rational basis for what is obviously a disruptive administrative process.

MANAGEMENT INFORMATION SYSTEMS (MIS)

One of the vital components of the planning and control processes of an organization is the management information system (MIS). Obviously organizations cannot function without information. Obtaining this information through observation of operations, interaction with others, and standard accounting statements is adequate in an organization of only a few people; but, as organizations grow in size, formalized means of apprising managers are required. The managers of each major function like marketing, production, and engineering need specific information related to their operations. Management information systems are designed to meet the broader needs of upper management and thus involve the compilation and integration of summary data from functional or subsidiary systems. However, MIS is not simply a summation of specialized information input but, is designed to provide information so managers can make effective decisions—which means they should be designed from the top down, based on the particular information input required.

Definition and Scope of MIS

The Management Information Systems Committee of the Financial Executives Institute defines MIS as follows:

> MIS is a system designed to provide selected decision-oriented information needed by management to plan, control, and evaluate the activities of the corporation. It is designed within a framework that emphasizes profit planning, performance planning, and control at all levels. It contemplates the ultimate integration of required business information subsystems, both financial and nonfinancial, within the company.[2]

Accurate, timely information contributes to making good decisions, which is in turn essential to sound management. The basic problem is designing systems that will meet the decision needs of managers. In designing MIS, questions like the following have to be asked:

What major decisions does the manager make?

How and when are these decisions made?

What historical data is needed as a basis for making these decisions?

What major trade-offs are involved in selecting from among the likely alternatives associated with the decision?

What ramifications will the decisions have on factors internal and external to the organization?

What major uncontrollable variables are associated with the situation relating to the decision, and how will their status influence the results achieved?

In effect, MIS should be designed to provide information inputs based on a management model such as the contingency approach we have used in this text. Once information of this sort is gathered, a system can be developed to aid managers in the decision process. The problem with most systems is that they are not rooted in the realities of management, because this process is not followed. Functional reports filter up from the bottom, rather than management's planning, control, and decision-making needs dictating the design.

MIS and Planning

It will be recalled from chapter 22 that the first step in planning involves "determining where you stand today." This includes obtaining information on a firm's market standing, its financial status, the condition of its human resources, and overall assessments relating to growth rates, strengths and weaknesses in relation to competitors, and other such data. The MIS should provide all of this information to management as a basis for initiating the planning cycle and making day-to-day decisions. Step two involves making a forecast of the future conditions likely to affect the firm. MIS should provide comparisons of actual conditions, as they occur, versus these forecasts. Methods should also be provided for updating estimates when necessary. MIS reports an organization's progress in relation to its goals and budgets. In fact, probably the primary purpose of MIS is to provide input for planning and to report progress against plans once they are established.

MIS and Control

In one sense MIS can be considered as a control function, since the first phase of control is to measure performance against the plan or standard.

The MIS is set up to help managers make decisions, but following the implementation of the decision, the system should also provide feedback so managers can be aware of what transpires. If the outcomes are not as anticipated, then adjustments should be made. As large as organizations are today, control is virtually impossible without a computerized MIS. The entire control function is dependent on the timeliness, accuracy, and relevance of the feedback from such a system.

QUESTIONS FOR MANAGERS RELATING TO INFORMATION

Where do I get my information and how?

Can I make greater use of my contacts to get information?

Can other people do some of my scanning for me?

In what areas is my knowledge weakest, and how can I get others to provide me with the information I need?

Do I have powerful enough mental models of those things I must understand within the organization and in its environment?

What information do I disseminate in my organization?

Do I keep too much information to myself because dissemination of it is time-consuming or inconvenient?

How can I get more information to others so they can make better decisions?

Do I balance information collecting with action taking?

Do I tend to act before information is in?

Or do I wait so long for all the information that opportunities pass me by and I become a bottleneck in my organization?

Reprinted from Henry Mintzberg, "The Manager's Job: Folklore and Fact," *Harvard Business Review,* July–August 1975, p. 58.

MIS and Decision Making

Contingency theory warns that the information needs of each type of manager are different. There are no universal decision variables and universal MIS that will be appropriate for all managers. For illustrative purposes in this chapter and for use in providing detailed examples of programming in chapter 24, the example of decision variables in a manufacturing organization will be used. Even though universal variables are lacking, the ones used in this example are indicative of those that are dominant in most business firms, so with few exceptions these are appropriate.

In making decisions relating to manufacturing goods or providing services, there are four major areas of top management concern that typically involve trade-offs for the decision maker. These are the *cost* of the product (or service), the *time* required to provide it, the *quantity* to be provided, and the *quality* of the end item. These four factors, reflected in figure 23-2, are more simply stated as cost, schedule, quantity, and performance (or quality) variables. If managers have a system that provides information on these four variables, they normally have the information they need to make product-oriented decisions. (These are also some of the primary concerns of other organizations. A university is concerned with its costs, number of students, time required to train students, and the quality of the graduates in terms of skills and training.)

MIS tends to be structured around these variables. One of the most significant points for the design of MIS is that decisions typically involve trade-offs relating to these variables, and therefore MIS should be designed to assist the manager in evaluating these trade-offs. For instance, if a firm is behind schedule, it can use overtime to catch up. (The trade-off is higher labor costs for getting the product out faster.) If a firm wants to reduce costs, it can use cheaper materials or simplify the product, which is usually trading-off quality for lower costs. If fixed costs are a major portion of total costs, increasing quantity can reduce average unit costs. There is also an obvious relationship between quantity and cost, as well as between quantity and the schedule.

A college can find many of the same trade-offs in its decisions. It can reduce the length of a semester and reduce costs, but the trade-off is in the quality of education provided. Costs also can be reduced by bringing in less-qualified instructors, but this will affect quality too. The quantity of students in each class can be increased, but this will also normally be detrimental to quality.

The problem with most current information systems is that the manager receives information on each of these four variables separately. He receives a cost report from the controller, a production report from manufacturing, and a quality control report from yet another organization. The manager is left the job of performing the analysis necessary to integrate this information in the form he needs for decision making. An MIS is not a single summation of middle-management reports covering each function, program, or resource area. It should reflect the perspective of top management in integrating functions and processes and in evaluating decision alternatives. In the next chapter, formats will be provided showing how these four variables can be interrelated. Our concern at this

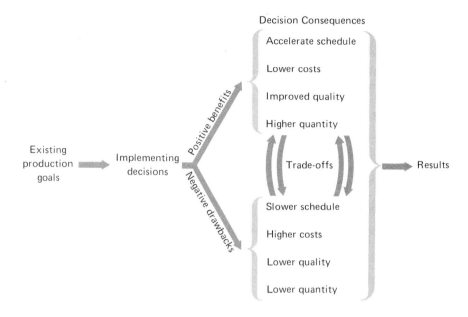

Fig. 23-2. Decision variables for manufacturing organizations, indicating the trade-offs involved

point is recognizing that a manager overseeing the production of goods or services needs to concentrate on the quantity, quality, cost, and scheduling of this output. It is also to recognize that a MIS is not a mere aggregation of information derived from lower-level units or programs.

Other Characteristics of MIS

In addition to providing information relevant in decision making, MIS should be designed as follows:

- Information should be provided promptly—especially in dynamic situations. Late information received after a decision is to be made is little better than no information.
- The data provided should be reliable. Inconsistent information will cause the manager to look elsewhere for his input.
- Common formats and a common data base should be used where possible so that short and long-range plans and all related reports will be similar. Managers will be more inclined to use MIS if they are familiar with the formats and do not have to study each one to gain understanding.

- Information overload should be avoided. This is one of the common weaknesses of existing systems. The objective should be only to provide the manager the information he needs. Reports should be kept as simple as possible. Generally, what is required is not more information, but improved methods for presenting and evaluating it.

- A successful system should be flexible and adaptive to change. This is one of the perpetual problems with MIS. Continuity and structure are important in providing consistent data, so flexibility always requires some negative trade-offs.

- The information provided and formats used should be determined by management. Dominance by data processing or financial personnel should be avoided.

Problems and Contingency Considerations

Even though MIS has been proclaimed as one of the new wonder tools of the manager, in many respects results have been discouraging. One analyst observes, "No tool has ever aroused so much hope at its creation as MIS, and no tool has proved so disappointing in use."[3] It again results from underestimating the complexity of management. As we have noted throughout this book, many variables are involved in managing an organization, and the significance and intensity of these tend to differ with organizations and situations. Also, upper-management decision making is involved with opinions, values, social influence systems, and unstructured situations—all of which are difficult to measure, quantify, and evaluate. However, some progress is being made in these areas, so MIS should gradually become more useful and appropriate.

Other contingency considerations are reflected in the nature of the information available at different levels within the organization and the type of information required to make decisions at these different levels. These information requirements vary, depending on whether they relate to short-range planning, annual operating plans, or strategic plans. The relationships shown in figure 23-3 are from an analysis developed by G. Anthony Gorry and Michael S. Scott Morton. Their three headings (operational control, management control, and strategic planning) are essentially the same as the three types of plans (operational or short-range, annual operating, and strategic) presented in chapter 21 and included in table 21-1. Gorry and Morton note that operational control is based on information that is largely internal, narrow in scope, detailed, historical, highly current, accurate, and in frequent use. Longer-range strategic planning is based on external information that is broad in scope, future oriented, not as current, low in accuracy, and infrequently required. This is consistent with many of the generalizations made in table

Characteristics of Information	Operational Control	Management Control	Strategic Planning
Source	Largely internal →→→→		External
Scope	Well defined, narrow →→→		Very wide
Level of aggregation	Detailed →→→→→		Aggregate
Time horizon	Historical →→→→		Future
Currency	Highly current →→→		Quite old
Required accuracy	High →→→→→		Low
Frequency of use	Very frequent →→→		Infrequent

Source: G. Anthony Gorry and Michael S. Scott Morton, "A Framework
          For Management Information Systems," *Sloan Management Review,* Fall, 1971, p. 58.

Fig. 23-3.   Information requirements by decision category

21-1 and again confirms that management systems must be designed to meet the needs of managers, at different levels, who are faced with making different types of decisions.

SUMMARY

Budgets are plans expressed in quantitative, usually financial, terms. Budgeting involves resource allocation, which is one of the primary responsibilities of management. Those who control resource allocation wield power in an organization. Budgets are of three basic types: organizational, resource, and program. Organizational budgets constitute the plans and resources of each organization unit. Resource budgets are summaries of total resources by type (manpower, raw materials, components, etc.). Program or product budgets are the plans and resources related to a major objective, such as manufacturing a product or conducting an activity (constructing a highway or improving health services).

There are two different methods of budgeting. Flexible budgets automatically adjust to different levels of activity, and fixed budgets remain stationary unless management changes them. Fixed budgets are used:

in organizations with nonstructured operations, when fixed sums are available, such as in governments, and in forecasting sales, cash requirements, etc.

PPBS (planning-programming-budgeting system) has been widely adopted in governments since 1965. It is a system emphasizing long-range planning, program budgeting, a uniform information system, and decision techniques like cost-benefit analysis of alternatives and analytical methods emphasizing modeling and quantitative analysis.

Management information systems (MIS) are an integral part of the planning and control functions of organizations. They are designed to provide managers feedback on the status of an organization's operations so that planning can be conducted and the implementation of plans monitored. MIS should be developed to aid managers in decision making. Because of the many variables involved, the development of viable systems has been slower than anticipated following the computer revolution in information services.

QUESTIONS FOR STUDY AND DISCUSSION

1. How does budgeting relate to resource allocation? To the distribution of power in an organization?
2. Why does the significance of budgeting differ in private and public institutions?
3. How should a company organize to handle the budgeting process?
4. What are the basic types of budgets that exist in organizations?
5. Calculate what the budget variances would be if fixed or flexible budgets were used in the following example: The company has an established standard cost of $200.00 to fabricate a typewriter. They planned to manufacture 1000 in April, but as a result of shifts in product lines they manufactured 1100. Actual costs were $210,000.
6. In question 5, how would you explain the difference between the two variances?
7. What is a zero-base budget? A 90-percent base budget? When is each used?
8. What human problems are experienced in budgeting? How do people respond to the pressures to conform to budgets?
9. Why has PPBS become so popular? What management concepts are involved in PPBS? Why has progress been slow?
10. How does MIS relate to planning? Control? Decision making?
11. What contingency considerations are involved in designing information systems?
12. What are the trade-offs if a company:

    A. Decides to have a product that will out-perform any product available on the market?

B. Substitutes plastic for metal parts?

C. Cuts back research and development expenditures?

Case Study:
BUDGETING IN HIGHER EDUCATION

The Board of Regents of higher education in a state system had been dissatisfied with the budgeting, reporting, and management systems used by member institutions. As a result, three years ago a major study was conducted, and more modern methods were adopted. The budgeting system was changed from one based on allocating resources by departments to one budgeting specific academic programs. The budget process was much more detailed, with estimates developed for each departmental activity. Participation was also broadened, in that each department prepared its own budget requests. Historical data on number of classes, student-credit hours taught, cost per student-credit hour, and student-faculty ratios were also developed. However, the data to meet the requirements of the new system was several times greater than previous budget submissions. Monthly reports also tripled in length because of the numerous cost codes.

After a budget session, two department heads were discussing the situation. "I really don't see where this new system has made much change except in the amount of time required from department heads," one observed. "We put all of that effort into budget preparation and collecting data on faculty and students, but I don't see that the results are much different. The State Legislature still increases our appropriation annually about 8 percent, and the president and his assistants take the easy way out by spreading it back across the colleges on the same basis. The results would have been the same one way or the other."

"Yes, I'm afraid you're right," the other professor replied. "They want all of this information, but what good is information unless it is used? If they would take last year's figure and mark it up by 20 percent to provide the necessary fudge factor, it surely would have saved a lot of time. These fancy systems may work in industry, but I don't think we need them at a university."

Are the two professors right?

What advantages are there to program budgets in higher education?

Can flexible budgets be used in any aspects of higher education?

On what basis should the central administration of a university allocate funds to colleges and departments?

Case Incident:
COMPETITION IN SKI ACCESSORIES

Snowline Ski Equipment Inc. has been producing ski bindings since the mid 1960's. They developed a type of step-in binding that immediately became popular, and within five years the company grew to sales of over $5 million. Just five years ago, their engineers came up with a type of car ski rack that has a locking feature, making it theft proof. This product also immediately swept the market, and within three years Snowline sold 60 percent of all ski racks in the United States.

Two years ago a larger ski manufacturer that specializes in skis and poles came out with a ski rack similar to Snowline's, although it did not violate any of their patents. The competitive rack had essentially the same features, but it was priced 5 percent cheaper. The first year in operation, they captured 28 percent of the market and Snowline's sales dropped by 12 percent. Snowline the next year reduced their price 5 percent assuming that this would return them to their previous market leadership. However, Snowline's sales again went down by 5 percent and their competitor's went up by a like amount.

This year Snowline is attempting to determine what other changes to make. They have thought of introducing some design changes to reduce the price, improving the quality through replacing some of the aluminum with stainless steel, achieving economies through mass producing them on even a larger basis, and other changes of this sort.

What information does management need to make the planning decisions on the ski rack?
How can this information be obtained?
What trade-offs are involved in the alternatives under consideration?
What other alternatives would you consider?
How does budgeting relate to this decision? What type of budgets should be used in manufacturing ski racks?

Footnotes

1. Roswell Gilpatrick, "Defense—How Much Will It Cost?" *California Management Review*, Winter 1962, p. 53.
2. Robert W. Holmes, "Twelve Areas to Investigate for Better MIS," *Financial Executive*, July 1970, p. 24.
3. William M. Zani, "Blueprint for MIS," *Harvard Business Review*, Nov.–Dec. 1970, p. 95.

Planning and Control: Programming and Contingencies

What steps need to be undertaken to ensure that goals are accomplished?

What techniques are available for programming operations?

How can a manager select appropriate programming techniques?

What financial measures are used for control purposes?

How is control over quality achieved?

What contingency considerations are involved in selecting and using the different methods for planning and controlling?

A group of scientists and engineers started a small research and development company in aerospace. Within a few years it grew to annual sales of over $40 million, derived primarily from government contracts. On many of the contracts, the firm was experiencing cost overruns and was behind on completion dates. The president felt the company lacked adequate controls, so he decided to hire several outsiders from another industry where "modern control processes" were used. Accordingly, he employed some cost analysts and industrial engineers from the automotive industry because of its reputation for tight control systems.

After the new employees had been with the firm for six months, two of the company's original design engineers were discussing the situation:

"Was that a laugh! Those industrial engineers went around using a stopwatch on the people in our model shop. Why, we never have any reason to build two models identically the same. I'd like to see what standard they come up with. How can they develop a standard when there isn't any repetition? They act like designing a new prototype is assembling an automobile. I've never seen anything so comical."

"What's even worse," the second engineer replied, "is that they wanted to develop a new budget system based on standard costs. They came around asking about the standard man-hours to complete the design of a nozzle, and I told them it's never the same. If we were going to use the same design on each nozzle we developed, we wouldn't have to repeat the design process. They wanted to know how we arrived at estimates when we bid on proposals, and I showed them our task breakdown using a milestone chart.* They'd never used one before. Talk about a duck out of water! They just don't understand why all of those control techniques used in an automotive plant won't work in research operations!"

"They're learning, though. I saw one of them carrying around a book on network planning and the critical-path method.* Give them a little time and they'll come around to how we plan and control in this industry."

PROGRAMMING CONCEPTS

In chapter 22, the third step of planning was identified as programming to achieve strategies and objectives, and the fourth step was determining the support resources required to conduct the prescribed activity. This chapter is devoted to exploring these programming concepts, analyzing certain complementary control methods, and relating contingency theory to the selection of planning and control methods.

---

*To be explained in this chapter.

Definition of Programming

Programming involves the specific determination of the tasks required to accomplish established goals, the time intervals associated with these tasks, and the resources necessary to carry them out. Programming comprises some of the most significant and difficult steps in planning. Goals are all too often not achieved because the detailed programming necessary to plan and schedule the implementing effort is never accomplished. Goal setting can be achieved with a minimum of effort, but programming requires a major commitment of time and resources to detail the operations necessary to attain desired results.

Steps in Programming

Programming does not begin until strategies and objectives have been established (step three in the planning progress). Programming lays out the specific steps involved in accomplishing these objectives. Programming encompasses determining the following:

1. *The nature and sequencing of tasks and operations to be performed.* If the goal is to open a district office in San Francisco, the first step is to determine the sequence of tasks and activities that are necessary to accomplish this plan. In which part of the city will the office be located? How will it be staffed? How will operations be transferred? Who will conduct the training?

2. *The scheduling or the timing of the tasks and operations.* Programming is often considered to be the same as scheduling, but estimating the timing associated with tasks and operations is only one phase of it. In the relocation of a district office, the schedule involves the time to find an office, arrange for personnel transfers, provide for training, and set up all other activities involved in the move.

3. *The resources (manpower, materials, facilities, etc.) necessary to accomplish the outlined tasks.* When standard methods and costs exist for performing known tasks, programming is relatively straightforward. However, when the tasks, time, and resource requirements involve new projects and nonrepetitive actions, programming is difficult and uncertain. Accordingly, different programming techniques are used in each of these situations. In the example of office relocation, the costs of the new space, moving employees, training, startup, equipment, and other requirements will need to be estimated. These are all "one-time" estimates where standard costs are not available.

PROGRAMMING FOR NONREPETITIVE OPERATIONS

The first set of programming techniques to be explored are those associated with nonrepetitive action. These are often referred to as one-of-a-kind, or single-use, projects. A contractor building bridges will most likely find each bridge a different problem, but a contractor building a subdivision of five hundred identical houses will find the tasks highly repetitive after the first few are constructed. There is some repetition in all organizational tasks, but organizations are also constantly changing as they adapt to an evolving environment. A professor will teach classes from year to year, but the students and subject matter are constantly changing. Employees in a job shop will perform the same operations, but the sequencing, timing, and resources will change with each special order received from customers. This is to be contrasted with repetitive operations where employees on an assembly line consecutively put together 10,000 typewriters of the same model.

Programming techniques for nonrepetitive action involve Gantt charts, milestone charts, IMPACT charts, and network approaches like PERT (Program Evaluation and Review Technique). Each of these will briefly be explained and evaluated. The evaluation will be primarily on how adequately each covers the quantity, quality, cost, and timing variaables (see chapter 23) essential in operations management. The sequence in which the charting methods are presented represents the evolution from simple to more complex techniques.

Gantt Charts

H. L. Gantt, one of the pioneers in management, developed the Gantt chart in approximately 1910. Since then it has been the most widely used planning and control technique in nonrepetitive operations. It has been the cornerstone of planning in the aerospace industry and is a favorite planning tool in construction, machine shops, and intermittent production. In recent years, it has been superseded in some instances by network planning and other methods, but it is still in wide use, especially in relatively nontechnical operations.

A typical Gantt chart is shown in figure 24-1. It is two dimensional, with time on the top scale and the series of operations involved in the activity or program listed on the vertical axis. In figure 24-1, the sequence of operations necessary to develop and produce a new product are shown. In this instance the example is hydraulic stools. The firm contemplates developing a hydraulic mechanism for use in raising and lowering seating such as found in dentist's chairs, draftsmen's stools, and secretarial chairs. By stepping on a lever located at the base of the stool,

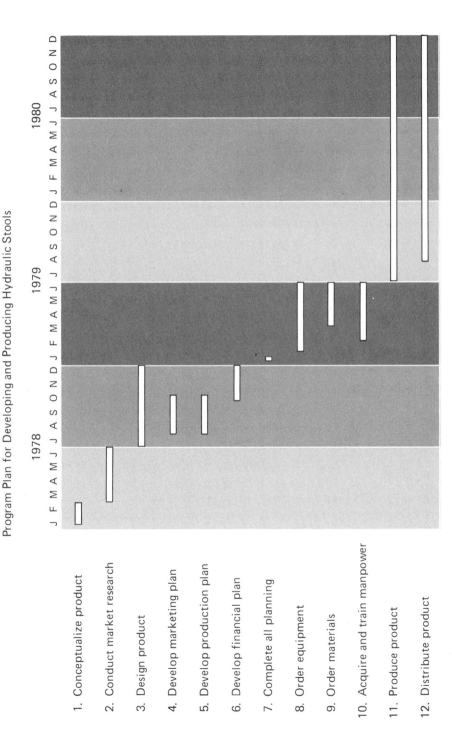

Fig. 24-1. Example of a Gantt chart

it can automatically be adjusted. Twelve phases are involved in conceptualizing, designing, producing, and distributing the product, as shown in
figure 24-1.

The advantage of this form of chart for planning purposes is the
ease in visualizing the contemplated activities and the associated time
requirements. The chart is also useful for control purposes. As phases of
the program are completed, the time bar is filled in solid to the point that
represents actual completion (as in figure 24-2). The observer can then
relate the planned completion of the work versus actual completion. The
wide use of Gantt charts can also be attributed to their flexibility. They
can be used for man or machine loadings, program phases, inventory
usage, or almost any activity that is time related. Where time factors are
already known, such as in repetitive production, they serve little use.
Their value is when uncertainty is involved in scheduling, such as with
"one-time" programs. Because of their simplicity, they are inexpensive
and easy to update.

The limitations of the Gantt chart are that it provides little detail on
activities spread over broad time spans (e.g., activity 11, "produce product," in figure 24-1 extends over eighteen months); it does not show dependent relationships between activities represented on different horizontal lines; it reflects the time variable adequately, but it completely
ignores costs; and it is somewhat awkward to explicitly show quality and
quantity considerations. In the latter instance, it must be assumed that as
work progresses to the next phase, the previous phases have been completed at quality and quantity standards, but if deviations exist they are
not identified.

The Milestone Chart

The milestone chart is an outgrowth of the Gantt chart and was developed to add detail to the events or control items listed on the vertical axis.
A *milestone* is the completion of a significant phase of an activity or program. Once that phase is completed, that activity ends, and the project
moves on to the next phase. For a student, passing an examination in a
course is a milestone. He or she has completed one hurdle or phase in the
chain of events involved in achieving the goal of successfully completing
the course. In constructing a house, completing the foundation, flooring,
and plumbing would all be separate milestones.

A sample milestone chart is shown in figure 24-3. The milestones are
indicated by the twenty-nine numerically numbered triangles that are
shown on the time bars. Milestone charts are always supported by a
legend, such as in table 24-1, which explains each of the milestones. Milestones 1, 2, and 3, involving phase 2, "conduct market research," indicate
the dates when the marketing research survey will be mailed, returns

Program Plan for Developing and Producing Hydraulic Stools

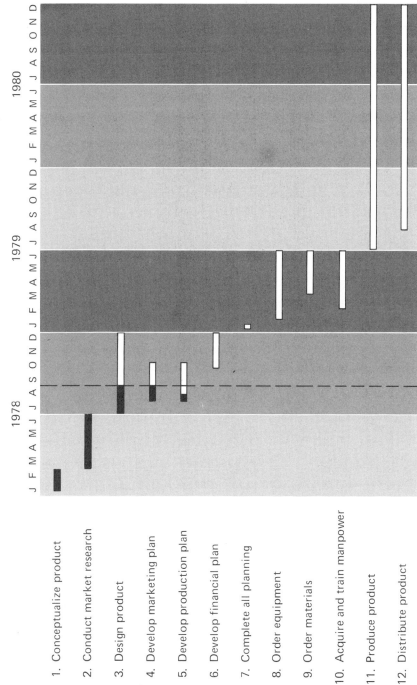

1. Conceptualize product
2. Conduct market research
3. Design product
4. Develop marketing plan
5. Develop production plan
6. Develop financial plan
7. Complete all planning
8. Order equipment
9. Order materials
10. Acquire and train manpower
11. Produce product
12. Distribute product

1978   1979   1980

J F M A M J J A S O N D J F M A M J J A S O N D J F M A M J J A S O N D

Reporting Date

Fig. 24-2. Example of a Gantt chart marked up to show accomplishment

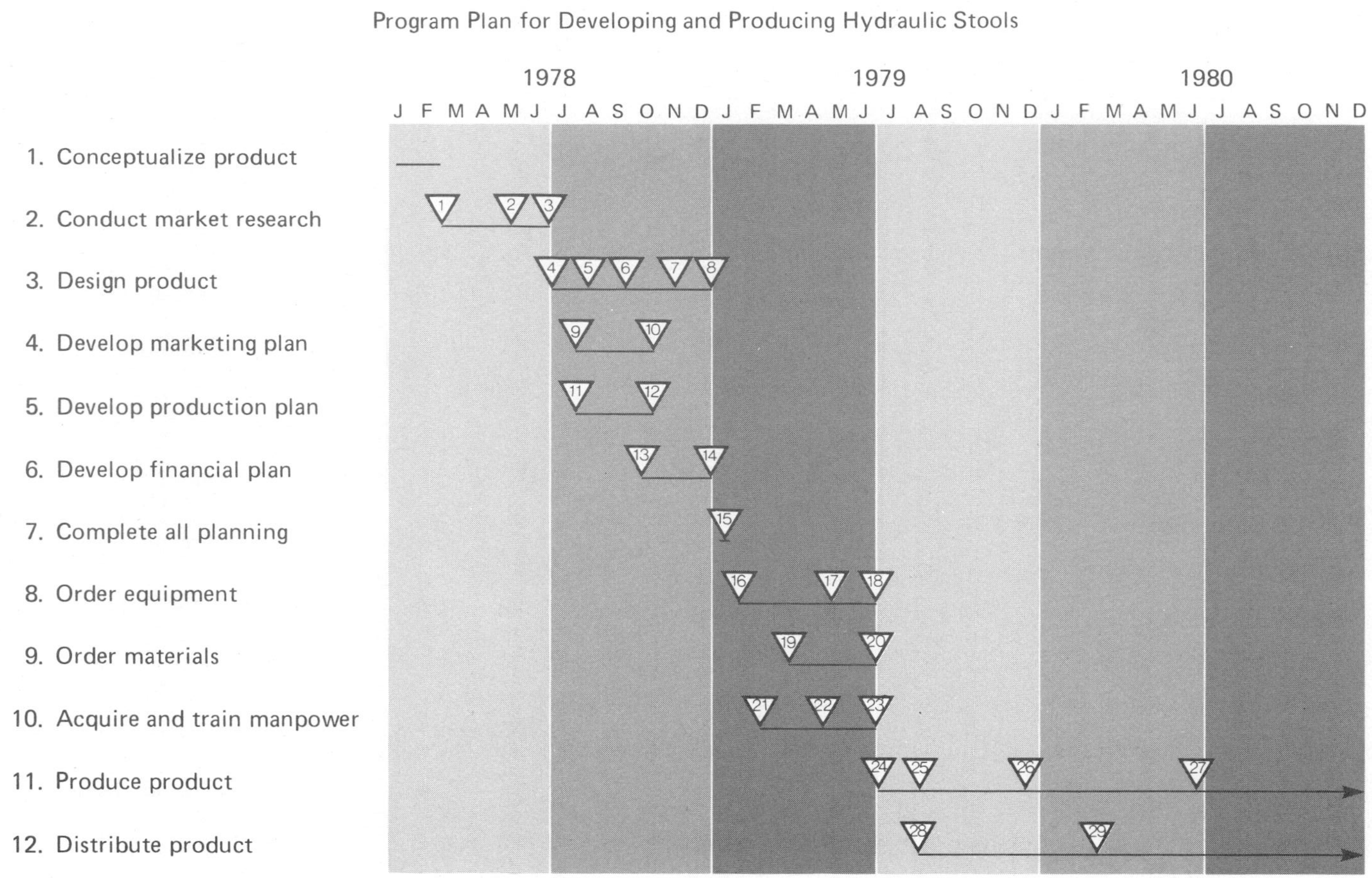

Program Plan for Developing and Producing Hydraulic Stools
1978
1979
1980
J F M A M J J A S O N D J F M A M J J A S O N D J F M A M J J A S O N D
1. Conceptualize product
2. Conduct market research
3. Design product
4. Develop marketing plan
5. Develop production plan
6. Develop financial plan
7. Complete all planning
8. Order equipment
9. Order materials
10. Acquire and train manpower
11. Produce product
12. Distribute product
1
2
3
4
5
6
7
8
9
10
11
12
13
14
15
16
17
18
19
20
21
22
23
24
25
26
27
28
29

Fig. 24-3. Example of a milestone chart

Table 24-1. Milestones for Developing and Producing Hydraulic Stools (supports figure 24-3.)

1. Send survey.
2. Receive returns.
3. Summarize returns and make decision.
4. Start preliminary design.
5. Complete preliminary design.
6. Start fabricating mock-ups.
7. Test mock-ups.
8. Obtain design approval.
9. Start marketing plan.
10. Complete marketing plan.
11. Start production plan.
12. Complete production plan.
13. Start financial plan.
14. Complete financial plan.
15. Complete all planning.
16. Place equipment orders.
17. Receive equipment.
18. Complete installation of equipment.
19. Order materials.
20. Receive materials.
21. Advertise job openings.
22. Hire manpower.
23. Complete training of manpower.
24. Start production shakedown.
25. Complete production shakedown.
26. Reach level of 50 per day.
27. Reach level of 100 per day.
28. Start delivery to local wholesalers.
29. Start delivery to eastern wholesalers.

received, results summarized, and a decision made, regarding whether to proceed with the design and production of hydraulic stools. Figure 24-3 is much simpler than the typical milestone chart. A normal chart would show thirty horizontal lines and perhaps as many as one-hundred milestones.

A primary advantage of the milestone chart, as presented in figure 24-3, is that the twenty-nine milestones add twenty-nine more check points in the twelve phases of the program. Thus it more than doubles the detailed information relating to the plans for developing and producing hydraulic stools. This advantage becomes especially significant when related to control. Figure 24-4 projects the value of milestones in program control. Actual progress in relation to the plan is recorded through the reporting date of September 1, 1978. Actuals are shown by reversing the triangles and pointing them up on the bottom of the time bar.

Using milestones in this manner makes it possible to specifically relate actual progress to planned accomplishment. In figure 24-4, it can be determined that the survey was mailed out approximately two weeks later than scheduled, and the return dates and decision dates (milestones 2 and 3) also slipped two weeks. However, the start of preliminary design was completed on time. The marketing plan got underway as scheduled, but the start of the production plan has slipped one month, which is a signal to management that a potential major problem exists. This slippage sets into action the control cycle. The report shows the discrepancy, and it is now up to management to determine what corrective action, if any, should be taken (such as authorizing the production planners overtime to catch up).

Milestone charts constitute the basic planning and control methods used in many organizations. Firms often have a chart room where this information is graphically portrayed. Regular staff meetings are held in the room to evaluate progress on the major programs of the organization. When managers become familiar with the charting approach, thirty or forty programs involving hundreds of milestones can be reviewed in a morning or afternoon. The review is normally handled on an exception basis, where only the major deviations from the plan are considered in detail.

Milestone charts have approximately the same advantages and disadvantages as Gantt charts, but they do overcome the primary weakness of too little detail. Milestone charts handle time, quality, and quantity variables, but they also have the limitation of not including associated costs. To know if the program is ahead or behind schedule can be deceptive to the manager unless he also knows if his program is over or under on costs. Quality is implied in the completion of a milestone. If the foundation is completed and the flooring is being added to the house, the foundation obviously met the quality standards—or work would not have

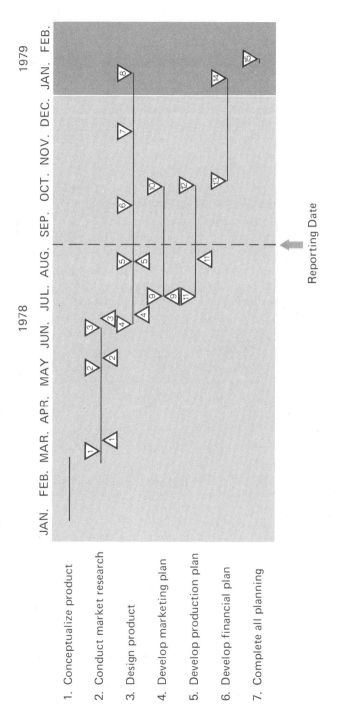

Fig. 24-4. **Example of a milestone chart with actual progress reported**

progressed to the flooring. When quantities are appropriate, they can be shown above the line and actuals noted below. For instance, in phase 11 when production starts, the estimated number to be produced each month can be listed on top of the time bar line and actual production below.

Milestone charts, like Gantt charts, do not show vertical dependencies. In figure 24-4, milestones 10 and 12, representing completion of the marketing and production plans, must be completed before the financial plan can be initiated, but this is not necessarily evident from the chart.

The IMPACT Chart[1]

The IMPACT (Integrated Management Program Analysis and Control Technique) is essentially the same as the milestone chart, except that it includes the cost dimension. However, this is an exceedingly important addition since a manager is receiving only part of the story he needs to know if costs are excluded.

The distinctive feature of an IMPACT chart (figure 24-5) is that it is split in half, so that the top portion represents technical or operational performance, and the bottom half shows in the same time period the costs associated with the activity. Now it is possible to evaluate all four variables in one chart: time, quantity, quality (or performance), and cost. On the bottom portion, the P stands for "planned cost" and A is for "actual cost." The reporting date is September 1, so actual costs are shown through this date.

The significance of the IMPACT chart is being able to correlate planned schedule, cost, and performance with actual schedule, cost, and performance. The planned costs represent a forecast or fixed budget in this particular instance. It was planned to start the marketing research in late February, but it was delayed (as shown by the slippage of the first milestone). No costs were recorded in February, so a temporary savings of $500 is shown. However, a cost overrun on this phase of the project ($500 projected versus $870 actual) occurred in March as more intensive activity took place caused by the delay.

By projecting cost performance with technical performance, it is possible to determine the reasons for not meeting cost projections. With no means of relating operational progress to cost incurred, it is impossible to make sense out of the cost figures. Also, showing only one set of data is deceptive. If a firm is ahead on its technical progress on a program, this explains why costs in excess of the forecast have been incurred. The budgeted and actual figures for phase 5, "develop production plan," will be misleading through August ($4300 projected on a cumulative basis versus $1320 actual), until it is recognized that a four-week delay was experienced in starting the program. This can be easily deciphered from the chart.

Program Plan and Costs for Developing and Producing Hydraulic Stools

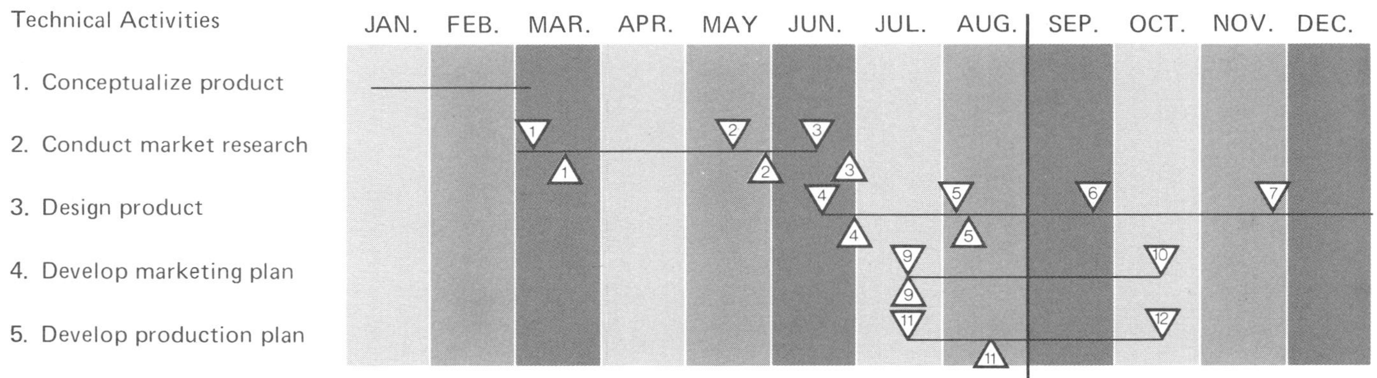

Technical Activities

1. Conceptualize product
2. Conduct market research
3. Design product
4. Develop marketing plan
5. Develop production plan

Associated Costs:

		JAN.	FEB.	MAR.	APR.	MAY	JUN.	JUL.	AUG.	SEP.	OCT.	NOV.	DEC.
1. Conceptualize product	P	2000	4000										
	A	1800	3500										
2. Conduct market research	P		500	500	500	2000	2000						
	A		0	870	650	2200	2300						
3. Design product	P						3000	5000	7000	9900	9000	8000	5000
	A						1200	7150	7320				
4. Develop marketing plan	P							1500	3750	3500	2000		
	A							1370	3840				
5. Develop production plan	P							1500	2800	2800	2400		
	A							0	1320				

P = Planned
A = Actual

Reporting Date

Fig. 24-5. **Milestone chart including associated costs (IMPACT-Integrated Management Program Analysis and Control Technique)**

Another advantage of IMPACT charting is flexibility. Cost can be shown by organization, cost element, or activity—depending on which is of concern to the particular manager involved. Also, manpower figures can be portrayed graphically on the top half and the corresponding tabular information on the bottom, reflecting both projected and actual data. The primary advantage of splitting the chart in half is that it makes it possible to show three variables rather than only two.

When the cost, time, quantity, and quality status of a program can be projected on one chart, as is the case with IMPACT, it permits the evaluation of trade-offs essential to decision making. However, IMPACT charts contain the major weakness of Gantt charts: sequential dependencies are difficult to show, especially for these milestones vertically distributed on the chart.

Network Plans

The first attempt to overcome this primary deficiency of Gantt charts was to draw vertical lines between milestones where these dependencies existed. Figure 24-6 shows such lines for the example of developing and producing hydraulic stools. The problem of doing this is, of course, that if thirty separate horizontal time bars are shown for thirty different phases of a program, and if a similar number of lines are drawn vertically it makes the chart imcomprehensive because of the crisscrossing of the lines. Accordingly, planners decided that one set of lines needed to be dropped. Since time can be shown either as a linear scale or as a number (one week, six weeks, etc.) it was decided to drop this linear scale and show time on the dependency line in numerical form. Out of this change evolved a family of planning and control techniques referred to as *network planning*. Each particular technique is identified by its own acronym.

PERT Networks

The first network system was PERT (Program Evaluation and Review Technique).[2] PERT was developed in 1958 by a team of individuals consisting of representatives from the Special Projects Office of the Navy, industrial contractors, and a group of consultants. They were working on the planning and control system for the Polaris missile to be used in nuclear submarines. Through the use of this technique, it was claimed that over two years were saved on the development of this weapon system. The success of PERT on the Polaris missile project let to its widespread adoption on other programs under development by the Department of Defense, and its expansion to other industries like construction. In the 1960's, it was acclaimed as one of the significant breakthroughs in plan-

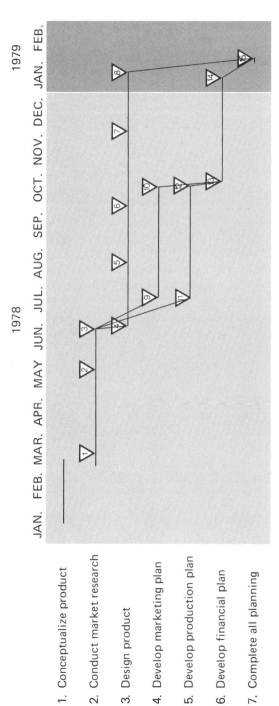

Fig. 24-6. Milestone chart showing vertical and horizontal dependent relationships

ning and control for single-use or nonrepetitive programs. During that time, many other variations were developed, particularly the *Critical Path Method* for use in the construction industry.[3]

ESTABLISHING A PERT NETWORK.   A simplified form of PERT will be used to demonstrate network analysis based on the example of developing and producing hydraulic stools. Two different symbols are used in PERT networks. A circle represents an event. (An *event* is essentially the same as a milestone.) It constitutes an accomplishment at a particular point in time. *Activity* is the work necessary to achieve an event. Performing the engineering work directed at completing the preliminary design of a product is activity. The event is when the preliminary design is accomplished.

In order to demonstrate the progression from milestone charts to PERT networks, the same milestones enumerated in table 24-1 are shown in PERT chart form in figure 24-7. Milestones 1 through 25 are now the events in the network. Activity is represented by the lines that connect the events. Activity requires time and resources. Accordingly, the figure on the line is the time estimate, in this instance, in weeks, to accomplish the activity necessary to achieve the event. Time is shown on the activity line rather than in the event circle, because activity is time consuming; an event (point in time) is not.

The significance of the PERT network is the dependency considerations represented by the interconnecting lines. PERT planning involves determining the sequence of events necessary to accomplish major milestones and eventually the entire program. If there is a connecting line between two events such as 8 and 15, it means that event 8 (design approval) must be attained before event 15 (completion of all planning) can be accomplished. When there is no connecting activity line between two events, such as numbers 17 and 20, it means that the completion of event 20 (receipt of materials) is not dependent on event 17 (receipt of equipment).

Network methods fostered two improvements in planning. First, using a network forces a consideration of planning details. It is difficult to be superficial if planning steps must be formulated in terms of the series of events and activities necessary to achieve a goal. It also forced planners to concentrate on identifying dependent relationships which are the most important ones in the chain of events involved in accomplishing a plan.

The Critical Path and Slack

When a total PERT network is established, it permits other types of analysis that are extremely important. Since all of the different series of

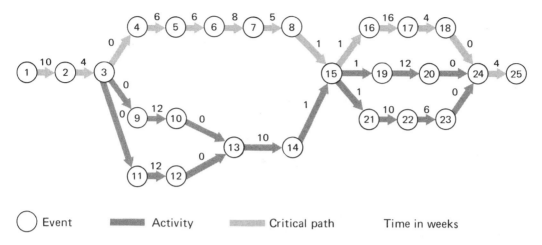

Event   Activity   Critical path   Time in weeks

Fig. 24-7. Network analysis for producing and developing hydraulic stools

events and activities necessary to accomplish a plan have been determined, it is now possible to identify the slowest such series, known as the *critical path*. (Since the critical path is also "activity," it is often represented in diagrams as a line twice the size of the activity lines. However, to avoid confusion, in figure 24-7 we have shown it as the lighter shaded line through the upper series of events and activities.)

The critical path is another example of management by exception. If management wants to speed up the project, they do not need to accomplish all activities and events more quickly but only those involved in the critical path. The difference between the required date for completion of the project and the time involved in each series of events and activities is known as *slack*. Assuming the required completion date in figure 24-7 is sixty-five weeks (in this instance the same as the critical path), slack can be determined by working backward from the completion date. An example is considering the three paths from event 15 to 25. The critical path involves twenty-one weeks in going from event 15 to 24 (upper loop). The middle path (events 15, 19, 20, 24) requires thirteen weeks, leaving a slack of eight weeks (21 minus 13). The lower loop (15, 21, 22, 23, 24) requires seventeen weeks and therefore has four weeks of slack.

An example of how PERT aids in decision making is illustrated by events 19 and 20. If the suppliers of the materials are three weeks behind schedule and the traffic department requests that air rather than rail transportation be used to get parts in on time, the request should be turned down, because this more expensive form of transportation is not required when there are already eight weeks of slack in this loop. Network models permit the transfer of resources to the critical path when speeding up the project is critical. If the company is behind on the marketing plan (events 9 and 10), overtime should not be authorized here, because there is already slack in this loop. Overtime should be authorized only for activity involved in the critical path and only then if the delays would cause the entire project to slip the required completion date—when meeting the completion date is considered critical.

TIME AND COST FACTORS IN PERT.   As indicated, figure 24-7 is a simplified form of PERT. Three time factors are normally used: *optimistic*, *most likely*, and *pessimistic*. The titles accurately reflect the difference between the estimates. Optimistic assumes everything will proceed with no problems; pessimistic assumes problems will be incurred; and most likely time is the normal situation in terms of the typical number of problems or obstacles. These three estimates provide parameters for visualizing the extremes of what could happen during the work on a project. By using probability factors, they can also be mathematically combined into one figure representing "expected time."

The one major deficiency of PERT is that is does not cover the cost variable. However, methods called PERT/Cost are available for doing this. The resources required to complete the activity associated with an event can be estimated, and actual costs can be collected in relation to the accomplishment of each event. This is often cumbersome, because it is contrary to established, proven methods of cost collection—but it is feasible. The cost information is not portrayed visually on the chart. Complex networks are normally computerized. Accordingly, printout reports are issued containing—in tabular form—the status of cost performance, along with the schedule and technical performance on the project.

ADVANTAGES AND LIMITATIONS OF PERT.   PERT has many advantages, as noted: it forces planning, highlights task-dependent relationships, and is schematic, comprehensive, and beneficial for control purposes. In planning, PERT almost serves the same function as dollars in budgeting. With PERT all planning and control activities can be represented in the same manner on one common schedule or network.

The limitations of PERT relate primarily to its misapplication. It is not a universal planning tool, because it was developed for nonrepetitive operations in which time and cost figures are not known. However, if too much uncertainty exists in the situation (conducting research on a cure for cancer), it is also of little value because time and event variables cannot be predicted within a sufficient range of accuracy to make them useful. After its use on Polaris, PERT became hailed as a panacea and was required on a large portion of the work contracted by the Department of

Defense and some other organizations. Frequently planners were forced to go into considerable detail when the project parameters and specifications were not firm or when uncertainty made detailed estimating futile. In some instances, a network could not be updated as rapidly as technical changes made it obsolete. Therefore, many organizations experienced problems with PERT and disregarded the concept when it would have proven valuable if properly applied.

The lesson is a basic postulate of contingency theory. It is just as important to know under what circumstances a method or technique is appropriate as it is to know how to "work" the method or technique. PERT, under any circumstances, is a time-consuming and costly planning device. Because of the three time estimates and the complexities of identifying and schematically interlocking dependencies, it requires at least initially twice as much effort as more typical planning techniques. However, under the proper circumstances the benefits will more than offset these extra costs.

PROGRAMMING FOR REPETITIVE OPERATIONS

The planning and control techniques used when operations are repetitive are considerably different from Gantt charts and network planning. Under repetition it is possible to predict with high accuracy the time and resources required to perform operations, so that a system is not required to specifically estimate and track the planned events and activities. In automation, time factors are fixed in relation to the speed of the machinery. Of greater concern in repetitive operations is being aware of deviations from standard times and resource requirements, so corrective action can be taken when necessary. Two examples of systems used in repetitive operations will be presented.

Programmed Scheduling

Planning and control can be reduced to digital data and processed electronically when the following conditions exist: time factors are known; resource input is established; and the sequence of operations is set and regulated. This applies to maintaining miles of highway, custodial services for office space, and scheduling of classes, as well as the operations of highly automated industries like automobile assembly. When the total requirements are established in terms of miles of highway, square feet of office space, number of classes, and quantity of automobiles to be produced, the resources and time requirements can easily be determined based on existing unit standards.

Flow Control

In assembly type operations, where the speed of the conveyer belts or overhead cranes determines the timing of the work performed and where sequencing is established by the physical layout of equipment, the primary scheduling problem is the inflow of parts to the appropriate end product. There are many different combinations of subassemblies or parts that can comprise an automobile. It can be with or without power brakes, power steering, custom upholstery, radios, air conditioning, radial tires, tilt-up steering, or vinyl top. Also, the colors of the exterior and all of the accessories must match. Therefore the scheduling problem is to have the parts and subassemblies flow into the final assembly line so that the end item meets required specifications. Because this again involves known conditions, it can be computerized to provide the necessary sequencing.

FINANCIAL AND OPERATING CONTROLS

In order to explore the full range of control techniques, a few brief examples will be provided of types of controls other than those relating to tracking operations or performance against a plan. Financial and operating ratios are a common means of assessing whether an organization is within or out of control. A ratio can be expressed as a proportion (10:1), a fraction ($\frac{1}{2}$), or as a percentage (20%). Whichever method is shown, the measurement is still the relationship between two quantities. Comparing two measures is significant, because one alone is usually not very meaningful. If a firm has a net income of $50,000, it is difficult to evaluate whether this is good performance until this figure is compared with the sales of the firm or the firm's total assets. Five examples of the many ratios that exist will be presented as illustrations of how ratios are used to measure operations and activate controls.[4]

Return on Total Assets

One of the primary measures of the effectiveness of a firm is the profit return it provides on total assets. If a firm has assets of $1 million and a net annual profit after taxes of $60,000, the return on total assets is 6 percent. Such a return would be considered low for many companies, but the acceptable percentage will vary, based on the industry, general economic conditions, the maturity of the firm, the desires of owners, and other factors.

Return on Net Worth

Another return-on-investment-type ratio is the return on net worth. In this instance, the net profit after taxes is divided by the net worth (stockholders' equity) rather than by the total assets. This would reduce the total assets by the portion offset by short- and long-term liabilities. This ratio reveals how well the owners' equity is being used in making a profit return. This return can then be compared with the potential returns from alternative forms of investment using the same amount of capital.

Profit Margin on Sales

The profit margin is also expressed as a percentage and is found by dividing the net profit after taxes by the amount of sales. If a firm has $1.5 million in annual sales and a $60,000 net profit, the profit margin on sales would be 4 percent. This again is a very important indicator of effectiveness when compared with the performance of other firms in the same industry. If the percentage is lower than the industry average, it is a signal to management that a problem exists in its operations, and some action is probably necessary.

Inventory Turnover

The inventory turnover is called an activity ratio. It measures the number of times annually that an inventory is sold or turned over. It is found by dividing the cost of goods sold during the year by the cost of the inventory at the end of the fiscal year (or the average over the year). If a firm had an inventory of $150,000 and the cost of goods sold was $1.5 million, the turnover would be ten times. Such a ratio will reveal whether inventories are too high when compared with industry averages.

Current Ratio

The current ratio is a "liquidity ratio." It is a measure of short-term solvency or liquidity in terms of the company's ability to pay its immediate debts (those payable within the next year). It is found by dividing current liabilities (accounts payable, short-term notes payable, etc.) into current assets (cash, accounts receivable, etc.). The capacity of a company to pay its bills promptly is of concern to debtors and business associates. A current ratio of 2:1 ($2.00 in current assets for every $1.00 in current liabilities) is considered adequate, but determining acceptable ratios is much more complex than this and relates to many situational variables associated with the firm and its operations.

Interpreting Ratios

Ratios are relatively easy to calculate—the problem is with proper interpretation. Accounting data can be subject to many interpretations, and acceptable averages will vary considerably by industry and product line. There is no precise means of determining what constitutes a satisfactory ratio. Also, it is not always easy to determine causes when ratios change. However, ratios are vital to the control process, because they provide feedback to the manager on many key profitability and operating factors that need to be monitored if management is to be alerted to changing conditions that require attention.

QUALITY CONTROL

Quality control will be used as an example of direct control over operations. One major purpose of quality control is to ensure that the output of the firm meets specifications. In order to do this, various inspections are made during processing and of the final unit. Each unit is not usually inspected, since statistical methods are available to draw conclusions from sampling a specified number of units out of each batch. Our concern here is not determining how this formula is arrived at but in establishing a process to achieve control over quality. The usual method is to state a standard as an acceptable range, rather than as an absolute. For instance, if a firm manufactures desks, and the drawers in width must be 14 inches $\pm$ .010th of an inch, the tolerance of $14 \pm .010$ makes any drawer between 13.99 and 14.01 acceptable.

Control charts, such as shown in figure 24-8, are developed to determine if processing is under control. Based on samples of drawers on the production line, upper and lower control limits are established. These limits typically represent three standard deviations from the mean, so that if a sample exceeds the limits there are only a few chances in a thousand that this could be due to chance. Thus in figure 24-8 the measurements in the inspection sample marked as point F warn that the process is probably out of control. Accordingly, changes are necessary to correct the situation. This would most likely require an adjustment in the equipment involved in the processing or in the methods used by a worker if this is the cause.

CONTINGENCY ASPECTS OF PLANNING AND CONTROL METHODS

Many of the contingency considerations in planning, control, and programming have already been identified. The primary contingency vari-

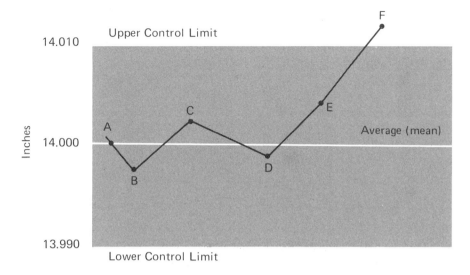

Fig. 24-8. Quality-control chart for desk drawers—represents measurements of samples taken for inspection purposes

ables relating to programming tend to be the same ones dominating all steps in the planning and control process. These will be summarized in this section, and answers to the following questions will be considered: What variables determine which types of programming systems are appropriate in a particular organization? What factors determine the depth of detail and degree of structure that are appropriate in planning and control? What match is necessary between planning and control systems and other organizational variables such as structure, technology, and organizational climate? How much planning is appropriate in an organization? What determines how much control is necessary?

Selecting Programming Systems

Earlier in this chapter, programming systems were divided into two types, based on whether the operations of the organization were repetitive or nonrepetitive. Programmed scheduling and flow control were identified as being appropriate for continuous production; Gantt charts, milestone charts, the IMPACT technique, and network planning are used in nonrepetitive operations, such as intermittent production or research and development.

A more thorough analysis of situational variables as they relate to planning, control, and cost systems is shown in table 24-2. When repe-

Table 24-2. Contingency Variables in Programming and Business Systems

Factor	Dimension	Evaluation	Gantt Chart	Milestone Chart	Network (PERT)	Flow Control	Programmed Scheduling	Fixed Budget	Variable Budget	Standard Cost	Actual Cost
						Planning and Scheduling		Budget and Accounting			
Task	Repetition	High				x	x		x	x	
		Low	x	x	x						x
	Time range	Short				x	x		x	x	
		Long	x	x	x						x
	Throughput	Low	x	x	x						x
		High				x	x		x	x	
	Functional nature	Prod'n				x	x		x	x	
		R&D	x	x	x			x			x
Technology	Technical content of operations	High	x	x	x			x			x
		Low				x	x		x	x	
	Automation	High				x	x		x	x	
		Low	x	x	x						x
External	Technological change	Slow				x	x		x	x	
		Rapid	x	x	x						x

tition is high in tasks (continuous production), flow control, programmed scheduling, variable budgets, and standard-cost systems are most effective. When repetition is low, Gantt charts, milestone charts, network planning, and actual-cost systems should be used. Other characteristics of continuous production, such as a short time cycle and a rapid throughput rate, call for the same systems as those involved in task repetition—with the opposite characteristics being associated with the systems for nonrepetitive tasks.

The two characteristics of technology that affect the need for different systems are the degree of automation and the technical complexity of the operations. Low automation and high technical complexity (e.g., research and development), involve considerable uncertainty, so programming methods like Gantt charts and milestone charts are useful in dealing with time, cost, and performance unknowns. Automated, certain operations lend themselves to standard-cost systems, variable budgets, and programmed scheduling based on these concepts. If technological change in the external environment is slow, systems associated with repetitive operations become appropriate, but if change is rapid, the more flexible systems like milestone charts and network planning are used.

Different Modes of Planning and Control

The central issue in selecting planning and control systems relates to characteristics such as comprehensiveness, rigidity, and required detail. When should an organization have comprehensive, detailed plans and when should merely general guides prevail, as in expediency planning? Obviously not all organizations should adopt the same planning premises and systems as Ford Motor Company has, nor should a manager start out with no better plan of where he was going than Christopher Columbus did. Certain variables control how—and the degree to which—organizations and managers will find it feasible to plan and control.

The two most important general factors influencing planning and control are the *certainty* of the environment and the *level* in the organization where the planning is to be conducted and applied. In more certain environments, planning is more predictable, and therefore detailed planning is of more value. In dynamic environments, planning is difficult, and factual information essential to detailed planning is not normally available. As indicated in chapter 21 (see table 21-1), there is more predictability, certainty, and control over internal operations, so detailed systems are appropriate for these purposes. Top-management strategic planning is directed at the environment, which increases uncertainty and forces planning to be more generalized.

Figure 24-9 contains ten of the most significant organization-related variables that determine the desirability of different planning and control systems. These variables are divided into three groupings, relating to certainty, organization structure, and behavioral factors.

CERTAINTY AND PLANNING. Variables 1 through 3 in figure 24-9 have been explained previously. Repetitive tasks, constant technology and a stable external environment all make it possible to conduct detailed, specific planning, especially of internal operations. The opposite conditions

Planning Systems		
	specific, detailed	general, flexible
Certainty of Planning:		
1. Nature of tasks		
	repetitive	varied
2. Nature of technology		
	constant	changing
3. External environment		
	stable	dynamic
4. Dependence on outside groups		
	independent	dependent
Organization Structure:		
5. Level in hierarchy		
	lower level supervisors	top management
6. Power distribution		
	centralized	divided
7. Type of structure		
	mechanistic	organic
Behavioral Factors:		
8. Acceptance of objectives by group		
	totally accepted	little concensus
9. Organizational climate		
	detailed controls accepted	detailed controls rejected
10. Leadership styles		
	directive	participative

Fig. 24-9. Contingency factors affecting appropriateness of different planning and control systems

normally make it mandatory to constantly adjust plans and seek redirection, so that intermittent, more vague directional planning is necessary. Production and research and development serve as the two contrasting examples.

The fourth variable under certainty is dependence on outside groups. If an organization is dependent on outside groups, planning becomes meaningless without direction from the outside source. An entrepreneur who operates his own business and sells to many customers can be independent and structured in his planning. Examples of organizations where planning is difficult because of dependence on outside groups is an industrial supplier selling to only one or two major manufacturers, an aerospace firm with 90 percent of its sales to the government, a state agency dependent on the state legislature for funding, and a state highway department, where 90 percent of the construction funds come from the federal government. These conditions do not prohibit these organizations from planning, but since they have limited control over their own destiny, it is more a forecasting than planning exercise.

One last example is appropriate relating the certainty of the environment to planning. In Latin America, which is noted for its political upheavals, one chief executive commented: "Planning is great. But how can you plan—let alone plan long-term—if you don't know what kind of government you'll have next year?"[5]

ORGANIZATION STRUCTURE AND PLANNING.   The three primary variables of organization structure that affect planning have also received earlier attention. Internal planning, such as that performed by middle managers in production control and quality control, can be detailed, exact, and certain in terms of predictability. The external planning of top management tends to have the opposite characteristics. When power in the organization is centralized, planning is easier to conduct and carryout. In totalitarian governments with authority centralized, such as the Soviet Union, five-year plans dominate the administrative process. In democratic governments where power is deliberately divided between the three branches of government, centralized planning is more difficult. All organizations with a high degree of power equalization, such as universities, find that central planning is usually general in nature, and subunits are free to pursue their own goals and interests within a broad framework. In organizations where power keeps shifting back and forth, as in many representative assemblies, planning will obviously be erratic.

The relationship between mechanistic or organic structures and planning is more associative than causal. Mechanistic structures thrive in stable environments as do methods for detailed planning. Dynamic environments are conducive to organic structures and adaptive planning.

BEHAVIORAL FACTORS AND PLANNING.   Three of the many behavior factors that affect planning are the degree to which the group accepts common objectives, the existing organizational climate, and the prevailing leadership styles. If the group is totally committed to organizational goals, then planning becomes more certain, arguing for greater detail and the need to set a pattern for action. When the organization climate is such that detailed controls and plans are accepted, they can also be easily implemented. In institutions like universities, where the climate is resistant to controls, plans and limitations that restrict activity tend to be rejected. If prevailing leadership styles are directive, more detailed planning and control tend to be part of the environment.

Many other people-related factors (not shown in figure 24-9) also affect planning. As an example, people who seek more stable, predictable job environments will accept plans and controls, while individuals who prefer variety and freedom of action will resist them.

Contingency Profiles in Planning and Control

Developing profiles to relate organizational associated characteristics with the appropriateness of different types of planning and control systems is a useful technique to aid managerial decision making. Figure 24-10 provides such an example. The top half of the figure represents the characteristics of a large family corporation that cans a variety of vegetables. Since it is a family corporation, it is likely to be centralized and independent. Canning vegetables involves repetitive tasks, constant technology, and a relatively stable environment. All of these factors encourage the use of specific, detailed, planning and control systems.

The family corporation is contrasted with the Environmental Protection Agency. Since the EPA is controlled by political considerations and is reliant on presidential direction and legislative support, the guidelines and resources provided the organization are often changing. No predictable product is produced, and the associated technology is rapidly evolving, which means that tasks and operations are varied in nature. However, existing environmental laws do provide some structure. In general, these factors would indicate that plans are often adjusted, and contingency plans should be developed.

Planning requirements are, of course, not consistent throughout an organization. The production function will plan in one fashion, while research and development will plan in another. Also, marketing will use one approach, purchasing another. Therefore, a manager should be attuned to the variables associated with his particular organization and what these imply in terms of the planning and control approaches that should be used.

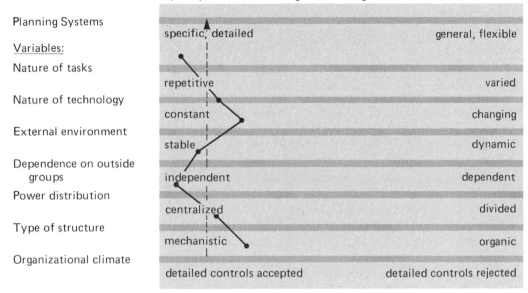

Family Corporation Producing Canned Vegetables

Planning Systems

specific, detailed   general, flexible

Variables:

Nature of tasks

repetitive   varied

Nature of technology

constant   changing

External environment

stable   dynamic

Dependence on outside groups

independent   dependent

Power distribution

centralized   divided

Type of structure

mechanistic   organic

Organizational climate

detailed controls accepted   detailed controls rejected

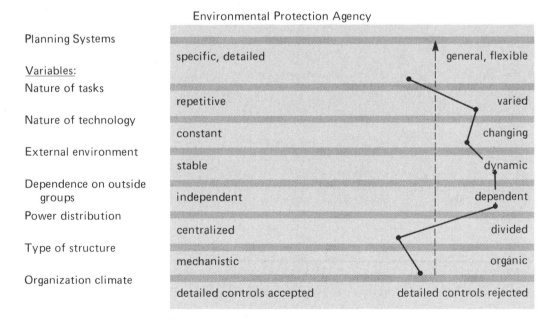

Environmental Protection Agency

Planning Systems

specific, detailed   general, flexible

Variables:
Nature of tasks

repetitive   varied

Nature of technology

constant   changing

External environment

stable   dynamic

Dependence on outside groups

independent   dependent

Power distribution

centralized   divided

Type of structure

mechanistic   organic

Organization climate

detailed controls accepted   detailed controls rejected

Fig. 24-10. Profiles of two situations relating contingency
variables to the need for different types of planning and control systems

SUMMARY

Programming involves the determination of the tasks required to accomplish established goals, the time intervals associated with the tasks, and the resources necessary to carry them out.

In programming for nonrepetitive actions, methods such as Gantt charts, milestone charts, the IMPACT chart, and network planning are appropriate. Each of these techniques represents progressive improvements over the others. Milestone charts show more detail than Gantt charts, and IMPACT charts add cost information. Network techniques reflect dependencies among the events involved in a particular program, and they highlight the critical path or slowest series of events and activities. However, network methods are often misapplied, so that even though they are one of the most complete forms of planning, problems are frequently experienced in their usage.

Programming in repetitive operations involves programmed scheduling and methods such as flow control.

Two other control techniques are financial and operating ratios and the charting associated with inspection in quality control. Each method measures some aspect of a company's operations in which information is generated to know when operations are out of control or deviating from plans.

There are no universal planning and control systems that are useful for all organizations. The methods are normally differentiated on the basis of the amount of detail and the flexibility of the system. Certainty associated with repetitive tasks, constant technology, a stable environment, and independence of operation permits the use of more detailed, structured systems. Uncertainty generated by varied tasks, changing technology, a dynamic environment, and dependence on outside groups forces more general planning that is frequently intermittent and makeshift in nature.

Internal, operational planning is more controlled and structured, while top-management external planning is long range and general. Mechanistic structures rely on fixed planning approaches, while organic structures are characterized by adaptive planning. Behavioral factors affecting the appropriateness of different plans are the degree of group acceptance of goals, the prevailing organizational climate, and leadership styles.

QUESTIONS AND EXERCISES

1. What steps are involved in programming?
2. Planning methods in organizations with nonrepetitive operations involve Gantt charts, milestone charts, IMPACT charts, and network

planning. In relation to these different methods explain the following:
   A. How they are used for planning.
   B. How they are used for control.
   C. What advantages does each technique have over the others?
   D. Are the systems more useful at one level of management than another?
3. In network methods of planning explain the following:
   A. Why are numerically sequenced milestones in milestone charts not an adequate reflection of dependencies?
   B. Why is the critical path of significance in planning?
   C. What does *slack* represent?
   D. In figure 24-7, why does event 13 follow events 10 and 12?
4. Develop a Gantt chart showing the balance of the course work you require to complete a degree.
5. Convert the Gantt chart developed in question 4 into a PERT network.
6. In figure 24-5, what would you conclude if actual costs in August for developing the marketing plan were $4500?
7. Answer the following questions regarding financial and operating ratios:
   A. In which industries are the profit margins on sales normally lower? Why?
   B. Why is a high inventory-turnover ratio considered desirable?
   C. If a firm has a low return on investment, what does this tell the manager?
8. How will the appropriateness of different planning and control systems vary depending on:
   A. The certainty of a firm's internal operations and external environment?
   B. The level in the organization where they are used?
   C. Whether the organization is a governmental agency or business firm?
   D. Existing leadership styles?
9. Draw a profile similar to 24-10 for a college. Also, draw one for a hospital.

Case Problem:
SMEDLEY BOOKSTORE

Two brothers are investigating the possibility of opening a bookstore in a location near a college campus. They have spent several weeks obtaining the information necessary to make a decision. As a result, they arrived at the following planning and cost data:

Planning: It will require 30 days to establish a corporation; 30 days to find a store location and sign a lease; 45 days to make arrangements with publishers and suppliers; 30 days to order and receive books; 7 days to unpackage and display the books and merchandise; 15 days to find a supplier and obtain a lease on shelving, display cases, and office equipment; 30 days to receive the shelving; 15 days for shelving installation; 30 days to establish a credit line and obtain necessary funds; 20 days to hire two clerks; and 5 days to train the clerks.

Cost: The building rent is estimated at $300.00 per month; the equipment lease will run $75.00 per month for three years; the salary for each clerk is estimated at $500.00 per month; overhead costs (lights, insurance, fringe benefits, heat, etc.) are estimated at $300.00 per month; in order to build up an inventory, they estimate that the difference between the costs of books and supplies versus income from their sale will require $3000 the first month of operation, $2000 the second, and they should break even the third. Costs of incorporating are $500.000.

Develop a Gantt chart to project their planning activities. (Note that many steps can be concurrent.)

Develop an IMPACT chart and show the planning and cost information.

Develop a PERT network and show the critical path.

Assuming that together they have $5000 to invest in the company, how much would they have to borrow during the first three months of operation?

What type of budget system should they use?

Case Study:
ULTRASYSTEMS CONSULTANTS

The ABC Atomics Company has a consulting contract with Ultrasystems to obtain their assistance in improving internal and long-range planning. ABC Atomics was established in 1960 to develop and produce atomic reactors for sale to power companies. The firm experienced rather limited growth in the sixties as the use of atomic reactors fell below national predictions. However, sales more than doubled during the early 1970's, and the company is now concerned with its management capability as it prepares for the big expansion forecast for the decade following. The firm currently builds seven reactors per year. These are often similar, but rarely identical—especially in size.

ABC Atomics has two main operating divisions: an engineering department that handles the design and development of reactors, and the production department that fabricates and assembles them. The engineering department has 125 engineers, scientists, and administrative support, and the production department employs approximately 400. There is also a small marketing division, and the usual financial, purchasing, and other administrative groups.

Ultrasystems is to develop recommendations encompassing planning systems for the two operating divisions (engineering and production), and procedures and formats for a five-year company plan.

What types of systems will Ultrasystems most likely recommend for the production department? For the engineering department?

Explain the need for different systems in each organization, based on variables similar to figure 24-9.

How will the formats and methods for the long-range plan be likely to differ from the operational plans?

What types of budgets can be used?

Footnotes

1. For a more detailed discussion of this technique see Howard M. Carlisle, "Systems Approach to Integrating Cost and Technical Data," *Management Services,* July–August 1967, pp. 34–41.
2. For a more complete explanation of PERT see Harry Evarts, *Introduction to PERT* (Boston: Allyn and Bacon, Inc., 1964).
3. For an explanation of the critical path method see K. G. Lockyer, *An Introduction to Critical Path Analysis* (New York: Pitman Publishing Corporation, 1964).
4. For additional ratios and a more thorough explanation see chapter 2, "Ratio Analysis," in J. Fred Weston and Eugene F. Brigham, *Managerial Finance* (Hinsdale, Illinois: Dryden Press, 5th edition, 1975).
5. Quoted by H. Stieglitz, *The Chief Executive and His Job* (New York: National Industrial Conference Board, Personnel Policy Study Number 214, 1969), p. 22.

Management and the Future

How will the environment of business change
in the future?

What trends of the past will carry over into the
future?

Will it be necessary to manage differently because
of these trends?

What changes can be expected in management
practices?

What are the likely trends in management theory?

How will contingency theory evolve?

THE PERILS OF FORECASTING

Many forecasts are available on the future of organizations and management. The hazards of forecasting are represented in the well-known predictions made in 1958 by Leavitt and Whisler in an article entitled, "Management in the 1980's."[1] Because of the new technology epitomized by the high-speed computer and the emergence of operations research methods, they projected a drastic change in the roles and functions of middle and upper management. Middle-management tasks would become more structured, because a greater portion of the work at that level would be programmed. The line between middle and upper management would become more distinct as certain middle-management jobs moved downward in the hierarchy, and former middle management tasks relating to innovation, planning, and creativity would rise to become essentially the exclusive domain of top management. In effect, they were projecting a move toward recentralization in organizations.

Even though electronic data processing has influenced organization structure and the tasks of managers, it has not resulted in the withering away of middle-management positions and a major return to centralization. On the contrary, within ten years leading industrial psychologists were predicting that "Adaptive, temporary systems of diverse specialists . . . linked together by coordinating and task-evaluative specialists in organic flux, will gradually replace bureaucracy as we know it."[2] More specifically, in 1973 another noted analyst made the following projection: "The manager of the future will deal with highly complex organizations. The organizational vehicle will not be the hierarchical pyramid in which decisions are centralized and most of the planning and control are done at the top."[3]

WORLD BREADBASKET: FEAST OR FAMINE?

Probably the most controversial aspect of futurology is the issue of population versus limited raw materials and the questioned capacity of science and technology to supply expanding energy needs. On the one hand, it is predicted that there will be a continually rising standard of living, more leisure, and a golden age of productivity. George Danzig sees the future as follows:

"We are witnessing a computer revolution in which nearly all tasks of man—be it manual labor or simple control, pattern recognition or complex higher order decision making—all are being reduced to mathematical terms and their solution delegated to computers.

"I believe this process is moving ahead so rapidly that the entire fabric of our present society will, in one generation, become a superficial fluff of busywork keeping us occupied whilst our slaves, the machines, will be doing all the real work for us. So rapid is this evolution in my opinion, that I wonder whether our government, industries, research centers, universities, and professional, societies are moving ahead fast enough to prepare us for this new world."[4]

Contrary predictions are provided by many environmentalists and social critics. Reich, in *The Greening of America,*[5] sees the social fabric of society disintegrating and views technology and production as uncontrolled instruments that pulverize everything in their path. Ehrlich, in *The Population Bomb,*[6] observes that we are strangling ourselves with overpopulation, resulting in food shortages, the energy crisis, and a deteriorating environment. A team at the Massachusetts Institute of Technology in 1972 reached the conclusion based on a computer model of the globe that, barring an unlikely change in human values, goals, and arrangements, the twenty-first century will witness a worldwide collapse.[7] Heilbroner, a noted economist, states that the ecological issue may "constitute the most dangerous and difficult challenge that humanity has ever faced."[8]

Heilbroner's balanced view provides reasons for both pessimism and optimism. He notes the possibility that "the ecological crisis will simply result in the decline, or even destruction, of Western civilization" and asks, "Can we really persuade the citizens of the Western world, who are just now entering the heady atmosphere of a high-consumption way of life, that conservation, stability, frugality, and a deep concern for the distant future must take priority over the personal indulgence for which they have been culturally prepared and which they are about to experience for the first time?"[9]

On the other hand, he offers the following as a possible alternative:

". . . it seems to me that the ecological enthusiasts may be right when they speak of the deteriorating environment as providing the *possibility* for a new political rallying ground. If a new New Deal, capable of engaging both the efforts and beliefs of this nation, is the last great hope to which we cling in the face of what seems otherwise to be an inevitable gradual worsening and coarsening of our style of life, it is possible that a determined effort to arrest the ecological decay might prove to be its underlying theme . . . I cannot estimate the likelihood of such a political awakening, dependent as these matters are on the dice of personality and the outcome of events at home and abroad. But however slim the possibility of bringing about such a change, it does at least make the ecological crisis, unquestionably the gravest long-run threat of our times, potentially the sources of its greatest short-term promise."[10]

As interesting and significant as these issues are to society, our primary concern in this chapter is *management* in the future—which is our next topic for consideration.

TRENDS IN THE MANAGEMENT OF ORGANIZATIONS

The student of today is the manager of tomorrow, and accordingly, the training of today should meet the needs of tomorrow. Trying to provide students with an understanding of future trends and attempting to equip them with the skills to manage in the future requires an evaluation of what managing organizations in the years ahead will be like. Irving Kristol's statement that, "The beginning of wisdom, for any social analyst or critic, is to know that the future is unknowable"[11] is undoubtedly correct, but at the same time the past has proven to be the prologue to the future. Any future forecast first involves an evaluation of the momentum of present forces. Changes undoubtedly will occur. The seeds of future developments are often buried in obscurity. Events, personalities, and power shifts are far too capricious to provide the reliability necessary for safe prediction. It is therefore with some trepidation that we shall look at some of the trends that are likely to shape the world of the manager in the years ahead.

Trends Evident in the Past Forty Years

In attempting to look at the problem of managing organizations in the future, a link will be made with the past by examining the major trends affecting organizations that are evident in the period from the mid 1930's to the mid 1970's. These trends will also be evaluated based on the likelihood of their continuing into the future.

SIZE OF ORGANIZATIONS.   The size of organizations of all types has tended to increase. The federal government is much larger than it was forty years ago; automotive manufacturers are bigger; major business corporations have become worldwide; and virtually all organizations that dominate society have tended to experience expansion. Organizations will undoubtedly become larger in the future, but this trend should show a definite slackening as the rate of population growth decreases and as the associated rising demand for goods and services tapers off. (There are also signs that antitrust action will be pursued more vigorously.)

Alfred P. Sloan, Jr., former President of General Motors Corporation, explains the problems of bigness in his statement of over thirty years ago: "In practically all our activities we seem to suffer from the inertia resulting from our great size. . . . Sometimes I am almost forced to the conclusion that General Motors is so large and its inertia so great that it is impossible for us to be leaders."[12] With organizations growing larger, the challenge of managing those organizations to achieve joint goals will continue to be one of the great enigmas of the future.

THE PACE OF CHANGE.   Probably the most distinguishing feature of managing organizations forty years ago compared with today is that change occurs more rapidly. The social, political, economic, and technological environment of business has become more turbulent, which has forced adaptive internal changes. Alvin Toffler, in *Future Shock*, has warned that we may be reaching the limits of man's capacity to adapt.[13] His argument for building "future-shock absorbers" into society has some validity. Many facets of the change dynamics experienced by organizations have been identified throughout this book. Accelerated change will be a feature of future society, so the manager's role will increasingly be one of keeping the organization adaptive and flexible.

MORE COMPLEX FORCES.   The forces of change will not only maintain a pace that defies control, but they will tend to increase in complexity. The manager of the 1970's faces the same variables as the manager of the 1930's—they are simply more complex today. For instance, government regulations regarding the hiring and utilization of manpower existed in the 1930's, but today they are far more extensive and involved. As business and society grows and expands, it forces more interdependence upon the existing units in the superstructure. The early homesteader on the prairie had few neighbors and few restrictions on his activities. As neighbors came and society closed in around him, the parties became dependent on each other, and laws and other restrictions came into existence to regulate and facilitate this interdependence. Acts that were previously private now became public. As "spaceship earth" continues to be more completely enveloped and dominated by man and organizations, this interdependence becomes ever greater and the web of relationships more entwined.

CHANGE FROM INTERNAL TO EXTERNAL EMPHASIS.   Because of a rapidly changing environment and the increased control of government, the focus of top management has switched more from internal control to an emphasis on external relations. Management literature of the 1930's was devoted almost entirely to making an organization more efficient through planning and control of internal operations. As the external environment has made the challenge of adaptation critical to success, dealing with external forces and conditions has received wider attention. Thus in the past twenty years, strategic planning, the social responsibilities of business, and organic organization structures have all received emphasis.

THE ROLE OF BUSINESS IN POLITICS

Businessmen could develop a more logical and more effective political stance by approaching politics in the spirit that guides their daily work. They spend most of their time at work trying to improve something: they are reorganizing a process to cut its cost, or trying to expand sales volume, or modifying a product, or clearing tangled lines of corporate communication. Every step of the innovative process is made between the hope that a change will result in betterment and the fear that a change will make things worse. Typically, the margin between the hope and fear is thin.

Businessmen have much practice in the calculus of improvement. They have no special competence in political philosophy. If they made fewer speeches defending "freedom" and paid more attention to the substantive issues that shape the actual course of government, they might contribute significantly to the rescue of U.S. politics.

. . . business may find millions of allies, at all income and educational levels, if it brings to politics the same spirit of progress that it routinely brings to its own management problems. The electorate won't tolerate a business stance that seems to say, "Nobody is allowed to make any changes—except us. And we will continue to change every nook and cranny of American life." It is by showing a willingness to cooperate with the American people in the management of change that business may regain the political influence it once had.

Reprinted from Max Ways, "Business Needs a Different Political Stance," *Fortune,* September, 1975, pp. 98 and 193.

INCREASED INFLUENCE OF GOVERNMENT.   Any executive who has managed an organization over several decades will readily relate that one of the biggest changes in managing a business is the increased number of laws and regulations, and the increased control of government over the marketplace. Starting with the New Deal in the 1930's, there has been a continual expansion of the power of government, and even though the rate of increase may decline, governments will continue to be more important in the society of the future. New technologies bring on the need for new regulations, and as social and ecological concerns gain importance in the public's eye, the growing dominance by government is inevitable. Problems with major industries like the railroads as well as international energy shortages also threaten certain features of the free-enterprise system.

Pluralism will continue to typify society, so that no one institution or group will dominate; but the lines between the different institutions will continue to fade. Business will most likely broaden its goals to give greater recognition to social and humanitarian considerations—which are also the concerns of government. Business will use its management skills to grapple with the major problems of society, such as pollution, urban blight, unemployment, public transportation, and education. Ideally, government will establish the goals, and business will provide the management and technical know-how. Business strategies will no longer be restricted to the economic aspects of the marketplace.

THE EXPECTATIONS SOCIETY HAS FOR BUSINESS.   In the 1930's the firm was still considered primarily as an economic entity. Business was supposed to efficiently produce the goods and services required by a materially oriented nation. As society has tended to emphasize protecting the environment, urban renewal, consumerism, and equal opportunities for minorities, the business firm has been viewed as having the capacity and responsibility for making contributions in these areas. This growth of the social responsibilities of business remains controversial, but it is evident that the basic charter and values of business are undergoing gradual change. This makes managing a firm more demanding and requires a wider range of knowledge and sensitivity to social and political issues.

INCREASED MATERIAL AND ENERGY SHORTAGES.   Shortages existed in the 1930's primarily as a result of general economic conditions—the inability of customers to pay or an inability of business to produce. However by the 1970's, a growing population, increased consumption by the consumer, and greater use of mechanical devices started to stretch the availability of the existing world supplies of raw materials. Greater effort will have to be placed on new energy sources (such as heat from the sun). The worldwide expansion of the units that consume resources and use energy will continue to make resource availability one of the major issues affecting the growth and transfer of world power centers and the rise and decline of business firms. A firm will have to be much more concerned with obtaining and using the factors of production that represent input from the environment. People involved in acquiring and maintaining adequate sources of supply will hold more status and power in organizations. Old methodologies will be re-examined and revised, based on shortages and the need for conservation.

ACCEPTANCE OF A "NO-GROWTH" PSYCHOLOGY.   One of the most difficult changes that managers and organizations are coming to cope with is a no-growth or slow-growth orientation. Growth has been as much a part of the American way of life as the Puritan work ethic or the sanctity of private property. Organizations that are not growing are considered to be failing. Growth is viewed as the concomitant of all the rewards available through business enterprise, such as profit, leadership, and power. The recent no-growth status of institutions like colleges and universities has forced a change in planning approaches, hiring policies, tenure considerations, and other methods and values associated with managing these organizations.

Many markets in the future will have to adjust to no-growth or limited-growth patterns that will significantly alter the assumptions and methods of managers. Static-growth markets should not, however, be confused with static-change markets. Consumer tastes, technology, new life styles, and political events will be sure to keep markets dynamic. Organizations will be more difficult to manage under these conditions because scarity creates conflict, and growing organizations have more flexibility that those in a steady state.

REVOLUTION IN MECHANIZATION AND IN INFORMATION SYSTEMS.   In contrasting the 1930's with the 1970's, one of the most obvious changes is the revolution caused by the computer and automation. More and more of the tasks performed by people are now being handled by machines. As already noted, in the 1950's, it was popular to predict that electronic data processing would eliminate the need for middle managers. Routine decisions would be programmed, and most of the analysis formerly conducted by middle managers would be by machines, resulting in the middle manager becoming obsolete. Also the tremendous input of information systems would make it possible for top-level managers to make more of the significant decisions because of their access to the necessary information. Even though these predictions have been found to be far overstated, one would hope that machines will eventually replace man in performing routine, drudgery-type tasks, and the more routine decisions will be programmed. However, organizations will probably be more, rather than less, reliant on the skill and foresight of managers because of the increased complexity associated with the environment of the future.

BETTER-TRAINED AND EDUCATED POPULACE.   The average level of education represented in the background of workers and managers has risen rapidly in the past few decades. Over 90 percent of the executives at the top of American corporations today have attended college, versus less than 50 percent thirty years ago.[14] By 1985, college graduates will out-

MANAGERS OF THE FUTURE

Managers in the future will be expected to create wealth, generate profits, and provide employment for the fulfillment of the public policy outlined in the Employment Act of 1946. Furthermore, they will be expected to utilize the human resources of the nation in accordance with the spirit of equal economic opportunity, civil rights, equal employment opportunity, and, at the same time, adhere to the clean air and clean water guidelines of the Environmental Protection Agency within the Occupational Health and Safety Act standards. Managers will be challenged to create almost two million new employment opportunities a year with people working fewer hours per week. The four-day work week is on the horizon with "gliding work time" a probability. A 28-hour work week has been predicted for the turn of the century, compared with 37.3 hours in 1970, 49 hours in 1930, 57 hours in 1900, 70 hours in 1850, and 84 hours in 1800.

Future managers will be expected to create more goods and services with more profits and more employment, and to deal with employees' demands for more leisure, more services, and more conveniences in a technological economy in a scientific society. The role of future managers will be complicated further by energy and power shortages and pressure to guard the environment from damage.

Quoted from John F. Mee, "The Manager of the Future," *Business Horizons*, June 1973, p. 8.

number those without a high school education in the U.S. work force.[15] Each year the new entrants into the work force tend to be better educated and trained. More knowledgeable employees make it possible to further decentralize and to expand the use of participative leadership styles. The increasing availability of education has resulted in higher educational requirements for many positions, and it has often placed college training as a prerequisite for attaining top-level jobs. It has also resulted in a better informed consumer, which has contributed to the upgrading of products, advertising, and sales efforts. Another factor is technology, which is becoming more knowledge-intensive as opposed to capital-intensive. This has placed greater emphasis on turning management into a profession and filling executive positions with scientists or technocrats. The improved level of knowledge and training in the work force has many implications that will affect organizations of the future.

TRADITIONAL THEORY EVOLVING INTO CONTINGENCY THEORY.   One of the important developments affecting organizations and the management of them has been the evolution of traditional management theories into contingency theories. Management theorists in the 1930's were disciples of Frederick Taylor and searching for "the one best way" to handle business operations and to manage organizations. Management processes were considered universal, and across-the-board principles were the foundation on which a science of management could be built.

In more recent years, it has been recognized that different strategies and concepts are appropriate in different situations, and that use of principles are normally restricted to common classes of situations. Greater knowledge of the forces and conditions that influence organizations has been developed, and attempts have been made to match organization structures, leadership styles, and planning and control concepts with the needs of the situation. The complexity of managing organizations has been recognized, and a more viable, theoretical structure has been developed to deal with this complexity.

IMPLICATIONS FOR MANAGING

What do all of these changing conditions mean for the manager? How is he or she to manage differently? How are concepts of planning, organizing, staffing, directing, and control to be changed or modified in application? What management practices will tend to be dropped, and which ones will receive greater emphasis? Obviously the trends and their influence on management will vary by culture and type of organization. However, their likely impact can be generalized by relating them to the five management functions.

Staffing Requirements

The trends in the skills required of managers can be predicted with some confidence. Managers will be more broadly trained. They will need to be attuned to social, economic, political, and technological changes, because the goals of business will be broadened to encompass these areas, and the manager will be called on to solve related problems. Because of the dynamic environment, emphasis will be on the flexibility and adaptive skills of the manager. He or she will act more as a change agent in directing the organization. Technical knowledge will be important, but changing the organization will be dependent on understanding people.

Emphasis will be on diagnostic skills, especially in relation to contingency variables. More women and minority members will be managers, and improved instruments will be available to identify managerial skills. Renewal through training and seminars will become more significant, because the manager's job will grow in complexity and importance, rather than diminish as some have predicted. Life-long training and education will undoubtedly receive greater emphasis.

Change in Directing

Participative styles of leadership will continue to be used more widely in organizations. There will also be greater emphasis on group decisions and personal involvement in the decisions that affect them. (This will not necessarily make the organization more efficient, but it will make it more democratic.) The increased knowledge of the worker and the increased emphasis on the quality of life in organizations will underwrite the trend toward diminished authoritarianism. There will be improved quantitative tools to aid in decision making. More useful information made available through MIS will represent one of the greatest advances. (MIS should eventually live up to some of the impressive predictions that have been made in the past.) The directing responsibilities of the manager will be away from running operations and more toward evaluating the long-range objectives and strategies of the firm. The executive will be less concerned with day-to-day decisions and more concerned with programs like organization development, aimed at making the entire organization more effective. The manager will have much greater knowledge of how to motivate subordinates, but it will not extend to the point of being able to manipulate individuals as many fear.

Organizing Concepts

To meet the needs of a changing environment, organizations will continue the trend toward beginning open, organic, and adaptive structures. The predictions of Warren Bennis on the need for temporary, flexible structures and of Alvin Toffler on the emergence of ad hoc organizations (or *Ad-hocracy*, as he refers to it), will be a primary concern of managers. This does not mean that bureaucracy will fade away or that there will be no need for rigid structures. It is essentially a recognition of the fact that the environment will be more conducive to organizations that can adapt. Specifically, there will be more use of project groups and temporary task forces to handled problems. The matrix form of organization also will become increasingly common—because of its greater capacity to handle a variety of problems. There will be more power equalization in organizations and less emphasis on the hierarchy. Distinctions like line and staff will continue to have reduced meaning as knowledge-based influence will receive more emphasis than will position-based influence.

Expertise in being able to divide up or differentiate organizations will continue to grow faster than our capacity to develop effective integrative mechanisms. As organizations become larger and more complex, the problem of coordinating and integrating all of the parts so that the common good is emphasized will require new innovations in organization design. The historical need for more effective organizations has never been greater, but the difficulty of obtaining integration is also reaching its apex. Loose federations of semiautonomous units are going to be more common.

The final change evident in future organization structure is the plural executive. The complexity of managing major organizations will be such that it will be beyond the capacity of any one individual to handle the whole job. As John F. Mee notes, "Collective Leadership is not for the expression of democratic feelings; it is an imperative of size and complexity."[16] Thus multiple executives or an "office of the president," such as is found in the federal government, will gradually replace the chief executive officer of the past. Again, no one structure will apply to all organizations. Some will still use the single executive, but the trend will be in the opposite direction, even though a central office (and sometimes a central personality) will tend to dominate.

Planning Systems and Concepts

Planning will become more, rather than less, important in the future. Some of this will be brought on by resource and energy shortages, but the primary factor is the growing interdependence of society. Land-use planning and public policies toward protecting the environment and related business expansion will become more critical. Strategic planning for the firm will be mandatory, as product lines and investment opportunities rapidly come and go. Planning will be more widespread, sophisticated, and farsighted. Methods for forecasting will experience improvement, and forecasting of newer areas such as technology and social change will become more refined. Planning will continue to be a primary means the firm will have to adapt to the environment—making contingency planning and the broad evaluation of alternatives a greater necessity.

Controlling Systems and Concepts

Controlling will duplicate planning in terms of growth, sophistication, and scope. However, control will be influenced more by electronic data processing. Feedback and adjustment will be commonly handled by the computer. Control over people will be less detailed in terms of activity, but more detailed as it relates to results or goals. Many new social measures and indicators will be available, making social audits and social accounting widespread. Greater reliance will be placed on people to evaluate their own performance and to meet their own goals, so control systems will switch to emphasizing the monitoring and regulating of total organizational performance.

Overall Management Knowledge

Even though there are many justified causes for concern about the future, there are also many reasons for optimism, especially in relation to the development of management knowledge. All indications are that the dramatic advances since 1930 in management theory and practice will continue in the future, heralding improvements in the effectiveness of organizations and in the quality of life that they afford.

SUMMARY

Ten trends are evident in organizations and their management:

1. The size of organizations will continue to increase.
2. The pace of change will continue to accelerate.
3. The forces affecting organizations will display increased complexity.
4. External forces and variables will be more important in managing.
5. The influence of government will increase.
6. The social responsibility and other noneconomic roles of business will take on greater significance.
7. More material and energy shortages will be experienced.
8. The acceptance and application of a "no-growth" psychology will continue.
9. People (representing both employees and customers) will be better trained and educated.
10. Traditional management theory will continue to evolve into contingency approaches.

These trends will influence the management process in the following ways: managers will need to be more broadly trained with an expanded orientation covering social, economic, political, and technological considerations; participative styles of leadership will become more widespread as will movements toward power equalization in organizations; organizations will be characterized by temporary groups that are frequently realigned; integration will continue to be one of the most significant structural problems; planning, especially strategic planning, will increase in importance; planning effectiveness will be improved through better tools and methods; and control will become more automated and extended to areas such as the social audit.

Management theory will evolve toward a contingency orientation. Improved means will be developed for categorizing and evaluating situational differences—heralding a major advance in establishing a science of management.

QUESTIONS AND EXERCISES

1. Interpret the quotations from Heilbroner found at the beginning of the chapter. Do you feel he is correct?
2. What problems in management occur because organizations are becoming larger?
3. Give some examples of how the major variables affecting organizations have become more complex.
4. What evidence is there that the influence of government is increasing?
5. How will material and energy shortages affect business firms and competition?
6. What differences in managing will a "no-growth" psychology bring?
7. Why will supervisors manage differently if employees are better trained?

Footnotes

1. Harold J. Leavitt and Thomas L. Whisler, "Management in the 1980's," *Harvard Business Review,* November–December, 1958, pp. 41–48.
2. Warren G. Bennis, *Changing Organizations* (New York: McGraw-Hill Book Company, 1966), p. 12.
3. John F. Mee, "The Manager of the Future," *Business Horizons,* June 1973, p. 9.
4. George B. Dantzig, "Management Science in the World of Today and Tomorrow," *Management Science,* February, 1967, p. C-111.
5. Charles A. Reich, *The Greening of America* (New York: Random House, 1970).
6. Paul R. Ehrlich, *The Population Bomb* (New York: Ballantine Books, 1968).
7. Dennis Meadows, et. al., *The Limits of Growth* (New York: Universe Books, 1972).
8. Robert L. Heilbroner, *Between Capitalism and Socialism* (New York: Vintage Books, 1970), p. 270.
9. *Ibid.,* p. 284.
10. *Ibid.,* p. 285.
11. Irving Kristol, "The New Era of Innovation," *Fortune,* February 1969, p. 189.
12. As quoted in Ernest Dale, *Management: Theory and Practice,* third edition (New York: McGraw-Hill Company, 1973), p. 713.

13. Alvin Toffler, *Future Shock* (New York: Bantam Books, 1970).
14. F. A. Bond and A. W. Swinyard, *Report on Management Succession: Top Executive Positions,* January-December 1972 (Ann Arbor: Graduate School of Business Administration, University of Michigan, 1973.)
15. John F. Mee, *op. cit.,* p. 11.
16. John F. Mee, *Ibid.,* p. 9.

Acknowledgments

(continued from page ii)

p. 281—From Frederick Herzberg, "One More Time: How do you Motivate Employees?", *Harvard Business Review,* January–February 1968, pp. 56–57. Chapter 12: pp. 304, 305—Reprinted with permission of *The Wall Street Journal,* © Dow Jones & Company, Inc. All Rights Reserved. pp. 313, 314—Reprinted with permission of *The Wall Street Journal,* © Dow Jones & Company, Inc. All Rights Reserved. Chapter 13: p. 340—Abstracted from Harold Stieglitz, "What's Not on the Organization Chart," *The Conference Board RECORD* (November 1964), pp. 7–10. p. 342—Reprinted with the special permission of *Dun's Review,* April 1968. Copyright, 1968, Dun & Bradstreet Publications Corporation. Chapter 14: pp. 371, 372—From *The Human Side of Enterprise* by Douglas McGregor. Copyright © 1960 by McGraw-Hill, Inc. Used with permission of McGraw-Hill Book Company. Chapter 16: pp. 415, 416—Edgar H. Schein, "Organizational Socialization and the Profession of Management," *Sloan Man-*

agement Review, Vol. 9, no. 2, pp. 2, 3. Chapter 17: pp. 454, 455—From Richard Beckhard, "The Confrontation Meeting," *Harvard Business Review,* March–April 1967, pp. 149–155. Chapter 18: p. 474—Fig. 18-1, reprinted by permission of the publisher from *Advanced Management Journal,* July 1966 © 1966 by S.A.M., a division of American Management Associations. p. 476—Table 18-2, adapted from table 4, page 140 of *Situational Management* by Howard M. Carlisle, American Management Associations, 1973. Chapter 19: p. 491—Fig. 19-1, from "How to Choose a Leadership Pattern," *Harvard Business Review* March–April 1958, by Tannenbaum and Schmidt. p. 493—Fig. 19-2, from "How to Choose a Leadership Pattern," *Harvard Business Review,* May–June 1973, by Tannenbaum and Schmidt. p. 495—Fig. 19-3, from "Engineer the Job to Fit the Manager," *Harvard Business Review,* Sept.–Oct. 1965, p. 117, by Fred E. Fiedler. p. 496—Fig. 19-4, copyright © 1969 Ziff-Davis Publishing Company Reprinted by permission of *Psychology Today Maga-*

zine. p. 499—Reprinted from *Leadership and Decision-Making* by Victor H. Vroom and Philip W. Yetton by permission of the University of Pittsburgh Press. © 1973 by the University of Pittsburgh Press. Chapter 22: pp. 587, 588—Reprinted with permission of *The Wall Street Journal,* © Dow Jones & Company, Inc. All Rights Reserved. Chapter 23: p. 631—From Henry Mintzberg, "The Manager's Job: Folklore and Fact," *Harvard Business Review,* July–August 1975, p. 58. p. 635—Fig. 23-3, from G. Anthony Gorry and Michael S. Scott Morton, "A Framework for Management Information Systems, *Sloan Management Review,* Vol. 13, no. 1, p. 58. Chapter 24: p. 664—Table 24-2, from *Situational Management* by Howard M. Carlisle. Used by permission from American Management Associations. Chapter 25: p. 677—From *Between Capitalism and Socialism* by Robert L. Heilbroner, by permission from Random House, Inc. p. 680—From Max Ways, "Business Needs a Different Political Stance," *Fortune* September 1975, pp. 98 and 193.

Selected Bibliography

General Management, History of Management, and Systems

BARNARD, CHESTER I.: *The Functions of the Executive.* Cambridge, Mass: Harvard University Press, 1938.

BECKETT, JOHN A.: *Management Dynamics: The New Synthesis.* New York: McGraw-Hill Book Company, 1971.

BENNIS, WARREN G.: *Changing Organizations.* New York: McGraw-Hill Book Company, 1966.

BOULDING, KENNETH: "General Systems Theory—The Skeleton of Science," *Management Science,* April 1956, pp. 197–208.

CARLISLE, HOWARD M.: *Situational Management.* New York: American Management Associations, 1973.

DALE, ERNEST: *Management: Theory and Practice,* 3rd ed., New York: McGraw-Hill Book Company, 1973; "Some Foundations of Organization Theory," *California Management Review,* Fall 1959, pp. 71–84.

DRUCKER, PETER: *The Practice of Management.* New York: Harper and Row, Publishers, Inc., 1954; *Management: Tasks, Responsibilities, Practices.* New York: Harper & Row, Publishers, Inc., 1974.

EMERY, F. E. (ed.): *Systems Thinking.* Middlesex, England: Penguin Books Ltd., 1969.

ENTHOVEN, ALAIN C. and K. WAYNE SMITH: *How Much Is Enough? Shaping the Defense Program 1961–1969.* New York: Harper and Row Publishers, Inc., 1971.

FAYOL, HENRI: *General and Industrial Management.* London: Sir Isaac Pitman & Sons Ltd., 1949.

FILLEY, ALAN C. and ROBERT J. HOUSE: *Managerial Process and Organizational Behavior.* Glenview, Ill: Scott, Foresman and Company, 1969.

GEORGE, JR., CLAUDE: *The History of Management Thought.* Englewood Cliffs, N. J: Prentice-Hall, Inc., 1968.

GULICK, L. and L. URWICK (eds.): *Papers on the Science of Administration.* New York: Institute of Public Administration, 1937.

HAMPTON, DAVID R., CHARLES E. SUMMER, and ROSS A. WEBBER: *Organization Behavior and the Practice of Management.* Glenview, Ill: Scott, Foresman and Company, 1973.

JOHNSON, RICHARD, FREMONT E. KAST, and JAMES E. ROSENZWEIG: *The Theory and Management of Systems.* 3rd ed., New York: McGraw-Hill Book Company, 1973.

KAST, FREMONT E. and JAMES E. ROSENZWEIG: *Organization and Management.* 2nd ed., New York: McGraw-Hill Book Company, 1974.

KOONTZ, HAROLD: "The Management Theory Jungle," *Academy of Management Journal,* December 1961, pp. 174–188; with Cyrill O'Donnell: *Principles of Management.* 5th ed., New York: McGraw-Hill Book Company, 1972.

McGREGOR, DOUGLAS: *The Human Side of Enterprise.* New York: McGraw-Hill Book Company, 1960.

McGUIRE, JOSEPH W. (ed.): *Contemporary Management: Issues and Viewpoints.* Englewood Cliffs, N.J: Prentice-Hall, Inc., 1974.

MARCH, JAMES G. (ed.): *Handbook of Organizations.* Chicago: Rand McNally & Company, 1965; with HERBERT A. SIMON: *Organizations.* New York; John Wiley and Sons, Inc., 1958.

METCALF, HENRY and L. URWICK (eds.): *Dynamic Administration, The Collected Papers of Mary Parker Follett.* London: Harper & Brothers Publishers, 1942.

MINTZBERG, HENRY: "The Manager's Job: Folklore and Fact," *Harvard Business Review,* July–August 1975, pp. 49–61.

MOONEY, J. D. and A. C. REILEY: *Onward Industry!* New York: Harper & Brothers Publishers, 1931.

NEWMAN, WILLIAM H., CHARLES E. SUMMER, and E. KIRBY WARREN: *The Process of Management.* 3rd ed., Englewood Cliffs, N. J: Prentice-Hall, Inc., 1972.

SIMON, HERBERT: *Administrative Behavior.* New York: Macmillan Company, 1957.

TAYLOR, FREDERICK WINSLOW: *The Principles of Scientific Management.* New York: Harper & Brothers Publishers, 1916.

WEBBER, ROSS A.: *Management.* Homewood, Ill: Richard D. Irwin, Inc., 1975.

Contingency Approaches

BURNS, TOM and G. M. STALKER: *The Management of Innovation.* London: Tavistock Publications, 1961.

CARLISLE, HOWARD M.: *Situational Management.* New York: American Management Associations, 1973.

DALTON, GENE W., PAUL R. LAWRENCE, and LARRY E. GREINER: *Organizational Change and Development.* Homewood, Ill: Richard D. Irwin, Inc., 1970; with PAUL R. LAWRENCE, and JAY W. LORSCH: *Organizational Structure and Design.* Homewood, Ill: Richard D. Irwin, Inc., 1970.

FIEDLER, FRED E. and MARTIN M. CHEMERS: *Leadership and Effective Management.* Glenview, Ill: Scott, Foresman and Company, 1974; *A Theory of Leadership Effectiveness.* New York: McGraw-Hill Book Company, 1967.

HELLRIEGEL, DON and JOHN W. SLOCUM, JR.: *Management: A Contingency Approach.* Reading, Mass: Addison-Wesley Publishing Company, 1974.

KAST, FREMONT E. and JAMES E. ROSENZWEIG (eds.): *Contingency Views of Organization and Management.* Palo Alto, Calif: Science Research Associates, Inc., 1973.

LAWRENCE, PAUL R. and J. W. LORSCH: *Organization and Environment.* Homewood, Ill: Richard D. Irwin, Inc., 1969.

LORSCH, JAY and PAUL R. LAWRENCE: *Studies in Organizational Design.* Homewood, Ill: Richard D. Irwin, Inc., 1970; with JOHN J. MORSE: *Organization and Their Members: A Contingency Approach.* New York: Harper and Row, Inc., 1974.

LUTHANS, FRED: "The Contingency Theory of Management, A Path Out of the Jungle," *Business Horizons,* June 1973, pp. 67–72.

MORSE, JOHN J. and JAY W. LORSCH: "Beyond Theory Y," *Harvard Business Review,* May–June 1970, pp. 61–68.

NEWSTROM, JOHN W., WILLIAM E. REIF, and ROBERT M. MONCZKA (eds.): *A Contingency Approach to Management: Readings.* New York: McGraw-Hill Book Company, 1975.

PERROW, CHARLES: *Organizational Analysis: A Sociological View.* Belmont, Calif: Wadsworth Publishing Company, Inc., 1970.

SHERMAN, HARVEY: *It All Depends.* University, Alabama: University of Alabama Press, 1966.

TOSI, HENRY L. and W. CLAY HAMNER: *Organizational Behavior and Management: A Contingency Approach.* Chicago, Ill: St. Clair Press, 1974.

THOMPSON, JAMES D.: *Organizations in Action.* New York: McGraw-Hill Book Company, 1967.

WOLF, WILLIAM B. (ed.): *Management: Readings Towards a General Theory.* Belmont, Calif: Wadsworth Publishing Company, Inc., 1964.

WOODWARD, JOAN: *Industrial Organization: Theory and Practice.* London: Oxford University Press, 1965.

Management Science and Decision Making

ACKOFF, R., and M. SASIENI: *Fundamentals of Operations Research.* New York: John Wiley and Sons, 1968.

CHURCHMAN, C., R. ACKOFF, and E.

ARNOFF: *Introduction to Operations Research.* New York: John Wiley and Sons, 1957.

GRAYSON, C. JACKSON, JR.: "Management Science and Business Practice," *Harvard Business Review,* July–August 1973, pp. 41–48.

HEIN, LEONARD W.: *The Quantitative Approach to Managerial Decisions.* Englewood Cliffs, N.J: Prentice-Hall, Inc., 1967.

MILLER, D. and M. STARR: *Executive Decisions and Operations Research.* Englewood Cliffs, N.J: Prentice-Hall, Inc., 1970.

RAIFFA, HOWARD: *Decision Analysis.* Reading, Mass: Addison-Wesley Publishing Company, 1966.

SCHLAIFER, ROBERT: *Analysis of Decisions under Uncertainty.* New York: McGraw-Hill Book Company, 1967.

STARR, MARTIN: *Management: A Modern Approach.* New York: Harcourt Brace Jovanovich, Inc., 1971.

WAGNER, HARVEY M.: *Principles of Operations Research with Applications to Managerial Decisions.* Englewood Cliffs, N. J: Prentice-Hall, Inc., 1969.

External Environment, Technology, and Social Responsibility

BRIGHT, JAMES D.: *Research, Development and Technological Innovation.* Homewood, Ill: Richard D. Irwin, Inc., 1964.

CHAMBERLAIN, NEIL W.: *Enterprise and Environment: The Firm in Time and Place.* New York: McGraw-Hill Book Company, 1968.

COMMITTEE for ECONOMIC DEVELOPMENT: *Social Responsibilities of Business Corporations.* New York: Committee for Economic Development, 1971.

DAVIS, KEITH and ROBERT L. BLOMSTROM: *Business, Society and Environment.* 2nd ed., New York: McGraw-Hill Book Company, 1971.

ELLUL, JACQUES: *The Technological Society.* John Wilkinson (trans.), New York: Alfred A. Knopf, Inc., 1964.

FRIEDMAN, MILTON: *Capitalism and Freedom.* Chicago: University of Chicago Press, 1962.

HEILBRONER, ROBERT L.: *Between Capitalism and Socialism.* New York: Vintage Books, 1970.

JACOBY, NEIL: *Corporate Power and Social Responsibility.* New York: Macmillan Publishing Company, Inc., 1973.

JANTSCH, E.: *Technological Forecasting in Perspective.* Paris: Organization for Economic Cooperation and Development, 1967.

MESTHENE, EMMANUEL G.: *Technological Change.* Cambridge, Mass: Harvard University Press, 1970.

RICHMAN, BARRY: "New Paths to Corporate Social Responsibility," *California Management Review,* Spring 1973, pp. 20–36.

SETHI, S. PRAKASH (ed.): *The Unstable Ground: Corporate Social Policy In A Dynamic Society.* Los Angeles: Melville Publishing Company, 1974.

STEINER, GEORGE A.: *Business and Society.* 2nd ed., New York: Random House, Inc., 1975.

TOFFLER, ALVIN: *Future Shock.* New York: Bantam Books, Inc., 1970.

People and Motivation

ALLPORT, GORDON W.: *Personality.* New York: Henry Holt and Company, Inc., 1937.

ARGYRIS, CHRIS: *Organization and Innovation.* Homewood, Ill: Richard D. Irwin, Inc., 1965.

BERELSON, BERNARD and GARY A. STEINER: *Human Behavior: An Inventory of Scientific Findings.* New York: Harcourt, Brace and World, Inc., 1964.

DAVIS, KEITH: *Human Behavior at Work.* 4th ed., New York: McGraw-Hill Book Company, 1972.

FILLEY, ALAN C.: *Interpersonal Conflict Resolution.* Glenview, Ill: Scott Foresman and Company, 1974.

GELLERMAN, S. W.: *Motivation and Productivity.* New York: American Management Associations, 1968.

HERZBERG, FREDERICK: *Work and the Nature of Man.* Cleveland: The World Publishing Company, 1966; with BERNARD MAUSNER and BARBARA SNYDERMAN: *The Motivation to Work.* New York: John Wiley & Sons, Inc., 1959.

HULIN, CHARLES L. and MILTON R. BLOOD: "Job Enlargement, Individual Differences, and Worker Responses," *Psychological Bulletin,* Vol. 69, 1968, pp. 41–55.

LEAVITT, HAROLD J.: *Managerial Psychology.* Chicago: University of Chicago Press, 1958.

LIKERT, RENSIS: *New Patterns of Management.* New York: McGraw-Hill Book Company, 1961.

LUTHANS, FRED and ROBERT KREITNER: *Organizational Behavior Modification.* Glenview, Ill: Scott, Foresman and Company, 1975.

MASLOW, ABRAHAM H.: *Motivation and Personality.* New York: Harper & Row Publishers, Inc., 1954; "A Theory of Human Motivation," *Psychological Review,* July 1943, pp. 370–396.

McGREGOR, DOUGLAS: *The Human Side of Enterprise.* New York: McGraw-Hill Book Company, 1960.

PORTER, LYMAN W. and EDWARD E. LAWLER, III: *Managerial Attitudes and Performance.* Homewood, Ill: Richard D. Irwin, Inc., 1968.

ROETHLISBERGER, FRITZ J. and WILLIAM J. DICKSON: *Management and the Worker.* Cambridge, Mass: Harvard University Press, 1939.

SCHEIN, EDGAR H.: *Organizational Psychology.* 2nd ed., Englewood Cliffs, N.J.: Prentice-Hall, Inc., 1970.

VROOM, VICTOR H.: *Work and Motivation.* New York: John Wiley and Sons, Inc., 1964.

Organization Structure and Behavior

BLAKE, R. R. and JANE S. MOUTON: *Corporate Excellence Through Grid Organization Development.* Houston, Texas: Gulf Publishing Co., 1968.

BLAU, P. M., and W. R. SCOTT: *Formal Organizations.* San Francisco: Chandler Publishing Company, 1962.

BROWN, ALVIN: *Organization of Industry.* Englewood Cliffs, N. J: Prentice-Hall, Inc., 1947.

CAMPBELL, JOHN P., MARVIN D. DUNNETTE, EDWARD E. LAWLER III, and KARL E. WEICH, JR.: *Managerial Behavior, Performance, and Effectiveness.* New York: McGraw-Hill Book Company, 1970.

ETZIONI, AMATI: *Modern Organizations.* Englewood Cliffs, N. J: Prentice-Hall, Inc., 1964.

FRENCH, WENDELL L. and CECIL H. BELL, JR.: *Organization Development.* Englewood Cliffs, N. J: Prentice-Hall, Inc., 1973.

HAAS, J. EUGENE and THOMAS E. DRABEK: *Complex Organizations: A Sociological Perspective.* New York: The Macmillan Company, 1973.

HALL, RICHARD H.: *Organizations: Structure and Process.* Englewood Cliffs, N. J: Prentice-Hall, Inc., 1972.

HINTON, BERNARD L. and H. JOSEPH REITZ (eds.): *Groups and Organizations: Integrated Readings in the Analysis of Social Behavior.* Belmont, Calif: Wadsworth Publishing Company, Inc., 1971.

HOMANS, GEORGE C.: *The Human Group.* New York: Harcourt, Brace and World, Inc., 1950.

MARCH, JAMES G. and HERBERT A. SIMON: *Organizations.* New York: John Wiley and Sons, Inc., 1958.

MAYNTZ, RENATE: "The Study of Organizations: A Trend Report and Bibliography," *Current Sociology,* Vol. XII, 1965, pp. 95–118.

SCOTT, W. E. and L. L. CUMMINGS (eds.): *Readings in Organizational Behavior and Human Performance.* Homewood, Ill: Richard D. Irwin Inc., 1973.

SCOTT, WILLIAM G. and TERENCE R. MITCHELL: *Organization Theory: A Structural and Behavioral Analysis.* Homewood, Ill: Richard D. Irwin, Inc., 1972.

THOMPSON, JAMES D.: *Organizations in Action.* New York: McGraw-Hill Book Company, 1967.

VROOM, VICTOR H. (ed.): *Methods of Organizational Research*. Pittsburgh, University of Pittsburgh Press, 1967.

WOODWARD, JOAN: *Industrial Organization: Theory and Practice*. London: Oxford University Press, 1965.

Leadership

BLAKE, ROBERT R. and JANE S. MOUTON: *The Managerial Grid*. Houston: Gulf Publishing Company, 1964.

FIEDLER, FRED E.: *A Theory of Leadership Effectiveness*. New York: McGraw-Hill Book Company, 1967; with MARTIN M. CHEMERS: *Leadership and Effective Management*. Glenview, Ill: Scott, Foresman and Company, 1974.

FLEISHMAN, EDWIN A. and JAMES G. HUNT (eds.): *Current Developments in the Study of Leadership*. Carbondale, Ill: Southern Illinois University Press, 1973.

GRAEN, G., J. ORRIS, and K. ALVARES: "Contingency Model of Leadership Effectiveness: Some Experimental Results," *Journal of Applied Psychology*, 1971, Vol. 55, pp. 196–201.

HOUSE, ROBERT J.: "A Path-Goal Theory of Leadership Effectiveness," *Administrative Science Quarterly*, 1971, Vol. 16, pp. 321–340; with TERENCE R. MITCHELL, "Path-Goal Theory of Leadership," *Journal of Contemporary Business*, Autumn 1974, pp. 81–97.

HUNT, JAMES G. and LARS L. LARSON (eds.): *Contingency Approaches to Leadership*. Carbondale, Ill: Southern Illinois University Press, 1974.

JENNINGS, EUGENE E.: *An Anatomy of Leadership*. New York: Harper & Brothers, 1960.

LIKERT, RENSIS: *New Patterns of Management*. New York: McGraw-Hill Book Company, 1961.

MCGREGOR, DOUGLAS: *The Human Side of Enterprise*. New York: McGraw-Hill Book Company, 1960.

STOGDILL, RALPH M.: *Handbook of Leadership*. New York: The Free Press, 1974; "Personal Factors Associated with Leadership: A Survey of the Literature,"

Journal of Psychology, January 1948, pp. 64–65.

TANNENBAUM, ROBERT and WARREN H. SCHMIDT: "How to Choose a Leadership Pattern," *Harvard Business Review*, March–April 1958, pp. 95–101.

VROOM, V. H. and P. W. YETTON: *Leadership and Decision-Making*. Pittsburgh: University of Pittsburgh Press, 1974.

Planning, Control and Reporting

ACKOFF, R. L.: *A Concept of Corporate Planning*. New York: John Wiley and Sons, 1970.

ANSOFF, H. IGOR: *Corporate Strategy*. New York: McGraw-Hill Book Company, 1965.

ANTHONY, ROBERT: *Planning and Control Systems*. Boston: Harvard University Press, 1965.

BRANCH, MELVILLE C.: *Planning: Aspects and Applications*. New York: John Wiley & Sons, Inc., 1966.

CAMILLUS, J. C.: "Formal Planning Systems: Their Place in the Framework of Planning and Control," *Economic and Political Weekly*, February 1972, pp. M-2 through M-6.

CARLISLE, HOWARD M.: "Management-By-Objectives: Making It Work," *Chemical Engineering*, October 28, 1974, pp. 124, 126, and 128; "Systems Approach to Integrating Cost and Technical Data," *Management Services*, July–August 1967, pp. 24–41.

GORRY, G. A. and M. S. S. MORTON: "A Framework for Management Information Systems," *Sloan Management Review*, Fall 1971, pp. 55–70.

GREENE, JAMES H.: *Operations Planning and Control*. Homewood, Ill: Richard D. Irwin, Inc., 1967.

HOLMES, ROBERT W.: "Twelve Areas to Investigate for Better MIS," *Financial Executive*, July 1970, pp. 26–31.

LINDBLOM, CHARLES E.: "The Science of Muddling Through," *Public Administration Review,* Spring 1959, pp. 79–88.

McCASKEY, MICHAEL B.: "A Contingency Approach to Planning: Planning with Goals and Planning Without Goals," *Academy of Management Journal,* June 1974, pp. 281–291.

MINTZBERG, HENRY: "Strategy-Making in Three Modes," *California Management Review,* Winter 1973, pp. 44–53.

MORRISEY, GEORGE L.: "Without Control, MBO Is a Waste of Time," *Management Review,* February 1975, pp. 11–17.

NOVICK, DAVID (ed.): *Program Budgeting.* New York: Holt, Rinehart and Winston, Inc., 1969.

ODIORNE, GEORGE: *Management By Objectives.* New York: Pitman Publishing Corporation, 1965.

SCHLEH, EDWARD: *Management By Results.* New York: McGraw-Hill Book Company, 1961.

STEINER, GEORGE: *Top Management Planning.* New York: The Macmillan Company, 1969.

TANNENBAUM, ARNOLD S.: *Control in Organizations.* New York: McGraw-Hill Book Company, 1968.

WHEELWRIGHT, STEVEN C. and SPYROL MAKRIDAKIS: *Forecasting Methods for Management.* New York: John Wiley and Sons, Inc., 1973.

ZANI, WILLIAM M.: "Blueprint for MIS," *Harvard Business Review,* November–December 1970, pp. 95–100.

Name Index

Subject Index

Edited by   James C. Budd

Designed by   Rick Chafian

Management Editor   Bruce Caldwell

Management: Concepts and Situations is
set in 10 on 12 Medallion; display type
is Medallion Semibold, Medallion Bold
Condensed, and Melior Semibold Outline,
set by Applied Typographic Systems.
Photography for chapter opener 1 is by
Tom Tracy; chapters 5, 6, 15, 17, 19, 20,
and 22 are by Connie and C. P. Peri; the
remainder is by Larry Keenan, Jr. Artwork
is by House of Graphics, and the cover
photo is from Tom Tracy. The book was
printed in PMS 455 green by R. R. Don-
nelley and Sons Company.